THE
CAMBRIDGE EDITION OF
THE LETTERS AND WORKS OF
D. H. LAWRENCE

THE WORKS OF D. H. LAWRENCE

EDITORIAL BOARD

THE PLUMED SERPENT
(QUETZALCOATL)

D. H. LAWRENCE

EDITED BY
L. D. CLARK

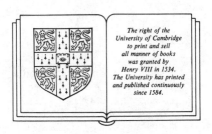

The right of the
University of Cambridge
to print and sell
all manner of books
was granted by
Henry VIII in 1534.
The University has printed
and published continuously
since 1584.

CAMBRIDGE UNIVERSITY PRESS

CAMBRIDGE
NEW YORK   NEW ROCHELLE
MELBOURNE   SYDNEY

Published by the Press Syndicate of the University of Cambridge
The Pitt Building, Trumpington Street, Cambridge CB2 1RP
32 East 57th Street, New York, NY 10022, USA
10 Stamford Road, Oakleigh, Melbourne 3166, Australia

Printed in Great Britain at the University Press, Cambridge

British Library cataloguing in publication data
Lawrence, D. H.
The plumed serpent: (quetzalcoatl). –
(The Cambridge edition of the
letters and works of D. H. Lawrence)
I. Title. II. Clark, L. D.
823'.912[F]   PR6023.A93

Library of Congress cataloguing in publication data
Lawrence, D. H. (David Herbert), 1885–1930.
The plumed serpent (Quetzalcoatl).
(The Cambridge edition of the
letters and works of D. H. Lawrence)
I. Clark, L. D. II. Title. III. Series:
Lawrence, D. H. (David Herbert), 1885–1930. Works. 1979.
PR6023.A93P53   1987   823'.912   86-32674

ISBN 0 521 22262 1 hard covers
ISBN 0 521 29422 3 paperback

CE

CONTENTS

GENERAL EDITORS' PREFACE

D. H. Lawrence is one of the great writers of the twentieth century – yet the texts of his writings, whether published during his lifetime or since, are, for the most part, textually corrupt. The extent of the corruption is remarkable; it can derive from every stage of composition and publication. We know from study of his MSS that Lawrence was a careful writer, though not rigidly consistent in matters of minor convention. We know also that he revised at every possible stage. Yet he rarely if ever compared one stage with the previous one, and overlooked the errors of typists or copyists. He was forced to accept, as most authors are, the often stringent house-styling of his printers, which overrode his punctuation and even his sentence-structure and paragraphing. He sometimes overlooked plausible printing errors. More important, as a professional author living by his pen, he had to accept, with more or less good will, stringent editing by a publisher's reader in his early days, and at all times the results of his publishers' timidity. So the fear of Grundyish disapproval, or actual legal action, led to bowdlerisation or censorship from the very beginning of his career. Threats of libel suits produced other changes. Sometimes a publisher made more changes than he admitted to Lawrence. On a number of occasions in dealing with American and British publishers Lawrence produced texts for both which were not identical. Then there were extraordinary lapses like the occasion when a compositor turned over two pages of MS at once, and the result happened to make sense. This whole story can be reconstructed from the introductions to the volumes in this edition; cumulatively they will form a history of Lawrence's writing career.

The Cambridge edition aims to provide texts which are as close as can now be determined to those he would have wished to see printed. They have been established by a rigorous collation of extant manuscripts and typescripts, proofs and early printed versions; they restore the words, sentences, even whole pages omitted or falsified by editors or compositors; they are freed from printing-house conventions which were imposed on Lawrence's style; and interference on the part of frightened publishers has been eliminated. Far from doing violence to the texts Lawrence would have wished to see published, editorial intervention is essential to recover them. Though we have to accept that some cannot now be recovered in their entirety because early states have not survived, we must be glad that so much evidence remains. Paradoxical as it may seem, the outcome of this recension will be texts which differ, often radically and certainly frequently, from those seen by the author himself.

Editors have adopted the principle that the most authoritative form of the text is to be followed, even if this leads sometimes to a 'spoken' or a 'manuscript' rather than a 'printed' style. We have not wanted to strip off one house-styling in order to impose another. Editorial discretion has been allowed in order to regularise Lawrence's sometimes wayward spelling and punctuation in accordance with his most frequent practice in a particular text. A detailed record of these and other decisions on textual matters, together with the evidence on which they are based, will be found in the textual apparatus or an occasional explanatory note. These give significant deleted readings in manuscripts, typescripts and proofs; and printed variants in forms of the text published in Lawrence's lifetime. We do not record posthumous corruptions, except where first publication was posthumous.

In each volume, the editor's introduction relates the contents to Lawrence's life and to his other writings; it gives the history of composition of the text in some detail, for its intrinsic interest, and because this history is essential to the statement of editorial principles followed. It provides an account of publication and reception which will be found to contain a good deal of hitherto unknown information. Where appropriate, appendixes make available extended draft manuscript readings of significance, or important material, sometimes unpublished, associated with a particular work.

Though Lawrence is a twentieth-century writer and in many respects remains our contemporary, the idiom of his day is not invariably intelligible now, especially to the many readers who are not native speakers of British English. His use of dialect is another difficulty, and further barriers to full understanding are created by now obscure literary, historical, political or other references and allusions. On these occasions explanatory notes are supplied by the editor; it is assumed that the reader has access to a good general dictionary and that the editor need not gloss words or expressions that may be found in it. Where Lawrence's letters are quoted in editorial matter, the reader should assume that his manuscript is alone the source of eccentricities of phrase or spelling. An edition of the letters is still in course of publication: for this reason only the date and recipient of a letter will be given if it has not so far been printed in the Cambridge edition.

ACKNOWLEDGEMENTS

Help in preparing this edition has come to me from a number of people and institutions. I would like them to know my gratitude:

Patricia Brandt, for her unfailing editorial assistance; Lindeth Vasey, for careful corrections and comments; Warren Roberts and James T. Boulton, for their part as General Editors in the Cambridge edition of Lawrence; Michael Black, Andrew Robertson and John Worthen, for their support and patience; Paul Rosenblatt and Edgar Dryden, for helping me find research funds; the late Alfred A. Knopf, for recalling publication practices of the 1920s; Michael Squires, John McElroy and Carl Ketcham, for discussion of editorial practices; Lawrence Clark Powell, for information on manuscripts; Lois Olsrud, Elaine Livermore, Mirene Hazebrouck, Andrew Makuch and the late Paul Barton, all of the University of Arizona Library, for helping me search out details; Ellen Dunlap, for help in research. To others I am indebted for indispensable if more general aid: the late Harry T. Moore, Marshall Best, Émile Delavenay, Donald Dickinson, David Farmer, R. R. Hackford, William Koshland, Gerald Lacy, Gerald Pollinger, the late Martin Secker and Jeremy Treglown.

I would also like to express my thanks to the National Endowment for the Humanities for a grant which gave me a year free to pursue the task of editing this volume, and the University of Arizona Foundation for a grant to purchase photocopies. The following libraries have been most generous in allowing me to make use of research materials in their collections: the manuscripts of 'Quetzalcoatl' and *The Plumed Serpent*, the typescript and proofs of *The Plumed Serpent*, Harry Ransom Humanities Research Center, University of Texas at Austin; the typescript of 'Quetzalcoatl', Houghton Library, Harvard University; the typescripts of Chapters VI and VII of *The Plumed Serpent*, Bancroft Library, University of California at Berkeley; the typescript of Chapter VII of *The Plumed Serpent*, Clark Library, University of California at Los Angeles; the letter-books of Martin Secker, University Library, University of Illinois at Urbana-Champaign; a manuscript of the music for *David*, Dartmouth College Library; Lawrence's drawing for the cover and Dorothy Brett's drawings for the dust jacket of *The Plumed Serpent*, Butler Library, Columbia University.

September 1986   L.D.C.

CHRONOLOGY

11 September 1885	Born in Eastwood, Nottinghamshire
September 1898 – July 1901	Pupil at Nottingham High School
1902–1908	Pupil teacher; student at University College, Nottingham
7 December 1907	First publication: 'A Prelude', in *Nottinghamshire Guardian*
October 1908	Appointed as teacher at Davidson Road School, Croydon
November 1909	Publishes five poems in *English Review*
3 December 1910	Engagement to Louie Burrows; broken off on 4 February 1912
9 December 1910	Death of his mother, Lydia Lawrence
19 January 1911	*The White Peacock* published in New York (20 January in London)
19 November 1911	Ill with pneumonia; resigns his teaching post on 28 February 1912
March 1912	Meets Frieda Weekley; they elope to Germany on 3 May
23 May 1912	*The Trespasser*
September 1912 – March 1913	At Gargnano, Lago di Garda, Italy
February 1913	*Love Poems and Others*
29 May 1913	*Sons and Lovers*
June–August 1913	In England
August 1913 – June 1914	In Germany, Switzerland and Italy
July 1914 – December 1915	In London, Buckinghamshire and Sussex
13 July 1914	Marries Frieda Weekley in London
26 November 1914	*The Prussian Officer*
30 September 1915	*The Rainbow*; suppressed by court order on 13 November
February 1916	Begins reading American literature: Melville, Dana, Crèvecoeur, Cooper and others
June 1916	*Twilight in Italy*

July 1916	*Amores*
January 1917	Plans essays on 'classic' (nineteenth-century) American literature
August 1917 – October 1918	Works on early version of American literature essays
15 October 1917	After twenty-one months' residence in Cornwall, ordered to leave by military authorities
October 1917 – November 1919	In London, Berkshire and Derbyshire
December 1917	*Look! We Have Come Through!*
October 1918	*New Poems*
November 1918 – June 1919	Eight American literature essays in *English Review*
September–October 1919	Revises American literature essays
November 1919 – February 1922	In Italy, then Capri and Sicily
20 November 1919	*Bay*
June 1920	Continues revising American literature essays
September 1920	Writes 'America, Listen to Your Own', 'Turkey-Cock' and 'The Revolutionary'
November 1920	Private publication of *Women in Love* (New York), *The Lost Girl*
10 May 1921	*Psychoanalysis and the Unconscious* (New York)
May 1921	Writes 'The Evening Land'
12 December 1921	*Sea and Sardinia* (New York)
26 February 1922	Sail from Naples for Ceylon
March–April 1922	In Ceylon
14 April 1922	*Aaron's Rod* (New York)
4 May – August 1922	In Australia
Late May – early July 1922	Writes *Kangaroo*
4 September 1922	Arrive in San Francisco
September 1922 – March 1923	In New Mexico
11 September 1922	Arrive in Taos
6 October 1922	Working on and soon abandons a novel based on the life of Mabel Dodge Luhan: 'The Wilful Woman'
Early October 1922	Revises *Kangaroo*, adding new last chapter
23 October 1922	*Fantasia of the Unconscious* (New York)

24 October 1922	*England, My England* (New York)
November–December 1922	Rewrites essays on American literature for the last time
March 1923	*The Ladybird, The Fox, The Captain's Doll*
23 March 1923	Arrive in Mexico City
27 April 1923	Arrive in Chapala, Jalisco
10 May – late June 1923	Writes 'Quetzalcoatl'
9 July 1923	Leave Chapala by train for New York
19 July – August 1923	In New York
27 August 1923	*Studies in Classic American Literature* (New York)
30 August – September 1923	In Los Angeles area; begins revising *The Boy in the Bush*
September 1923	*Kangaroo*
25 September 1923	Leaves Los Angeles by train to travel down west coast of Mexico
9 October 1923	*Birds, Beasts and Flowers* (New York)
17 October 1923	Arrives in Guadalajara
21 October – November 1923	In Jalisco and Mexico City; finishes *The Boy in the Bush*
22 November 1923	Sails from Veracruz for England
December 1923 – March 1924	In England, France and Germany
11 March 1924	Arrive in New York
March–October 1924	At Taos, New Mexico, mostly at Kiowa Ranch
April 1924	Writes 'Indians and Entertainment', 'The Dance of the Sprouting Corn' and probably 'The Overtone'
22–3 April 1924	Attend Santo Domingo corn dance
June 1924	Writes 'The Woman Who Rode Away', the second version of 'Pan in America' and probably early version of *St. Mawr*
Late June – 13 September 1924	Writes second, longer version of *St. Mawr*
17–18 August 1924	Attend Hopi Snake Dance, Hotevilla, Arizona

Late August 1924	Writes 'The Hopi Snake Dance'
28 August 1924	*The Boy in the Bush* (with Mollie Skinner)
10 September 1924	Death of his father, John Arthur Lawrence
Late September – 8 October 1924	Writes 'The Princess'
16 October 1924	Leave Taos for Mexico City
9 November 1924 – February 1925	In Oaxaca
19 November 1924	Begins second version of *The Plumed Serpent*
Mid-December 1924	Writes the four 'Mornings in Mexico' sketches
by 2 February 1925	Finishes manuscript of *The Plumed Serpent*; falls gravely ill
26 February – 25 March 1925	In Mexico City
29 March 1925	Arrive in New Mexico
March – ?late May 1925	Writes *David*
14 May 1925	*St. Mawr Together with The Princess*
June – ?early July 1925	Revises typescript of *The Plumed Serpent*
September 1925 – June 1928	In England and, mainly, Italy
7 December 1925	*Reflections on the Death of a Porcupine* (Philadelphia)
21 January 1926	*The Plumed Serpent* published in London (5 February in New York)
June 1927	*Mornings in Mexico*
24 May 1928	*The Woman Who Rode Away and Other Stories*
June 1928 – March 1930	In Switzerland and, principally, in France
July 1928	*Lady Chatterley's Lover* privately published (Florence)
September 1928	*Collected Poems*
July 1929	Exhibition of paintings in London raided by police. *Pansies* (manuscript earlier seized in mail)
September 1929	*The Escaped Cock* (Paris)
2 March 1930	Dies at Vence, Alpes Maritimes, France

CUE-TITLES

(The place of publication, here and throughout, is London unless otherwise stated.)

Bernal Díaz   Bernal Díaz del Castillo. *The True History of the Conquest of New Spain*, trans. Alfred Percival Maudslay. 5 volumes. Hakluyt Society, 1908–16

Blavatsky   H. P. Blavatsky. *The Secret Doctrine*. 2 volumes. Pasadena, California: Theosophical University Press, 1952 (first published London, 1888)

Brundage   Burr Cartwright Brundage. *The Fifth Sun*. Austin: University of Texas Press, 1979

Bynner   Witter Bynner. *Journey with Genius: Recollections and Reflections Concerning the D. H. Lawrences*. New York: Day, 1951

Calderón de la Barca   Frances Calderón de la Barca. *Life in Mexico*. J. M. Dent & Sons, 1913 (first published 1843)

Caso   Alfonso Caso. *The Aztecs: People of the Sun*, trans. Lowell Dunham. Norman: University of Oklahoma Press, 1958

Clark   L. D. Clark. *Dark Night of the Body*. Austin: University of Texas Press, 1964

Complete Poems   Vivian de Sola Pinto and Warren Roberts, eds. *The Complete Poems of D. H. Lawrence*. 2 volumes. Heinemann, 1964

Lacy, *Seltzer*   Gerald M. Lacy, ed. *D. H. Lawrence: Letters to Thomas and Adele Seltzer*. Santa Barbara: Black Sparrow Press, 1976

Letters, iv.   Warren Roberts, James T. Boulton and Elizabeth Mansfield, eds. *The Letters of D. H. Lawrence*. Volume IV. Cambridge: Cambridge University Press, 1987

Mornings in Mexico   D. H. Lawrence. *Mornings in Mexico*. New York: Knopf, 1927

xiv

Nehls, ii.   Edward Nehls, ed. *D. H. Lawrence: A Composite Biography*. Volume II, 1919–25. Madison: University of Wisconsin Press, 1958

Nuttall   Zelia Nuttall. *The Fundamental Principles of Old and New World Civilizations: A comparative research based on a study of the ancient Mexican religious, sociological and calendrical systems*. Cambridge, Mass., 1901

Phoenix   Edward D. McDonald, ed. *Phoenix: The Posthumous Papers of D. H. Lawrence*. Heinemann, 1936

'Q'   'Quetzalcoatl', first and unpublished version of *The Plumed Serpent*, written May–June 1923, Chapala (Jalisco), Mexico

Roberts   Warren Roberts. *A Bibliography of D. H. Lawrence*, 2nd edn. Cambridge: Cambridge University Press, 1982

Seler   Eduard Seler. *Gesammelte Abhandlungen zür Amerikanischen Spräch- und Alterthumskunde*. 5 volumes. Berlin: A. Asher v. Co., 1902–15

Spence   Lewis Spence. *The Gods of Mexico*. New York: Frederick A. Stokes, 1923

Studies   D. H. Lawrence. *Studies in Classic American Literature*. New York: Seltzer, 1923

Symbolic Meaning D. H. Lawrence. *The Symbolic Meaning*, ed. Armin Arnold. Fontwell, Arundel: Centaur Press, 1962

Terry   T. Philip Terry. *Terry's Guide to Mexico*, rev. edn. New York: Houghton Mifflin, 1923

INTRODUCTION

INTRODUCTION

Soon after beginning his Mexican novel in May 1923, Lawrence declared that he had wanted all his life to write this book.[1] A few weeks later, nearing the end of a first draft and confident of his achievement, he could say: 'I like my new novel best of all – much' and 'this is my real novel of America'.[2]

Even so, he was to hesitate over the work for more than two years, to rewrite it entirely, to revise through final proofs and still to dread how it would fare in print. Behind his apprehension that the public could not appreciate his achievement, doubts apparently lingered in Lawrence's mind as to whether he had really created in *The Plumed Serpent* the novel he envisaged. Yet he was still ready to maintain, till it was out of his hands, that this was his 'most important novel, so far'.[3]

During the four years of life remaining to him after the novel appeared, Lawrence spoke little of *The Plumed Serpent*. Plainly, he ceased before long to think of this novel as the crowning accomplishment of his career, the fulfilment of a long-held ambition to write a book about 'America'. He even came to believe, insofar as the work embodies a political ideal, that he had made a mistake.[4]

How far back the impulse behind his American novel went in Lawrence's life is difficult to ascertain. It can be traced at least to his disillusionment with Europe during the First World War and his fascination with America as a haven for the rebirth of self and society.[5] In his wartime analysis of American literature (much revised, and published as

---

[1] *Letters*, iv. 446; MS unlocated but summarised in a House of Books, Ltd. catalogue (1970).
[2] Letters to Adele and Thomas Seltzer (*Letters*, iv. 455, 457). The Seltzers published DHL in America from the foundation of the firm (Thomas Seltzer, Inc.) in 1920, and did much to build his reputation. DHL left Seltzer for Alfred A. Knopf, Inc. in 1925. See Alexandra Lee Levin and Lawrence L. Levin, 'The Seltzers and D. H. Lawrence', in *D. H. Lawrence: Letters to Thomas and Adele Seltzer*, ed. Gerald M. Lacy (Santa Barbara, 1976), pp. 169–201.
[3] Letter to Curtis Brown, 23 June 1925. See also letters to Edward D. McDonald, 29 June and 26 October 1925; to Martin Secker, 18 June and 16 October 1925.
[4] Letter to Witter Bynner, 13 March 1928; see p. xlvi below.
[5] George J. Zytaruk and James T. Boulton, eds., *The Letters of D. H. Lawrence* (Cambridge, 1981), ii. 379, 420–1, 431–2, 436–8. All through the war and until the time of his departure from Europe in 1922, DHL's attitude toward America followed an attraction-repulsion rhythm. For America as a refuge both actual and symbolic, see *Twilight in Italy* (1916), in particular 'San Gaudenzio' and 'John'.

Studies in Classic American Literature in 1923), he found the 'perfect but untranslatable consciousness' of the blood ready to come to the surface of American society through the democratic overlay imported from Europe.[6] From 1917, when he first undertook these essays, Lawrence's endeavours to discover 'a new science of psychology' always seemed in some way connected with America.[7] In an epilogue addressed to American readers of *Fantasia of the Unconscious* (1922), for example, he wrote, 'I reckon this book of mine is a real American book. If there had been no America I should never have written it.'[8]

Aaron's Rod, over which Lawrence laboured for several years, often concurrently with the essays on American literature, is the first of his novels to touch upon concerns that emerge fully in *The Plumed Serpent*. Josephine Ford of *Aaron's Rod* is the earliest of his characters to claim aboriginal American blood, but her identity is familiar from distinctions already drawn in the American studies. Beneath 'a certain Parisian *chic* and mincingness', she moves 'like some savage squaw' to threaten Aaron's aloofness and endanger his quest for self-possession.[9] As the novel draws to a close, a dream of Aaron's culminates near 'a lake-city, like Mexico' in a vision of aboriginal deity both regenerative and dangerous: a 'roadside Astarte' with eggs 'in her open lap'.[10] *Aaron's Rod* is also Lawrence's first novel to suggest the political dimension of blood-consciousness, in the charismatic power of leadership that Lilly exerts over Aaron.

The Lost Girl, dating from 1920 between revisions of *Aaron's Rod*, first presents sustained American Indian themes, though without political overtones. A company of European actors performs as 'strictly a Red Indian troupe', in a Midlands village, anticipating the ritual scenes of *The Plumed Serpent*. Alvina is captivated by Ciccio masquerading as an Indian, 'velvety and alive on horseback'.[11] In their marriage, Lawrence created the joining of dark race and light race he thought essential to the restoration of humanity. Arriving in Ciccio's native valley in Italy, Alvina stands enthralled, like Kate in the Valley of Mexico, by the 'grand, pagan twilight of the

---

[6] 'The Two Principles' (*Symbolic Meaning* 187); Zytaruk and Boulton, *Letters of D. H. Lawrence*, ii. 469–71. (An earlier version of most of the essays was published in *English Review*, 1918–19 and reprinted in *Symbolic Meaning*.)

[7] James T. Boulton and Andrew Robertson, eds., *The Letters of D. H. Lawrence* (Cambridge, 1984), iii. 400.

[8] Harry T. Moore, *The Priest of Love*, revised edn (New York, 1974), p. 338.

[9] Chap. VII.

[10] Chap. XXI.

[11] *The Lost Girl*, ed. John Worthen (Cambridge, 1981), pp. 120, 140. See DHL's view of Cooper's Sioux Indians, who 'cleave close to their horses, almost in one flesh' (*Symbolic Meaning* 100).

valleys, savage, cold, with a sense of ancient gods who knew the right for human sacrifice'.[12]

In Italy in November 1921, when Lawrence received an invitation from Mabel Dodge Sterne to come and live on her estate in Taos, New Mexico, and to contribute by his writing to the preservation of American Indian culture, his immediate reaction was: 'I want to go. The Indian, the Aztec, old Mexico – all that fascinates me and has fascinated me for years.'[13] Some months of wavering followed, however, and then a decision which led to a short stay in Ceylon and a longer one in Australia. His reason for taking this circuitous route was: 'I shall be fulfilling my real desire to approach America from the west, over the Pacific.'[14] He looked upon his three months in Australia and the writing of *Kangaroo* as preparatory to the challenge of creating fiction about America. As he put it: 'I have learned a lot coming here', and 'I should like very much to write an American novel, after this Australian one: on something the same lines.'[15] Then just as he was completing *Kangaroo*, he declared that he would like 'to write a New Mexico novel with Indians in it'.[16]

Kangaroo is Lawrence's first novel to take as a point of departure the politics of a nation. Like *The Plumed Serpent*, it explores magnetism and loyalty between men, most of all male leadership by blood authority. In *Kangaroo*, Richard Somers must finally reject what Australia offers: an incarnation of the Australian spirit of place, the man Kangaroo, who has in his make-up too much of that Old World abomination we call 'charity', which long ago usurped the primacy of 'the old dark gods, who had waited so long in the outer dark'.[17] At the end of the novel Somers is ready to pursue his way over the Pacific to encounter these gods in America.

According to Mabel Sterne, Lawrence had scarcely arrived in Taos in September 1922, when he set out to realise his hope of writing an 'American novel'.[18] He cannot have begun before 19 September, when he wrote to his American publisher, Thomas Seltzer: 'I wonder if I'll get a novel out of here? It would be interesting if I could.' Then on 6 October he informed his American agent Robert Mountsier: 'Am doing a M[abel] Sterne novel of *here*: with her Indian: she makes me notes. Wonder how we

---

[12] *The Lost Girl*, ed. Worthen, p. 315. At the end of the novel, Alvina expects to emigrate to America if her husband survives the First World War. Three poems from just after the war also express the magnetism of America: 'The Revolutionary', 'Turkey-Cock' and 'The Evening Land' (*Complete Poems*, i. 287–9, 369–72, 289–93).

[13] *Letters*, iv. 125; see also pp. 110–12.   [14] Ibid., 225.   [15] Ibid., 260, 259.

[16] Ibid., 274.

[17] Chaps. XI, XIII and XVII.

[18] Mabel Dodge Luhan, *Lorenzo in Taos* (New York, 1932), p. 52.

shall get on with it. I don't let her see my stuff.'[19] The story was to be based
on her life, which appeared to fulfil Lawrence's requirements for a subject.
The novel never got past an incomplete narration of her journey west, with
a few notes indicating that once arrived in a village like Taos, she would
become involved with an Indian lover.[20]

After this abortive attempt, Lawrence's urge to write an American novel
diminished for a time. His last revision of the American essays took
precedence over fiction. On 18 November he thought that when he had
finished these, he might 'try a Taos novel. I'll see.'[21] He produced a few
poems for *Birds, Beasts and Flowers*, three essays on the Indians and his first
essay on the art of the novel.[22]

One of the Indian essays, 'Indians and an Englishman', recreates the
bewilderment Lawrence felt on first contact with Indian ceremonial at an
Apache festival. What he sees in the Indian now is not far from what he had
imagined in the original essays on James Fenimore Cooper.[23] More
surprisingly, the revolutionary who had seen from afar his destiny as 'Lord
of the dark and moving hosts' now declines to 'cluster at the drum any
more'.[24] Perplexity before a great force long contemplated from a distance
is the prevalent emotion, along with another feeling prominent in the last
revision of the Leatherstocking essay: in the sketch it is 'a jeering
malevolent vibration' in the air around the Apache encampment, and in the
essay 'a certain slightly devilish resistance in the American landscape'.[25]
This resistance was still powerful shortly before Lawrence began his
American novel: 'I should never be able to write on this continent –
something in the spirit opposes one's going forth.'[26] He even thought of

---

[19] *Letters*, iv. 298, 319. 'Her Indian' was Tony Luhan, eventually her husband.

[20] Luhan, *Lorenzo in Taos*, pp. 65–6. The fragment is published as 'The Wilful Woman' in
St. Mawr and Other Stories, ed. Brian Finney (Cambridge, 1983), pp. 197–203.

[21] *Letters*, iv. 341.

[22] 'Eagle in New Mexico', 'The Blue Jay', 'Bibbles', etc. (*Complete Poems*, ii. 372–5,
394–414); 'Indians and an Englishman' and 'Taos' (*Phoenix* 92–103); 'The Future of the
Novel' (*Study of Thomas Hardy and Other Essays*, ed. Bruce Steele (Cambridge, 1985),
pp. 151–5); 'Certain Americans and an Englishman' (*Phoenix II: Uncollected, Unpublished
and Other Prose Works by D. H. Lawrence*, ed. Warren Roberts and Harry T. Moore (1968),
pp. 238–43). 'Certain Americans', first published in the *New York Times Magazine* (24
December 1922), was DHL's contribution to an effort to save Indian lands from seizure;
see also *Letters*, iv. 331–2.

[23] DHL's refusal to cross the ages between his own 'stream of conscious human blood' and
the 'frenzy of the old mystery' in the Apaches is like Deerslayer's acknowledging the
mystery of the Indian while remaining true to the white race (*Phoenix* 99; *Symbolic Meaning*
100).

[24] 'The Revolutionary' (*Complete Poems*, ii. 289); *Phoenix* 99.   [25] *Phoenix* 96; *Studies* 81.
[26] *Letters*, iv. 426.

the modern American Indians as being 'up against a dead wall, even more than we are' – survivors of a culture beyond recovery.[27]

During this period Lawrence wrote his first essay on the novel in general. Aware of the crisis that America imposed upon his own experiments in fiction, he now demanded that the novel should avoid Joyce's 'self-analytical stunts'.[28] The novelist must reach beyond the articulate individual ego into the 'primary human psyche', a theory which Lawrence had drawn up in the original American studies.[29] The novelist should 'go back to the Greek philosophers' to 'find a new impulse for new things in mankind', back before 'philosophy and fiction got split'.[30] He was plainly addressing his own next move in fiction. The first draft of *The Plumed Serpent* assimilates a great deal of the discussion present in his essays, and both it and the published novel incorporate much philosophical discourse.

In early December 1922, the Lawrences left Mabel Sterne's cottage in Taos for Del Monte Ranch in the mountains to the north. Thomas and Adele Seltzer came for a visit during the Christmas holidays. Lawrence talked with Seltzer about travelling to Mexico, though not necessarily about writing a novel there.[31] He feared that he might be shirking a responsibility in abandoning his own continent for the New World, and spoke of going to Russia in the summer, or even to Greenland.[32] But he had been studying Spanish and, from December onward, made increasingly definite plans for a trip to Mexico.[33] In a letter to Adele Seltzer in early February, Frieda wrote: 'Lawr wants to go to Mexico, he thinks he might write his American novel there – You know he would like to write a novel of each continent'.[34]

'Quetzalcoatl'

The Lawrences arrived in Mexico City on 23 March 1923, where he wrote of this trip as the gratification of an old wish: 'Do you remember, during the war I always wanted to come to Mexico.'[35] Once there, he went through his usual alterations of attitude: the country was 'very pleasant, rather like South Italy' or else it put 'a strain on the temper' or, after a few

[27] Ibid., 310.
[28] 'The Future of the Novel' (*Study of Thomas Hardy*, ed. Steele, p. 154). See also *Letters*, iv. 345, 340.
[29] *Symbolic Meaning* 176. See also Zytaruk and Boulton, *Letters of D. H. Lawrence*, ii. 182–4.
[30] 'The Future of the Novel' (*Study of Thomas Hardy*, ed. Steele, p. 154).
[31] *Letters*, iv. 367.
[32] Ibid., 362, 361.   [33] Ibid., 364, 383.   [34] Ibid., 385.   [35] Ibid., 420.

weeks, it was at times unbearable.[36] He was nevertheless at the 'solar plexus of North America'. He found the 'gruesome Aztec carvings' in the National Museum distasteful, but when he went out to San Juan Teotihuacán and observed the 'huge gnashing heads' of serpent deities, he was pleased that in Mexico 'the gods bit'. North of the Border the gods were thought to be tamed, though in reality, underneath, 'the same old American dragon's blood' flowed.[37]

With Witter Bynner and Willard ('Spud') Johnson, friends from Santa Fe, the Lawrences explored the capital and other cities, while Lawrence vacillated between staying in Mexico and going back to the USA or to England. Zelia Nuttall, the American anthropologist, offered him a house in Coyoacán, a southern suburb of Mexico City, but that was too urban for Lawrence.[38] On 9 April he mentioned that he might look around Guadalajara and that he 'would like to settle down and do a novel'.[39] Within a month the Lawrences had moved to a house in Chapala, on the lake, with Bynner and Johnson in a hotel nearby.[40]

Lawrence at once launched into a novel, made 'two false starts' – neither, apparently, has survived – and then on 10 May began the first version of *The Plumed Serpent* (Roberts E313a), with a zeal evident in several letters.[41] Lawrence chose 'Quetzalcoatl' as a title, and had later to be persuaded by his publishers to change it to *The Plumed Serpent*, which he thought sounded 'a bit silly'.[42] A recent hesitancy now overcome, his theme was the fruit of reflection maturing since his first preoccupation with America: the revival of the primordial spirit of the continent, now to be effected by religious and political revolution.[43]

Frieda reports that her husband went out regularly to write under the trees at the lakeside.[44] There, in his precise script, he advanced at a pace averaging 2,500 words a day. He had 250 pages by 30 May, and 415 by 15 June. By late June he had about 480 pages – some 120,000 words – all in two bound notebooks except for the first 56 pages on loose sheets torn from a similar notebook. Lawrence called this manuscript 'the first rough draft'.[45] By 27 June he had put it aside until a more propitious time: 'The

---

[36] Ibid., 414, 430; 'Au Revoir, U.S.A.' (*Phoenix* 104); see also Bynner 19–60.

[37] 'Au Revoir, U.S.A.' (*Phoenix* 105–6); *Letters*, iv. 416.

[38] *Letters*, iv. 422.   [39] Ibid., 419.   [40] Ibid., 436.   [41] Ibid., 442; see p. xix.

[42] Letter to Alfred Knopf, 4 May 1925; letter from Martin Secker to Curtis Brown, 23 February 1925 (University of Illinois at Urbana-Champaign, hereafter UIll); letter to George Conway, 10 June 1925.

[43] *Letters*, iv. 429.

[44] *"Not I, But the Wind . . ."* (Sante Fe, 1934), p. 155. See also Johnson's reminiscence in Nehls, ii. 236.

[45] *Letters*, iv. 450, 457, 454.

novel isn't finished – I must do it when my soul gets calmer.'[46] Cautious now, after his initial exuberance, he needed time and the advantage of seeing this manuscript turned into typescript before he could proceed with assurance. This 'first complete sketch', as he called it elsewhere, turned out to be not a text for revision but a first version eventually rejected in favour of a total rewriting.[47] 'Quetzalcoatl' differs from *The Plumed Serpent* much as the three versions of *Lady Chatterley's Lover* differ. The two works represent separate processes of creation, even though one is preliminary to the other. Comparisons made here and in the Explanatory notes relate the two processes within the whole of Lawrence's American experience.

Several aspects of Mexico gave Lawrence the stimulus to begin a novel. Lake Chapala provided a symbolic geography of rebirth in direct lineage from Cooper's Lake Glimmerglass, also appropriate in that the Aztecs had built a lake civilisation.[48] The Mexican gods had a power that could still be felt, and represented a tradition of the renewal of society through violence: the pre-Conquest human sacrifice. Lawrence responded at once to a degenerate form of blood ritual imported from Spain: the bull fight gave him an opening chapter that he changed little through the revisions that follow. The contemporary state of Mexican society was such that a radical upheaval of any sort was imaginable. The political turmoil of the Mexican Revolution going on since 1910 had in great part originated among the oppressed Indian majority.[49] But for Lawrence the struggle was mis-directed: the true revolution must be not economic and political, but religious. If a truly religious consciousness could be awakened by calling back the Mexican gods in a form appealing to moderns, then all other essential reshaping of society would follow. To make this point, the

---

[46] Ibid., 465.   [47] Ibid., 451 ('erste volle Skizze'); see also pp. 446–7.

[48] Cf. the versions of 'Fenimore Cooper's Leatherstocking Novels' in *Symbolic Meaning* and *Studies*. Cooper's symbolism is viewed with more scepticism in the later one, but DHL states that he first sensed in Cooper 'the myth of atonement' between the white man and the red.

[49] By this time DHL is known to have read the following works on Mexican history and culture: Bernal Díaz del Castillo, *The True History of the Conquest of New Spain* (first published in 1632; in Maudslay's five-volume translation, 1908–16); Frances Calderón de la Barca, *Life in Mexico* (1843); Hernán Cortés's letters to the Spanish emperor, of which the first complete publication in English was *Hernando Cortes: His Five Letters of Relation to the Emperor Charles V*, ed. and trans. by Francis Augustus MacNutt (1908); Charles Flandrau, *Viva Mexico!* (1908); L. Gutiérrez de Lara and Edgcumb Pinchon, *The Mexican People: Their Struggle for Freedom* (1914); William Hickling Prescott, *History of the Conquest of Mexico* (New York, 1843). DHL also made considerable use of a guidebook popular at the time: T. Philip Terry, *Terry's Guide to Mexico*, rev. edn (New York, 1923). DHL intended to re-read Bernal Díaz in 1923, but apparently did not obtain the book (*Letters*, iv. 445). See William York Tindall, *D. H. Lawrence and Susan His Cow* (New York, 1939), pp. 114–16 and Clark 103–12. See also footnote 89 and appendixes I and III.

chapter called 'Conversion' in 'Quetzalcoatl' lays out Ramón's background – parallel in some ways with that of José Vasconcelos, the Minister of Education.[50] Ramón, disillusioned with politics and with Europe and the United States as sources of hope, has remained silent during the first decade of the Revolution, writing a history of modern Mexico, and watching. Now he seeks to put into effect his matured conviction: that only a revival of the primitive religious consciousness can save mankind.

In 'Quetzalcoatl' the revolution is truly indigenous. Both Ramón and Cipriano speak as Indians who would tear the heart out of the white race and offer it to the sun: Lawrence had said in 'Fenimore Cooper's Anglo-American Novels' that 'the Aztec lives unappeased and destructive within the Mexican'.[51] But he is not specific about how Indian his chief characters are. Ramón looks and acts wholly like an Indian at Mrs Norris's tea party, but Kate can seriously ask him later whether he considers himself to be white. Cipriano is introduced in the first chapter as dark, but seeming 'Italian and friendly', yet near the end of the manuscript, when Kate sees him swimming in the lake at sunrise, he is 'nearly black like a negro'.[52] The novelist's indecision is reflected in Kate's and is never resolved, indecision concerning not only the ethnic authenticity of the chief male characters but also the relative identities of male and female in the new society.

Kate sees a potential salvation for herself in this patriarchal country, where such men as Ramón claim the right to do the thinking, and where he and Cipriano intend to foster a religion of men, not priests and women. Cipriano can even state privately to Ramón that he must have Kate and will detain her in Mexico by force if necessary.[53] The *machismo* theme is developed in part by contrast. The fussy and jealous Owen, the North American male, makes a poor show at rivalry with his Mexican counterparts.[54] Yet masculine dominance must be tempered by a powerful goddess. The god Quetzalcoatl had left Mexico primarily to seek a wife 'in the watery countries'. Early in the story there are hints that Kate may fill this role.[55] When the deification offered her instead is that of consort to Cipriano as Huitzilopochtli, the reasoning is still that the heavy dark

---

[50] Moore, *Priest of Love*, p. 397; Clark 29, 31–2. See also Bynner 117–22 and José Vasconcelos, *A Mexican Ulysses* (Indiana, 1963).

[51] *Symbolic Meaning* 80.   [52] 'Q' 135; 19; 448.

[53] 'Q' 56, 107, 110, 168, 181; 175–7, 242.

[54] 'Q' 55–63, 80.

[55] 'Q' 95; 99, but see also p. 97, where DHL crossed out 'They say the wife is a *gringuita*, a foreigner' and p. 212, where a similar remark occurs.

maleness of Mexico suffers from want of a female balance.[56] And as the novel draws to a close, the male bravado diminishes. Cipriano, conditioned to feminine influence through the Englishwoman who saw to his education and treated him as a foster son – in *The Plumed Serpent* it is a bishop who does this – almost pleads with Kate to marry him and accept apotheosis in the new pantheon.[57] But in the first version Kate steadfastly refuses, also declining a love affair with Cipriano. She cannot yet bring herself to unite her white blood with the Indian blood of Mexico. She will make a firm decision on this in Europe – so she promises Cipriano – and in the final scene she packs up to sail away: much as Lawrence shut his notebooks near the end of June and shortly thereafter took a train for New York.[58]

The key scene of Kate's resistance to male power in 'Quetzalcoatl' comes when Ramón all but forces her to take instruction in the occult lore of the new way, as well as the first step toward initiation.[59] Trying with help from Cipriano to teach Kate how the ancients thought in images, Ramón recounts in Neoplatonic terms the descent of the soul into the flesh. Ramón and Cipriano compel Kate to swirl wine in a glass into a vortex and drink it as a pledge to join them. She swallows the wine and almost faints into submission, but reacts at last by standing up and walking out of the room, throwing off their power. An authorial comment has it that she is left 'a miserable prisoner with all the appearance of freedom', but we are not allowed to forget that Ramón and Cipriano may be seen as 'mystical, life-destroying men, with their hateful abstraction and imagery'.[60] An instruction similar to the one just described, which Kate does not repudiate, forms the ending of her story in the second manuscript version of the novel, but Lawrence deleted it in the typescript.

'Quetzalcoatl' contains little invented myth and ceremony. When Lawrence acquired some of his eventually substantial knowledge of pre-Columbian American religion is difficult to determine, but what he used in the first version he could have constructed from reading Terry's guidebook or Prescott's *History of the Conquest of Mexico*.[61]

The Lawrences left Mexico in early July and went to New York, where

---

[56] 'Q' 313.   [57] 'Q' 58, 314; 370–3.
[58] 'Q' 449, 457, 459–60. DHL wrote on 27 June 1923 that his novel was *'nearly* finished – near enough to leave' (*Letters*, iv. 462). He could not have worked on it more than a few days longer: according to Bynner (p. 167), a group including the Lawrences left on a *canoa* trip around Lake Chapala on 5 July, and the Lawrences left for the USA on 9 July.
[59] 'Q' 428–48.   [60] 'Q' 441, 446–8; 448, 462.
[61] Pp. 42–3, 298–308, 496–7, 519–20; Book I, chap. III. See also Prescott's *History of the Conquest of Peru* (New York, 1847), Book I, chap. III, which DHL had read by 1919, perhaps earlier (Boulton and Robertson, *Letters of D. H. Lawrence*, iii. 327 and James T. Boulton, ed., *The Letters of D. H. Lawrence* (Cambridge, 1979), i. 86).

he delivered his manuscript to Thomas Seltzer to be typed. On the road again by 21 August – after a falling-out with Frieda that sent her off to England and him to California – Lawrence anxiously inquired from time to time whether the typing was done and what the Seltzers thought of the novel.[62] After an arduous trip down the west coast of Mexico with a friend, Kai Götzsche, though he still did not have the typescript Lawrence wrote to the Seltzers from Guadalajara that he would spend the winter in Mexico and 'finish "Quetzalcoatl"', aware already that he 'must go all over it again', after the easier task of reshaping *The Boy in the Bush* (from the manuscript written by Mollie Skinner), because 'this is much more important to me, my "Quetzalcoatl"'.[63]

Frieda's refusal to rejoin him decided Lawrence against staying in Mexico and proceeding with his American novel. To perform his heroic task in this 'black land' of Mexico 'full of man-strength', the presence and support of 'woman' was essential, not for love but for 'strength, strength, strength'.[64] So Lawrence sailed to England on 22 November, to make peace with Frieda and to persuade her to accompany him again to America.[65] Before he left Mexico, thinking that Seltzer was soon to visit England, he asked him to bring along the 'Quetzalcoatl' manuscript. But Seltzer did not come, nor did he send the manuscript; he had a typescript (Roberts E313b) finished in New York and held both texts until Lawrence returned to the USA.[66] Seltzer was now nearing bankruptcy and began ignoring Lawrence's letters; while in London, Lawrence made a contract with his literary agent Curtis Brown, to represent him in the USA, as he had since 1921 in England.[67] This arrangement led to a change of American publishers and to eventual publication of *The Plumed Serpent* by Knopf rather than by Seltzer.[68]

The Plumed Serpent

The winter of 1923–4 in Europe was long, cold and dismal. Lawrence was glad to set out for America with Frieda in the spring.[69] The Lawrences landed in New York on 11 March, where he picked up the 'Quetzalcoatl'

---

[62] *Letters*, iv. 495, 517; 523. [63] Ibid., 517. [64] Ibid., 531–2. [65] Ibid., 522.
[66] Ibid., 527, 544. [67] Ibid., 544, 588; 559.
[68] Letter to Curtis Brown, 10 January 1925.
[69] DHL wrote a 'London Letter' (to Willard Johnson, 9 January 1924; see *Letters*, iv. 555), which was published in Johnson's little magazine, *The Laughing Horse*, in May 1924. DHL wrote also for this publication 'Paris Letter' and 'A Letter from Germany' (*Phoenix* 119–22, 107–10). In the latter he reports on the emerging forces that later solidified into Nazism; see also *Letters*, iv. 574.

draft manuscript and typescript. They then headed west, meaning to pause briefly in Taos and then proceed to Mexico in order to finish the novel by autumn,[70] but the stay in Taos lasted through the whole summer. For one thing, as Lawrence put it, 'I shan't get the "Quetzalcoatl" novel done this year. I don't feel much like working at anything just now. The winter was a bad one.'[71] For another, the Lawrences acquired Kiowa Ranch from Mabel Luhan and went about establishing a home there.[72] The new access to primitive America in Lawrence's closer contact with the Indians and his exposure to the spring and summer landscape around the mountain ranch were to have a deep influence on the rewriting of his novel. Lawrence still had not communicated with anyone who had an intimate knowledge of Mexican culture. This summer he exchanged letters with Manuel Gamio, a pioneer of Mexican anthropology and archaeology. Gamio sent one of his books, probably *Forjando Patria* (1916), and invited Lawrence to visit him in Mexico.[73]

Lawrence attended dances at Santo Domingo, San Felipe, the Hopi village of Hotevilla and no doubt others at Taos Pueblo, observing as well the impromptu dances done in the evening by the Indians working on the ranch cabins. Out of all this he wrote four essays on primitive Indian rites.[74] In these essays Lawrence held as always to the 'vivid relatedness between the man and the living universe', only now he sought this in more definite expressive forms, in symbols such as Pan and in the drama of the sacred dance.[75] He had already written two stories centring on Pan, about the vengeance Pan wreaks on those who think him dead, and the futility of a world without him.[76] In the subconscious chant of one of the stories, 'The Overtone', which he seems to have finished in New Mexico, an attempt at mythical love poetry resembles that of the marriage ceremony in *The Plumed Serpent*.[77] In the essay 'Pan in America', first written in May 1924, Lawrence connects the god-urge of the Old World with that which he means to recreate in the New, sensing that Pan is more vividly alive

[70] *Letters*, iv. 591.   [71] Letter to Seltzer, 10 April 1924.

[72] Letter to Else Jaffe, 10 April 1924.

[73] Their correspondence is unlocated. See letters to Idella Purnell and Seltzer, 9 June and 18 May 1924.

[74] 'Pan in America' (*Phoenix* 22–31) and three essays later collected in *Mornings in Mexico* (1927): 'Indians and Entertainment', 'Dance of the Sprouting Corn' and 'The Hopi Snake Dance'.

[75] 'Pan in America' (*Phoenix* 27).

[76] In 'The Last Laugh' (collected in *The Woman Who Rode Away* (Secker, 1928)), Pan comes back to take vengeance on the modern male for his impiety against the chthonic powers.

[77] Cf. the marriage ceremony in chap. xx of *The Plumed Serpent* with Elsa's 'sing-song' invocation to a faun-like lover in *St. Mawr*, ed. Finney, pp. 15–17.

there than in Europe.[78] In 'Indians and Entertainment' he speculates on
the drama of these dances, recollecting the hypothesis he had adopted
after reading Jane Harrison's *Ancient Art and Ritual* in 1913: that drama
arose from 'religious yearning' through the old 'ceremonial dances'.[79]
Modern men have spoiled their instincts by splitting their identities into
selves of 'pure consciousness, pure spirit' who sit as gods at a play
'surveying those selves of clay who are so absurd or so tragic, below'. For
primitive man there was 'no individual, isolated experience'; all experience
came from the undifferentiated 'human bloodstream'. The 'little individual consciousness lording it' was outside his conception of the universe.
In dance, primitive man was in fact asserting his isolated being, though in a
manner unlike the modern. He was dancing 'the glory in power of the man
of single existence'. The difference is that he was a whole self partici-
pating, not a half-self acting and a half-self observing. Fundamentally,
Lawrence rejects the Aristotelian view of drama as 'imitation of an action'.
The ceremonial dance is 'not representing something, not even playing. It
is a soft, subtle *being* something'.[80]

In speaking so of imaginative representation, of 'literature', Lawrence
was still looking for a way to bring the 'primal consciousness' into his
American fiction. But the descriptive sketches brought him up against the
old dilemma. The first concession was simple: to admit that the Indian
consciousness and the white are radically different, that 'one man can
belong to one great way of consciousness only' and that 'acceptance of the
great paradox of human consciousness is the first step to a new accomplishment'.[81] This left him with the next step unresolved: how to find the
common ground of the red consciousness and the white that might open
the way to the new accomplishment.

The other two essays on Indian dance build on the same arguments.
Through dance the Santo Domingos call down the universal energies that
produce their corn, in a ritual of participation rather than invocation.[82]
The Hopis, conveying their message through the snakes they dance with,
put themselves 'into relation with the vast living convulsions of rain and
thunder and sun'.[83] The imagery of the Hopi piece is often near that of
The Plumed Serpent: 'the earth's dark centre holds its dark sun, our source
of isolated being, round which our world coils its folds like a great snake'.[84]

---

[78] *Phoenix* 24–6.   [79] Zytaruk and Boulton, *Letters of D. H. Lawrence*, ii. 90, 114.
[80] 'Indians and Entertainment', *Mornings in Mexico*.
[81] Ibid.   [82] 'Dance of the Sprouting Corn', *Mornings in Mexico*.
[83] 'The Hopi Snake Dance', *Mornings in Mexico*.
[84] Ibid.

The whole cycle of rain ceremonies in *The Plumed Serpent*, including the marriage ritual, issues directly out of these essays.

Of equal importance are three long American stories Lawrence was at last able to produce: 'The Woman Who Rode Away', *St. Mawr* and 'The Princess' serve as preliminary writings to Lawrence's last effort to grasp the meaning of 'America' in fiction.[85] All three heroines are variations on Kate Leslie. In *St. Mawr*, Lou Witt rejects the Indian as lover, and all other men too. She will become a hermit, cultivating union with the spirit of place about her mountain ranch, understanding all the while that this spirit may be devouring as well as sustaining. The 'princess', in her story, magnetised by the dark American lover and the genius of place, toys with both, courting destruction, and in retreating from it causes the death of the lover. In 'The Woman Who Rode Away' the unnamed woman goes to the farthest limit – she seeks out a wild Indian tribe in Mexico and submits as victim in a human sacrifice, a rite that may bring the native spirit of the continent into ascendancy once more.[86]

Lawrence left Taos in mid-October 1924, with Frieda and the Hon. Dorothy Brett, an artist who had been the only one of his friends to accept his offer to join him in starting a new life together in New Mexico. He had already said he must go deeper into Mexico than Chapala, and before leaving England had mentioned Oaxaca, the land of the Mixtecs and the Zapotecs.[87] Within a month of setting out from New Mexico, spending a little time in Mexico City again, he and the two women had arrived in Oaxaca, the Lawrences had taken a house, with Brett at a hotel close by, and he was ready to resume work on his Quetzalcoatl novel, now untouched for over a year.

On 19 November, writing the date on a fly-leaf of the new copybook in which he began, Lawrence went back to his American novel. He had brought with him the manuscript and the typescript of 'Quetzalcoatl'. Either here or earlier in Taos, he made scattered revisions in the typescript, not many in the second half. But the extensive changes already contemplated could not be accomplished, he must have decided, without a

---

[85] 'The Woman Who Rode Away' dates from June 1924, *St. Mawr* from June to September and 'The Princess' from September and October (the first was collected in *The Woman Who Rode Away* and the latter two in *St. Mawr*, ed. Finney, pp. 21–155, 159–96).

[86] DHL originally thought of these three long stories as belonging naturally in one volume (letter to Curtis Brown, 8 October 1924), but 'The Woman Who Rode Away' has always been published with short stories, not in a novelette group.

[87] *Letters*, iv. 541, 545. (The revolution mentioned in the latter was the de la Huerta rebellion.)

total rewriting. Neither the typescript nor the manuscript of 'Quetzalcoatl' has any further place in the composition of the novel.[88]

Changing little in the first two chapters but deepening his vision of Mexico greatly after these, Lawrence wrote his second version as rapidly as he had the first.[89] By 31 December he had filled the first notebook with twelve chapters and the beginning of what was then chapter XIII – 381 manuscript pages – and had begun a second notebook, on a fly-leaf of which he again wrote the date. When this notebook was full, nearing the end and perhaps having no other at hand, he turned the second notebook of 'Quetzalcoatl' upside down and wrote the last thirty-nine pages of the new version at the back. This version came to 806 manuscript pages (Roberts E313c, hereafter MS), compared with 479 for 'Quetzalcoatl'. The only interruption of any significance to the flow of work was four sketches on life around Oaxaca – later to be part of *Mornings in Mexico* – written in mid-December and touching on the character and cosmology of the Mexican Indian in ways closely paralleling Lawrence's pursuit of the same themes in *The Plumed Serpent*.[90]

The date on which Lawrence finished the novel is difficult to determine. On 16 January 1925 he reported that he was 'nearly done' with it, only to repeat that statement on 22 January.[91] Then on 29 January he wrote to Martin Secker, 'I have finished "Quetzalcoatl" – or at least am in the last chapter', and the same day informed Curtis Brown, 'I have done "Quetzal-

---

[88] This typescript is in the Houghton Library, Harvard University.

[89] At some time, besides the works he is known to have read by 1923 (see footnote 49), DHL acquainted himself with the following works, and perhaps others, dealing with the mythology he sought to reconstruct: 'several volumes' of the *Anales* of the National Museum of Mexico – these 'volumes' are monographs of a hundred pages or so; Adolph Bandelier, *The Delight Makers* (New York, 1890) and *The Gilded Man* (New York, 1893); Henry W. Bates, *The Naturalist in Nicaragua* (1863); Alexandre de Humboldt, *Vues des Cordillères et Monuments des Peuples Indigènes de l'Amérique* (Paris, 1810); Zelia Nuttall, *The Fundamental Principles of Old and New World Civilizations: A comparative research based on a study of the ancient Mexican religious, sociological and calendrical systems* (Cambridge, Mass., 1901); Lewis Spence, *The Gods of Mexico* (New York, 1923). DHL had long since read Edward B. Tylor, *Primitive Culture* (1889) and a great deal of James G. Frazer's *The Golden Bough*, 12 vols. (1890–1915). He probably gathered some ideas from Gilbert Murray, *Four Stages of Greek Religion* (1912) and John Burnet, *Early Greek Philosophy* (Edinburgh, 1907). Other works that DHL may have read are suggested in the Explanatory notes. DHL's use of mythology in *The Plumed Serpent* is best characterised by his own description (in 'Foreword' to *Fantasia of the Unconscious*) of how he proceeded in writing about 'cosmology': 'I have found hints, suggestions for what I say here in all kinds of scholarly books . . . I remember only hints – and I proceed by intuition'.

[90] 'Corasmin and the Parrots', 'Walk to Huayapa', 'The Mozo' and 'Market Day' are the 'Mornings in Mexico' as such. The volume that appeared under this title includes several sketches of the southwestern United States.

[91] Letters to Amy Lowell, 16 January 1925 and to Carlo Linati, 22 January 1925.

coatl"'.[92] Conclusive as these assertions appear, they disagree with another that Lawrence made later. In letters written on 30 and 31 January, no mention of the novel occurs, but then none of an illness either, of a sudden and severe attack of fever brought on, Lawrence later suspected, by his struggle with the novel: 'I managed to finish my Mexican novel "Quetzalcoatl" in Mexico: the very day I went down, as if shot in the intestines'.[93] This day may well have been the first of February.[94]

For a time Lawrence despaired of life in Oaxaca and in Mexico City, where he was told he had tuberculosis.[95] His illness was such that he was almost refused entry into the United States. And although during and just after the illness he began a story of a male exile returning to England, started one play and wrote the whole of another, he took a long time to overcome his unwillingness to touch the novel again: 'I daren't even look at the outside of the MS. It cost one so much'.[96]

In MS Lawrence made few changes: some words or lines crossed out, here and there an interlinear revision, a couple of chapter titles altered – some of which may have gone on during the initial composition. Significant revision began with the typescript, which he did not obtain in a complete text for some time. He had taken his own typewriter to Oaxaca, and from the time he began writing, Brett had transcribed some of it in her 'slow, painful typewriting'. She hurried to produce all she could prior to leaving Oaxaca, some two weeks before Lawrence finished MS.[97] Apparently she completed the first six chapters and six pages of the seventh, in a ribbon and a carbon copy.[98] Soon after returning to Taos, at the beginning of April, Lawrence mailed the notebooks containing MS to the New York office of Curtis Brown to be typed, in a ribbon and a carbon copy. Apparently, he did not ask that the first five chapters be done, since these chapters in the eventually complete typescript are still from the Brett typing. He was in no hurry to have the novel back. All through April and into May, still recuperating, he could only 'loathe the thought of having to

[92] Letters to Martin Secker and to Curtis Brown, 29 January 1925.
[93] Letters to A. D. Hawk, 30 January 1925; to Constantine Rickards, 31 January 1925; to Amy Lowell, 6 April 1925.
[94] For a detailed account of Lawrence's illness in Oaxaca, see Ross Parmenter, *Lawrence in Oaxaca* (Salt Lake City, 1984), chap. XII.
[95] Frieda Lawrence, *"Not I, But the Wind . . . "*, pp. 165–7.
[96] Letter to Amy Lowell, 6 April 1925; the writings are 'The Flying-Fish' (*St. Mawr*, ed. Finney, pp. 207–25, see also Earl and Achsah Brewster, *D. H. Lawrence: Reminiscences and Correspondence* (1934), p. 288); the fragment of 'Noah's Flood' (*Phoenix* 811–16); and *David* (begun either in Mexico City or in New Mexico and finished in New Mexico in May; published 1926).
[97] Dorothy Brett, *Lawrence and Brett: A Friendship* (Philadelphia, 1933), pp. 181, 204, 207.
[98] The first part of Roberts E313d and E313e, f and g.

go over it and prune and correct, in typescript'.[99] When he felt up to sustained writing, his first completed work was _David_ – he had felt earlier that he could take a wonderful and terrible play out of _The Plumed Serpent_, but the biblical subject now appealed to him more than the ancient American one.[100]

When the typescript came from New York, not long before 21 May, Lawrence was still in no mood to face revision: 'They urge me to go over the MS., but I feel still that I can't look at it. It smells too much of Oaxaca, which I hated so much because I was so ill.'[101] But some time during the next two weeks he did assemble a complete working typescript. For the first five chapters he used Brett's typescript fragment. These 118 pages are all carbon except for one ribbon page in chapters I, II and IV and four in chapter III; there is no clue as to why these seven ribbon pages were substituted, since the other copy is unlocated. Presumably a corresponding text of the first five chapters – chiefly ribbon with an interleaving of carbon – was held by the Curtis Brown office in New York, together with the carbon of the chapters they had typed, since a complete 'duplicate' typescript in their possession is later mentioned.[102] From the opening of chapter VI to the end, Lawrence utilised the text he had received from Curtis Brown, all of it ribbon copy. In the first five chapters the pages are numbered consecutively, while in the Curtis Brown typescript each chapter has a fresh page-numbering. This composite typescript of 724 pages (hereafter TS) is Roberts E313d.[103]

We do not know why Lawrence asked Curtis Brown to have a new chapter VI typed; he already had a complete text of it and the first six pages of chapter VII, which Brett had typed, in both a ribbon and a carbon copy. At some point, perhaps while waiting for the Curtis Brown transcription, Lawrence made a few changes in this remainder of the Brett fragment. He entered them first on either the ribbon or the carbon pages and then copied them, with further minor alterations, on the other copy. Since in TS, chapter VI and the early pages of chapter VII carry yet another, more extensive set of revisions, it appears that when he had assembled TS, he

[99] Letter to Mollie Skinner, 21 April 1925.

[100] For the dances performed in _David_ (see footnote 96) DHL wrote music heavily influenced by Pueblo Indian music and also by Koteliansky's Hebrew chant 'Ranani Zadikim'; see _Letters_, ii. 252 n. 3. Manuscripts of the _David_ music are in the Dartmouth College Library and the Harry Ransom Humanities Research Center, University of Texas at Austin (Roberts E87.2 a and b).

[101] Letter to Eduardo Rendón, 21 May 1925; see also letter to Blanche Knopf, 23 May 1925.

[102] See letter to Secker, 18 June 1925.

[103] Located at the Harry Ransom Humanities Research Center. The manuscripts of both versions are also there.

simply put aside the pages of the Brett fragment after the end of chapter v. The revisions in these pages have been recorded in the Textual apparatus of this edition but are treated as being superseded by the TS revisions.[104]

In England Secker, and in the USA the new publisher Knopf, wanted the revisions done as soon as possible. By 5 June Lawrence had at least conquered his repugnance so far as to examine the work: 'I went through the "Quetzalcoatl" MS [i.e. TS] – will do a few things to it, and send it on.'[105] Five days later he was saying he had finished the revisions.[106] But he must have reconsidered, for on 18 June he wrote to Secker that he had 'just revised' TS and would be mailing it right away to the New York office of Curtis Brown, and someone there was to enter the 'alterations' on 'the duplicate' and then send a copy to Secker. But even this statement was not conclusive, for on 23 June Lawrence wrote to Curtis Brown that he would be finished 'next week', that is, not before the 29th, since 23 June was a Tuesday. How much longer he worked on TS is uncertain; he may have kept it into July. In any event, Secker had just received it on 30 July – and only afterwards did he issue a written contract.[107] No record remains of a transference of Lawrence's changes to the duplicate of TS at Curtis Brown's New York office, and the duplicate itself has not survived. As later developments show, such a step would have been superfluous.

Despite his claims for the novel's importance, Lawrence was still unsure about the authenticity of his treatment of Mexican themes.[108] Acknowledging receipt of TS from Curtis Brown, Secker wrote: 'I have just had a letter from the author, asking me to have the book set up in slip [galleys], so that he may work on the proofs' – 'freely', according to another Secker letter – 'and I am therefore putting the work in hand forthwith.'[109] The Dunedin Press, Ltd., of Edinburgh, undertook the task at once, from TS (as can be seen by the galley breaks marked in it). By 24 August Secker spoke of 'beginning to send slip proofs to the author' – 'a large batch', as he

---

[104] Roberts E313e and f comprise the ribbon copy; Roberts E313g is the carbon. (E313e is at the Clark Library, University of California at Los Angeles; E313f and g are at the Bancroft Library, University of California at Berkeley.) The 'merely duplicate' fragment referred to in the letter of 14 September 1929 to Willard Johnson is probably one copy of these discarded chapters.

[105] Letter to Blanche Knopf.   [106] Letter to George Conway, 10 June 1925.

[107] Letter from Secker to Michael Joseph of Curtis Brown, London; UIll. The contract is dated 25 August 1925. DHL received an advance of £125 and a graduated scale of royalties from 15 to 25%.

[108] When DHL submitted TS, he wanted to seek advice from two men versed in Mexican culture, Eduardo Rendón and George Conway: he wished them to see proofs and give him their opinions (letters to Curtis Brown, Rendón and Anne Conway, 23 June, 17 and 28 August 1925). The plan proved impractical.

[109] Letters from Secker to Joseph and Knopf, 30 July and 11 September 1925; UIll.

later described them. As he understood Lawrence's intentions, 'until he has worked on these he will not be sending the book to Knopf'.[110] The American printer would thus be working from the corrected English setting, eliminating any need for the duplicate typescript. On 11 September, Secker wrote to Knopf that the last of the galleys had been mailed to Lawrence that day – probably in care of Curtis Brown of New York – adding, 'I believe he is, or shortly will be in New York, and it should be possible for him to leave the corrected proofs with you before he leaves America at the beginning of October.'[111] Secker must have intended to follow the same procedure with *The Plumed Serpent* as he had used the previous year, mailing two sets of proofs of *The Boy in the Bush* to Lawrence in America, with the understanding that he would write his alterations on both sets, return one to Secker, and send the other to Thomas Seltzer.[112] Presumably Lawrence was to deliver the corrected proofs of *The Plumed Serpent* to London himself in early October.

In this instance the timing went wrong. Lawrence had left New Mexico on 10 September. He arrived in New York on 13 September and sailed on the 22nd for England. With only eleven days between the mailing of the last proofs from London and Lawrence's departure from America, it is not likely that he saw a full set of slip galleys until he arrived in England on 30 September. Probably he did see at least the first large batch Secker mailed, since almost a month passed between the day they were sent from London and the day Lawrence sailed from New York, although he does not refer to any proofs of the novel when writing to Blanche Knopf while he was in New York, sending her the corrected proofs of an essay.[113] It is highly probable, also, that the two surviving sets of galleys (Roberts E313h, henceforth G), one set uncorrected and the other lightly gone over, are those which Secker expected Lawrence to revise in New York, not wholly assembled until after Lawrence was gone.[114] The few changes in the G text are faintly done in pencil and impossible to identify with certainty. They consist mainly of a few horizontal lines and brackets and sizeable X's in the margins, quite often at points where revisions were made in the final proofs. More puzzling is the presence of a few minor substantive changes

---

[110] Letters from Secker to Joseph and Knopf, 24 August and 11 September 1925; UIll.
[111] UIll.
[112] Letter from Secker to DHL, 3 April 1924; UIll (Martin Secker, ed., *Letters from a Publisher: Martin Secker to D. H. Lawrence and Others, 1911–1929* (1970), p. 20).
[113] Letter to Blanche Knopf, 21 September 1925; see also letter to her of 18 April 1925. The essay was 'Accumulated Mail' for Knopf's *Borzoi* of 1925, subtitled 'Being a sort of record of ten years publishing'.
[114] Located at the Harry Ransom Humanities Research Center.

pencilled in the margins in a hand that may be Lawrence's, though the evidence is not sufficient for such a conclusion. Most of these are essential corrections already incorporated into the published text. The only change accepted editorially in the present edition is that of a place-name, on other grounds than possible authorial revision.[115]

Lawrence must have begun to work on an entirely new set of galleys from Secker about 1 October, for he was on the verge of completing them by the 16th.[116] On 20 October he wrote to Knopf that he had mailed the finished proofs to Secker and that Knopf should be receiving 'a revised set very soon now'. Secker promptly had Lawrence's changes transferred to another set of galleys and mailed them to Knopf on 23 October, saying, 'your printers will now be able to go straight ahead. There is no occasion for Lawrence to see revises.'[117]

The complex process of *The Plumed Serpent*'s composition – Lawrence's moving about the world during the time, his reluctance to undertake any revision after illness struck, a decision to complete final proofs quickly after proposing to revise extensively – sometimes makes Lawrence's intentions regarding accidentals obscure. With underlining, hyphenation, even spelling, his practices often seem haphazard, and his offhand attitude in these matters is confirmed by two letters concerning final proofs. The first is to Martin Secker on 16 October 1925: 'In the proofs, the word *serape* is spelt half the time *sarape*. Both ways are correct, it's an Indian word. But ought one to stick to one form? God knows why I changed. I began sarape, wrote serape for thirty or forty galleys, then went back to sarape. Bore!' The second letter, to Alfred Knopf, is dated 20 October: 'Another thing is the word *serape*: which is spelt so often *sarape*, that I simply didn't face altering it. Both ways are correct: it's an Indian word for a blanket that you wear: but *serape* is now commoner. God knows why I changed from one to the other. If you think it matters, tell the printers to set the one form, will you?'

What happened was that Secker did not regularise, so that the E1 text contains both spellings as Lawrence wrote them – actually he shifted back and forth throughout the text. Knopf attempted regularisation to 'serape', but in a number of instances 'sarape' was overlooked. Lawrence's statement that 'serape' was 'now commoner' is misleading. The word in

---

115 See Explanatory note on 84:17.
116 Letter to Secker, 16 October 1925. While correcting the proofs at his sister Ada Clarke's home in Ripley, DHL discovered that the next-to-last galley, number 156, was missing from his set. He wrote asking Secker to send another at once. Since he did not ask for two of this galley, he was not himself making a copy of the proofs to be sent to Knopf.
117 Letter from Secker to Knopf; UIll.

Spanish is 'sarape'. The loan-word in English is 'serape' – though in rare instances the Spanish spelling also occurs. In the present edition 'sarape' has been silently adopted throughout, both because Lawrence wrote that form most often and because he employs the word in a Spanish context.

A close study of the novel's text makes it evident that Lawrence's indifference to spelling extended also to italicisation and hyphenation, leading to variations in form where no reasonable standards of judgment can discover any intended variations of meaning. The result often leads to mere distraction of the reader. Since the letters quoted clearly authorise an editor to regularise erratic practices if he thinks it 'matters', some regularisation has been adopted in the present edition, as formulated in the 'Note on the text'.

The two publishers had agreed that Knopf would produce the book as quickly as possible so that Secker would not have to delay his publication date too much.[118] By 6 November Knopf had received his copy of the final proofs and could confirm 23 January 1926 as a feasible date for simultaneous release in London and New York.[119] Knopf used the Vail-Ballou Press of Binghamton, New York, who set up new plates. Secker published the novel on 21 January, while Knopf, with only two and a half months for production, could not release the American edition until 5 February.[120]

Revisions and base-text

Brett's chapters of TS are filled with the mistakes of an inexpert typist: strike-overs, misspellings, letters dropped, omission of word endings and punctuation at the right-hand margin, changes of wording and omissions of text ranging from a word to a paragraph. The typists for Curtis Brown – at least two – turned out more professional copy, but still made many similar errors. They took greater liberties than Brett with punctuation,

---

[118] Letters from Secker to Curtis Brown, 24 September and 10 November 1925; UIll.

[119] Letter from Secker to Knopf, 17 November 1925.

[120] Roberts 87–8. Brett had made drawings for a dust jacket of *The Plumed Serpent*, based on motifs taken from Spence (opposite p. 118 and opposite p. 120). The front cover is a group of Mexicans in large sombreros surrounding a figure of Quetzalcoatl as he appears in an Aztec codex (see Roberts, p. 427). On the spine is also a figure of a Mexican god taken from a codex. DHL drew an emblem of a circular serpent with an eagle displayed inside the circle, as described in chap. XI (pp. 170–4). (All of these drawings are in Butler Library, Columbia University.) Knopf used the Brett dust jacket and stamped DHL's design on the front cover, but Secker issued his edition in his usual plain brown boards with a plain cream-coloured wrapper. See DHL's letters to Knopf, 4 May 1925 and to Brett, 25 November 1925 and 16 February 1926; P. P. Howe to Secker, 5 January 1926, University of Texas.

frequently replacing Lawrence's colons with semi-colons and dropping his dashes. As usual, working on TS without checking it against MS, Lawrence often missed the less evident but more significant errors, such as the omission or alteration of substantive text. And as long as the punctuation made sense, he did little toward restoring his own. If we take into account the house-styling by Secker and Knopf and further regularisation by the printers, it must be concluded that for punctuation MS is the most authoritative text.

Substantive revisions may be seen under two headings: those Lawrence made in accurately transcribed text, and those he made when inaccurate typing produced a reading not in accord with the sense of the text or else a nonsense reading. In revision in TS of accurately transcribed text – thus motivated purely by change of intention – Lawrence made many small changes and deleted some passages, few of them more than a page, sometimes writing a replacement passage (see Textual apparatus entries for 66:13, 73:13 and 348:25). The only deletion of any length until late in the book covers about three pages of typescript (see entry for 78:13). He was nominally busy with TS for more than a month – almost half as much time as he had spent in creating MS – but the number of changes does not point to this much actual time spent at work. Possibly, as a statement by Frieda suggests, Lawrence was some while in making up his mind about how to end the novel.[121] In the penultimate chapter he rejected about three pages of TS, and he rewrote nearly eighty per cent of the last chapter, scrapping TS and inserting new pages done on his own typewriter. When he came to the final proofs he made other extensive alterations in the last chapter, as well as a few earlier in the book (for the latter, see Textual apparatus entries for 136:12, 399:22 and 414:21). All these final changes are readily verifiable even though the Secker and the Knopf final proofs have both disappeared, since Secker's slightly corrected slip galley (G) is extant and has been collated with the published text of the first English edition (E1). Substantive variants between the G and E1 texts are assumed to be Lawrence's revisions. Revised punctuation in E1 has been given greater weight because it is possible that it was corrected by Lawrence.

The final chapter was totally reshaped. The first few paragraphs (426:3 – 427:7) remain nearly intact from MS to publication. Then, in MS, Ramón expounds a message in symbols to Kate similar to that in 'Quetzalcoatl', which she is to take to the European nations, on how to reawaken their primitive gods (see Textual apparatus entry for 427:9).

---

[121] See Frieda Lawrence, *"Not I, But the Wind . . ."*, p. 165.

The replacement in TS was a dialogue between Kate and Ramón, but Lawrence deleted in proof the middle third of this, a heated exchange that almost led to a parting of ways for them, and substituted Kate's self-questioning and her feeling of being compelled by Ramón and Cipriano (TS entry in 427:9). This revision leads more naturally to the ending of the passage, in which Ramón just goes quietly away. The next scene, the loading of the cow and the bull onto the *canoa*, is little changed from 'Quetzalcoatl'. Then MS had a brief passage stressing Kate's mission to the outer world, from which Teresa believes she will return fully committed to the reborn Mexico (see apparatus entry for 433:18). Lawrence inserted in TS the scene emphasising Kate's militancy and independence, and showed a clear rivalry between the two women. The following scene concerns Kate's absorption with the human and animal life in this lakeside land – again essentially from MS and little different from 'Quetzalcoatl'. But from 436:23 to the end of the novel, Lawrence replaced with the present ending the four closing pages of MS in which Ramón reiterates his charge to Kate in symbolic language (see apparatus entry for 436:23). He also made other, small changes at proof stage, but the only truly important one was to substitute 'You won't let me go!' for the French phrase 'Le gueux m'a plantée là' in the very last sentence.[122] Thus the original ending of the second version presented Kate about to leave Mexico with only the possibility of her return (much as in 'Quetzalcoatl') while the final revision shows Kate staying on, magnetised by Cipriano and Ramón, but still somewhat sceptical of their vision of the future.

These substantive changes are clearly authoritative: in each state of the text the author's later intention obviously supersedes the former. But those revisions that were influenced by errors in transmission are another matter. If Lawrence had had a correct transcription of MS in the TS text, we may assume that he would not have revised as he did at these points. At the time of writing MS, he had a concept of the novel as a whole which he no longer enjoyed during later revision, when he concentrated only on a few passages. When he made changes not from a desire to reshape his original text but because of extraneous influence, greater authority must be accorded to the original readings. MS should consequently take precedence over later states in instances where changes occurred without Lawrence's consent and also, in most cases, where his own substantive revisions were provoked by a typist's mistranscription from MS. Exceptions have been made to this procedure when Lawrence's changes extend

---

[122] G 157. The French phrase ('The rascal left me standing there') is described as 'the words of an old song', but it is unidentified.

beyond smoothing the text, into rewriting traceable to new intention. With all stages of change taken into consideration, MS has been chosen as base-text for the present edition, yielding only to later revisions in TS and E1 clearly attributable to a change of authorial purpose. Since Lawrence had no hand in Knopf's edition (A1), this text has no authority.

Reception

Even when he was writing *The Plumed Serpent*, Lawrence dreaded 'to think of its going out into the world'.[123] On the eve of publication he felt he 'could weep' to see it fall 'into the tuppenny hands of the tuppenny public'.[124] Yet he maintained that the novel would 'stand a lot of wear'.[125] And surely he was preparing a defence, when after revising TS he turned out four essays on the meaning and purpose of the modern novel – these, with the one written shortly before he began 'Quetzalcoatl', being all he ever produced on the art of fiction.[126] His publishers were no more optimistic than he was about how the book would be received, Secker writing to Knopf: 'I agree with you that it cannot be popular, but it is a book to which Lawrence himself attaches great importance'.[127]

Unsympathetic reviewers of *The Plumed Serpent* were not as numerous as Lawrence had feared. Only a few condemned it out of hand, and at least as many praised it as a strikingly original work. Between these limits, reviewers often applied superlatives to faults as well as to virtues in the same review.

J. W. Crawford in the *New York World* came close to unreserved admiration for the novel, and Charles Marriott in the *Manchester Guardian* was not far behind him. Crawford described Lawrence as 'a farouche intellectual pirate', and drew from his vision 'a hard, clear kernel of profound meditation upon the deeply inner significance of human conduct'. *The Plumed Serpent* was 'a challenge to profound reflection, a touching of all but submerged responses'.[128] The religious drama was also convincing to Marriott: 'all the passages treating of the relationship between the two religions are touched with extreme beauty of feeling'. For him 'the people and their surroundings are made extraordinarily real', and the novelist created

---

123 Letter to Carlo Linati, 22 January 1925.
124 Letter to Harold Mason, 1 February 1926.
125 Letter to Knopf, 20 October 1925.
126 'Morality and the Novel', 'Why the Novel Matters', 'The Novel and the Feelings' and 'The Novel' (*Study of Thomas Hardy*, ed. Steele, pp. 171–6, 193–205, 179–90).
127 23 October 1925; UIll.   128 *New York World*, 7 February 1926, p.6.

the impression that he was always on the verge of discovering all that he sought in the depths of human nature.[129]

On the opposite side of the question were C. H. Rickword's assessment in the *Calendar of Modern Letters* and an unsigned review in the *Spectator*. Rickword pronounced the work 'a continuous falsification of reality'. Its metaphysics was a 'sentimental vulgarization of the ordinary dualism of subject and object, togged up in the tawdry finery of emotive (often erotic) symbolism'. The affair between Kate and Cipriano might be 'made respectable by elevation' to heroic stature, but still the descriptions of it were 'nauseating in the extreme'. The language would not have mattered, even so, 'if the device of representing it as reported introspection were at all successful'. But here, as throughout the novel, the 'absence of detachment' prevented verisimilitude. Except for a few passages, the novel was a tract in which 'the fervour of the missionary overcame the integrity of the artist'.[130] The reviewer in the *Spectator*, who shared a widespread sentiment that Lawrence had been going downhill since *Sons and Lovers*, thought *The Plumed Serpent* 'bewilderingly romantic', and 'the all-important presence of sex' a sign of 'girlish hysteria'. Lawrence's characters were 'phantoms of his own fancy', and the message of the 'fanciful religious speculation' was 'paltry'. And surely the book did not mean to suggest that America could solve its problems 'by reviving folk-dances and invoking the old gods of the Indians'.[131] The political theme touched on in this review was seldom mentioned in others; such attention to the novel came largely after fascism emerged as a dominant force in the world.

A more balanced review appeared in *The Times Literary Supplement*, where A. S. McDowall stated perceptively that Lawrence had become a novelist for whom places were symbols in which he sought answers to the riddles of his spirit. In Mexico he had discovered 'a singular and apt embodiment for some of his conceptions', and the resulting novel was 'a remarkable *tour de force*'. McDowall granted what few others did: that the characters were credible. Further, Lawrence had 'deftly interwoven his drama of religion with the fates of all the characters'. But then came qualifications which, like those of other reviewers, border on contradiction. The novel had too much 'weight to carry' in ideas, with sexual symbols so abstract they were sometimes 'absurd'. And 'psychological subtlety' was strained in bringing Kate across a gulf to unite with Cipriano

---

[129] *Manchester Guardian*, 29 January 1926, p. 9. See R. P. Draper, ed., *D. H. Lawrence: The Critical Heritage* (1970), pp. 263–4.
[130] April 1926, pp. 77–9.   [131] 30 January 1926, p. 182.

– apparently an exception to the skill in character creation.[132] Lawrence thought this review 'rather feeble'.[133]

Reaching a balanced evaluation often meant an attempt to reconcile great disparities between the novel's elements. In the London *Saturday Review*, L. P. Hartley spoke of Lawrence as 'obsessed by the idea of fusion' between his characters, yet he gave us only a 'game of blind man's buff played by confirmed solipsists' condemned to 'mutual inaccessibility'. But though he might fail in writing of people, Lawrence was superb in the creation of things, as though 'he had the consciousness of a dozen men at his command'. Hartley gave hesitant approval to the religious vision. However obscure the rites and the 'tremendous apparatus of mysticism' might be, Lawrence made them 'almost credible'.[134]

Two other reviewers who dealt with the contradictions of *The Plumed Serpent* by appealing to the poetic genius behind the language were Edwin Muir in the *Nation and Athenæum* and Donald Douglas in the *Nation* (New York). According to Muir, the setting, the myth with its metaphysics and the story of Kate never reached coherence. The book read as though Nietzsche had chosen to express his philosophy in a novel, and had included a guide to the Riviera. A novel with a 'message' cannot succeed, whereas a long poem can. If the whole concept had been shaped into a volume of the hymns, with their 'greater profundity' than any of Lawrence's writing to date, the outcome might have been 'magnificent'. Then, with some inconsistency, Muir went further than Hartley in saying that the fictional religion did come through as credible, 'by sheer loftiness of inspiration'.[135] Douglas, who like Hartley judged the characters to be distorted, and who detested Lawrence's 'missionary zeal and his metaphysical divinations', could still assert that the book contained 'passages of miraculous wonder and words like arrows tipped with light borrowed from the sun'. Douglas's conclusion, echoing Blake, was that 'the crooked roads which cannot be made straight are the roads of genius.'[136]

The *Living Age* in its column 'Book of the Month' undertook to balance opinions of the novel in a context of Lawrence's artistic growth and reputation: 'Judgments of Mr. Lawrence's work have been, from the beginning, as various and irreconcilable as its judges'. The severe review from the *Spectator* and one classified as laudatory from the *Daily Telegraph* were then cited – in fact, the *Telegraph* reviewer qualified his general

132 21 January 1926, p. 41.   133 Letter to Dorothy Brett, 25 January 1926.
134 30 January 1926, p.129. See Draper, ed., *Critical Heritage*, pp. 265–6.
135 *Nation and Athenæum*, 20 February 1926, p. 719.
136 *Nation*, 17 March 1926, p. 291. See Blake's *The Marriage of Heaven and Hell*, plate 10, line 6.

admiration by judging Kate to be 'a hollow figure which Mr. Lawrence stuffs out with theory'.[137] The *Living Age* then reprinted in full H. C. Harwood's 'judicious' review from the *Outlook* (London). Harwood characterised *The Plumed Serpent* as 'profoundly obscure, and often tedious' but with moments of 'fierce, intuitional understanding, parallels with which can be found in no other living writer'. Plainly Harwood was uncertain about where the novel stood in Lawrence's development, suggesting that *Women in Love* was better than *Sons and Lovers*, but as for later work, he stated only that *The Plumed Serpent* showed no advance beyond *Kangaroo*.[138]

Disappointment with the progress of a prominent writer was often the tone of those looking back on Lawrence's career. The *Adelphi* reviewer wondered whether Lawrence had lost faith in his imagination, and the *Dial* saw nothing new in the book, implying a decline from previous accomplishment.[139] Reviewers like Elizabeth Shipley in the New York *Saturday Review of Literature* and 'M.H.' in the *New Republic* attributed the falling-off to Lawrence's inability to rise above his raging dissatisfaction. He was no longer a novelist, the reviewer in the *New Republic* wrote, but 'a frantic, agonized seeker after mysteries'.[140] Elizabeth Shipley followed the pattern of paying general tribute to Lawrence's power and originality, then lamenting the disappearance of the author of *Sons and Lovers* and *Sea and Sardinia*. She went on to deplore *The Plumed Serpent* as 'a book of hate, tense, parched, unsatisfied, full of deep rancor and unrest', a work that was 'less a picture of Mexico than an almost demented state of homesickness'.[141]

One reviewer who attempted to look more deeply into the probings of *The Plumed Serpent* was Percy Hutchinson in the *New York Times Book Review*. He saw the novel's analysis of human character as comparable to that of *Women in Love*, and understood the symbolic nature of its events, whose 'underlying purpose' was substantiated in another form in *Reflections on the Death of a Porcupine* (Philadelphia, 1925). Recognising in Lawrence the 'striving for something really important' in our time, he saw in the book's prophetic utterance the 'flashing color and austere passions of the books of the Hebrew prophets'. But for all their power, these utterances remained 'the fumblings of a powerful and brilliant, yet sadly befuddled, intellect'.[142]

---

[137] *Living Age* (Boston, 4 April 1926), p. 75; *Daily Telegraph*, 29 January 1926, p. 15.
[138] *Outlook*, 30 January 1926, p. 74.
[139] August 1926, p. 138; June 1926, p. 520.   [140] 17 February 1926, p. 363.
[141] *Saturday Review of Literature*, 24 April 1926, p. 735.
[142] 7 February 1926, p. 5.

One of the most important reviews was by Katherine Anne Porter, in the *New York Herald Tribune*, because of her own Mexican experience and the significant fiction she had written out of it. Lawrence was now in a new world of fiction, and Kate, in a 'last upsurge of romantic sex-hunger', could 'touch the darkly burning Indian mystery'. Yet she could not cross the gulf, and was only hampered by the 'fanatic vision' of Ramón, the 'cumbrous machinery' of the ritual, the 'high-sounding nonsense' of the poetry. None of this 'artificial Western mysticism' could bring the seeker any closer to the 'truly occult mind' of the Indian. When Porter went on to say, like several others, that since *Sons and Lovers* a 'catastrophe' had overtaken Lawrence, it might be expected that she would conclude that *The Plumed Serpent* was a failure. But she too was impressed by Lawrence's language: 'flexible as a whiplash, uneven and harmonious as breakers rolling on a beach, and the sound is music'. With this, Lawrence made the reader a 'radiant gift' of Mexico. In words reminiscent of Hartley and Muir, she asserted that 'out of his confusions, the divisions of his mind, he has gained by sheer poetic power to a fine order, a mystical truth above his obsessions and debased occult dogma'.[143]

Publishing history

Secker sold out the first printing of 3,000 copies of *The Plumed Serpent* before the end of 1926 and ordered a second printing of 500. In March 1927 he added the novel in the same setting to his Thin Paper Pocket Editions and kept both formats in print in succeeding years. It is difficult to tell which edition sold in larger numbers, but Secker reprinted the novel in one or the other in 1928, 1930, 1932 and 1933. Lawrence was not consulted about either of the first two reprints. When William Heinemann took over publication of most of Lawrence's titles in 1935, he issued only one format, again a reprint of the original English edition, but demand was so small by now that no new printing was needed until 1948.[144]

---

[143] 7 March 1926, pp. 1–2; see Draper, ed., *Critical Heritage*, pp. 268–71. *The Plumed Serpent* was also reviewed in *Booklist*, May 1926, p. 331; *The Bookman*, March 1926, p. 99; *Boston Transcript*, 24 February 1926, p. 4; *Cleveland Open Shelf*, April 1926, p. 53; *The Laughing Horse*, April 1926, pp. 23–9 – in this review Mabel Luhan writes about DHL the man versus DHL the artist, with little to say on the novel itself; *Literary Digest International Book Review*, March 1926, p. 247; *New York Evening Post Literary Review*, 20 February 1926, p. 3; *London Mercury*, April 1926, p. 549; *New Statesman*, 30 January 1926, p. 481.

[144] In March 1950 Penguin brought out an edition for which the text was reset. In 1955 Heinemann published *The Plumed Serpent* in their Phoenix edition, with an introduction by Richard Aldington, in a new setting. The Phoenix edition, which descends from E1, has remained in print to the present time. In 1983 Penguin issued a new edition in their English Library, edited by Ronald G. Walker.

In America, Knopf had to reprint the novel within a month of its publication, but did not reprint again until he issued his 'cheaper edition' in January 1933. Then in 1949 he allowed the work to go out of print, until April 1951 – less than three years before the American copyright would have expired under the United States law then in effect – when he published a new edition, from the same plates, with an introduction by William York Tindall.[145] None of the later printings was large, either in England or the USA, so that *The Plumed Serpent* has been, almost from the beginning, one of the least read of Lawrence's major works.

Lawrence's near-silence after publication of *The Plumed Serpent* was perhaps a sign that his belief in its importance was diminishing. Except for three comments, most of his remarks about the novel were oblique. In July 1926 he commented in a letter: 'They've translated *Plumed Serpent* into Swedish. Hope it'll bite 'em.'[146] And his reaction to Secker's Thin Paper Edition was 'I do like the little red books. Perhaps now the little dull people will manage to read them, in that cosy and familiar form.'[147]

The most emphatic statement Lawrence made about the novel after its appearance came in response to Witter Bynner's questioning of the book's political ideals:

I sniffed the red herring in your last letter a long time: then at last decide it's a live sprat. I mean about the *Plumed Serpent* and the 'hero.' On the whole, I think you're right. The hero is obsolete, and the leader of men is a back number. After all, at the back of the hero is the militant ideal: and the militant ideal, or the ideal militant, seems to me also a cold egg. We're sort of sick of all forms of militarism and militantism, and *Miles* is a name no more, for a man. On the whole I agree with you, the leader-cum-follower relationship is a bore. And the new relationship will be some sort of tenderness, sensitive, between men and men and men and women, and not the one up one down, lead on I follow, ich dien sort of business.[148]

This assertion is often taken as Lawrence's total repudiation of what he had attempted in his American novel, and is set off against another

---

[145] It was reprinted in February 1952, June 1959 and August 1963; the hardcover was available until 1978. Knopf also issued a Vintage paperback, in a new setting, in September 1955, which is still in print in the USA. All these editions derive from A1. It has not been possible to determine the size of any of these printings because when Knopf transferred the printing of the work to another company in 1952, Vail-Ballou destroyed the records of the title (letter to the editor, 6 April 1977).

[146] Letter to Dorothy Brett, 7 July 1926.

[147] Letter to Secker, 29 April 1927. (*Women in Love* and *Sea and Sardinia* were also being reissued in this format.)

[148] Letter to Bynner, 13 March 1928. DHL and Bynner had long been at odds over political matters, Bynner being a professed Socialist. Cf. also DHL's attempt at apology for portraying Bynner as he did in the novel, in his letter of 27 January 1926.

assertion made in a letter to Secker as the novel was about to appear: 'Tell the man, very nice man, in your office, I *do* mean what Ramón means – for all of us.'[149] Nevertheless, even though Lawrence's absorption in *Lady Chatterley's Lover* at the time of the letter to Bynner had tempered his political outlook, a declaration made in mid-1929 also has an important bearing on *The Plumed Serpent*. Lawrence had been discussing with Frieda's sister Else Jaffe the possibility of her translating the novel into German, and what he said about his work in general applies without question to *The Plumed Serpent*: 'You say *satanisch*. Perhaps you are right; Lucifer is brighter now than tarnished Michael or shabby Gabriel. All things fall in their turn, now Michael goes down, and whispering Gabriel, and the Son of the Morning will laugh at them all. Yes, I am all for Lucifer, who is really the Morning Star.'[150]

[149] 16 October 1925.
[150] 12 June 1929. See also letters of 12 October 1926 and 28 October 1927.

THE PLUMED SERPENT
(QUETZALCOATL)

Note on the text

The base-text for this edition is DHL's autograph manuscript (MS), completed in Oaxaca, Mexico at the end of January or beginning of February 1925. MS and the following texts are all in the possession of the Harry Ransom Humanities Research Center, University of Texas at Austin. MS has been emended as follows: (1) from DHL's revisions (TSR) in a typescript (TS) made from MS; (2) from the first English edition (E1), which incorporates DHL's changes in the unlocated final proofs; (3) for correction of errors and one editorial acceptance (84:17), from two sets of largely untouched galley proofs (G). Regularisation has been adopted as follows:

1 Inconsistent spelling, hyphenation and capitalisation have been regularised in accord with DHL's most frequent practice. With 'god' and its plural, since DHL's capital G's are hard to identify, the word is capitalised when a proper noun is plainly called for.

2 If DHL underlined a foreign word or phrase within an English sentence a number of times, with the apparent intention of making it stand out as a foreign expression, all such occurrences have been italicised. If he seldom underlined such a word or phrase, then all occurrences have been romanised. When reporting speech in Spanish, DHL sometimes underlined and sometimes not, for no apparent reason; all such speech has been italicised. For ritual prose and poetry, DHL's purpose in underlining is obscure. While his practice has been largely adhered to, regularisation has been imposed when he underlined elements early in long ritual passages and then discontinued underlining elements of identical structure later in the passage.

All the foregoing changes are recorded in the Textual apparatus.

The following emendations have been made silently:

1 In the English, obvious errors in spelling have been corrected. Incorrect spellings in Spanish and other foreign languages have been silently corrected in the final text, but if such misspellings occur in a preferred reading in the apparatus, correction by editorial intervention has been recorded.

2 DHL's majority practice of omitting internal quotation marks for speech within speech has been silently adopted throughout the text. For speech of more than one paragraph, DHL ordinarily placed double quotation marks only at the beginning of the first and the end of the last paragraph. Reminder quotation marks have been placed at the opening of

each intermediate paragraph. Quotation marks entered through house-styling of inset verse have been removed.

3 With poetry and ritual dialogue, spacing, indentation and line or stanza breaks have been silently restored to the most frequent practice of the base-text, except that when DHL revised these in a later text the variants have been recorded.

4 When drawing a line under a word, DHL rarely extended it under the following punctuation. Italicisation of such punctuation has been carried out as necessary.

5 Accidental omissions have been restored only in the case of incomplete quotation marks, final stops and apostrophes in colloquial contractions. Misplaced apostrophes have also been corrected.

6 DHL divided chapter XII in TSR, making a new chapter XIII. The resulting discrepancy in chapter numbering between MS and the other texts from here to the end of the book has not been recorded in the Textual apparatus. The house-styling of chapter numbers and titles in E1 and A1 has not been recorded. The form of DHL's chapter numbers and titles, and also hymn titles, has been silently restored, with stops added after the titles where he omitted them in MS.

7 DHL's corrections of typing errors, e.g. missing letters of words cut off at the right margin, have not been recorded unless they resulted in an error in transmission.

8 DHL's dashes following terminal punctuation and preceding capitals, e.g. 21:40 'taxi.—You', were frequently omitted in TS or in G; these have been silently restored.

9 DHL's 'today', 'tomorrow' and 'tonight', 'Labor' and 'Fifi' and 'Fifis' became 'to-day', 'to-morrow' and 'to-night', 'Labour' and 'fifi' and 'fifis' in G; his original form has been restored, and exceptions recorded.

Contents

Chapter I.

Beginnings of a Bull-fight.*

It was the Sunday after Easter, and the last bull-fight of the season in Mexico City. Four special bulls had been brought over from Spain for the occasion, since Spanish bulls are more fiery than Mexican. 5 Perhaps it is the altitude, perhaps just the spirit of the western continent which is to blame for the lack of "pep," as Owen put it, in the native animal.

Although Owen, who was a great socialist, disapproved of bull-fights, "We have never seen one. We shall have to go," he said. 10

"Oh yes, I think we must see it," said Kate.*

"And it's our last chance," said Owen.

Away he rushed to the place where they sold tickets, to book seats, and Kate went with him. As she came into the street, her heart sank. It was as if some little person inside her were sulking and resisting. 15 Neither she nor Owen spoke much Spanish, there was a fluster at the ticket place, and an unpleasant individual came forward to talk American for them.

It was obvious they ought to buy tickets for the "Shade." But they wanted to economise, and Owen said he preferred to sit among the 20 crowd, therefore, against the resistance of the ticket man and the onlookers, they bought reserved seats in the "Sun."

The show was on Sunday afternoon. All the tram-cars and the frightful little Ford omnibuses called *camiones* were labelled *Toreo*, and were surging away towards Chapultepec.* Kate felt that sudden 25 dark feeling, that she didn't want to go.

"I'm not very keen on going," she said to Owen.

"Oh but why not? I don't believe in them on principle, but we've never seen one, so we shall *have* to go."

Owen was an American, Kate was Irish. "Never having seen one" 30 meant "having to go." But it was American logic rather than Irish, and Kate only let herself be overcome.

Villiers of course was keen. But then he too was American, and he too had never seen one, and being younger, he more than anybody *had* to go. 35

They got into a Ford taxi and went. The busted car careered away down the wide dismal street of asphalt and stone and Sunday dreariness. Stone buildings in Mexico have a peculiar hard, dry dreariness.

5 The taxi drew up in a side street under the big iron scaffolding of the stadium. In the gutters, rather lousy men were selling pulque and sweets, cakes, fruit, and greasy food. Crazy motor-cars rushed up and hobbled away. Little soldiers in washed-out cotton uniforms, pinky drab, hung around an entrance. Above all loomed the network

10 iron frame of the huge, ugly stadium.

Kate felt she was going to prison. But Owen excitedly surged to the entrance that corresponded to his ticket. In the depths of him, he too didn't want to go. But he was a born American, and if anything was on show, he had to see it. That was "life."

15 The man who took tickets at the entrance suddenly, as they were passing in, stood in front of Owen, put both his hands on Owen's chest and pawed down the front of Owen's body. Owen startled, bridled, transfixed for a moment. The fellow stood aside. Kate remained petrified.

20 Then Owen jerked into a smiling composure as the man waved them on.

"Feeling for fire-arms!" he said, rolling his eyes with pleased excitement at Kate.

But she had not yet got over the shock of horror, fearing the lout

25 might paw her.

They emerged out of a tunnel in the hollow of the concrete-and-iron amphitheatre. A real gutter-lout came to look at their counter-slips, to see which seats they had booked. He jerked his head downwards, and slouched off. Now Kate knew she was in a trap—a

30 big concrete beetle-trap.

They dropped down the concrete steps till they were only three tiers from the bottom. That was their row. They were to sit on the concrete, with a loop of thick iron between each numbered seat. This was a reserved place in the "Sun."

35 Kate sat gingerly between her two iron loops, and looked vaguely around.

"I think it's thrilling!" she said.

Like most modern people, she had a will-to-happiness.

"Isn't it thrilling!" cried Owen, whose will-to-happiness was

40 almost a mania. "Don't you think so, Bud?"

"Why, yes, I think it may be," said Villiers, non-committal.

But then Villiers was young, he was only over twenty, while Owen was over forty. The younger generation calculates its "happiness" in a more business-like fashion. Villiers was out after a thrill, but he wasn't going to say he'd got one till he'd got it. Kate and Owen— Kate was also nearly forty—must enthuse a thrill, out of a sort of politeness to the great Show-man, Providence.

"Look here!" said Owen. "Supposing we try to protect our extremity on this concrete—" and thoughtfully he folded his rain-coat and laid it along the concrete ledge so that both he and Kate could sit on it.

They sat and gazed around. They were early. Patches of people mottled the concrete slope opposite, like eruptions. The ring just below was vacant, neatly sanded; and above the ring, on the encircling concrete, great advertisements for hats, with a picture of a city-man's straw hat, and advertisements for spectacles, with pairs of spectacles supinely folded, glared and shouted.

"Where is the 'Shade,' then?" said Owen, twisting his neck.

At the top of the amphitheatre, near the sky, were concrete boxes. This was the "Shade," where anybody who was anything sat.

"Oh but," said Kate, "I don't want to be perched right up there, so far away."

"Why no!" said Owen. "We're much better where we are, in our 'Sun,' which isn't going to shine a great deal after all."

The sky was cloudy, preparing for the rainy season.

It was nearly three o'clock in the afternoon, and the crowd was filling in, but still only occupied patches of the bare concrete. The lower tiers were reserved, so the bulk of the people sat in the mid-way levels, and gentry like our trio were more or less isolated.

But the audience was already a mob, mostly of fattish town men in black tight suits and little straw hats, and a mixing-in of the dark-faced laborers in big hats. The men in black suits were probably employees and clerks and factory hands. Some had brought their women, in sky-blue chiffon with brown chiffon hats and faces powdered to look like white marshmallows. Some were families with two or three children.

The fun began. The game was to snatch the hard straw hat off some fellow's head, and send it skimming away down the slope of humanity, where some smart bounder down below would catch it and send it skimming across in another direction. There were shouts

of jeering pleasure from the mass, which rose almost to a yell as
seven straw hats were skimming meteor-like at one moment, across
the slope of people.

"Look at that!" said Owen. "Isn't that fun!"

5   "No," said Kate, her little *alter ego* speaking out for once, in spite
of her will-to-happiness. "No, I don't like it. I really hate common
people."

As a socialist, Owen disapproved, and as a happy man, he was
disconcerted. Because his own real self, as far as he had any left,
10   hated common rowdiness just as much as Kate did.

"It's awfully smart though!" he said, trying to laugh in sympathy
with the mob. "There now, see that!"

"Yes, it's quite smart, but I'm glad it's not my hat," said Villiers.

"Oh, it's all in the game," said Owen largely.

15   But he was uneasy. He was wearing a big straw hat of native
make, conspicuous in the comparative isolation of the lower tiers.
After a lot of fidgeting, he took off this hat and put it on his knee.
But unfortunately he had a very definite bald spot on a sunburnt
head.

20   Behind, above, sat a dense patch of people in the unreserved
section. Already they were throwing things. *Bum!* came an orange,
aimed at Owen's bald spot, but hitting him on the shoulder. He
glared round rather ineffectually through his big shell spectacles.

"I'd keep my hat on if I were you," said the cold voice of Villiers.

25   "Yes, I think perhaps it's wiser," said Owen, with assumed nonchalance, putting on his hat again.

Whereupon a banana skin rattled on Villiers' tidy and ladylike
little panama. He glared round coldly, like a bird that would stab
with its beak if it got a chance, but which will fly away at the first
30   real menace.

"How I detest them!" said Kate.

A diversion was created by the entrance, opposite, of the military
bands, with their silver and brass instruments under their arms.
There were three sets. The chief band climbed and sat on the
35   right, in the big bare tract of concrete reserved for the Authorities.
These musicians wore dark-grey uniforms trimmed with rose
colour, and made Kate feel almost reassured, as if it were Italy and
not Mexico City. A silver band in pale buff uniforms sat opposite
our party, high up across the hollow distance, and still a third
40   *música* threaded away to the left, on the remote scattered hillside of

the amphitheatre. The newspapers had said that the President would attend.* But Presidents are scarce at bull-fights in Mexico, nowadays.

There sat the bands, in as much pomp as they could muster, but they did not begin to play. Great crowds now patched the slopes, but there were still bare tracts, especially in the Authorities' section.* Only a little distance above Kate's row was a mass of people, as it were impending: a very uncomfortable sensation.

It was three o'clock, and the crowd had a new diversion. The bands, due to strike up at three, still sat there in lordly fashion, sounding not a note.

"*La música! La música!*" shouted the mob, with the voice of mob authority. They were The People, and the revolutions had been their revolutions, and they had won them all. The bands were their bands, present for their amusement.

But the bands were military bands, and it was the army which had won all the revolutions. So the revolutions were *their* revolutions, and they were present for their own glory alone.

*Música pagada toca mal tono.**

Spasmodically, the insolent yelling of the mob rose and subsided. *La música! La música!* The shout became brutal and violent: Kate always remembered it. *La música!* The band peacocked its nonchalance. The shouting was a great yell: the degenerate mob of Mexico City!

At length, at its own leisure, the band in grey with dark rose facings struck up: crisp, martial, smart.

"That's fine!" said Owen. "But that's really good! And it's the first time I've heard a good band in Mexico, a band with any backbone."

The music was smart, but it was brief. The band seemed scarcely to have started, when the piece was over. The musicians took their instruments from their mouths with a gesture of dismissal. They played just to say they'd played, making it as short as possible.

Música pagada toca mal tono.

There was a ragged interval, then the silver band piped up. And at last it was half-past three, or more.

Whereupon, at some unknown signal, the masses in the middle, unreserved seats, suddenly burst and rushed down on to the lowest, reserved seats. It was a crash like a burst reservoir, and the populace in black Sunday suits poured down round and about our astonished, frightened trio. And in two minutes it was over. Without any pushing or shoving. Everybody careful, as far as possible, not to touch anybody else. You don't elbow your neighbour if he's got a pistol on his hip and a knife at his belly. So all the seats in the lower tiers filled in one rush, like the flowing of water.

5   Kate now sat among the crowd. But her seat, fortunately, was above one of the track-ways that went round the arena, so at least she would not have anybody sitting between her knees.

Men went uneasily back and forth along this gangway past her feet, wanting to get in next their friends, but never venturing to ask.
10   Three seats away, on the same row, sat a Polish bolshevist fellow* who had met Owen. He leaned over and asked the Mexican next to Owen if he might change seats with him. "No," said the Mexican. "I'll sit in my own seat."

"*Muy bien, Señor, muy bien!*"* said the Pole.
15   The show did not begin, and men like lost mongrels still prowled back and forth on the track that was next step down from Kate's feet. They began to take advantage of the ledge on which rested the feet of our party, to squat there.

Down sat a heavy fellow, plumb between Owen's knees.
20   "I hope they won't sit on *my* feet," said Kate anxiously.

"We won't let them," said Villiers, with bird-like decision. "Why don't you shove him off, Owen? Shove him off?"

And Villiers glared at the Mexican fellow ensconced between Owen's legs. Owen flushed, and laughed uncomfortably. He was not
25   good at shoving people off. The Mexicans began to look round at the three angry white people.

And in another moment, another fat Mexican in a black suit and a little black hat was lowering himself into Villiers' foot-space. But Villiers was too quick for him. He quickly brought his feet together
30   under the man's sinking posterior, so the individual subsided uncomfortably on to a pair of boots, and at the same time felt a hand shoving him quietly but determinedly on the shoulder.

"No!" Villiers was saying in good American. "This place is for my *feet*! Get off! You get *off*!"
35   And he continued, quietly but very emphatically to push the Mexican's shoulder, to remove him.

The Mexican half raised himself, and looked round murderously at Villiers. Physical violence was being offered, and the only retort was death. But the young American's face was so cold and
40   abstract, only the eyes showing a primitive, bird-like fire, that the

Mexican was nonplussed. And Kate's eyes were blazing with Irish contempt.

The fellow struggled with his Mexican city-bred inferiority complex. He muttered an explanation in Spanish that he was only sitting there for a moment, till he could join his friends—waving his hand towards a lower tier. Villiers did not understand a word, but he re-iterated:

"I don't care what it is. This place is for my *feet*, and you don't sit there."

Oh home of liberty! Oh land of the free! Which of these two men was to win in the struggle for conflicting liberty? Was the fat fellow free to sit between Villiers' feet, or was Villiers free to keep his foot-space?

There are all sorts of inferiority complex, and the city Mexican has a very strong sort, that makes him all the more aggressive, once it is roused. Therefore the intruder lowered his posterior with a heavy, sodden bounce on Villiers' feet, and Villiers, out of very distaste, had to extricate his feet from such a compression. The young man's face went pale at the nostrils, and his eyes took on that bright abstract look of pure democratic anger. He pushed the fat shoulder more decisively, repeating:

"Go away! Go away! You're not to *sit* there."

The Mexican, on his own ground, and heavy on his own base, let himself be shoved, oblivious.

"Insolence!" said Kate loudly. "Insolence!"

She glared at the fat back in the shoddily-fitting black coat, which looked as if a woman dressmaker had made it, with loathing. How could any man's coat-collar look so home-made, so *en famille*!

Villiers remained with a fixed, abstract look on his thin face, rather like a death's head. All his American will was summoned up, the bald eagle of the north bristling in every feather. The fellow *should not* sit there.—But how remove him?

The young man sat tense with will to annihilate his beetle-like intruder, and Kate used all her Irish malice to help him.

"Don't you wonder who was his tailor?" she asked, with a flicker in her voice.

Villiers looked at the femalish black coat of the Mexican, and made an arch grimace at Kate.

"I should say he hadn't one. Perhaps did it himself."

"Very likely!" Kate laughed venomously.

It was too much. The man got up and betook himself, rather diminished, to another spot.

"Triumph!" said Kate. "Can't you do the same, Owen?"

Owen laughed uncomfortably, glancing down at the man between
5   his knees as he might glance at a dog with rabies, when it had its back to him.

"Apparently not yet, unfortunately," he said, with some constraint, turning his nose away again from the Mexican who was using him as a sort of chair-back.

10   There was an exclamation. Two horsemen in gay uniforms and bearing long staffs had suddenly ridden into the ring. They went round the arena, then took up their posts, sentry-wise, on either side the tunnel entrance through which they had come in.

In marched a little column of four toreadors wearing tight
15   uniforms plastered with silver embroidery. They divided, and marched smartly in opposite directions, two and two, around the ring, till they came to the place facing the section of the Authorities, where they made their salutes.

So this was a bull-fight! Kate already felt a chill of disgust. In the
20   seats of the Authorities were very few people, and certainly no sparkling ladies in high tortoise-shell combs and lace mantillas. A few common-looking people, bourgeois with not much taste, and a couple of officers in uniform. The President had not come.

There was no glamour, no charm. A few commonplace people in
25   an expanse of concrete were the elect, and below, four grotesque and effeminate-looking fellows in tight, ornate clothes were the heroes. With their rather fat posteriors and their squiffs of pigtails and their clean-shaven faces, they looked like eunuchs, or women in tight pants, these precious toreadors.

30   The last of Kate's illusions concerning bull-fights came down with a flop. These were the darlings of the mob? These were the gallant toreadors! Gallant? Just about as gallant as assistants in a butcher's shop. Lady-killers? Ugh!

Then there was an *Ah!* of satisfaction from the mob. Into the ring
35   suddenly rushed a smallish, dun-coloured bull with long flourishing horns. He ran out, blindly, as if from the dark, probably thinking that now he was free. Then he stopped short, seeing he was not free, but surrounded in an unknown way. He was utterly at a loss.

A toreador came forward and switched out a pink cloak like a fan
40   not far from the bull's nose. The bull gave a playful little prance, neat

and pretty, and charged mildly on the cloak. The toreador switched
the cloak over the animal's head, and the neat little bull trotted on
round the ring, looking for a way to get out.

Seeing the wooden barrier around the arena, finding he was able
to look over it, he thought he might as well take the leap. So over he 5
went, into the corridor or passage-way which circled the ring, and in
which stood the servants of the arena.

Just as nimbly, these servants vaulted over the barrier into the
arena, that was now bull-less.

The bull in the gangway trotted enquiring round till he came to an 10
opening on to the arena again. So back he trotted into the ring.

And back into the gangway vaulted the servants, where they stood
again to look on.

The bull trotted waveringly and somewhat irritated. The
toreadors waved their cloaks at him, and he swerved on. Till his 15
vague course took him to where one of the horsemen with lances* sat
motionless on his horse.

Instantly, in a pang of alarm, Kate noticed that the horse was
thickly blindfolded with a black cloth. Yes, and so was the horse on
which sat the other picador. 20

The bull trotted suspiciously up to the motionless horse bearing
the rider with the long pole: a lean old horse that would never move
till Doomsday, unless someone shoved it.

Oh shades of Don Quixote! Oh four Spanish horsemen of the
Apocalypse!* This was surely one of them. 25

The picador pulled his feeble horse round slowly, to face the bull,
and slowly he leaned forward and shoved his lance-point into the
bull's shoulder. The bull, as if the horse were a great wasp that had
stung him deep, suddenly lowered his head in a jerk of surprise and
lifted his horns straight up into the horse's abdomen. And without 30
more ado, over went horse and rider, like a tottering monument
upset.

The rider scrambled from under the horse and went running away
with his lance. The old horse, in complete dazed amazement,
struggled to rise, as if overcome with dumb incomprehension. And 35
the bull, with a red place on his shoulder welling a trickle of dark
blood, stood looking around in equally hopeless amazement.

But the wound was hurting. He saw the queer sight of the horse
half reared from the ground, trying to get to its feet. And he smelled
blood and bowels. 40

So, rather vaguely, as if not quite knowing what he ought to do, the bull once more lowered his head and pushed his sharp, flourishing horns in the horse's belly, working them up and down inside there with a sort of vague satisfaction.

5   Kate had never been taken so completely by surprise in all her life. She had still cherished some idea of a gallant show. And before she knew where she was, she was watching a bull whose shoulder trickled blood goring his horns up and down inside the belly of a prostrate and feebly plunging old horse.

10 The shock almost overpowered her. She had come for a gallant show. This she had paid to see. Human cowardice and beastliness, a smell of blood, a nauseous whiff of bursten bowels! She turned her face away.

When she looked again, it was to see the horse feebly and dazedly
15 walking out of the ring, with a great ball of its own entrails hanging out of its abdomen and swinging reddish against its own legs as it automatically moved.

And once more, the shock of amazement almost made her lose consciousness. She heard the confused small applause of amuse-
20 ment from the mob. And that Pole, to whom Owen had introduced her, leaned across and said to her, in horrible English:

"Now, Miss Leslie, you are seeing *Life!* Now you will have something to write about, in your letters to England!"

She looked at his unwholesome face in complete repulsion, and
25 wished Owen would not introduce her to such sordid individuals.

She looked at Owen. His nose had a sharp look, like a little boy who may make himself sick, but who is watching at the shambles with all his eyes, knowing it is forbidden.

Villiers, the younger generation, looked intense and abstract,
30 getting the sensation. He would not even feel sick. He was just getting the thrill of it, without emotion, coldly and scientifically, but very intent.

And Kate felt a red pang of hatred against this Americanism which is coldly and unscrupulously sensational.

35 "Why doesn't the horse move? Why doesn't it run away from the bull?" she asked in repelled amazement, of Owen.

Owen cleared his throat.

"Didn't you see? It was blindfolded," he said.

"But can't it *smell* the bull?" she asked.

40 "Apparently not.—They bring the old wrecks here to finish them off.—I know it's awful: but it's part of the game."

How Kate hated phrases like "part of the game." What do they mean, anyhow? She felt utterly humiliated, crushed by a sense of human indecency, cowardice of two-legged humanity. In this "brave" show she felt nothing but reeking cowardice. Her breeding and her natural pride were outraged.

The ring servants had cleaned away the mess and spread new sand. The toreadors were playing with the bull, unfurling their foolish cloaks at arm's length. And the animal, with the red sore running on his shoulder, foolishly capered and ran from one rag to the other, here and there.

For the first time, a bull seemed to her a fool. She had always been afraid of bulls, fear tempered with reverence of the great Mithraic beast.* And now she saw how stupid he was, in spite of his long horns and his massive maleness. Blindly and stupidly he ran at the rag, each time, and the toreadors skipped like fat-hipped girls showing off. Probably it needed skill and courage, but it *looked* silly.

Blindly and foolishly the bull ran ducking its horns each time at the rag, just because the rag fluttered.

"Run at the *men*, idiot!" said Kate aloud, in her overwrought impatience. "Run at the men, not at the cloaks."

"They never do, isn't it curious!" replied Villiers, with cool scientific interest. "They say no toreador will face a cow, because a cow always goes for *him* instead of the cloak. If a bull did that there'd be no bull-fight. Imagine it!"

She was bored now. The nimbleness and the skipping tricks of the toreadors bored her. Even when one of the banderilleros reared himself on tiptoe, his plump posterior much in evidence, and from his slanting erectness pushed two razor-sharp darts with frills at the top into the bull's shoulder, neatly and smartly, Kate felt no admiration. One of the darts fell out, anyway, and the bull ran on with the other swaying and waggling in another bleeding place.

The bull now wanted to get away, really. He leaped the fence again, quickly, into the attendants' gangway. The attendants vaulted over into the arena. The bull trotted in the corridor, then nicely leaped back. The attendants vaulted once more into the corridor. The bull trotted round the arena, ignoring the toreadors, and leaped once more into the gangway. Over vaulted the attendants.

Kate was beginning to be amused, now that the mongrel men were skipping for safety.

The bull was in the ring again, running from cloak to cloak, foolishly. A banderillero was getting ready with two more darts. But

first another picador put nobly forward on his blindfolded old horse. The bull ignored this little lot too, and trotted away again, as if all the time looking for something, excitedly looking for something. He stood still and excitedly pawed the ground, as if he wanted some-
5 thing. A toreador advanced and swung a cloak. Up pranced the bull, tail in air, and with a prancing bound charged—upon the rag, of course. The toreador skipped round with a ladylike skip, then tripped to another point. Very pretty!

The bull, in the course of his trotting and prancing and pawing,
10 had once more come near the bold picador. The bold picador shoved forward his ancient steed, leaned forwards, and pushed the point of his lance in the bull's shoulder. The bull looked up, irritated and arrested. What the devil!

He saw the horse and rider. The horse stood with that feeble
15 monumentality of a milk horse, patient as if between the shafts, waiting while his master delivered milk. How strange it must have been to him when the bull, giving a little bound like a dog, ducked its head and dived its horns upward into his belly, rolling him over with his rider as one might push over a hat-stand.

20 The bull looked with irritable wonder at the incomprehensible medley of horse and rider kicking on the ground a few yards away from him. He drew near to investigate. The rider scrambled out and bolted. And the toreadors, running up with their cloaks, drew off the bull. He went caracoling round, charging at more silk-lined rags.

25 Meanwhile an attendant had got the horse on its feet again, and was leading it totteringly into the gangway and round to the exit under the Authorities. The horse crawled slowly. The bull, running from pink cloak to red cloak, rag to rag, and never catching anything, was getting excited, impatient at the rag game. He jumped once
30 more into the gangway, and started running, alas, on towards where the wounded horse was still limping its way to the exit.

Kate knew what was coming. Before she could look away, the bull had charged on the limping horse from behind, the attendants had fled, the horse was up-ended absurdly, one of the bull's horns
35 between his hind legs and deep in his inside. Down went the horse, collapsing in front, but his rear was still heaved up, with the bull's horn working vigorously up and down inside him, while he lay on his neck all twisted. And a huge heap of bowels coming out. And a nauseous stench. And the cries of pleased amusement among the
40 crowd.

This pretty event took place on Kate's side of the ring, and not far from where she sat, below her. Most of the people were on their feet, craning to look down over the edge to watch the conclusion of this delightful spectacle.

Kate knew that if she saw any more she would go into hysterics. 5 She was getting beside herself.

She looked swiftly at Owen, who looked like a guilty boy spell-bound.

"I'm going!" she said, rising.

"Going!" he cried, in wonder and dismay, his flushed round face 10 and his bald flushed forehead a picture, looking up at her.

But she had already turned, and was hurrying away towards the mouth of the exit-tunnel.

Owen came running after her, fluttered, and drawn in all directions. 15

"Really going!" he cried in chagrin, as she came to the high, vaulted exit-tunnel.

"I must. I've got to get out," she cried. "Don't you come."

"Really!" he echoed, torn all ways.

The scene was creating a very hostile attitude in the audience. To 20 leave the bull-fight is a national insult.

"Don't come! Really! I shall take a tram-car," she said hurriedly.

"Really! Do you really think you'll be all right?"

"Perfectly. You stay. Goodbye! I can't smell any more of this stink." 25

He turned like Orpheus looking back into hell,* and wavering made towards his seat again.

It was not so easy, because many people were now on their feet and crowding to the exit vault. The rain which had spattered a few drops suddenly fell in a downward splash. People were crowding to 30 shelter; but Owen, unheeding, fought his way back to his seat, and sat in his rain-coat with the rain pouring on his bald head. He was as nearly in hysterics as Kate. But he was convinced that this was life. He was seeing LIFE, and what can an American do more?

"They might just as well sit and enjoy somebody else's diarrhœa!" 35 was the thought that passed through Kate's distracted but still Irish mind.

There she was in the great concrete archway under the stadium, with the lousy press of the audience crowding in after her. Facing outwards, she saw the straight downpour of the rain, and a little 40 beyond, the great wooden gates that opened to the free street. Oh to be out, to be out of this, to be free!

But it was pouring tropical rain. The little shoddy soldiers were pressing back under the brick gateway, for shelter. And the gates
5　were almost shut. Perhaps they would not let her out. Oh horror!

She stood hovering in front of the straight downpour. She would have dashed out, but for the restraining thought of what she would look like when her thin gauze dress was plastered to her body by drenching rain. On the brink she hovered.

10　Behind her, from the inner end of the stadium tunnel, the people were surging in in waves. She stood horrified and alone, looking always out to freedom. The crowd was in a state of excitement, cut off in its sport, on tenterhooks lest it should miss anything. Thank goodness the bulk stayed near the inner end of the vault. She
15　hovered near the outer end, ready to bolt at any moment.

The rain crashed steadily down.

She waited on the outer verge, as far from the people as possible. Her face had that drawn, blank look of a woman near hysterics. She could not get out of her eyes the last picture of the horse lying twisted
20　on its neck with its hind-quarters hitched up and the horn of the bull goring slowly and rhythmically in its vitals. The horse so utterly passive and grotesque. And all its bowels slipping on to the ground.

But a new terror was the throng inside the tunnel entrance. The big arched place was filling up, but still the crowd did not come very
25　near her. They pressed towards the inner exit.

They were mostly loutish men in city clothes, the mongrel mass of a mongrel city. Two men stood making water against the wall, in the interval of their excitement. One father had kindly brought his little boys to the show, and stood in fat, sloppy paternal benevolence above
30　them. They were pale mites, the elder about ten years old, highly dressed up in Sunday clothes. And badly they needed protecting from that paternal benevolence, for they were oppressed, peaked and a bit wan from the horrors. To those children at least bull-fights did not come natural, but would be an acquired taste. There were other
35　children, however, and fat mammas in black satin that was greasy and grey at the edges with an overflow of face-powder. These fat mammas had a pleased, excited look in their eyes, almost sexual, and very distasteful in contrast to their soft, passive bodies.

Kate shivered a little in her thin frock, for the ponderous rain had
40　a touch of ice. She stared through the curtain of water at the big

ricketty gates of the enclosure surrounding the amphitheatre, at the midget soldiers cowering in their shoddy, pinky-white cotton uniforms, and at the glimpse of the squalid road outside, now running with dirty brown streams. The vendors had all taken refuge, in dirty-white clusters, in the pulque shops, one of which was sinisterly named: *A Ver que Sale.** 5

She was afraid more of the repulsiveness than of anything. She had been in many cities of the world, but Mexico had an underlying ugliness, a sort of squalid evil, which made Naples seem debonnaire in comparison. She was afraid, she dreaded the thought that anything might really touch her in this town, and give her the contagion of its crawling sort of evil. But she knew that the one thing she must do was to keep her head. 10

A little officer in uniform, wearing a big, pale-blue cape, made his way through the crowd. He was short, dark, and had a little black beard like an *impériale*. He came through the people from the inner entrance, and cleared his way with a quiet, silent unobtrusiveness, yet with the peculiar heavy Indian momentum. Even touching the crowd delicately with his gloved hand, and murmuring almost inaudibly the *Con permiso!** formula, he seemed to be keeping himself miles away from contact. He was brave too: because there was just a chance some lout might shoot him because of his uniform. The people knew him too. Kate could tell that, by the flicker of a jeering, self-conscious smile that passed across many faces, and the exclamation: "General Viedma! Don Cipriano!"* 15 20 25

He came towards Kate, saluting and bowing with a brittle shyness.

"I am General Viedma. Did you wish to leave? Let me get you an automobile," he said, in very English English, that sounded strange from his dark face, and a little stiff on his soft tongue. 30

His eyes were dark, quick, with the glassy darkness that she found so wearying. But they were tilted up with a curious slant, under arched black brows. It gave him an odd look of detachment, as if he looked at life with raised brows. His manner was superficially assured, underneath perhaps half savage, shy and farouche, and deprecating. 35

"Thank you so much," she said.

He called to a soldier in the gateway.

"I will send you in the automobile of my friend," he said. "It will be better than a taxi.—You don't like the bull-fight?" 40

"No! Horrible!" said Kate. "But do get me a yellow taxi.* That is quite safe."

"Well, the man has gone for the automobile.—You are English, yes?"

5   "Irish," said Kate.

"Ah Irish!" he replied, with the flicker of a smile.

"You speak English awfully well," she said.

"Yes. I was educated there. I was in England seven years."

"Were you!—My name is Mrs Leslie."

10   "Ah Leslie! I knew James Leslie in Oxford. He was killed in the war."

"Yes. That was my husband's brother."

"Oh really!"

"How small the world is!" said Kate.

15   "Yes, indeed!" said the general. There was a pause.

"And the gentlemen who are with you, they are—?"

"American," said Kate.

"Ah American! Ah yes!"

"The older one is my cousin—Owen Rhys."

20   "Owen Rhys! Ah yes! I think I saw in the newspaper you were here—in town—visiting Mexico."

He spoke in a peculiar quiet voice, rather suppressed, and his quick eyes glanced at her, and at his surroundings, like those of a man perpetually suspecting an ambush. But his face had a certain
25   silent hostility, under his kindness. He was saving his nation's reputation.

"They did put in a not very complimentary note," said Kate. "I think they don't like it that we stay in the Hotel San Remo.* It is too poor and foreign. But we are none of us rich, and we like it better
30   than those other places."

"The Hotel San Remo? Where is that?"

"In the Avenida del Perú. Won't you come and see us there, and meet my cousin and Mr Thompson?"*

"Thank you! Thank you! I hardly ever go out. But I will call if I
35   may, and then perhaps you will all come to see me at the house of my friend, Señor Ramón Carrasco."*

"We should like to," said Kate.

"Very well. And shall I call, then?"

She told him a time, and added:

40   "You mustn't be surprised at the hotel. It *is* small, and nearly all

Italians. But we tried some of the big ones, and there is such a
feeling of lowness about them, awful! I can't stand the feeling of
prostitution. And then the cheap insolence of the servants. No, my
little San Remo may be rough, but it is kindly and human, and it's
not rotten. It is like Italy as I always knew it, decent, and with a bit of   5
human generosity.—I do think Mexico City is evil, underneath."

"Well—" he said—"the hotels are bad. It is unfortunate—but the
foreigners seem to make the Mexicans worse than they are, naturally. And Mexico, or something in it, certainly makes the foreigners
worse than they are at home."   10

He spoke with a certain bitterness.

"Perhaps we should all stay away," she said.

"Perhaps!" he said, lifting his shoulders a little. "But I don't think
so."

He relapsed into a slightly blank silence. Peculiar how his feelings   15
flushed over him, anger, diffidence, wistfulness, assurance, and
anger again, all in little flushes, and somewhat naïve.

"It doesn't rain so much," said Kate. "When will the car come?"

"It is here. It has been waiting some time," he replied.

"Then I'll go," she said.   20

"Well—!" he replied, looking at the sky. "It is still raining, and
your dress is very thin. You must take my cloak."

"Oh!" she said, shrinking. "It is only two yards."

"It is still raining fairly fast. Better either wait—or let me lend you
my cloak."   25

He swung out of his cloak with a quick little movement, and held
it up to her. Almost without realising, she turned her shoulders to
him, and he put the cape on her. She caught it round her, and ran
out to the gate, as if escaping. He followed, with a light yet military
stride. The soldiers saluted rather slovenly, and he responded very   30
briefly.

A not very new Fiat stood at the gate, with a chauffeur in a short
red-and-black check coat. The chauffeur opened the door. Kate
slipped off the cloak as she got in, and handed it back. He stood with
it over his arm.   35

"Goodbye!" she said. "Thank you ever so much. And we shall
see you on Tuesday.—Do put your cape on."

"On Tuesday, yes.—Hotel San Remo, Calle del Perú—" he
added to the chauffeur. Then turning again to Kate: "The hotel,
no?"   40

"Yes," she said, and instantly changed. "No, take me to San-born's,* where I can sit in a corner and drink tea to comfort me."

"To comfort you after the bull-fight?" he said, with another quick smile. "To Sanborn's, González."

5   He saluted and bowed and closed the door. The car started.

Kate sat back, breathing with relief. Relief to get away from that beastly place. Relief even to get away from that nice man. He was awfully nice. But he made her feel she wanted to get away from him too. There was that heavy, black Mexican fatality about him, that put
10   a burden on her. His quietness, and his peculiar assurance, almost aggressive: and at the same time, a nervousness, an uncertainty. His heavy sort of gloom, and yet his quick, naïve, childish smile. Those black eyes, like black jewels, that you couldn't look into, and which were so watchful; yet which perhaps were waiting for some sign of
15   recognition and of warmth! Perhaps!

She felt again, as she had felt before, that Mexico lay in her destiny almost as a doom. Something so heavy, so oppressive, like the folds of some huge serpent that seemed as if it could hardly raise itself.

She was glad to get to her corner in the tea-house, to feel herself in
20   the cosmopolitan world once more, to drink her tea and eat strawberry shortcake and try to forget.

Chapter II.

Tea-party in Tlacolula.*

Owen came back to the hotel at about half-past six, tired, excited, a
little guilty, and a good deal distressed at having let Kate go alone.
And, now the whole thing was over, rather dreary in spirit.   5

"Oh, how did you get on?" he cried, the moment he saw her,
afraid almost like a boy of his own sin of omission.

"I got on perfectly. Went to Sanborn's for tea, and had strawberry
shortcake—so good!"

"Oh good for you!" he laughed in relief. "Then you weren't *too*   10
much overcome! I'm so glad. I had such awful qualms after I'd let
you go. Imagined all the things that are supposed to happen in
Mexico—chauffeur driving away with you into some horrible remote
region, and robbing you and all that—But then I *knew* really you'd be
all right.—Oh, the time I had—The rain!—and the people throwing   15
things at my bald patch—and those horses—wasn't that horrible?—I
wonder I'm still alive."—And he laughed with tired excitement,
putting his hand over his stomach and rolling his eyes.

"Aren't you drenched?" she said.

"Drenched!" he replied. "Or at least I was. I've dried off quite a   20
lot. My rain-coat is no good—I don't know why I don't buy
another.—Oh, but what a time! The rain *streaming* on my bald head,
and the crowd behind throwing oranges at it. Then simply *gored* in
my inside about letting you go alone.—Yet it was the only bull-fight I
shall *ever* see.— —I came then before it was over. Bud wouldn't   25
come. I suppose he's still there."

"Was it all as awful as the beginning?" she asked.

"No! No! It wasn't. The first was worst—that horse-shambles.
Oh, they killed two more horses. And *five* bulls! Yes, a regular
butchery. But some of it was very neat work; those toreadors did   30
some very pretty feats. One stood on his cloak while a bull charged
him—"

"I think," interrupted Kate, "if I knew that some of those
toreadors were going to be tossed by the bull, I'd go to another
bull-fight. Ugh, how I detest them! The longer I live the more   35

25

loathsome the human species becomes to me. *How* much nicer the bulls are!"

"Oh, quite!" said Owen vaguely. "Exactly.—But still, there was some very skilful work, very plucky."

5 "Yah!" snarled Kate. "Plucky! They, with all their knives and their spears and cloaks and darts—and they know just how a bull will behave! It's just a performance of human beings torturing animals, with those common fellows showing off, how smart they are at hurting a bull. Dirty little boys maiming flies—that's what they are.

10 Only being grown-up, they are bastards, not boys.—Oh, I wish *I* could be a bull, just for five minutes.—Bastard, that's what I call it!"

"Well—!" laughed Owen uneasily. "It is rather."

"Call that manliness!" cried Kate. "Then thank God a million times that I'm a woman, and know poltroonery and dirty-minded-

15 ness when I see it."

Again Owen laughed uncomfortably.

"Go upstairs and change," she said. "You'll die."

"I think I'd better.—I feel I might die any minute, as a matter of fact.—Well, till dinner then. I'll tap at your door in half an hour."

20 Kate sat trying to sew, but her hand trembled. She could not get the bull-ring out of her mind, and something felt damaged in her inside.

She straightened herself, and sighed. She was really very angry, too, with Owen. He was naturally so sensitive, and so kind. But he

25 had the insidious modern disease of tolerance. He must tolerate everything, even a thing that revolted him. He would call it Life! He would feel he had *lived* this afternoon. Greedy for even the most sordid sensations.

Whereas *she* felt as if she had eaten something which was giving

30 her ptomaine poisoning. If *that* was life!

Ah men, men! They all had this soft rottenness of the soul, a strange perversity which made even the squalid, repulsive things seem part of *life* to them. Life! And what is life? A louse lying on its back and kicking? Ugh!

35 At about seven o'clock Villiers came tapping. He looked wan, peaked, but like a bird that has successfully pecked a bellyful of garbage.

"Oh it was GREAT!" he said, lounging on one hip. "GREAT! —They killed *seven* BULLS—"*

40 "No calves, unfortunately," said Kate, suddenly furious again.

He paused to consider the point, then laughed. Her anger was another slight sensational amusement to him.

"No, no calves—" he said. "The calves have come home to be fattened.—But several more horses after you'd gone—"

"I don't want to hear," she said coldly.   5

He laughed, feeling rather heroic. After all, one must be able to look on blood and bursten bowels calmly: even with a certain thrill. The young hero! But there were dark rings round his eyes, like a debauch.

"Oh but!" he began, making a rather coy face. "Don't you want to   10
hear what I did after! I went to the hotel of the chief toreador, and saw him lying on his bed all dressed up, smoking a fat cigar.* Rather like a male Venus who is never undressed. So funny!"

"Who took you there?" she said.

"That Pole, you remember?—and a Spaniard who talked English.   15
The toreador was great, lying on his bed in all his get-up, except his shoes, and quite a crowd of men going over it all again—*wawawawa-wa!*—you never heard such a row!"

"Aren't you wet?" said Kate.

"No, not at all. I'm perfectly dry. You see I had my coat. Only my   20
head, of course. My poor hair was all streaked down my face like streaks of dye." He wiped his thin hair across his head with rather self-conscious humour. "Hasn't Owen come in?" he added.

"Yes, he's changing."

"Well, I'll go up. I suppose it's nearly supper time. Oh yes, it's   25
after!" At which discovery he brightened as if he'd received a gift. "Oh, by the way, how did you get on? Rather mean of us to let you go all alone like that," he said, as he hung poised in the open doorway.

"Not at all," she said. "You wanted to stay. And I can look after myself, at my time of life."   30

"We-ell!" he said, with an American drawl. "Maybe you can!—" Then he gave a little laugh. "But you *should* have seen all those men rehearsing in that bedroom, throwing their arms about, and the toreador lying on the bed like Venus with a fat cigar, listening to her lovers—"   35

"I'm glad I didn't," said Kate.

Villiers disappeared with a wicked little laugh.

And as she sat her hands trembled with outrage and passion. A-moral! How *could* one be a-moral, or non-moral, when one's soul was revolted! How could one be like these Americans, picking over   40 the garbage of sensations, and gobbling it up like carrion birds. At the moment, both Owen and Villiers seemed to her like carrion birds, repulsive.

5   She felt, moreover, that they both hated her just because she was a woman. It was all right so long as she fell in with them in every way. But the moment she stood out against them in the least, they hated her mechanically for the very fact that she was a woman. They hated her womanness.

10   And in this Mexico, with its great under-drift of squalor and heavy, reptile-like evil, it was hard for her to bear up.

She was really fond of Owen. But how could she respect him? So empty, and waiting for circumstance to fill him up. Swept with an American despair of having lived in vain, or of not having *really* lived. Having missed something. Which fearful misgiving would make him
15   rush like mechanical steel filings to a magnet, towards any crowd in the street. And then, all his poetry and philosophy gone with the cigarette-end he threw away, he would stand craning his neck in one more frantic effort to *see*—just to *see*. Whatever it was, he must see it. Or he might miss something. And then, after he'd seen an old ragged
20   woman run over by a motor-car and bleeding on the floor, he'd come back to Kate pale at the gills, sick, bewildered, daunted, and yet, yes, glad he'd seen it. It was Life!

"Well," said Kate, "I always thank God I'm not Argus.* Two eyes are often two too many for me, in all the horrors. I don't feed myself
25   on street-accidents."

At dinner they tried to talk of pleasanter things than bull-fights. Villiers was neat and tidy and very nicely mannered, but she knew he was keeping a little mocking laugh up his sleeve, because she could not stomach the afternoon's garbage. He himself had black rings
30   under his eyes: but that was because he had "lived."

The climax came with the dessert. In walked the Pole and that Spaniard who spoke American. The Pole was unhealthy and unclean-looking. She heard him saying to Owen, who of course had risen with automatic cordiality:
35   "We thought we'd come here to dinner—Well, how are you—"

Kate's skin was already goose-flesh. But the next instant she heard that dingy voice, that spoke so many languages dingily, assailing her with familiarity:

"Ah, Miss Leslie, you missed the best part of it.—You missed all
40   the fun! Oh, I say—"

Rage flew into her heart and fire into her eyes. She got up suddenly from her chair, and faced the fellow behind her.

"Thank you!" she said. "I don't want to hear. I don't want you to speak to me. I don't want to know you."

She looked at him once, then turned her back, sat down again, and took a pitahaya from the fruit plate. 5

The fellow went green, and stood a moment speechless.

"Oh, all right!" he said mechanically, turning away to the Spaniard who spoke American.

"Well—see you later!" said Owen rather hurriedly, and he went back to his seat at Kate's table. 10

The two strange fellows sat at another table. Kate ate her cactus fruit in silence, and waited for her coffee. By this time she was so angry, she was quite calm. And even Villiers hid his joy in a new sensation under a manner of complete quiet composure. 15

When coffee came, she looked at the two men at the other table, and at the two men at her own table.

"I've had enough of *canaille*, of any sort," she said.

"Oh, I understand, perfectly," said Owen.

After dinner, she went to her room. And through the night she could not sleep, but lay listening to the noises of Mexico City, then to the silence and the strange, grisly fear that so often creeps out on to the darkness of a Mexican night. Away inside her, she loathed Mexico City. She even feared it. In the daytime it had a certain spell—but at night, the underneath grisliness and evil came forth. 25

In the morning Owen also announced that he had not slept at all.

"Oh, I never slept so well since I was in Mexico," said Villiers, with a triumphant look of a bird that has just pecked a good morsel from the garbage-heap.

"Look at the frail aesthetic youth!" said Owen, in a hollow voice. 30

"His frailty and his aestheticism are both bad signs, to me," said Kate ominously.

"*And* the youth. Surely that's another!" said Owen, with a dead laugh.

But Villiers only gave a little snirt of cold, pleased amusement. 35

Someone was calling Miss Leslie on the telephone, said the Mexican chambermaid.—It was the only person Kate knew in the Capital—or in the Distrito Federal—a Mrs Norris, widow of an English ambassador of thirty years ago. She had a big, ponderous old house out in the village of Tlacolula.* 40

"Yes! Ye-es! This is Mrs Norris. How are you? That's right, that's
right. Now, Mrs Leslie, won't you come out to tea this afternoon and
see the garden? I wish you would. Two friends are coming in to see
me, two Mexicans: Don Ramón Carrasco and General Viedma.*
5   They are both *charming* men, and Don Ramón is a great scholar. I
assure you, they are both entirely the exception among Mexicans.
Oh, but *entirely* the exception!—So now, *dear* Mrs Leslie, won't you
come with your cousin? I wish you would."

"Thank you!" said Kate. "I should like to."

10   She remembered the little general: he was a good deal smaller
than herself. She remembered his erect, alert little figure, something
bird-like, and the face with the eyes slanting under arched eyebrows,
and the little black tuft of an *impériale* on the chin: a face with a
peculiar Chinese suggestion, without being Chinese in the least,
15   really. An odd, detached, yet cocky little man, a true little Indian,
speaking Oxford English in a rapid, low, musical voice, with
extraordinarily gentle intonations. Yet those black, inhuman eyes!

Till this minute, she had not really been able to recall him to
herself: to get any sharp impression. Now she had it.

20   He was an Indian pure and simple. And in Mexico, she knew,
there were more generals than soldiers. There had been three
generals in the Pullman coming down from El Paso,* two, more or
less educated, in the "drawing-room," and the third, a real peasant
Indian, travelling with a frizzy half-white woman who looked as if she
25   had fallen into a flour-sack, her face was so deep in powder, and her
frizzy hair and her brown silk dress so douched with the white dust of
it. Neither this "general" nor this woman had ever been in a Pullman
before. But the general was sharper than the woman. He was a tall,
wiry fellow with a reddened, pock-marked face and sharp little black
30   eyes. He followed Owen to the smoking room, and watched with
sharp eyes, to see how everything was done. And soon he knew. And
he would wipe his wash-bowl dry as neatly as anybody. There was
something of a real man about him. But the poor, half-white woman,
when she wanted the Ladies toilet, got lost in the passage and wailed
35   aloud: *I don't know where to go! No sé adonde! No sé adonde!*—until the
general sent the Pullman boy to direct her.

But it had annoyed Kate to see this general and this woman
eating chicken and asparagus and jelly in the Pullman, paying fifteen
pesos for a rather poor dinner, when for a peso-and-a-half apiece
40   they could have eaten a better meal, and real Mexican, at the meal-

stop station. And all the poor, barefoot people clamoring on the platforms, while this "general," who was a man of their own sort, nobly swallowed his asparagus on the other side of the window-pane.

But this is how they save the people, in Mexico and elsewhere. Some tough individual scrambles up out of the squalor and proceeds to save himself. Who pays for the asparagus and jelly and face-powder, nobody asks because everybody knows.

And so much for Mexican generals: as a rule, a class to be strictly avoided.

Kate was aware of all this. She wasn't much interested in any sort of Mexican in office. There is so much in the world that one wants to avoid, as one wants to avoid the lice that creep on the unwashed crowd.

Being rather late, Owen and Kate bumped out to Tlacolula in a Ford taxi. It was a long way, a long way through the peculiar squalid endings of the town, then along the straight road between trees, into the valley. The sun of April was brilliant, there were piles of cloud about the sky, where the volcanoes* would be. The valley stretched away to its sombre, atmospheric hills, in a flat dry bed, parched except where there was some crop being irrigated. The soil seemed strange, dry, blackish, artificially welted, and old. The trees rose high, and hung bare boughs, or withered shade. The buildings were either new and alien, like the Country Club, or cracked and dilapidated, with all the plaster falling off. The falling of thick plaster from cracked buildings—one could almost hear it.

Yellow tram-cars rushed at express speed away down the fenced-in car-lines, rushing round towards Xochimilco or Tlalpam.* The asphalt road ran outside these lines, and on the asphalt rushed incredibly dilapidated Ford omnibuses, crowded with blank dark natives in dirty cotton clothes and big straw hats. At the far edge of the road, on the dust-track under the trees, little donkeys under huge loads loitered towards the city, driven by men with blackened faces and bare, blackened legs. Three-fold went the traffic: the roar of the tram-trains, the clatter of the automobiles, the straggle of asses and of outside-seeming individuals.

Occasional flowers would splash out in colour from a ruin of falling plaster. Occasional women with strong, dark-brown arms would be washing rags in a drain. An occasional horseman would ride across to the herd of motionless, black-and-white cattle on the field. Occasional maize fields were already coming green. And the pillars that mark the water conduits passed one by one.

They went through the tree-filled plaza of Tlacolula, where natives were squatting on the ground, selling fruits or sweets, then
5 down a road between high walls. They pulled up at last at big gate-doors, beyond which was a heavy pink-and-yellow house, and beyond the house, high, dark cypress trees.

In the road two motor-cars were already standing. That meant other visitors. Owen knocked on the studded fortress doors, there
10 was an imbecile barking of dogs. At last a little footman with a little black moustache opened silently.

The square, inner patio, dark, with sun lying on the heavy arches of one side, had pots of red and white flowers, but was ponderous, as if dead for centuries. A certain dead, heavy strength and beauty
15 seemed there unable to pass away, unable to liberate itself and decompose. There was a stone basin of clear but motionless water, and the heavy reddish-and-yellow arches went round the courtyard with a warrior-like fatality, their bases in dark shadow. Dead, massive house of the Conquistadores,* with a glimpse of tall-grown
20 garden beyond, and further Aztec cypresses rising to strange dark heights. And dead silence, like the black, porous, absorptive lava rock. Save when the tram-cars battered past outside the solid wall.

Kate went up the jet-like stone stair-case and through the leather doors. Mrs Norris came forward on the terrace of the upper patio to
25 receive her guests.

"I'm so glad, my dear, that you came.—I should have rung you up before, but I've had such trouble with my heart. And the doctor wanting to send me down to a lower altitude! I said to him, I've no patience! If you're going to cure me, cure me at an altitude of seven
30 thousand feet, or else admit your incompetence at once. Ridiculous, this rushing up and down from one altitude to another. I've lived at this height all these years, I simply refuse to be bundled down to Cuernavaca or some other place where I don't want to go.—Well, my dear, and how are you—?"

35 Mrs Norris was an elderly woman, rather like a Conquistador herself, in her black silk dress and her little black shoulder-shawl of fine cashmere, with a short silk fringe, and her ornaments of black enamel. Her face had gone slightly grey, her nose was sharp and dusky, and her voice, hammered almost like metal, was slow,
40 distinct, and with a peculiar hard music of its own. She was an

archaeologist, and she had studied the Aztec remains so long, that now some of the black-grey look of the lava rock, and some of the expression of the Aztec idols, with sharp nose and slightly prominent eyes and an expression of tomb-like mockery, had passed into her face. A lonely daughter of culture, with a strong mind and a dense will, she had browsed all her life on the hard stones of archaeological remains, and at the same time she had retained a strong sense of humanity, and a slightly fantastic humorous vision of her fellow men.

From the first instant, Kate respected her for her isolation and her dauntlessness. The world is made up of a mass of people and a few individuals. Mrs Norris was one of the few individuals. True, she played her social game all the time. But she was an odd number; and all alone, she could give the even numbers a bad time.

"But come in. Do come in!" she said, after keeping her two guests out on the terrace that was lined with little black idols and dusty native baskets and shields and arrows and tapa, like a museum.

In the dark sitting-room that opened on to the terrace were three visitors: an old man in a black morning coat and white hair and beard, and a woman in black crêpe-de-chine, with the inevitable hat of her sort upon her grey hair: a stiff black satin turned up on three sides and with black ospreys underneath. She had the baby face and the faded blue eyes and the Middle-West accent inevitable.

"Judge and Mrs Burlap."

The third visitor was a youngish man, very correct and not quite sure. He was Major Law, American military attaché at the moment.

The three people eyed the newcomers with cautious suspicion. They might be shady. There are indeed so many shady people in Mexico that it is taken for granted, if you arrive unannounced and unexpected in the Capital, that you are probably under an assumed name, and have some dirty game up your sleeve.

"Been long in Mexico?" snapped the Judge: the police enquiry had begun.

"No!" said Owen, resonantly, his gorge rising. "About two weeks."

"You are an American?"

"*I*," said Owen, "am American. Mrs Leslie is English—or rather Irish."

"Been in the club yet?"

"No," said Owen, "I haven't. American clubs aren't much in my line. Though Garfield Spence gave me a letter of introduction."*

"Who? Garfield Spence?"—The Judge started as if he had been
stung. "Why the fellow's nothing better than a bolshevist. Why he
went to Russia!"

"I should rather like to go to Russia myself," said Owen. "It is
5 probably the most interesting country in the world today."

"But weren't you telling me," put in Mrs Norris, in her clear,
metal-musical voice, "that you loved China so much, Mr Rhys?"

"I *did* like China *very* much," said Owen.

"And I'm sure you made some wonderful collections. Tell me
10 now, what was your particular fancy?"

"Perhaps, after all," said Owen, "it was jade."

"Ah jade! Yes! Jade! Jade is beautiful! Those wonderful little
fairy-lands they carve in jade—!"

"And the stone itself! It was the delicate stone that fascinated
15 me," said Owen. "The wonderful quality of it—"

"Ah wonderful, wonderful—! Tell me now, dear Mrs Leslie, what
you have been doing since I saw you?"

"We went to a bull-fight, and hated it," said Kate. "At least I did.
We sat in the Sun, near the ring, and it was all horrible."

20 "Horrible, I am sure. I never went to a bull-fight in Mexico. Only
in Spain, where there is wonderful colour. Did you ever try a
bull-fight, Major?"

"Yes, I have been several times."

"You have! Then you know all about it.—And how are you liking
25 Mexico, Mrs Leslie?"

"Not much," said Kate. "It strikes me as evil."

"It does! It does!" said Mrs Norris. "Ah, if you had known Mexico
before the revolutions! It was different then.—What is the latest
news, Major?"

30 "About the same," said the Major. "There is a rumour that the
new President will be turned down by the army, a few days before he
comes into office.* But you never know."

"I think it would be a great shame not to let him have a try," put in
Owen hotly. "He seems a sincere man, and just because he is
35 honestly a Labor man, they want to shut him out."

"Ah, my dear Mr Rhys, they *all* talk so nobly beforehand. If only
their deeds followed their words, Mexico would be heaven on
earth."

"Instead of hell on earth," snapped the Judge.

40 A young man and his wife, also Americans, were introduced as
Mr and Mrs Henry. The young man was fresh and lively.

"We were talking about the new President," said Mrs Norris.

"Well why not!" said Mr Henry breezily. "I'm just back from Orizaba. And do you know what they've got pasted up on the walls? *Hosanna! Hosanna! Hosanna! Viva el Jesucristo de México, Sócrates Tomás Montes!*"

"Why, did you ever hear such a thing?" said Mrs Norris.

"*Hosanna! Hosanna! Hosanna!* To the new Labor President! I think it's rich," said Henry.

The Judge stamped his stick on the ground in a speechless access of irritability.

"They pasted on my luggage," said the Major, "when I came through Veracruz: *La degenerada media clase, Será regenerada, por mí, Montes.*—The degenerate middle class shall be regenerated by me, Montes."

"Poor Montes!" said Kate. "He seems to have got his work cut out."

"He has indeed!" said Mrs Norris. "Poor man, I wish he might come in peacefully and put a strong hand on the country. But there's not much hope, I'm afraid."

There was a silence, during which Kate felt that bitter hopelessness that comes over people who know Mexico well. A bitter barren hopelessness.

"How can a man who comes in on a Labor vote, even a doctored one, put a strong hand on a country!" snapped the Judge. "Why he came in on the very cry of *Down with the strong hand!*" And again the old man stamped his stick in an access of extreme irritability.

This was another characteristic of the old residents of the city: a state of intense, though often suppressed irritation, an irritation amounting almost to rabies.

"Oh, but mayn't it be possible that he will change his views a little on coming into power?" said Mrs Norris. "So many Presidents have done so."

"I should say very probable, if ever he gets into power," said young Henry. "He'll have all his work cut out saving Sócrates Tomás, he won't have much time left for saving Mexico."

"He's a dangerous fellow, and will turn out a scoundrel," said the Judge.

"Myself," said Owen, "as far as I have followed him, I believe he is sincere, and I admire him."

"I thought it was so nice," said Kate, "that they received him in

New York with loud music by the Street Sweepers Band. The Street
Sweepers Band they sent to receive him from the ship!"*

"But you see," said the Major, "no doubt the Labor people
themselves wished to send that particular band."

5   "But to be President Elect, and be received by the Street
Sweepers Band!" said Kate. "No, I can't believe it!"

"Oh, it actually was so," said the Major. "But that is Labor hailing
Labor, surely."

"The latest rumour," said Henry, "is that the army will go over *en*
10 *bloc* to General Ayala about the twenty-third, a week before the
inauguration."*

"But how is it possible?" said Kate. "When Montes is so
popular?"

"Montes popular!" they all cried at once. "Why!" snapped the
15 Judge. "He's the most unpopular man in Mexico."

"Not with the Labor Party," said Owen, almost at bay.

"The Labor Party!" the Judge fairly spat like a cat. "There is no
such thing. What is the Labor Party in Mexico? A bunch of isolated
factory hands here and there, mostly in the State of Veracruz. The
20 Labor Party! They've done what they could already. We know
them."

"That's true," said Henry. "The Laboristas* have tried every little
game possible. When I was in Orizaba they marched up to the Hotel
Francia to shoot all the gringos and the gachupines.* The hotel
25 manager had pluck enough to harangue them, and they went off to
the next hotel. When the man came out there to talk to them, they
shot him before he got a word out. It's funny really! If you have to go
to the Town Hall, and you're dressed in decent clothes, they let you
sit on a bench for hours. But if a street-sweeper comes in, or a fellow
30 in dirty cotton drawers, it is *Buenos Días! Señor! Pase Usted! Quiere
Usted algo?*—while you sit there waiting their pleasure. Oh, it's quite
funny."

The Judge trembled with irritation like an access of gout. The
party sat in gloomy silence, that sense of doom and despair
35 overcoming them as it seems to overcome all people who talk
seriously about Mexico. Even Owen was silent. He too had come
through Veracruz, and had had his fright: the porters had charged
him twenty pesos to carry his trunk from the ship to the train.
Twenty pesos is ten dollars, for ten minutes work.* And when Owen
40 had seen the man in front of him arrested and actually sent to jail, a

Mexican jail at that, for refusing to pay the charge, "the legal charge," he himself had stumped up without a word.

"I walked into the National Museum the other day," said the Major quietly. "Just into that room on the patio where the stones are. It was rather a cold morning, with a Norte blowing. I'd been there 5 about ten minutes when somebody suddenly poked me on the shoulder. I turned round, and it was a lout in tight boots. *You spik English?* I said *Yes!* Then he motioned me to take my hat off: I'd got to take my hat off. *What for?* said I, and I turned away and went on looking at their idols and things: ugliest set of stuff in the world, I 10 believe. Then up came the fellow with the attendant—the attendant of course wearing his cap. They began gabbling at me that this was the National Museum and I must take off my hat to their national monuments. Imagine it: those dirty stones! I laughed at them and jammed my hat on tighter and walked out.*—They are really only 15 monkeys, when it comes to nationalism."

"Exactly!" cried Henry. "When they forget all about the Patria and Méjico* and all that stuff, they're as nice a people as you'd find. But as soon as they get national, they're just monkeys.—A man up from Mixcoac* told me a nice story. Mixcoac is a capital way in the 20 South, and they've got a sort of Labor bureau there. Well the Indians come in from the hills, as wild as rabbits. And they get them into that bureau, and the Laboristas, the agitator fellows, say to them: *Now Señores, haven't you anything to report from your native village? Haven't you anything for which you would like redress?* Then of 25 course the Indians start complaining about one another, and the Secretary says: *Wait a minute, gentlemen! Let me ring up the Governor and report this.* So he goes to the telephone and starts ringing: ringing: *Ah! Is that the Palace? Is the Governor in? Tell him Señor Fulano* wants to speak to him!* The Indians sit gaping with open 30 mouths. To them it's a miracle. *Ah! Is that you, Governor! Good morning! How are you! Can I have your attention for a moment? Many thanks! Well I've got some gentlemen here down from Apaxtle, in the hills: José García, Jesús Querido, etc.—and they wish to report so-and-so. Yes! Yes! That's it! Yes! What? You will see that justice is 35 done and the thing is made right? Ah Señor, many thanks! In the name of these gentlemen from the hills, from the village of Apaxtle, many thanks.*

"There sit the Indians staring as if heaven had opened and the Virgin of Guadalupe* was standing tiptoe on their chins.—And what 40 do you expect? The telephone is a dummy. It isn't connected with anywhere.—Isn't that rich? But it's Mexico."*

The moment's fatal pause followed this funny story.

"Oh but!" said Kate. "It's wicked! It *is* wicked. I'm sure the
5 Indians would be all right, if they were left alone—"

"Well!" said Mrs Norris. "Mexico isn't like any other place in the world."

But she spoke with fear and despair in her voice.

"They seem to *want* to betray everything," said Kate. "They seem
10 to *love* criminals and ghastly things. They seem to *want* the ugly things to come up to the top. All the foulness that lies at the bottom, they want to stir it up to the top. They seem to enjoy it. To enjoy making everything fouler. Isn't it curious!"

"It *is* curious," said Mrs Norris.

15 "But that's what it is," said the Judge. "They want to turn the country into one big crime. They don't like anything else. They don't like honesty and decency and cleanliness. They want to foster lies and crime. What they call liberty here is just freedom to commit crime. That's what Labor means, that's what they all mean. Free
20 crime, nothing else."

"I wonder all the foreigners don't go away," said Kate.

"They have their occupations here," snapped the Judge.

"And the good people *are* all going away. They have nearly all gone—those that have anything left to go to," said Mrs Norris.
25 "Some of us, who have our property here, and who have made our lives here, and who know the country, we stay out of a kind of tenacity. But we know it's hopeless. The more it changes, the worse it is.—Ah, here is Don Ramón and Don Cipriano. So pleased to see you. Let me introduce you—"

30 Don Ramón Carrasco was a tall, big, handsome man who gave the effect of bigness. He was middle aged, with a large black moustache and large, rather haughty eyes under straight brows. The General was in civilian clothes, looking very small beside the other man, and very smartly built, almost cocky.

35 "Come," said Mrs Norris. "Let us go across and have tea."

The Major excused himself, and took his departure.

Mrs Norris gathered her little shawl round her shoulders and led through a sombre antechamber to a little terrace, where creepers and flowers bloomed thick on the low walls. There was a bell-flower, red
40 and velvety, like blood that is drying: and clusters of white roses: and tufts of bougainvillea, papery magenta colour.

"How lovely it is here!" said Kate. "Having the great dark trees beyond."

But she stood in a kind of dread.

"Yes, it *is* beautiful," said Mrs Norris, with the gratification of a possessor—"I have such a time trying to keep these apart." And going across in her little black shawl, she pushed the bougainvillea away from the rust-scarlet bell-flower, stroking the little white roses to make them intervene.

"I think the two reds together are interesting," said Owen.

"Do you really!" said Mrs Norris, automatically, paying no heed to such a remark.

The sky was blue overhead, but on the lower horizon was a thick, pearly haze. The clouds had gone.

"One never sees Popocatepetl nor Ixtaccihuatl," said Kate, disappointed.

"No, not at this season.—But look, through the trees there, you see Ajusco!"*

Kate looked at the sombre-seeming mountain, between the huge dark trees.

On the low stone parapet were Aztec things, obsidian knives, grimacing, squatting idols in black lava, and a queer thickish stone stick, or bâton. Owen was balancing the latter: it felt murderous even to touch.

Kate turned to the General, who was near her, his face expressionless yet alert.

"Aztec things oppress me," she said.

"They *are* oppressive," he answered, in his beautiful cultured English, that was nevertheless a tiny bit like a parrot talking.

"There is no hope in them," she said.

"Perhaps the Aztecs never asked for hope," he said, somewhat automatic.

"Surely it is hope that keeps one going?" she said.

"You, maybe. But not the Aztec, nor the Indian today."

He spoke like a man who has something in reserve, who is only half attending to what he hears, and even to his own answer.

"What do they have, if they don't have hope?" she said.

"They have some other strength, perhaps," he said evasively.

"I would like to give them hope," she said. "If they had hope, they wouldn't be so sad, and they would be cleaner, and not have vermin."

"That of course would be good," he said, with a little smile. "But

I think they are not so very sad. They laugh a good deal, and are gay."

"No," she said. "They oppress me, like a weight on my heart. They make me irritable, and I want to go away."

5 "From Mexico?"

"Yes. I feel I want to go away from it and never, never see it again. It is so oppressive and gruesome."

"Try it a little longer," he said. "Perhaps you will feel differently. But perhaps not—" he ended vaguely, driftingly.

10 She could feel in him a sort of yearning towards her. As if a sort of appeal came to her from him, from his physical heart in his breast. As if the very heart gave out dark rays of seeking and yearning. She glimpsed this now for the first time, quite apart from the talking, and it made her shy.

15 "And does everything in Mexico oppress you?" he asked, almost shyly, but with a touch of mockery, looking at her with a troubled naïve face that had its age heavy and resistant beneath the surface.

"Almost everything!" she said. "It *always* makes my heart sink. Like the eyes of the men in the big hats—I call them the peons.

20 Their eyes have no middle to them. Those big handsome men, under their big hats, they aren't really there. They have no centre, no real *I*. Their middle is a raging black hole, like the middle of a maelstrom."

She looked with her troubled grey eyes into the black, slanting, 25 watchful, calculating eyes of the small man opposite her. He had a pained expression, puzzled, like a child. And at the same time something obstinate and mature, a demonish maturity, opposing her in an animal way.

"You mean we aren't real people, we have nothing of our own, 30 except killing and death," he said, quite matter of fact.

"I don't know," she said, startled by his interpretation. "I only say how it makes me feel."

"You are very clever, Mrs Leslie," came Don Ramón's quiet, but rich and teasing voice behind her. "It is quite true. Whenever a 35 Mexican cries *Viva!* he ends up with *Muera!* When he says *Viva!* he really means *Death for Somebody or Other!* If I think of all the Mexican revolutions, I see a skeleton walking ahead of a great number of people, waving a black banner with *Viva la Muerte!* written in large white letters. *Long live Death!* Not *Viva Cristo Rey!* 40 but *Viva Muerte Rey! Vamos! Viva!!*"*

Kate looked round. Don Ramón was flashing his knowing, brown Spanish eyes, and a little sardonic smile lurked under his moustache. Instantly Kate and he, Europeans in essence, understood one another. He was waving his arm to the last *Viva!*

"But," said Kate, "I don't want to say *Viva la Muerte!*" 5

"But when you are a real Mexican—," he said, teasing.

"I *never* could be," she said hotly, and he laughed.

"I'm afraid *Viva la Muerte!* hits the nail on the head," said Mrs Norris, rather stonily. "But won't you come to tea! Do!"

She led the way in her black little shawl and neat grey hair, going 10 ahead like a Conquistador herself, and turning to look with her Aztec eyes, through her pince-nez, to see if the others were coming.

"We are following," said Don Ramón in Spanish, teasing her. Stately in his black suit, he walked behind her on the narrow terrace, and Kate followed, with the small, strutting Don Cipriano, also in a 15 black suit, lingering oddly near her.

"Do I call you General or Don Cipriano or Señor?" she asked, turning to him.

An amused little smile quickly lit his face, though his eyes did not smile. They looked at her with a black, sharp look. 20

"As you wish," he said. "You know *General* is a term of disgrace in Mexico. Shall we say *Don Cipriano?*"

"Yes, I like that much the best," she said.

And he seemed pleased.

It was a round tea-table, with shiny silver tea-service, and silver 25 kettle with a little flame, and pink and white oleanders. The little, neat young foot-man carried the tea-cups, in white cotton gloves. Mrs Norris poured tea and cut cakes with a heavy hand.

Don Ramón sat on her right hand, the Judge on her left. Kate was between the Judge and Mr Henry. Everybody except Don Ramón 30 and the Judge was a little nervous. Mrs Norris always put her visitors uncomfortably at their ease, as if they were captives and she the chieftainess who had captured them. She rather enjoyed it, heavily, archaeologically queening at the head of the table. But it was evident that Don Ramón, by far the most impressive person present, liked 35 her. Cipriano on the other hand remained mute and disciplined, perfectly familiar with the tea-table routine, superficially quite at ease, but underneath remote and unconnected. He glanced from time to time at Kate.

She was a beautiful woman, in her own unconventional way, and 40

with a certain richness. She was going to be forty next week. Used to all kinds of society, British, continental, and American, she read the social world as one reads the pages of a novel, with a certain disinterested amusement. She was never *in* any society: too Irish, too
5 wise.

"But of course nobody lives without hope," Mrs Norris was saying banteringly to Don Ramón. "If it's only the hope of a *real* to buy a litre of pulque."

"Ah Mrs Norris!" he replied in his quiet, yet curiously deep voice,
10 like a violincello: "If pulque is the highest happiness!"

"Then we are fortunate, because a *tostón* will buy paradise," she said.

"It is a *bon mot, Señora mía,*"* said Don Ramón, laughing and drinking his tea.

15 "Now won't you try these little native cakes with sesame seeds on them!" said Mrs Norris to the table at large. "My cook makes them, and her national feeling is flattered when anybody likes them. Mrs Leslie, do take one."

"I will," said Kate. "Does one say *Open Sesame!*"*
20 "If one wishes," said Mrs Norris.

"Won't you have one?" said Kate, handing the plate to Judge Burlap.

"Don't want any," he snapped, turning his face away as if he had been offered a plate of Mexicans, and leaving Kate with the dish
25 suspended.

Mrs Norris quietly but definitely took the plate, saying:

"Judge Burlap is afraid of *Sesame seed*, he prefers the cave shut."—And she handed the dish quietly to Cipriano, who was watching the old man's bad manners with black, snake-like eyes.

30 "Did you read that article by Willis Rice Hope, in the *Excelsior?*"* suddenly snarled the Judge, to his hostess.

"I did. I thought it very sensible."

"The *only* sensible thing that's been said about these Agrarian Laws. Sensible! I should think so. Why Rice Hope came to me, and I
35 put him up to a few things. But his article says *everything*, doesn't miss an item of importance."

"Quite!" said Mrs Norris, with rather stony attention. "If only *saying* would alter things, Judge Burlap."

"Saying the wrong thing has done all the mischief!" snapped the
40 Judge. "Fellows like Garfield Spence coming down here and talking

a lot of criminal talk. Why the town's full of socialists and *sinvergüen-zas** from New York."

Mrs Norris adjusted her pince-nez.

"Fortunately," she said, "they don't come out to Tlacolula, so we needn't think about them.—Mrs Henry, let me give you some more 5
tea."

"Do you read *Spanish?*" the Judge spat out, at Owen. Owen, in his big shell spectacles, was evidently a red rag to his irritated fellow-countryman.

"No!" said Owen, round as a cannon-shot. 10

Mrs Norris once more adjusted her eye-glasses.

"It's such a relief to hear someone who is altogether innocent of Spanish, and altogether unashamed," she said. "My father had us all speaking four languages by the time we were twelve, and we have none of us ever quite recovered. My stockings were all dyed blue for 15
me before I put my hair up.—By the way, how have you been for walking, Judge?—You heard of the time I had with my ankle?"

"Of course we heard!" cried Mrs Burlap, seeing dry land at last. "I've been trying *so* hard to get out to see you, to ask about it. We were so *grieved* about it." 20

"What happened?" said Kate.

"Why, I foolishly slipped on a piece of orange peel in town—just at the corner of San Juan de Letrán and Madero.* And I fell right down. And of course, the first thing I did when I got up was to push the piece of orange peel into the gutter. And would you believe it, that lot 25
of Mex—" she caught herself up—"that lot of fellows standing there at the corner laughed heartily at me, when they saw me doing it. They thought it an excellent joke."

"Of course they would," said the Judge. "They were waiting for the next person to come along and fall." 30

"Did nobody help you?" asked Kate.

"Oh no! If anyone has an accident in this country, you must never, *never* help. If you touch them even, you may be arrested for causing the accident."

"That's the law!" said the Judge. "If you touch them before the 35
police arrive, you are arrested for complicity. Let them lie and bleed, is the motto."

"Is that true?" said Kate to Don Ramón.

"Fairly true," he replied. "Yes, it is true you must not touch the one who is hurt." 40

"How disgusting!" said Kate.

"Disgusting!" cried the Judge. "A great deal is disgusting in this country, as you'll learn if you stay here long. I nearly lost my life on a banana skin; lay in a darkened room for days, between life and death, and lame for life from it."

"How awful!" said Kate. "What did you do when you fell?"

"What did I do? Just smashed my hip."

It had truly been a terrible accident, and the man had suffered bitterly.

"You can hardly blame Mexico for a banana skin," said Owen, elated. "I fell on one in Lexington Avenue:* but fortunately I only bruised myself on a soft spot."

"That wasn't your head, was it?" said Mrs Henry.

"No," laughed Owen. "The other extreme."

"We've got to add banana skins to the list of public menaces," said young Henry. "I'm an American, and I may any day turn bolshevist, to save my pesos, so I can repeat what I heard a man saying yesterday. He said there are only two great diseases in the world today, Bolshevism and Americanism: and Americanism is the worst of the two, because Bolshevism only smashes your house or your business or your skull, but Americanism smashes your soul."

"Who was he?" snarled the Judge.

"I forget," said Henry, wickedly.

"One wonders," said Mrs Norris slowly, "what he meant by Americanism."

"He didn't define it," said Henry. "Cult of the dollar, I suppose."

"Well," said Mrs Norris. "The cult of the dollar, in my experience, is far more intense in the countries that haven't got the dollar, than in the United States."

Kate felt that the table was like a steel disc to which they were all, as victims, magnetised and bound.

"Where *is* your garden, Mrs Norris?" she asked.

"Why," said Mrs Norris, rising, "let us go and look at it."

They trooped out, gasping with relief, to the terrace. The Judge hobbled behind, and Kate had to linger sympathetically to keep him company.

They were on the little terrace.

"Isn't this strange stuff!" said Kate, picking up one of the Aztec stone knives on the parapet. "Is it a sort of jade?"

"Jade!" snarled the Judge. "Jade's *green*, not black. That's obsidian."*

"Jade *can* be black," said Kate. "I've got a lovely little black tortoise of jade, from China."

"You can't have. Jade's bright green." 5

"But there's white jade too. I know there is."

The Judge was silent from exasperation for a few moments, then he snapped:

"Jade's bright green."

Owen, who had the ears of a lynx, had heard. 10

"What's that?" he said.

"Surely there's more than green jade!" said Kate.

"What!" cried Owen. "More! Why there's every imaginable tint. White, rose, lavender—"

"And black?" said Kate. 15

"Black, oh yes, quite common. Why you should see my collection. —The most beautiful range of colour! *Only green jade!* Ha-ha-ha!"—and he laughed a rather stage laugh.

They had come to the stairs, which were old stone waxed and polished in some way till they were of a glittering black. 20

"I'll catch hold of your arm down here," said the Judge to young Henry. "This stair-case is a death-trap."

Mrs Norris heard without comment. She only tilted her pince-nez on her sharp nose.

In the archway downstairs, Don Ramón and the General took 25 their leave. The rest trailed on into the garden.

Evening was falling. The garden was drawn up tall, under the huge dark trees on the one side and the tall, reddish-and-yellow house on the other. It was like being at the bottom of some dusky, flowering garden down in Hades. Hibiscus hung scarlet from the 30 bushes, putting out yellow, bristling tongues. Some roses were scattering scentless petals on the twilight, and lonely-looking carnations hung on weak stalks. From a huge dense bush the mysterious white bells of the datura were suspended large and silent, like the very ghosts of sound. And the datura scent was moving thick and 35 noiseless from the tree, into the little alleys.

Mrs Burlap had hitched herself on to Kate, and from her silly, social baby-face was emitting searching questions.

"What hotel are you staying at?"

Kate told her. 40

"I don't know it. Where is it?"

"In the Avenida del Perú. You wouldn't know it, it is a little Italian hotel."

"Are you staying long?"

5   "We aren't certain."

"Is Mr Rhys on a newspaper?"

"No, he's a poet."

"Does he make a living by poetry?"

"No, he doesn't try to."

10   It was the sort of secret service investigation one is submitted to, in the Capital of shady people, particularly shady foreigners.

Mrs Norris was lingering by a flowering arch of little white flowers.

Already a firefly was sparking. It was night.

15   "Well, goodbye, Mrs Norris! *Won't* you come and lunch with us. I don't mean come out to our house. Only let me know, and lunch with me *anywhere you like*, in town."

"Thank you my dear! Thank you so much! Well! I'll see!"

Mrs Norris was almost regal, stonily, Aztec-regal.

20   At last they had all made their adieus, and the great doors were shut behind them.

"How did you come out?" Mrs Burlap asked, impertinent.

"In an old Ford taxi—but where is it?" said Kate, peering into the dark.

25   It should have been under the *fresno* trees opposite, but it wasn't.

"What a curious thing!" said Owen, and he disappeared into the night.

"Which way do you go?" said Mrs Burlap.

"To the Zócalo,"* said Kate.

30   "We have to take a tram, the opposite way," said the baby-faced withered woman from the Middle-West.

The Judge was hobbling along the pavement like a cat on hot bricks, to the corner. Across the road stood a group of natives in big hats and white calico clothes, all a little the worse for the pulque they

35   had drunk. Nearer, on this side of the road, stood another little gang, of workmen in town clothes.

"There you have 'em," said the Judge, flourishing his stick with utter vindictiveness. "There's the two lots of 'em."

"What two lots?" said Kate, surprised.

40   "Those peon fellows and those obreros, all drunk, the lot of them.

The lot of them!"—And in a spasm of pure, frustrated hate he turned his back on her.

At the same moment they saw the bright lights of a tram-car rushing dragon-like up the dark road, between the high walls and the huge trees.

"Here's our car!" said the Judge, beginning to scramble excitedly with his stick.

"You go the other way," flung the baby-faced faded woman in the three-cornered satin hat, also beginning to fluster as if she were going to swim off the pavement.

The couple clambered avidly into the brightly-lighted car, first class; hobbling up. The natives crowded into the second class.

Away whizzed the *tren*. The Burlap couple had not even said Goodnight! They were terrified lest they might have to know somebody whom they might not want to know: whom it might not *pay* to know.

"You commonplace little woman!" said Kate aloud, looking after the retreating tram-car. "You awful ill-bred little pair."

She was a bit afraid of the natives, not quite sober, who were waiting for the car in the opposite direction. But stronger than her fear was a certain sympathy with these dark-faced silent men in their big straw hats and naïve little cotton blouses. Anyhow they had blood in their veins: they were columns of dark blood.

Whereas that other bloodless, acidulous couple from the Middle-West, with their nasty whiteness——!

She thought of the little tale the natives tell.—When the Lord was making the first men, he made them of clay and put them into the oven to bake. They came out black. *They're baked too much!* said the Lord. So he made another batch, and put them in. They came out white. *They're baked too little!* he said. So he had a third try. These came out a good warm brown. *They're just right!* said the Lord.

That couple from the Middle-West, that withered baby-face and that limping Judge, they weren't baked. They were hardly baked at all.

Kate looked at the dark faces under the arc-lamp. They frightened her. They were a sort of menace to her. But she felt they were at least baked hot and to a certain satisfactory colour.

The taxi came lurching up, with Owen poking his head out and opening the door.

"I found the man in a *pulquería*," he said. "But I don't think he's *quite* drunk. Will you risk driving back with him?"

"The *pulquería* was called *La Flor de un Día*—the Flower of a Day," said Owen, with an apprehensive laugh.

5   Kate hesitated, looking at her man.

"We may as well," she said.

Away gallivanted the Ford, full speed to Hell.

"Do tell him not so fast," said Kate.

"I don't know how," said Owen.

10   He shouted in good English:

"Hey! Chauffeur! Not so fast! Don't drive so fast."

"No presto. Troppo presto. Va troppo presto!"* said Kate.

The man looked at them with black, dilated eyes of fathomless incomprehension. Then he put his foot on the accelerator.

15   "He's only going faster!" laughed Owen nervously.

"Ah! Let him alone!" said Kate, with utter weariness.

The fellow drove like a devil incarnate, as if he had the devil in his body. But also, he drove with the devil's own nonchalant skill. There was nothing to do but let him rip.

20   "Wasn't that a ghastly tea-party!" said Owen.

"Ghastly!" said Kate.

Chapter III.

Fortieth Birthday.

Kate woke up one morning, aged forty. She did not hide the fact from herself, but she kept it dark from the others.

It was a blow, really. To be forty! One had to cross a dividing line. 5 On this side was youth and spontaneity and "happiness." On the other side was something different: reserve, responsibility, a certain standing back from "fun."

She was a widow, and a lonely woman now. Having married young, her two children were grown up. The boy was twenty-one, 10 and her daughter nineteen. They stayed chiefly with their father, from whom she had been divorced ten years before, in order to marry James Joachim Leslie. Now Leslie was dead, and all that half of life was over.

She climbed up to the flat roofs of the hotel. It was a brilliant 15 morning, and for once, under the blue sky of the distance, Popocatepetl stood aloof, a heavy giant presence under heaven, with a cape of snow. And rolling a long dark roll of smoke like a serpent.

Ixtaccihuatl, the White Woman, glittered and seemed near, but the other mountain, Popocatepetl, stood further back, and in 20 shadow, a pure cone of atmospheric shadow, with glinting flashes of snow. There they were, the two monsters, watching gigantically and terribly over this lofty, bloody cradle of men, the Valley of Mexico. Alien, ponderous, the white-hung mountains seemed to emit a deep purring sound, too deep for the ear to hear, and yet audible on the 25 blood, a sound of dread. There was no soaring or uplift or exaltation, as there is in the snowy mountains of Europe. Rather a ponderous white-shouldered weight, pressing terribly on the earth, and murmuring like two watchful lions.

Superficially, Mexico might be all right: with its suburbs of villas, 30 its central fine streets, its thousands of motor-cars, its tennis and its bridge-parties. The sun shone brilliantly every day, and big bright flowers stood out from the trees. It was a holiday.

Until you were alone with it. And then the undertone was like the low, angry, snarling purring of some jaguar spotted with night.* 35

49

There was a ponderous, down-pressing weight upon the spirit: the great folds of the dragon of the Aztecs, the dragon of the Toltecs* winding around one and weighing down the soul. And on the bright sunshine was a dark steam of angry, impotent blood, and the flowers
5 seemed to have their roots in spilt blood. The spirit of place was cruel, down-dragging, destructive.

Kate could so well understand the Mexican who had said to her: *El Grito mexicano es siempre el Grito del Odio.* The Mexican shout is always a shout of hate.—The famous revolutions, as Don Ramón
10 said, began with *Viva!* but ended always with *Muera!* Death to this, Death to the other, it was all death! death! death! as insistent as the Aztec sacrifices. Something forever gruesome and macabre.

Why had she come to this high plateau of death? As a woman, she suffered even more than men suffer: and in the end, practically all
15 men go under. Once, Mexico had had an elaborate ritual of death. Now it has death ragged, squalid, vulgar, without even the passion of its own mystery.*

She sat on a parapet of the old roof. The street beyond was like a black abyss, but around her was the rough glare of uneven flat roofs,
20 with loose telephone wires trailing across, and the sudden deep, dark wells of the patios, showing flowers blooming in shade.

Just behind was a huge old church, its barrel roof humping up like some crouching animal, and its domes, like bubbles inflated, glittering with yellow tiles, and blue and white tiles,* against the intense
25 blue heaven. Quiet native women in long skirts were moving on the roofs, hanging out washing or spreading it on the stones. Chickens pecked here and there. An occasional bird soared huge overhead, trailing a shadow. And not far away stood the brownish tower-stumps of the Cathedral, the profound old bell trembling huge and
30 deep, so soft as to be almost inaudible, upon the air.

It ought to have been all gay, allegro, allegretto, in that sparkle of bright air and old roof surfaces. But no! There was the dark undertow, the black, serpent-like fatality all the time.

It was no good Kate's wondering why she had come. Over in
35 England, in Ireland, in Europe, she had heard the *consummatum est* of her own spirit. It was finished, in a kind of death agony. But still this heavy continent of dark-souled death was more than she could bear.

She was forty: the first half of her life was over. The bright page,
40 with its flowers and its love and its stations of the Cross ended with a

grave. Now she must turn over, and the page was black, black and empty.

The first half of her life had been written on the bright smooth vellum of hope, with initial letters all gorgeous upon a field of gold. But the glamour had gone from station to station of the Cross, and the last illumination was the tomb.

Now the bright page was turned, and the dark page lay before her. How could one write on a page so profoundly black?

She went down, having promised to go and see the frescoes in the University and schools. Owen and Villiers and a young Mexican* were waiting for her. They set off through the busy streets of the town, where automobiles and the little omnibuses called *camiones* run wild, and where the natives in white cotton clothes and sandals and big hats linger like heavy ghosts in the street, among the bourgeoisie, the young ladies in pale pink crêpe-de-chine and high heels, the men in little shoes and American straw hats. A continual hustle in the glitter of sunshine.

Crossing the great shadeless plaza in front of the Cathedral, where the tram-cars gather as in a corral, and slide away down their various streets, Kate lingered again to look at the things spread for sale on the pavement: the little toys, the painted gourd-shells, brilliant in a kind of lacquer, the *novedades* from Germany, the fruits, the flowers. And the natives squatting with their wares, large-limbed, silent, handsome men looking up with their black, centreless eyes, speaking so softly, and lifting, with small, sensitive brown hands the little toys they had so carefully made and painted. A strange gentle appeal and wistfulness, strange male voices, so deep, yet so quiet and gentle. Or the women, the small, quick women in their blue rebozos, looking up quickly with dark eyes, and speaking in their quick, coaxing voices. The man just setting out his oranges, wiping them with a cloth so carefully, almost tenderly, and piling them in bright tiny pyramids, all neat and exquisite. A certain sensitive tenderness of the heavy blood, a certain chirping charm of the bird-like women, so still and tender with a bud-like femininity. And at the same time, the dirty clothes, the unwashed skin, the lice, and the peculiar hollow glint of the black eyes, at once so fearsome and so appealing. Something serpent-like, something also patient and appealing.

Kate knew the Italian fruit vendors, vigorously polishing their oranges on their coat-sleeves. Such a contrast the big, handsome Indian, sitting so soft and as it were lonely by the kerb, softly,

lingeringly polishing his yellow oranges to a clean gleam, and
lingeringly, delicately arranging the little piles, the pyramids for two
or three cents each.

Queer work, for a big, handsome, male-looking man. But they
5   seemed to prefer these childish little jobs.

The University was a Spanish building that had been done up
spick and span, and given over to the young artists to decorate. Since
the revolutions, nowhere had authority and tradition been so finally
overthrown as in the Mexican fields of science and of art. Science
10 and art are the sport of the young.—Go ahead, my boys!*

The boys had gone ahead. But even then the one artist of
distinction was no longer a boy, and he had served a long apprentice-
ship in Europe.

Kate had seen the reproductions of some of Ribera's frescoes.
15 Now she went round the patios of the University, looking at the
originals. They were interesting: the man knew his craft.

But the impulse was the impulse of the artist's hate. In the many
frescoes of the Indians, there was sympathy with the Indian, but
always from the ideal, social point of view. Never the spontaneous
20 answer of the blood. These flat Indians were symbols in the great
script of modern socialism, they were figures of the pathos of the
victims of modern industry and capitalism. That was all they were
used for: symbols in the weary script of socialism and anarchy.

Kate thought of the man polishing his oranges half-an-hour
25 before: his peculiar beauty, a certain richness of physical being, a
ponderous power of blood within him, and a helplessness, a
profound unbelief that was fatal and demonish. And all the Liberty,
all the Progress, all the Socialism in the world would not help him.
Nay, it would only help further to destroy him.

30 On the corridors of the University, young misses in bobbed hair
and boys' jumpers were going smartly around, their chins pushed
forward with the characteristic, deliberate youth-and-eagerness of
our day. Very much aware of their own youth and eagerness. And
very American. Young professors were passing in soft amiability,
35 young and apparently harmless.

The artists were at work on the frescoes, and Kate and Owen were
introduced to them. But they were men—or boys—whose very
pigments seemed to exist only to *épater le bourgeois*.* And Kate was
weary of *épatisme*, just as much as of the bourgeoisie. She wasn't
40 interested in *épatant le bourgeois*. The *épateurs* were as boring as the
bourgeois, two halves of one dreariness.

The little party passed on to the old Jesuit convent* now used as a secondary school. Here were more frescoes.

But these were by another man. And they were caricatures so crude and so ugly that Kate was merely repelled. They were meant to be shocking, but perhaps the very deliberateness prevents them from being as shocking as they might be. But they are ugly and vulgar. Strident caricatures of the Capitalist, and the Church, and of the Rich Woman, and of Mammon painted life-size and as violently as possible, round the patio of the grey old building, where the young people are educated. To anyone with the spark of human balance, the things are a misdemeanour.

"Oh, but how wonderful!" cried Owen.

His susceptibilities were shocked, therefore, as at the bull-fight, he was rather pleased. He thought it was novel and stimulating to decorate your public buildings in this way.

The young Mexican who was accompanying the party was a professor in the University too: a rather short, soft young fellow of twenty-seven or eight, who wrote the inevitable poetry of sentiment, had been in the government, even as a member of the House of Deputies, and was longing to go to New York. There was something fresh and soft, petulant, about him. Kate liked him. He could laugh with real hot young amusement, and he was no fool.

Until it came to these maniacal ideas of socialism, politics, and La Patria. Then he was as mechanical as a mousetrap. Very tedious.

"Oh no!" said Kate in front of the caricatures. "They are too ugly. They defeat their own ends."

"But they are meant to be ugly," said young García. "They must be ugly, no? Because capitalism is ugly, and Mammon is ugly, and the priest holding his hand to get the money from the poor Indians is ugly, no?"—He laughed rather unpleasantly.

"But," said Kate. "These caricatures are too intentional. They are like vulgar abuse, not art at all."

"Isn't that true?" said García, pointing to a hideous picture of a fat female in a tight short dress, with hips and breasts as protuberances, walking over the faces of the poor.* "That is how they are, no?"

"Who is like that?" said Kate. "It bores me. One must keep a certain balance."

"Not in Mexico!" said the young Mexican brightly, his plump cheeks flushing. "In Mexico you can't keep a balance, because things are so bad. In other countries, yes, perhaps you can remain balanced, because things are not so bad as they are here. But here they are so very bad, you can't be human. You have to be Mexican. You have to be *more* Mexican than human—no? You can't do no other. You have to hate the capitalist, you have to, in Mexico, or nobody can live. We can't live. Nobody can live. If you are Mexican you can't be human, it is impossible. You have to be a socialist Mexican, or you have to be a capitalist Mexican, and you hate. What else is there to be done? We hate the capitalist because he ruins the country and the people. We *must* hate him."

"But after all," said Kate, "what about the twelve million poor—mostly Indians—whom Montes talks about? You can't make them all rich, whatever you do. And they don't understand the very words, capital and socialism. They are Mexico, really, and nobody ever looks at them, except to make a *casus belli** of them. Humanly, they never exist for you."

"Humanly they can't exist, they are too ignorant!" cried García. "But when we can kill all the capitalists, then—"

"You'll find somebody killing *you*," said Kate. "No, I don't like it. *You* aren't Mexico. You aren't even Mexicans, really. You are just half-Spaniards full of European ideas, and you care for asserting your own ideas and nothing else. You have no real bowels of compassion. You are no good."

The young man listened with round eyes, going rather yellow in the face. At the end he lifted his shoulders and spread his hands in a pseudo-Mediterranean gesture.

"Well! It may be!" he said, with a certain jeering flippancy. "Perhaps you know everything. Maybe! Foreigners, they usually know everything about Mexico." And he ended on a little cackling laugh.

"I know what I *feel*," said Kate. "And now I want a taxi and I want to go home. I don't want to see any more stupid ugly pictures."

Off she drove back to the hotel, once more in a towering rage. She was amazed at herself. Usually she was so good-tempered and easy. But something about this country irritated her and put her into such violent anger she felt she would die. Burning, furious rage.

And perhaps, she thought to herself, the white and half-white Mexicans suffered some peculiar reaction in their blood which made them that they too were almost always in a state of suppressed irritation and anger, for which they *must* find a vent. They *must* spend their lives in a complicated game of frustration, because the very blood in their veins was frustrated in its ebbing and flowing.

Perhaps something came out of the earth, the dragon of the earth, some effluence, some vibration which militated against the very composition of the blood and nerves in human beings. Perhaps it came from the volcanoes. Or perhaps even from the silent, serpent-like dark resistance of those masses of ponderous natives whose 5 blood was principally the old, heavy, resistant Indian blood.

Who knows? But something there was, and something very potent. Kate lay on her bed and brooded her own organic rage. There was nothing to be done.

But young García was really nice. He called in the afternoon and 10 sent up his card. Kate, feeling sore, received him unwillingly.

"I came," he said, with a little stiff dignity, like an ambassador on a mission, "to tell you that I too don't like those caricatures. I too don't like them. I don't like the young people, boys and girls, no?—to be seeing them all the time. I too don't like it. But I think, also, that here 15 in Mexico, we can't help it. People are very bad, very greedy, no?—they only want to get money here, and they don't care. So we must hate them. Yes, we must. But I too, I don't like it."

He held his hat in his two hands, and twisted his shoulders in a conflict of feelings. 20

Kate suddenly laughed, and he laughed too, with a certain pain and confusion in his laughter.

"That's awfully nice of you to come and say so," she said, warming to him.

"No, not nice," he said, frowning. "But I don't know what to *do*. 25 Perhaps you think I am—different—I am not the thing that I am. And I don't want it."

He flushed, and was uncomfortable. There was a curious naïve sincerity about him, since he was being sincere. If he had chosen to play a game of sophistication, he could have played it better. But with 30 Kate he wanted to be sincere.

"I know, really," laughed Kate, "you feel a good deal like I do about it. I know you only pretend to be fierce and hard."

"No!" he said, suddenly making solemn, flashing eyes. "I do also feel fierce. I do hate those men who take, only take everything from 35 Mexico—money, and all—*everything*!"—he spread his hands with finality. "I hate them because I *must*, no? But also, I am sorry—I am sorry I have to hate so much. Yes, I think I am sorry. I think so—"

He knitted his brows rather tense. And over his plump, young, fresh face was a frown of resentment and hatred, quite sincere too. 40

Kate could see he wasn't really sorry. Only the two moods, of natural gay flow and of heavy resentment and hate, alternated inside him like shadow and shine on a cloudy day, in swift, unavoidable succession. What was nice about him was his simplicity, in spite of
5 the complication of his feelings, and the fact that his resentments were not personal, but beyond persons, even beyond himself.

She went out with him to tea, and while she was out, Don Ramón called and left cards with the corners turned down,* and an invitation to dinner, for her and Owen. There seemed an almost old-fashioned
10 correctness in those cards.

Looking over the newspaper, she came on an odd little item. She could read Spanish without much difficulty: the trouble lay in talking it, when Italian got in her way and caused a continual stumble. She looked on the English page of the *Excelsior* or the *Universal** for the
15 news—if there was any. Then she looked through the Spanish pages for bits of interest.

This little item was among the Spanish information, and was headed: The Gods of Antiquity Return to Mexico.*

"There was a ferment in the village of Sayula, Jalisco, on the Lake
20 of Sayula,* owing to an incident of more or less comic nature, yesterday morning towards mid-day. The women who inhabit the shores of the lake are to be seen each day soon after sunrise descending to the water's edge with large bundles. They kneel on the rocks and stones, and in little groups like water-fowl they wash their
25 dirty linen in the soft water of the lake, pausing at times as an old *canoa* sails by with large single sail. The scene is little changed since the days of Montezuma,* when the natives of the lake worshipped the spirit of the waters, and threw in little images and idols of baked clay, which the lake sometimes returns to the descendants of the dead
30 idolaters, to keep them in mind of practices not yet altogether forgotten.*

As the hot sun rises in the sky, the women spread their washing on the sand and pebbles of the shore, and retire to the shade of the willow trees that grow so gracefully and retain their verdant hue
35 through the dryest season of the year. While thus reposing after their labors, these humble and superstitious women were astonished to see a man of great stature rise naked from the lake and wade towards the shore. His face, they said, was dark and bearded, but his body shone like gold.*
40 As if unaware of any watchful eyes, he advanced calmly and

majestically towards the shore. There he stood a moment, and selecting with his eye a pair of the loose cotton pants worn by the peasants in the fields, that was spread whitening in the sun, he stooped and proceeded to cover his nakedness with the said garment.

The woman who thus saw her husband's apparel robbed beneath her eye, rose, calling to the man and summoning the other women. Whereupon the stranger turned his dark face upon them, and said in a quiet voice: Why are you crying? Be quiet! It will be given back to you. Your gods are ready to return to you. Quetzalcoatl and Tlaloc,* the old gods, are minded to come back to you. Be quiet, don't let them find you crying and complaining. I have come from out of the lake to tell you, the gods are coming back to Mexico, they are ready to return to their own home—*

Little comforted by this speech, the woman who had lost her washing was overcome and said no more. The stranger then appropriated a cotton blouse, which he donned, and disappeared.

After a while, the simple women gathered courage to return to their humble dwellings. The story thus reached the ears of the police, who at once set out to search for the thief.

The story, however, is not yet concluded. The husband of the poor woman of the lake-shore, returning from his labors in the field, approached the gates of the village towards sunset, thinking, no doubt, of nothing but repose and the evening meal. A man in a black sarape stepped towards him, from the shadow of a broken wall, and asked: Are you afraid to come with me? The laborer, a man of spirit, promptly replied: No Señor! He therefore followed the unknown man through the broken wall and through the bushes of a deserted garden. In a dark room or cellar a small light was burning, revealing a great basin of gold, into which four little men smaller than children were pouring sweet-scented water.* The astounded peasant was now told to wash and put on clean clothes, to be ready for the return of the gods. He was seated in the golden basin and washed with sweet-smelling soap, while the dwarfs poured water over him. *This*, they said, *is the bath of Quetzalcoatl. The bath of fire is yet to come.*￼* They gave him clean clothing of pure white cotton, and a new hat with star embroidery, and sandals with straps of white leather. But besides this, a new blanket, white with bars of blue and black, and flowers like stars at the centre, and two pieces of silver money. *Go*, he was told. *And when they ask you, where did you get your blanket? answer that*

Quetzalcoatl is young again. The poor fellow went home in sore fear,
lest the police should accuse him of possessing stolen goods.

The village is full of excitement, and Don Ramón Carrasco, our
eminent historian and archaeologist,* whose hacienda lies in the
5 vicinity, has announced his intention of proceeding as soon as
possible to the spot, to examine the origin of this new legend.
Meanwhile the police are watching attentively the development of
affairs, without taking any steps for the moment. Indeed, these little
fantasies create a pleasant diversion in the regular order of banditry,
10 murder, and outrage which it is usually our duty to report."

Kate wondered what was back of this: if anything more than a
story. Yet, strangely, a different light than the common light seemed
to gleam out of the words of even this newspaper paragraph.

She wanted to go to Sayula. She wanted to see the big lake where
15 the gods had once lived, and whence they were due to emerge. Amid
all the bitterness that Mexico produced in her spirit, there was still a
strange beam of wonder and mystery, almost like hope. A strange
darkly-iridescent beam of wonder, of magic.

The name Quetzalcoatl too fascinated her. She had read bits
20 about the god. Quetzal is the name of a bird that lives high in the
mists of tropical mountains, and has very beautiful tail-feathers,
precious to the Aztecs. Coatl is a serpent. Quetzalcoatl is the Plumed
Serpent, so hideous in the fanged, feathered, writhing stone of the
National Museum.

25 But Quetzalcoatl was, she vaguely remembered, a sort of fair-
faced, bearded god; the wind, the breath of life, the eyes that see and
are unseen, like the stars by day. The eyes that watch behind the
wind, as the stars beyond the blue of day. And Quetzalcoatl must
depart from Mexico, to merge again into the deep bath of life. He
30 was old. He had gone eastwards, perhaps into the sea, perhaps he
had sailed into heaven, like a meteor returning, from the top of the
Volcano of Orizaba: gone back as a peacock streaming into the night,
or as a bird of Paradise, its tail gleaming like the wake of a meteor.
Quetzalcoatl! Who knows what he meant to the dead Aztecs, and to
35 the older Indians, who knew him before the Aztecs raised their
deities to heights of horror and vindictiveness?*

All a confusion of contradictory gleams of meaning, Quetzalcoatl.
But why not? Her Irish spirit was weary to death of definite
meanings, and a god of one fixed purport. Gods should be iri-
40 descent, like the rainbow in the storm. Man creates a god in his own

image, and the god grows old along with the men that made him. But storms sway in heaven, and the god-stuff sweeps high and angry over our heads. Gods die with men who have conceived them. But the god-stuff roars eternally, like the sea, with too vast a sound to be heard. Like the sea in storm, that beats against the rocks of living, 5 stiffened men, slowly to destroy them. Or like the sea of the glimmering, ethereal plasm of the world, that bathes the feet and the knees of men as earth-sap bathes the roots of trees.—Ye must be born again.* Even the gods must be born again. We must be born again. 10

In her vague, woman's way, Kate knew this. She had lived her life. She had had her lovers, her two husbands. She had her children.

Joachim Leslie, her dead husband, she had loved as much as a woman can love a man: that is, to the bounds of human love. Then she had realised that human love has its limits, that there is a beyond. 15 And Joachim dead, willy nilly her spirit had passed the bounds. She was no longer in love with love. She no longer yearned for the love of a man, or the love even of her children. Joachim had gone into eternity in death, and she had crossed with him into a certain eternity in life. There, the yearning for companionship and sympathy and 20 human love had left her. Something infinitely intangible but infinitely blessed took its place: a peace that passes understanding.*

At the same time, a wild and angry battle raged between her and the thing that *Owen* called Life: such as the bull-fight, the tea-parties, the enjoyments, the arts in their modern aspect of hate 25 effusions. The powerful, degenerate thing called Life, wrapping one or other of its tentacles round her.

And then, when she could escape into her true loneliness, the influx of peace and soft, flower-like potency which was beyond understanding. It disappeared even if you thought about it, so 30 delicate, so fine. And yet, the only reality.

Ye must be born again. Out of the fight with the octopus of Life, the dragon of degenerated or of incomplete existence, one must win this soft bloom of being, that is damaged by a touch.

No, she no longer wanted love, excitement, and something to fill 35 her life. She was forty, and in the rare, lingering dawn of maturity, the flower of her soul was opening. Above all things, she must preserve herself from worldly contacts. Only she wanted the silence of other unfolded souls around her, like a perfume. The presence of that which is forever unsaid. 40

And in this horror and climax of death-rattles which is Mexico, she thought she could feel as well the silence of souls in bud. She thought she could see it in the black eyes of the Indians. She felt that Don Ramón and Don Cipriano both had heard the soundless call,

5   across all the hideous choking.

Perhaps this had brought her to Mexico: away from England and her mother, away from her children, away from everybody. To be alone with the unfolding flower of her own soul, in the delicate, chiming silence that is at the midst of things.

10   The thing called "Life" is just a mistake we have made in our own minds. Why persist in the mistake any further?

Owen was the mistake itself: so was Villiers: so was that vile Mexico City.

She wanted to get out, to disentangle herself again.

15   They had promised to go out to dinner to the house of Don Ramón. His wife was away in the United States with her two boys, one of whom had been ill, not seriously, at his school in California. But Don Ramón's aunt would be hostess.

The house was way out at Tlalpam.* It was May, the weather was

20   hot, the rains were not yet started. The shower at the bull-fight had been a sort of accident.

"I wonder," said Owen, "whether I ought to put on a dinner-coat. Really, I feel humiliated to the earth every time I put on evening dress."

25   "Then don't do it!" said Kate, who was impatient of Owen's kicking at these very little social pricks, and swallowing the whole porcupine.*

She herself came down in a simple gown with a black velvet top and a loose skirt of delicate brocaded chiffon, of a glimmering green

30   and yellow and black. She also wore a long string of jade and crystal.

It was a gift she had, of looking like an Ossianic goddess,* a certain feminine strength and softness glowing in the very material of her dress. But she was never "smart."

"Why you're dressed up to the eyes!" cried Owen in chagrin,

35   pulling at his soft collar. "Bare shoulders notwithstanding!"

They went out to the distant suburb in the tram-car, swift in the night, with big clear stars overhead, dropping and hanging with a certain gleam of menace. In Tlalpam there was a heavy scent of night flowers, a feeling of ponderous darkness, with a few sparks of

40   intermittent fireflies. And always the heavy calling of night-flower

scents. To Kate, there seemed a faint whiff of blood in all tropical-scented flowers: of blood or sweat.

It was a hot night. They banged on the iron doors of the entrance, dogs barked, and a mozo opened to them, warily, closing fast again the moment they had entered the dark garden of trees.

Don Ramón was in white, a white dinner jacket: Don Cipriano the same. But there were other guests, young García, another pale young man called Mirabal, and an elderly man in a black cravat, named Toussaint. The only other woman was Doña Isabel, aunt to Don Ramón. She wore a black dress with a high collar of black lace, and some strings of pearls, and seemed shy, frightened, absent as a nun before all those men. But to Kate she was very kind, caressive, speaking English in a plaintive, faded voice. This dinner was a sort of ordeal and ritual combined, to the cloistered, elderly soul.

But it was soon evident that she was trembling with fearful joy. She adored Ramón with an uncritical, nun-like adoration. It was obvious she hardly heard the things that were said. Words skimmed the surface of her consciousness without ever penetrating. Under-neath, she was trembling in nun-like awareness of so many men, and in an almost sacred excitement at facing Don Ramón as hostess.

The house was a fairly large villa, quietly and simply furnished, with natural taste.

"Do you always live here?" said Kate to Don Ramón. "Never at your hacienda?"

"How do you know I have a hacienda?" he asked.

"I saw it in the newspaper—near Sayula."

"Ah!" he said, laughing at her with his eyes. "You saw about the returning of the Gods of Antiquity."

"Yes," she said. "Don't you think it is interesting?"

"I think so," he said.

"I love the *word* Quetzalcoatl."

"The *word?*" he repeated.

His eyes laughed at her teasingly all the time.

"What do you think, Mrs Leslie," cried the pale-faced young Mirabal, in curiously resonant English, with a French accent. "Don't you think it would be wonderful if the gods came back to Mexico: our own gods?"—He sat in intense expectation, his blue eyes fixed on Kate's face, his soup-spoon suspended.

Kate's face was baffled with incomprehension.

"Not those Aztec horrors!" she said.

"The Aztec horrors! The Aztec horrors! Well, perhaps they were
not so horrible after all. But if they were, it was because the Aztecs
were all tied up. They were in a cul de sac, so they saw nothing but
death. Don't you think so?"

5   "I don't know enough!" said Kate.

"Nobody knows any more. But if you like the *word* Quetzalcoatl,
don't you think it would be wonderful if he came back again?—Ah,
the *names* of the gods! Don't you think the *names* are like seeds, so
full of magic, of the unexplored magic? *Huitzilopochtli!*—how won-

10   derful! And *Tlaloc!** Ah! I love them! I say them over and over, like
they say *Mani padma Om!** in Thibet. I believe in the fertility of
sound. *Itzpapalotl*—the Obsidian Butterfly! *Itzpapalotl!* But say it,
and you will see it does good to your soul. *Itzpapalotl!*
Tezcatlipoca!*—They were old when the Spaniards came, they

15   needed the bath of life again. But now, re-bathed in youth, how
wonderful they must be! Think of *Jahveh! Jehovah!* Think of *Jesus
Christ!* How thin and poor they sound! Or *Jesucristo!* They are dead
names, all the life withered out of them. Ah, it is time now for Jesus
to go back to the place of the death of the gods, and take the long bath

20   of being made young again. He is an old-old young god, don't you
think?"—He looked long at Kate, then dived for his soup.

Kate widened her eyes in amazement at this torrent from the
young Mirabal. Then she laughed.

"I think it's a bit overwhelming!" she said, non-committal.

25   "Ah! Yes! Exactly! Exactly! But how good to be overwhelmed!
How splendid if something will overwhelm me! Ah, I am so glad!"

The last word came with a clapping French resonance, and the
young man dived for his soup again. He was lean and pale, but
burning with an intense, crazy energy.

30   "You see," said young García, raising his full, bright dark eyes to
Kate, half-aggressive and half-bashful: "we must do something for
Mexico. If we don't, it will go under, no? You say you don't like
socialism. I don't think I do either. But if there is nothing else but
socialism, we will have socialism. If there is nothing better. But

35   perhaps there is—"

"Why should Mexico go under?" said Kate. "There are lots of
children everywhere."

"Yes. But the last census of Porfirio Díaz* gave seventeen million
people in Mexico, and the census of last year gave only thirteen

40   millions. Maybe the count was not quite right. But you count four

million people fewer, in twenty years, then in sixty years there will be no Mexicans:* only foreigners, who don't die."

"Oh, but figures always lie!" said Kate. "Statistics are always misleading."

"Maybe two and two don't make four," said García. "I don't know if they do. But I know, if you take two away from two, it leaves none."

"Do you think Mexico might die out?" she said to Don Ramón.

"Why!" he replied. "It might. Die out and become Americanised."

"I quite see the danger of Americanisation," said Owen. "That *would* be ghastly. Almost better die out."

Owen was so American, he invariably said these things.

"But!" said Kate. "The Mexicans look so strong!"

"They are strong to carry heavy loads," said Don Ramón. "But they die easily. They eat all the wrong things, they drink the wrong things, and they don't mind dying. They have many children, and they like their children very much. But when the child dies, the parents say: *Ah, he will be an angelito!*—So they cheer up and feel as if they had been given a present. Sometimes I think they enjoy it when their children die. Sometimes I think they would like to transfer Mexico *en bloc* into Paradise, or whatever lies behind the walls of death.* It would be better there!"

There was a silence.

"But how sad you are!" said Kate, afraid.

Doña Isabel was giving hurried orders to the man-servant.

"Whoever knows Mexico below the surface, is sad!" said Julio Toussaint rather sententiously, over his black cravat.

"Well," said Owen, "it seems to me, on the contrary, a gay country. A country of gay, irresponsible children. Or rather, they *would* be gay, if they were properly treated. If they had comfortable homes, and a sense of real freedom. If they felt that they could control their own lives and their own country. But being in the grip of outsiders, as they have been for hundreds of years, life of course seems hardly worth while to them. Naturally they don't care if they live or die. They don't feel *free*."

"Free what for?" asked Toussaint.

"To make Mexico their own. Not to be so poor and at the mercy of outsiders."

"They are at the mercy of something worse than outsiders," said Toussaint. "Let me tell you. They are at the mercy of their own

natures. It is this way. Fifty percent of the people in Mexico are pure
Indians: more or less. Of the rest, a small proportion are foreigners
or Spaniards. You have then the mass which is on top, of mixed
blood, Indian and Spaniard mixed, chiefly. These are the real
5 Mexicans, those with the mixed blood. Now you take us at this table.
Don Cipriano is pure Indian. Don Ramón is almost pure Spaniard,
but most probably he has the blood of Tlaxcalan Indians* in his veins
as well. Señor Mirabal is mixed French and Spanish. Señor García
most probably has a mixture of Indian blood with Spanish. I myself
10 have French, Spanish, Austrian and Indian blood. Very well! Now
listen to me. You may mix Spanish and French blood, and it may be
all right. Europeans are all of Aryan stock, the race is the same. But
when you mix European and American Indian, you mix different
blood races, and you produce the half-breed. Now the half-breed is a
15 calamity. For why? He is neither one thing nor another, he is divided
against himself. His blood of one race tells him one thing, his blood
of another race tells him another. He is an unfortunate, a calamity to
himself. And it is hopeless.

"And this is Mexico. The Mexicans of mixed blood are hopeless.
20 Well then! There are only two things to be done. All the foreigners
and the Mexicans clear out and leave the country to the Indians, the
pure-blooded Indians.—But already you have a difficulty. How can
you distinguish the pure-blooded Indian, after so many gener-
ations?—Or else the half-breed, or mixed-blood Mexicans who are
25 all the time on top shall continue to destroy the country till the
Americans from the United States flood in and we are as California
and New Mexico now are, swamped under the dead white sea.

"But let me tell you something further. I hope we are not Puritans.
I hope I may say that it all depends on the moment of coition. At the
30 moment of coition, either the spirit of the father fuses with the spirit
of the mother, to create a new being with a soul, or else nothing fuses
but the germ of procreation.

"Now consider. How have these Mexicans of mixed blood been
begotten, for centuries? In what spirit? What was the moment of
35 coition like?—Answer me that, and you have told me the reason for
this Mexico which makes us despair and which will go on making
everybody despair, till it destroys itself. In what spirit have the
Spanish and other foreign fathers gotten children of the Indian
women? What sort of spirit was it? What sort of coition?—And then,
40 what sort of race do you expect?"*

"But what sort of a spirit is there between white men and white women!" said Kate.

"At least," replied the didactic Toussaint, "the blood is homogeneous, so the consciousness automatically unrolls in continuity."

"I hate its unrolling in automatic continuity," said Kate.   5

"Perhaps! But it makes life possible. Without developing continuity in consciousness, you have chaos. And this comes of mixed blood."

"And then," said Kate, "surely the Indian men are fond of their women! The men seem manly, and the women seem very lovable   10
and womanly."

"It is possible that the Indian children are pure blooded, there is the continuity of blood. But the Indian consciousness is swamped under the stagnant water of the white man's Dead Sea consciousness. Take a man like Benito Juárez,* a pure Indian. He floods his   15
old consciousness with the new white ideas, and there springs up a whole forest of verbiage, new laws, new constitutions and all the rest. But it is a sudden weed. It grows like a weed on the surface, saps the strength of the Indian soil underneath, and helps the process of ruin.—No madam! There is no hope for Mexico short of a miracle."   20

"Ah!" cried Mirabal, flourishing his wine glass. "Isn't that wonderful, when only the miracle will save us? When we must produce the miracle? *We! We!* We must make the miracle!" He hit his own breast emphatically. "Ah, I think that is marvellous!"—And he returned to his turkey in black sauce.*   25

"Look at the Mexicans!" Toussaint flared on. "They don't care about anything. They eat food so hot with chile it burns holes in their insides. And it has no nourishment. They live in houses that a dog would be ashamed of, and they lie and shiver with cold. But they don't *do* anything. They could make, easily, easily, a bed of maize   30
leaves or similar leaves. But they don't do it. They don't do anything. They roll up in a thin sarape and lie on a thin mat on the bare ground, whether it is wet or dry. And Mexican nights are cold. But they lie down like dogs, anywhere, as if they lay down to die. I say dogs! But you will see the dogs looking for a dry sheltered place. The   35
Mexicans, no! Anywhere, with a terrible indifference. They don't care, about nothing, nothing, nothing! And it is terrible. It is terrible, terrible! As if they wanted to punish themselves for being alive."

"But then why do they have so many children?" said Kate.

"Why do they? The same, because they don't care. They don't   40

care about money, they don't care about making anything, they don't
care about nothing, nothing, nothing. Only they get an excitement
out of women, as they do out of chile. They like to feel the red pepper
burning holes in their insides, and they like to feel the other thing,
5   the sex, burning holes in them too. But after the moment, they don't
care. They don't care a bit.

"And that is bad. I tell you, excuse me, but all, everything,
depends on the moment of coition. At that moment many things can
come to a crisis: all a man's hope, his honour, his faith, his trust, his
10 belief in life and creation and God, all these things can come to a
crisis at the moment of coition. And these things will be handed on in
continuity to the child.—Believe me, I am a crank on this idea, but it
is true. It is certainly absolutely true."

"I believe it is true," said Kate, rather coldly.

15 "Ah! you do! Well then! Look at Mexico! The only *conscious*
people are half-breeds, people of mixed blood, begotten in greed and
selfish brutality."

"Some people believe in the mixed blood," said Kate.

"Ah! They do, do they? Who?"

20 "Some of your serious-minded men.* They say the half-breed is
better than the Indian."

"Better! Well! The Indian has his hopelessness. The moment of
coition is his moment of supreme hopelessness, when he throws
himself down the pit of despair."

25 The Austrian, European blood, which fans into fire of conscious
understanding, died down again, leaving what was Mexican in Julio
Toussaint sunk in irredeemable gloom.

"It is true," said Mirabal, out of the gloom. "The Mexicans who
have any feeling always prostitute themselves, one way or another,
30 and so they can never *do* anything. And the Indians can never do
anything either, because they haven't got hope in anything.—But it is
always darkest before the dawn. We must make the miracle come.
The miracle is superior even to the moment of coition."

It seemed, however, as if he said it by an effort of will.

35 The dinner was ending in silence. During the whirl of talk, or of
passionate declamation, the servants had carried round the food and
wine. Doña Isabel, completely oblivious of the things that were being
said, watched and directed the servants with nervous anxiety and
excitement, her hands with their old jewellery trembling with
40 agitation. Don Ramón had kept his eye on his guests' material

comfort, at the same time listening, as it were, from the back of his head. His big brown eyes were inscrutable, his face impassive. But when he had anything to say, it was always with a light laugh and a teasing accent. And yet his eyes brooded and smouldered with an incomprehensible, unyielding fire. 5

Kate felt she was in the presence of men. Here were men face to face, not with death and self-sacrifice, but with the life-issue. She felt, for the first time in her life, a pang almost like fear, of men who were passing beyond what she knew, beyond her depth.

Cipriano, his rather short but intensely black, curved eyelashes 10 lowering over his dark eyes, watched his plate, only sometimes looking up with a black, brilliant glance, either at whomsoever was speaking, or at Don Ramón, or at Kate. His face was changeless and intensely serious, serious almost with a touch of childishness. But the curious blackness of his eyelashes lifted so strangely, with such 15 intense unconscious maleness from his eyes, the movement of his hand was so odd, quick, light, as he ate, so easily a movement of shooting, or of flashing a knife into the body of some adversary, and his dark-coloured lips were so helplessly savage, as he ate or briefly spoke, that her heart stood still. There was something undeveloped 20 and intense in him, the intensity and the crudity of the semi-savage. She could well understand the potency of the snake upon the Aztec and Maya imagination. Something smooth, undeveloped, yet vital in this man suggested the heavy-ebbing blood of reptiles in his veins. That was what it was, the heavy-ebbing blood of powerful reptiles, 25 the dragon of Mexico.

So that unconsciously she shrank when his black, big, glittering eyes turned on her for a moment. They were not, like Don Ramón's, *dark* eyes. They were black as black jewels into which one could not look without a sensation of fear. And her fascination was tinged with 30 fear. She felt somewhat as the bird feels when the snake is watching it.

She wondered almost that Ramón was not afraid. Because she had noticed that usually, when an Indian looked at a white man, both men stood back from actual contact, from actual meeting of each 35 other's eyes. They left a wide space of neutral territory between. But Cipriano looked at Ramón with a curious intimacy, glittering, steady, warrior-like, and at the same time betraying an almost menacing trust in the other man.

Kate realised that Ramón had a good deal to stand up to. But he 40 kept a little, foiling laugh on his face, and lowered his beautiful head with the black hair touched with grey, as if he would put a veil before his countenance.

"Do you think one can make the miracle come?" she asked of him.

5   "The miracle is always there," he said, "for the man who can pass his hand through to it, to take it."

They finished dinner, and went to sit out on the verandah, looking into the garden where the light from the house fell uncannily on the blossoming trees and the dark tufts of yucca and the strange great
10   writhing trunks of the *laurel de la India.*

Cipriano had sat down next to her, smoking a cigarette.

"It is a strange darkness, the Mexican darkness!" she said.

"Do you like it?" he asked.

"I don't know yet," she said. "Do you?"

15   "Yes. Very much. I think I like best the time when the day is falling, and the night coming on like something else. Then, one feels more free, don't you think? Like the flowers that send out their scent at night, but in the daytime they look at the sun and don't have any smell."*

20   "Perhaps the night here scares me," she laughed.

"Yes. But why not? The smell of the flowers at night may make one feel afraid, but it is a good fear. One likes it, don't you think?"

"I am afraid of fear," she said.

He laughed shortly.

25   "You speak such English English," she said. "Nearly all the Mexicans who speak English speak American English. Even Don Ramón does, rather."

"Yes. Don Ramón graduated in Columbia University. But I was sent to England, to school in London, and then to Oxford."

30   "Who sent you?"

"My god-father. He was an Englishman: Bishop Severn, Bishop of Oaxaca.* You have heard of him?"

"No," said Kate.

"He was a very well-known man. He died only about ten years
35   ago. He was very rich too, before the Revolution. He had a big hacienda in Oaxaca, with a very fine library. But they took it away from him in the Revolution, and they sold the things, or broke them. They didn't know the value of them, of course."

"And did he adopt you?"

40   "Yes! In a way. My father was one of the overseers on the

hacienda. When I was a little boy I came running to my father, when the Bishop was there, with something in my hands—so!"—and he made a cup of his hands. "I don't remember. This is what they tell me. I was a small child—three, four years of age—somewhere there. What I had in my hands was a yellow scorpion, one of the small ones, 5 very poisonous, no?"

And he lifted the cup of his small, slender, dark hands, as if to show Kate the creature.

"Well the Bishop was talking to my father, and he saw what I had got before my father did. So he told me at once, to put the scorpion in 10 his hat—the Bishop's hat, no? Of course I did what he told me, and I put the scorpion in his hat, and it did not bite me. If it had stung me I should have died, of course. But I didn't know, so I suppose the alacrán was not interested.—The Bishop was a very good man, very kind. He liked my father, so he became my god-father. Then he 15 always took an interest in me, and he sent me to school, and then to England.—He hoped I should be a priest. He always said that the one hope for Mexico was if she had really fine native priests—" He ended rather wistfully.

"And didn't you want to become a priest?" said Kate. 20

"No!" he said sadly. "No!"

"Not at all?" she asked.

"No! When I was in England it was different from Mexico. Even God was different, and the Blessed Mary. They were changed so much, I felt I didn't know them any more. Then I came to 25 understand better—and when I understood I didn't believe any more. I used to think it was the images of Jesus, and the Virgin, and the saints, that were doing everything in the world. And the world seemed to me so strange, no? I couldn't see that it was bad, because it was all so very strange and mysterious. Everything that happened 30 was strange and mysterious, when I was a child, in Mexico. Only in England I learned about the laws of life, and some science. And then, when I knew why the sun rose and set, and how the world really was—I felt quite different."

"Was your god-father disappointed?" 35

"A little, perhaps. But he asked me if I would rather be a soldier, so I said I would. Then when the Revolution came, and I was twenty-two years old, I had to come back to Mexico."

"Did you like your god-father?"

"Yes, very much.—But the revolutions carried everything away. I 40

felt I must do what my god-father wished. But I could see that
Mexico was not the Mexico he believed in. It was different. He was
too English, and too good to understand. In the revolutions, I tried to.
help the man I believed was the best man.—So you see, I have always
5 been half a priest and half a soldier."

"You never married?"

"No. I couldn't marry, because I always felt my god-father was
there, and I felt I had promised him to be a priest—all those things,
you know. When he died he told me to follow my own conscience,
10 and to remember that Mexico and all the Indians were in the hands
of God, and he made me promise never to take sides against God.
He was an old man when he died, seventy-five."

Kate could see the spell of the old Bishop's strong, rather
grandiose personality upon the impressionable Indian. She could see
15 the curious recoil into chastity, perhaps characteristic of the savage.
And at the same time she felt the intense masculine yearning,
coupled with a certain male ferocity, in the man's breast.

"Your husband was James Joachim Leslie, the famous Irish
leader?" he asked her: and added:
20 "You had no children?"

"No. I wanted Joachim's children so much, but I didn't have any.
But I have a boy and a girl from my first marriage. My first husband
was a lawyer, and I was divorced from him for Joachim."

"Did you like him—that first one?"
25 "Yes. I liked him. But I never felt anything very deep for him. I
married him when I was young, and he was a good deal older than I. I
was fond of him, in a way. But I had never realised that one could be
more than just fond of a man, till I knew Joachim. I thought that was
all one could ever expect to feel—that you just liked a man, and that
30 he was in love with you. It took me years to understand that a woman
can't love a man—at least a woman like I am can't—if he is only the
sort of good decent citizen. With Joachim I came to realise that a
woman like me *can* only love a man who is fighting to *change* the
world, to make it freer, more alive. Men like my first husband, who
35 are good and trustworthy and who work to keep the world going on
well in the same state they found it in, they let you down horribly,
somewhere. You feel so terribly sold. Everything is just a sell: it
becomes so small.—A woman who isn't quite ordinary herself can
only love a man who is fighting for something beyond the ordinary
40 life."

"And your husband fought for Ireland."

"Yes—for Ireland, and for something he never quite realised. He ruined his health. And when he was dying, he said to me: *Kate, perhaps I've let you down. Perhaps I haven't really helped Ireland. But I couldn't help myself. I feel as if I'd brought you to the doors of life, and was leaving you there. Kate, don't be disappointed in life because of me. I didn't really get anywhere. I haven't really got you anywhere. I feel as if I'd made a mistake. But perhaps when I'm dead I shall be able to do more for you than I have done while I was alive. Say you'll never feel disappointed!"*

There was a pause. The memory of the dead man was coming over her again, and all her grief.

"And I don't feel disappointed," she went on, her voice beginning to shake. "But I loved him. And it was bitter, that he had to die, feeling he hadn't—hadn't—"

She put her hands before her face, and the bitter tears came through her fingers.

Cipriano sat motionless as a statue. But from his breast came that dark, surging passion of tenderness the Indians are capable of. Perhaps it would pass, leaving him indifferent and fatalistic again. But at any rate for the moment he sat in a dark, fiery cloud of passionate male tenderness. He looked at her soft, wet white hands over her face, and at the one big emerald on her finger, in a sort of wonder. The wonder, the mystery, the magic that used to flood over him as a boy and a youth, when he kneeled before the babyish figure of the Santa María de la Soledad,* flooded him again. He was in the presence of the goddess, white-handed, mysterious, gleaming with a moon-like power and the intense potency of grief.

Then Kate hastily took her hands from her face and with head ducked, looked for a handkerchief. Of course she hadn't got one. Cipriano lent her his, nicely folded. She took it without a word, and rubbed her face and blew her nose.

"I want to go and look at the flowers," she said in a strangled voice.

And she dashed into the garden with his handkerchief in her hand. He stood up and drew aside his chair, to let her pass, then stood a moment looking at the garden, before he sat down and lighted a cigarette.

Chapter IV.

To Stay or Not To Stay.*

Owen had to return to the United States, and he asked Kate whether she wanted to stay on in Mexico.

5   This put her into a quandary. It was not an easy country for a woman to be alone in. And she had been beating her wings in an effort to get away. She felt like a bird round whose body a snake has coiled itself. Mexico was the snake.

The curious influence of the country, pulling one down, pulling
10   one down. She had heard an old American, who had been forty years in the Republic, saying to Owen: "No man who hasn't a strong moral backbone should try to settle in Mexico. If he does, he'll go to pieces, morally and physically, as I've seen hundreds of young Americans do."

15   To pull one down. It was what the country wanted to do all the time, with a slow, reptilian insistence, to pull one down. To prevent the spirit from soaring. To take away the free, soaring sense of liberty.

"There is no such thing as liberty," she heard the quiet, deep,
20   dangerous voice of Don Ramón repeating. "There is no such thing as liberty. The greatest liberators are usually slaves of an idea. The freest people are slaves to convention and public opinion, and more still, slaves to the industrial machine. There is no such thing as liberty. You only change one sort of domination for another. All we
25   can do is to choose our master."

"But surely that *is* liberty—for the mass of people."

"They don't choose. They are tricked into a new form of servility, no more. They go from bad to worse."

"You yourself—aren't you free?" she asked.
30   "I?" he laughed. "I spent a long time trying to pretend. I thought I could have my own way. Till I realised that having my own way meant only running about smelling all the things in the street, like a dog that will pick up something. Of myself, I have no way. No man has any way in himself. Every man who goes along a way is led by one of three

72

things: by an appetite—and I class ambition among appetite; or by an idea; or by an inspiration."

"I used to think my husband was inspired about Ireland," said Kate doubtfully.

"And now?"

"Yes! Perhaps he put his wine in old, rotten bottles that wouldn't hold it. No!—Liberty is a rotten old wine-skin,* it won't hold one's wine of inspiration or passion any more," she said.

"And Mexico!" he said. "Mexico is another Ireland.—Ah no, no man can be his own master. If I must serve, I will not serve an idea, which cracks and leaks like an old wine-skin. I will serve the God that gives me my manhood. There is no liberty for a man, apart from the God of his manhood. Free Mexico is a bully, and the old, colonial-ecclesiastical Mexico was another sort of bully. When man has nothing but his *will* to assert—even his good-will—it is always bullying. Bolshevism is one sort of bullying, capitalism another: and Liberty is a change of chains—"

"Then what's to be done?" said Kate. "Just nothing?"

And with her own will, she wanted nothing to be done. Let the skies fall!

"One is driven, at last, back to the far distance, to look for God," said Ramón uneasily.

"I rather hate this search-for-God business, and religiosity," said Kate.

"I know!" he said, with a laugh. "I've suffered from would-be-cocksure religion myself."

"And you can't *really* 'find God'!" she said. "It's a sort of sentimentalism, and creeping back into old, hollow shells."

"No!" he said slowly. "I can't *find God*, in the old sense. I know it's a sentimentalism, if I pretend to. But I am nauseated with humanity and the human will: even with my own will. I have realised that *my will*, no matter how intelligent I am, is only another nuisance on the face of the earth, once I start exerting it. And other people's *wills* are even worse."

"Oh! isn't human life horrible!" she cried. "Every human being exerting his will all the time—over other people, and over himself—and nearly always self-righteous!"

Ramón made a grimace of repulsion.

"To me," he said, "that is just the weariness of life! For a time, it can be amusing: exerting your own will, and resisting all the other people's wills, that they try to put over you. But at a certain point, a nausea sets in at the very middle of me: my *soul* is nauseated. My soul is nauseated, and there is nothing but death ahead, unless I find something else."

Kate listened in silence. She knew the road he had gone, but she herself had not yet come to the end of it. As yet she was still strong in the pride of her own—her very own *Will*.

"Oh, people are repulsive!" she cried.

"My own will becomes even more repulsive, at last," he said. "My own will, merely as my own will, is even more distasteful to me than other people's wills. From being the God in my own machine, I must either abdicate, or die of disgust—self-disgust, at that."

"How amusing!" she cried.

"It is rather funny," he said sardonically.

"And then?" she asked, looking at him with a certain malevolent challenge.

He looked back at her slowly, with an ironical light in his eyes.

"Then!" he repeated. "Then!—I ask, what else is there in the world, besides human will, human appetite?—because ideas and ideals are only instruments of human will and appetite."

"Not entirely," said Kate. "They may be disinterested."

"May they? If the appetite *isn't* interested, the *will* is."

"Why not?" she mocked. "We can't be mere detached blocks."

"It nauseates me.—I look for something else."

"And what do you find?"

"My own manhood!"

"What does that mean?" she cried, jeering.

"If you looked, and found your own womanhood, you would know."

"But I *have* my own womanhood!" she cried.

"And then—when you find your own manhood—your womanhood," he went on, smiling faintly at her—"then you know it is not your own, to do as you like with. You don't have it of your own will. It comes from—from the middle—from the God. Beyond me, at the middle, is the God. And the God gives me my manhood, then leaves me to it. I have nothing but my manhood. The God gives it me, and leaves me to do further."

Kate would not hear any more—She broke off, into banalities.

The immediate question, for her, was whether she would stay in

Mexico or not. She was not really concerned with Don Ramón's
soul—or even her own. She was concerned with her immediate
future. Should she stay in Mexico? Mexico meant the dark-faced
men in cotton clothes and big hats: the peasants, peons, pelados,
Indians, call them what you will. The mere natives!   5

Those pale-faced Mexicans of the Capital, politicians, artists,
professionals, and business people, they did not interest her. Neither
did the hacendados and the ranch-owners, in their tight trousers and
weak, soft sensuality, pale victims of their own emotional
undiscipline.—Mexico still meant the mass of silent peons, to her.   10
And she thought of them again, these silent, stiff-backed men,
driving their strings of asses along the country roads, in the dust of
Mexico's infinite dryness, past broken walls, broken houses, broken
haciendas, along the endless desolation left by the revolutions; past
the vast stretches of maguey, the huge cactus, or aloe, with its   15
gigantic rosette of upstarting, pointed leaves, that in its iron rows
covers miles and miles of ground in the Valley of Mexico, cultivated
for the making of that bad-smelling drink, pulque. The Mediterranean has the grape, old Europe has malted beer, and China has
opium from the white poppy. But out of the Mexican soil a bunch of   20
black-tarnished swords* bursts up, and a great unfolded bud of the
once-flowering monster begins to thrust at the sky. They cut the
great phallic bud and crush out the sperm-like juice for the pulque.
Agua miel! Pulque!

But better pulque than the fiery white brandy distilled from the   25
maguey: mescal, tequila: or in the low lands, the hateful sugar-cane
brandy, aguardiente.

And the Mexican burns out his stomach with these beastly
fire-waters, and cauterises the hurt with red-hot chile. Swallowing
one hell-fire to put out another.   30

Tall fields of wheat and maize. Taller, more brilliant fields of
bright-green sugar cane. And threading in white cotton clothes, with
dark, half-visible face, the eternal *peón* of Mexico, his great wide
calico drawers flopping round his ankles as he walks, or rolled up
over his dark, handsome legs.   35

The wild, sombre, erect men of the north! The too-often
degenerate men of Mexico Valley, their heads through the middle of
their ponchos! The big men in Tlaxcala, selling ice-cream or huge
half-sweetened buns and fancy bread! The quick little Indians,
quick as spiders, down in Oaxaca! The queer-looking half-Chinese   40

natives towards Veracruz! The dark faces and the big black eyes on the coast of Sinaloa! The handsome men of Jalisco, with a scarlet blanket folded on one shoulder!

They were of many tribes and many languages, and far more alien
5 to one another than Frenchmen, English, and Germans are. Mexico! It is not really even the beginnings of a nation: hence the rabid assertion of nationalism in the few. And it is not a race.

Yet it is a people. There is some Indian quality which pervades the whole.* Whether it is men in blue overalls and a slouch, in Mexico
10 City, or men with handsome legs in skin-tight trousers, or the floppy white cotton-clad laborers in the fields, there is something mysteriously in common. The erect, prancing walk, stepping out from the base of the spine, with lifted knees and short steps. The jaunty balancing of the huge hats. The thrown-back shoulders with a folded
15 sarape like a royal mantle. And most of them handsome, with dark, warm-bronze skin so smooth and living, their proudly-held heads whose black hair gleams like wild, rich feathers. Their big, bright black eyes that look at you wonderingly, and have no centre to them. Their sudden charming smile, when you smile first. But the eyes
20 unchanged.

Yes, and she had to remember too a fair proportion of smaller, sometimes insignificant looking men, some of them scaly with dirt, who looked at you with a cold, mud-like antagonism as they stepped cattishly past. Poisonous, thin, stiff little men, cold and unliving like
25 scorpions, and as dangerous.

And then the truly terrible faces of some creatures in the city, slightly swollen with the poison of tequila, and with black, dimmed, swivel eyes swinging in pure evil. Never had she seen such faces of pure brutish evil, cold and insect-like, as in Mexico City.

30 The country gave her a strange feeling of hopelessness and of dauntlessness. Unbroken, eternally resistant, it was a people that lived without hope, and without care. Gay even, and laughing with indifferent carelessness.

They were something like her own Irish, but gone to a much
35 greater length. And also, they did what the self-conscious and pretentious Irish rarely do, they touched her bowels with a strange fire of compassion.

At the same time, she feared them. They would pull her down, pull her down to the dark depths of nothingness.

40 It was the same with the women. In their full long skirts and bare

feet, and with the big, dark-blue scarf or shawl called a rebozo over their womanly small heads and tight round their shoulders, they were images of wild submissiveness, the primitive womanliness of the world, that is so touching and so alien. Many women kneeling in a dim church, all hooded in their dark-blue rebozos, the pallor of their skirts on the floor, their heads and shoulders wrapped dark and tight, as they swayed with devotion of fear and ecstasy! A churchful of dark-wrapped women sunk there in wild, humble supplication of dread and of bliss filled Kate with tenderness and revulsion. They crouched like people not quite created.

Their soft, untidy black hair, which they scratched for lice: the round-eyed baby joggling like a pumpkin in the shawl slung over the woman's shoulder: the never-washed feet and ankles, again somewhat reptilian under the long, flounced, soiled cotton skirt; and then, once more, the dark eyes of half-created women, soft, appealing, yet with a queer void insolence! Something lurking, where the womanly centre should have been: lurking snake-like. Fear! The fear of not being able to find full creation. And the inevitable mistrust and lurking insolence, insolent against a higher creation, the same thing that is in the striking of a snake.

Kate, as a woman, feared the women more than the men. The women were little and insidious, the men were bigger and more reckless. But in the eyes of each, the uncreated centre, where the evil and the insolence lurked.

And sometimes she wondered whether America really was the great death-continent, the great *No!* to the European and Asiatic and even African *Yes!* Was it really the great melting pot, where men from the creative continents were smelted back again, not to a new creation, but down into the homogeneity of death? Was it the great continent of the undoing, and all its peoples the agents of the mystic destruction? Plucking, plucking at the created soul in a man, till at last it plucked out the growing germ, and left him a creature of mechanism and automatic reaction, with only one inspiration, the desire to pluck the quick out of every living, spontaneous creature.

Was that the clue to America, she sometimes wondered. Was it the great death-continent, the continent that destroyed again what the other continents had built up. The continent whose spirit of place fought purely to pick the eyes out of the face of God. Was that America?

And all the people who went there, Europeans, negroes, Japanese,

Chinese, all the colours and the races, were they the spent people, in whom the god impulse had collapsed, so they crossed to the great continent of the negation, where the human will declares itself "free," to pull down the soul of the world? Was it so? And did this account for the great drift to the New World, the drift of spent souls passing over to the side of godless democracy, energetic negation? The negation which is the life-breath of materialism.—And would the great negative pull of the Americas at last break the heart of the world?*

This thought would come to her, time and again.

She herself, what had she come to America for?

Because the flow of her life had broken, and she knew she could not re-start it, in Europe.*

These handsome natives! Was it because they were death-worshippers, Moloch-worshippers,* that they were so uncowed and handsome? Their pure acknowledgement of death, and their undaunted admission of nothingness kept them so erect and reckless.

White men had had a soul, and lost it. The pivot of fire had been quenched in them, and their lives had started to spin in the reversed direction, widdershins. That reversed look which is in the eyes of so many white people, the look of nullity, and life wheeling in the reversed direction. Widdershins.

But the dark-faced natives, with their strange soft flame of life wheeling upon a dark void: were they centreless and widdershins too, as so many white men now are?

The strange, soft flame of courage in the black Mexican eyes. But still it was not knit to a centre, that centre which is the soul of a man.

And all the efforts of white men to bring the soul of the dark men of Mexico into final clinched being has resulted in nothing but the collapse of the white men. Against the soft, dark flow of the Indian the white man at last collapses, with his god and his energy he collapses. In attempting to convert the dark man to the white man's way of life, the white man has fallen helplessly down the hole he wanted to fill up. Seeking to save another man's soul, the white man lost his own, and collapsed upon himself.

Mexico! The great, precipitous, dry, savage country, with a handsome church in every landscape, rising as it were out of nothing. A revolution-broken landscape, with lingering, tall, handsome churches whose domes are like inflations that are going to burst, and whose pinnacle towers are like the trembling pagodas of an unreal race. Gorgeous churches waiting, above the huts and straw hovels of the natives, like ghosts to be dismissed.

And noble ruined haciendas, with ruined avenues approaching their broken splendour.

And the cities of Mexico, great and small, that the Spaniards conjured up out of nothing. Stones live and die with the spirit of the builders. And the spirit of Spaniards in Mexico dies, and the very stones in the buildings die. The natives drift into the centre of the plazas again, and in unspeakable empty weariness the Spanish buildings stand around, in a sort of dry exhaustion.

Ah the conquered race! Cortés* came with his iron heel and his iron will, a conqueror. But a conquered race, unless grafted with a new inspiration, slowly sucks the blood of the conquerors, in the silence of a strange night and the heaviness of a hopeless will. So that now, the race of the conquerors in Mexico is soft and boneless, children crying in helpless hopelessness.

Was it the dark negation of the continent?

Kate could not look at the stones of the National Museum in Mexico without depression and dread. Snakes coiled like excrement, snakes fanged and feathered beyond all dreams of dread. And that was all.

The ponderous pyramids of San Juan Teotihuacán, the House of Quetzalcoatl wreathed with the Snake of all snakes, his huge fangs white and pure* today as in the lost centuries when his makers were alive. He has not died. He is not so dead as the Spanish churches, this all-enwreathing dragon of the horror of Mexico.

Cholula, with its church where the altar was! And the same ponderousness, the same unspeakable sense of weight and down- ward pressure, of the blunt pyramid. Down-sinking pressure and depression. And the great market-place with its lingering dread and fascination.*

Mitla under its arid hills, in the parched valley where a wind blows the dust and the dead souls of the vanished race in terrible gusts.* The carved courts of Mitla, with a hard, sharp-angled, intricate fascination but the fascination of fear and repellance. Hard, four- square, sharp-edged, cutting, zig-zagging Mitla, like continual blows of a stone axe. Without gentleness or grace or charm. Oh America, with your unspeakable hard lack of charm, what then is your final meaning? Is it forever the knife of sacrifice, as you put out your tongue at the world?*

Charmless America! With your hard, vindictive beauty, are you waiting forever to smite to death? Is the world your everlasting
5 victim?

So long as it will let itself be victimised.

But yet! But yet! The gentle voices of the natives. The voices of the boys like birds twittering among the trees of the plaza of Tehuacán! The soft touch, the gentleness. Was it the dark-fingered
10 quietness of death, and the music of the presence of death in their voices?

She thought again of what Don Ramón had said to her.

"They pull you down! Mexico pulls you down, the people pull you down like a great weight! But it may be they pull you down as the
15 earth's pull of gravitation does, that you can balance on your feet. Maybe they draw you down as the earth draws down the roots of a tree, so that it may be clinched deep in soil. Men are still part of the Tree of Life, and the roots go down to the centre of the earth. Loose leaves, and aeroplanes, blow away on the wind, in what they call
20 freedom. But the Tree of Life has fixed, deep, gripping roots.

"It may be you need to be drawn down, down, till you send roots into the deep places again. Then you can send up the sap and the leaves back to the sky, later.

"And to me, the men in Mexico are like trees, forests that the
25 white men felled in their coming. But the roots of the trees are deep and alive, and forever sending up new shoots. And each new shoot that comes up overthrows a Spanish church or an American factory. And soon the dark forest will rise again, and shake the Spanish buildings from the face of America.*

30 "All that matters to me are the roots that reach down beyond all destruction. The roots and the life are there. What else it needs is the word, for the forest to begin to rise again—And some man among men must speak the word."

The strange doom-like sound of the man's words! But in spite of
35 the sense of doom on her heart, she would not go away yet. She would stay longer in Mexico.

Chapter V.

The Lake.*

Owen left, Villiers stayed on a few days to escort Kate to the lake. If
she liked it there, and could find a house, she could stay by herself.
She knew sufficient people in Mexico and in Guadalajara to prevent   5
her from being lonely. But she still shrank from travelling alone, in
this country.

She wanted to leave the city. The new President had come in
quietly enough, but there was an ugly feeling of uppishness in the
lower classes, the bottom dog clambering mangily to the top. Kate   10
was no snob. Man or woman, she cared nothing about the social
class. But meanness, sordidness she hated. She hated bottom dogs.
They all were mangy, they all were full of envy and malice, many had
the rabies. Ah no, let us defend ourselves from the bottom dog, with
its mean growl and its yellow teeth.*   15

She had tea with Cipriano before leaving.

"How do you get along with the government?" she asked.

"I stand for the law and the constitution," he said. "They know I
don't want anything to do with cuartelazos or revolutions. Don
Ramón is my chief."   20

"In what way?"

"Later, you will see."

He had a secret, important to himself, on which he was sitting
tight. But he looked at her with shining eyes, as much as to say that
soon she would share the secret, and then he would be much   25
happier.

He watched her so curiously, from under his wary black lashes.
She was one of the rather plump Irishwomen, with soft brown hair
and hazel eyes, and a beautiful, rather distant repose. Her great
charm was her soft repose, and her gentle, unconscious inaccessibi- 30
lity. She was taller and bigger than Cipriano: he was almost boyishly
small. But he was all energy, and his eyebrows tilted black and with a
barbarian conceit, above his full, almost insolent black eyes.

He watched her continually, with a kind of fascination: the same
spell that the absurd little figures of the doll Madonnas had cast over 35

81

him as a boy. She was the mystery, and he the adorer, under the semi-ecstatic spell of the mystery. But once he rose from his knees, he rose in the same strutting conceit of himself as before he knelt: with all his adoration in his pocket again. But he had a good deal of
5 magnetic power. His education had not diminished it. His education lay like a film of white oil on the black lake of his barbarian consciousness. For this reason, the things he said were hardly interesting at all. Only what he *was*. He made the air around him seem darker, but richer and fuller. Sometimes his presence was
10 extraordinarily grateful, like a healing of the blood. And sometimes he was an intolerable weight on her, she gasped to get away from him.

"You think a great deal of Don Ramón?" she said to him.

"Yes," he said, his black eyes watching her. "He is a very fine
15 man."

How trivial the words sounded! That was another boring thing about him: his English seemed so trivial. He wasn't really expressing himself. He was only flipping at the white oil that lay on his surface.

"You like him better than the Bishop, your god-father?"
20 He lifted his shoulders in a twisted, embarrassed shrug.

"The same!" he said. "I like him the same."

Then he looked away into the distance, with a certain *hauteur* and insolence.

"Very different, no?" he said. "But in some ways, the same. He
25 knows better what is Mexico. He knows better what I am. Bishop Severn did not know the real Mexico: how could he, he was a sincere Catholic! But Don Ramón knows the real Mexico, no?"

"And what is the real Mexico?" she asked.

"Well—you must ask Don Ramón. I can't explain."
30 She asked Cipriano about going to the lake.

"Yes!" he said. "You can go! You will like it. Go first to Orilla, no?—you take a ticket on the railway to Ixtlahuacan. And in Orilla is an hotel with a German manager. Then from Orilla you can go in a motor-boat, in a few hours, to Sayula. And there you will find a
35 house to live in."

He wanted her to do this, she could tell.

"How far is Don Ramón's hacienda from Sayula?" she asked.

"Near! About an hour in a boat. He is there now. And at the beginning of the month I am going with my division to Guadalajara:
40 now there is a new governor.* So I shall be quite near too."

"That will be nice," she said.

"You think so?" he asked quickly.

"Yes," she said, on her guard, looking at him slowly. "I should be sorry to lose touch with Don Ramón and you."

He had a little tension on his brow, haughty, unwilling, conceited, and at the same time, yearning and desirous.

"You like Don Ramón very much?" he said. "You want to know him more?"

There was a peculiar anxiety in his voice.

"Yes," she said. "One knows so few people in the world nowadays, that one can respect—and fear a little. I am a little afraid of Don Ramón: and I have the *greatest* respect for him—" she ended on a hot note of sincerity.

"It is good!" he said. "It is very good. You may respect him more than any man in the world."

"Perhaps that is true," she said, turning her eyes slowly to his.

"Yes! Yes!" he cried impatiently. "It is true. You will find out later.—And Ramón likes you. He told me to ask you to come to the lake. When you come to Sayula, when you are coming, write to him, and no doubt he can tell you about a house, and all those things."

"Shall I?" she said, hesitant.

"Yes, Yes! Of course! We say what we mean."

Curious little man, with his odd, inflammable *hauteur* and conceit, something burning inside him, that gave him no peace! He had an almost childish faith in the other man. And yet she was not sure that he did not, in some corner of his soul, resent Ramón somewhat.

Kate set off on the night train for the west, with Villiers. The one Pullman coach was full: people going to Guadalajara and Colima and the coast. There were three military officers, rather shy in their new uniforms, and rather swaggering at the same time, making eyes at the empty air, as if they felt they were conspicuous, and sitting quietly in their seats, as if to obliterate themselves. There were two country farmers or rancheros, in tight trousers and cart-wheel hats stitched with silver.* One was a tall man with a big moustache, the other was a smaller, grey man. But they both had the handsome, alive legs of the Mexicans, and the rather quenched faces. There was a widow buried in crape, accompanied by a criada, a maid. The rest were townsmen, Mexicans on business, at once shy and fussy, unobtrusive and self-important.

The Pullman was clean and neat, with its hot green-plush seats.

But, full of people, it seemed empty compared with a Pullman in the United States. Everybody was very quiet, very soft and guarded. The farmers folded their beautiful sarapes and laid them carefully on the seats, sitting as if their section were a lonely little place. The officers folded their cloaks and arranged dozens of little parcels, little cardboard hatboxes and heterogeneous bundles, under the seats and on the seats. The business men had the oddest luggage, canvas hold-alls embroidered in wool, with long, touching mottoes.

And in all the crowd, a sense of guardedness and softness and self-effacement: a curious soft *sensibilité*, touched with fear. It was already a somewhat conspicuous thing to travel in the Pullman, you had to be on your guard.

The evening for once was grey: the rainy season really approaching. A sudden wind whirled dust and a few spots of rain. The train drew out of the formless, dry, dust-smitten areas fringing the city, and wound mildly on for a few minutes, only to stop in the main street of Tacuba,* the suburb-village. In the grey approach of evening the train halted heavily in the street, and Kate looked out at the men who stood in groups, with their hats tilted against the wind and their blankets folded over their shoulders and up to their eyes, against the dust, motionless standing like sombre ghosts, only a glint of eyes showing between the dark sarape and the big hat-brim; while donkey-drivers in a dust-cloud ran frantically, with lifted arms like demons, uttering short, sharp cries to prevent their donkeys from poking in between the coaches of the train. Silent dogs trotted in and out under the train, women, their faces wrapped in their blue rebozos, came to offer tortillas folded in a cloth to keep them warm, or pulque in an earthern mug, or pieces of chicken smothered in red, thick, oily sauce: or oranges or bananas or pitahayas, anything. And when few people bought, because of the dust, the women put their wares under their arm, under the blue rebozo, and covered their faces and motionless watched the train.

It was about six o'clock. The earth was utterly dry and stale. Somebody was kindling charcoal in front of a house. Men were hurrying down the wind, balancing their great hats curiously. Horsemen on quick, fine little horses, guns slung behind, trotted up to the train, lingered, then trotted quickly away again into nowhere.

Still the train stood in the street. Kate and Villiers got down. They watched the sparks blowing from the charcoal which a little girl was kindling in the street, to cook the tortillas.

The train had a second-class coach and a first-class. The second-class was jam full of peasants, Indians, piled in like chickens with their bundles and baskets and bottles, endless things. One woman had a fine peacock under her arm. She put it down and in vain tried to suppress it beneath her voluminous skirts. It refused to 5 be suppressed. She took it up again and balanced it on her knee, and looked round again over the medley of jars, baskets, pumpkins, melons, guns, bundles and human beings.

In the front was a steel car with a guard of little scrubby soldiers in their dirty cotton uniforms. Some soldiers were mounted on top of 10 the train with their guns: the look-out.

And the whole train, seething with life, was curiously still, subdued. Perhaps it is the perpetual sense of danger which makes the people so hushed, without clamour or stridency. And with an odd, hushed politeness among them. A sort of demon-world. 15

At last the train moved on. If it had waited forever, no-one would have been deeply surprised. For what might not be ahead? Rebels, bandits, bridges blown up—anything.

However, quietly, stealthily, the train moved out and along the great weary valley. The circling mountains, so relentless, were 20 invisible save near at hand. In a few broken adobe huts, a bit of fire sparked red. The adobe was grey-black, of the lava dust, and depressing. Into the distance the fields spread dry, with here and there patches of green irrigation. There was a broken hacienda with columns that supported nothing. Darkness was coming, dust still 25 blew in the shadow, the valley seemed encompassed in a dry, stale, weary gloom.

Then there came a heavy shower. The train was passing a pulque hacienda. The rows of the giant maguey stretched bristling their iron-black barbs in the gloom. 30

All at once, the lights came on, the Pullman attendant came swiftly lowering the blinds, so that the brilliance of the windows should attract no bullets from the darkness outside.

There was a poor little meal at exorbitant prices, and when this was cleared away, the attendants came with a clash to make the beds, 35 pulling down the upper berths. It was only eight o'clock, and the passengers looked up in resentment. But no good. The pug-faced Mexican in charge, and his small-pox-pitted assistant insolently came in between the seats, inserted the key over-head, and brought down the berth with a crash. And the Mexican passengers humbly 40 crawled away to the smoking room or the toilet, like whipped dogs.

At half-past eight everybody was silently and with intense discretion going to bed. None of the collar-stud-snapping bustle and "homely" familiarity of the United States—Like subdued animals they all crept in behind their green serge curtains.

Kate hated a Pullman, the discreet indiscretion, the horrible nearness of other people, like so many larvae in so many sections, behind the green serge curtains. Above all, the horrible intimacy of the noises of going to bed. She hated to undress, struggling in the oven of her berth, with her elbow butting into the stomach of the attendant who was buttoning up the green curtain outside.

And yet, once she was in bed and could put out her light and raise the window blind, she had to admit it was better than a *wagon-lit* in Europe: and perhaps the best that can be done for people who will or must travel through the night in trains.

There was a rather cold wind, after the rain, up there on that high plateau. The moon had risen, the sky was clear. Rocks, and tall organ cactus, and more miles of maguey. Then the train stopped at a dark little station on the rim of a slope, where men swathed dark in sarapes held dusky, ruddy lanterns that lit up no faces at all, only dark gaps. Why did the train stay so long? Was something wrong?

At last they were going again. Under the moon she saw beyond her a long downslope of rocks and cactus, and in the distance below, the lights of a town. She lay in her berth watching the train wind slowly down the wild, rugged slope. Then she dozed.

To wake at a station that looked like a quiet inferno, with dark faces coming near the windows, glittering eyes in the half-light, women in their rebozos running along the train balancing dishes of meat, tamales, tortillas on one hand, black-faced men with fruit and sweets, and all calling in a subdued, intense, hushed hubbub. Strange and glaring, she saw eyes at the dark screen of the Pullman, sudden hands thrusting up something to sell. In fear, Kate dropped her window. The wire screen was not enough.

The platform below the Pullman was all dark. But at the back of the train she could see the glare of the first-class windows, on the dark station. And a man selling sweetmeat—*Cajetas! Cajetas! La de Celaya!*

She was safe inside the Pullman, with nothing to do but to listen to an occasional cough behind the green curtains, and to feel the faint bristling apprehension of all the Mexicans in their dark berths. The dark Pullman was full of a subdued apprehension, fear lest there might be some attack on the train.

She went to sleep and woke at a bright station: probably Querétaro. The green trees looked theatrical in the electric light. *Ópalos!** 5 she heard the men calling softly. If Owen had been there he would have got up in his pyjamas to buy opals. The call would have been too strong.

She slept fitfully, in the shaken saloon, vaguely aware of stations and the deep night of the open country. Then she started from a 10 complete sleep. The train was dead still, no sound. Then a tremendous jerking as the Pullman was shunted. It must be Irapuato, where they branched to the west.

She would arrive at Ixtlahuacan soon after six in the morning. The man woke her at daybreak, before the sun had risen. Dry country 15 with mesquite bushes, in the dawn: then green wheat alternating with ripe wheat. And men already in the pale, ripened wheat reaping with sickles, cutting short little handfuls from the short straw. A bright sky, with a bluish shadow on earth. Parched slopes with ragged maize stubble. Then a forlorn hacienda and a man on 20 horseback, in a blanket, driving a silent flock of cows, sheep, bulls, goats, lambs, rippling a bit ghostly in the dawn, from under a tottering archway. A long canal beside the railway, a long canal paved with bright green leaves from which poked the mauve heads of the *lirio*, the water-hyacinth. The sun was lifting up, red. In a moment, it 25 was the full, dazzling gold of a Mexican morning.

Kate was dressed and ready, sitting facing Villiers, when they came to Ixtlahuacan. The man carried out her bags. The train drifted in to a desert of a station. They got down. It was a new day.

In the powerful light of morning, under a turquoise blue sky, she 30 gazed at the helpless-looking station, railway lines, some standing trucks, and a remote lifelessness. A boy seized their bags and ran across the lines to the station yard, which was paved with cobble stones but overgrown with weeds. At one side stood an old tram-car with two mules, like a relic. One or two men, swathed up to the eyes 35 in scarlet blankets, were crossing on silent white legs.

"*Adonde?*" said the boy.

But Kate went to see her big luggage taken out. It was all there.

"Orilla Hotel," said Kate.

The boy said they must go in the tram-car, so in the tram-car they 40

went. The driver whipped his mules, they rolled in the still, heavy morning light away down an uneven, cobbled road with holes in it, between walls with falling mortar and low, black adobe houses, in the peculiar *vacuous* depression of a helpless little Mexican town,
5 towards the plaza. The strange emptiness, everything empty of life!

Occasional men on horseback clattered subduedly by, occasional big men in scarlet sarapes went noiselessly on their own way, under the big hats. A boy on a high mule was delivering milk from red
10 globe-shaped jars slung on either side his mount. The street was stony, uneven, vacuous, sterile. The stones seemed dead, the town seemed made of dead stone. The human life came with a slow, sterile unwillingness, in spite of the low-hung power of the sun.

At length they were in the plaza where brilliant trees flowered in a
15 blaze of pure scarlet, and some in pure lavender, around the basins of milky-looking water. Milky-dim the water bubbled up in the basins, and women bleary with sleep, uncombed, came from under the dilapidated arches of the *portales*, and across the broken pavement, to fill their water-jars.

20 The tram stopped, and they got down. The boy got down with the bags, and told them they must go to the river to take a boat.

They followed obediently down the smashed pavements, where every moment you might twist your ankle or break your leg. Everywhere the same weary indifference and brokenness, a sense of
25 dirt and of helplessness, squalor of far-gone indifference, under the perfect morning sky, in the pure sunshine and the pure Mexican air. The sense of life ebbing away, leaving dry ruin.

They came to the edge of the town, to a dusty, humped bridge, a broken wall, a pale-brown stream flowing full. Below the bridge a
30 cluster of men.

Each one wanted her to hire his boat. She demanded a motor-boat: the boat from the hotel. They said there wasn't one. She didn't believe it. Then a dark-faced fellow with his black hair down his forehead, and a certain intensity in his eyes, said: Yes, yes! The hotel
35 had a boat, but it was broken. She must take a row-boat. In an hour and a half he would row her there.

"How long?" said Kate.

"An hour and a half."

"And I am so hungry!" cried Kate. "How much do you charge?"
40 "Two pesos."—He held up two fingers.

Kate said yes, and he ran down to his boat. Then she noticed he was a cripple, with inturned feet. But how quick and strong!

She climbed with Villiers down the broken bank to the river, and in a moment they were in the boat. Pale green willow trees fringed from the earthen banks to the full-flowing, pale-brown water. The river was not very wide, between deep banks. They slipped under the bridge, and past a funny high barge with rows of seats. The boatman said it went up the river to Jocotlán: and he waved his hand to show the direction. They were slipping down-stream, between lonely banks of willow trees.

The crippled boatman was pulling hard, with great strength and energy. When she spoke to him in her bad Spanish and he found it hard to understand, he knitted his brow a little, anxiously. And when she laughed, he smiled at her with such a beautiful gentleness, sensitive, wistful, quick. She felt he was naturally honest and truthful, and generous. There was a beauty in these men, a wistful beauty and a great physical strength. Why had she felt so bitterly about the country?

Morning was still young on the pale buff river, between the silent earthen banks. There was a blue dimness in the lower air, and black water-fowl ran swiftly, unconcernedly back and forth from the river's edge, on the dry, baked banks that were treeless now, and wider. They had entered a wide river, from the narrow one. The blueness and moistness of the dissolved night seemed to linger under the scattered pepper trees of the far shore.

The boatman rowed short and hard upon the flimsy, soft, sperm-like water, only pausing at moments swiftly to smear the sweat from his face with an old rag he kept on the bench beside him. The sweat ran from his bronze-brown skin like water, and the black hair on his high-domed, Indian head smoked with wetness.

"There is no hurry," said Kate, smiling to him.

"What does the Señorita say?"

"There is no hurry," she repeated.

He paused, smiling, breathing deeply, and explained that now he was rowing against stream. This wider river flowed out of the lake, full and heavy. See! even as he rested a moment, the boat began to turn and drift!—He quickly took his oars.

Kate looked at it in wonder, the rather wide stream of soft, full-flowing buff water,* that carried little tufts of floating water-hyacinth. Some willow trees stood near the edge, and some pepper

trees of most delicate green foliage. Beyond the trees and the level of the shores, big hills rose up to high, blunt points, baked incredibly dry, like biscuit. The blue sky settled against them nakedly, they were leafless and lifeless save for the iron-green shafts of the organ
5 cactus, that glistened blackly, yet atmospherically, in the ochreous aridity. This was Mexico again, stark-dry and luminous with powerful light, cruel and unreal.

On the flat near the river a peon, perched on the rump of his ass, was slowly driving five luxurious cows towards the water to drink.
10 The big black-and-white animals stepped in a dream-pace past the pepper trees to the bank, like moving pieces of light-and-shade: the dun cows trailed after, in the incredible silence and brilliance of the morning.

Earth, air, water were all silent with new light, the last blue of
15 night dissolving like a breath. No sound, even no life. The great light was stronger than life itself. Only, up in the blue, some turkey-buzzards were wheeling with dirty-edged wings, as everywhere in Mexico.

"Don't hurry!" Kate said again to the boatman, who was again
20 mopping his face, while his black hair ran sweat. "We can go slowly."

The man smiled deprecatingly.

"If the Señorita will sit in the back," he said.

Kate did not understand his request at first.—He had rowed in towards a bend in the right bank, to be out of the current. On the left
25 bank Kate had noticed some men bathing: men whose wet skins flashed with the beautiful brown-rose colour and glitter of the naked natives, and one stout man with the curious creamy-biscuit skin of the city Mexicans. Low against the water across-stream she watched the glitter of naked men half-immersed in the river.

30 She rose to step back into the stern of the boat, where Villiers was. As she did so, she saw a dark head and the flashing ruddy shoulders of a man swimming towards the boat. She wavered—and as she was sitting down, the man stood up in the water and was wading near, the water washing at the loose little cloth he had round his loins. He was
35 smooth and wet and of a lovely colour, with the rich smooth-muscled physique of the Indians. He was coming towards the boat, pushing back his hair from his forehead.

The boatman watched him transfixed, without surprise, a little subtle half-smile, perhaps of mockery, round his nose. As if he had
40 expected it.

"Where are you going?" asked the man in the water, the brown river running softly at his strong thighs.

The boatman waited a moment for his patrons to answer, then, seeing they were silent, replied in a low, unwilling tone:

"Orilla."

The man in the water took hold of the stern of the boat, as the boatman softly touched the water with the oars to keep her straight, and he threw back his longish black hair with a certain effrontery.

"Do you know whom the lake belongs to?" he asked, with the same effrontery.

"What do you say?" asked Kate, haughty.

"If you know whom the lake belongs to?" the young man in the water repeated.

"To whom?" said Kate, flustered.

"To the old Gods of Mexico," the stranger said. "You have to make a tribute to Quetzalcoatl, if you go on the lake."

The strange calm effrontery of it! But truly Mexican.

"How?" said Kate.

"You can give me something," he said.

"But why should I give something to you, if it is a tribute to Quetzalcoatl?" she stammered.

"I am Quetzalcoatl's man, I," he replied, with calm effrontery.

"And if I don't give you anything?" she said.

He lifted his shoulders and spread his free hand, staggering a little, losing his footing in the water as he did so.

"If you wish to make an enemy of the lake!—" he said, coolly, as he recovered his balance.

And then for the first time he looked straight at her. And as he did so, the demonish effrontery died down again, and the peculiar American tension slackened and left him.

He gave a slight wave of dismissal with his free hand, and pushed the boat gently forward.

"But it doesn't matter," he said, with a slight insolent jerk of his head sideways, and a faint, insolent smile. "We will wait till the Morning Star rises."*

The boatman softly but powerfully pulled the oars. The man in the water stood with the sun on his powerful chest, looking after the boat in half-seeing abstraction. His eyes had taken again the peculiar gleaming far-awayness, suspended between the realities, which Kate suddenly realised as the central look in the native eyes. The boatman,

rowing away, was glancing back at the man who stood in the water, and his face too had the abstracted, transfigured look of a man perfectly suspended between the world's two strenuous wings of energy. A look of extraordinary, arresting beauty, the silent, vulner-
5   able centre of all life's quivering, like the nucleus gleaming in tranquil suspense, within a cell.

"What does he mean," said Kate, "by *We will wait till the Morning Star rises?*"

The man smiled slowly:
10   "It is a name," he said.

And he seemed to know no more. But the symbolism had evidently the power to soothe and sustain him.

"Why did he come and speak to us?" asked Kate.

"He is one of those of the god Quetzalcoatl, Señorita."
15   "And you?—are you one too?"

"Who knows!" said the man, putting his head on one side. Then he added: "I think so. We are many."

He watched Kate's face with that gleaming, intense semi-abstraction, a gleam that hung unwavering in his black eyes, and
20   which suddenly reminded Kate of the morning star, or the evening star, hanging perfect between night and the sun.

"You have the morning star in your eyes," she said to the man.

He flashed her a smile of extraordinary beauty.

"The Señorita understands," he said.
25   His face changed again to a dark-brown mask, like semi-transparent stone, and he rowed with all his might. Ahead, the river was widening, the banks were growing lower, down to the water's level, like shoals planted with willow trees and with reeds. Above the willow trees a square white sail was standing, as if erected on the
30   land.

"Is the lake so near?" said Kate.

The man hastily mopped his running wet face.

"Yes Señorita! The sailing-boats are waiting for the wind, to come into the river. We will pass by the canal—"
35   He indicated with a backward movement of the head a narrow, twisting passage of water between deep reeds. It made Kate think of the little river Anapo:* the same mystery unbroken. The boatman, with creases half of sadness and half of exaltation in his bronze, still face, was pulling with all his might. Water-fowl went swimming into
40   the reeds, or rose on wing and wheeled into the blue air. Some

willow trees hung a dripping, vivid green, in the stark dry country. The stream was narrow and winding. With a nonchalant motion, first of the right then of the left hand, Villiers was guiding the boatman, to keep him from running aground in the winding narrow water-way. 5

And this put Villiers at his ease, to have something practical and slightly mechanical to do and to assert. He was striking the American note once more, of mechanical dominance.

All the other business had left him incomprehending, and when he asked Kate, she had pretended not to hear him. She sensed a 10 certain delicate, tender mystery in the river, in the naked man of the water, in the boatman, and she could not bear to have it subjected to the tough American flippancy. She was weary to death of American automatism and American flippant toughness. It gave her a feeling of nausea. 15

"Quite a well-built fellow, that one who laid hold of the boat. What did he want, anyway?" Villiers insisted.

"Nothing!" said Kate.

They were slipping out past the clay-coloured, loose stony edges of the land, through a surge of ripples, into the wide white light of the 20 lake. A breeze was coming from the east, out of the upright morning, and the surface of the shallow, flimsy, dun-coloured water was in motion. Shoal water rustled near at hand. Out to the open, large, square white sails were stepping gingerly forward, and beyond the buff-coloured, pale stretch of water rose far-away blue sharp hills of 25 the other side, many miles away, pure pale blue with distance, yet sharp-edged and clear in form.

"Now," said the boatman, smiling to Kate, "it is easier. Now we are out of the current."

He pulled rhythmically through the frail-rippling, sperm-like 30 water, with a sense of peace. And for the first time Kate felt she had met the mystery of the natives, the strange and mysterious gentleness between a scylla and a charybdis of violence; the small, poised, perfect body of the bird that waves wings of thunder and wings of fire and night, in its flight.* But central between the flash of 35 day and the black of night, between the flash of lightning and the break of thunder, the still, soft body of the bird poised and soaring, forever. The mystery of the evening star brilliant in silence and distance between the downward-surging plunge of the sun and the vast hollow seething of inpouring night. The magnificence of the 40

watchful morning star, the watcher between the night and the day,
the gleaming clue to the two opposites.

This kind of frail, pure sympathy she felt at the moment between
herself and the boatman, between herself and the man who had
5 spoken from the water. And she was not going to have it broken by
Villiers' American jokes.

There was a sound of breaking water. The boatman drew away,
and pointed across to where a *canoa*, a native sailing-boat, was lying
at an angle. She had run aground in a wind, and now must wait till
10 another wind would carry her off the submerged bank again.
Another boat was coming down the breeze, steering cautiously
among the shoals, for the river outlet. She was piled high with *petates*,
the native leaf mats, above her hollowed black sides. And barelegged
men with loose white drawers rolled up, and brown chests showing,
15 were running with poles as the shallows heaved up again, pushing
her off, and balancing their huge hats with small, bird-like shakes of
the head.

Beyond the boats, sea-wards, were rocks outcropping, and strange
birds like pelicans standing in silhouette, motionless.

20 They had been crossing a bay of the lake-shore, and were nearing
the hotel. It stood on a parched dry bank above the pale-brown
water, a long, low building amid a tender green of bananas and
pepper trees. Everywhere the shores rose up pale and cruelly dry,
dry to cruelty, and on the little hills the dark statues of the organ
25 cactus poised in nothingness.

There was a broken-down landing-place and boat-house in the
distance, and someone in white flannel trousers was standing on the
broken masonry. Upon the filmy water ducks and black water-fowl
bobbed like corks. The bottom was stony. The boatman suddenly
30 backed the boat, and pulled round. He pushed up his sleeve and
hung over the bows, reaching into the water. With a quick motion he
grabbed something, and scrambled into the boat again. He was
holding in the pale-skinned hollow of his palm a little earthenware
pot, crusted by the lake-deposit.

35 "What is it?" she said.

"Ollita of the gods," he said. "Of the old dead gods. Take it,
Señorita."

"You must let me pay for it," she said.

"No Señorita. It is yours," said the man, with that sensitive,
40 masculine sincerity which comes sometimes so quickly from a native.

It was a little, rough round pot with protuberances.

"Look!" said the man, reaching again for the little pot. He turned it upside-down, and she saw cut-in eyes and the sticking-out ears of an animal. The little cooking-pot was also an animal's head.

"A cat!" she exclaimed. "It is a cat." 5

"Or a coyote," he said.

"A coyote!"

"Let's look!" said Villiers. "Why how awfully interesting! Do you think it's *old*?"

"It is old?" Kate asked. 10

"The time of the old gods," said the boatman. Then with a sudden smile: "The dead gods don't eat much rice, they only want little casseroles, while they are bone under the water."

And he looked her in the eyes.

"While they are bone?" she repeated. And she realised he meant 15 the skeletons of gods that cannot die.*

They were at the landing stage: or rather, at the heap of collapsed masonry which had once been a landing stage. The boatman got out and held the boat steady while Kate and Villiers landed. Then he scrambled up with the bags. 20

The man in white trousers, and a mozo appeared. It was the hotel manager. Kate paid her boatman.

"*Adios, Señorita!*" he said with a smile. "May you go with Quetzalcoatl."

"Yes!" she cried. "Goodbye!" 25

They went up the slope between the tattered bananas, whose ragged leaves were making a hushed, distant patter in the breeze. The green fruit curved out its bristly-soft bunch, the purple flower-bud depending stiffly.

The German manager came to talk to them: a young man of about 30 forty, with his blue eyes going opaque and stony behind his spectacles, though the centres were keen. Evidently a German who had been many years out in Mexico—out in the lonely places. The rather stiff look, the slight look of fear in the *soul*—not physical fear—and the look of defeat, characteristic of the European who has 35 been long subjected to the unbroken spirit of place! But the defeat was in the soul, not in the will.

He showed Kate to her room in the unfinished quarter, and ordered her breakfast. The hotel consisted of an old low ranch-house with a verandah—and this was the dining-room, lounge, 40 kitchen and office. Then there was a two-storey new wing, with a smart bath-room between each two bedrooms, and almost up-to-date fittings: very incongruous.

But the new wing was unfinished—had been unfinished for a
5 dozen years and more, the work abandoned when Porfirio Díaz fled. Now it would probably never be finished.

And this is Mexico. Whatever pretentiousness and modern improvements it may have, outside the Capital, they are either smashed or raw and unfinished, with rusty bones of iron girders
10 sticking out.

Kate washed her hands and went down to breakfast. Before the long verandah of the old ranch-house, the green pepper trees drooped like green light, and small cardinal birds, with scarlet bodies and blazing impertinent heads like poppy buds flashed among the
15 pinkish pepper-beads, closing their brown wings upon the audacity of their glowing redness. A train of geese passed in the glaring sun, automatic, towards the eternal tremble of pale, earth-coloured water beyond the stones.

It was a place with a strange atmosphere: stony, hard, broken, with
20 round cruel hills and the many-fluted bunches of the organ cactus behind the old house, and an ancient road trailing past, deep in ancient dust. A touch of mystery and cruelty, the stonyness of fear, a lingering cruel sacredness.

Kate loitered hungrily, and was glad when the Mexican in
25 shirt-sleeves and patched trousers, another lingering remnant of Don Porfirio's day, brought her her eggs and coffee.

He was muted as everything about the place seemed muted, even the very stones and the water. Only those poppies on wing, the cardinal birds, gave a sense of liveliness: and they were uncanny.

30 So swiftly one's mood changed! In the boat, she had glimpsed the superb rich stillness of the morning star, the poignant intermediate flashing its quiet between the energies of the cosmos. She had seen it in the black eyes of the natives, in the sunrise of the man's rich, still body, Indian-warm.

35 And now again already the silence was of vacuity, arrest, and cruelty: the uncanny empty unbearableness of many Mexican mornings. Already she was uneasy, suffering from the malaise which tortures one inwardly in that country of cactuses.

She went up to her room, pausing at the corridor window to look
40 at the savage little hills that stood at the back of the hotel in desiccated heaps, with the dark-green bulks of organ cactus sticking

up mechanically and sinister, sombre in all the glare. Grey ground-squirrels like rats slithered ceaselessly around. Sinister, strangely dark and sinister, in the great glare of the sun!

She went to her room to be alone. Below her window, in the bricks and fallen rubble of unfinished masonry, a huge white turkey-cock, dim-white, strutted with his brown hens. And sometimes he stretched out his pink wattles and gave vent to fierce, powerful turkey-yelps, like some strong dog yelping; or else he ruffled all his feathers like a great, soiled white peony, and chuffed hissing here and there, raging the metal of his plumage.*

Below him, the eternal tremble of pale-earth, unreal waters, far beyond which rose the stiff resistance of mountains losing their pristine blue. Distinct, frail distances far off on the dry air, dim-seeming, yet sharp and edged with menace.

Kate took her bath in the filmy water that was hardly like water at all. Then she went and sat on the collapsed masonry, in the shade of the boat-house below. Small white ducks bobbed about on the shallow water below her, or dived, raising clouds of submarine dust. A canoe came paddling in: a lean fellow with sinewy brown legs. He answered Kate's nod with the aloof promptness of an Indian, made fast his canoe inside the boat-house, and was gone, stepping silent and barefoot over the bright green water-stones, and leaving a shadow, cold as flint, on the air behind him.

No sound on the morning save a faint touching of water, and the occasional powerful yelping of the turkey-cock. Silence, an aborigi-nal, empty silence, as of life *withheld*. The vacuity of a Mexican morning. Resounding sometimes to the turkey-cock.

And the great, lymphatic expanse of water, like a sea, trembling, trembling, trembling to a far distance, to the mountains of sub-stantial nothingness.

Near at hand, a ragged shifting of banana trees, bare hills with immobile cactus, and to the left, a hacienda with peons' square mud boxes of houses. An occasional ranchero in skin-tight trousers and big hat, rode trotting through the dust on a small horse, or peons on the rump of their asses, in floppy white cotton, going like ghosts.

Always something ghostly. The morning passing all of a piece, empty, vacuous. All sound withheld, all life withheld, everything *holding back*. The land so dry as to have a quality of invisibility, the water flimsy and earth-filmy, hardly water at all. The lymphatic milk of fishes, somebody said.*

Chapter VI.

The Move Down the Lake.*

In Porfirio Díaz' day, the Lake-side began to be the Riviera of Mexico, and Orilla was to be the Nice, or at least, the Mentone of the
5 country.* But revolutions started erupting again, and in 1911 Don Porfirio fled to Paris with, it is said, thirty million gold pesos in his pocket: a peso being half a dollar, nearly half-a-crown.*—But we need not believe all that is said, especially by a man's enemies.

During the subsequent revolutions, Orilla, which had begun to be
10 a winter Paradise for the Americans, lapsed back into barbarism and broken brick-work. In 1921 a feeble new start* had been made.

The place belonged to a German-Mexican family, who also owned the adjacent hacienda. They acquired the property from the American Hotel Company, who had undertaken to develop the
15 lake-shore, and who had gone bankrupt during the various revolutions.

The German-Mexican owners were not popular with the natives. An angel from heaven would not have been popular, these years, if he had been known as the owner of property. However, in 1921 the
20 hotel was very modestly opened again, with an American manager.

Towards the end of the year José, son of the German-Mexican owner, came to stay with his wife and children in the hotel: in the new wing. José was a bit of a fool, as most foreigners are, after the first generation in Mexico. Having business to settle, he went into
25 Guadalajara to the bank and returned with a thousand gold pesos in a bag: keeping the matter, as he thought, a dead secret.

Everyone had just gone to bed, on a brilliant moonlight night in winter, when two men appeared in the yard calling for José: they had to speak to him. José, suspecting nothing, left his wife and two
30 children, and went down. In a moment he called for the American manager. The manager, thinking it was some bargaining to be done, also came down. As he came out of the door, two men seized him by the arms, and said: *Don't make a noise!*

"What's amiss?" said Bell, who had built up Orilla, and had been
35 twenty years on the lake.

Then he noticed that two other men had hold of José. "Come," they said.

There were five Mexicans—Indians, or half-Indians—and the two captives. They went, the captives in slippers and shirt-sleeves, to the little office away at the end of the other part of the hotel, which 5 had been the old ranch-house.

"What do you want?" said Bell.

"Give us the money," said the bandits.

"Oh all right," said the American.—There were a few pesos only in the safe. He opened, showed them, and they took the money. 10

"Now give us the rest," they said.

"There is no more," said the manager, in all sincerity: for José had not confessed to the thousand pesos.

The five peons then began to search the poor little office. They found a pile of red blankets—which they appropriated—and a few 15 bottles of red wine—which they drank.

"Now," they said, "give us the money."

"I can't give you what there isn't to give," said the manager.

"Good!" they said, and pulled out the hideous machetes, the heavy knives of the Mexicans. 20

José, intimidated, produced the suit-case with the thousand pesos. The money was wrapped up in the corner of a blanket.

"Now come with us," said the bandits.

"Where to?" asked the manager, beginning at last to be scared.

"Only out on to the hill, where we will leave you, so that you 25 cannot telephone to Ixtlahuacan before we have time to get away," said the Indians.

Outside, in the bright moon, the air was chill. The American shivered, in his trousers and shirt and a pair of bedroom slippers.

"Let me take a coat," he said. 30

"Take a blanket," said the tall Indian.

He took a blanket, and with two men holding his arms, he followed José, who was likewise held captive, out of the little gate, across the dust of the road, and up the steep little round hill on which the organ cactus thrust up their sinister clumps, like bunches of cruel fingers, 35 in the moonlight. The hill was stony and steep, the going slow. José, a fat young man of twenty-eight, protested in the feeble manner of the well-to-do Mexicans.

At last they came to the top of the hill. Three men took José apart, leaving Bell alone near a cactus clump. The moon shone in a perfect 40

Mexican heaven. Below, the big lake glimmered faintly, stretching its length towards the west. The air was so clear, the mountains across, thirty miles away, stood sharp and still in the moonlight. And not a sound nor a motion anywhere!—At the foot of the hill was the
5   hacienda, with the peons asleep in their huts. But what help was there in them?

José and the three men had gone behind a cactus tree that stuck up straight like a great black bundle of poles, poised on one central foot, and cast a sharp, iron shadow. The American could hear the voices,
10 talking low and rapidly, but could not distinguish the words. His two guards drew away from him a little, to hear what the others were saying, behind the cactus.

And the American, who knew the ground he stood on and the sky that hung over him, felt again the black vibration of death in the air,
15 the black thrill of the death-lust. Unmistakeable he felt it seething on the air, as any man may feel it, in Mexico. And the strange aboriginal fiendishness, awake now in the five bandits, communicated itself to his blood.

Loosening his blanket, he listened tensely in the moonlight. And
20 came the *thud! thud! thud!* of a machete striking with lust in a human body, then the strange voice of José: *Perdóneme!—Forgive me!* the murdered man cried as he fell.

The American waited for no more. Dropping his blanket, he jumped for the cactus cover, and stooping, took the downslope like a
25 rabbit. The pistol-shots rang out after him, but the Mexicans don't as a rule take good aim. His bedroom slippers flew off, and barefoot the man, thin and light, sped down over the stones and the cactus, down to the hotel.

When he got down, he found everyone in the hotel awake and
30 shouting.

"They are killing José!" he said, and he rushed to the telephone, expecting every moment the five bandits would be on him.

The telephone was in the old ranch-building, in the dining-room. There was no answer—no answer—no answer. In her little bedroom
35 over the kitchen, the cook-woman, the traitress, was yelling. Across in the new wing, a little distance away, José's Mexican wife was screaming. One of the servant boys appeared.

"Try and get the police in Ixtlahuacan," said the American, and he ran to the new wing, to get his gun and to barricade the doors. His
40 daughter, a motherless girl, was crying with José's wife.

There was no answer on the telephone. At dawn, the cook, who said the bandits would not hurt a woman, went across to the hacienda to fetch the peons. And when the sun rose, a man was sent for the police.

They found the body of José, pierced with fourteen holes.—The American was carried to Ixtlahuacan, and kept in bed having cactus spines dug out of his feet by two native women.

The bandits fled across the marshes. Months later, they were identified by the stolen blankets, away in Michoacán: and, pursued, one of them betrayed the others.*

After this, the hotel was closed again, and had been re-opened only three months, when Kate arrived.

But Villiers came with another story. Last year the peons had murdered the manager of one of the estates across the lake. They had stripped him and left him naked on his back, with his sexual organs cut off and put into his mouth, his nose slit and pinned back, the two halves, to his cheeks, with long cactus spines.

"Tell me no more!" said Kate.

She felt there was doom written on the very sky, doom and horror.

She wrote to Don Ramón in Sayula, saying she wanted to go back to Europe. True, she herself had seen no horrors, apart from the bull-fight. And she had had some exquisite moments, as coming to this hotel in the boat. The natives had a certain mystery and beauty, to her. But she could not bear the unease, and the latent sense of horror.

True, the peons were poor. They used to work for twenty cents, American, a day: and now the standard price was fifty cents, or one peso. But then in the old days they received their wage all the year round. Now only at harvest time or sowing time. No work, no pay. And in the long dry season, it was mostly no work.

"Still," said the German manager of the hotel, a man who had run a rubber plantation in Tabasco, a sugar plantation in the state of Veracruz, and a hacienda growing wheat, maize, oranges, in Jalisco: "Still, it isn't a question of money with the peons. It doesn't start with the peons. It starts in Mexico City, with a lot of malcontents who want to put their spoke in the wheel, and who lay hold of pious catchwords, to catch the poor. There's no more in it than that.— Then the agitators go round and infect the peons. It is nothing but a sort of infectious disease, like syphilis, all this revolution and socialism."

"But why does no-one oppose it?" said Kate. "Why don't the hacendados put up a fight, instead of caving in and running away?"

"The Mexican hacendado!" The man's German eyes gave out a
5 spark. "The Mexican *gentleman* is such a brave man, that while the soldier is violating his wife on the bed, he is hiding under the bed and holding his breath so they shan't find him. He's as brave as that."

Kate looked away uncomfortably.

"They all want the United States to intervene.* They hate the
10 Americans: but they want the United States to intervene, to save them their money and their property. That's how brave they are! They hate the Americans personally, but they love them because they can look after money and property. So they want the United States to annex Mexico, the beloved Patria: leaving the marvellous
15 green and white and red flag, and the eagle with the snake in its claws, for the sake of appearances and *honour*! They're simply bottled full of *honour*: of that sort."

Always the same violence of bitterness, Kate thought to herself. And she was so weary of it. How, how weary she was of politics, of
20 the very words "Labor!" and "*socialism!*" and all that rant! It suffocated her.

"Have you heard of the Men of Quetzalcoatl?" asked Kate.

"Quetzalcoatl!" exclaimed the manager, giving a little click of the final 'l,' in a peculiar native fashion. "That's another try-on of the
25 bolshevists. They thought socialism needed a god, so they're going to fish him out of this lake. He'll do for another pious catchword in another revolution."

The man went away, unable to stand any more.

"Oh dear!" thought Kate. "It really is hard to bear."
30 But she wanted to hear more of Quetzalcoatl.

"Did you know," she said to the man later, showing him the little pot, "that they find these things in the lake?"

"They're common enough!" he said. "They used to throw them in, in the idolatrous days. May still do so, for what I know. Then get
35 them out again to sell to tourists."

"They call them ollitas of Quetzalcoatl."

"That's a new invention."

"Why, do you think?"

"They're trying to start a new thing, that's all. They've got this
40 society on the lake here, of the Men of Quetzalcoatl, and they go

round singing songs. It's another dodge for national-socialism, that's all."

"What do they do, the Men of Quetzalcoatl?"

"I can't see they do anything, except talk and get excited over their own importance."

"But what's the idea?"

"I couldn't say. Don't suppose they have any. But if they have, they won't let on to you. You're a gringo—or a gringuita, at the best. And this is for pure Mexicans. For los señores, the workmen, and los caballeros, the peons. Every *peón* is a *caballero* nowadays, and every workman is a señor. So I suppose they're going to get themselves a special god, to put the final feather in their caps."

"Where did it start, the Quetzalcoatl thing?"

"Down in Sayula. They say Don Ramón Carrasco is at the back of it. Maybe he wants to be the next President—or maybe he's aiming higher, and wants to be the first Mexican Pharaoh."

Ah, how tired it made Kate feel: the hopelessness, the ugliness, the cynicism, the emptiness. She felt she could cry aloud, for the unknown gods to put the magic back into her life, and to save her from the dry-rot of the world's sterility.

She thought again of going back to Europe. But what was the good? She knew it! It was all politics or jazzing or slushy mysticism or sordid spiritualism. And the magic had gone. The younger generation, so smart and *interesting*, but so without any mystery, any background. The younger the generation, the flatter and more jazzy, more and more devoid of wonder.

No, she could not go back to Europe.

And no!—she refused to take the hotel manager's estimate of Quetzalcoatl. How should an hotel manager judge?—even if he was not really an hotel manager, but a ranch-overseer. She had seen Ramón Carrasco, and Cipriano. And they were men. They wanted something beyond. She would believe in them. Anything, anything rather than this sterility of nothingness which was the world, and into which her life was drifting.

She would send Villiers away, too. He was nice, she liked him. But he too was widdershins. When he was not automatic and factory-made, he was widdershins, unwinding the sensations of disintegration and anti-life. No, she must send him away. She must, she must free herself from these mechanical connections.

Even one of them, like Villiers, was like a cog-wheel in contact with which all one's workings were reversed. Everything he said, everything he did reversed her real life flow, made her go against the sun.

And she did not want to go against the sun. After all, in spite of the
5 horrors latent in Mexico, when you got these dark-faced people away from wrong contacts like agitators and socialism, they made one feel that life was vast, if fearsome, and death was fathomless.

Horrors might burst out of them. But something must burst out, sometimes, if men are not machines.

10 *No! no! no! no! no!* she cried to her own soul. *Let me still believe in some human contact. Let it not be all cut off for me!*

But she made up her mind, to be alone, and to cut herself off from all the mechanical widdershins contacts. Villiers must go back to his United States. She would be alone in her own milieu. Not to be
15 touched by any, any of the mechanical cog-wheel people. To be left alone, not to be touched. To hide, and be hidden, and never really be spoken to.

Yet at the same time, with her blood flowing softly sunwise, to let the sunwise sympathy of unknown people steal in to her. To shut
20 doors of iron against the mechanical world. But to let the sunwise world steal across to her, and add its motion to her, the motion of the stress of life, with the big sun and the stars, like a tree holding out its leaves.

She wanted an old Spanish house, with its inner patio of flowers
25 and water. Turned inwards, to the few flowers walled in by shadow. To turn one's back on the cog-wheel world. Not to look out any more on to that horrible machine of the world. To look at one's own quiet little fountain and one's own little orange trees, with only heaven above.

30 So, having soothed her heart, she wrote Don Ramón again, that she was coming to Sayula to look for a house. She sent Villiers away. And the next day she set off with a man-servant, in the old motor-boat of the hotel, down to the village of Sayula.

It was thirty-five miles to travel, down the long lake. But the
35 moment she set off, she felt at peace. A tall dark-faced fellow sat in the stern of the boat, steering and attending to the motor. She sat on cushions in the middle. And the young man-servant perched in the prow.

They started before sunrise, when the lake was bathed in motion-
40 less light. Odd tufts of water-hyacinth were travelling on the soft

spermy water, holding up a green leaf like a little sail of a boat, and nodding a delicate, mauve blue flower.

Give me the mystery and let the world live again for me! Kate cried to her own soul. *And deliver me from man's automatism.*

The sun rose, and a whiteness of light played on the tops of the 5 mountains. The boat hugged the north shore, turning the promontory on which the villas had started so jauntily, twenty years ago, but now were lapsing back to wilderness. All was still and motionless in the light. Sometimes, on the little bare patches high up on the dry hills were white specks: birds? No, men in their white cotton, peons 10 hoeing. They were so tiny and so distinct, they looked like white birds settled.

Round the bend were the hot springs, the church,* the inaccessible village of the pure Indians, who spoke no Spanish. There were some green trees, under the precipitous dry mountain-side. 15

So on and on, the motor-boat chugging incessantly, the man in the bows coiled up like a serpent, watching; the fish-milk water gleaming and throwing off a dense light, so that the mountains away across were fused out. And Kate, under the awning, went into a kind of sleep. 20

They were passing the island, with its ruins of fortress and prison.* It was all rock and dryness, with great broken walls and the shell of a church among its hurtful stones and its dry grey herbage. For a long time the Indians had defended it against the Spaniards. Then the Spaniards used the island as a fortress against the Indians. 25 Later, as a penal settlement. And now the place was a ruin, repellant, full of scorpions, and otherwise empty of life. Only one or two fishermen lived in the tiny cove facing the mainland, and a flock of goats, specks of life creeping among the rocks. And an unhappy fellow put there by the government to register the weather. 30

No, Kate did not want to land. The place looked too sinister. She took food from the basket, and ate a little lunch, and dozed.

In this country, she was afraid. But it was her soul more than her body that knew fear. She had realised, for the first time, with finality and fatality, what was the illusion she labored under. She had 35 thought that each individual had a complete self, a complete soul, an accomplished I. And now she realised as plainly as if she had turned into a new being, that this was not so. Men and women had incomplete selves, made up of bits assembled together loosely and somewhat haphazard. Man was not created ready-made. Men today 40 were half-made, and women were half-made. Creatures that existed and functioned with certain regularity, but which ran off into a hopeless jumble of inconsequence.

Half-made, like insects that can run fast and be so busy and
5 suddenly grow wings, but which are only winged grubs after all. A world full of half-made creatures on two legs, eating food and degrading the one mystery left to them, sex. Spinning a great lot of words, burying themselves inside the cocoons of words and ideas that they spin round themselves, and inside the cocoons, mostly
10 perishing inert and overwhelmed.

Half-made creatures, rarely more than half-responsible and half-accountable, acting in terrible swarms like locusts.

Awful thought!—And with a collective insect-like will, to avoid the responsibility of achieving any more perfected being or identity.
15 The queer, rabid hate of being urged on into purer self. The morbid fanaticism of the non-integrate.

In the great seething light of the lake, with the terrible blue-ribbed mountains of Mexico beyond, she seemed swallowed by some grisly skeleton, in the cage of his death-anatomy. She was afraid, mysti-
20 cally, of the man crouching there in the bows with his smooth thighs and supple loins like a snake, and his black eyes watching. A half-being, with a will to disintegration and death. And the tall man behind her at the tiller, he had the curious smoke-grey phosphorus eyes under black lashes, sometimes met among the Indians. Hand-
25 some, he was, and quiet and seemingly self-contained. But with that peculiar devilish half-smile lurking under his face, the half jeering look of a part-thing, which knows its power to destroy the purer thing.

And yet, Kate told herself, both these men were manly fellows.
30 They would not molest her, unless she communicated the thought to them, and by a certain cowardliness, prompted them. Their souls were nascent, there was no fixed evil in them. They could sway both ways.

So in her soul she cried aloud to the greater mystery, the higher
35 power that hovered in the interstices of the hot air, rich and potent. It was as if she could lift her hands and clutch the silent, stormless potency that roved everywhere, waiting. "Come then!" she said, drawing a long slow breath, and addressing the silent life-breath which hung unrevealed in the atmosphere, waiting.
40 And as the boat ran on, and her fingers rustled in the warm

water of the lake, she felt the fulness descend into her once more, the peace, and the power. The fulfilment filling her soul like the fulness of ripe grapes. And she thought to herself: "Ah, how wrong I have been, not to turn sooner to the other presence, not to take the life-breath sooner! How wrong to be afraid of these two men."

She did what she had been half-afraid to do before: she offered them the oranges and sandwiches still in the basket. And each of the men looked at her, the smoke-grey eyes looked her in the eyes, and the black eyes looked her in the eyes. And the man with the smoke-grey eyes, who was cunninger than the other man, but also prouder, said to her with his eyes: *We are living! I know your sex, and you know mine. The mystery we are glad not to meddle with. You leave me my natural honour, and I thank you for the grace.*

In his look, so quick and proud, and in his quiet *Muchas gracias!* she heard the touch of male recognition, a man glad to retain his honour, and to feel the communion of grace. Perhaps it was the Spanish word *Gracias!* But in her soul she was thinking of the communion of grace.

With the black-eyed man it was the same. He was humbler. But as he peeled his orange and dropped the yellow peel on the water, she could see the stillness, the humility, and the pathos of grace in him: something very beautiful and truly male, and very hard to find in a civilised white man. It was not of the spirit. It was of the dark, strong, unbroken blood, the flowering of the soul.

Then she thought to herself: After all, it is good to be here. It is very good to be in this boat on this lake with these two silent, semi-barbarous men. They can receive the gift of grace, and we can share it like a communion, they and I. I am very glad to be here. It is so much better than love: the love I knew with Joachim. This is the fulness of the vine.

"Sayula!" said the man in the bows, pointing ahead.

She saw, away off, a place where there were green trees, where the shore was flat, and a biggish building stood out.

"What is the building?" she asked.

"The railway station."

She was suitably impressed, for it was a new-looking imposing structure.

A little steamer was smoking, lying off from a wooden jetty in the loneliness, and black, laden boats were poling out to her, and

merging back to shore. The vessel gave a hoot, and slowly yet busily
set off on the bosom of the water, heading in a slanting line across the
lake, to where the tiny high white twin-towers of Tuliapán* showed
above the water-line, tiny and far-off, on the other side.

5   They had passed the jetty, and rounding the shoal where the
willows grew, she could see Sayula: white fluted twin-towers of the
church, obelisk shaped above the pepper trees: beyond, a mound of a
hill standing alone, dotted with dry bushes, distinct and Japanese
looking; beyond this, the corrugated, blue-ribbed, flat-flanked
10   mountains of Mexico.

It looked peaceful, delicate, almost Japanese. As she drew nearer
she saw the beach with the washing spread on the sand: the fleecy
green willow trees and pepper trees, and the villas in foliage and
flowers, hanging magenta curtains of bougainvillea, red dots of
15   hibiscus, pink abundance of tall oleander trees: occasional palm-
trees sticking out.

The boat was steering round a stone jetty, on which in black letters
was painted an advertisement for motor-car tyres. There were a few
seats, some deep fleecy trees growing out of the sand, a booth for
20   selling drinks, a little promenade, and white boats on a sandy beach.
A few women sitting under parasols, a few bathers in the water, and
trees in front of the few villas deep in green or blazing scarlet
blossoms.

"This is very good," thought Kate. "It is not too savage, and not
25   over civilised. It isn't broken, but it is rather out of repair. It is in
contact with the world, but the world has got a very weak grip on it."

She went to the hotel, as Don Ramón had advised her.

"Do you come from Orilla?—You are Mrs Leslie?—Don Ramón
Carrasco sent us a letter about you."

30   There was a house. Kate paid her boatmen and shook hands with
them. She was sorry to be cut off from them again. And they looked
at her with a touch of regret as they left. She said to herself:

"There is something rich and alive in these people. They want to
be able to breathe the Great Breath.* They are like children,
35   helpless. And then they're like demons.—But somewhere, I believe
they want the breath of life and the communion of the brave, more
than anything."

She was surprised at herself, suddenly using this language. But
her weariness and her sense of devastation had been so complete,
40   that the Other Breath in the air, and the bluish dark power in the

earth had become, almost suddenly, more real to her than so-called reality. Concrete, jarring, exasperating reality had melted away, and a soft world of potency stood in its place, the velvety dark flux from the earth, the delicate yet supreme life-breath in the inner air. Behind the fierce sun the dark eyes of a deeper sun were watching, 5 and between the bluish ribs of the mountains a powerful heart was secretly beating, the heart of the earth.*

Her house was what she wanted: a low L-shaped, tiled building with rough red floors and deep verandah, and the other two sides of the patio completed by the thick, dark little mango-forest outside the 10 low wall. The square of the patio, within the precincts of the house and the mango trees, was gay with oleanders and hibiscus, and there was a basin of water in the seedy grass. The flower-pots along the verandah were full of flowering geranium and foreign flowers. At the far end of the patio, the chickens were scratching under the silent 15 motionlessness of ragged banana trees.

There she had it: her stone, cool, dark house, every room opening on to the verandah: her deep, shady verandah, or piazza, or corridor, looking out to the brilliant sun, the sparkling flowers and the seed-grass, the still water and the yellowing banana trees, the dark 20 splendour of the shadow-dense mango trees.*

With the house went a Mexican Juana with two thick-haired daughters and one son.* This family lived in a den at the back of the projecting bay of the dining-room. There, half screened, was the well and the toilet, and a little kitchen and a sleeping room where the 25 family slept on mats on the floor. There the paltry chickens paddled, and the banana trees made a chitter as the wind came.

Kate had four bedrooms to choose from. She chose the one whose low, barred window opened on the rough, grass and cobble-stone street, closed her doors and windows, and went to sleep, saying to 30 herself as she lay down: Now I am alone. And now I have only one thing to do: not to get caught up into the world's cog-wheels any more, and not to lose my hold on the hidden greater thing.

She was tired with a strange weariness, feeling she could make no further effort. She woke up at tea-time, but there was no tea. Juana 35 hastened off to the hotel to buy a bit.

Juana was a woman of about forty, rather short, with full dark face, centreless dark eyes, untidy hair and a limping way of walking. She spoke rapidly, a rather plum-in-the-mouth Spanish, adding 'n' to all her words. Something of a sloven, down to her speech. 40

"*No, Niña, no hay másn*"*—*másn* instead of *más*. And calling Kate,
in the old Mexican style, *Niña*, which means *Child*. It is the
honorable title for a mistress.

Juana was going to be a bit of a trial. She was a widow of doubtful
5   antecedents, a creature with passion, but not much control, strong
with a certain indifference and looseness. The hotel owner assured
Kate that she was honest, but that if Kate would rather find another
criada, all well and good.

There was a bit of a battle to be fought between the two women.
10 Juana was obstinate and reckless: she had not been treated very well
by the world. And there was a touch of bottom-dog insolence about
her.

But also, sudden touches of passionate warmth and the peculiar
selfless generosity of the natives. She would be honest out of rough
15 defiance and indifference, so long as she was not in a state of
antagonism.

As yet, however, she was cautiously watching her ground, with
that black-eyed touch of malice and wariness to be expected. And
Kate felt that the cry: *Niña—Child!* by which she was addressed,
20 held in it a slight note of malevolent mockery.

But there was nothing to do but to go ahead and trust the
dark-faced, centreless woman.

The second day, Kate had the energy to cast out one suite of
bent-wood and cane furniture from her salon, remove pictures and
25 little stands.

If there is one social instinct more dreary than all the other social
instincts in the world, it is the Mexican. In the centre of Kate's
red-tiled salon were two crescents: a black bent-wood cane settee
flanked on each side by two black bent-wood cane chairs exactly
30 facing a brown bent-wood cane settee flanked on each side by two
brown bent-wood cane chairs. It was as if the two settees and the
eight chairs were occupied by the ghosts of all the Mexican banalities
ever uttered, sitting facing one another with their knees towards one
another, and their feet on the terrible piece of green-with-red-roses
35 carpet, in the weary centre of the salon. The very sight of it was
frightening.

Kate shattered this face to face symmetry, and had the two girls,
María and Concha, assisted by the ironic Juana, carrying off the
brown bent-wood chairs and the bamboo stands into one of the spare
40 bedrooms. Juana looked on cynically, and assisted officiously. But

when Kate had her trunk, and fished out a couple of light rugs and a couple of fine shawls and a few things to make the place human, the criada began to exclaim:

"*Qué bonita! Qué bonita, Niña! Mire qué bonita!*"*

Chapter VII.

The Plaza.

Sayula was a little lake resort: not for the idle rich, for Mexico has
few left; but for tradespeople from Guadalajara, and week-enders.
5 Even of these, there were few.

Nevertheless, there were two hotels, left over, really, from the safe
quiet days of Don Porfirio, as were most of the villas. The outlying
villas were shut up, some of them abandoned. Those in the village
lived in a perpetual quake of fear. There were many terrors, but the
10 two regnant were bandits and bolshevists.

Bandits are merely men who, in the outlying villages, having very
often no money, no work, and no prospects, take to robbery and
murder for a time—occasionally for a life-time—as a profession.
They live in their wild villages until troops are sent after them, when
15 they retire into the savage mountains, or the marshes.

Bolshevists somehow seem to be born on the railway. Wherever
the iron rails run, and passengers are hauled back and forth in
railway coaches, there the spirit of rootlessness, of transitoriness, of
first and second class in separate compartments, of envy and malice,
20 and of iron and demonish panting engines, seems to bring forth the
logical children of materialism, the bolshevists.

Sayula had her little branch of railway, her one train a day. The
railway did not pay, and fought with extinction.* But it was enough.

Sayula also had that real insanity of America, the automobile. As
25 men used to want a horse and a sword, now they want a car. As
women used to pine for a home and a box at the theatre, now it is a
"machine." And the poor follow the middle class. There was a
perpetual rush of "machines," motor-cars and motor-buses—called
camiones—along the one forlorn road coming to Sayula from
30 Guadalajara. One hope, one faith, one destiny:* to ride in a *camión*, to
own a car.

There was a little bandit scare when Kate arrived in the village,
but she did not pay much heed. At evening she went into the plaza, to
be with the people. The plaza was a square with big trees and a
35 disused bandstand in the centre, a little promenade all round, and

then the cobbled street where the donkeys and the *camiones* passed. There was a further little section of real market-place, on the north side.

The band played no more in Sayula, and the *elegancia* strolled no more on the inner pavement around the plaza, under the trees. But the pavement was still good, and the benches were still more-or-less sound. Oh Don Porfirio's day! And now it was the peons and Indians, in their blankets and white clothes, who filled the benches and monopolised the square. True, the law persisted that the peons must wear trousers in the plaza, and not the loose great floppy drawers* of the fields. But then the peons also *wanted* to wear trousers, instead of the drawers that were the garb of their humble labor.

The plaza now belonged to the peons. They sat thick on the benches, or slowly strolled round in their sandals and blankets. Across the cobbled road on the north side, the little booths selling soup and hot food were crowded with men, after six o'clock: it was cheaper to eat out, at the end of a day's work.—The women at home could eat tortillas, never mind the *caldo*, the soup or the meat mess. At the booths which sold tequila, men, women, boys sat on the benches with their elbows on the board. There was a mild gambling game, where the man in the centre turned the cards, and the plaza rang to his voice: *Cinco de Espadas! Rey de Copas!* A large, stout, imperturbable woman, with a cigarette on her lip and danger in her lowering black eye, sat on into the night, selling tequila. The sweetmeat man stood by his board and sold sweets at one centavo each. And down on the pavement, small tin torch-lamps flared upon tiny heaps of mangoes or nauseous tropical red plums, two or three centavos the little heap, while the vendor, a woman in the full wave of her skirt, or a man with curious patient humility, squatted waiting for a purchaser, with that strange fatal indifference and that gentle sort of patience so puzzling to a stranger. To have thirty cents worth of little red plums to sell: to pile them on the pavement in tiny pyramids, five in a pyramid: and to wait all day and on into the night, squatting on the pavement and looking up from the feet to the far-off face of the passer-by and potential purchaser, this, apparently, is an occupation and a living. At night by the flare of the tin torch, blowing its flame on the wind.

Usually there would be a couple of smallish young men with guitars of different sizes, standing close up facing one another like

two fighting cocks that are uttering a long, endless swan song, singing in tense subdued voices the eternal ballads, not very musical, mournful, endless, intense, audible only within close range: keeping on and on till their throats were scraped. And a few tall, dark men in
5   red blankets standing around, listening casually, and rarely, very rarely making a contribution of one centavo.

In among the food-booths would be another trio, this time two guitars and a fiddle, and two of the musicians blind: the blind ones singing at a high pitch, full speed, yet not very audible. The very
10 singing seemed secretive, the singers pressing close in face to face, as if to keep the wild, melancholy ballad re-echoing in their private breasts, their backs to the world.

And the whole village was in the plaza, it was like a camp, with the low, rapid sound of voices. Rarely, very rarely a voice rose above the
15 deep murmur of the men, the musical ripple of the women, the twitter of children. Rarely any quick movement: the slow promenade of men in sandals, the sandals, called huaraches, making a slight cockroach shuffle on the pavement. Sometimes, darting among the trees, barelegged boys went sky-larking in and out of the shadow, in
20 and out of the quiet people. They were the irrepressible boot-blacks, who swarm like tiresome flies in a barefooted country.

At the south end of the plaza, just across from the trees and cornerwise to the hotel was a struggling attempt at an out-door café, with little tables and chairs on the pavement. Here, on week days, the
25 few who dared flaunt their prestige would sit and drink a beer or a glass of tequila. They were mostly strangers. And the peons, sitting immobile on the seats in the background, looked on with basilisk eyes from under the great hats.

But on Saturdays and Sundays there was something of a show.
30 Then the *camiones* and motor-cars came in lurching and hissing. And, like strange birds alighting, you had slim and charming girls in organdie frocks and face-powder and bobbed hair, fluttering into the plaza. There they strolled, arm in arm, brilliant in red organdie and blue chiffon and white muslin and pink and mauve and tangerine
35 frail stuffs, their black hair bobbed out, their dark slim arms interlaced, their dark faces curiously macabre in the heavy make-up, approximating to white, but the white of a clown or a corpse.

In a world of big, handsome peon men, these flappers flapped with butterfly brightness and an incongruous shrillness, manless. The
40 supply of Fifis, the male young elegants who are supposed to equate

the flappers, was small. But still, Fifis there were, in white flannel trousers and white shoes, dark jackets, correct straw hats, and canes. Fifis far more ladylike than the reckless flappers: and far more nervous, wincing. But Fifis none the less, gallant, smoking a cigarette with an elegant flourish, talking elegant Castilian, as near as possible, 5 and looking as if they were going to be sacrificed to some Mexican god within a twelvemonth: when they were properly plumped and perfumed. The sacrificial calves* being fattened.

On Saturday, the Fifis and the flappers and the motor-car people from town—only a forlorn few, after all—tried to be butterfly-gay, in 10 sinister Mexico. They hired the musicians with guitars and fiddle, and the jazz music began to quaver, a little too tenderly, without enough kick.

And on the pavement under the trees of the alameda—under the trees of the plaza, just near the little tables and chairs of the café, the 15 young couples began to gyrate *à la mode*. The red and the pink and the yellow and the blue organdie frocks were turning sharply with all the white flannel trousers available, and some of the white flannel trousers had smart shoes, white with black strappings or with tan brogue bands.* And some of the organdie frocks had green legs and 20 green feet, some had legs *à la nature*, and white feet. And the slim, dark arms went around the dark blue Fifi shoulders—or dark blue with a white thread. And the immeasurably soft faces of the males would smile with a self-conscious fatherliness at the whitened, pretty, reckless little faces of the females, soft, fatherly, sensuous 25 smiles, suggestive of a victim's luxuriousness.

But they were dancing on the pavement of the plaza, and on this pavement the peons were slowly strolling, or standing in groups watching with black, inscrutable eyes the uncanny butterfly twitching of the dancers. Who knows what they thought?—whether they felt 30 any admiration and envy at all, or only just a silent, cold, dark-faced opposition. Opposition there was.

The young peons in their little white blouses, and the scarlet sarape folded jauntily on one shoulder, strolled slowly on under their big, heavy, poised hats, with a will to ignore the dancers. Slowly, with 35 a heavy calm balance they moved irresistibly through the dance, as if the dance did not exist. And the Fifis in white trousers, with organdie in their arms, steered as best they might, to avoid the heavy relentless passage of the young peons, who went on talking to one another, smiling and flashing powerful white teeth, in a black, heavy sang 40 froid that settled like a blight even on the music. The dancers and the passing peons never touched, never jostled. In Mexico you do not run into people accidentally. But the dance broke against the invisible opposition.

5 The Indians on the seats, they too watched the dancers for a while. Then they turned against them the heavy negation of indifference, like a stone on the spirit. The mysterious faculty of the Indians, as they sit there so quiet and dense, for killing off any ebullient life, for quenching any light and colourful effervescence.

10 There was indeed a little native dance-hall. But it was shut apart within four walls. And the whole rhythm and meaning was different, heavy, with a touch of violence. And even there, the dancers were artizans and mechanics or railway-porters, the half-urban people. No peons at all—or practically none.

15 So, before very long, the organdie butterflies and the flannel-trouser Fifis gave in, succumbed, crushed once more beneath the stone-heavy passivity of resistance in the demonish peons.

The curious, radical opposition of the Indians to the thing we call the Spirit. It is Spirit which makes the flapper flap her organdie 20 wings like a butterfly. It is Spirit, which creases the white flannel trousers of the Fifi and makes him cut his rather pathetic dash. They try to talk the elegancies and flippancies of the modern Spirit.

But down on it all, like a weight of obsidian, comes the passive negation of the Indian. He understands Soul, which is of the blood. 25 But Spirit, which is superior, and is the quality of our civilisation, this, in the mass, he darkly and barbarically repudiates. Not until he becomes an artizan or connected with machinery does the modern Spirit get him.

And perhaps it is this ponderous repudiation of the modern Spirit 30 which makes Mexico what it is.

But perhaps the automobile will make roads even through the inaccessible soul of the Indian.

Kate was rather sad, seeing the dance swamped. She had been sitting at a little table, with Juana for dueña, sipping a glass of 35 absinthe.

The motor-cars returning to town left early, in a little group. If bandits were out, they had best keep together. Even the Fifis had a pistol on their hips.

But it was Saturday, so some of the young "elegance" was staying 40 on, till the next day: to bathe and flutter in the sun.

It was Saturday, so the plaza was very full, and along the cobble streets stretching from the square, many torches fluttered and wavered upon the ground, illuminating a dark salesman and an array of straw hats, or a heap of straw mats called *petates*, or pyramids of oranges from across the lake.

It was Saturday, and Sunday morning was market. So, as it were suddenly, the life in the plaza was dense and heavy with potency. The Indians had come in from all the villages, and from far across the lake. And with them they brought the curious heavy potency of life which seems to hum deeper and deeper when they collect together.

In the afternoon, with the wind from the south, the big *canoas*, sailing-boats with black hulls and one huge sail, had come drifting across the waters, bringing the market-produce and the natives to their gathering ground. All the white specks of villages on the far shore, and on the far-off slopes, had sent their wild quota to the throng.

It was Saturday, and the Indian instinct for living on into the night, once they are gathered together, was now aroused. The people did not go home. Though market would begin at dawn, men had no thought of sleep.

At about nine o'clock, after the Fifi dance was shattered, Kate heard a new sound, the sound of a drum, or tom-tom, and saw a drift of the peons away to the dark side of the plaza, where the side market would open tomorrow. Already places had been taken, and little stalls set up, and huge egg-shaped baskets, big enough to hold two men, were lolling against the wall.

There was a rippling and a pulse-like thudding of the drum, strangely arresting on the night air, then the long note of a flute playing a sort of wild, unemotional melody, with the drum for a syncopated rhythm. Kate, who had listened to the drums and the wild singing of the Red Indians in Arizona and New Mexico, instantly felt that timeless, primeval passion of the prehistoric races, with their intense and complicated religious significance,* spreading on the air.

She looked enquiringly at Juana, and Juana's black eyes glanced back at her furtively.

"What is it?" said Kate.

"Musicians, singers," said Juana evasively.

"But it's *different*," said Kate.

"Yes, it is new."

"New?"

"Yes. It has only been coming for a short time."

"Where does it come from?"

5   "Who knows!" said Juana, with an evasive shrug of her shoulders.

"I want to hear," said Kate.

"It's purely men," said Juana.

"Still one can stand a little way off."

Kate moved towards the dense, silent throng of men in big hats.
10   They all had their backs to her.

She stood on the step of one of the houses, and saw a little clearing
at the centre of the dense throng of men, under the stone wall over
which bougainvillea and plumbago flowers were hanging, lit up by
the small, brilliantly flaring torches of sweet-smelling wood, which a
15   boy held in his two hands.

The drum was in the centre of the clearing, the drummer standing
facing the crowd. He was naked from the waist up, wore snow-white
cotton drawers, very full, held round the waist by a red sash, and
bound at the ankles with red cords. Round his uncovered head was a
20   red cord, with three straight scarlet feathers rising from the back of
his head, and on his forehead, a turquoise ornament, a circle of blue
with a round blue stone in the centre.* The flute player was also
naked to the waist, but over his shoulder was folded a fine white
sarape with blue-and-dark edges, and fringe. Among the crowd,
25   men with naked shoulders were giving little leaflets to the onlookers.
And all the time, high and pure, the queer clay flute was repeating a
savage, rather difficult melody, and the drum was giving the
blood-rhythm.

More and more men were drifting in from the plaza. Kate stepped
30   from her perch and went rather shyly forward. She wanted one of the
papers. The man gave her one without looking at her. And she went
into the light to read. It was a sort of ballad, but without rhyme, in
Spanish. At the top of the leaflet was a rough print of an eagle within
the ring of a serpent that had its tail in its mouth: a curious deviation
35   from the Mexican emblem, which is an eagle standing on a nopal, a
cactus with great flat leaves, and holding in its beak and claws a
writhing snake.

This eagle stood slim upon the serpent, within the circle of the
snake, that had black markings round its back, like short black rays
40   pointing inwards. At a little distance, the emblem suggested an eye.*

In the place of the west
In peace, beyond the lashing of the sun's bright tail,
In the stillness where waters are born
Slept I, Quetzalcoatl.

In the cave which is called Dark Eye,   5
Behind the sun, looking through him as a window
Is the place. There the waters rise,
There the winds are born.*

On the waters of the after-life
I rose again, to see a star falling, and feel a breath on my face.   10

The breath said: Go! And lo!
I am coming.

The star that was falling was fading,
Was dying.

I heard the star singing like a dying bird: 15
My name is Jesus, I am Mary's Son.
I am coming home.
My mother the moon is dark.

Oh brother, Quetzalcoatl
Hold back the dragon of the sun,   20
Bind him with shadow while I pass
Homewards. Let me come home.

I bound the bright fangs of the sun
And held him while Jesus passed
Into the lidless shade,   25
Into the eye of the Father,
Into the womb of refreshment.*

And the breath blew upon me again.
So I took the sandals of the Saviour*
And started down the long slope   30
Past the mount of the sun.

Till I saw beneath me
White breast-tips of my Mexico
My bride.

Jesus the Crucified   35
Sleeps in the healing waters
The long sleep.

Sleep, sleep, my brother, sleep.

My bride between the seas*
Is combing her dark hair,
Saying to herself: Quetzalcoatl.

5   There was a dense throng of men gathered now, and from the
centre, the ruddy glow of ocote torches rose warm and strong, and
the sweet scent of the cedar-like resin was on the air. Kate could see
nothing, for the mass of men in big hats.

The flute had stopped its piping, and the drum was beating a slow,
10 regular thud, acting straight on the blood. The incomprehensible
hollow barking of the drum was like a spell on the mind, making the
heart burst each stroke, and darkening the will.

The men in the crowd began to subside, sitting and squatting on
the ground, with their hats between their knees. And now it was a
15 little sea of dark, proud heads leaning a little forward above the soft,
strong male shoulders.

Near the wall was a clear circle, with the drum in the centre. The
drummer with the naked torso stood tilting his drum towards him,
his shoulders gleaming smooth and ruddy in the flare of light. Beside
20 him stood another man holding a banner that hung from a light rod.
On the blue field of the banneret was the yellow sun with a black
centre, and between the four greater yellow rays, four black rays
emerging, so that the sun looked like a wheel spinning with a
dazzling motion.*

25 The crowd having all sat down, the six men with naked torsos, who
had been giving out the leaflets and ordering the crowd, now came
back and sat down in a ring, of which the drummer, with the drum
tilted between his knees as he squatted on the ground, was the key.
On his right hand sat the banner-bearer, on his left the flautist. They
30 were nine men in the ring, the boy, who sat apart watching the two
ocote torches, which he had laid upon a stone supported on a long
cane tripod,* being the tenth.

The night seemed to have gone still. The curious seed-rattling
hum of voices that filled the plaza was hushed. Under the trees, on
35 the pavements, people were still passing unconcerned, but they
looked curiously lonely, isolated figures drifting in the twilight of the
electric lamps, and going about some exceptional business. They
seemed outside the nucleus of life.

Away on the north side, the booths were still flaring, people were buying and selling. But this quarter too looked lonely, and outside the actual reality, almost like memory.

When the men sat down, the women began to drift up shyly, and seat themselves on the ground at the outer rim, their full cotton skirts flowering out around them, and their dark rebozos drawn tight over 5 their small, round, shy heads, as they squatted on the ground. Some, too shy to come right up, lingered on the nearest benches of the plaza. And some had gone away. Indeed, a good many men and women had disappeared as soon as the drum was heard.

So that the plaza was curiously void. There was the dense clot of 10 people round the drum, and then the outer world, seeming empty and hostile. Only in the dark little street that gave on to the darkness of the lake, people were standing like ghosts, half lit-up, the men with their sarapes over their faces, watching erect and silent and concealed, from the shadow. 15

But Kate, standing back in a doorway, with Juana sitting on the doorstep at her feet, was fascinated by the silent, half-naked ring of men in the torchlight. Their heads were black, their bodies soft and ruddy with the peculiar Indian beauty that has at the same time something terrible in it. The soft, full, handsome torsos of silent men 20 with heads softly bent a little forward: the soft, easy shoulders, that are yet so broad, and which balance upon so powerful a backbone; shoulders drooping a little, with the relaxation of slumbering, quiescent power; the beautiful ruddy skin, gleaming with a dark fineness; the strong breasts, so male and so deep, yet without the 25 muscular hardening that belongs to white men; and the dark, closed faces, closed upon a darkened consciousness, the black moustaches and delicate beards framing the closed silence of the mouth: all this was strangely impressive, moving strange, frightening emotions in the soul. Those men who sat there in their dark, physical tenderness, 30 so still and soft, they looked at the same time frightening. Something dark, heavy, and reptilian in their silence and their softness. Their very naked torsos were clothed with a subtle shadow, a certain secret obscurity. White men sitting there would have been strong-muscled and frank, with an openness in their very physique, a certain 35 ostensible presence.—But not so these men. Their very nakedness only revealed the soft, heavy depths of their natural secrecy, their eternal invisibility. They did not belong to the realm of that which comes forth.

Everybody was quite still: the expectant hush deepened to a kind 40

of dead, night silence. The naked-shouldered men sat motionless,
sunk into themselves, and listening with the dark ears of the blood.
The red sash went tight round their waists, the wide white trousers,
starched rather stiff, were bound round the ankles with red cords,
5   and the dark feet in the glare of the torch looked almost black, in
huaraches that had red thongs. What did they want then, in life,
these men who sat so softly and without any assertion, yet whose
weight was so ponderous, arresting?

   Kate was at once attracted and repelled. She was attracted, almost
10 fascinated by the strange *nuclear* power of the men in the circle. It
was like a darkly glowing, vivid nucleus of new life. Repellant the
strange heaviness, the sinking of the spirit into the earth, like dark
water. Repellant the silent, dense opposition to the pale-faced
spiritual direction.

15   Yet here and here alone, it seemed to her, life burned with a deep
new fire. The rest of life, as she knew it, seemed wan, bleached and
sterile. The pallid wanness and weariness of her world! And here,
the dark, ruddy figures in the glare of a torch, like the centre of the
everlasting fire, surely this was a new kindling of mankind!

20   She knew it was so. Yet she preferred to be on the fringe,
sufficiently out of contact. She could not bear to come into actual
contact.

   The man with the banner of the sun lifted his face as if he were
going to speak. And yet he did not speak. He was old: in his sparse
25 beard were grey hairs, grey hairs over his thick dark mouth. And his
face had the peculiar thickness, with a few deep-scored lines, of the
old among these people. Yet his hair rose vigorous and manly from
his forehead, his body was smooth and strong. Only, perhaps, a little
smoother, heavier, softer than the shoulders of the younger men.

30   His black eyes gazed sightless for some time. Perhaps he was
really blind; perhaps it was a heavy abstraction, a sort of heavy
memory working in him, which made his face seem sightless.

   Then he began, in a slow, clear, far-off voice, that seemed
strangely to echo the vanished barking of the drum:

35   "Listen to me, men! Listen to me, women of these men!—A long
time ago, the lake started calling for men, in the quiet of the night.
And there were no men. The little charales were swimming round
the shore, looking for something, and the bagres and the other big
fish would jump out of the water, to look around. But there were no
40 men.

   "So one of the gods with hidden faces walked out of the water,* and climbed the hill—" he pointed with his hand in the night towards the invisible round hill at the back of the village—"and looked about. He looked up at the sun, and through the sun he saw the dark sun, the same that made the sun and the world, and will swallow it* again like a draught of water.

"He said: Is it time? And from behind the bright sun the four dark arms of the greater sun shot out, and in the shadow men arose. They could see the four dark arms of the sun in the sky. And they started walking.

"The man on the top of the hill, who was a god, looked at the mountains and the flat places, and saw men very thirsty, their tongues hanging out. So he said to them: Come! Come here! Here is my sweet water!*

"They came like dogs running with their tongues out, and kneeled on the shore of the lake. And the man on the top of the hill heard them panting with having drunk much water. He said to them: Have you drunk too much into yourselves? Are your bones not dry enough?*

"The men made houses on the shore, and the man on the hill, who was a god, taught them to sow maize and beans, and build boats. But he said to them: No boat will save you, when the dark sun ceases to hold out his dark arms abroad in the sky.

"The man on the hill said: I am Quetzalcoatl, who breathed moisture on your dry mouths. I filled your breasts with breath from beyond the sun. I am the wind that whirls from the heart of the earth, the little winds that whirl like snakes round your feet and your legs and your thighs, lifting up the head of the snake of your body, in whom is your power. When the snake of your body lifts its head, beware! It is I, Quetzalcoatl, rearing up in you, rearing up and reaching beyond the bright day, to the sun of darkness beyond, where is your home at last. Save for the dark sun at the back of the day-sun, save for the four dark arms in the heavens, you were bone, and the stars were bone, and the moon an empty sea-shell on a dry beach, and the yellow sun were an empty cup, like the dry thin bone of a dead coyote's head. So beware!

"Without me you are nothing. Just as I, without the sun that is back of the sun, am nothing.

"When the yellow sun is high in the sky, then say: Quetzalcoatl will lift his hand and screen me from this, else I shall burn out, and the land will wither.

"For, say I, in the palm of my hand is the water of life, and on the back of my hand is the shadow of death. And when men forget me, I lift the back of my hand, farewell! Farewell, and the shadow of death.

"But men forgot me. Their bones were moist, their hearts weak. When the snake of their body lifted its head, they said: This is the tame snake that does as we wish. And when they could not bear the fire of the sun, they said: The sun is angry. He wants to drink us up. Let us give him blood of victims.

"And so it was, the dark branches of shade were gone from heaven, and Quetzalcoatl mourned and grew old, holding his hand before his face, to hide his face from men.

"He mourned and said: Let me go home. I am old, I am almost bone. Bone triumphs in me, my heart is a dry gourd. I am weary in Mexico.

"So he cried to the Master-Sun, the dark one, of the unuttered name: I am withering white like a perishing gourd-vine. I am turning to bone. I am denied of these Mexicans. I am waste and weary and old. Take me away.

"Then the dark sun reached an arm, and lifted Quetzalcoatl into the sky. And the dark sun beckoned with a finger, and brought white men out of the east. And they came with a dead god on a cross, saying: Lo! This is the Son of God! He is dead, he is bone! Lo, your god is bled and dead, he is bone. Kneel and sorrow for him, and weep. For your tears he will give you comfort again, from the dead, and a place among the scentless rose-trees of the after-life, when you are dead.

"Lo! His mother weeps, and the waters of the world are in her hands. She will give you drink, and heal you, and lead you to the land of God. In the land of God you shall weep no more. Beyond the gates of death, when you have passed from the house of bone, into the garden of white roses.

"So the weeping Mother brought her Son who was dead on the Cross to Mexico, to live in the temples. And the people looked up no more, saying: The Mother weeps. The Son of her womb is bone. Let us hope for the place of the west, where the dead have peace among the scentless rose-trees, in the Paradise of God.

"For the priests would say: It is beautiful beyond the grave.

"And then the priests grew old, and the tears of the Mother were exhausted, and the Son on the Cross cried out to the dark sun far beyond the sun: What is this that is done to me? Am I dead forever, and only dead? Am I always and only dead, but bone on a cross of bone?

"So this cry was heard in the world, and beyond the stars of the night, and beyond the sun of the day.

"Jesus said again: Is it time? My mother is old like a sinking moon, the old bone of her can weep no more. Are we perished beyond redeem?

"Then the greatest of the great suns spoke aloud from the back of the sun: I will take my Son to my bosom, I will take his mother on my lap. Like a woman I will put them in my womb,* like a mother I will lay them to sleep, in mercy I will dip them in the bath of forgetting and peace and renewal.—

"That is all.—So hear now, you men, and you women of these men. Jesus is going home, to the Father, and Mary is going back, to sleep in the belly of the Father. And they both will recover from death, during the long long sleep.

"But the Father will not leave us alone. We are not abandoned.

"The Father has looked around, and has seen the Morning Star, fearless between the rush of the oncoming yellow sun, and the backward reel of the night. So the Great One, whose name has never been spoken, says: Who art thou, bright watchman? And the Dawn Star answering: It is I, the Morning Star, who in Mexico was Quetzalcoatl. It is I, who look at the yellow sun from behind, have my eye on the unseen side of the moon. It is I, the star, midway between the darkness and the rolling of the sun. I, called Quetzalcoatl, waiting in the strength of my days.

"The Father answered: It is well. It is well. And again: It is time.

"Thus the big word was spoken behind the back of the world. The Nameless said: It is time.—

"Once more the word has been spoken: It is time.

"Listen, men and the women of men: It is time. Know now it is time. Those that left us are coming back. Those that came are leaving again. Say welcome, and then farewell!

"Welcome! Farewell!"

The old man ended with a strong, suppressed cry, as if really calling to the gods:

"*Bienvenido! Bienvenido! Adios! Adios!*"

And the people, half starting to their feet, cried with a startled, irregular cry:

"*Bienvenido! Adios! Bienvenido! Adios!*"

Even Juana, seated at Kate's feet, cried out without knowing what
she did:

"*Bienvenido! Bienvenido! Adios! Adios! Adios-n!*"

On the last adios! she trailed out to a natural, human 'n.'

5   The drum began to beat with an insistent, intensive rhythm, and
the flute, or whistle, lifted its odd, far-off calling voice. It was playing
again and again the peculiar melody Kate had heard at first.

Then one of the men in the circle lifted his voice, and began to
sing the hymn. He sang in the fashion of the old Red Indians, with
10 intensity and restraint, singing inwardly, singing to his own soul, not
outward to the world, nor yet even upward to God, as the Christians
sing. But with a sort of suppressed, tranced intensity, singing to the
inner mystery, singing not into space, but into the other dimension of
man's existence, where he finds himself in the infinite room that lies
15 inside the axis of our wheeling space. Space, like the world, cannot
but move. And like the world, there is an axis. And the axis of our
worldly space, when you enter, is a vastness where even the trees
come and go, and the soul is at home in its own dream, noble and
unquestioned.

20 The strange, inward pulse of the drum, and the singer singing
inwardly, swirled the soul back into the very centre of time, which is
older than age. He began on a high, remote note, and holding the
voice at a distance, ran on in subtle, running rhythms, apparently
unmeasured, yet pulsed underneath by the drum, and giving throb-
25 bing, three-fold lilts and lurches. For a long time, no melody at all
was recognisable: it was just a lurching, running, far-off crying,
something like the distant faint howling of a coyote. It was really the
music of the old American Indian.

There was no recognisable rhythm, no recognisable emotion, it
30 was hardly music. Rather a far-off, perfect crying in the night. But it
went straight through to the soul, the most ancient and everlasting
soul of all men, where alone can the human family assemble in
immediate contact.

Kate knew it at once, like a sort of fate. It was no good resisting.
35 There was neither urge nor effort, nor any speciality. The sound
sounded in the innermost far-off place of the human core, the
ever-present, where there is neither hope nor emotion, but passion
sits with folded wings on the nest, and faith is a tree of shadow.

Like fate, like doom. Faith is the Tree of Life itself, inevitable, and
40 the apples are upon us, like the apples of the eye, the apples of the

chin, the apple of the heart, the apples of the breast, the apple of the belly, with its deep core, the apples of the loins, the apples of the knees, the little, side-by-side apples of the toes. What do change and evolution matter. We are the Tree with the fruit forever upon it. And we are faith forever. Verbum Sat.*

My bride between the seas
Is combing her dark hair,
Saying to herself: Quetzalcoatl!

The one singer had finished, and only the drum kept on, touching the sensitive membrane of the night subtly and knowingly. Then a voice in the circle rose again on the song, and like birds flying from a tree, one after the other the individual voices arose, till there was a strong, intense, curiously weighty soaring and sweeping of male voices, like a dark flock of birds flying and dipping in unison. And all the dark birds seemed to have launched out of the heart, in the inner forest of the masculine chest.

In the place of the west
In peace, beyond the lashing of the sun's bright tail,
In the stillness where waters are born
Slept I, Quetzalcoatl.

And one by one, voices in the crowd broke free, like birds launching and coming in from a distance, caught by the spell. The words did not matter. Any verse, any words, no words, the song remained the same: a strong, deep wind rushing from the caverns of the breast, from the everlasting soul! Kate herself was too shy and wincing to sing: too blenched with disillusion. But she heard the answer away back in her soul, like a far-off mocking-bird at night. And Juana was singing in spite of herself, in a crooning feminine voice, making up the words unconsciously.

The half-naked men began to reach for their sarapes: white sarapes, with borders of blue and earth-brown bars, and dark fringe. A man rose from the crowd and went towards the lake. He came back with ocote and with faggots that a boat had brought over. And he started a little fire. After a while, another man went for fuel, and started another fire in the centre of the circle, in front of the drum. Then one of the women went off soft and barefoot, in her full cotton skirt. And she made a little bonfire among the women.

The air was bronze with the glow of flame, and sweet with smoke like incense. The song rose and fell, then died away. Rose, and died. The drum ebbed on, faintly touching the dark membrane of the night. Then ebbed away. In the absolute silence could be heard the soundless stillness of the dark lake.

5   Then the drum started again, with a new, strong pulse. One of the seated men, in his white poncho with the dark blackish-and-blue border, got up, taking off his sandals as he did so, and began softly to dance the dance step. Mindless, dancing heavily and with a curious bird-like sensitiveness of the feet, he began to tread the earth with

10   his bare soles, as if treading himself deep into the earth. Alone, with a curious pendulum rhythm, leaning a little forward from a powerful backbone, he trod to the drum-beat, his white knees lifting and lifting alternately against the dark fringe of his blanket, with a queer dark splash. And another man put his huaraches into the centre of

15   the ring, near the fire, and stood up to dance. The man at the drum lifted up his voice in a wild, blind song. The men were taking off their ponchos. And soon, with the firelight on their breasts and on their darkly abstracted faces, they were all afoot, with bare torsos and bare feet, dancing the savage bird-tread.

20   "Who sleeps shall wake! Who sleeps shall wake! Who treads down the path of the snake in the dust shall arrive at the place; in the path of the dust shall arrive at the place and be dressed in the skin of the snake; shall be dressed in the skin of the snake of the earth, that is father of stone; that is father of stone and the timber of earth; of the

25   silver and gold, of the iron, the timber of earth from the bone of the father of earth, of the snake of the world, of the heart of the world, that beats as a snake beats the dust in its motion on earth, from the heart of the world—

"Who slee-eeps, sha-all wake! Who slee-eeps, sha-all wake! Who

30   sleeps, sha-all wake in the way of the snake of the dust of the earth, of the stone of the earth, of the bone of the earth—"

The song seemed to take new wild flights, after it had sunk and rustled to a last ebb. It was like waves that rise out of the invisible, and rear up into foam and a flying, disappearing whiteness and a

35   rustle of extinction. And the dancers, after dancing in a circle in a slow, deep absorption, each man changeless in his own place, treading the same dust with the soft churning of bare feet, slowly, slowly began to revolve, till the circle was slowly revolving round the fire, with always the same soft, down-sinking, churning tread. And

40   the drum kept the changeless living beat, like a heart, and the song

rose and soared and fell, ebbed and ebbed to a sort of extinction, then heaved up again.

Till the young peons could stand it no more. They put off their sandals and their hats and their blankets, and shyly, with inexpert feet that yet knew the old echo of the tread, they stood behind the wheeling dancers, and danced without changing place. Till soon the revolving circle had a fixed yet throbbing circle of men outside.

Then suddenly one of the naked-shouldered dancers from the inner circle stepped back into the outer circle, and with a slow leaning, slowly started the outer circle revolving in the reverse direction from the inner. So now there were two wheels of the dance, one within the other, and revolving in different directions.

They kept on and on, with the drum and the song, revolving like wheels of shadow-shapes around the fire. Till the fire died low, and the drum suddenly stopped, and the men suddenly dispersed, returning to their seats again.

There was silence, then the low hum of voices and the sound of laughter. Kate had thought, so often, that the laughter of the peons broke from them in a sound almost like pain. But now the laughs came like little invisible flames, suddenly from the embers of the talk.

Everybody was waiting, waiting. Yet nobody moved at once, when the thud of the drum struck again like a summons. They sat still talking, listening with a second consciousness. Then a man arose and threw off his blanket, and threw wood on the central fire. Then he walked through the seated men to where the women clustered in the fulness of their skirts. There he waited, smiling with a look of abstraction. Till a girl rose and came with utmost shyness towards him, holding her rebozo tight over her lowered head with her right hand, and taking the hand of the man in her left. It was she who lifted the motionless hand of the man in her own, shyly, with a sudden shy snatching.* He laughed, and led her through the now risen men, towards the inner fire. She went with dropped head, hiding her face in confusion. But side by side and loosely holding hands, they began to tread the soft, heavy dance-step, forming the first small segment of the inner, stationary circle.

And now all the men were standing facing outwards, waiting to be chosen. And the women quickly, their shawled heads hidden, were slipping in and picking up the loose right hand of the man of their choice. The inner men with the naked shoulders were soon chosen.

The inner circle, of men and women in pairs, hand in hand, was closing.*

"Come, Niña, come!" said Juana, looking up at Kate with black, gleaming eyes.

5 "I am afraid!" said Kate. And she spoke the truth.

One of the bare-breasted men had come across the street, out of the crowd, and was standing waiting, near the doorway in which Kate stood, silently, with averted face.

"Look! Niña! This master is waiting for you. Then come! Oh
10 Niña, come!"

The voice of the criada had sunk to the low, crooning, almost magical appeal of the women of the people, and her black eyes glistened strangely, watching Kate's face. Kate, almost mesmerised, took slow, reluctant steps forward, towards the man who was
15 standing with averted face.

"Do you mind?" she said in English, in great confusion. And she touched his fingers with her own.

His hand, warm and dark and savagely suave, loosely, almost with indifference, and yet with the soft barbaric nearness held her fingers,
20 and he led her to the circle. She dropped her head, and longed to be able to veil her face. In her white dress and green straw hat, she felt a virgin again, a young virgin. This was the quality these men had been able to give back to her.

Shyly, awkwardly, she tried to tread the dance-step. But in her
25 shoes she felt inflexible, insulated, and the rhythm was not in her. She moved in confusion.

But the man beside her held her hand in the same light, soft grasp, and the slow, pulsing pendulum of his body swayed untrammeled. He took no notice of her. And yet he held her fingers in his soft, light
30 touch.

Juana had discarded her boots and stockings, and, with her dark, creased face like a mask of obsidian, her eyes gleaming with the timeless female flame, dark and unquenchable, she was treading the step of the dance.

35 "As the bird of the sun treads the earth at the dawn of the day like a brown hen under his feet, like a hen and the branches of her belly droop with the apples of birth, with the eggs of gold, with the eggs that hide the globe of the sun in the waters of heaven, in the purse of the shell of earth that is white from the fire of the blood, tread the
40 earth, and the earth will conceive like the hen 'neath the feet of the

bird of the sun; 'neath the feet of the heart, 'neath the heart's twin feet. Tread the earth, tread the earth that squats as a pullet with wings closed in—"

The circle began to shift, and Kate was slowly moving round between two silent and absorbed men, whose arms touched her arms. And the one held her fingers softly, loosely, but with transcendent nearness. And the wild song rose again like a bird that had alighted for a second, and the drum changed rhythm incomprehensibly.

The outer wheel was all men. She seemed to feel the strange dark glow of them upon her back. Men, dark, collective men, nonindividual. And herself woman, wheeling upon the great wheel of womanhood.

Men and women alike danced with faces lowered and expressionless, abstract, gone in the deep absorption of men into the greater manhood, women into the great womanhood. It was sex, but the greater, not the lesser sex. The waters over the earth wheeling upon the waters under the earth,* like an eagle silently wheeling above its own shadow.

She felt her sex and her womanhood caught up and identified in the slowly revolving ocean of nascent life, the dark sky of the men lowering and wheeling above. She was not herself, she was gone, and her own desires were gone in the ocean of the great desire. As the man whose fingers touched hers was gone in the ocean that is male, stooping over the face of the waters.

The slow, vast, soft-touching revolution of ocean above upon ocean below, with no vestige of rustling or foam. Only the pure sliding conjunction. Herself gone into her greater self, her womanhood consummated in the greater womanhood. And where her fingers touched the fingers of the man, the quiet spark, like the dawn star, shining between her and the greater manhood of men.

How strange, to be merged in desire beyond desire, to be gone in the body beyond the individualism of the body, with the spark of contact lingering like a morning star between her and the man, her woman's greater self, and the greater self of man. Even of the two men next to her. What a beautiful slow wheel of dance, two great streams streaming in contact, in opposite directions.

She did not know the face of the man whose fingers she held. Her personal eyes had gone blind, his face was the face of dark heaven, only the touch of his fingers a star that was both hers and his.

Her feet were feeling the way into the dance-step. She was beginning to learn softly to loosen her weight, to loosen the uplift of all her life, and let it pour slowly, darkly, with an ebbing gush, rhythmical in soft, rhythmic gushes from her feet into the dark body of the earth. Erect, strong like a staff of life, yet to loosen all the sap of her strength and let it flow down into the roots of the earth.

She had lost count of time. But the dance of itself seemed to be wheeling to a close, though the rhythm remained exactly the same to the end.

The voice finished singing, only the drum kept on. Suddenly the drum gave a rapid little shudder, and there was silence. And immediately the hands were loosened, the dance broke up into fragments. The man gave her a quick, far-off smile, and was gone. She would never know him by sight. But by presence she might know him.

The women slipped apart, clutching their rebozos tight round their shoulders. The men hid themselves in their blankets. And Kate turned to the darkness of the lake.

"Already you are going, Niña?" came Juana's voice of mild, aloof disappointment.

"I must go now," said Kate hurriedly.

And she hastened towards the dark of the lake, Juana running behind her with shoes and stockings in her hand.

Kate wanted to hurry home with her new secret, the strange secret of her greater womanhood, that she could not get used to. She would have to sink in to this mystery.

She hastened along the uneven path of the edge of the lake-shore, that lay dark in shadow, though the stars gave enough light to show the dark hulks and masts of the sailing-*canoas* against the downy obscurity of the water. Night, timeless, hourless night. She would not look at her watch. She would lay her watch face down, to hide its phosphorus figures. She would not be timed.

And as she sank into sleep, she could hear the drum again, like a pulse inside a stone beating.

Chapter VIII.

Night in the House.

Over the gateway of Kate's house was a big tree called a cuenta tree, because it dropped its fruits, that were little, round, hard balls like little dark marbles, perfect in shape, for the natives to gather up and string for beads, cuentas, or more particularly, for the Pater Noster beads of the rosary. At night, the little road outside was quite dark, and the dropping of the cuentas startled the silence.

The nights, which at first had seemed perfectly friendly, began to be full of terrors. Fear had risen again. A band of robbers had gathered in one of the outlying villages on the lake, a village where the men had bad characters, as being ready to turn bandit at any moment. And this gang, invisible in the daytime, consisting during the day of lake fishermen and laborers on the land, at night would set off on horseback to sack any lonely, or insufficiently-protected house.

Then the fact that a gang of bandits was out always set the isolated thieves and scoundrels in action. Whatever happened, it would be attributed to the bandits. And so, many an unsuspected, seemingly honest man, with the old lust in his soul, would steal out by night with his machete and perhaps a pistol, to put his fingers in the pie of the darkness.

And again Kate felt the terror clot and thicken in the black silence of the Mexican night, till the sound of a cuenta falling was terrible. She would lie and listen to the thickening darkness. A little way off would sound the long, shrill whistle of the police watch. And in a while, the police patrol, on horseback, would go clattering lightly by. But the police in most countries are never present save where there is no trouble.

The rainy season was coming, and the night-wind rose from the lake, making strange noises in the trees, and shaking the many loose doors of the house. The servants were away in their distant recess. And in Mexico, at night, each little distance isolates itself absolutely, like a man in a black cloak turning his back.

In the morning, Juana would appear from the plaza, her eyes

blob-like and inky, and the old, weary, monkey look of subjection to fear, settled on her bronze face. A race old in subjection to fear, and unable to shake it off.—She would immediately begin to pour forth to Kate, in a babbling, half-intelligent stream, some story of a house
5   broken into and a woman stabbed. And she would say, the owner of the hotel had sent word that it was not safe for Kate to sleep alone in the house. She must go to the hotel to sleep.

The whole village was in that state of curious, reptile apprehension which comes over dark people. A panic fear, a sense of
10 devilment and horror thick in the night air. When blue morning came they would cheer up. But at night, like clotting blood the air would begin to thicken again.

The fear, of course, was communicated from one person to another. Kate was sure that if Juana and her family had not been
15 huddled in reptile terror away at the far end of the house, she herself would have been unafraid. As it was, Juana was like a terror-struck lizard.

There was no man about the place. Juana had two sons, Jesús, who was about twenty, and Ezequiel, about seventeen. But Jesús—she
20 pronounced it *Hezoosn*—ran the little gasoline motor for the electric light, and he and Ezequiel slept together on the floor of the little engine house. So that Juana huddled with her two girls, Concha and María, in the den at the end of Kate's house, and seemed to sweat a rank odour of fear.

25 The village was submerged. Usually the plaza kept alive till ten o'clock, with the charcoal fires burning and the ice-cream man going round with his bucket on his head, endlessly crying: *Nieve! Nieve!*,* and the people gossiping on the seats or listening to the young men with guitars.

30 Now, by nine o'clock, the place was deserted, curiously stony and vacuous. And the Jefe* sent out the order that anybody in the streets after ten o'clock would be arrested.

Kate hurried to her house and locked herself in. It is not easy to withstand the panic fear of a black-eyed, semi-barbaric people. The
35 thing communicates itself like some drug on the air, wringing the heart and paralysing the soul with a sense of evil, black, horrible evil.

She would lie in her bed in the absolute dark: the electric light was cut off completely, everywhere, at ten o'clock, and primitive dark-
40 ness reigned. And she could feel the demonish breath of evil moving on the air in waves.

She thought of the grisly stories of the country, which she had heard. And she thought again of the people, outwardly so quiet, so nice, with a gentle smile. But even Humboldt had said of the Mexicans, that few people had such a gentle smile, and at the same time, such fierce eyes.* It was not that their eyes were exactly fierce. 5 But their blackness was inchoate, with a dagger of white light in it. And in the inchoate blackness the blood-lust might arise, out of the sediment of the uncreated past.

Uncreated, half-created, such a people was at the mercy of old black influences that lay in a sediment at the bottom of them. While 10 they were quiet, they were gentle and kindly, with a sort of limpid naïveté. But when anything shook them at the depths, the black clouds would arise, and they were gone again in the old grisly passions of death, blood-lust, incarnate hate. A people incomplete, and at the mercy of old, upstarting lusts. 15

Somewhere at the bottom of their souls, she felt, was a fathomless resentment, like a raw wound. The heavy, bloody-eyed resentment of men who have never been able to win a soul for themselves, never been able to win themselves a nucleus, an individual integrity, out of the chaos of passions and potencies and death. They are caught in 20 the toils of old lusts and old activities as in the folds of a black serpent that strangles the heart. The heavy, evil-smelling weight of an unconquered past.

And under this weight they live and die, not really sorry to die. Clogged and tangled in the elements, never able to extricate 25 themselves. Blackened under a too-strong sun, surcharged with the heavy, sundering electricity of the Mexican air, and tormented by the bubbling of volcanoes away below the feet. The tremendous potent elements of the American continent, that give men powerful bodies, but which weigh the soul down and prevent its rising into birth. Or, if 30 a man arrives with a soul, the maleficent elements gradually break it, gradually, till he decomposes into ideas and mechanistic activities, in a body full of mechanical energy, but with his blood-soul dead and putrescent.

So, these men unable to overcome the elements, men held down 35 by the serpent tangle of sun and electricity and volcanic emission, they are subject to an ever-recurring, fathomless lust of resentment, a demonish hatred of life itself. Then, the instriking thud of a heavy knife, stabbing into a living body, this is the best. No lust of women can equal that lust. The clutching throb of gratification as the knife 40 strikes in and the blood spurts out!

It is the inevitable *supreme* gratification of a people entangled in the past, and unable to extricate itself. A people that has never been redeemed, that has not known a Saviour.

For Jesus is no Saviour to the Mexicans. He is a dead god in their
5 tomb. As a miner who is entombed underground by the collapsing of the earth in the gangways, so do whole nations become entombed under the slow subsidence of their Past. Unless there comes some Saviour, some redeemer to drive a new way out, to the sun.

But the white men brought no salvation to Mexico. On the
10 contrary, they find themselves at last shut in the tomb along with their dead god and the conquered race.

Which is the *status quo*.

Kate lay and thought hard, in the black night. At the same time, she was listening intensely, with a clutch of horror. She could not
15 control her heart. It seemed wrenched out of place, and really hurt her. She was, as she had never been before, absolutely physically afraid, blood afraid. Her blood was wrenched in a paralysis of fear.

In England, in Ireland, during the war and the revolution she had known *spiritual* fear. The ghastly fear of the rabble—and during the
20 war, nations were nearly all rabble. The terror of the rabble that, mongrel-like, wanted to break the free *spirit* in individual men and women. It was the cold, collective lust of millions of people, to break the spirit in the outstanding individuals. They wanted to break this spirit, so that they could start the great downhill rush back to old
25 underworld levels, old gold worship and murder lust. The rabble.

In those days, Kate had known the agony of cold social fear, as if a democracy were a huge, huge cold centipede which, if you resisted it, would dig every claw into you. And the flesh would mortify around every claw.

30 That had been her worst agony of fear. And she had survived.

Now she knew the real heart-wrench of blood fear. Her heart seemed pulled out of place, in a stretched pain.

She dozed, and wakened suddenly, at a small noise. She sat up in bed. Her doors on to the verandah had shutters. The doors
35 themselves were fastened, but the shutters were open for air, leaving the upper space, like the window of the door, open. And against the dark grey of the night she saw what looked like a black cat crouching on the bottom of the panel-space.

"What is that?" she said automatically.

40 Instantly, the thing moved, slid away, and she knew it was the arm

of a man that had been reaching inside to pull the bolt of the door. She lay for a second paralysed, prepared to scream. There was no movement. So she leaned and lit a candle.

The curious panic fear was an agony to her. It paralysed her and wrenched her heart out of place. She lay prostrate in the anguish of 5 night-terror. The candle blazed duskily. There was a far-off mutter of thunder. And the night was horrible, horrible, Mexico was ghastly to her beyond description.

She could not relax, she could not get her heart into place. "Now," she thought to herself, "I am at the mercy of this thing, and I 10 have lost myself." And it was a terrible feeling, to be lost, scattered, as it were, from herself in a horror of fear.

"What can I do?" she thought, summoning her spirit. "How can I help myself?" She knew she was all alone.

For a long time she could do nothing. Then a certain relief came 15 to her as she thought: "I am believing in evil. I mustn't believe in evil. Panic and murder never start unless the leading people let slip the control. I don't really believe in evil. I don't believe the old Pan can wrench us back into the old, evil forms of consciousness,* unless we wish it. I do believe there is a greater power, which will give us the 20 greater strength, while we keep the faith in it, and the spark of contact. Even the man who wanted to break in here, I don't think he really had the power. He was just trying to be mean and wicked, but something in him would have to submit to a greater faith and a greater power." 25

So she reassured herself, till she had the courage to get up and fasten her door-shutters at the top. After which she went from room to room, to see that all was made fast. And she was thankful to realise that she was afraid of scorpions on the floor, as well as of the panic horror. 30

Now she had seen that the five doors and the six windows of her wing of communicating rooms were fast. She was sealed inside the darkness, with her candle. To get to the other part of the house, the dining-room and kitchen, she had to go outside on to the verandah. 35

She grew quieter, shut up with the dusky glow of her candle. And her heart, still wrenched with the pain of fear, was thinking: "Joachim said that evil was the lapsing back to old life-modes that have been surpassed in us. This brings murder and lust.—But the drums of Saturday night are the old rhythm, and that dancing round 40

the drum is the old savage form of expression. Consciously reverting
to the savage. So perhaps it is evil."

But then again her instinct to believe came up.

"No! It's not a helpless, panic reversal. It is conscious, carefully
5   chosen. We must go back to pick up old threads. We must take up
the old, broken impulse that will connect us with the mystery of the
cosmos again, now we are at the end of our own tether. We must do
it. Don Ramón is right. He must be a great man, really. I thought
there *were* no really great men any more: only great financiers and
10 great artists and so on, but no great *men*. He must be a great man."

She was again infinitely reassured by this thought.

But again, just as she had blown out the candle, vivid flares of
white light spurted through all the window-cracks, and thunder
broke in great round balls smashing down. The bolts of thunder
15 seemed to fall on her heart. She lay absolutely crushed, in a kind of
quiescent hysterics, tortured. And the hysterics held her listening
and tense and abject, until dawn. And then she was a wreck.*

In the morning came Juana, also looking like a dead insect, with
the conventional phrase: "How have you passed the night, Niña?"

20 "Badly!" said Kate. Then she told the story of the black cat, or the
man's arm.

"*Mire!*"* said Juana, in a hushed voice. "The poor innocent will
be murdered in her bed. No, Niña, you must go and sleep in the
hotel. No no, Niña, you can't leave your window-shutter open. No,
25 no, impossible. See now, will you go to the hotel to sleep? The other
señora* does it."

"I don't want to," said Kate.

"You don't want to, Niña? Ah! *Entonces! Entonces,** Niña, I will tell
Ezequiel to sleep here outside your door, with his pistol. He has a
30 pistol, and he will sleep outside your door. Jesúsn can sleep alone in
the *planta*—" the little hole where the engine was—"and Ezequiel
will sleep outside your door, and you can leave your shutter open, for
air in the hot night. Ah Niña, we poor women, we need a man and a
pistol. We ought not to be left alone all the night. We are afraid, the
35 children are afraid. And imagine it, that there was a robber trying to
open the bolt of your door! Imagine it to yourself! No Niña, we will
tell Ezequiel at mid-day—"

Ezequiel came striding proudly in, at mid-day. He was a wild shy
youth, very erect and proud, and half savage. His voice was breaking,
40 and had a queer resonance.

He stood shyly while the announcement was being made to him. Then he looked at Kate with flashing black eyes, very much the man to the rescue.

"Yes! Yes!" he said. "I will sleep here on the corridor. Don't have any fear. I shall have my pistol."

He marched off, and returned with the pistol, an old, long-barreled affair.

"It has five shots," he said, showing the weapon. "If you open the door in the night, you must say a word to me first. Because if I see anything move, I shall fire five shots. *Pst! Pst!*"

She saw by the flash of his eyes *what* satisfaction it would give him to fire five shots at some thing moving in the night. The thought of shots being fired at *him* gave him not the least concern.

"And Niña," said Juana, "if you come home late, after the light is out, you must call *Ezequiel!* Because if not, *Brumm! Brumm!*—and who knows who will be killed!"

Ezequiel slept on a straw mat on the brick verandah outside Kate's door, rolled up in his blanket, and with the pistol at his side. So she could leave her shutter open for air. And the first night she was kept awake once more by his fierce snoring. Never had she heard such a tremendous resonant sound! What a chest that boy must have! It was sound from some strange, savage other-world. The noise kept her awake, but there was something in it which she liked. Some sort of wild strength.

Chapter IX.

Casa de las Cuentas.

Kate was soon fond of her limping, untidy Juana, and of the girls. Concha was fourteen, a thick, heavy, barbaric girl with a mass of black waving hair which she was always scratching. María was eleven, a shy thin bird-like thing with big eyes that seemed almost to *absorb* the light round her.

It was a reckless family. Juana admitted a different father for Jesús, but to judge from the rest, one would have suspected a different father for each of them. There was a basic, sardonic carelessness in the face of life, in all the family. They lived from day to day, a stubborn, heavy, obstinate life of indifference, careless about the past, careless about the present, careless about the future. They had even no interest in money. Whatever they got they spent in a minute, and forgot it again.

Without aim or purpose, they lived absolutely *à terre*,* down on the dark, volcanic earth. They were not animals, because men and women and their children *cannot* be animals. It is not granted us.—*Go, for once gone, thou never canst return!* says the great Urge which drives us creatively on. When man tries brutally to return to the older, previous levels of evolution, he does so in the spirit of cruelty and misery.

So in the black eyes of the family, a certain viscous fear, and wonder, and misery. The misery of human beings who squat helpless outside their own unbuilt selves, unable to win their souls out of the chaos, and indifferent to all other victories.

White people are becoming soulless too. But they have conquered the lower worlds of metal and energy, so they whizz around in machines, circling the void of their own emptiness.

To Kate, there was a great pathos in her family. Also a certain repulsiveness.

Juana and her children, once they accepted their Niña as their own, were honest with intensity. Point of honour, they were honest to the least little plum in the fruit bowl. And almost intensely eager to serve.

140

Themselves indifferent to their surroundings, they would live in squalor. The earth was the great garbage bowl. Everything discarded was flung on the earth, and they did not care. Almost they liked to live in a milieu of fleas and old rags, bits of paper, banana skins and mango stones.—Here's a piece torn off my dress! Earth, take it. 5 Here's the combings of my hair! Earth, take them!

But Kate could not bear it. She *cared*. And immediately, the family was quite glad, thrilled that *she* cared. They swept the patio with the twig brooms till they swept the very surface of the earth away. Fun! The Niña had feelings about it. 10

She was a source of wonder and amusement to them. But she was never a class superior. She was a half-incomprehensible, half-amusing wonder-being.

The Niña wanted the *aguador* to bring two *botes* of hot water, quick, from the hot springs, to wash herself all over every morning. 15 Fun! Go, María, tell the *aguador* to *run* with the Niña's water.

Then they almost resented it that she shut herself off to have her bath. She was a sort of goddess to them, to provide them with fun and wonder: but she ought always to be accessible. And a god who is forever accessible to human beings has an unenviable time of it, Kate 20 soon discovered.

No, it was no sinecure, being a Niña. At dawn began the scrape-scrape of the twig broom outside. Kate stayed on in bed, doors fastened but shutters open. Flutter outside! Somebody wanted to sell two eggs. Where is the Niña?—She is sleeping! The visitor 25 does not go. Continual flutter outside.

The *aguador*! Ah, the water for the Niña's bath! She is sleeping, she is sleeping. "No!" called Kate, slipping into a dressing gown and unbolting the door. In come the children with the bath tub, in comes the *aguador* with the two square kerosene cans full of hot water. 30 Twelve centavos! Twelve centavos for the *aguador*! *No hay!** We haven't got twelve centavos. Later! Later! Away trots the *aguador*, pole over his shoulder. Kate shuts her doors and shutters, and starts her bath.

"Niña? Niña?" 35
"What do you want?"
"Eggs boiled or fried or *rancheros*?* Which do you want?"
"Boiled."
"Coffee or chocolate?"
"Coffee." 40

"Or do you want tea?"

"No, coffee."

Bath proceeds.

"Niña?"

5   "Yes."

"There is no coffee. We are going to buy some."

"I'll take tea."

"No Niña! I am going. Wait for me."

"Go then."

10   Kate comes out to breakfast on the verandah. The table is set, heaped with fruit, and white bread and sweet buns.

"Good morning, Niña. How have you passed the night? Well! Ah, praised be God!—María, the coffee. I'm going to put the eggs in the water. Oh Niña, that they may not be boiled hard!—Look, what feet
15 of the Madonna! Look! *Bonitos!*"

And Juana stooped down fascinated to touch with her black finger Kate's white soft feet, that were thrust in light sandals, just a thong across the foot.

The day had begun. Juana looked upon herself as dedicated
20 entirely to Kate. As soon as possible she shooed her girls away, to school. Sometimes they went: mostly they didn't. The Niña said they must go to school. Listen! Listen now! Says the Niña that you must go to school! Away! Walk!

Juana would limp back and forth down the long verandah from
25 kitchen to the breakfast table, carrying away the dishes one by one. Then, with a great splash, she was washing up.

Morning! Brilliant sun pouring into the patio, on the hibiscus flowers and the fluttering yellow and green rags of the banana trees. Birds swiftly coming and going, with tropical suddenness. In the
30 dense shadow of the mango-grove, white clad Indians going like ghosts. The sense of fierce sun, and almost more impressive, of dark, intense shadow. A twitter of life, yet a certain heavy weight of silence. A dazzling flicker and brilliance of light, yet the feeling of weight.

Kate would sit alone, rocking on her verandah, pretending to sew.
35 Silently appears an old man with one egg held up mysteriously, like some symbol. Would the *patrona* buy it for five centavos.—La Juana only gives four centavos.* All right? Where is Juana?

Juana appears from the plaza with more purchases. The egg! The four centavos! The account of the spendings. *Entonces! Entonces!*
40 *Luego! Luego! Ah, Niña, no tengo memoria!**—Juana could not read

nor write. She scuffled off to the market with her pesos, bought endless little things at one or two centavos each, every morning. And every morning there was a reckoning up. Ah! Ah! Where are we? I have no memory. Well then—ah—yes—I bought ocote for three centavos! How much? How much, Niña? How much is it now?

It was a game which thrilled Juana to the marrow, reckoning up the centavos to get it just right. If she was a centavo short in the change, she was paralysed. Time after time she would re-appear. *There is a centavo short, Niña? Ah, how stupid I am! But I will give you one of mine!*

"Don't bother," said Kate. "Don't think of it any more."

"But yes. But yes!"—and away she limped in distraction.

Till an hour later, loud cry from the far end of the house. Juana waving a scrap of greenery.

"*Mire! Niña! Compré perejil a un centavo*—I bought parsley for one cent. Is it right?"

"It is right," said Kate.

And life could proceed once more.

There were two kitchens, the one next the dining-room, belonging to Kate, and the narrow little shed under the banana trees, belonging to the servants. From her verandah Kate looked away down to Juana's kitchen shed. It had a black window-hole.

Clap! Clap! Clap! Clap!—Why I thought Concha was at school!—said Kate to herself.

No!—there, in the darkness of the window-hole was Concha's swarthy face and mane, peering out like some animal from a cave, as she made the tortillas. Tortillas are flat pancakes of maize dough, baked dry on a flat earthenware plate over the fire. And the making consists of clapping a bit of raw dough from the palm of one hand to the palm of the other, till the tortilla is of the requisite thinness, roundness, and so-called lightness.

Clap! Clap! Clap! Clap! Clap! Clap! Clap!—it was as inevitable as the tick of some spider, the sound of Concha making tortillas in the heat of the morning, peering out of her dark window-hole. And some time after mid-day, the smoke would be coming out of the window-hole; Concha was throwing the raw tortillas on the big earthen plate over the slow wood fire.

Then Ezequiel might or might not stride in, very much the man, sarape poised over one shoulder and big straw hat jauntily curled, to eat the mid-day tortillas. If he had work in the fields at any distance,

he would not appear till nightfall. If he appeared, he sat on the
doorstep and the women served him his tortillas and fetched him his
drink of water as if he was a king, boy though he might be. And his
rough, breaking voice was heard in quiet command.

5 Command was the word. Though he was quiet and gentle, and
very conscientious, there was calm, kingly command in his voice
when he spoke to his mother or sisters. The old male prerogative.
Somehow, it made Kate want to ridicule him.

Came her own meal: one of her trials. Hot, rather greasy soup.
10 Inevitable hot, greasy, rather peppery rice. Inevitable meat in hot,
thick, rather greasy sauce. Boiled calabacitas or egg-plant, salad,
perhaps some *dulce* made with milk—and the big basket of fruit.
Overhead, the blazing tropical sun of late May.

Afternoon, and greater heat. Juana set off with the girls and the
15 dishes. They would do the washing up in the lake. Squatting on the
stones, they would dabble the plates one by one, the spoons and the
forks one by one in the filmy water of the lake, then put them in the
sun to dry. After which Juana might wash a couple of towels in the
lake, and the girls might bathe. Sauntering the day away—sauntering
20 the day away.

Jesús, the eldest son, a queer, heavy, greasy fellow, usually
appeared in the afternoon, to water the garden. But he ate his meals
at the hotel, and really lived there, had his home there. Not that he
had any home, any more than a zopilote had a home. But he ran the
25 *planta*, and did odd jobs about the hotel, and worked every day in the
year till half-past ten at night, earning twenty-two pesos, eleven
dollars, a month. He wore a black shirt, and his thick, massive black
hair dropped over his low brow. Very near to an animal. And though,
to order, he wore a black Fascista shirt,* he had the queer, animal
30 jeering of the socialists, an instinct for pulling things down.

His mother and he had a funny little intimacy of quiet and
indifferent mutual taunting of one another. He would give her some
money if she were in a strait. And there was a thin little thread of
blood-bondage between them. Apart from that, complete
35 indifference.

Ezequiel was a finer type. He was slender and so erect that he
almost curved backwards. He was very shy, farouche. Proud also,
and more responsible to his family. He would not go to work in an
hotel. No. He was a worker in the fields, and he was proud of it. A
40 man's work. No equivocal sort of half-service for him.

Though he was just a hired laborer, yet, working on the land he never felt he was working for a master. It was the land he worked for. Somewhere inside himself he felt that the land was his, and he belonged in a measure to it. Perhaps a lingering feeling of tribal, communal land-ownership and service.

When there was work, he was due to earn a peso a day. There was often no work: and often only seventy-five centavos a day for wage. When the land was dry, he would try to get work on the road, though this he did not like. But he earned his peso a day.

Often, there was no work. Often, for days, sometimes for weeks, he would have to hang about, nothing to do, nothing to do. Only, when the socialist government had begun giving the peasants bits of land, dividing up the big haciendas, Ezequiel had been allotted a little piece outside the village.* He would go and gather the stones together there, and prepare to build a little hut. And he would break the earth with a hoe, his only implement, as far as possible.—But he had no blood connection with this square allotment of unnatural earth, and he could not get himself into relations with it. He was fitful and diffident about it. There was no incentive, no urge.

On workdays he would come striding in about six o'clock, shyly greeting Kate as he passed. He was a gentleman in his barbarism. Then, away in the far recess, he would rapidly fold tortilla after tortilla, sitting on the floor with his back to the wall, rapidly eating the leathery things that taste of mortar, because the maize is first boiled with lime to loosen the husk, and accepting another little pile, served on a leaf, from the cook, Concha. Juana, cook for the Niña, would no longer condescend to cook for her own family. And sometimes there was a mess of meat and chile for Ezequiel to scoop up out of the earthenware casserole, with his tortillas. And sometimes there was not. But always, he ate with a certain blind, rapid indifference, that also seems to be Mexican. They seem to *eat* even with a certain hostile reluctance, and have a strange indifference to what or when they eat.

His supper finished, as a rule he was off again like a shot, to the plaza, to be among men. And the women would sit desultorily about, on the ground. Sometimes Kate would come in at nine o'clock to an empty place—Ezequiel in the plaza, Juana and María disappeared somewhere or other, and Concha lying asleep like a heap of rag on the gravel of the patio. When Kate called her, she would raise her head, stupefied and hopeless; then get up like a dog and crawl away to the gate. The strange stupor of boredom and hopelessness that was always sinking upon them would make Kate's heart stand still with dread.

The peculiar indifference to everything, even to one another. Juana washed a cotton shirt and a pair of cotton trousers for each of her sons, once a week, and there her maternal efforts ended. She saw hardly anything of them, and was often completely unaware of what Ezequiel was doing, where he was working, or at what. He had just gone off to work, no more.

Yet again, sometimes she had hot, fierce pangs of maternal protectiveness, when the boy was unjustly treated, as he often was. And if she thought he were ill, a black sort of fatalistic fear came over her. But Kate had to rouse her into getting some simple medicine.

Like animals, yet not at all like animals. For animals are complete in their isolation and their insouciance. With them it is not indifference. It is completeness in themselves. But with the family there was always a kind of bleeding of incompleteness, a terrible stupor of boredom settling down.

The two girls could not be apart: they must always be running after one another. Yet Concha continually teased the big-eyed, naïve simpleton of a María. And María was always in tears. Or the two were suddenly throwing stones at one another. But with no real aim to hit. And Juana was abusing them with sudden vehemence, that flickered out in a minute to complete indifference again.

Queer, the savage ferocity with which the girls would suddenly be throwing stones at one another. But queerer still, they always aimed *just to miss*. Kate noticed the same in the savage attacks the boys made on one another, on the beach: hurling large stones with intense, terrible ferocity. But almost always, aiming with a curious cast in the eyes, just to miss.

But sometimes not. Sometimes hitting with a sharp cut. And then the wounded one would drop right down, with a howl, as if dead. And the other boys would edge away, in a silent kind of dread. And the wounded boy would lie prostrate, not really much hurt, but as if he was killed.

Then, maybe, suddenly he would be up, with a convulsion of murder in his face, pursuing his adversary with a stone. And the adversary would abjectly flee.

Always the same thing among the young: a ceaseless, endless

taunting and tormenting. The same as among the Red Indians. But the Pueblo Indians rarely lapsing from speech into violence. The Mexican boys almost always. And almost always, one boy in murderous rage, pursuing his taunter till he had hurt him: then an abject collapse of the one hurt. Then, usually, a revival of the one hurt, the murderous frenzy transferred to him, and the first attacker fleeing abjectly, in terror. One or the other always abject.

They were a strange puzzle to Kate. She felt something must be done. She herself was inspired to help. So she had the two girls for an hour a day, teaching them to read, to sew, to draw. María wanted to learn to read: that she did want. For the rest, they began well. But soon, the regularity and the slight insistence of Kate on their attention made them take again that peculiar invisible jeering tone, something peculiar to the American continent. A quiet, invisible, malevolent mockery, a desire to wound. They would press upon her, trespassing upon her privacy, and with a queer effrontery, doing all they could to walk over her. With their ugly little wills, trying to pull her will down.

"No, don't lean on me, Concha. Stand on your own feet!"

The slight grin of malevolence on Concha's face, as she stood on her own feet. Then:

"Do you have lice in your hair, Niña?"

The question asked with a peculiar subtle, Indian insolence.

"No!" said Kate, suddenly angry. "And now go! Go! Go away from me! Don't come near me."

They slunk out, abject. So much for educating them.

Kate had visitors from Guadalajara: great excitement. But while the visitors were drinking tea with Kate on the verandah, at the other side of the patio, full in view, Juana, Concha, María, and Felipa, a cousin of about sixteen, squatted on the gravel with their splendid black hair down their backs, displaying themselves as they hunted in each other's hair for lice. They wanted to be full in view. And they were it. They wanted the basic fact of lice to be thrust under the noses of those white people.

Kate strode down the verandah.

"If you must pick lice," she said in a shaking voice to Juana, shaking with anger, "pick them there, in your own place, where you can't be seen."

One instant, Juana's black inchoate eyes gleamed with a malevolent ridicule, meeting Kate's. The next instant, humble and abject, the four with their black hair down their backs slunk into the recess out of sight.

But it pleased Juana that she had been able to make Kate's eyes blaze with anger. It pleased her. She felt a certain low power in herself. True, she was a little afraid of that anger. But that was what she wanted. She would have no use for a Niña of whom she was not a bit afraid. And she wanted to be able to provoke that anger, of which she felt a certain abject twinge of fear.

Ah the dark races! Kate's own Irish were near enough, for her to have glimpsed some of the mystery. The dark races belong to a bygone cycle of humanity. They are left behind in a gulf out of which they have never been able to climb. And on to that particular white man's levels they never will be able to climb. They can only follow as servants.

While the white man keeps the impetus of his own proud onward march, the dark races will yield and serve, perforce. But let the white man once have a misgiving about his own leadership, and the dark races will at once attack him, to pull him down into the old gulfs. To engulph him again.

Which is what is happening. For the white man, let him bluster as he may, is hollow with misgiving about his own supremacy.

Full speed ahead, then, for the débâcle.

But once Kate had been roused to a passion of revulsion from these lice-picking, down-dragging people, they changed again, and served her with a certain true wistfulness that could not but touch her. Juana cared really about nothing. But just that last thread of relationship that connected her with Kate and the upper world of daylight and fresh air, she didn't want to break. No no, she *didn't* want finally to drive her Niña away. No no, the only one thing she did want, ultimately, was to serve her Niña.

But at the same time, she cherished a deep malevolent grudge against rich people, white people, superior people. Perhaps the white man has finally betrayed his own leadership: who knows! But it is a thing of the brave, on-marching soul, and perhaps this has been betrayed already by the white man. So that the dark are rising upon him.

Juana would come to Kate, telling her stories from the past. And the sinister mocking film would be on her black eyes, and her lined, copper face would take on its reptile mask as she would continue: "*Usted sabe, Niña, los gringos, los gringuitos llevan todo*—You know, Niña, the gringos and the gringuitos take away everything— — —"

The gringos are the Americans. But Kate herself was included by Juana in the gringuitos: the white foreigners. The woman was making another sliding, insolent attack.

"It is possible," said Kate coldly. "But tell me what I take away from Mexico."

"No, Niña! No!"—The subtle smile of satisfaction lurked under the bronze tarnish of Juana's face. She had been able to get at the other woman, touch the raw. "I don't speak of you, Niña—!" But there was too much protest in it.

Almost, they wanted to drive her away: to insult her and drag her down and make her want to go away. They couldn't help it. Like the Irish, they would cut off their nose to spite their face.

The backward races!

At the same time there was a true pathos about them. Ezequiel had worked for a man for two months, building a house, when he was a boy of fourteen, in order to get a sarape. At the end of the two months, the man had put him off, and he had not got the sarape: had never got it. A bitter disappointment.*

But then, Kate was not responsible for that. And Juana seemed almost to make her so.

A people without the energy of *getting on*, how could they fail to be hopelessly exploited. They had been hopelessly and cruelly exploited, for centuries. And their backbones were locked in male-volent resistance.

"But," as Kate said to herself, "*I* don't want to exploit them. Not a bit. On the contrary, I am willing to give more than I get. But that nasty insinuating insultingness is not fair in the game. I never insult them. I am so careful not to hurt them. And then they *deliberately* make these centipede attacks on me, and are pleased when I am hurt—"

But she knew her own Irish at the game. So she was able to put Juana and the girls away from her, and isolate herself from them. Once they were put away, their malevolence subsided and they remembered what Kate wanted. While she stayed amiable, they forgot. They forgot to sweep the patio, they forgot to keep them-selves clean. Only when they were shoved back, into isolation, did they remember again.

The boy, Ezequiel, seemed to her to have more honour than the women. He never made these insidious attacks.

And when her house was clean and quiet, and the air seemed cleansed again, the soul renewed, her old fondness for the family came back. Their curious flitting coming-and-going, like birds: the busy clap-clap-clapping of tortillas, the excited scrunching of tomatoes and chile on the metate, as Juana prepared sauce. The noise of the bucket in the well—Jesús, come to water the garden.

5 The game, the game of it all! Everything they did must be *fun*, or they could not do it. They could not abstract themselves to a routine. Never. Everything must be fun, must be variable, must be a bit of an adventure. It was confusion, but after all, a living confusion, not a dead, dreary thing. Kate remembered her English servants in the

10 English kitchens: so mechanical and somehow inhuman. Well, this was the other extreme.

Here there was no discipline or method at all. Although Juana and her brats really wanted to do the things Kate wished, they must do them their own way. Sometimes Kate felt distracted: after all, the

15 mechanical lines are so much *easier* to follow. But as far as possible, she let the family be. She had to get used, for example, to the vagaries of her dining table: a little round table that always stood on the verandah. At breakfast time it would be discreetly set under the *plantas* by the salon; for dinner, at one o'clock, it would have travelled

20 way down the verandah; for tea it might be under a little tree on the grass. And then Juana would decide that the Niña must take supper, two eggs *rancheros*, in the dining-room itself, isolated at the corner of the long dining table meant for fourteen people.

The same with the dishes. Why they should, after washing up in

25 the big bowls in the kitchen for several days, suddenly struggle way down to the lake with the unwashed pots in a basket on Concha's shoulder, Kate never knew. Except for the fun of the thing.

Children! But then, not at all children. None of the wondering *insouciance* of childhood. Something dark and cognisant in their souls

30 all the time: some heavy weight of resistance. They worked in fits and starts, and could be very industrious; then came days when they lay about on the ground like pigs. At times they were merry, seated round on the ground in groups, like Arabian nights, and laughing away. Then suddenly resisting even merriment in themselves,

35 relapsing into the numb gloom. When they were busily working, suddenly, for no reason, throwing away the tool, as if resenting having given themselves. Careless in their morals, always changing their loves, the men at least resisted all the time any real giving of themselves. They didn't even want the thing they were pursuing. It

40 was the women who drew them on. And a young man and a girl going

down the road from the lake in the dark, teasing and poking each
other in excitement, would startle Kate because of their unusual-
ness—the men and women never walked their sex abroad, as white
people do. And the sudden, sexual laugh of the man, so strange a
sound of pain and desire, obstinate reluctance and helpless passion, 5
a noise as of something tearing in his breast, was a sound to
remember.

Kate felt her household a burden. In a sense, they were like
parasites, they wanted to live on her life, and pull her down, pull her
down. Again, they were so generous with her, so good and gentle, 10
she felt they were wonderful. And then once more she came up
against that unconscious, heavy, reptilian indifference in them,
indifference and resistance.

Her servants were the clue to all the native life, for her. The men
always together, erect, handsome, balancing their great hats on the 15
top of their heads, and sitting, standing, crouching with a snake-like
impassivity. The women together separately, soft, and as if *hidden*,
wrapped tight in their dark rebozos. Men and women seemed always
to be turning their backs on one another, as if they didn't want to see
one another. No flirting, no courting. Only an occasional quick, dark 20
look, the signal of a weapon-like desire, given and taken.*

The women seemed, on the whole, softly callous and determined
to go their own way: to change men if they wished. And the men
seemed not to care very profoundly. But it was the women who
wanted the men. 25

The native women, with their long black hair streaming down
their full, ruddy backs, would bathe at one end of the beach, usually
wearing their chemise, or a little skirt. The men took absolutely no
notice. They didn't even look the other way. It was the women
bathing, that was all. As if it were, like the charales swimming, just a 30
natural part of the lake life. The men just left that part of the lake to
the women. And the women sat in the shallows of the lake, isolated in
themselves like moor-fowl, pouring water over their heads and over
their ruddy arms from a gourd scoop.

The quiet, unobtrusive, but by no means down-trodden women of 35
the peon class. They went their own way, enveloped in their rebozos
as in their own darkness. They hurried nimbly along, their full
cotton skirts swinging, chirping and quick like birds. Or they sat in
the lake with long hair streaming, pouring water over themselves:
again like birds. Or they passed with a curious slow inevitability up 40

the lake-shore, with a heavy red jar of water perched on one
shoulder, one arm over the head, holding the rim of the jar. They
had to carry all water from the lake to their houses. There was no
town supply. Or, especially on Sunday afternoons, they sat in their
5 doorways lousing one another. The most resplendent *belles*, with
magnificent black wavy hair, were most thoroughly loused. It was as
if it were a meritorious public act.

The men were the obvious figures. They assert themselves on the
air. They are the dominant. Usually they are in loose groups, talking
10 quietly, or silent: always standing and sitting apart, rarely touching
one another. Often a single man would stand alone at a street-corner
in his sarape, motionless for hours, like some powerful spectre. Or a
man would lie on the beach as if he had been cast up dead from the
waters. Impassive, motionless they would sit side by side on the
15 benches of the plaza, not exchanging a word. Each one isolated in his
own fate, his eyes black and quick like a snake's, and as blank.

It seemed to Kate that the highest thing this country might
produce would be some powerful relationship of man to man.
Marriage itself would always be a casual thing. Though the men
20 seemed very gentle and protective to the little children. Then they
forgot them.

But sex itself was a powerful, potent thing, not to be played with or
paraded. The one mystery. And a mystery greater than the individual. The individual hardly counted.

25 It was strange to Kate to see the Indian huts on the shore, little
holes built of straw or corn-stalks, with half-naked children squatting on the naked earth floor, and a lousy woman-squalor around,
litter of rags and bones, and a sharp smell of human excrement. The
people have no noses.—And standing silent and erect not far from
30 the hole of the doorway, the man, handsome and impassive. How
could it be, that such a fine-looking human male should be so
absolutely indifferent, content with such paltry squalor?

But there he was, unconscious. He seemed to have life and
passion in him. And she knew he was strong. No men in the world
35 can carry heavier loads on their backs, for longer distances, than
these Indians. She had seen an Indian trotting down a street with a
piano on his back: holding it, also, by a band round his forehead.
From his forehead, and on his spine he carried it, trotting along.—
The women carry with a band round the breast.

40 So there is strength. And *apparently*, there is passionate life. But

no energy. Nowhere in Mexico is there any sign of energy. This is, as it were, switched off.

Even the new artizan class, though it imitates the artizan class of the United States, has no real energy. There are workmen's clubs. The workmen dress up and parade a best girl on their arm. But somehow, it seems whàt it is, only a weak imitation.

Kate's family was increased, without her expecting it. One day arrived from Ocotlán a beautiful ox-eyed girl of about fifteen, wrapped in her black cotton rebozo, and somewhat towny in her Madonna-meekness: María del Carmen. With her, Julio, a straight and fierce young man of twenty-two. They had just been married, and had come to Sayula for a visit. Julio was Juana's cousin.

Might they sleep in the patio with herself and the girls, was Juana's request. They would stay only two days.

Kate was amazed. María del Carmen must have had some Spanish blood, her beauty was touched with Spain. She seemed even refined and superior. Yet she was to sleep out on the ground like a dog, with her young husband. And he, so erect and proud-looking, possessed nothing in the world but an old sarape.

"There are three spare bedrooms," said Kate. "They may sleep in one of those."

The beds were single beds. Would they need more blankets? she asked Juana.

No! They would manage with the one sarape of Julio's.

The new family had arrived. Julio was a bricklayer. That is to say, he worked building the adobe walls of the little houses. He belonged to Sayula, and had come back for a visit.

The visit continued. Julio would come striding in at mid-day and at evening: he was looking for work. María del Carmen, in her one black dress, would squat on the floor and pat tortillas. She was allowed to cook them in Juana's kitchen-hole. And she talked and laughed with the girls. At night, when Julio was home, he would lie on the ground with his back to the wall, impassive, while María del Carmen fondled his thick black hair.

They were in love. But even now, he was not yielding to his love. She wanted to go back to Ocotlán, where she was at home, and more a señorita than here in Sayula. But he refused. There was no money: the young ménage lived on about five American cents a day.

Kate was sewing. María del Carmen, who didn't know how to put even a chemise together, watched with great eyes. Kate taught her, and bought a length of cotton material. María del Carmen was sewing herself a dress!

Julio had got work at a peso a day. The visit continued. Kate thought Julio wasn't very nice with María del Carmen: his quiet voice was so overbearing in command when he spoke to her. And María del Carmen, who was a bit towny, did not take it well. She brooded a little.

The visit stretched into weeks. And now Juana was getting a bit tired of her relatives.

But Julio had got a bit of money: he had rented a little one-room adobe house, at one peso fifty per week. María del Carmen was going to move into her own home.

Kate saw the new outfit got together. It consisted of one straw mat, three cooking plates of earthenware, five bits of native crockery, two wooden spoons, one knife, and Julio's old blanket. That was all. But María del Carmen was moving in.

Kate presented her with a large old eiderdown, whose silk was rather worn, a couple of bowls, and a few more bits of crockery. María del Carmen was set up. *Good! Good! Oh good!* Kate heard her voice down the patio. *I have got a coverlet! I have got a coverlet!*

In the rainy season, the nights can be very cold, owing to evaporation. Then the natives lie through the small hours like lizards, numb and prostrate with cold. They are lying on the damp earth on a thin straw mat, with a corner of an old blanket to cover them. And the same terrible inertia makes them endure it, without trying to make any change. They could carry in corn husks or dry banana leaves for a bed. They could even cover themselves with banana leaves.

But no! On a thin mat on damp cold earth they lie and tremble with cold, night after night, night after night, night after night.

But María del Carmen was a bit towny. *Oh good! Oh good! I've got a coverlet!*

Chapter X.

Don Ramón and Doña Carlota.

Kate had been in Sayula ten days before she had any sign from Don
Ramón. She had been out in a boat on the lake, and had seen his
house, round the bend of the western point. It was a reddish-and-   5
yellow two-storey house with a little stone basin for the boats, and a
mango-grove between it and the lake.* Among the trees away from
the lake were the black adobe huts, two rows, of the peons.

The hacienda had once been a large one. But it had been irrigated
from the hills, and the revolutions had broken all the aqueducts.   10
Only a small supply of water was available. Then Don Ramón had
had enemies in the government. So that a good deal of his land was
taken away to be divided among the peons. Now, he had only some
three hundred acres. The two hundred acres along the lake-shore
were mostly lost to him. He worked a few acres of fruit land round   15
the house, and in a tiny valley just in the hills, he raised sugar cane.
On the patches of the mountain slope, little patches of maize were to
be seen.

But Doña Carlota had money. She was from Torreón, and drew
still a good income from the mines.   20

A mozo came with a note from Don Ramón: might he bring his
wife to call on Kate.

Doña Carlota was a thin, gentle, wide-eyed woman with a slightly
startled expression, and soft, brownish hair. She was pure European
in extraction, of a Spanish father and French mother: very different   25
from the usual stout, over-powdered, ox-like Mexican matron. Her
face was pale, faded, and without any make-up at all. Her thin, eager
figure had something English about it, but her strange, wide brown
eyes were not English. She spoke only Spanish—or French. But her
Spanish was so slow and distinct and slightly plaintive, that Kate   30
understood her at once.

The two women understood one another quickly, but were a little
nervous of one another. Doña Carlota was delicate and sensitive like
a Chihuahua dog, and with the same slightly prominent eyes. Kate
felt she had rarely met a woman with such a doglike finesse of   35

155

gentleness. And the two women talked. Ramón, large and muted, kept himself in reserve. It was as if the two women rushed together to unite against his silence and his powerful, different significance.

Kate knew at once that Doña Carlota loved him, but with a love that was now nearly all *will*. She had worshipped him, and she had had to leave off worshipping him. She had had to question him. And she would never now cease from questioning.

So he sat apart, a little constrained, his handsome head hanging a little, and his dark, sensitive hands dangling between his thighs.

"I had such a wonderful time!" Kate said suddenly to him. "I danced a dance round the drum with the Men of Quetzalcoatl."

"I heard," he said, with a rather stiff smile.

Doña Carlota understood English, though she would not speak it.

"You danced with the Men of Quetzalcoatl!" she said in Spanish, in a pained voice. "But, Señora, why did you do such a thing? Oh why?"

"I was fascinated," said Kate.

"No, you must not be fascinated. No! No! It is not good. I tell you, I am *so sorry* my husband interests himself in this thing. I am so sorry."

Juana was bringing a bottle of vermouth: all that Kate had to offer her visitors, in the morning.

"You went to see your boys in the United States?" said Kate to Doña Carlota. "How were they?"

"Oh better, thank you. They are well; that is the younger is very delicate—"

"You didn't bring him home?"

"No! No! I think they are better at school. Here—! Here—there are so many things to trouble them. No! But they will come home next month, for the vacation."

"How nice!" said Kate. "Then I shall see them.—They will be here, won't they?—on the lake?"

"Well!—I am not sure. Perhaps for a little while. You see I am so busy in Mexico with my Cuna."

"What is a Cuna?" said Kate: she only knew it was the Spanish for cradle.

It turned out to be a foundlings home, run by a few obscure Carmelite sisters.* And Doña Carlota was the director. Kate gathered that Don Ramón's wife was an intense, almost exalted Catholic. She exalted herself in the Church, and in her work for the Cuna.

"There are so many children born in Mexico," said Doña Carlota, "and so many die. If only we could save them, and equip them for life. We do a little, all we can."

It seemed, the waste, unwanted babies could be delivered in at the door of the Cuna, like parcels. The mother had only to knock, and hand in the little living bundle.

"It saves so many mothers from neglecting their babies, and letting them die," said Doña Carlota. "Then we do what we can. If the mother doesn't leave a name, I name the child. Very often I do. The mothers just hand over a little naked thing, sometimes without a name or a rag to cover it. And we never ask."

The children were not all kept in the Home. Only a small number. Of the others, some decent Indian woman was paid a small sum to take the child into her home. Every month she must come with the little one to the Cuna, to receive her wage. The Indians are so very rarely unkind to children. Careless, yes. But rarely, rarely unkind.

In former days, Doña Carlota said, nearly every well-born lady in Mexico would receive one or more of these foundlings into her home, and have it brought up with the family. It was the loose, patriarchal generosity innate in the bosoms of the Spanish-Mexicans. But now, few children were adopted. Instead, they were taught as far as possible to be carpenters or gardeners or house-servants, or, among the girls, dress-makers, even school-teachers.

Kate listened with uneasy interest. She felt there was so much real human feeling in this Mexican charity: she was almost rebuked. Perhaps what Doña Carlota was doing was the best that could be done, in this half-wild, helpless country. At the same time, it was such a forlorn hope, it made one's heart sink.

And Doña Carlota, confident as she was in her good works, still had just a bit the look of a victim: a gentle, sensitive, slightly startled victim. As if some secret enemy drained her blood.

Don Ramón sat there impassive, listening without heeding; solid and unmoving *against* the charitable quiver of his wife's emotion. He let her do as she would. But against her work and against her flow he was in silent, heavy, unchanging opposition. She knew this, and trembled in her nervous eagerness as she talked to Kate about the Cuna, and won Kate's sympathy. Till it seemed to her that there was something cruel in Don Ramón's passive, masked poise. An impassive male cruelty, changeless as a stone idol.

"Now won't you come and spend the day with me while I am here

with Don Ramón?" said Doña Carlota. "The house is very poor and
rough. It is no longer what it used to be. But it is your house if you
will come."

Kate accepted, and said she would prefer to walk out. It was only
5 four miles, and surely she would be safe, with Juana.

"I will send a man to come with you," said Don Ramón. "It might
not be quite safe."

"Where is General Viedma?" asked Kate.

"We shall try to get him out when you come," replied Doña
10 Carlota. "I am so very fond of Don Cipriano, I have known him for
many years, and he is the god-father of my younger son. But now he
is in command of the Guadalajara division, he is not very often able
to come out."

"I wonder why he is a general?" said Kate. "He seems to me too
15 human."

"Oh, but he is very human too. But he is a general: yes, yes, he
wants to be in command of the soldiers. And I tell you, he is very
strong. He has great power with his regiments. They believe in him,
oh they believe in him. He has that power, you know, that some of
20 the higher types of Indians have, to make many others want to follow
them and fight for them. You know? Don Cipriano is like that. You
can never change him.—But I think a woman might be wonderful for
him. He has lived so without any woman in his life. He won't care
about them."

25 "What does he care about?" asked Kate.

"Ah!" Doña Carlota started as if stung. Then she glanced quickly,
involuntarily at her husband, as she added: "I don't know. Really, I
don't know."

"The Men of Quetzalcoatl," said Don Ramón heavily, with a little
30 smile.

But Doña Carlota seemed to be able to take all the ease and the
banter out of him. He seemed stiff and a bit stupid.

"Ah, there! There! There you have it! The Men of Quetzalcoatl,
that is a nice thing for him to care about! A nice thing, I say—"
35 fluttered Doña Carlota, in her gentle, fragile, scolding way. And it
was evident to Kate that she adored both the men, and trembled in
opposition to their wrongness, and would never give in to them.

To Ramón it was a terrible burden, his wife's quivering, absolute,
blind opposition, taken in conjunction with her helpless adoration.

40 A man-servant appeared at nine o'clock one morning, to accom-

pany Kate to the hacienda, which was called Jamiltepec. He had a basket, and had been shopping in the market. An elderly man, with grey in his moustache, he had bright young eyes and seemed full of energy. His bare feet in the huaraches were almost black with exposure, but his clothes were brilliantly white.

Kate was glad to be walking. The one depressing thing about life in the villages was that one could not walk out into the country. There was always the liability to be held up or attacked. And she had walked already as far as possible in every direction, in the neighbour-hood of the village, accompanied usually by Ezequiel. Now she was beginning to feel a prisoner.

She was glad, then, to be setting off. The morning was clear and hot, the pale brown lake quite still, like a phantom. People were moving on the beach, in the distance tiny, little dots of white: white dots of men following the faint dust of donkeys. She wondered often why humanity was like specks in the Mexican landscape: just specks of life.

They passed from the lake-shore to the rough, dusty road going west, between the steep slope of the hills and the bit of flat by the lake. For almost a mile there were villas, most of them shut up fast, some of them smashed, with broken walls and smashed windows. Only flowers bloomed in masses above the rubble.

In the empty places were flimsy straw huts of the natives, hap-hazard, as if blown there. By the road under the hill, were black-grey adobe huts, like boxes, and fowls running about, and brown pigs or grey pigs spotted with black careered and grunted, and half-naked children, dark orange-brown, trotted or lay flat on their faces in the road, their little naked posteriors hutched up, fast asleep. Already asleep again.

The houses were many of them being re-thatched, or the tiled roofs were being patched by men who assumed a great air of importance at having undertaken such a task. They were pretending to hurry, too, because the real rains might begin any day. And in the little stony levels by the lake, the land was being scratch-ploughed by a pair of oxen and a lump of pointed wood.

But this part of the road Kate knew. She knew the fine villa on the knoll, with its tufts of palms, and the laid-out avenues that were laid out indeed, as the dead are, to crumble back again. She was glad to be past the villas, where the road came down to the lake again, under big shady trees that had twisted, wiggly beans. On the left was the

water, the colour of turtle doves, lapping the pale fawn stones. At a
water-hole of a stream in the beach, a cluster of women were busily
washing clothes. In the shallows of the lake itself two women sat
bathing, their shoulders heavy and womanly and of a fine orange-
5 brown colour, their black hair hanging dense and wet. A little further
along, a man was wading slowly, stopping to throw his round net
skilfully upon the water, then slowly stooping and gathering it in,
picking out the tiny, glittery fish called charales. Strangely silent and
remote everything, in the gleaming morning, as if it were some
10 distant period of time.

A little breeze was coming from the lake, but the deep dust
underfoot was hot. On the right the hill rose precipitous, baked and
yellowish, giving back the sun and the intense dryness, and exhaling
the faint, desiccated, peculiar smell of Mexico, that smells as if the
15 earth had sweated itself dry.

All the time strings of donkeys trotted laden through the dust,
their drivers stalking erect and rapid behind, watching with eyes like
black holes, but always answering Kate's salute with a respectful
Adios! And Juana echoed her laconic *Adiosn!* She was limping, and
20 she thought it horrible of Kate to walk four miles, when they might
have struggled out in an old hired motor-car, or gone in a boat, or
even ridden donkey-back.

But to go on foot! Kate could hear all her criada's feelings in the
drawled, sardonic *Adiosn!* But the man behind strode bravely and
25 called cheerfully. His pistol was prominent in his belt.

A bluff of yellow rock came jutting at the road. The road wound
round it, and into a piece of flat open country. There were fields of
dry stone, and hedges of dusty thorn and cactus. To the left the
bright green of the willows by the lake-shore. To the right the hills
30 swerved inland, to meet the sheer, fluted sides of dry mountains.
Away ahead, the hills curved back at the shore, and a queer little
crack or niche showed. This crack in the hills led from Don Ramón's
shore-property to the little valley where he grew the sugar cane. And
where the hills approached the lake again, there was a dark
35 clustering of mango trees, and the red upper-storey of the hacienda
house.

"There it is!" cried the man behind. "*Jamiltepec, Señorita. La
hacienda de Don Ramón!*"

And his eyes shone as he said the name. He was a proud peon, and
40 he really seemed happy.

"Look! how far!" cried Juana.

"Another time," said Kate, "I shall come alone, or with Ezequiel."

"No, Niña! Don't say so. Only my foot hurts this morning."

"Yes. Better not to bring you."

"No Niña! I like to come, very much!"

The tall windmill fan for drawing up water from the lake was spinning gaily. A little valley came down from the niche in the hills, and at the bottom a little water running. Towards the lake, where this valley flattened out, was a grove of banana plants, screened a little from the lake breeze by a vivid row of willow trees. And on the top of the slope, where the road ran into the shade of mango trees, were the two rows of adobe huts, like a village, set a little back from the road.

Women were coming up between the trees, on the path from the lake, with jars of water on their shoulders; children were playing around the doors, squatting with little naked posteriors in deep dust; and here and there a goat was tethered. Men in soiled white clothes were lounging, with folded arms and one leg crossed in front of the other, against the corner of a house, or crouching under the walls. Not by any means *dolce far niente*. They seemed to be waiting, eternally waiting for something.

"That way, Señorita!" called the man with the basket, running to her side and indicating the smoother road sloping down between some big trees, towards the white gate of the hacienda. "We are here!"

Always he spoke with pleased delight, as if the place were a wonder-place to him.

The big doors of the zaguán, the entrance, stood open, and in the shade of the entrance-way a couple of little soldiers were seated. Across the cleared, straw-littered space in front of the gates two peons were trotting, each with a big bunch of bananas on his head. The soldiers said something, and the two peons halted in their trotting, and slowly turned under their yellow-green load, to look back at Kate and Juana and the man Martín, approaching down the road. Then they turned again and trotted into the courtyard, barefoot.

The soldiers stood up. Martín, trotting at Kate's side again, ushered her into the arched entrance, where the ox wagons rumbling through had worn deep ruts. Juana came behind, making a humble nose.

Kate found herself in a big, barren yard, that seemed empty. There were high walls on the three sides, with sheds and stables. The fourth side, facing, was the house, with heavily-barred windows looking on to the courtyard, but with no door. Instead, there was
5 another zaguán or passage with closed doors, piercing the house.

Martín trotted ahead to knock on the closed doors. Kate stood looking round at the big yard. In a shed in one corner, four half-naked men were packing bunches of bananas. A man in the shade was sawing poles, and two men in the sun were unloading tiles
10 from a donkey. In a corner was a bullock wagon, and a pair of big black-and-white oxen standing with heads pressed down, waiting.

The big doors opened, and Kate entered the second zaguán. It was a wide entrance-way, with stairs going up on one side, and Kate lingered to look through the open iron gates in front of her, down a
15 formal garden hemmed in with huge mango trees, to the lake, with its little artificial harbour where two boats were moored. The lake seemed to give off a great light, between the dark walls of mango.

At the back of the new-comers the servant woman closed the big doors on to the yard, then waved Kate to the stairs.
20 "Pass this way, Señorita."

A bell tinkled above. Kate climbed the stone stairs. And there above her was Doña Carlota, in white muslin and with white shoes and stockings, her face looking curiously yellow and faded by contrast. Her soft brown hair was low over her ears, and she held out
25 her thin brownish arms with queer effusiveness.

"So, you have come! And you have walked, walked all the way? Oh, imagine walking in so much sun and dust! Come, come in and rest."

She took Kate's hands and led her across the open terrace at the
30 top of the stairs.

"It is beautiful here," said Kate.

She stood on the terrace, looking out past the mango trees at the lake. A distant sailing-*canoa* was going down the breeze, on the pallid, unreal water. Away across rose the bluish, grooved moun-
35 tains, with the white speck of a village: far away in the morning it seemed, in another world, in another life, in another mode of time.

"What is that village?" Kate asked.

"That one? That one there? It is San Ildefonso," said Doña Carlota, in her fluttering eagerness.
40 "But it is beautiful here!" Kate repeated.

"*Hermoso—sí! Sí, bonito!*"* quavered the other woman uneasily, always answering in Spanish.

The house, reddish and yellow in colour, had two short wings towards the lake. The terrace, with green plants on the terrace wall, went round the three sides, the roof above supported by big square   5
pillars that rose from the ground. Down below, the pillars made a sort of cloisters around the three sides, and in the little stone court was a pool of water. Beyond, the rather neglected formal garden with strong sun and deep mango-shade.

"Come, you will need to rest!" said Doña Carlota.   10

"I would like to change my shoes," said Kate.

She was shown into a high, simple, rather bare bedroom with a red-tiled floor. There she changed into the shoes and stockings Juana had carried, and rested a little.

As she lay resting, she heard the dulled thud-thud of the tom-tom   15
drum, but, save the crowing of a cock in the distance, no other sound on the bright, yet curiously hollow Mexican morning. And the drum, thudding with its dulled, black insistence, made her uneasy. It sounded like something coming over the horizon.

She rose, and went into the long, high salon where Doña Carlota   20
was sitting talking to a man in black. The salon, with its three window-doors open on to the terrace, its worn, red floor tiled with old square bricks, its high walls colour-washed a faint green, and the many-beamed ceiling whitewashed, and with its bareness of furniture, seemed like part of the out-of-doors, like some garden-arbor   25
put for shade. The sense, which houses have in hot climates, of being just three walls wherein one lingers for a moment, then goes away again.

As Kate entered the room, the man in black rose and shook hands with Doña Carlota, bowing very low and deferential. Then with a   30
deferential sideways sort of bow to Kate, he vanished out-of-doors.

"Come!" said Doña Carlota to Kate. "Are you sure now you are rested?"—And she pulled forward one of the cane rocking-chairs that had poised itself in the room, en route to nowhere.

"Perfectly!" said Kate. "How still it seems here! Except for the   35
drum. Perhaps it is the drum that makes it seem so still. Though I always think the lake *makes* a sort of silence."

"Ah, the drum!" cried Doña Carlota, lifting her hand with a gesture of nervous, spent exasperation. "I cannot hear it. No, I cannot, I cannot bear to hear it."   40

And she rocked herself in a sudden access of agitation.

"It does hit one rather below the belt," said Kate. "What is it?"

"Ah, do not ask me! It is my husband."

She made a gesture of despair, and rocked herself almost into
unconsciousness.

"Is Don Ramón drumming?"

"Drumming?"—Doña Carlota seemed to start. "No! Oh no! He
is not drumming, himself. He brought down two Indians from the
north to do that."

"Did he!" said Kate, non-committal.

But Doña Carlota was rocking in a sort of semi-consciousness.
Then she seemed to pull herself together.

"I *must* talk to somebody, I must!" she said, suddenly straighten-
ing herself in her chair, her face creamy and creased, her soft brown
hair sagging over her ears, her brown eyes oddly desperate. "May I
talk to you?"

"Do!" said Kate, rather uneasy.

"You know what Ramón is doing?" she said, looking at Kate
almost furtively, suspiciously.

"Does he want to bring back the old gods?" said Kate vaguely.

"Ah!" cried Doña Carlota, again with that desperate, flying jerk of
her hand. "As if it were *possible*! As if it were possible!—The old gods!
Imagine it, Señora! The old gods! Why what are they? Nothing but
dead illusions. And ugly, repulsive illusions!—Ah! I always thought
my husband such a clever man, so superior to me! Ah, it is terrible to
have to change one's idea!—This is such *nonsense*. How dare he!
How dare he take such nonsense seriously! How does he dare!"

"Does he believe in it himself?" asked Kate.

"Himself? But Señora—" and Doña Carlota gave a pitiful, pitying
smile of contempt. "How could he! As if it were possible! After all he
is an educated man! How could he believe in such nonsense!"

"Then why does he do it?"

"Why? Why?" There was a tone of unspeakable weariness in
Doña Carlota's voice. "I wish I knew. I think he has gone insane, as
Mexicans do. Insane like Francisco Villa, the bandit."

Kate thought of the pug-faced, notorious Pancho Villa in wonder,
unable to connect him with Don Ramón.*

"All the Mexicans, as soon as they rise above themselves, go that
way," said Doña Carlota. "Their pride gets the better of them. And
then they understand nothing, nothing but their own foolish will,

their will to be very very important. It is just the male vanity. Don't you think, Señora, that the beginning and the end of a man is his vanity? Don't you think it was just against this danger that Christ came, to teach men a proper humility? To teach them the sin of pride?—But that is why they hate Christ so much, and his teaching.—First and last, they want their own vanity."

Kate had often thought so herself. Her own final conclusion about men was that *they* were the vanity of vanities,* nothing but vanity. They must be flattered and made to feel great: Nothing else.

"And now, my husband wants to go to the other extreme of Jesus. He wants to exalt pride and vanity higher than God. Ah, it is terrible, terrible! And foolish like a little boy! Ah, what is a man but a little boy who needs a nurse and a mother! Ah Señora, I can't bear it."

Doña Carlota covered her face with her hand, as if swooning.

"But there is something wonderful, too, about Don Ramón," said Kate coaxingly: though at the moment she hated him.

"Wonderful! Ah yes, he has gifts. He has great gifts! But what are gifts to a man who perverts them!"

"Tell me what you think he really wants," said Kate.

"Power! Just power! Just foolish, wicked power. As if there had not been enough horrible, wicked power let loose in this country. But he—he—he wants to go beyond them all. He—he—he wants to be worshipped. To be worshipped! To be worshipped! A God! He, whom I've held in my arms! He is a child, as all men are children. And now he wants—to be worshipped—!" She went off into a shrill, wild laughter, covering her face with her hands, and laughing shrilly, her laughter punctuated by hollow, ghastly sobs.

Kate sat in absolute dismay, waiting for the other woman to recover herself. She felt cold against these hysterics, and exerted all her heavy female will to stop them.

"After all," she said, when Doña Carlota became quiet, her face in her hands, "it isn't your fault. We can't be responsible, even for our husbands. I know *that*, since my husband died, and I couldn't prevent him dying.—And then—then I learned that no matter how you love another person, you can't really do anything, you are helpless when it comes to the last things. You have to leave them to themselves, when they want to die: or when they want to do things that seem foolish, so, so foolish, to a woman."

Doña Carlota looked up at the other woman.

"You loved your husband very much—and he died?" she said softly.

"I *did* love him. And I shall never, never love another man. I couldn't. I've lost the power."

5　　"And why did he die?"

"Ah, even that was really his own fault. He broke his own soul and spirit, in those Irish politics. I knew it was wrong. What does Ireland matter, what does nationalism and all that rubbish matter, really! And revolutions! They are so, so stupid and *vieux jeu*. Ah—! It would

10　have been *so* much better if Joachim had been content to live his life in peace, with me. It could be so jolly, so lovely. And I tried and tried and tried with him. But it was no good. He *wanted* to kill himself with that beastly Irish business, and I tried in vain to prevent him—"

Doña Carlota stared slowly at Kate.

15　　"As a woman *must* try to prevent a man, when he is going wrong," she said. "As I try to prevent Ramón. As he will get himself killed, as surely as they all do, down to Francisco Villa. And when they are dead, what good is it all?"

"When they *are* dead," said Kate, "then you *know* it's no good."

20　　"You do!—Oh, Señora, if you think you can help me with Ramón, *do* help me, *do!* For it means the death either of me or him. And *I* shall die, though he is wrong. Unless he gets killed."

"Tell me what he wants to do," said Kate. "What does he *think* he wants to do, anyhow?—Like my husband thought he wanted to make

25　a free Ireland and a great Irish people.—But I knew all the time, the Irish aren't a great people any more, and you *can't* make them free. They are only good at destroying—just mere stupid destroying. How can you make a people free, if they *aren't* free. If something inside them compels them to go on destroying!"

30　　"I know! I know!—And that is Ramón. He wants to destroy even Jesus and the Blessed Virgin, for this people. Imagine it! To destroy Jesus and the Blessed Virgin: the last thing they've got!"

"But what does he say himself, that he wants to do?"

"He says he wants to make a new connection between the people

35　and God. He says himself, God is always God. But man loses his connection with God. And then he can never recover it again, unless some new Saviour comes to give him his new connection. And every new connection is different from the last, though God is always God.—And now, Ramón says, the people have lost God, and the

40　Saviour cannot lead them to him any more. There must be a new

Saviour with a new vision.—But ah, Señora, that is not true for me.
God is love, and if Ramón would only submit to love, he would know
that he had found God. But he is perverse.—Ah, if we could be
together, quietly loving, and enjoying the beautiful world, and
waiting in the love of God!—Ah, Señora, *why*, why, why can't he see   5
it? Oh, why can't he see it! Instead of doing all these—"

The tears came to Doña Carlota's eyes, and spilled over her
cheeks. Kate also was in tears, mopping her face.

"It's no good!" she said, sobbing. "I know it's no good, no matter
what we do. They don't *want* to be happy and peaceful. They *want*   10
this strife and these other false, horrible connections. It's no good
whatever we do! That's what's so bitter, so bitter—!"

The two women sat in their bent-wood rocking-chairs and just
sobbed. And as they sobbed, they heard a step coming along the
terrace, the faint swish of the sandals of the people.   15

It was Don Ramón, drawn unconsciously by the emotional
disturbance of the two women.

Doña Carlota hastily dabbed her eyes and her sniffing nose, Kate
blew her nose like a trumpet, and Don Ramón stood in the doorway.

He was dressed in white, dazzling, in the costume of the *peones*,   20
the white blouse jacket and the white, wide pantaloon trousers. But
the white was linen, slightly starched, and brilliant, almost unnatural
in its whiteness. From under his blouse, in front, hung the ends of a
narrow woolen sash, white, with blue and black bars, and a fringe of
scarlet. And on his naked feet were the plaited huaraches, of blue   25
and black stripes of leather, with thick, red-dyed soles. His loose
trousers were bound round the ankles with blue, red, and black
woolen braids.

Kate glanced at him as he stood in the sun, so dazzlingly white,
that his black hair and dark face looked like a hole in the atmosphere.   30
He came forward, the ends of his sash swinging against his thighs,
his sandals slightly swishing.

"I am pleased to see you," he said, shaking hands with Kate.
"How did you come?"

He dropped into a chair, and sat quite still. The two women hung   35
their heads, hiding their faces. The presence of the man seemed to
put their emotion out of joint. He ignored all the signs of their
discomfort, overlooking it with a powerful will. There was a certain
strength in his presence. They all cheered up a bit.

"You didn't know my husband had become one of the people—a   40 real *peón*—a *Señor Peón*, like Count Tolstoy became a *Señor Moujik?*"* said Doña Carlota, with an attempt at raillery.

"Anyway it suits him," said Kate.

"There!" said Don Ramón. "Give the devil his dues."

5   But there was something unyielding, unbending about him. He laughed and spoke to the women only from a surface self. Underneath, powerful and inscrutable, he made no connection with them.

So it was at lunch. There was a flitting conversation, with intervals of silence. And in the silence, it was evident that Ramón was thinking
10   in another world. And the ponderous stillness of his will, working in another sphere, made the women feel overshadowed.

"The Señora is like me, Ramón," said Doña Carlota. "She cannot bear the sound of that drum. Must it play any more this afternoon?"

There was a moment's pause, before he answered:
15   "After four o'clock only."

"*Must* we have that noise today?" Carlota persisted.

"Why not today like other days!" he said. But a certain darkness was on his brow, and it was evident he wanted to leave the presence of the two women.
20   "Because the Señora is here: and I am here: and we neither of us like it. And tomorrow the Señora will not be here, and I shall be gone back to Mexico. So why not spare us today! Surely you can show us this consideration."

Ramón looked at her, and then at Kate. There was anger in his
25   eyes. And Kate could almost feel, in his powerful chest, the big heart swelling with a suffocation of anger. Both women kept mum. But it pleased them, anyhow, that they could make him angry.

"Why not row with Mrs Leslie on the lake!" he said, with quiet control.
30   But under his dark brows was a level, indignant anger.

"We may not want to," said Carlota.

Then he did what Kate had not known anyone to do before. He withdrew his consciousness away from them as they all three sat at table, leaving the two women, as it were, seated outside a closed
35   door, with nothing more happening. Kate felt for the time startled and forlorn, then a slow anger burned in her warm ivory cheek.

"Oh yes," she said. "I can start home before then."

"No! No!" said Doña Carlota, with a Spanish wail. "Don't leave me. Stay with me till evening, and help me to amuse Don Cipriano.
40   He is coming to supper."

Chapter XI.

Lords of the Day and Night.*

When lunch was over, Ramón went to his room, to sleep for an hour. It was a hot, still afternoon. Clouds were standing erect and splendid, at the west end of the lake, like messengers. Ramón went into his room and closed the window-doors and the shutters, till it was quite dark, save for yellow pencils of light that stood like substance on the darkness, from the cracks of the shutters.

He took off his clothes, and in the darkness thrust his clenched fists upwards above his head, in a terrible tension of stretched, upright prayer. In his eyes was only darkness, and slowly the darkness revolved in his brain too, till he was mindless. Only a powerful will stretched itself and quivered from his spine in an immense tension of prayer. Stretched the invisible bow of the body in the darkness with inhuman tension, erect, till the arrows of the soul, mindless, shot to the mark, and the prayer reached its goal.

Then suddenly, the clenched and quivering arms dropped, the body relaxed into softness. The man had reached his strength again. He had broken the cords of the world, and was free in the other strength.

Softly, delicately, taking great care not to think, not to remember, not to disturb the poisonous snakes of mental consciousness, he picked up a thin, fine blanket, wrapped it round him, and lay down on the pile of mats on the floor. In an instant he was asleep.

He slept in complete oblivion for about an hour. Then suddenly he opened his eyes wide. He saw the velvety darkness, and the pencils of light gone frail. The sun had moved. Listening, there seemed not a sound in the world: there was no world.

Then he began to hear. He heard the faint rumble of an ox wagon: then leaves in a wind: then a faint tapping noise: then the creak of some bird calling.

He rose and quickly dressed in the dark, and threw open the doors. It was mid-afternoon, with a hot wind blowing, and clouds reared up dark and bronze in the west, the sun hidden. But the rain would not fall yet. He took a big straw hat and balanced it on his

head. It had a round crest of black and white and blue feathers, like
an eye, or a sun, in front.

He heard the low sound of women talking. Ah, the strange
woman! He had forgotten her. And Carlota! Carlota was here! He
thought of her for a moment, and of her curious opposition. Then,
before he could be angry, he lifted his breast again in the black,
mindless prayer, his eyes went dark, and the sense of opposition left
him.

He went quickly, driftingly along the terrace to the stone stairs
that led down to the inner entrance-way. Going through to the
courtyard, he saw two men packing bales of bananas upon donkeys,
under a shed. The soldiers were sleeping in the zaguán. Through the
open doors, up the avenue of trees, he could see an ox wagon slowly
retreating. Within the courtyard there was the sharp ringing of metal
hammered on an anvil. It came from a corner where was a smithy,
where a man and a boy were working. In another shed, a carpenter
was planing wood.

Don Ramón stood a moment to look round. This was his own
world. His own spirit was spread over it like a soft, nourishing
shadow, and the silence of his own power gave it peace.

The men working were almost instantly aware of his presence.
One after the other the dark, hot faces glanced up at him, and
glanced away again. They were men, and his presence was wonderful to them; but they were afraid to approach him, even by staring at
him. They worked the quicker for having seen him, as if it gave them
new life.

He went across to the smithy, where the boy was blowing the
old-fashioned bellows, and the man was hammering a piece of metal,
with quick, light blows. The man worked on without lifting his head,
as the *patrón* drew near.

"It is the bird?" said Ramón, standing watching the piece of metal,
now cold upon the anvil.

"Yes, *Patrón*! It is the bird. Is it right?"—And the man looked up
with black, bright, waiting eyes.

The smith lifted with the tongs the black, flat, tongue-shaped
piece of metal, and Ramón looked at it a long time.

"I put the wings on after," said the smith.

Ramón traced with his dark, sensitive hand an imaginary line,
outside the edge of the iron. Three times he did it. And the
movement fascinated the smith.

"A little more slender—so!" said Ramón.

"Yes, *Patrón*! Yes! Yes! I understand," said the man eagerly.

"And the rest?"

"Here it is!"—The man pointed to two hoops of iron, one smaller than the other, and to some flat discs of iron, triangular in shape. 5

"Lay them on the ground."

The man put the hoops on the ground, one within the other. Then, taking the triangular discs, he placed them with quick, sensitive hands, so that their bases were upon the outer circle, and their apices touched the inner. There were seven. And thus they 10 made a seven-pointed sun of the space inside.

"Now the bird," said Ramón.

The man quickly took the long piece of iron: it was the rudimentary form of a bird, with two feet, but as yet without wings. He placed it in the centre of the inner circle, so that the feet touched the circle 15 and the crest of the head touched opposite.

"So! It fits," said the man.

Ramón stood looking at the big iron symbol on the ground. He heard the doors of the inner entrance: Kate and Carlota walking across the courtyard. 20

"I take it away?" asked the workman quickly.

"Never mind," Ramón answered quietly.

Kate stood and stared at the great wreath of iron on the ground.

"What is it?" she asked brightly.

"The bird within the sun." 25

"Is that a bird?"

"When it has wings."

"Ah yes! When it has wings. And what is it for?"

"For a symbol to the people."

"It is pretty." 30

"Yes."

"Ramón!" said Doña Carlota. "Will you give me the key for the boat! Martín will row us out."

He produced the key from under his sash.

"Where did you get that beautiful sash?" asked Kate. 35

It was the white sash with blue and brown-black bars, and with a heavy red fringe.

"This!" he said. "We wove it here."

"And did you make the sandals too?"

"Yes! They were made by Manuel. Later I will show you." 40

"Oh, I should like to see!—They are beautiful, don't you think, Doña Carlota?"

"Yes! Yes! It is true. But whether beautiful things are wise things, I don't know. So much I don't know, Señora. Ay, so much!—And you, do you know what is wise?"

"I!" said Kate. "I don't care very much."

"Ah! You don't care!—You think Ramón is wise, to wear the peasants' clothes, and the huaraches?"—For once Doña Carlota was speaking in slow English.

"Oh yes!" cried Kate. "He looks so handsome!—Men's clothes are so hideous, and Don Ramón looks so handsome in those!" With the big hat poised on his head, he had a certain air of nobility and authority.

"Ah!" cried Doña Carlota, looking at the other woman with intelligent, half-scared eyes, and swinging the key of the boat. "Shall we go to the lake?"

The two women departed. Ramón, laughing to himself, went out of the gate and across the outer yard, to where a big, barn-like building stood near the trees. He entered the barn, and gave a low whistle. It was answered from the loft above, and a trap-door opened. Don Ramón went up the steps, and found himself in a sort of studio and carpenter's shop. A fattish young man with curly hair, wearing an artist's blouse, and with mallet and chisels in his hand, greeted him.

"How is it going?" asked Ramón.

"Yes—well—"

The artist was working on a head, in wood. It was larger than life, conventionalised. Yet under the conventional lines the likeness to Ramón revealed itself.

"Sit for me for half an hour," said the sculptor.

Ramón sat in silence, while the other man bent over his model, working in silent concentration. And all the time, Ramón sat erect, almost motionless, with a great stillness of repose and concentration, thinking about nothing, but throwing out the dark aura of power, in the spell of which the artist worked.

"That is enough," he said at last, quietly rising.

"But give me the pose before you go," said the artist.

Ramón slowly took off his blouse-shirt, and stood with naked torso, the sash with its blue and black bars tight round his naked waist. For some moments he stood gathering himself together. Then suddenly, in a concentration of intense, proud prayer, he flung his right arm up above his head, and stood transfixed, his left arm hanging softly by his side, the fingers touching his thigh. And on his face that fixed, intense look of pride which was at once a prayer.

The artist gazed with wonder, and with an appreciation touched with fear. The other man, large and intense, with big dark eyes staring with intense pride, yet prayerful, beyond the natural horizons, sent a thrill of dread and of joy through the artist. He bowed his head as he looked.

Don Ramón turned to him.

"Now you!" he said.

The artist was afraid. He seemed to quail. But he met Ramón's eyes. And instantly, that stillness of concentration came over him, like a trance. And then suddenly, out of the trance, he shot his arm aloft, and his fat, pale face took on an expression of peace, a noble, motionless transfiguration, the blue-grey eyes calm, proud, reaching into the beyond, with prayer. And though he stood in his blouse, with a rather pudgy figure and curly hair, he had the perfect stillness of nobility.

"It is good!" said Ramón, bowing his head.

The artist suddenly changed; Ramón held out his two hands, the artist took them in his two hands. Then he lifted Ramón's right hand and placed the back of it on his brow.

"*Adios!*" said Ramón, taking his blouse again.

"*Adios Señor!*" said the artist.

And with a proud, white look of joy in his face, he turned again to his work.

Ramón visited the adobe house, its yard fenced with cane and overshadowed by a great mango tree, where Manuel and his wife and children, and two assistants, were spinning and weaving. Two little girls were assiduously carding white wool and brown wool under a cluster of banana trees: the wife and a young maiden were spinning fine, fine thread. On the line hung dyed wool, red, and blue, and green. And under the shed stood Manuel and a youth, weaving at two heavy hand-looms.

"How is it going?" called Don Ramón.

"*Muy bien! Muy bien!*" answered Manuel, with that curious look of transfiguration glistening in his black eyes and in the smile of his face. "It is going well, very well, Señor!"

Ramón paused to look at the fine white sarape on the loom.* It had

a zig-zag border of natural black wool and blue, in little diamonds,
and the ends a complication of blackish and blue diamond-pattern.
The man was just beginning to do the centre—called the *boca*, the
mouth: and he looked anxiously at the design that was tacked to the
5   loom. But it was simple: the same as the iron symbol the smith was
making: a snake with his tail in his mouth, the black triangles on his
back being the outside of the circle: and in the middle, a blue eagle
standing erect, with slim wings touching the belly of the snake with
their tips, and slim feet upon the snake, within the hoop.

10   Ramón went back to the house, to the upper terrace, and round to
the short wing where his room was. He put a folded sarape over his
shoulder, and went along the terrace. At the end of this wing,
projecting to the lake, was a square terrace with a low, thick wall and
a tiled roof, and a coral-scarlet bignonia dangling from the massive
15   pillars. The terrace, or loggia, was strewn with the native palm-leaf
mats, *petates*, and there was a drum in one corner, with the
drum-stick upon it. At the far inner corner, went down an enclosed
stone stair-case, with an iron door at the bottom.

Ramón stood a while looking out at the lake. The clouds were
20   dissolving again, the sheet of water gave off a whitish light. In the
distance he could see the dancing speck of a boat, probably Martín
with the two women.

He took off his hat and his blouse, and stood motionless, naked to
the waist. Then he lifted the drum-stick, and after waiting a moment
25   or two, to become still in soul, he sounded the rhythmic summons,
rather slow, yet with a curious urge in its strong-weak, one-two
rhythm. He had got the old barbaric power into the drum.

For some time he stood alone, the drum, or tom-tom, lifted by its
thong against his legs, his right hand drumming, his face expres-
30   sionless. A man entered, bareheaded, running from the inner
terrace. He was in the white cotton clothes, snow white, but with a
dark sarape folded on his shoulder, and he held a key in his hand. He
saluted Ramón by putting the back of his right hand in front of his
eyes for a moment, then he went down the stone stairway and opened
35   the iron door.

Immediately men were coming up, all dressed alike, in the white
cotton clothes and the huaraches, each with a folded sarape over his
shoulder. But their sashes were all blue, and their sandals blue and
white. The sculptor came too, and Mirabal was there, also dressed in
40   the cotton clothes.

There were seven men, besides Ramón. At the top of the stairs, one after another, they saluted. Then they took their sarapes, dark brown, with blue eyes filled with white,* along the edges, and threw them down along the wall, their hats beside them. Then they took off their blouses, and flung them on their hats. 5

Ramón left the drum, and sat down on his own sarape, that was white with the blue and black bars, and the scarlet fringe. The drummer sat down and took the drum. The circle of men sat cross-legged, naked to the waist, silent. Some were of a dark, ruddy coffee-brown, two were white, Ramón was of a soft creamy brown. 10 They sat in silence for a time, only the monotonous, hypnotic sound of the drum pulsing, touching the inner air. Then the drummer began to sing, in the curious, small, inner voice, that hardly emerges from the circle, singing in the ancient falsetto of the Indians: 15

"Who sleeps—shall wake! Who sleeps—shall wake! Who treads down the path of the snake shall arrive at the place; in the path of the dust shall arrive at the place and be dressed in the skin of the snake—"

One by one the voices of the men joined in, till they were all 20 singing in the strange, blind infallible rhythm of the ancient barbaric world. And all in the small, inward voices, as if they were singing from the oldest, darkest recess of the soul, not outwards, but inwards, the soul singing back to herself.

They sang for a time, in the peculiar unison like a flock of birds 25 that fly in one consciousness.* And when the drum shuddered for an end, they all let their voices fade out, with the same broad, clapping sound in the throat.

There was silence. The men turned speaking to one another, laughing in a quiet way. But their daytime voices, and their daytime 30 eyes had gone.

Then Ramón's voice was heard, and the men were suddenly silent, listening with bent heads. Ramón sat with his face lifted, looking far away, in the pride of prayer.

"There is no Before and After, there is only Now,"* he said, 35 speaking in a proud, but inward voice.

"The great Snake coils and uncoils the plasm of his folds, and stars appear, and worlds fade out. It is no more than the changing and easing of the plasm.

"*I always am*, says his sleep. 40

"As a man in a deep sleep knows not, but is, so is the Snake of the coiled cosmos, heaving its plasm.

"As a man in a deep sleep has no tomorrow, no yesterday nor today, but only *is*, so is the limpid, far-reaching Snake of the eternal
5 Cosmos, Now, and forever Now.

"Now, and only Now, and forever Now.

"But dreams arise and fade in the sleep of the Snake.

"And worlds arise as dreams, and are gone as dreams.

"And man is a dream in the sleep of the Snake.

10 "And only the sleep that is dreamless breathes *I Am!*＊

"In the dreamless Now, *I Am*.

"Dreams arise as they must arise, and man is a dream arisen.

"But the dreamless plasm of the Snake is the plasm of a man, of his body, his soul, and his spirit at one.

15 "And the perfect sleep of the Snake *I Am* is the plasm of a man, who is whole.

"When the plasm of the body, and the plasm of the soul, and the plasm of the spirit are at one, in the Snake *I Am*.

"I am Now.

20 "Was-not is a dream, and shall-be is a dream, like two separate, heavy feet.

"But Now, *I Am*.

"The trees put forth their leaves in their sleep, and flowering emerge out of dreams, into pure *I Am*.

25 "The birds forget the stress of their dreams, and sing aloud in the Now, *I Am! I Am!*

"For dreams have wings and feet, and journeys to take, and efforts to make.

"But the glimmering Snake of the Now is wingless and footless,
30 and undivided, and perfectly coiled.

"It is thus the cat lies down, in the coil of Now, and the cow curves round her nose to her belly, lying down.

"On the feet of a dream the hare runs uphill. But when he pauses, the dream has passed, he has entered the timeless Now, and his eyes
35 are the wide *I Am*.

"Only man dreams, dreams, and dreams, and changes from dream to dream, like a man who tosses on his bed.

"With his eyes and his mouth he dreams, with his hands and his feet, with phallos and heart and belly, with body and spirit and soul,
40 in a tempest of dreams.

"And rushes from dream to dream, in the hope of the perfect dream.

"But I, I say to you, there is no dream that is perfect, for every dream has an ache and an urge, an urge and an ache.

"And nothing is perfect, save the dream pass out into the sleep, *I Am*.   5

"When the dream of the eyes is darkened, and encompassed with Now.

"And the dream of the mouth resounds in the last *I Am*.

"And the dream of the hands is a sleep like a bird on the sea, that   10
sleeps and is lifted and shifted, and knows not.

"And the dreams of the feet and the toes touch the core of the world, where the Serpent sleeps.

"And the dream of the phallos reaches the great I Know Not.

"And the dream of the body is the stillness of a flower in the dark.   15

"And the dream of the soul is gone in the perfume of Now.

"And the dream of the spirit lapses, and lays down its head, and is still with the Morning Star.

"For each dream starts out of Now, and is accomplished in Now.   20

"In the core of the flower, the glimmering, wakeless Snake.

"And what falls away is a dream, and what accrues is a dream. There is always and only Now, Now, and *I Am*."

There was silence in the circle of men. Outside, the sound of the bullock wagon could be heard, and from the lake, the faint knocking   25
of oars. But the seven men sat with their heads bent, in the semi-trance, listening inwardly.

Then the drum began softly to beat, as if of itself. And a man began to sing, in a small voice:

> The Lord of the Morning Star   30
> Stood between the day and the night:
> As a bird that lifts its wings, and stands
> With the bright wing on the right
> And the wing of the dark on the left,
> The Dawn Star stood into sight.   35
>
> Lo! I am always here!
> Far in the hollow of space
> I brush the wing of the day
> And put light on your face.

The other wing brushes the dark.
But I, I am always in place.

Yea, I am always here. I am Lord
In every way. And the lords among men
5   See me through the flashing of wings.
They see me and lose me again.
But lo! I am always here
Within ken.

The multitudes see me not.
10   They see only the waving of wings,
The coming and going of things.
The cold and the hot.

But ye that perceive me between
The tremors of night and the day,
15   I make you the Lords of the Way
Unseen.

The path between gulfs of the dark and steeps of the light;
The path like a snake that is gone, like the length of a fuse to
    ignite
20   The substance of shadow, that bursts and explodes into
    sight.

I am here undeparting. I sit tight
Between wings of the endless flight,
At the depths of the peace and the fight.

25   Deep in the moistures of peace,
And far down the muzzle of the fight
You shall find me, who am neither increase
Nor destruction, different quite.

I am far beyond
30   The horizons of love and strife.
Like a star, like a pond
That washes the lords of life.

"Listen!" said Ramón, in the stillness. "We will be masters among men, and lords among men. But lords of men, and masters of men
35 we will not be. Listen! We are lords of the day, and lords of the night. Lords of the day and night. Sons of the Morning Star, sons of the Evening Star. Men of the Morning and the Evening Star.

"We are not lords of men: how can men make us lords? Nor are we masters of men, for men are not worth it.

"But I am the Morning and the Evening Star, and lord of the day and the night. By the power that is put in my left hand, and the power that I grasp in my right, I am lord of the two ways.

"And my flower on earth is the jasmine flower, and in heaven the flower Hesperus.

"I will not command you, nor serve you, for the snake goes crooked to his own house.

"Yet I will be with you, so you depart not from yourselves.

"There is no giving, and no taking. When the fingers that give touch the fingers that receive, the Morning Star shines at once, from the contact, and the jasmine gleams between the hands. And thus there is neither giving nor taking, nor hand that proffers nor hand that receives, but the star between them is all, and the dark hand and the light hand are invisible on each side. The jasmine takes the giving and the receiving in her cup, and the scent of the oneness is fragrant on the air.

"Think neither to give nor to receive, only let the jasmine flower.

"Let nothing spill from you in excess, let nothing be reived from you.

"And reive nothing away. Not even the scent from the rose, nor the juice from the pomegranate, nor the warmth from the fire.

"But say to the rose: Lo! I take you away from your tree, and your breath is in my nostrils, and my breath is warm in your depths. Let it be a sacrament between us.

"And beware when you break the pomegranate: it is sunset you take in your hands. Say: I am coming, come thou. Let the Evening Star stand between us.

"And when the fire burns up and the wind is cold and you spread your hands to the blaze, listen to the flame saying: Ah! Is it thou? Comest thou to me? Lo, I was going the longest journey, down the path of the greatest Snake. But since thou comest to me, I come to thee. And where thou fallest into my hands, fall I into thine, and jasmine flowers on the burning bush between us.* Our meeting is the burning bush, whence the jasmine flowers.—

"Reive nothing away, and let nothing be reived from you. For reiver and bereaved alike break the root of the jasmine flower, and spit upon the Evening Star.

"Take nothing, to say: *I have it!* For you can possess nothing, not even peace.

"Nought is possessible, neither gold, nor land nor love, nor life, nor peace, nor even sorrow nor death, nor yet salvation.

"Say of nothing: It is mine.

"Say only: It is with me.

"For the gold that is with thee lingers as a departing moon, looking across space thy way, saying: Lo! We are beholden of each other. Lo! for this little while, to each other thou and I are beholden.

"And thy land says to thee: Ah, my child of a far-off father! Come, lift me, lift me a little while, that poppies and wheat may blow on the level wind that moves between my breast and thine. Then sink with me, and we will make one mound.

"And listen to thy love saying: Beloved! I am mown by thy sword like mown grass, and darkness is upon me, and the tremble of the Evening Star. And to me thou art darkness and nowhere.—Oh thou, when thou risest up and goest thy way, speak to me, only say: The star rose between us.

"And say to thy life: Am I thine? Art thou mine? Am I the blue curve of day around thine uncurved night? Are my eyes the twilight of neither of us, where the star hangs? Is my upper lip the sunset and my lower lip the dawn, does the star tremble inside my mouth?

"And say to thy peace: Ah! risen, deathless star! Already the waters of dawn sweep over thee, and wash me away on the flood!

"And say to thy sorrow: Axe, thou art cutting me down!

"Yet did a spark fly from out of thy edge and my wound!

"Cut then, while I cover my face, father of the Star.

"And say to thy strength: Lo, the night is foaming up my feet and my loins, day is foaming down from my eyes and my mouth to the sea of my breast. Lo they meet! My belly is a flood of power, that races in down the sluice of bone at my back, and a star hangs low on the flood, over a troubled dawn.

"And say to thy death: Be it so! I, and my soul, we come to thee, Evening Star. Flesh, go thou into the night. Spirit, farewell, 'tis thy day. Leave me now. I go in last nakedness now to the nakedest Star."

Chapter XII.

The First Waters.*

The men had risen and covered themselves, and put on their hats, and covered their eyes for a second, in salute before Ramón, as they departed down the stone stair. And the iron door at the bottom had 5 clanged, the doorkeeper had returned with the key, laid it on the drum, and softly, delicately departed.

Still Ramón sat on his sarape, leaning his naked shoulders on the wall, and closing his eyes. He was tired, and in that state of extreme separateness which makes it very hard to come back to the world. On 10 the outside of his ears he could hear the noises of the hacienda, even the tinkle of tea-spoons, and the low voice of women, and later, the low, laboring sound of a motor-car struggling over the uneven road, then swirling triumphantly into the courtyard.

It was hard to come back to these things. The noise of them 15 sounded on the outside of his ears, but inside him was the slow, vast, inaudible roar of the cosmos, like in a sea-shell. It was hard to have to bear the contact of commonplace daily things, when his soul and body were naked to the cosmos.

He wished they would leave him the veils of his isolation awhile. 20 But they would not: especially Carlota. She wanted him to be present to her: in familiar contact.

She was calling: "Ramón! Ramón! Have you finished? Cipriano is here." And even so, in her voice was fear, and an over-riding temerity. 25

He pushed back his hair and rose, and very quickly went out, as he was, with naked torso. He didn't want to dress himself into everyday familiarity, since his soul was unfamiliar.

They had a tea-table out on the terrace, and Cipriano, in uniform, was there. He got up quickly, and came down the terrace with 30 outstretched arms, his black eyes gleaming with an intensity almost like pain, upon the face of the other man. And Ramón looked back at him with wide, seeing, yet unchanging eyes.

The two men embraced, breast to breast, and for a moment Cipriano laid his little blackish hands on the naked shoulders of the 35 bigger man, and for a moment was perfectly still on his breast. Then very softly, he stood back and looked at him, saying not a word.

Ramón abstractly laid his hand on Cipriano's shoulder, looking down at him with a little smile.

5   "*Qué tal?*" he said, from the edge of his lips. "How goes it?"

"*Bien! Muy bien!*" said Cipriano, still gazing into the other man's face with black, wondering, childlike, searching eyes, as if he, Cipriano, were searching for *himself* in Ramón's face. Ramón looked back into Cipriano's black, Indian eyes with a faint, kind smile of
10   recognition, and Cipriano hung his head as if to hide his face, the black hair, which he wore rather long and brushed sideways, dropping over his forehead.

The women watched in absolute silence. Then, as the two men began slowly to come along the terrace to the tea-table, Carlota
15   began to pour tea. But her hand trembled so much, the teapot wobbled as she held it, and she had to put it down and clasp her hands in the lap of her white muslin dress.

"You rowed on the lake?" said Ramón abstractedly, coming up.

"It was lovely!" said Kate. "But hot when the sun came."

20   Ramón smiled a little, then pushed his hand through his hair. Then, leaning one hand on the parapet of the terrace wall, he turned to look at the lake, and a sigh lifted his shoulders unconsciously.

He stood thus, naked to the waist, his black hair ruffled and splendid, his back to the women, looking out at the lake. Cipriano
25   stood lingering beside him.

Kate saw the sigh lift the soft, quiescent, cream-brown shoulders. The soft, cream-brown skin of his back, of a smooth, *pure* sensuality, made her shudder. The broad, square, rather high shoulders, with neck and head rising steep, proudly. The full-fleshed, deep-chested,
30   rich body of the man made her feel dizzy. In spite of herself, she could not help imagining a knife stuck between those pure, male shoulders. If only to break the arrogance of their remoteness.

That was it. His nakedness was so aloof, far-off and intangible, in another day. So that to *think* of it was almost a violation, even to look
35   at it with prying eyes. Kate's heart suddenly shrank in her breast. This was how Salome had looked at John.* And this was the beauty of John, that he had had, like a pomegranate on a dark tree in the distance, naked, but not undressed. Forever still and clothe-less, and with another light about it, of a richer day than our paltry, prying,
40   sneak-thieving day.

The moment Kate had imagined a knife between his shoulders, her heart shrank with grief and shame, and a great stillness came over her. Better to take the hush into one's heart, and the sharp, prying beams out of one's eyes. Better to lapse away from one's own prying, assertive self, into the soft, untrespassing self, to whom nakedness is neither shame nor excitement, but clothed like a flower in its own deep, soft consciousness, beyond cheap awareness.

The evening breeze was blowing very faintly. Sailing-boats were advancing through the pearly atmosphere, far off, the sun above had a golden quality. The opposite shore, twenty miles away, was distinct, and yet there seemed an opalescent, sperm-like haze in the air, the same quality as in the filmy water. Kate could see the white specks of the far-off church-towers of Tuliapán.

Below, in the garden below the house, was a thick grove of mango trees. Among the dark and reddish leaves of the mangos, scarlet little birds were bustling, like suddenly-opening poppy-buds, and pairs of yellow birds, yellow underneath as yellow butter-flies, so perfectly clear, went skimming past. When they settled for a moment and closed their wings, they disappeared, for they were grey on top. And when the cardinal birds settled, they too disappeared, for the outside of their wings was brown. Like a sheath.

"Birds in this country have all their colour below," said Kate.

Ramón turned to her suddenly.

"They say the word *Mexico* means *Below this!*"* he said, smiling, and sinking into a rocking-chair.

Doña Carlota had made a great effort over herself, and with eyes fixed on the tea-cup, she poured out the tea. She handed him his cup without looking at him. She did not trust herself to look at him. It made her tremble with a strange, hysterical anger: she, who had been married to him for years, and knew him, ah, knew him: and yet, and yet, had not got him at all. None of him.

"Give me a piece of sugar, Carlota," he said, in his quiet voice.

But at the sound of it, his wife stopped as if some hand had suddenly grasped her.

"Sugar! Sugar!" she repeated abstractedly to herself.

Ramón sat forward in his rocking-chair, holding his cup in his hand, his breasts rising in relief. And on his thighs the thin linen seemed to reveal him almost more than his own dark nakedness revealed him. She understood why the cotton pantaloons were forbidden on the plaza. The living flesh seemed to emanate through them.

He was handsome, almost horribly handsome, with his black head poised as it were without weight, above his darkened, smooth neck. A pure sensuality, with a powerful purity of its own, hostile to her sort of purity. With the blue sash round his waist, pressing a fold in the flesh, and the thin linen seeming to gleam with the life of his hips and his thighs, he emanated a fascination almost like a narcotic, asserting his pure, fine sensuality against her. The strange, soft, still sureness of him, as if he sat secure within his own dark aura. And as if this dark aura of his militated against her presence, and against the presence of his wife. He emitted an effluence so powerful, that it seemed to hamper her consciousness, to bind down her limbs.

And he was utterly still and quiescent, without desire, soft and unroused, within his own *ambiente*. Cipriano going the same, the pair of them so quiet and dark and heavy, like a great weight bearing the women down.

Kate knew now how Salome felt. She knew now how John the Baptist had been, with his terrible, aloof beauty, inaccessible yet so potent.

"Ah!" she said to herself. "Let me close my eyes to him, and open only my soul. Let me close my prying, *seeing* eyes, and sit in dark stillness along with these two men. They have got more than I, they have a richness that I haven't got. They have got rid of that itching of the eye, and the desire that works through the eye. The itching, prurient, *knowing*, imagining eye, I am cursed with it, I am hampered up in it. It is my curse of curses, the curse of Eve. The curse of Eve* is upon me, my eyes are like hooks, my knowledge is like a fish-hook through my gills, pulling me in spasmodic desire. Oh, who will free me from the grappling of my eyes, from the impurity of sharp sight! Daughter of Eve, of greedy vision,* why don't these men save me from the sharpness of my own eyes—!"

She rose and went to the edge of the terrace. Yellow as daffodils underneath, two birds emerged out of their own invisibility. In the little shingle bay, with a small break-water, where the boat was pulled up and chained, two men were standing in the water, throwing out a big, fine round net, catching the little silvery fish called charales, which flicked out of the brownish water sometimes like splinters of glass.

"Ramón!" Kate heard Doña Carlota's voice. "Won't you put something on?"

The wife had been able to bear it no more.

"Yes! Thank you for the tea," said Ramón, rising.

Kate watched him go down the terrace, in his own peculiar 5
silence, his sandals making a faint swish on the tiles.

"Oh, Señora Caterina!" came the voice of Carlota. "Come and drink your tea. Come!"

Kate returned to the table, saying:

"It seems so wonderfully peaceful here." 10

"Peaceful!" echoed Carlota. "Ah, I do not find it peaceful. There is a horrible stillness, which makes me afraid."

"Do you come out very often?" said Kate, to Cipriano.

"Yes. Fairly often. Once a week. Or twice," he replied, looking at her with a secret consciousness which she could not understand, 15
lurking in his black eyes.

These men wanted to take her *will* away from her, as if they wanted to deny her the light of day.

"I must be going home now," she said. "The sun will be setting." 20

"*Ya va?*" said Cipriano, in his soft, velvety Indian voice, with a note of distant surprise and reproach. "Will you go already?"

"Oh no, Señora!" cried Doña Carlota. "Stay until tomorrow. Oh yes, stay until tomorrow, with me."

"They will expect us home," she said, wavering. 25

"Ah no! I can send a boy to say you will come tomorrow.—Yes? You will stay? Ah good, good!"

And she laid her hand caressively on Kate's arm, then rose to hurry away to the servants.

Cipriano had taken out his cigarette case. He offered it to Kate. 30

"Shall I take one?" she said. "It is my vice."

"Do take one," he said. "It isn't fair, to be perfect."

"It isn't, is it?" she laughed, puffing her cigarette.

"Now do you call it peace?" he asked, with incomprehensible irony. 35

"Why?" she cried.

"Why do white people always want peace?" he asked.

"Surely peace is natural! Don't all people want it? Don't you?"

"Peace is only the rest after war," he said. "So it is not more natural than fighting: perhaps not so natural." 40

"No, but there is another peace: the peace that passes all understanding. Don't you know that?"

"I don't think I do," he said.

"What a pity!" she cried.

5 "Ah!" he said. "You want to teach me!—But to me it is different. Each man has two spirits in him. The one is like the early morning in the time of rain, very quiet and sweet, moist, no?—with the mocking-bird singing, and birds flying about, very fresh.—And the other is like the dry season, the steady, strong hot light of the day, 10 which seems as if it will never change."

"But you like the first better," she cried.

"I don't know!" he replied. "The other lasts longer."

"I am sure you like the fresh morning better," she said.

"I don't know! I don't know!" He smiled a crumpled sort of smile, 15 and she could tell he really did *not* know. "In the first time, you can feel the flowers on their stem, the stem very strong and full of sap, no?—and the flower opening on top like a face that has the perfume of desire. And a woman might be like that.—But this passes, and the sun begins to shine very strong, very hot, no? Then everything inside 20 a man changes, goes dark, no! And the flowers crumple up, and the breast of a man becomes like a steel mirror. And he is all darkness inside, coiling and uncoiling like a snake. All the flowers withered up on shrunk stems, no? And then women don't exist for a man. They disappear like the flowers."

25 "And then what does he want?" said Kate.

"I don't know. Perhaps he wants to be a very big man, and master all the people."

"Then why doesn't he?" said Kate.

He lifted his shoulders.

30 "And you," he said to her. "You seem to me like that morning I told you about."

"I am just forty years old," she laughed shakily.

Again he lifted his shoulders.

"It doesn't matter," he said. "It is the same. Your body seems to 35 me like the stem of the flower I told you about, and in your face it will always be morning, of the time of the rains."

"Why do you say that to me?" she said, as an involuntary, strange shudder shook her.

"Why not say it!" he replied. "You are like the cool of the 40 morning, very fresh. In Mexico, we are the end of the hot dry day."

He watched her, with a strange lingering desire in his black eyes,
and what seemed to her a curious, lurking sort of insolence. She
dropped her head to hide from him, and rocked in her chair.

"I would like to marry you," he said; "if ever you will marry, I
would like to marry you."   5

"I don't think I shall *ever* marry again," she flashed, her bosom
heaving like suffocation, and a dark flush suffusing over her face,
against her will.

"Who knows!" said he.

Ramón was coming down the terrace, his fine white sarape folded   10
over his naked shoulder, with its blue-and-dark pattern at the
borders, and its long scarlet fringe dangling and swaying as he
walked. He leaned against one of the pillars of the terrace, and
looked down at Kate and Cipriano. Cipriano glanced up with that
peculiar glance of primitive intimacy.   15

"I told the Señora Caterina," he said, "if ever she wanted to marry
a man, she should marry me."

"It is plain talk," said Ramón, glancing at Cipriano with the same
intimacy, and smiling.

Then he looked at Kate, with a slow smile in his brown eyes, and a   20
shadow of curious knowledge on his face. He folded his arms over
his breast, as the natives do when it is cold and they are protecting
themselves; and the cream-brown flesh, like opium, lifted the bosses
of his breast, full and smooth.

"Don Cipriano says that white people always want peace," she   25
said, looking up at Ramón with haunted eyes. "Don't you consider
yourselves white people?" she asked, with a slight, deliberate
impertinence.

"No whiter than we are," smiled Ramón. "Not lily-white, at
least."   30

"And don't you want peace?" she asked.

"I? I shouldn't think of it. The meek have inherited the earth,
according to prophecy.* But who am I, that I should envy them their
peace! No Señora. Do I look like a gospel of peace?—or a gospel of
war either? Life doesn't split down that division, for me."   35

"I don't know *what* you want," she said, looking up at him with
haunted eyes.

"We only half know ourselves," he replied, smiling with changeful
eyes. "Perhaps not so much as half."

There was a certain vulnerable kindliness about him, which made   40 her wonder, startled, if she had ever realised what real fatherliness meant. The mystery, the nobility, the inaccessibility, and the vulnerable compassion of man in his separate fatherhood.

"You don't like brown-skinned people?" he asked her gently.

5   "I think it is beautiful to look at," she said. "But"—with a faint shudder—"I am glad I am white."

"You feel there could be no contact?" he said, simply.

"Yes!" she said. "I mean that."

"It is as you feel," he said.

10 And as he said it, she knew he was more beautiful to her than any blond white man, and that, in a remote, far-off way, the contact with him was more precious than any contact she had known.

But then, though he cast over her a certain shadow, he would never encroach on her, he would never seek any close contact. It was

15 the incompleteness in Cipriano that sought her out, and seemed to trespass on her.

Hearing Ramón's voice, Carlota appeared uneasily in a doorway. Hearing him speak English, she disappeared again, on a gust of anger. But after a little while, she came once more, with a little vase

20 containing the creamy-coloured, thick flowers that are coloured like freesias, and that smell very sweet.

"Oh how nice!" said Kate. "They are temple flowers! In Ceylon the natives tiptoe in to the little temples and lay one flower on the table at the foot of the big Buddha statues. And the tables of offering

25 are all covered with these flowers, all put so neatly. The natives have that delicate oriental way of putting things down."

"Ah!" said Carlota, setting the vase on the table. "I did not bring them for any gods, especially strange ones. I have brought them for you, Señora. They smell so sweet."

30 "Don't they!" said Kate.

The two men went away, Ramón laughing.

"Ah Señora!" said Carlota, sitting down tense at the table. "Could you follow Ramón? Could *you* give up the Blessed Virgin?—I could sooner die!"

35 "Ha!" said Kate, with a little weariness. "Surely we don't want any *more* gods."

"More gods, Señora!" said Doña Carlota, shocked. "But how is it possible!—Don Ramón is in mortal sin."

Kate was silent.

40 "And he wants to lead more and more people into the same,"

continued Carlota. "It is the sin of pride. Men wise in their own conceit!—The cardinal sin of men.* Ah, I have told him.—And I am so glad, Señora, that you feel as I feel. I am so afraid of American women, women like that. They wish to have men's minds, so they accept all the follies and wickedness of men.—You are Catholic, 5 Señora?"

"I was educated in a convent," said Kate.

"Ah, of course! Of course!—Ah Señora, as if a woman who had ever known the Blessed Virgin could ever part from her again. Ah, Señora, what woman would have the heart to put Christ back on the 10 Cross, to crucify him twice! But men, men! This Quetzalcoatl business! What buffoonery, Señora; if it were not horrible sin! And two clever, well-educated men! Wise in their own conceit!"

"Men usually are," said Kate.

It was sunset, with a big level cloud like fur overhead, only the 15 sides of the horizon fairly clear. The sun was not visible. It had gone down in a thick, rose-red fume, behind the wavy ridge of the mountains. Now the hills stood up bluish, all the air was a salmon-red flush, the fawn water had pinkish ripples. Boys and men, bathing a little way along the shore, were the colour of deep flame. 20

Kate and Carlota had climbed up to the azotea, the flat roof, from the stone stairway at the end of the terrace. They could see the world: the hacienda with its courtyard like a fortress, the road between deep trees, the black mud huts near the broken high-road, and little naked fires already twinkling outside the doors. All the air 25 was pinkish, melting to a lavender blue, and the willows on the shore, in the pink light, were apple-green and glowing. The hills behind rose abruptly, like mounds, dry and pinky. Away in the distance, down the lake, the two white obelisk towers of Sayula glinted among the trees, and villas peeped out. Boats were creeping in to the 30 shadow, from the outer brightness of the lake.

And in one of these boats was Juana, being rowed disconsolate home.

Chapter XIII.

The First Rain.*

Ramón and Cipriano were out by the lake. Cipriano also had changed into the white clothes and sandals, and he looked better than when in
5 uniform.

"I had a talk with Montes when he came to Guadalajara," Cipriano said to Ramón—Montes was the President of the Republic.

"And what did he say?"
10 "He is careful. But he doesn't like his colleagues. I think he feels lonely. I think he would like to know you better."

"Why?"

"Perhaps that you could give him your moral support.—Perhaps that you might be Secretary, and President* when Montes' term is
15 up."

"I like Montes," said Ramón. "He is sincere and passionate. Did you like him?"

"Yes!" said Cipriano. "More or less. He is suspicious, and jealous for fear anyone else might want to share in his power. He has the
20 cravings of a dictator.—He wanted to find out if I would stick to him."

"You let him know you would?"

"I told him that all I cared for was for you and for Mexico."

"What did he say?"
25 "Well, he is no fool.—He said: Don Ramón sees the world with different eyes from mine. Who knows which of us is right. I want to save my country from poverty and unenlightenment, he wants to save its soul. I say, a hungry and ignorant man has no place for a soul. An empty belly grinds upon itself, so does an empty mind, and the soul
30 doesn't exist.—Don Ramón says, if a man has no soul, it doesn't matter whether he is hungry or ignorant.—Well, he can go his way, and I mine. We shall never hinder one another, I believe. I give you my word I won't have him interfered with. He sweeps the patio and I sweep the street."
35 "Sensible!" said Ramón. "And honest in his convictions."*

"Why should you not be Secretary, in a few months' time? And follow to the Presidency?" said Cipriano.

"You know I don't want that. I must stand in another world, and act in another world.—Politics must go their own way, and society must do as it will. Leave me alone, Cipriano. I know you want me to 5 be another Porfirio Díaz, or something like that. But for me, that would be failure pure and simple."

Cipriano was watching Ramón with black, guarded eyes, in which was an element of love, and of fear, and of trust, but also of incomprehension, and the suspicion that goes with incom- 10 prehension.

"I don't understand, myself, *what* you want," he muttered.

"Yes, yes, you do. Politics, and all this *social* religion that Montes has got is like washing the outside of the egg, to make it look clean. But I, myself, I want to get inside the egg, right to the middle, to start 15 it growing into a new bird. Ay! Cipriano! Mexico is like an old, old egg that the bird of Time laid long ago; and she has been sitting on it for centuries, till it looks foul in the nest of the world. But still, Cipriano, it is a good egg. It is not addled. Only the spark of fire has never gone into the middle of it, to start it.—Montes wants to clean 20 the nest and wash the egg. But meanwhile, the egg will go cold and die. The more you save these people from poverty and ignorance, the quicker they will die: like a dirty egg that you take from under the hen-eagle, to wash it. While you wash the egg, it chills and dies. Poor old Montes, all his ideas are American and European. And the old 25 Dove of Europe will never hatch the egg of dark-skinned America. The United States can't die, because it isn't alive. It is a nestful of china eggs, made of pot. So they can be kept clean.—But here, Cipriano, here, let us hatch the chick before we start cleaning up the nest." 30

Cipriano hung his head. He was always testing Ramón, to see if he could change him. When he found he couldn't, then he submitted, and new little fires of joy sprang up in him. But meanwhile, he had to try, and try again.

"It is no good, trying to mix the two things. At this stage of affairs, 35 at least, they won't mix. We have to shut our eyes and sink down, sink away from the surface, away, like shadows, down to the bottom. Like the pearl divers.—But you keep bobbing up like a cork."

Cipriano smiled subtly. He knew well enough.

"We've got to open the oyster of the cosmos, and get our manhood 40 out of it. Till we've got the pearl, we are only gnats on the surface of the ocean," said Ramón.

"My manhood is like a devil inside me," said Cipriano.

"It's very true," said Ramón. "That's because the old oyster has him shut up, like a black pearl. You must let him walk out."

"Ramón," said Cipriano, "wouldn't it be good to be a serpent, and be big enough to wrap one's folds round the globe of the world, and crush it like that egg?"

Ramón looked at him and laughed.

"I believe we could do that," said Cipriano, a slow smile curling round his mouth. "And wouldn't it be good?"

Ramón shook his head, laughing.

"There would be *one* good moment, at least," he said.

"Who asks for more!" said Cipriano.

A spark flashed out of Ramón's eyes too.—Then he checked himself, and gathered himself together.

"What would be the good!" he said heavily. "If the egg was crushed, and we remained, what could we do but go howling down the empty passages of darkness. What's the good, Cipriano?"

Ramón got up and went away. The sun had set, the night was falling. And in his soul the great, writhing anger was alive again. Carlota provoked it into life: the two women seemed to breathe life into the black monster of his inward rage, till it began to lash again. And Cipriano stirred it up till it howled with desire.

"My manhood is like a demon howling inside me," said Ramón to himself, in Cipriano's words.

And he admitted the justice of the howling, his manhood being pent up, humiliated, goaded with insult inside him. And rage came over him, against Carlota, against Cipriano, against his own people, against all mankind, till he was filled with rage like the devil.

His people would betray him, he knew that. Cipriano would betray him. Given one little vulnerable chink, they would pierce him. They would leap at the place out of nowhere, like a tarantula, and bite in the poison.

While ever there was one little vulnerable chink. And what man can be invulnerable?

He went upstairs, by the outer stairway, through the iron door at the side of the house, under the heavy trees, up to his room, and sat on his bed. The night was hot, heavy, and ominously still.

"The waters are coming," he heard a servant say.

He shut the doors of his room till it was black dark inside. Then he threw aside his clothing, saying: I put off the world with my clothes. And standing nude and invisible in the centre of his room he thrust his clenched fist upwards, with all his might, feeling he would break the walls of his chest. And his left hand hung loose, the fingers softly 5 curving downwards.

And tense like the gush of a soundless fountain, he thrust up and reached down in the invisible dark, convulsed with passion. Till the black waves began to wash over his consciousness, over his mind, waves of darkness broke over his memory, over his being, like an 10 incoming tide, till at last it was full tide, and he trembled, and fell to rest. Invisible in the darkness, he stood soft and relaxed, staring with wide eyes at the dark, and feeling the dark fecundity of the inner tide washing over his heart, over his belly, his mind dissolved away in the greater, dark mind, which is undisturbed by thoughts. 15

He covered his face with his hands, and stood still, in pure unconsciousness, neither hearing nor feeling nor knowing, like a dark sea-weed deep in the sea. With no Time and no World, in the deeps that are timeless and worldless.

Then when his heart and his belly were restored, his mind began 20 to flicker again softly, like a soft flame flowing without departing.

So he wiped his face with his hands, and put his sarape over his head, and, silent inside an aura of pain, he went out and took the drum, carrying it downstairs.

Martín, the man who loved him, was hovering in the zaguán. 25

"*Ya, Patrón?*" he said.

"*Ya!*"* said Ramón.

The man ran indoors, where a lamp was burning in the big, dark kitchen, and ran out again with an armful of the woven straw mats.

"Where, *Patrón?*" he said. 30

Ramón hesitated in the centre of the courtyard, and looked at the sky.

"*Viene el agua?*" he said.

"*Creo que sí, Patrón.*"*

They went to the shed where the bananas had been packed and 35 carried away on donkeys. There the man threw down the *petates*. Ramón arranged them. Martín ran with canes. He was going to make lights, the simplest possible. Three pieces of thick cane, tied at the neck with a cord, stood up three-legged, waist high. In the three-pronged fork at the top he laid a piece of flat, slightly hollow lava 40 stone. Then he came running from the house with a bit of burning ocote wood. Three or four bits of ocote, each bit no bigger than a long finger, flickered and rose up in quick flames from the stone, and the courtyard danced with shadow.

5 Ramón took off his sarape, folded it, and sat upon it. Martín lit another tripod-torch. Ramón sat with his back to the wall, the firelight dancing on his dark brows, that were sunk in a sort of frown. His breast shone like gold in the flame. He took the drum and sounded the summons, slow, monotonous, rather sad. In a moment

10 two or three men came running. The drummer came, Ramón stood up and handed him the drum. He ran with it to the great outer doorway, and out into the dark lane, and there sounded the summons, quick, sharp.

Ramón put on his sarape, whose scarlet fringe touched his knees,

15 and stood motionless, with ruffled hair. Round his shoulders went the woven snake, and his head was through the middle of the blue, woven bird.

Cipriano came from the house. He was wearing a sarape all scarlet and dark brown, a great scarlet sun at the centre, deep scarlet

20 zig-zags at the borders, and dark brown fringe at his knees. He came and stood at Ramón's side, glancing up into Ramón's face. But the other man's brows were low, his eyes were fixed in the darkness of the sheds away across the courtyard. He was looking into the heart of the world; because the faces of men, and the hearts of men are

25 helpless quicksands. Only into the heart of the cosmos man can look for strength. And if he can keep his soul in touch with the heart of all the world, then from the heart of the world new blood will beat in strength and stillness into him, fulfilling his manhood.

Cipriano turned his black eyes to the courtyard. His soldiers had

30 drawn near, in a little group. Three or four men were standing, in dark sarapes, round the fire. Cipriano stood brilliant like a cardinal bird, next to Ramón. Even his sandals were bright, sealing-wax red, and his loose linen trousers were bound at the ankles with red and black bands.—His face looked very dark and ruddy in the firelight,

35 his little black tuft of a beard hung odd and devilish, his eyes were glittering sardonically. But he caught Ramón's hand in his small hand, and stood holding it.

The peons were coming through the entrance-way, balancing their big hats. Women were hurrying barefoot, swishing their full

40 skirts, carrying babies inside the dark wrap of their rebozos, children

running after. They all clustered towards the flame-light, like wild animals gazing in at the circle of men in dark sarapes, Ramón, magnificent in his white and blue and shadow, poising his beautiful head, Cipriano at his side like a glittering cardinal bird.

Carlota and Kate emerged from the inner doorway of the house. But there Carlota remained, wrapped in a black silk shawl, seated on a wooden bench where the soldiers usually sat, looking across at the ruddy flare of light, the circle of dark men, the tall beauty of her husband, the poppy-petal glitter of red, of Cipriano, the group of little, dust-coloured soldiers, and the solid throng of peons and women and children, standing gazing like animals. While through the gate men still came hurrying, and from outside, the drum sounded, and a high voice sang again and again:

Someone will enter between the gates,
Now, at this moment, Ay!
See the light on the man that waits.
Shall you? Shall I?

Someone will come to the place of fire,
Now, at this moment, Ay!
And hark to the words of their heart's desire.
Shall you? Shall I?

Someone will knock when the door is shut,
Ay! in a moment, Ay!
Hear a voice saying: I know you not!
Shall you! Shall I!*

There was a queer, wild yell each time on the *Ay!* and like a bugle the refrain: *Shall you? Shall I?* It made Carlota shiver.

Kate, wrapping her yellow shawl round her, walked slowly towards the group.

The drum outside gave a rapid shudder, and was finished. The drummer came in, the great doors were shut and barred, the drummer took his place in the ring of standing men. A dead silence supervened.

Ramón continued to gaze from under lowered brows, into space. Then in a quiet, inward voice, he said:

"As I take off this cover, I put away the day that is gone from upon me."

He took off his sarape, and stood with it over his arm. All the men in the circle did the same, till they stood with naked breasts and shoulders, Cipriano very dark and strong-looking, in his smallness, beside Ramón.

"I put away the day that is gone," Ramón continued, in the same still, inward voice, "and stand with my heart uncovered in the night
5　of the gods."

Then he looked down at the ground.

"Serpent of the earth," he said; "snake that lies in the fire at the heart of the world, come! Come! Snake of the fire of the heart of the world, coil like gold round my ankles, and rise like life around my
10　knee, and lay your head against my thigh. Come, put your head in my hand, cradle your head in my fingers, snake of the deeps. Kiss my feet and my ankles with your mouth of gold, kiss my knees and my inner thigh, snake branded with flame and shadow, come! and rest your head in my finger-basket! So!"

15　The voice was soft and hypnotic. It died upon a stillness. And it seemed as if really a mysterious presence had entered unseen from the underworld. It seemed to the *peones* as if really they saw a snake of brilliant gold and living blackness softly coiled around Ramón's ankle and knee, and resting its head in his fingers, licking his palm
20　with forked tongue.

He looked out at the big, dilated, glittering eyes of his people, and his own eyes were wide and uncanny.

"I tell you," he said, "and I tell you truly. At the heart of this earth sleeps a great serpent, in the midst of fire. Those that go down in
25　mines feel the heat and the sweat of him, they feel him move. It is the living fire of the earth, for the earth is alive. The snake of the world is huge, and the rocks are his scales, trees grow between them. I tell you the earth you dig is alive as a snake that sleeps. So vast a serpent you walk on, this lake lies between his folds as a drop of rain in the
30　folds of a sleeping rattlesnake. Yet he none the less lives. The earth is alive.

"And if he died, we should all perish. Only his living keeps the soil sweet, that grows your maize. From the roots of his scales we dig silver and gold, and the trees have root in him, as the hair of my face
35　has root in my lips.

"The earth is alive. But he is very big, and we are very small, smaller than dust. But he is very big in his life, and sometimes he is angry. *These people, smaller than dust,* he says, *they stamp on me and say I am dead. Even to their asses they speak, and shout* Arre! Burro! *But to*
40　*me they speak no word. Therefore I will turn against them, like a woman*

*who lies angry with her man in bed, and eats away his spirit with her
anger, turning her back to him.*

"That is what the earth says to us. He sends sorrow into our feet,
and depression into our loins.

"Because as an angry woman in the house can make a man heavy, 5
taking his life from him, so the earth can make us heavy, make our
souls cold, and our life dreary in our feet.

"Speak then to the snake of the heart of the world, put oil on your
fingers and lower your fingers for him to taste the oil of the earth, and
let him send life into your feet and ankles and knees, like sap in the 10
young maize pressing against the joints and making the milk of the
maize bud among its hair.

"From the heart of the earth man feels his manhood rise up in
him, like the maize that is proud, turning its green leaves outwards.
Be proud like the maize, and let your roots go deep, deep, for the 15
rains are here, and it is time for us to be growing, in Mexico—"

Ramón ceased speaking, the drum softly pulsed. All the men of
the ring were looking down at the earth and softly letting their left
hands hang.

Carlota, who had not been able to hear, drifted up to Kate's side, 20
spell-bound by her husband. Kate unconsciously glanced down at
the earth, and secretly let her fingers hang softly against her dress.
But then she was afraid of what might happen to her, and she caught
her hand up into her shawl.

Suddenly the drum began to give a very strong note, followed by a 25
weak: a strange, exciting thud.

Everybody looked up. Ramón had flung his right arm tense into
the air, and was looking at the black dark sky. The men of the ring
did the same, and the naked arms were thrust aloft like so many
rockets. 30

"Up! Up! Up!" said a wild voice.

"Up! Up!" cried the men of the ring, in a wild chorus.

And involuntarily the men in the crowd twitched, then shot their
arms upwards, turning their faces to the dark heavens. Even some of
the women boldly thrust up their naked arms, and relief entered 35
their hearts as they did so.

But Kate would not lift her arm.

There was dead silence, even the drum was silent. Then the voice
of Ramón was heard, speaking upwards to the black sky:

"Your big wings are dark, Bird, you are flying low tonight. You are 40 flying low over Mexico, we shall soon feel the fan of your wings on our face.

"Ay, Bird! You fly about where you will. You fly past the stars, and you perch on the sun. You fly out of sight, and are gone beyond the white river of the sky. But you come back like the ducks of the north, looking for water and winter.

"You sit in the middle of the sun, and preen your feathers. You crouch in the river of stars, and make the star-dust rise around you. You fly away into the deepest hollow place of the sky, whence there seems no return.

"Yet you come back to us, and hover overhead, and we feel your wings fanning our faces—"

Even as he spoke the wind rose, in sudden gusts, and a door could be heard slamming in the house, with a shivering of glass, and the trees gave off a tearing sound.

"Come then, Bird of all the great sky!" Ramón called wildly. "Come! Oh Bird, settle a moment on my wrist, over my head, and give me power of the sky, and wisdom. Oh Bird! Bird of all the wide heavens, even if you drum your feathers in thunder, and drop the white snake of fire from your beak back to the earth again, where he can run in, deep down the rocks again, home: even if you come as the Thunderer, come! settle on my wrist a moment, with the clutch of the power of thunder, and arch your wings over my head, like a shadow of clouds, and bend your breast to my brow, and bless me with the sun. Bird, roaming Bird of the Beyond, with thunder in your pinions and the snake of lightning in your beak, with blue heaven in the socket of your wings and cloud in the arch of your neck, with sun in the burnt feathers of your breast and power in your feet, with terrible wisdom in your flight, swoop to me a moment, swoop!"*

Sudden gusts of wind tore at the little fires of flame, till they could be heard to rustle, and the lake began to speak in a vast hollow noise, beyond the tearing of trees. Distant lightning was beating far off, over the black hills.

Ramón dropped his arm, which had been bent over his head. The drum began to beat. Then he said:

"Sit down a moment, before the Bird shakes water out of his wings. It will come soon. Sit down."

There was a stir. Men put their sarapes over their faces, women clutched their rebozos tighter, and all sat down on the ground. Only Kate and Carlota remained standing, on the outer edge. Gusts of wind tore at the flames, the men put their hats on the ground in front of them.

"The earth is alive, and the sky is alive," said Don Ramón in his natural voice, "and between them, we live. Earth has kissed my knees, and put strength in my belly. Sky has perched on my wrist, and sent power into my breast.

"But as in the morning the Morning Star stands between earth and sky, a star can rise in us, and stand between the heart and the loins.

"That is the manhood of man, and for woman, her womanhood.

"You are not yet men. And women, you are not yet women.

"You run about and toss about and die, and still you have not found the star of your manhood rise within you, the star of your womanhood shine out serene between your breasts, women.

"I tell you, for him that wishes it, the star of his manhood shall rise within him, and he shall be proud, and perfect even as the Morning Star is perfect.

"And the star of a woman's womanhood can rise at last, from between the heavy rim of the earth and the lost grey void of the sky.

"But how? How shall we do it? How shall it be?

"How shall we men become Men of the Morning Star? And the women the Dawn-Star Women?

"Lower your fingers to the caress of the Snake of the earth.

"Lift your wrist for a perch to the far-flying Bird.

"Have the courage of both, the courage of lightning and the earthquake.

"And wisdom of both, the wisdom of the snake and the eagle.

"And the peace of both, the peace of the serpent and the sun.

"And the power of both, the power of the innermost earth and the outermost heaven.

"But on your brow, Men! the undimmed Morning Star, that neither day nor night, nor earth nor sky can swallow and put out.

"And between your breasts, Women! the Dawn Star, that cannot be dimmed.

"And your home at last is the Morning Star. Neither heaven nor earth shall swallow you up at the last, but you shall pass into the place beyond both, into the bright star that is lonely yet feels itself never alone.—

"The Morning Star is sending you a messenger, a god who died in Mexico. But he slept his sleep, and the invisible Ones washed his

body with water of resurrection. So he has risen, and pushed the stone from the mouth of the tomb, and has stretched himself. And now he is striding across the horizons even quicker than the great stone from the tomb is tumbling back to the earth, to crush those that
5　rolled it up.

"The Son of the Star is coming back to the sons of men, with big, bright strides.

"Prepare to receive him. And wash yourselves, and put oil on your hands and your feet, on your mouth and eyes and ears and nostrils,
10　on your breast and navel and on the secret places of your body, that nothing of the dead days, no dust of skeletons and evil things may pass into you and make you unclean.

"Do not look with the eyes of yesterday, nor like yesterday listen, nor breathe, nor smell, nor taste, nor swallow food and drink. Do not
15　kiss with the mouths of yesterday, nor touch with the hands, nor walk with yesterday's feet. And let your navel know nothing of yesterday, and go into your women with a new body, enter the new body in her.

"For yesterday's body is dead, and carrion, the zopilote is hovering above it.
20　"Put yesterday's body from off you, and have a new body. Even as your god who is coming, Quetzalcoatl, is coming with a new body, like a star, from the shadow of death.

"Yes, even as you sit upon the earth this moment, with the round of your body touching the round of the earth, say: Earth! Earth! you
25　are alive as the globes of my body are alive. Breathe the kiss of the inner earth upon me, even as I sit upon you.

"And so, it is said. The earth is stirring beneath you, the sky is rushing its wings above. Go home to your houses, in front of the waters that will fall and cut you off forever from your yesterdays.
30　"Go home, and hope to be Men of the Morning Star, Women of the Star of Dawn.

"You are not yet men and women——"

He rose up and waved to the people to be gone. And in a moment they were on their feet, scurrying and hastening with the quiet
35　Mexican hurry, that seems to run low down upon the surface of the earth.

The black wind was all loose in the sky, tearing with the thin shriek of torn fabrics, in the mango trees. Men held their big hats on their heads and ran with bent knees, their sarapes blowing. Women
40　clutched their rebozos tighter and ran barefoot to the zaguán.

The big doors were open, a soldier stood with a gun across his back, holding a hurricane lamp. And the people fled like ghosts through the doors, and away up the black lane like bits of paper veering away into nothingness, blown out of their line of flight. In a moment, they had all silently gone.

Martín barred the great doors. The soldier put down his lamp on the wooden bench, and he and his comrades sat huddled in their dark shawls, in a little bunch like toadstools in the dark cavern of the zaguán. Already one had curled himself up on the wooden bench, wrapped like a snail in his blanket, head disappeared.

"The water is coming!" cried the servants excitedly, as Kate went upstairs with Doña Carlota.

The lake was quite black, like a great pit. The wind suddenly blew with violence, with a strange ripping sound in the mango trees, as if some membrane in the air were being ripped. The white-flowered oleanders in the garden below leaned over quite flat, their white flowers ghostly, going right down to the earth, in the pale beam of the lamp—like a street-lamp—that shone on the wall at the front entrance. A young palm-tree bent and spread its leaves on the ground. Some invisible juggernaut car rolling in the dark over the outside world.*

Away across the lake, south-west, lightning blazed and ran down the sky like some portentous writing. And soft, velvety thunder broke inwardly, strangely.

"It frightens me!" cried Doña Carlota, putting her hand over her eyes and hastening into a far corner of the bare salon.

Cipriano and Kate stood on the terrace, watching the coloured flowers in the pots shake and fly to bits, disappearing up into the void of darkness. Kate clutched her shawl. But the wind suddenly got under Cipriano's blanket, and lifted it straight up in the air, then dropped it in a scarlet flare over his head. Kate watched his deep, strong Indian chest lift as his arms quickly fought to free his head. How dark he was, and how primitively physical, beautiful and deep-breasted, with soft, full flesh! But all, as it were, for himself. Nothing that came forth from him to meet with one outside. All oblivious of the outside, all for himself.

"Ah! the water!" he cried, holding down his sarape.

The first great drops were flying darkly at the flowers, like arrows. Kate stood back into the doorway of the salon. A pure blaze of lightning slipped three-fold above the black hills, seemed to stand a moment, then slip back into the dark.

Down came the rain with a smash, as if some great vessel had

broken.* With it, came a waft of icy air. And all the time, first in one
part of the sky, then in another, in quick succession the blue
lightning, very blue, broke out of heaven and lit up the air for a blue,
breathless moment, looming trees and ghost of a garden, then was
gone, while thunder dropped and exploded continually.

Kate watched the dropping masses of water in wonder. Already, in
the blue moments of lightning, she saw the garden below a pond, the
walks were rushing rivers. It was cold. She turned indoors.

A servant was going round the rooms with a lantern, to look if
scorpions were coming out. He found one scuttling across the floor
of Kate's room, and one fallen from the ceiling beams on to Carlota's
bed.

They sat in the salon in rocking-chairs, Carlota and Kate, and
rocked, smelling the good wetness, breathing the good, chilled air.
Kate had already forgotten what really chill air was like. She wrapped
her shawl tighter round her.

"Ah yes, you feel cold! You must take care in the nights, now.
Sometimes in the rainy season the nights are very cold. You must be
ready with an extra blanket. And the servants, poor things, they just
lie and shudder, and they get up in the morning like corpses.—But
the sun soon warms them again, and they seem to think they must
bear what comes—So they complain sometimes, but still they don't
provide."

The wind had gone, suddenly. Kate was uneasy, uneasy, with the
smell of water, almost of ice, in her nostrils, and her blood still hot
and dark. She got up and went again to the terrace. Cipriano was still
standing there, motionless and inscrutable, like a monument, in his
red and dark sarape.

The rain was abating. Down below in the garden, two barefoot
women-servants were running through the water, in the faint light of
the zaguán lamp, running across the garden and putting ollas, and
square gasoline cans under the arching spouts of water that seethed
down from the roof, then darting away while they filled, then
struggling in with the frothy vessel.—It would save making trips to
the lake, for water.

"What do you think of us?" Cipriano said to her.

"It is strange to me," she replied, wondering and a little awed by
the night.

"Good, no?" he said, in an exultant tone.

"A little scaring," she replied, with a slight laugh.

"When you are used to it," he said, "it seems natural, no? It seems natural so—as it is. And when you go to a country like England, where all is so safe and ready-made, then you miss it. You keep saying to yourself: What am I missing? What is it that is not here?"

He seemed to be gloating in his native darkness. It was curious, that though he spoke such English English, it seemed always foreign to her, more foreign than Doña Carlota's Spanish.

"I can't understand that people want to have everything, all life, no?—so safe and ready-made as in England and America. It is good to be *awake*. On the *qui vive*, no?"

"Perhaps," she said.

"So I like it," he said, "when Ramón tells the people the earth is alive, and the sky has a big bird in it, that you don't see. I think it is true. Certainly! And it is good to know it, because then one is on the *qui vive*, no?"

"But it's tiring to be always on the *qui vive*," she said.

"Why? Why tiring? No, I think, on the contrary, it is refreshing.—Ah, you should marry, and live in Mexico. At last, I am sure, you would like it. You would keep waking up more and more to it."

"Or else going more and more deadened," she said. "That is how most foreigners go, it seems to me."

"Why deadened!" he said to her. "I don't understand. Why deadened? Here you have a country where night is night, and rain comes down and you know it. And you have a people with whom you must be on the *qui vive* all the time, all the time. And that is very good, no? You don't go sleepy. Like a pear! Don't you say a pear goes sleepy, no?—*cuando se echa a perder?*"*

"Yes!" she said.

"And here you have also Ramón. How does Ramón seem to you?"

"I don't know. I don't want to say anything. But I do think he is almost too much: too far.—And I *don't* think he is Mexican."

"Why not? Why not Mexican? He is Mexican."

"Not as you are."

"How not as I am? He is Mexican."

"He seems to me to belong to the old, old Europe," she said.

"And he seems to me to belong to the old, old Mexico—and also to the new," he added quickly.

"But you don't believe in him."

"How?"

5

10

15

20

25

30

35

40

"You—yourself. You don't believe in him. You think it is like everything else, a sort of game. Everything is a sort of game, a put-up job, to you Mexicans. You don't *really* believe, in anything."

"How not believe? I not believe in Ramón?—Well, perhaps not, in
5 that way of kneeling before him and spreading out my arms and shedding tears on his feet. But I—I believe in him, too. Not in your way, but in mine. I tell you why. Because he has the power to compel me. If he hadn't the power to *compel* me, how should I believe?"

"It is a queer sort of belief, that is compelled," she said.

10 "How else should one believe, except by being compelled?—I like Ramón for that, that he can compel me. When I grew up, and my god-father could not compel me to believe, I was very unhappy. It made me very unhappy.—But Ramón *compels* me, and that is very good. It makes me very happy, when I know I can't escape. It would
15 make you happy too."

"To know I could not escape from Don Ramón?" she said ironically.

"Yes, that also. And to know you could not escape from Mexico. And even from such a man, as me."

20 She paused in the dark before she answered, sardonically:

"I don't think it would make me happy to feel I couldn't escape from Mexico. No, I feel, unless I was sure I could get out any day, I couldn't bear to be here."

In her mind she thought: And perhaps Ramón is the only one I
25 couldn't quite escape from, because he really touches me some-where inside. But from you, you little Cipriano, I should have no need even to escape, because I could not be caught by you.

"Ah!" he said quickly. "You think so. But then you don't know. You can only think with American thoughts. It is natural. From your
30 education, you have only American thoughts, U.S.A. thoughts to think with. Nearly all women are like that: even Mexican women of the Spanish-Mexican class. They are all thinking nothing but U.S.A. thoughts, because those are the ones that go with the way they dress their hair. And so it is with you. You think like a modern
35 woman, because you belong to the Anglo-Saxon or Teutonic world, and dress your hair in a certain way, and have money, and are altogether free.—But you only think like this because you have had these thoughts put in your head, just as in Mexico you spend centavos and pesos, because that is the Mexican money you have put
40 in your pocket. It's what they give you at the bank.—So when you say

you are free, you are *not* free. You are compelled all the time to be
thinking U.S.A. thoughts—*compelled*, I must say. You have not as
much choice as a slave. As the *peones* must eat tortillas, tortillas,
tortillas, because there is nothing else, you must think these U.S.A.
thoughts, about being a woman and being free. Every day you must   5
eat those tortillas, tortillas.—Till you don't know how you would like
something else."

"What else should I like?" she said, with a grimace at the
darkness.

"Other thoughts, other feelings.—You are afraid of such a man as   10
me, because you think I should not treat you *à l'américaine*. You are
quite right. I should not treat you as an American woman must be
treated. Why should I? I don't wish to. It doesn't seem good to me."

"You would treat a woman like a real old Mexican, would
you?—keep her ignorant, and shut her up?" said Kate sarcastically.   15

"I could not keep her ignorant if she did not start ignorant.—But
what more I had to teach her wouldn't be in the American style of
teaching."

"What then?"

"*Quién sabe!* Ça reste à voir."   20

"Et continuera à y rester,"* said Kate, laughing.

Chapter XIV.

Home to Sayula.

The morning came perfectly blue, with a freshness in the air and a blue luminousness over the trees and the distant mountains, and birds so bright, absolutely like new-opened buds sparking in the air.

Cipriano was returning to Guadalajara in the automobile, and Carlota was going with him. Kate would be rowed home on the lake.

To Ramón, Carlota was still, at times, a torture. She seemed to have the power still to lacerate him, inside his bowels. Not in his mind or spirit, but in his old emotional, passional self: right in the middle of his belly, to tear him and make him feel he bled inwardly.

Because he had loved her, he had cared for her: for the affectionate, passionate, whimsical, sometimes elfish creature she had been. He had made much of her, and spoiled her, for many years.

But all the while, gradually, his nature was changing inside him. Not that he ceased to care for her, or wanted other women. That she could have understood. But inside him was a slow, blind imperative, urging him to cast his emotional and spiritual and mental self into the slow furnace, and smelt them into a new, whole being.

But he had Carlota to reckon with. She loved him, and that, to her, was the outstanding factor. She loved him, emotionally. And spiritually, she loved mankind. And mentally, she was sure she was quite right.

Yet as time went on, he had to change. He had to cast that emotional self, which she loved, into the furnace, to be smelted down to another self.

And she felt she was robbed, cheated. Why couldn't he go on being gentle, good, and loving, and trying to make the whole world more gentle, good, and loving?

He couldn't, because it was borne in upon him that the world had gone as far as it could go in the good, gentle, and loving direction, and anything further in that line meant perversity. So the time had come for the slow great change, to something else—what, he didn't know.

The emotion of love, and the greater emotion of Liberty for mankind seemed to go hard and congeal upon him, like the shell on a chrysalis. It was the old caterpillar stage of Christianity evolving into something else.

But Carlota felt this was all she had, this emotion of love, for her husband, her children, for her people, for the animals and birds and trees of the world. It was her all, her Christ and her Blessed Virgin. How could she let it go?

So she continued to love him, and to love the world, steadily, pathetically, obstinately and devilishly. She prayed for him, and she engaged in works of charity.

But her love had turned from being the spontaneous flow, subject to the unforeseen comings and goings of the Holy Ghost, and had turned into will. She loved now with her *will*: as the white world now tends to do. She became filled with charity: that cruel kindness.

Her winsomeness and her elvishness departed from her, she began to wither, she grew tense. And she blamed him, and prayed for him. Even as the spontaneous mystery died in her, the will hardened, till she was nothing but a will: a love-will.

She soon succeeded in drawing the life of her young boys all to herself, with her pathos and her subtle will. Ramón was too proud and angry to fight for them. They were her children. Let her have them.

They were the children of his old body. His new body had no children: would probably never have any.

"But remember," he said to her, with southern logic, "you do not love, save with your will. I don't like the love you have for your god: it is an assertion of your own will. I don't like the love you have for me: it is the same. I don't like the love you have for your children. If ever I see in them a spark of desire to be saved from it, I shall do my best to save them. Meanwhile have your love, have your will. But you know I dislike it. I dislike your insistence. I dislike your monopoly of one feeling, I dislike your charity works. I disapprove of the whole trend of your life. You are weakening and vitiating the boys. You do *not* love them, you are only putting your love-will over them. One day they will turn and hate you for it.—Remember I have said this to you."

Doña Carlota had trembled in every fibre of her body, under the shock of this. But she went away to the chapel of the Annunciation Convent, and prayed. And praying for his soul, she seemed to gain a victory over him, in the odour of sanctity. She came home in frail, pure triumph, like a flower that blooms on a grave: his grave.

And Ramón henceforth watched her in her beautiful, rather fluttering, rather irritating gentleness, as he watched his closest
5   enemy.

Life had done its work on one more human being, quenched the spontaneous life and left only the will. Killed the god in the woman, or the goddess, and left only charity, with a will.

"Carlota," he had said to her, "how happy you would be if you
10 could wear deep, deep mourning for me.—I shall not give you this happiness."

She gave him a strange look from her hazel-brown eyes.

"Even that is in the hands of God," she had replied; as she hurried away from him.

15   And now, on this morning after the first rains, she came to the door of his room as he was sitting writing. As yesterday, he was naked to the waist, the blue-marked sash tied round his middle confined the white linen, loose trousers—like big, wide pyjama trousers crossed in front and tied round his waist.

20   "May I come in?" she said nervously.

"Do!" he replied, putting down his pen and rising.

There was only one chair—he was offering it her, but she sat down on the unmade bed, as if asserting her natural right. And in the same way she glanced at his naked breast—as if asserting her natural
25 right.

"I am going with Cipriano after breakfast," she said.

"Yes, so you said."

"The boys will be home in three weeks."

"Yes."
30   "Don't you want to see them?"

"If they want to see me."

"I am sure they do."

"Then bring them here."

"Do you think it is pleasant for me?" she said, clasping her hands.
35   "You do not make it pleasant for me, Carlota."

"How can I? You know I think you are wrong. When I listened to you last night—there is something so beautiful in it all—and yet so monstrous. So *monstrous!*—Oh! I think to myself: What is this man doing! This man of all men, who might be such a blessing to his
40 country and mankind—"

"Well," said Ramón. "And what is he instead?"

"You know! You know! I can't bear it.—It *isn't* for you to save Mexico, Ramón. Christ has already saved it."

"It seems to me not so."

"He has! He has! And He made you the wonderful being that you are, so that you should *work out* the salvation, in the name of Christ and of love. Instead of which—"

"Instead of which, Carlota, I try something else.—But believe me, if the real Christ has not been able to save Mexico,—and He hasn't; then I am sure, the white Anti-Christ* of charity, and socialism, and politics, and reform, will only succeed in finally destroying her. That, and that alone makes me take my stand.—You, Carlota, with your charity works and your *pity*: and men like Benito Juárez, with their Reform and their Liberty: and all the rest of the benevolent people, politicians and socialists and so-forth, surcharged with pity for living men, in their mouths, but really with hate—the hate of the materialist *have-nots* for the materialist *haves*: they are the Anti-Christ. The old world, that's just the world. But the new world, that wants to save the People, this is the Anti-Christ. This is Christ with real poison in the communion cup.—And for this reason, I step out of my ordinary privacy and individuality. I don't want everybody poisoned. About the great mass I don't care. But I don't want everybody poisoned."

"How can you be so sure that you yourself are not a poisoner of the people?—I think you are."

"Think it then. I think of you, Carlota, merely, that you have not been able to come to your complete, final womanhood: which is a different thing from the old womanhoods."

"Womanhood is always the same."

"Ah no it isn't! Neither is manhood."

"But what do you think you can do? What do you think this Quetzalcoatl nonsense amounts to?"

"Quetzalcoatl is just a living word, for these people, no more.—All I want them to do is to find the beginnings of the way to their own manhood, their own womanhood. Men are not yet men in full, and women are not yet women. They are all half and half, incoherent, part horrible, part pathetic, part good creatures. Half arrived.—I mean you as well, Carlota. I mean all the world.—But these people don't *assert* any righteousness of their own, these Mexican people of ours. That makes me think that grace is still with them. And so, having got hold of some kind of clue to my own whole manhood, it is part of me now to try with them."

"You will fail."

"I shan't. Whatever happens to me, there will be a new vibration, a
5 new call in the air, and a new answer inside some men."

"They will betray you.—Do you know what even your friend Toussaint said of you?—Ramón Carrasco's future is just the past of mankind."

"A great deal of it is the past. Naturally Toussaint sees that
10 part."

"But the boys don't believe in you. *Instinctively*, they disbelieve. Cyprian said to me, when I went to see him: Is father doing any more of that silly talk about old gods coming back, mother? I wish he wouldn't. It would be pretty nasty for us if he got himself into the
15 newspapers with it."

Ramón laughed.

"Little boys," he said, "are like little gramophones. They only talk according to the record that's put into them."

"*You* don't believe—out of the mouths of babes and sucklings,"*
20 said Carlota bitterly.

"Why Carlota, the babes and sucklings don't get much chance. Their mothers and their teachers turn them into little gramophones from the first, so what can they do, but say and feel according to the record the mother and teacher puts into them. Perhaps in the time of
25 Christ, babes and sucklings were not so perfectly exploited by their elders."

Suddenly, however, the smile went off his face. He rose up, and pointed to the door:

"Go away!" he said in a low tone. "Go away! I have smelt the smell
30 of your spirit long enough."

She sat on the bed, spell-bound, gazing at him with frightened, yet obstinate, insolent eyes, wincing from his outstretched arm as if he had threatened to strike her.

Then again the fire went out of his eyes, and his arm sank. The
35 still, far-away look came on his face.

"What have I to do with it!" he murmured softly.

And taking up his blouse and his hat, he went silently out on to the terrace, departing from her in body and in soul. She heard the soft swish of his sandals. She heard the faint resonance of the iron door
40 to the terrace, to which he alone had access. And she sat like a heap

of ash on his bed, ashes to ashes, burnt out, with only the coals of her
will still smouldering.

Her eyes were very bright, as she went to join Kate and Cipriano.

After breakfast, Kate was rowed home down the lake. She felt a
curious depression at leaving the hacienda: as if, for her, life now was
there, and not anywhere else.

Her own house seemed empty, banal, vulgar. For the first time in
her life, she felt the banality and emptiness even of her own milieu.
Though the Casa de las Cuentas was not purely her own milieu.

"Ah, Niña, how good! How good that you have come! Ay, in the
night, how much water! Much! Much! But you were safe in the
hacienda, Niña.—Ah, how nice, that hacienda of Jamiltepec. Such a
good man, Don Ramón—isn't he, Niña? He cares a great deal for his
people. And the Señora, ah, how sympathetic she is!"

Kate smiled and was pleasant. But she felt more like going into her
room and saying: For God's sake, leave me alone, with your cheap
rattle.

She suffered again from her servants. Again that quiet, subterranean insolence against life, which seems to belong to modern life.
The unbearable note of flippant jeering, which is underneath almost
all modern utterance. It was underneath Juana's constant cry "Niña!
Niña!"

At meal-times Juana would seat herself on the ground at a little
distance from Kate, and talk, talk in her rapid mouthfuls of
conglomerate words with trailing, wistful endings: and all the time
watch her mistress with those black, unseeing eyes on which the
spark of light would stir with the peculiar slow, malevolent jeering of
the Indian.

Kate was not rich—she had only her moderate income.

"Ah, the rich people—!" Juana would say.

"I am not rich," said Kate.

"You are not rich, Niña?" came the singing, caressive, bird-like
voice: "Then, you are poor?"—this with indescribable irony.

"No, I am not poor either. I am not rich, and I am not poor," said
Kate.

"You are not rich, and you are not poor, Niña!"—repeated Juana,
in her bird-like voice, that covered the real bird's endless, vindictive
jeering.

For the words meant nothing to her. To her, who had nothing,
could never have anything, Kate was one of that weird class, the rich.

And, Kate felt, in Mexico it was a crime to be rich, or to be classed with the rich. Not even a crime, really, so much as a freak. The rich class was a freak class, like dogs with two heads or calves with five legs. To be looked upon, not with envy, but with the slow, undying antagonism and curiosity which "normals" have towards "freaks." The slow, powerful, corrosive Indian mockery, issuing from the lava-rock Indian nature, against anything which strives to be above the grey, lava-rock level.

"Is it true, Niña, that your country is through there?" Juana asked, jabbing her finger downwards, towards the bowels of the earth.

"Not quite!" said Kate. "My country is more *there*—" and she slanted her finger at the earth's surface.

"Ah—that way!" said Juana. And she looked at Kate with a subtle leer, as if to say: what could you expect from people who came out of the earth sideways, like sprouts of camote!

"And is it true, that over there, there are people with only one eye—here!"—Juana punched herself in the middle of the forehead.

"No. That isn't true. That is just a story."

"Ah!" said Juana. "Isn't it true? Do you know? Have you been to the country where they are, these people?"

"Yes," said Kate. "I have been to all the countries, and there are no such people."

"*Verdad! Verdad!*"* breathed Juana, awestruck. "You have been to all the countries, and there are no such people!—But in your country, they are all gringos? Nothing but gringos?"

She meant, no real people and salt of the earth like her own Mexican self.

"They are all people like me," said Kate coldly.

"Like you, Niña? And they all talk like you?"

"Yes! Like me."

"And there are many?"

"Many! Many!"

"Look now!" breathed Juana, almost awestruck to think that there could be whole worlds of these freak, mockable people.

And Concha, that young, belching savage, would stare through her window-grating at the strange menagerie of the Niña and the Niña's white visitors. Concha, slapping tortillas, was real.

Kate walked down towards the kitchen. Concha was slapping the *masa*, the maize dough which she bought in the plaza at eight centavos a kilo.

"Niña!" she called in her raucous voice. "Do you eat tortillas?"

"Sometimes," said Kate.

"Eh?" shouted the young savage.

"Sometimes."

"Here! Eat one now!" And Concha thrust a brown paw with a 5
pinkish palm, and a dingy-looking tortilla, at Kate.

"Not now," said Kate.

She disliked the heavy plasters that tasted of lime.

"Don't you want it? Don't you eat it?" said Concha, with an
impudent, strident laugh. And she flung the rejected tortilla on the 10
little pile.

She was one of those who won't eat bread: say they don't like it,
that it is not food.

Kate would sit and rock on her terrace, while the sun poured in
the green square of the garden, the palm-tree spread its great fans 15
translucent at the light, the hibiscus dangled great double-red
flowers, rosy red, from its very dark tree, and the dark-green oranges
looked as if they were sweating as they grew.

Came lunch time, madly hot: and greasy hot soup, greasy rice,
splintery little fried fishes, bits of boiled meat and boiled egg-plant 20
vegetables, a big basket piled with mangoes, papayas, zapotes—all
the tropical fruits one did not want, in hot weather.

And the barefoot little María, in a limp, torn, faded red frock, to
wait at table. She was the loving one. She would stand by Juana as
Juana bubbled with talk, like dark bubbles in her mouth, and she 25
would stealthily touch Kate's white arm; stealthily touch her again.
Not being rebuked, she would stealthily lay her thin little black arm
on Kate's shoulder, with the softest, lightest touch imaginable, and
her strange, wide black eyes would gleam with ghostly black
beatitude, very curious, and her childish, pock-marked, slightly 30
imbecile face would take on a black, arch, beatitudinous look. Then
Kate would quietly remove the thin, dark, pock-marked arm, the
child would withdraw half a yard, the beatitudinous look foiled, but
her very black eyes still shining exposed and absorbedly, in a rapt,
reptilian sort of ecstasy. 35

Till Concha came to hit her with her elbow, making some brutal,
savage remark which Kate could not understand. So the glotzing
black eyes of the child would twitch, and María would break into
meaningless tears, Concha into a loud, brutal, mocking laugh, like
some violent bird. And Juana interrupted her black and gluey flow of 40

words to glance at her daughters and throw out some ineffectual remark.

The victim, the inevitable victim, and the inevitable victimiser.

5 The terrible, terrible hot emptiness of the Mexican mornings, the weight of black *ennui* that hung in the air! It made Kate feel as if the bottom had fallen out of her soul. She went out to the lake, to escape that house, that family.

Since the rains, the trees in the broken gardens of the lake-front had flamed into scarlet, and poured themselves out into lavender 10 flowers. Rose-red, scarlet and lavender, quick, tropical flowers. Wonderful splashes of colour. But that was all: splashes! They made a splash, like fireworks.

And Kate thought of the black-thorn puffing white, in the early year, in Ireland, and hawthorn with coral grains, in a damp still 15 morning in the lanes, and foxgloves by the bare rock, and tufts of ling and heather, and a ravel of harebells. And a terrible, terrible longing for home came over her. To escape from these tropical brilliancies and meaninglessnesses.

In Mexico, the wind was a hard draught, the rain was a sluice of 20 water, to be avoided, and the sun hit down on one with hostility, terrific and stunning. Stiff, dry, unreal land, with sunshine beating on it like metal. Or blackness and lightning and crashing violence of rain.

No lovely fusion, no communion. No beautiful mingling of sun 25 and mist, no softness in the air, never. Either hard heat or hard chill. Hard, straight lines and zig-zags, wounding the breast. No soft, sweet smell of earth. The smell of Mexico, however subtle, suggested violence and things in chemical conflict.

And Kate felt herself filled with an anger of resentment. She 30 would sit under a willow tree by the lake, reading a Pío Baroja novel that was angry and full of No! No! No!—ich bin der Geist der stets verneint!* But she herself was so much angrier and fuller of repudiation than Pío Baroja. Spain cannot stand for No! as Mexico can.

35 The tree hung fleecy above her. She sat on the warm sand in the shadow, careful not to let even her ankles lie in the biting shine of the sun. There was a faint, old smell of urine. The lake was so still and filmy as to be almost invisible. In the near distance, some dark women were kneeling on the edge of the lake, dressed only in their 40 long wet chemises in which they had bathed. Some were washing

garments, some were pouring water over themselves, scooping it up in gourd scoops and pouring it over their black heads and ruddy-dark shoulders, in the intense pressure of the sunshine. On her left were two big trees, and a cane fence, and little straw huts of Indians. There the beach itself ended, and the little Indian plots of land went down to the lake-front.

Glancing around in the great light, she seemed to be sitting isolated in a dark core of shadow, while the world moved in inconsequential specks through the hollow glare.

She noticed a dark urchin, nearly naked, marching with naked, manly solemnity down to the water's edge. He would be about four years old, but more manly than an adult man. With sex comes a certain vulnerability which these round-faced, black-headed, stiff-backed infant men have not got. Kate knew the urchin. She knew his tattered rag of a red shirt, and the weird rags that were his little-man's white trousers. She knew his black round head, his stiff, sturdy march of a walk, his round eyes, and his swift, scuttling run, like a bolting animal.

"What's the brat got," she said to herself, gazing at the moving little figure within the great light.

Dangling from his tiny outstretched arm, held by the webbed toe, head down and feebly flapping its out-sinking wings, was a bird, a water-fowl. It was a black mud-chick with a white bar across the under-wing, one of the many dark fowl that bobbed in little flocks along the edge of the sun-stunned lake.

The urchin marched stiffly down to the water's edge, holding the upside-down bird, that seemed big as an eagle in the tiny fist. Another brat came scuttling after. The two infant men paddled a yard into the warm, lapping water, under the great light, and gravely stooping, like old men, set the fowl on the water. It floated, but could hardly paddle. The lift of the ripples moved it. The urchins dragged it in, like a rag, by a string tied to its leg.

So quiet, so still, so dark, like tiny, chubby little infant men, the two solemn figures with the rag of a bird!

Kate turned uneasily to her book, her nerves on edge. She heard the splash of a stone. The bird was on the water, but apparently the string that held it by the leg was tied to a stone. It lay wavering, a couple of yards out. And the two little he-men, with sober steadfast-ness and a quiet, dark lust, were picking up stones, and throwing them with the fierce Indian aim at the feebly fluttering bird: right down upon it. Like a little warrior stood the mite in the red rag, his arm upraised, to throw the stone with all his might down on the tethered bird.

In a whiff, Kate was darting down the beach.

5 "Ugly boys! Ugly children! Go! Go away, ugly children, ugly boys!" she said on one breath, with quiet intensity.

The round-headed dot gave her one black glance from his manly eyes, then the two of them scuttled up the beach into invisibility.

Kate went into the water, and lifted the wet, warm bird. The bit of
10 coarse fibre string hung from its limp, greenish, water-fowl's ankle. It feebly tried to bite her.

She rapidly stepped out of the water and stood in the sun to unfasten the string. The bird was about as big as a pigeon. It lay in her hand with the absolute motionlessness of a caught wild thing.

15 Kate stooped and pulled off her shoes and stockings. She looked round. No sign of life from the reed huts dark in the shadow of the trees. She lifted her skirts and staggered out barefoot in the hot shallows of the water, almost falling on the cruel stones under the water. The lake-side was very shallow. She staggered on and on, in
20 agony, holding up her skirts in one hand, holding the warm, wet, motionless bird in the other. Till at last she was up to her knees. Then she launched the greeny-black bird, and gave it a little push to the uprearing expanse of filmy water, that was almost dim, invisible with the glare of light.

25 It lay wet and draggled on the pale, moving sperm of the water, like a buoyant rag.

"Swim then! Swim!" she said, trying to urge it away into the lake. Either it couldn't or wouldn't. Anyhow it didn't.

But it was out of reach of those urchins. Kate struggled back from
30 those stones, to her tree, to her shade, to her book, away from the rage of the sun. Silent with slow anger, she kept glancing up at the floating bird, and sideways at the reed huts of the Indians in the black shadow.

Yes, the bird was dipping its beak in the water, and shaking its
35 head. It was coming to itself. But it did not paddle. It let itself be lifted, lifted on the ripples, and the ripples would drift it ashore.

"Fool of a thing!" said Kate nervously, using all her consciousness to make it paddle away into the lake.

Two companions, two black dots with white specks of faces, were
40 coming out of the pale glare of the lake. Two mud-chicks swam

busily forward. The first swam up and poked its beak at the inert bird, as if to say: *Hello! What's up?* Then immediately it turned away and paddled in complete oblivion to the shore, its companion following.

Kate watched the rag of feathered misery anxiously. Would it not rouse itself, wouldn't it follow?

No! There it lay, slowly, inertly drifting on the ripples, only sometimes shaking its head.

The other two alert birds waded confidently, busily among the stones.

Kate read a bit more.

When she looked again, she could not see her bird. But the other two were walking among the stones, jauntily.

She read a bit more.

The next thing was a rather loutish youth of eighteen or so, in overall trousers, running with big strides towards the water, and the stiff little man-brat scuttling after with determined bare feet. Her heart stood still.

The two busy mud-chicks rose in flight and went low over the water into the blare of light. Gone!

But the lout in the big hat, and overall trousers, and those stiff Indian shoulders she sometimes hated so much, was peering among the stones. She, however, was sure her bird had gone.

No! Actually no! The stiff-shouldered lout stooped and picked up the damp thing. It had let itself drift back.

He turned, dangling it like a rag from the end of one wing, and handed it to the man-brat. Then he stalked self-satisfied up the shore.

Ugh! and at that moment how Kate hated these people: their terrible lowness, *à terre, à terre.* Their stiff broad American shoulders, and high chests, and above all, their walk, their prancing, insentient walk. As if some motor-engine drove them at the bottom of their back.

Stooping rather forward and looking at the ground so that he could turn his eyes sideways to her, without showing her his face, the lout returned to the shadow of the huts. And after him, diminutive, the dot of a man marched stiffly, hurriedly, dangling the wretched bird, that stirred very feebly, downwards from the tip of one wing. And from time to time turning his round, black-eyed face in Kate's direction, vindictively, apprehensively, lest she should swoop down on him again. Black, apprehensive male defiance of the great white, weird female.

Kate glared back from under her tree.

"If looks would kill you, brat, I'd kill you," she said. And the urchin turned his face like clockwork at her from time to time, as he strutted palpitating towards the gap in the cane hedge, into which the youth had disappeared.

Kate debated whether to rescue the foolish bird again. But what was the good!

This country would have its victim. America would have its victim. As long as time lasts, it will be the continent divided between Victims and Victimisers. What is the good of trying to interfere!

She rose up in detestation of the flabby bird, and of the sulky-faced brat turning his full moon on her in apprehension—

Lumps of women were by the water's edge. Westwards, down the glare, rose the broken-looking villas and the white twin-towers of the church, holding up its two fingers in mockery above the scarlet flame-trees and the dark mangoes. She saw the rather lousy shore, and smelt the smell of Mexico, come out in the hot sun after rains: excrement, human and animal, dried in the sun on a dry, dry earth; and dry leaves; and mango leaves; and pure air with a little refuse-smoke in it.

"But the day will come when I shall go away," she said to herself.

And sitting rocking once more on her verandah, hearing the clap-clap of tortillas from the far end of the patio, the odd, metallic noises of birds, and feeling the clouds already assembling in the west, with a weight of unborn thunder upon them, she felt she could bear it no more: the vacuity, and the pressure: the horrible uncreate elementality, so uncouth, even sun and rain uncouth, uncouth.

And she wondered over the black vision in the eyes of that urchin. The curious void.

He could not see that the bird was a real living creature with a life of its own. This, his race had never seen. With black eyes they stared out on an elemental world, where the elements were monstrous and cruel, as the sun was monstrous, and the cold, crushing black water of the rain was monstrous, and the dry, dry, cruel earth.

And among the monstrosity of the elements flickered and towered other presences: terrible uncouth things called Gringos, white people, and dressed up monsters of rich people, with powers like gods, but uncouth, demonish gods. And uncouth things like birds that could fly and snakes that could crawl and fish that could swim and bite. An uncouth, monstrous universe of monsters big and little, in which man held his own by sheer resistance and guardedness, never, never going forth from his own darkness.

And sometimes, it was good to have revenge on the monsters that fluttered and strode. The monsters big and the monsters little. Even the monster of that bird, which had its own monstrous bird-nature. On this the mite could wreck the long human vengeance, and for once be master.

Blind to the creature as a soft, struggling thing finding its own fluttering way through life. Seeing only another monster of the outer void.

Walking forever through a menace of monsters, blind to the sympathy in things, holding one's own, and not giving in, nor going forth. Hence the lifted chests and the prancing walk. Hence the stiff, insentient spines, the rich physique, and the heavy, dreary natures, heavy like the dark-grey mud bricks, with a terrible obstinate ponderosity and a dry sort of gloom.

Chapter XV.

The Written Hymns of Quetzalcoatl.

The electric light in Sayula was as inconstant as everything else. It
would come on at half-past six in the evening, and it *might* bravely
5 burn till ten at night, when the village went dark with a click. But
usually it did no such thing. Often it refused to sputter into being till
seven, or half-past, or even eight o'clock. But its worst trick was that
of popping out just in the middle of supper, or just when you were
writing a letter. All of a sudden, the black Mexican night came down
10 on you with a thud. And then everybody running blindly for matches
and candles, with a calling of frightened voices. Why were they
always frightened?—Then the electric light, like a wounded thing,
would try to revive, and a red glow would burn in the bulbs, sinister.
All held their breath—was it coming or not? Sometimes it expired for
15 good, sometimes it got its breath back and shone, rather dully, but
better than nothing.

Once the rainy season had set in, it was hopeless. Night after night
it collapsed. And Kate would sit with her weary, fluttering candle,
while blue lightning revealed the dark shapes of things in the patio.
20 And half-seen people went swiftly down to Juana's end of the patio,
secretly.

On such a night Kate sat on her verandah facing the deepness of
the black night. A candle shone in her desert salon. Now and again
she saw the oleanders and the papaya in the patio garden, by the blue
25 gleam of lightning that fell with a noiseless splash into the pitch
darkness. There was a distant noise of thunders, several storms
prowling round like hungry jaguars, above the lake.

And several times the gate clicked, and crunching steps came
along the gravel, someone passed on the gravel walk, saluting her,
30 going down to Juana's quarters, where the dull light of a floating oil
wick shone through the grated window-hole. Then there was a low,
monotonous sound of a voice, reciting or reading. And as the wind
blew and the lightning alighted again like a blue bird among the
plants, there would come the sharp noise of the round cuentas falling
35 from the cuenta tree.

220

Kate was uneasy and a bit forlorn. She felt something was happening down in the servants' corner, something secret, in the dark. And she was stranded in her isolation on her terrace.

But after all, it was her house, and she had a right to know what her own people were up to. She rose from her rocking-chair and walked down the verandah and round the dining-room bay. The dining-room, which had its own two doors on the patio, was already locked up.

In the far corner beyond the well, she saw a group sitting on the ground, outside the doorway of Juana's kitchen-hole. Out of this little kitchen-shed shone the light of the floating-wick lamp, and a voice was slowly intoning, all the faces were looking into the dim light, the women dark-hooded in rebozos, the men with their hats on, their sarapes over their shoulders.

When they heard Kate's footsteps, the faces looked her way, and a voice murmured in warning. Juana struggled to her feet.

"It is the Niña!" she said. "Come, then, Niña, you poor innocent all alone in the evening."

The men in the group rose to their feet—she recognised the young Ezequiel, taking his hat off to her. And there was María del Carmen, the bride. And inside the little shed, with the wick-lamp on the floor, was Julio, the bridegroom of a few weeks ago. Concha and little María were there, and a couple of strangers.

"I could hear the voice—" said Kate. "I didn't know it was you, Julio. How do you do?—And I wondered so much what it was."

There was a moment's dead silence. Then Juana plunged in.

"Yes, Niña! Come! It's very nice that you come. Concha, the chair for the Niña!"

Concha got up rather unwillingly, and fetched the little low chair which formed Juana's sole article of furniture, save the one bed.

"I don't disturb you?" said Kate.

"No, Niña. You are a friend of Don Ramón, *verdad*?"

"Yes," said Kate.

"And we—we are reading the Hymns."

"Yes?" said Kate.

"The Hymns of Quetzalcoatl," said Ezequiel, in his barking young voice, with sudden bravado.

"Do go on! May I listen!"

"You hear! The Niña wants to listen. Read, Julio, read! Read then."

They all sat down once more on the ground, and Julio sat down by the lamp, but he hung his head, hiding his face in the shadow of his big hat.

"*Entonces!*—Read then," said Juana.

5   "He is afraid," murmured María del Carmen, laying her hand on the young man's knee. "However, read, Julio! Because the Niña wants to hear."

And after a moment's struggle, Julio said in a muffled voice:

"Do I begin from the beginning?"

10   "Yes, from the beginning! Read!" said Juana.

The young man took a sheet of paper, like an advertisement leaflet, from under his blanket. At the top it had the Quetzalcoatl symbol, called the Eye, the ring with the bird-shape standing in the middle.

15   He began to read in a rather muffled voice:

"I am Quetzalcoatl with the dark face, who lived in Mexico in other days.

"Till there came a stranger from over the seas, and his face was white, and he spoke with strange words. He showed his hands and

20   his feet, that in both there were holes. And he said: My name is Jesus, and they called me Christ. Men crucified me on a cross till I died. But I rose up out of the place where they put me, and I went up to heaven to my Father. Now my Father has told me to come to Mexico.

25   "*Quetzalcoatl said:* You alone?

"*Jesus said:* My mother is here. She shed many tears for me, seeing me crucify. So she will hold the Sons of Mexico on her lap, and soothe them when they suffer, and when the women of Mexico weep, she will take them on her bosom and comfort them. And when

30   she cries to the Father for her people, He will make everything well.

"*Quetzalcoatl said:* That is well. And Brother with the name Jesus, what will you do in Mexico?

"*Jesus said:* I will bring peace into Mexico. And on the naked I will put clothes, and food between the lips of the hungry, and gifts in all

35   men's hands, and peace and love in their hearts.

"*Quetzalcoatl said:* It is very good. I am old. I could not do so much. I must go now. Farewell, people of Mexico! Farewell, strange brother called Jesus. Farewell, woman called Mary. It is time for me to go.

40   "So Quetzalcoatl looked at his people; and he embraced Jesus, the

Son of Heaven; and he embraced María, the Blessed Virgin, the
Holy Mother of Jesus, and he turned away. Slowly he went. But in
his ears was the sound of the tearing down of his temples in Mexico.
Nevertheless he went on slowly, being old, and weary with much
living. He climbed the steep of the mountain, and over the white   5
snow of the volcano. As he went, behind him rose a cry of people
dying, and a flame of places burning. He said to himself: Surely
those are Mexicans crying! Yet I must not hear, for Jesus has come to
the land, and he will wipe the tears from all eyes, and his mother will
make them all glad.   10

"He also said: Surely that is Mexico burning. But I must not look,
for all men will be brothers, now Jesus has come to the land, and the
women will sit by the blue skirts of Mary, smiling with peace and
with love.

"So the old god reached the top of the mountain, and looked up   15
into the blue house of heaven. And through a door in the blue wall he
saw a great darkness, and stars and a moon shining. And beyond the
darkness he saw one great star, like a bright gateway.

"Then fire rose from the volcano around the old Quetzalcoatl, in
wings and glittering feathers. And with the wings of fire and the   20
glitter of sparks Quetzalcoatl flew up, up, like a wafting fire, like a
glittering bird, up, into the space, and away to the white steps of
heaven, that lead to the blue walls, where is the door to the dark. So
he entered in and was gone.

"Night fell, and Quetzalcoatl was gone, and men in the world saw   25
only a star travelling back into heaven, departing under the low
branches of darkness.*

"Then men in Mexico said: Quetzalcoatl has gone. Even his star
has departed. We must listen to this Jesus, who speaks in a foreign
tongue.   30

"So they learned a new speech from the priests that came from
upon the great waters to the east. And they became Christians—"

Julio, who had become absorbed, ended abruptly, as the tale of the
leaflet was ended.

"It is beautiful," said Kate.   35

"And it is true!" cried the sceptical Juana.

"It seems to me true," said Kate.

"Señora!" yelled Concha. "Is it true that heaven is up there, and
you come down steps like clouds to the edge of the sky, like the steps
from the mole into the lake? Is it true that El Señor comes and stands 40

on the steps and looks down at us like we look down into the lake to
see the charales?"

Concha shoved up her fierce swarthy face, and shook her masses
of hair, glaring at Kate, waiting for an answer.

5   "I don't know everything," laughed Kate. "But it seems to me
true."

"She believes it," said Concha, turning her face to her mother.

"And is it true," asked Juana, "that El Señor, el Cristo del
Mundo, is a gringo, and that He comes from your country, with his
10 Holy Mother?"

"Not from my country, but from a country near."

"Listen!" exclaimed Juana, awestruck. "El Señor is a gringuito,
and his Holy Mother is a gringuita. Yes, one really knows. Look!
Look at the feet of the Niña! Pure feet of the Santísima!* Look!"—
15 Kate was barefoot, wearing sandals with a simple strap across the
foot. Juana touched one of the Niña's white feet, fascinated. "Feet of
the Santísima. And She, the Holy Mary, is a gringuita, She came
over the sea, like you, Niña?"

"Yes, She came over the sea!"

20   "Ah! You know it?"

"Yes. We know that."

"Think of it! The Santísima is a gringuita, and She came over the
sea like the Niña, from the countries of the Niña!" Juana spoke in a
wicked wonder, horrified, delighted, mocking.

25   "And the Lord is a gringuito—pure gringuito?" barked Concha.

"And Niña—It was the gringos who killed El Señor? It wasn't the
Mexicans? It was those other gringos who put Him on the Cross?"

"Yes!" said Kate. "It wasn't the Mexicans."

"The gringos?"

30   "Yes, the gringos."

"And He himself was a gringo?"

"Yes!" said Kate, not knowing what else to say.

"Look!" said Juana, in her hushed, awed, malevolent voice. "He
was a gringo, and the gringos put him on the Cross."

35   "But a long time ago," said Kate hastily.

"A long time ago, says the Niña," echoed Juana, in her awed voice.

There was a moment of silence. The dark faces of the girls and
men seated on the ground were turned up to Kate, watching her
fixedly, in the half light, counting every word. In the outer air,
40 thunder muttered in different places.

"And now, Niña," came the cool, clear voice of María del Carmen, "El Señor is going back again to his Father, and our Quetzalcoatl is coming back to us?"

"And the Santísima is leaving us?" put in the hurried voice of Juana. "Think of it! The Santísima is leaving us, and this Quetzalcoatl is coming! He has no mother, he!"

"Perhaps he has a wife," said Kate.

"*Quién sabe!*" murmured Juana.

"They say," said the bold Concha, "that in Paradise he has grown young."

"Who?" asked Juana.

"I don't know how they call him," muttered Concha, ashamed to say the word.

"Quetzalcoatl!" said Ezequiel, in his barking, strong young voice. "Yes, he is young. He is a god in the flower of life, and finely built."

"They say so! They say so!" murmured Juana. "Think of it!"

"Here it says so!" cried Ezequiel. "Here it is written. In the Second Hymn."

"Read it then, Julio."

And Julio, now nothing loth, took out a second paper.

"I, Quetzalcoatl, of Mexico, I travelled the longest journey.*

"Beyond the blue outer wall of heaven, beyond the bright place of the sun, across the plains of darkness where the stars spread out like trees, like trees and bushes, far away to the heart of all the worlds, low down like the Morning Star.

"And at the heart of all the worlds those were waiting whose faces I could not see. And in voices like bees they murmured among themselves: *This is Quetzalcoatl whose hair is white with fanning the fires of life. He comes alone, and slowly.*

"Then with hands I could not see, they took my hands, and in their arms that I could not see, at last I died.

"But when I was dead, and bone, they cast not my bones away, they did not give me up to the four winds, nor to the six.* No, not even to the wind that blows down to the middle of earth, nor to him that blows upward like a finger pointing, did they give me.

"*He is dead*, they said, *but unrelinquished.*

"So they took the oil of the darkness, and laid it on my brow and my eyes, they put it in my ears and nostrils and my mouth, they put it on the two-fold silence of my breasts, and on my sunken navel, and on my secret places, before and behind: and in the palms of my hands, and on the mounds of my knees, and under the tread of my feet.

"Lastly, they anointed all my head with the oil that comes out of the darkness. Then they said: He is sealed up. Lay him away.

5   "So they laid me in the fountain that bubbles darkly at the heart of all the worlds, far, far behind the sun, and there lay I, Quetzalcoatl, in warm oblivion.

"I slept the great sleep, and dreamed not.

"Till a voice was calling: Quetzalcoatl!

10   "I said: Who is that?

"No-one answered, but the voice said: Quetzalcoatl!

"I said: Where art thou?

"Lo! he said. I am neither here nor there. I am thyself. Get up.

"Now all was very heavy upon me, like a tomb-stone of darkness.

15   "I said: Am I not old? How shall I roll this stone away?

"How art thou old, when I am new man? I will roll away the stone. Sit up!

"I sat up, and the stone went rolling, crashing down the gulfs of space.

20   "I said to myself: I am new man. I am younger than the young and older than the old. Lo! I am unfolded on the stem of time like a flower, I am at the midst of the flower of my manhood. Neither do I ache with desire, to tear, to burst the bud; neither do I yearn away like a seed that floats into heaven. The cup of my flowering is
25   unfolded, in its middle the stars float balanced with array. My stem is in the air, my roots are in all the dark, the sun is no more than a cupful within me.

"Lo! I am neither young nor old, I am the flower unfolded, I am now.

30   "So I rose and stretched my limbs and looked around. The sun was below me in a daze of heat, like a hot humming-bird hovering at mid-day over the worlds. And his beak was long and very sharp, he was like a dragon.*

"And a faint star was hesitating wearily, wanting to pass.

35   "I called aloud, saying: Who is that?

My name is Jesus, I am Mary's son.
I am coming home.
My mother the moon is dark.

Brother, Quetzalcoatl,
40   *Hold back the wild hot sun.*

Bind him with shadow while I pass.
Let me come home.

"I caught the sun and held him, and in my shade the faint star slipped past, going slowly into the dark reaches beyond the burning of the sun. Then on the slope of silence he sat down and took off his sandals, and I put them on.

"How do they wear the wings of love, Jesus, the Mexican people?

"The souls of the Mexican people are heavy for the wings of love, they have swallowed the stone of despair.

"Where is your Lady Mother in the mantle of blue, she with comfort in her lap?

"Her mantle faded in the dust of the world, she was weary without sleep, for the voices of people cried night and day, and the knives of the Mexican people were sharper than the pinions of love, and their stubbornness was stronger than hope. Lo! the fountain of tears dries up in the eyes of the old, and the lap of the aged is comfortless, they look for rest. Quetzalcoatl, Sir, my mother went even before me, to her still white bed in the moon.*

"She is gone, and thou art gone, Jesus, the Crucified. Then what of Mexico?

"The images stand in their churches, Oh Quetzalcoatl, they don't know that I and my mother have departed. They are angry souls, Brother, my Lord! They vent their anger. They broke my churches, they stole my strength, they withered the lips of the Virgin. They drove us away, and we crept away like a tottering old man and a woman tearless and bent double with age. So we fled while they were not looking. And we seek but rest, to forget forever the children of men who have swallowed the stone of despair.

"Then said I: It is good, pass on. I, Quetzalcoatl, will go down. Sleep thou the sleep without dreams. Farewell at the cross-roads, Brother Jesus.

"He said: Oh Quetzalcoatl! They have forgotten thee. The feathered snake! The serpent-silent bird! They are asking for none of thee.

"I said: Go thy way, for the dust of earth is in thy eyes and on thy lips. For me the serpent of middle-earth sleeps in my loins and my belly, the bird of the outer air perches on my brow and sweeps her bill across my breast. But I, I am lord of two ways. I am master of up and down. I am as a man who is a new man, with new limbs and life, and the light of the Morning Star in his eyes. Lo! I am I! the lord of both ways. Thou wert lord of the one way. Now it leads thee to the sleep. Farewell!

"So Jesus went on towards the sleep. And Mary the Mother of Sorrows lay down on the bed of the white moon, weary beyond any more tears.

"And I, I am on the threshold. I am stepping across the border. I am Quetzalcoatl, lord of both ways, star between day and the dark."

There was silence as the young man finished reading.

Chapter XVI.

Cipriano and Kate.

On Saturday afternoons the big black *canoas* with their large square sails came slowly approaching out of the thin haze across the lake, from the west, from Tlapaltepec, with big straw hats and with blankets and earthenware stuff, from Ixtlahuacan and Jaramay and Las Yemas with mats and timber and charcoal and oranges, from Tuliapán and Cuxcueco and San Cristóbal* with boat-loads of dark-green, globular water-melons, and piles of red tomatoes, mangoes, vegetables, oranges: and boat-loads of bricks and tiles, burnt red, but rather friable; then more charcoal, more wood, from the stark dry mountains over the lake.

Kate nearly always went out about five o'clock, on Saturdays, to see the boats, flat-bottomed, drift up to the shallow shores, and begin to unload in the glow of the evening. It pleased her to see the men running along the planks with the dark-green melons, and piling them in a mound on the rough sand, melons dark-green like creatures with pale bellies. To see the tomatoes all poured out into a shallow place in the lake, bobbing about while the women washed them, a bobbing scarlet upon the water.

The long, heavy bricks were piled in heaps along the scrap of demolished break-water, and little gangs of donkeys came trotting down the rough beach, to be laden, pressing their little feet in the gravelly sand, and flopping their ears.

The cargadores were busy at the charcoal boats, carrying out the rough sacks.

"Do you want charcoal, Niña?" shouted a grimy cargador, who had carried her trunks from the station on his back.

"At how much?"

"Twenty-five reales the two sacks."

"I pay twenty reales."

"At twenty reales then, Señorita. But you give me two reales for the transport?"

"The owner pays the transport," said Kate. "But I will give you twenty centavos."

229

Away went the man, trotting barelegged, barefoot over the stony ground, with two large sacks of charcoal on his shoulders. The men carry huge weights, without seeming even to think they are heavy. Almost as if they liked to feel a huge weight crushing on their iron
5   spines, and to be able to resist it.

Baskets of spring guavas, baskets of sweet lemons called limas, baskets of tiny green and yellow lemons, big as walnuts; orange-red and greenish mangoes, oranges, carrots, cactus fruits in great abundance, a few knobby potatoes, flat, pearl-white onions, little
10 calabacitas and speckled green calabacitas like frogs, camotes cooked and raw—she loved to watch the baskets trotting up the beach past the church.

Then, rather late as a rule, big red pots, bulging red ollas for water-jars, earthenware casseroles and earthenware jugs with cream
15 and black scratched pattern in glaze, bowls, big flat earthenware discs for cooking tortillas—much earthenware.

On the west shore, men running up the beach wearing twelve enormous hats at once, like a trotting pagoda. Men trotting with finely woven huaraches and rough strip sandals. And men with a few
20 dark sarapes, with gaudy rose-pink patterns, in a pile on their shoulders.

It was fascinating. But at the same time, there was a heavy, almost sullen feeling on the air. These people came to market to a sort of battle. They came, not for the joy of selling, but for the sullen contest
25 with those who wanted what they had got. The strange, black resentment always present.

By the time the church bells clanged for sunset, the market had already begun. On all the pavements round the plaza squatted the Indians with their wares, pyramids of green water-melons, arrays of
30 rough earthenware, hats in piles, pairs of sandals side by side, a great array of fruit, a spread of collar-studs and knick-knacks, called *novedades*, little trays with sweets. And people arriving all the time out of the wild country, with laden asses.

Yet never a shout, hardly a voice to be heard. None of the
35 animation and the frank wild clamour of a Mediterranean market. Always the heavy friction of the will: always, always, grinding upon the spirit, like the grey-black grind of lava-rock.

When dark fell, the vendors lighted their tin torch-lamps, and the flames wavered and streamed as the dark-faced men squatted on the
40 ground in their white clothes and big hats, waiting to sell. They never

asked you to buy. They never showed their wares. They didn't even look at you. It was as if their static resentment and indifference would hardly let them sell at all.

Kate sometimes felt the market cheerful and easy. But more often she felt an unutterable weight slowly, invisibly sinking on her spirits. And she wanted to run. She wanted, above all, the comfort of Don Ramón and the Hymns of Quetzalcoatl. This seemed to her the only escape from a world gone ghastly.

There was talk of revolution again, so the market was uneasy and grinding the black grit into the spirit. Foreign-looking soldiers were about, with looped hats, and knives and pistols, and savage northern faces: tall, rather thin figures. They would loiter about in pairs, talking in a strange northern speech, and seeming more alien even than Kate herself.

The food-stalls were brilliantly lighted. Rows of men sat at the plank boards, drinking soup and eating hot food with their fingers. The milkman rode in on horseback, his two big cans of milk slung before him, and he made his way slowly through the people to the food-stalls. There, still sitting unmoved on horseback, he delivered bowls of milk from the can in front of him, and then, on horseback like a monument, took his supper, his bowl of soup, and his plate of tamales, or of minced, fiery meat spread on tortillas. The peons drifted slowly round. Guitars were sounding, half-secretly. A motor-car worked its way in from the city, choked with people, girls, young men, city papas, children, in a pile.

The thick press of life, above the flare of torches upon the ground! The throng of white-clad, big-hatted men circulating slowly, the women with dark rebozos slipping silently. Dark trees overhead. The doorway of the hotel bright with electricity. Girls in organdie frocks, white, cherry-red, blue, from the city. Groups of singers singing inwardly. And all the noise subdued, suppressed.

The sense of strange, heavy suppression, the dead black power of negation in the souls of the peons. It was almost pitiful to see the pretty, pretty slim girls from Guadalajara going round and round, their naked arms linked together, so light in their gauzy, scarlet, white, blue, orange dresses, looking for someone to look at them, to take note of them. And the *peón* men only emitting from their souls the black vapor of negation, that perhaps was hate. They seemed, the natives, to have the power of blighting the air with their black, rock-bottom resistance.

Kate almost wept over the slim eager girls, pretty as rather papery flowers, eager for attention, but thrust away, victimised.

Suddenly there was a shot. The market-place was on its feet in a moment, scattering, pouring away into the streets and the shops. 5 Another shot! Kate, from where she stood, saw across the rapidly-emptying plaza a man sitting back on one of the benches, firing a pistol into the air. He was a lout from the city, and he was half drunk. The people knew what it was. Yet any moment he might lower the pistol and start firing at random. Everybody hurried silently, melting 10 away, leaving the plaza void.

Two more shots, pap-pap! still into the air. And at the same moment a little officer in uniform darted out of the dark street where the military station was, and where now the big hats were piled on the ground; he rushed straight to the drunkard, who was spreading his 15 legs and waving the pistol: and before you could breathe, *slap!* and again *slap!* He had slapped the pistol-firer first on one side of the face, then on the other, with slaps that resounded almost like shots. And in the same breath he seized the arm that held the pistol, and wrested the weapon away.

20 Two of the strange soldiers instantly rushed up and seized the man by the arms. The officer spoke two words, they saluted and marched off their prisoner.

Instantly the crowd was ebbing back into the plaza, unconcerned. Kate sat on a bench with her heart beating. She saw the prisoner pass 25 under a lamp, streaks of blood on his cheek. And Juana, who had fled, now came scuttling back and took Kate's hand, saying:

"Look! Niña! It is the General!"

She rose startled to her feet. The officer was saluting her.

"Don Cipriano!" she said.

30 "The same!" he replied. "Did that drunken fellow frighten you?"

"Not much! Only startled me. I didn't *feel* any evil intention behind it."

"No, only drunk."

"But I shall go home now."

35 "Shall I walk with you?"

"Would you care to?"

He took his place at her side, and they turned down by the church, to the lake-shore. There was a moon above the mountains, and the air was coming fresh, not too strong, from the west. From the Pacific. 40 Little lights were burning ruddy by the boats at the water's edge,

some outside, and some inside, under the roof-tilt of the boat's little
inward shed. Women were preparing a mouthful of food.

"But the night is beautiful," said Kate, breathing deep.

"With the moon clipped away just a little," he said.

Juana was following close on her heels: and behind, two soldiers in
slouched hats.

"Do the soldiers escort you?"

"I suppose so," said he.

"But the moon," she said, "isn't lovely and friendly as it is in
England or Italy."

"It is the same planet," he replied.

"But the moonshine in America isn't the same. It doesn't make
one feel glad as it does in Europe. One feels it would like to hurt
one."

He was silent for some moments. Then he said:

"Perhaps there is in you something European, which hurts our
Mexican moon."

"But I come in good faith."

"European good faith. Perhaps it is not the same as Mexican."

Kate was silent, almost stunned.

"Fancy your Mexican moon objecting to me!" she laughed
ironically.

"Fancy your objecting to our Mexican moon!" said he.

"I wasn't," said she.*

They came to the corner of Kate's road. At the corner was a group
of trees, and under the trees, behind the hedge, several reed huts.
Kate often laughed at the donkey looking over the dry-stone low
wall, and at the black sheep with curved horns, tied to a bitten tree,
and at the lad, naked but for a bit of a shirt, fleeing into the corner
under the thorn screen. The corner, of course, was an improvised
W.C., and there was always a smell of human excrement.*

Kate and Cipriano sat on the verandah of the House of the
Cuentas. She offered him vermouth, but he refused.

They were still. There came the faint pip!—pip!—pip! from the
little electric plant just up the road, which Jesús tended. Then a cock
from beyond the bananas crowed powerfully and hoarsely.

"But how absurd!" said Kate. "Cocks don't crow at this hour."

"Only in Mexico," laughed Cipriano.

"Yes! Only here!"

"He thinks your moon is the sun, no?" he said, teasing her.

The cock crowed powerfully, again and again.

"This is very nice, your house, your patio," said Cipriano.

But Kate was silent.

"Or don't you like it?" he said.

5   "You see," she answered. "I have nothing to *do!* The servants won't let me do anything. If I sweep my room, they stand round and say *Qué Niña!** *Qué Niña!* as if I was standing on my head for their benefit. I sew, though I've no interest in sewing.—What is it, for a life?"

"And you read!" he said, glancing at the magazines and books.

10   "Ah, it is all such stupid, lifeless stuff, in the books and papers," she said.

There was a silence. After which he said:

"But what would you like to do? As you say, you take no interest in sewing.—You know the Navajo women, when they weave a blanket,

15 leave a little place for their soul to come out, at the end: not to weave their soul into it.*—I always think England has woven her soul into her fabrics, into all the things she has made. And she never left a place for it to come out. So now all her soul is in her goods, and nowhere else."

20   "But Mexico *has* no soul," said Kate. "She's swallowed the stone of despair, as the hymn says."

"Ah! You think so? I think not. The soul is also a thing you make, like a pattern in a blanket. It is very nice while all the wools are rolling their different threads and different colours, and the pattern

25 is being made. But once it is finished—then finished. It has no interest any more. Mexico hasn't started to weave the pattern of her soul. Or she is only just starting: with Ramón. Don't you believe in Ramón?"

Kate hesitated before she answered:

30   "Ramón, yes! I do!—But whether it's any good trying here in Mexico, as he is trying—" she said slowly.

"He *is* in Mexico. *He* tries here. Why should not you?"

"I?"

"Yes! You! Ramón doesn't believe in womanless gods, he says.

35 Why should you not be the woman in the Quetzalcoatl pantheon? If you will, the goddess!"

"I, a goddess in the Mexican pantheon?" cried Kate, with a burst of startled laughter.

"Why not?" said he.

40   "But I am not Mexican," said she.

"You may easily be a goddess," said he, "in the same pantheon with Don Ramón and me."

A strange, inscrutable flame of desire seemed to be burning on Cipriano's face, as his eyes watched her glittering. Kate could not help feeling that it was a sort of intense, blind *ambition*, of which she was partly an object: a passionate object also: which kindled the Indian to the hottest pitch of his being.

"But I don't feel like a goddess in a Mexican pantheon," she said. "Mexico is a bit horrible to me. Don Ramón is *wonderful*: but I'm so afraid they will destroy him."

"Come, and help to prevent it."

"How?"

"You marry me.—You complain you have nothing to do. Then marry me. Marry me, and help Ramón and me. We need a woman, Ramón says, to be with us. And you are the woman. There is a great deal to do."

"But can't I help without marrying anybody?" said Kate.

"How can you?" he said simply.

And she knew it was true.

"But you see," she said, "I have no *impulse* to marry you, so how can I?"

"Why?" he said.

"You see, Mexico is *really* a bit horrible to me. And the black eyes of the people *really* make my heart contract, and my flesh shrink. There's a bit of horror in it. And I don't want horror in my soul."

He was silent and unfathomable. She did not know in the least what he was thinking, only a black cloud seemed over him.

"Why not?" he said at last. "Horror is real. Why not a bit of horror, as you say, among all the rest?"

He gazed at her with complete, glittering earnestness, something heavy upon her.

"But—" she stammered in amazement.

"You feel a bit of horror for me too—But why not? Perhaps I feel a bit of horror for you too, for your light-coloured eyes and your strong white hands. But that is good."

Kate looked at him in amazement. And all she wanted was to flee, to flee away beyond the bounds of this gruesome continent.

"Get used to it," he said. "Get used to it that there must be a bit of fear, and a bit of horror in your life. And marry me, and you will find many things that are not horror. The bit of horror is like the sesame seed in the nougat, it gives the sharp, wild flavour. It is good to have it there."

He sat watching her with black, glittering eyes, and talking with strange, uncanny reason. His desire seemed curiously impersonal, physical, and yet not personal at all. She felt as if, for him, she had some other name, she moved within another species. As if her name were, for example, Itzpapalotl, and she had been born in unknown places, and was a woman unknown to herself.*

Yet surely, surely he was only putting his will over her!

She was breathless with amazement, because he had made her see the physical possibility of marrying him: a thing she had never even glimpsed before. But surely, surely it would not be *herself* who could marry him. It would be some curious female within her, whom she did not know and did not own.

He was emanating a dark, exultant sort of passion.

"I can't believe," she said, "that I could do it."

"Do it," he said. "And then you will know."

She shuddered slightly, and went indoors for a wrap. She came out again in a silk Spanish shawl, brown, but deeply embroidered in silver-coloured silk. She tangled her fingers nervously in the long brown fringe.

Really, he seemed sinister to her, almost repellant. Yet she hated to think that she merely was afraid: that she had not the courage. She sat with her head bent, the light falling on her soft hair and on the heavy, silvery-coloured embroidery of her shawl, which she wrapped round her tight, as the Indian women do their rebozos. And his black eyes watched her, and watched the rich shawl, with a peculiar intense glitter. The shawl, too, fascinated him.

"Well!" he said suddenly. "When shall it be?"

"What?" she said, glancing up into his black eyes with real fear.

"The marriage."

She looked at him, almost hypnotised with amazement that he should have gone so far. And even now, she had not the power to make him retreat.

"I don't know," she said.

"Will you say in August? on the first of August?"

"I won't say any time," she said.

Suddenly the black gloom and anger of the Indians came over him. Then again he shook it off, with a certain callous indifference.

"Will you come to Jamiltepec tomorrow to see Ramón?" he asked.
"He wants to speak with you."

Kate also wanted to see Ramón: she always did.

"Shall I?" she said.

"Yes! Come with me in the morning in the automobile. Yes?"

"I would like to see Don Ramón again," she said.

"You are not afraid of him, eh?—not the bit of horror, eh?"—he said, smiling peculiarly.

"No. But Don Ramón isn't really Mexican," she said.

"Not really Mexican?"

"No! He feels European."

"Really! To me he is—Mexico."

She paused and gathered herself together.

"I will row in a boat to Jamiltepec tomorrow—or I will take Alonso's motor-boat. I will come about ten o'clock."

"Very good!" said Cipriano, rising to leave.

When he had gone, she heard the sound of the drum from the plaza. It would be another meeting of the Men of Quetzalcoatl. But she had not the desire nor the courage to set out afresh that day.

Instead, she went to bed, and lay breathing the inner darkness. Through the window-cracks she saw the whiteness of the moon, and through the walls she heard the small pulse of the drum. And it all oppressed her and made her afraid. She lay forming plans to escape. She must escape. She would hurriedly pack her trunks and disappear: perhaps take the train to Manzanillo, on the coast, and thence sail up to California, to Los Angeles or to San Francisco. Suddenly escape, and flee away to a white man's country, where she could once more breathe freely. How good it would be!—Yes, this was what she would do.

The night grew late, the drum ceased, she heard Ezequiel come home and lie down on the mattress outside her door. The only sound was the hoarse crowing of cocks in the moonlit night. And in her room, like someone striking a match, came the greenish light of a firefly, intermittent, now here, now there.

Thoroughly uneasy and cowed, she went to sleep. But then she slept deeply.

And curiously enough, she awoke in the morning with a new feeling of strength. It was six o'clock, the sun was making yellow pencils through her shutter-cracks. She threw open her window to the street, and looked through the iron grating at the little lane with

deep shadow under the garden wall, and above the wall, banana
leaves fraying translucent green, and shaggy mops of palm-trees
perching high, towards the twin white tower-tips of the church,
crowned by the Greek cross, with four equal arms.

5   In the lane it was already motion: big cows marching slowly to the
lake, under the bluish shadow of the wall, and a small calf, big-eyed
and adventurous, trotting aside to gaze through her gate at the
green-watered grass and the flowers. The silent peon, following,
lifted his two arms with a sudden swoop upwards, noiselessly, and
10   the calf careered on. Only the sound of feet of calves.

Then two boys vainly trying to urge a young bull-calf to the lake. It
kept on jerking up its sharp rump, and giving dry little kicks, from
which the boys ran away. They pushed its shoulder, and it butted
them with its blunt young head. They were in the state of semi-
15   frenzied bewilderment which the Indians fall into when they are
opposed and frustrated. And they took the usual recourse of running
to a little distance, picking up heavy stones, and hurling them
viciously at the animal.

"No!" cried Kate from her window. "Don't throw stones. Drive it
20   sensibly!"

They started as if the skies had opened, dropped their stones, and
crept very much diminished after the see-sawing bull-calf.

An ancient crone appeared at the window with a plate of chopped-
up young cactus leaves, for three centavos. Kate didn't like cactus
25   vegetable,* but she bought it. An old man was thrusting a young
cockerel through the window-bars.

"Go," said Kate, "into the patio."

And she shut her window on the street, for the invasion had
begun.

30   But it had only changed doors.

"Niña! Niña!" came Juana's voice. "Says the old man that you buy
this chicken?"

"At how much?" shouted Kate, slipping on a dressing gown.

"At ten reales."

35   "Oh no!" said Kate, flinging open her patio doors, and appearing
in her fresh wrap of pale pink cotton crape, embroidered with heavy
white flowers. "Not more than a peso!"

"A peso and ten centavos!" pleaded the old man, balancing the
staring-eyed young red cock between his hands. "He is nice and fat,
40   Señorita. See!"

And he held out the cock for Kate to take it and balance it between her hands, to try its weight.—She motioned to him to hand it to Juana. The red cock fluttered, and suddenly crowed in the transfer. Juana balanced him, and made a grimace.

"No, only a peso!" said Kate.

The man gave a sudden gesture of assent, received the peso, and disappeared like a shadow. Concha lurched up and took the cock, and instantly she bawled in derision:

"*Está muy flaco!* He is very thin."

"Put him in the pen," said Kate. "We'll let him grow."

The patio was liquid with sunshine and shadows. Ezequiel had rolled up his mattress and gone. Great rose-coloured hibiscus dangled from the tips of their boughs, there was a faint scent from the half-wild, creamy roses. The great mango trees were most sumptuous in the morning, like cliffs, with their hard green fruits dropping like the organs of some animal from the new bronze leaves, so curiously heavy with life.

"*Está muy flaco!*" the young Concha was bawling still in derision as she bore off the young cock to the pen under the banana trees. "He's very scraggy."

Everybody watched intent while the red cock was put in among the few scraggy fowls. The grey cock, elder, retreated to the far end of the pen, and eyed the new-comer with an eye of thunder. The red cock, *muy flaco*, stood diminished in a dry corner. Then suddenly he stretched himself and crowed shrilly, his red gills lifted like an aggressive beard. And the grey cock stirred around, preparing the thunders of his vengeance. The hens took not the slightest notice.

Kate laughed, and went back to her room to dress, in the powerful newness of the morning. Outside her window the women were passing quietly, the red water-jar on one shoulder, going to the lake for water. They always put one arm over their head, and held the jar on the other shoulder. It had a contorted look, different from the proud way the women carried water in Sicily.

"Niña! Niña!" Juana was crying outside.

"Wait a minute," said Kate.

It was another of the hymn-sheets, with a Hymn of Quetzalcoatl.

"See, Niña, the new hymn from last evening."

Kate took the leaflet and sat upon her bed to read it.

Quetzalcoatl Looks Down on Mexico.

Jesus had gone far up the dark slope, when he looked back.
Quetzalcoatl, my brother! he called. Send me my images.
And the images of my mother, and the images of my saints.
5   Send me them by the swift way, the way of the sparks,
That I may hold them like memories in my arms when I go to
    sleep.

And Quetzalcoatl called back: I will do it.

Then he laughed, seeing the sun dart fiercely at him.
10   He put up his hand, and held back the sun with his shadow.

So he passed the yellow one, who lashed like a dragon in
    vain.
And having passed the yellow one, he saw the earth beneath.
And he saw Mexico lying like a dark woman with white
15   breast-tips.

Wondering, he stepped nearer, and looked at her—
At her ruins, at her railways and her automobiles,
At her cities of stone and her huts of straw.
And he said: Surely this looks very curious!

20   He sat within the hollow of a cloud, and saw the men that
    worked in the fields, with foreign overseers.
He saw the men that were blind, reeling with aguardiente.
He saw the women that were not clean.
He saw the hearts of them all, that were black, and heavy,
25   with a stone of anger at the bottom.

Surely, he said, this is a curious people I have found!

So leaning forward on his cloud, he said to himself:
I will call to them.
Holá! Holá! Mexicanos! Glance away a moment towards me.
30   *Just turn your eyes this way, Mexicanos!*

They turned not at all, they glanced not one his way.

Holálá! Mexicanos! Holálá!
Quetzalcoatl sat on a cloud and dangled his feet, singing
    Holálá, Mexicanos!
35   They have gone stone deaf! he said.

So he blew down on them, to blow his breath in their faces.
But in the weight of their stupefaction, none of them knew.

Holálá! What a pretty people!
All gone stupefied!

A falling star was running like a white dog over a plain.
He whistled to it loudly, twice, till it fell to his hand.
In his hand it lay and went dark.
It was the Stone of Change.

This is the Stone of Change! he said.

So he tossed it awhile in his hand, and played with it.
Then suddenly he spied the old lake, and he threw it in.
It fell in.
And two men looked up.

Holálá! he said. *Mexicanos!*
Are there two of you awake?
So he laughed, and one heard him laughing.

Why are you laughing? asked the First Man of Quetzalcoatl.

I hear the voice of my First Man ask me why I am laughing.
Holálá, Mexicanos! It is funny!
To see them so glum and so lumpish!

Hey! First Man of my name! Hark here!
Here is my sign.
Get a place ready for me.
Send Jesus his images back, Mary and the saints and all.
Wash yourself, and rub oil in your skin.
On the seventh day, let every man wash himself, and put oil
    on his skin: let every woman.
Let him have no animal walk on his body, nor through the
    shadow of his hair. Say the same to the women.
Tell them they all are fools, that I'm laughing at them.
The first thing I did when I saw them, was to laugh at the
    sight of such fools.
Such lumps, such frogs with stones in their bellies.
Tell them they are like frogs with stones in their bellies, can't
    hop!

Tell them they must get the stones out of their bellies,
Get rid of their heaviness,
Their lumpishness,
Or I'll smother them all.

I'll shake the earth, and swallow them up, with their cities.
I'll send fire and ashes upon them, and smother them all.
I'll turn their blood like sour milk rotten with thunder,*
They will bleed rotten blood, in pestilence.
5   Even their bones shall crumble.

Tell them so, First Man of my name.

For the sun and the moon are alive, and watching with
    gleaming eyes.
And the earth is alive, and ready to shake off his fleas.
10 And the stars are ready with stones to throw in the faces of
    men.
And the air that blows good breath in the nostrils of people
    and beasts
Is ready to blow bad breath upon them, to perish them all.

15 The stars and the earth and the sun and the moon and the
    winds
Are about to dance the war dance round you, men!
When I say the word, they will start.
For sun and stars and earth and the very rains are weary
20 Of tossing and rolling the substance of life to your lips.
They are saying to one another: Let us make an end
Of these ill-smelling tribes of men, these frogs that can't
    jump,
These cocks that can't crow
25 These pigs that can't grunt
This flesh that smells
These words that are all flat
These money-vermin.
These white men, and red men, and yellow men, and brown
30   men, and black men
That are neither white, nor red, nor yellow, nor brown, nor
    black
But every one of them dirtyish.
Let us have a spring cleaning in the world.
35 For men upon the body of the earth are like lice,
Devouring the earth into sores.

This is what stars and sun and earth and moon and winds
    and rain

Are discussing with one another; they are making ready to
  start.

So tell the men I am coming to,
To make themselves clean, inside and out.
To roll the grave-stone off their souls, from the cave of their   5
  bellies,
To prepare to be men.

Or else prepare for the other things.

Kate read this long leaflet again, and again, and again, and a swift
darkness like a whirlwind seemed to envelop the morning. She drank 10
her coffee on the verandah, and the heavy papayas in their grouping
seemed to be oozing like great drops from the invisible spouting of
the fountain of non-human life. She seemed to see the great
sprouting and urging of the cosmos, moving into weird life. And men
only like green-fly clustering on the tender tips, an aberration there. 15
So monstrous the rolling and unfolding of the life of the cosmos, as if
even iron could grow like lichen deep in the earth, and cease
growing, and prepare to perish. Iron and stone render up their life,
when the hour comes. And men are less than the green-fly sucking
the stems of the bush, so long as they live by business and bread 20
alone. Parasites on the face of the earth.

She strayed to the shore. The lake was blue in the morning light,
the opposite mountains pale and dry and ribbed like mountains in
the desert. Only at their feet, next the lake, the dark strip of trees and
white specks of villages. 25

Near her against the light five cows stood with their noses to the
water, drinking. Women were kneeling on the stones, filling red jars.
On forked sticks stuck up on the foreshore, frail fishing-nets were
hung out, drying, and on the nets a small bird sat facing the sun; he
was red as a drop of new blood, from the arteries of the air. 30

From the straw huts under the trees, her urchin of the mud-chick
was scuttling towards her, clutching something in his fist. He opened
his hand to her, and on the palm lay three of the tiny cooking-pots,
the ollitas which the natives had thrown into the water long ago, to
the gods. 35

"*Muy chiquitas!*"* he said, in his brisk way, a little, fighting
tradesman. "Do you buy them?"

"I have no money. Tomorrow!" said Kate.

"Tomorrow!" he said, like a pistol shot.

"Tomorrow."

He had forgiven her, but she had not forgiven him.

Somebody in the fresh Sunday morning was singing rather beautifully, letting the sound, as it were, produce itself.

5　A boy was prowling with a sling, prowling like a cat, to get the little birds. The red bird like a drop of new blood twittered upon the almost invisible fish-nets, then in a flash was gone. The boy prowled under the delicate green of the willow trees, stumbling over the great roots in the sand.

10　Along the edge of the water flew four dark birds, their necks pushed out, skimming silent near the silent surface of the lake, in a jagged level rush.

Kate knew these mornings by the lake. They hypnotised her almost like death. Scarlet birds like drops of blood, in very green

15　willow trees. The *aguador* trotting to her house with a pole over his shoulder, and two heavy square gasoline cans, one at each end of the pole, filled with hot water. He had been to the hot spring for her daily supply. Now barefoot, with one bare leg, the young man trotted softly beneath the load, his dark, handsome face sunk beneath the

20　shadow of the big hat, as he trotted in a silence, a mindlessness that was like death.

Dark heads out on the water in little groups, like black water-fowl bobbing. Were they birds? Were they heads? Was this human life, or something intermediate, that lifted its orange, wet, glistening

25　shoulders a little out of the lake, beneath the dark head?

She knew so well what the day would be. Slowly the sun thickening and intensifying in the air overhead. And slowly the electricity clotting invisibly as afternoon approached. The beach in the blind heat, strewn with refuse, smelling of refuse and the urine of

30　creatures.

Everything going vague in the immense sunshine, as the air invisibly thickened, and Kate could feel the electricity pressing like hot iron on the back of her head. It stupefied her like morphine. Meanwhile the clouds rose like white trees from behind the moun-

35　tains, as the afternoon swooned in silence, rose and spread black branches, quickly, in the sky, from which the lightning stabbed like birds.

And in the midst of the siesta stupor, the sudden round bolts of thunder, and the crash and the chill of rain.

40　Tea-time, and evening coming. The last sailing-boats making to

depart, waiting for the wind. The wind was from the west, the boats
going east and south had gone, their sails were lapsing far away on
the lake. But the boats towards the west were waiting, waiting, while
the water ruttled* under their black, flat keels.

The big boat from Tlapaltepec, bringing many people from the   5
west, waited on into the night. She was anchored a few yards out, and
in the early night her passengers came down the dark beach, weary
of the day, to go on board. They clustered in a group at the edge of
the flapping water.

The big, wide, flat-bottomed *canoa* with her wooden awning and   10
her one straight mast lay black, a few yards out, in the dark night. A
lamp was burning under the wooden roof; one looked in, from the
shore. And this was home for the passengers.

A short man with trousers rolled up came to carry the people on
board. The men stood with their backs to him, legs apart. He   15
suddenly dived at them, ducked his head between the fork of their
legs, and rose, with a man on his shoulders. So he waded out through
the water to the black boat, and heaved his living load on board.

For a woman, he crouched down before her, and she sat on one of
his shoulders. He clasped her legs with his right arm, she clasped his   20
dark head. So he carried her to the ship, as if she were nothing.

Soon the boat was full of people. They sat on the mats of the floor,
with their backs to the sides of the vessel, baskets hanging from the
pent roof, swaying as the vessel swayed. Men spread their sarapes
and curled up to sleep. The light of the lantern lit them up, as they sat   25
and lay, and slept, or talked in murmurs.

A little woman came up out of the darkness: then suddenly ran
back again. She had forgotten something. But the vessel would not
sail without her, for the wind would not change yet.

The tall mast stood high, the great sail lay in folds along the roof,   30
ready. Under the roof, the lantern swayed, the people slept and
stretched. Probably they would not sail till midnight. Then down the
lake to Tlapaltepec, with its reeds at the end of the lake, and its dead,
dead plaza, its dead dry houses of black adobe, its ruined streets, its
strange, buried silence, like Pompeii.   35

Kate knew it. So strange and deathlike, it frightened her, and
mystified her.

But today! Today she would not loiter by the shore all morning.
She must go to Jamiltepec in a motor-boat, to see Ramón. To talk to
him even about marrying Cipriano.   40

Ah, how could she marry Cipriano, and give her body to this death? Take the weight of this darkness on her breast, the heaviness of this strange gloom. Die before dying, and pass away whilst still beneath the sun?

5   Ah no! Better to escape back to the white men's lands.

But she went to arrange with Alonso for the motor-boat.

Chapter XVII.

Fourth Hymn and the Bishop.*

The President of the Republic, as a new broom, had been sweeping perhaps a little too clean for the common liking, so there was a "rebellion."* It was not a very large one. But it meant, of course, 5 banditry, robbery, and cowed villages.

Ramón was determined to keep free from the taint of politics. But already the Church, and with the Church, the Knights of Cortés* and a certain "black" faction, was preparing against him. The priests began to denounce him from the pulpits—but not very loudly—as an 10 ambitious Anti-Christ. With Cipriano beside him, however, and with Cipriano the army of the west, he had not much to fear.

But it was possible Cipriano would have to march away in defence of the government.

"Above all things," said Ramón, "I don't want to acquire a 15 political smell. I don't want to be pushed in the direction of any party. Unless I can stand uncontaminated, I had better abandon everything. But the Church will push me over to the socialists—and the socialists will betray me on the first opportunity.—It is not myself. It is the new spirit. The surest way to kill it—and it can be killed, like 20 any other living thing—is to get it connected with any political party."

"Why don't you see the Bishop?" said Cipriano. "I will see him too. Am I to be chief of the division in the west, for nothing?"

"Yes," said Ramón slowly. "I will see Jiménez. I have thought of 25 it. Yes, I intend to use every means in my power.—Montes will stand for us, because he hates the Church and hates any hint of dictation from outside. He sees the possibility of a 'national' church.* Though myself, I don't care about national churches. Only one has to speak the language of one's own people.—You know the priests are 30 forbidding the people to read the Hymns?"

"What does that matter?" said Cipriano. "These people are nothing if not perverse, nowadays. They will read them all the more."

"Maybe!—I shall take no notice. I'll let my new legend, as they call 35 it, grow while the earth is moist.—But we have to keep our eye very close on all the little bunches of 'interests'."

"Ramón!" said Cipriano. "If you can turn Mexico entirely into a Quetzalcoatl country, what then?"

"I shall be First Man of Quetzalcoatl—I know no more."

"You won't trouble about the rest of the world?"

Ramón smiled. Already he saw in Cipriano's eye the gleam of a Holy War.

"I would like," he said, smiling, "to be one of the Initiates of the Earth. One of the Initiators. Every country its own Saviour, Cipriano: or every people its own Saviour. And the First Men of every people, forming a Natural Aristocracy of the World. One must have aristocrats, that we know. But natural ones, not artificial. And in some way the world must be organically united: the world of man. But in the concrete, not in the abstract. Leagues and Covenants and International Programmes: Ah! Cipriano! it's like an international pestilence. The leaves of one great tree can't hang on the boughs of another great tree. The races of the earth are like trees, in the end they neither mix nor mingle. They stand out of each other's way, like trees. Or else they crowd on one another, and their roots grapple, and it is the fight to the death.—Only from the flowers there is commingling. And the flowers of every race are the natural aristocrats of that race. And the spirit of the world can fly from flower to flower, like a hummingbird, and slowly fertilise the great trees in their blossoms.—Only the Natural Aristocrats can rise above their nation into the upper air, like flowers above the leaves of a tree. And even then, they do not rise beyond their race. Only the Natural Aristocrats of the World* can be international, or cosmopolitan, or cosmic. It has always been so. The peoples are no more capable of it, than the leaves of the mango tree are capable of attaching themselves to the pine.—So if I want Mexicans to learn the name of Quetzalcoatl, it is because I want them to speak with the tongues of their own blood. I wish the Teutonic world would once more think in terms of Thor and Wotan, and the tree Igdrasil. And I wish the Druidic world would see, honestly, that in the mistletoe is their mystery, and that they themselves are the Tuatha De Danaan, alive, but submerged. And a new Hermes should come back to the Mediterranean, and a new Ashtaroth to Tunis; and Mithras again to Persia, and Brahma unbroken to India, and the oldest of dragons to China.—Then I, Cipriano, I, First Man of Quetzalcoatl, with you, First Man of

Huitzilopochtli, and perhaps your wife, First Woman of Itzpapalotl, could we not meet, with sure souls, the other great aristocrats of the world, the First Man of Wotan and the First Woman of Freya,* First Lord of Hermes, and the Lady of Astarte, the Best-Born of Brahma, and the Son of the Greatest Dragon? I tell you, Cipriano, then the earth might rejoice, when the First Lords of the West met the First Lords of South and East, in the Valley of the Soul. Ah, the earth has Valleys of the Soul, that are not cities of commerce and industry. And the mystery is one mystery, but men must see it differently. The hibiscus and the thistle and the gentian all flower on the Tree of Life, but in the world they are far apart: and they must be. And I am hibiscus and you are a yucca flower, and your Caterina is a wild daffodil, and my Carlota is a white pansy. Only four of us, yet we make a curious bunch. So it is. The men and women of the earth are not manufactured goods, to be interchangeable. But the Tree of Life is one tree, as we know when our souls open in the last blossoming. We can't change ourselves, and we don't want to. But when our souls open out in the final blossoming, then as blossoms we share one mystery with all blossoms, beyond the knowledge of any leaves and stems and roots: something transcendent.

"But it doesn't matter. At the present time I have to fight my way in Mexico, and you have to fight yours. So let us go and do it."

He went away to his workshops and his men who were laboring under his directions, while Cipriano sat down to his correspondence, and his military planning.

They were both interrupted by the thudding of a motor-boat entering the little bay. It was Kate, escorted by the black-scarved Juana.

Ramón, in his white clothes with the blue-and-black figured sash, and the big hat with the turquoise-inlaid Eye of Quetzalcoatl, went down to meet her. She was in white, too, with a green hat and the shawl of pale yellow silk.

"I was so glad to come again," she said, holding out her hand to him. "Jamiltepec has become a sort of Mecca to me, my inside yearns for it."

"Then why don't you come oftener? I wish you would come."

"I am afraid of intruding."

"No! You could help if you would."

"Oh!" she said. "I am so frightened, and so sceptical of big undertakings. I think it is because, at the very bottom of me, I dislike the masses of people—anywhere. I'm afraid I rather despise people; I don't want them to touch me, and I don't want to touch them.—So how could I pretend to join any—any—any sort of Salvation Army?—which is a horrid way of putting it."

5   Don Ramón laughed.

"I do myself," he said. "I detest and despise masses of people. But these are my own people."

"I, ever since I was a child, since I can remember.—They say of me, when I was a little girl of four, and my parents were having a big

10 dinner party, they had the nurse bring me in to say goodnight to all the people they had there dressed up and eating and drinking. And I suppose they all said nice things to me, as they do. I only answered: *You are all monkeys!* It was a great success!—But I felt it even as a child, and I feel it now. People are all monkeys to me, performing in

15 different ways."

"Even the people nearest you?"

Kate hesitated. Then she confessed, rather unwillingly:

"Yes! I'm afraid so. Both my husbands—even Joachim—they seemed, somehow, so *obstinate* in their little stupidities—rather like

20 monkeys. I felt a terrible revulsion from Joachim when he was dead. I thought: What peaked monkey is that, that I have been losing my blood about.—Do you think it's rather awful?"

"I do! But then I think we *all* feel like that, at moments. Or we would if we dared. It's only one of our moments."

25   "Sometimes," said she, "I think that is my *permanent* feeling, towards people.—I like the world, the sky and the earth and the greater mystery beyond. But people—yes, they are all monkeys to me."

He could see that, at the bottom of her soul, it was true.

30   "*Puros monos!*" he said to himself in Spanish. "*Y lo que hacen, puras monerías.*"

"Pure monkeys! And the things they do, sheer monkeydom!" Then he added: "Yet you have children?"

"Yes! Yes!" she said, struggling with herself. "My first husband's

35 children."

"And they?—*monos y no más?*"*

"No!" she said, frowning and looking angry with herself. "Only partly."

"It is bad," he said, shaking his head. "But then," he added,

40 "what are my own children to me, but little monkeys? And their

mother—and their mother—Ah no! Señora Caterina! It is no good. One must be able to disentangle oneself from persons, from people. If I go too near even to a rose-bush, it is a nasty thing that hurts me. One must disentangle oneself from persons and personalities, and see people as one sees the trees in the landscape. People in some way *dominate* you. In some way, humanity dominates your consciousness. So you must hate people and humanity, and you want to escape. But there is only one way of escape: to turn beyond them, to the greater life."

"But I do!" cried Kate. "I do nothing else. When I was with Joachim absolutely alone in a cottage, doing all the work myself, and knowing nobody at all, just living, and *feeling* the greater thing all the time: then I was free, I was happy."

"But he?" said Ramón. "Was he free and happy?"

"He was *really*. But that's where the monkeyishness comes in. He wouldn't let himself be content. He insisted on having *people* and a *cause*, just to torture himself with."

"Then why didn't you live in your cottage *quite* alone, and without him?" he said. "Why do you travel, and see people?"

She was silent, very angry. She knew she could not live quite alone. The vacuity crushed her. She needed a man there, to stop the gap, and to keep her balanced. But even when she had him, in her heart of hearts she despised him, as she despised the dog and the cat. Between herself and humanity there was the bond of subtle, helpless antagonism.

She was naturally quite free-handed and she left people their liberty. Servants would get attached to her, and casual people all liked and admired her. She had a strong life-flow of her own, and a certain assertive *joie de vivre*.

But underneath it all was the unconquerable dislike, almost *disgust* of people. More than hate, it was disgust. Whoever it was, wherever it was, however it was, after a little while this disgust overcame her. Her mother, her father, her sisters, her first husband, even her children whom she loved, and Joachim, for whom she had felt such passionate love, even these, being near her, filled her with a certain disgust and repulsion after a little while, and she longed to fling them down the great and final oubliette.

But there is no great and final oubliette: or at least, it is never final, until one has flung *oneself* down.

So it was with Kate. Till she flung herself down the last dark

oubliette of death, she would never escape from her deep, her
bottomless disgust with human beings. Brief contacts were all right,
thrilling even. But close contacts, or long contacts, were short and
long revulsions of violent disgust.

5　　　　She and Ramón had sat down on a bench under the white-
flowering oleander of the garden downstairs. His face was impassive
and still. In the stillness, with a certain pain and nausea, he realised
the state she was in, and realised that his own state, as regards
personal people, was the same. Mere *personal* contact, mere human
10　contact filled him too with disgust. Carlota disgusted him. Kate
herself disgusted him. Sometimes, Cipriano disgusted him.

But this was because, or when, he met them on a merely human,
personal plane. To do so was disaster: it filled him with disgust of
them and loathing of himself.

15　　　He had to meet them on another plane, where the contact was
different: intangible, remote, and without *intimacy*. His soul was
concerned elsewhere. So that the quick of him need not be bound to
anybody. The quick of a man must turn to God alone: in some way or
other.

20　　　With Cipriano he was most sure. Cipriano and he, even when they
embraced each other with passion, when they met after an absence,
embraced in the recognition of each other's eternal and abiding
loneliness: like the Morning Star.

But women would not have this. They wanted intimacy—and
25　intimacy means disgust. Carlota wanted to be eternally and closely
identified with Ramón, consequently she hated him and hated
anything which she thought drew him away from this eternal close
identification with herself. It was just a horror, and he knew it.

Men and women should know that they cannot, absolutely, meet
30　on earth. In the closest kiss, the dearest touch, there is the small gulf
which is none the less complete because it is so narrow, so *nearly*
non-existent. They must bow and submit in reverence, to the gulf.
Even though I eat the body and drink the blood of Christ, Christ is
Christ and I am I, and the gulf is impassable. Though a woman be
35　dearer to a man than his own life, yet he is he and she is she, and the
gulf can never close up. Any attempt to close it is a violation and the
crime against the Holy Ghost.*

That which we get from the beyond, we get it alone. The final me I
am, comes from the farthest off, from the Morning Star. The rest is
40　assembled. All that of me which is assembled from the mighty

cosmos can meet and touch all that is assembled in the beloved. But this is never the quick. Never can be.

If we would meet in the quick, we must give up the assembled self, the daily I, and putting off our selves one after the other, meet unconscious in the Morning Star. Body, soul and spirit can be transfigured into the Morning Star. But without transfiguration we shall never get there. We shall gnash at the leash.

Ramón knew what it was to gnash at his leashes. He had gnashed himself almost to pieces, before he had found the way to pass out in himself, in the quick of himself, to the Quick of all being and existence, which he called the Morning Star, since men must give all things names. To pass in the quick of himself, with transfiguration, to the Morning Star, and there, there alone meet his fellow man.

He knew what it was to fail even now, and to keep on failing. With Carlota he failed absolutely. She claimed him and he strained himself in resistance. Even his very naked breast, when Carlota was there, was self-conscious and assertively naked. But then that was because she claimed it as her property.

When men meet at the quick of all things, they are neither naked nor clothed; in the transfiguration they are just complete, they are not seen in part. The final perfect strength has also the power of innocence.

Sitting on the seat beside Kate, Ramón was sad with the sense of heaviness and inadequacy. His third Hymn was angry and bitter. Carlota almost embittered his soul. In Mexico, turbulent fellows had caught at his idea and burlesqued it. They had invaded one of the churches of the city, thrown out the sacred images, and hung in their place the grotesque papier-mâché Judas figures which the Mexicans explode at Easter time.* This of course made a scandal. And Cipriano, whenever he was away on his own for some time, slipped back into the inevitable Mexican general, fascinated by the opportunity for furthering his own personal ambition and imposing his own personal will. Then came Kate, with this centre of sheer repudiation deep in the middle of her, the will to explode the world.

He felt his spirits sinking again, his limbs going like lead. There is only one thing that a man really wants to do, all his life: and that is, to find his way to his God, his Morning Star, and be alone there. Then afterwards, in the Morning Star, salute his fellow man, and enjoy the woman who has come the long way with him.

But to find the way, far, far along, to the bright Quick of all things, this is difficult, and requires all a man's strength and courage, for himself. If he breaks a trail alone, it is terrible. But if every hand pulls at him, to stay him in the human places: if the hands of love drag at his entrails and the hands of hate seize him by the hair, it becomes 5 almost impossible.

This was how Ramón felt at the moment:—I am attempting the impossible. I had better either go and take my pleasure of life while it lasts, hopeless of the pleasure which is beyond all pleasures. Or else I had better go into the desert and take my way all alone, to the Star 10 where at last I have my wholeness, holiness. The way of the anchorites and the men who went into the wilderness to pray.—For surely my soul is craving for her consummation, and I am weary of the thing men call life. Living, I want to depart to where *I am*.

Yet, he said to himself, the woman that was with me in the 15 Morning Star, how glad I should be of her! And the man that was with me there, what a delight his presence would be! Surely the Morning Star is a meeting-ground for us, for the joy!

Sitting side by side on the bench, Ramón and Kate forgot one another, she thinking back on the past, with the long disgust of it all, 20 he thinking on into his future, and trying to revive his heavy spirits.

In the silence, Cipriano came out on to the balcony above, looking round. He almost started as he saw the two figures seated on the bench below, under the white oleander tree, miles apart, worlds apart, in their silence.

25 Ramón heard the step, and glanced up.

"We are coming up!" he called, rising and looking round at Kate. "Shall we go upstairs? Will you drink something cool, tepache, or squeezed oranges? There is no ice."

"I would like orange juice and water," she said.

30 He called to his servant and gave the order.

Cipriano was in the white pantaloons and blouse, like Ramón. But his sash was scarlet, with black curves, something like the markings on a snake.

"I heard you come. I thought perhaps you had gone away again," 35 he said, looking at her with a certain black reproachfulness: an odd, hesitating wistfulness of the barbarian, who feels himself at a loss. Then also a certain resentment.

"Not yet," she said.

Ramón laughed, and flung himself into a chair.

40 "The Señora Caterina thinks we are all monkeys, but perhaps this

particular monkey-show is the most amusing after all," he said. "So she will see a little more of it."

Cipriano, a real Indian, was offended in his pride, and the little black *impériale* on his chin seemed to become portentous.

"That's *rather* an unfair way of putting it!" laughed Kate.

The black eyes of Cipriano glanced at her in hostility. He thought she was laughing at him. And so, at the depths of her female soul, she was. She was jeering at him inwardly. Which no man can stand, least of all, a dark-skinned man.

"No!" she said. "There's something else besides that."

"Ah!" said Ramón. "Take care! A little mercy is a dangerous thing."

"No! Not mercy!" she said, flushing. "Why are you being horrid to me?"

"Monkeys always end by being horrid to the spectators," said Ramón.

She looked up at him, and caught the flash of anger in his eyes.

"I came," she said, "to hear about the Mexican pantheon. I was even given to understand I might be admitted."

"Ah, that is good!" laughed Ramón. "A rare specimen of the female monkey has been added to the Ramón menagerie!—I am sure you would be a good draw. There have been some pretty goddesses, I assure you, in the Aztec pantheon."

"How horrid!" she said.

"Come! Come!" he cried. "Let us keep to the bedrock of things, *Señora mía*. We are all monkeys. *Monos somos.—Ihr seid alle Affen!** Out of the mouths of babes and sucklings was it spoken, as Carlota said. You see that little male monkey, Cipriano. He had the monkey's idea of marrying you. Say the word. Marriage is a monkey's game. Say the word. He will let you go when you've had enough: and he's had enough: He is a *general* and a very great *jefe*. He can make you monkey-queen of monkey-Mexico, if it please you. And what should monkeys do, but amuse themselves! *Vamos! Embobémonos!*—Shall I be priest? *Vamos! Vamos!**"

He rose with sudden volcanic violence, and rushed away.

Cipriano looked at Kate in wonder. She had gone pale.

"What have you been saying to him?" he asked.

"Nothing!" she said, rising. "I'd better go now."

Juana was collected, and Alonso, and Kate set off back down the lake. She sat with a certain obstinate offendedness under the awning of the boat. The sun was terrifically hot, and the water blinded her. She put on black spectacles, in which she looked a monster.

"*Mucho calor, Niña! Mucho calor!*"* Juana was repeating behind her. The criada had evidently imbibed tepache.

On the pale-brown water little tufts of water-hyacinth were vaguely sailing, holding up the hand of a leaf for a sail. Everywhere the lake was dotted with these sailing tufts. The heavy rains had washed in flood down the Lerma river into the lake, washing the acres of *lirio* loose from the marshy end of the waters, thirty miles away, and slowly setting them travelling over all the expanse of the inland sea, till the shores began to be piled, and the far-off Santiago river, which flowed out of the lake, was choked.

That day Ramón wrote his Fourth Hymn.

What Quetzalcoatl Saw in Mexico.

Who are these strange faces in Mexico?
Palefaces, yellowfaces, blackfaces? These are no Mexicans!
Where do they come from, and why?

Lord of the Two Ways, these are the foreigners.
They come out of nowhere.
Sometimes they come to tell us things,
Mostly they are the greedy ones.

What then do they want?

They want gold, they want silver from the mountains,
And oil, much oil from the coast.
They take sugar from the tall tubes of the cane,
Wheat from the high lands, and maize;
Coffee from the bushes in the hot lands, even the juicy
    rubber.
They put up tall chimneys that smoke,
And in the biggest houses they keep their machines, that talk
And work iron elbows up and down,
And hold myriad threads from their claws!
Wonderful are the machines of the greedy ones!

And you, Mexicans and peons, what do you do?

We work with their machines, we work in their fields,
They give us pesos made of Mexican silver.
They are the clever ones.

Do you love them then?

We love them not, and never.
Their faces are ugly, yet they make wonderful things.
And their wills are like their machines of iron.
What can we do?

I see dark things rushing across the country.   5

Yea, Lord! Even trains and *camiones* and automobiles.

Trains and *camiones*, automobiles and aeroplanes.
How nice! says the *peón*, to go rushing in a train!
How nice, to get in the *camión*, and for twenty centavos, to be
     gone!   10
How nice, in the great cities, where all things rush, and huge
     lights flare bright, to wander and do nothing!
How nice to sit in the *cine*, where the picture of all the world
     dances before the eyes!
How nice if we could take all these things away from the   15
     foreigners, and possess them!
Take back our lands and silver and oil, take the trains and the
     factories and the automobiles
And play with them all the time!
How nice!   20

Oh fools! Mexicans and peons!
Who are you, to be masters of machines which you cannot
     make?
Which you can only break!
Those that can make are masters of these machines.   25
Not you, poor boobs.

How have these palefaces, yellowfaces crossed the waters of
     the world?
Oh fools! Mexicans and peons, with muddy hearts!
Did they do it by squatting on their hams?   30
You do nothing but squat on your hams, and stare with
     vacant eyes, and drink fire-waters, and quarrel and stab.
And then run like surly dogs at the bidding of paleface
     masters.

Oh dogs and fools, Mexicans and peons!   35
Watery-hearted, with wishy-washy knees.
Sulky in spirit, and inert.
What are you good for, but to be slaves, and rot away?

You are not worth a god!   .
Lo! the universe tangles its great dragons,
The dragons in the cosmos are stirring with anger again.
The dragon of the disappointed dead, that sleeps in the
5   snow-white north
Is lashing his tail in his sleep: the winds howl, the cold rocks
    round.
The spirits of the cold dead whistle in the ears of the world.*
Prepare for doom.

10 For I tell you, there are no dead dead, not even your dead.
There are dead that sleep in the waves of the Morning Star,
    with freshening limbs.
There are dead that weep in bitter rains.
There are dead that cluster in the frozen north, shuddering
15   and chattering among the ice
And howling with hate.
There are dead that creep through the burning bowels of the
    earth,
Stirring the fires to acid of bitterness.
20 There are dead that sit under the trees, watching with
    ash-grey eyes for their victims.
There are dead that attack the sun like swarms of black flies,
    to suck his life.
There are dead upon the moon, whistling at you.
25 There are dead that stand upon you, when you go in to your
    women,
And they dart to her womb, they fight for the chance to be
    born, they struggle at the gate you have opened,
They gnash when it closes, and hate the one that got in, to be
30   born again,
Child of the living dead, the dead that live and are not
    refreshed.

I tell you, sorrow upon you: you shall all die.
And being dead, you shall not be refreshed.
35 There are no dead dead.
Being dead, you shall rove like dogs with broken haunches
Seeking the offal and garbage of life, in the invisible lanes of
    the air.

The dead that have mastered fire live on, salamanders, in
40   fire.*

The dead of the water-lords rock and glimmer in the seas.
The dead of the steel machines go up in motion, *away!*
The dead of electric masters are electricity itself.

But the dead of those who have mastered nothing, nothing at all,   5
Crawl like masterless dogs in the back streets of the air,
Creeping for the garbage of life, and biting with venomous mouths.

Those that have mastered the forces of the world, die into the forces, they have homes in death.   10
But you! what have you mastered, among the dragon hosts of the cosmos?

There are dragons of sun and ice, dragons of the moon and the earth, dragons of salty waters, dragons of thunder;
There is the spangled dragon of the stars at large.   15
And far at the centre, with one unblinking eye, the dragon of the Morning Star.

Conquer! says the Morning Star. Pass the dragons, and pass on to me.
For I am sweet, I am the last and the best, the pool of new   20
life.

But lo! you inert ones, I will set the dragons upon you.
They shall crunch your bones.
And even then they shall spit you out, as broken-haunched dogs,   25
You shall have nowhere to die into.

Lo! in the back streets of the air, dead ones are crawling like curs!
Lo! I release the dragons! The great white one of the north,
Him of the disappointed dead, he is lashing and turning   30
round.
He is breathing cold corruption upon you, you shall bleed in your chests.

I am going to speak to the dragon of the inner fires,
He who housels the dead of the guns,   35
To withdraw his warmth from your feet, so your feet turn cold with death.

I am about to tell the dragon of the waters to turn round on you

And spue out corrosion into your streams, on your rains.

And I wait for the final day, when the dragon of thunder,
     waking under the spider-web nets
     Which you've thrown upon him, shall suddenly shake with
5   rage,
And dart his electric needles into your bones, and curdle your
     blood like milk with electric venom.

Wait! Only wait! Little by little it all shall come upon you.

Ramón put on his black city clothes, and a black hat, and went
10 himself with this hymn to the printer in the city. The sign of
Quetzalcoatl he had printed in black and red, and the sign of the
dragon,* at the end, in green and black and red. And the sheet was
folded.

Six soldiers of Cipriano's command took the bundles of hymns by
15 train: one to the Capital, one to Puebla and Jalapa, one to Tampico
and Monterrey, one to Torreón and Chihuahua, one to Sinaloa and
Sonora, and one to the mines in Pachuca, Guanajuato, and the
central region. Each soldier took only a hundred sheets. But in every
town there was a recognised Reader of the Hymns; or two, or three,
20 or four, or even ten Readers in one city. And Readers who went
round to the villages.

Because there was a strange, submerged desire in the people for
things beyond the world. They were weary of events, and weary of
news and the newspapers, weary even of the things that are taught
25 in education. Weary is the spirit of man with man's importunity.
Of all things human, and humanly invented, we have had enough,
they seemed to say. And though they took not much active notice
of the Hymns, they craved for them, as men crave for alcohol, as a
relief from the weariness and ennui of mankind's man-made
30 world.

Everywhere, in all towns and villages, at night-time the little
flames would be seen flickering, a cluster of people was seen,
sometimes standing, sometimes sitting upon the ground, listening to
the slow voice of some Reader.

35 More rarely, in some small, out-of-the-way plaza, would sound
the sinister thud of the tom-tom, beating out of the hollow of the
ages. And there would be two men with white sarapes barred with
blue and black, two more in dark sarapes with the blue edges. Then
the singing of the Songs of Quetzalcoatl, and perhaps the slow round

dance, with the ancient rhythm of the feet on the earth, belonging to aboriginal America.

For the old dances of the Aztecs and the Zapotecs, of all the submerged Indian races, are based upon the old, sinking bird-step of the Red Indians of the north. It is in the blood of the people: they cannot quite forget it. It comes back to them, with a sense of fear, and joy, and relief.

Of themselves, they dared not revive the old motion, nor stir the blood in the old way. The spell of the past is too terrible. But in the Songs and the Hymns of Quetzalcoatl, there spoke a new voice, the voice of a master and an authority. And though they were slow to trust, the slowest and the most untrusting, they seized upon the new-old thrill, with a certain fear, and joy, and relief.

The Men of Quetzalcoatl avoided the great market-places and centres of activity. They took their stand in the little, side places. On the rim of a fountain a man in a dark blanket with blue borders, or with the sign of Quetzalcoatl in his hat, would sit down and begin to read aloud. It was enough. The people lingered to listen. He would read to the end, then say: I have finished this reading of the Fourth Hymn of Quetzalcoatl. Now I will begin again.

In this way, by a sort of far-away note in the voice, and by the slow monotony of repetition, the thing would drift darkly into the consciousness of the listeners.

Already in the beginning there had been the scandal of the Judases. Holy Week, in Mexico City, is, to all appearance, the great week of Judas. Everywhere you see men carrying home in triumph the great, gaudily-varnished dolls of papier-mâché. They are all men-dolls, more or less lifelike grotesque. Most frequently it is a fat Mexican-Spanish hacendado, landowner and big farmer, who is represented with his tight trousers, sticking-out belly, and huge up-turned moustaches. The old-fashioned *patrón*. Some of the figures are like Punch, some are like harlequin.* But they all have rosy faces and the white man's get-up. You never see the dark-faced image of a native-blooded Mexican: always a stiff, haughty grotesque of a white man.

And all these are Judases. Judas is the fun of the fair, the victim, the big man of Holy Week, just as the skeleton, and the skeleton on horseback, is the idol of the first week in November, the days of the dead* and of all the saints.

On Easter Saturday the Judases are hung from the balconies, the string is lighted, and at length, *bang!* Shrieks of joy, Judas has exploded into nothingness, from a big cracker in the middle of him!—All the town is popping with Judases.

5   There was the scandal of the Holy Images* thrown out of one of the churches in Mexico City, and these Judases put in their place. The Church began to move.

But then the Church in Mexico has to move gingerly: it is not popular, and its claws are cut. The priests may not ring the church bells for more than three minutes. Neither priests nor monks may
10 wear any habit in the street, beyond the hideous black vest and white collar of the Protestant clergy. So that the priest shows himself as little as possible in the street, and practically never in the chief streets and the chief plazas.

Nevertheless, he still has influence. Processions in the streets are
15 forbidden, but not sermons from the pulpit, nor advice from the confessional. Montes, the President, had no love for the Church, and was meditating the expulsion of all foreign priests. The Archbishop himself was an Italian.* But he was also a fighter.

He gave orders to all the priests, to forbid the people from
20 listening to anything concerned with Quetzalcoatl, to destroy any hymn-sheet that might fall into their hands, and to prevent as far as possible the Hymns from being read, and the Songs from being sung, in the parishes.

But Montes had given orders to the police and the military, to
25 afford such protection to the Men of Quetzalcoatl as was accorded to any other law-abiding citizen.

Mexico is not Mexico for nothing, however, and already blood had been shed on both sides. This Ramón particularly wanted to avoid, as he felt that violent death was not so easily wiped out of the air and
30 out of the souls of men, as spilt blood was washed off the pavements.

Therefore, when he was in the city, he asked the Bishop of the West if he would consent to an interview with himself and Don Cipriano, and would he name the place. The Bishop—who was an old friend and adviser of Carlota, and who knew Ramón well
35 enough, replied that he should be pleased to see Don Ramón and the *Señor General* the next day, if they would be so good as to come to his house.

The Bishop no longer occupied the great episcopal palace. This was turned into the post-office building. But he had a large house
40 not far from the Cathedral, which had been presented by the faithful.

Ramón and Cipriano found the thin old man in a dusty, un-interesting library, waiting. He wore a simple black cassock, not too clean, with purple buttons. He received Ramón, who was in a black town suit, and Cipriano, who was in uniform, with an affable manner and suspicious looks. But he played at being the lively, genial old bird.

"Ah, Don Ramón, it is long since I saw you! How goes it, eh? Well, well? That is good! That is very good!"—And he patted Ramón on the sleeve like a fussy old uncle. "Ah, my General, much honour, much honour! Welcome to this poor house of yours. It is the house of your Honour! To serve you! Gentlemen! Won't you take a seat?"

They all sat down, in the dusty, dreary room, in the old leather chairs. The Bishop nervously looked at his thin old hands, at the fine, but rather dull amethyst ring he wore.

"Good! Señores!" he said, glancing up with his little black eyes. "At your service! Entirely at the service of your Honours!"

"Doña Carlota is in the city, Father. You have seen her?" said Ramón.

"Yes, son of mine," said the Bishop.

"Then you know the latest news about me. She told you everything."

"Somewhat! Somewhat! She spoke somewhat of you, the poor little thing. Thanks to God she has her sons with her. They are safely back in their native country, in good health."

"Did you see them?"

"Yes! Yes! Two of my dearest children! Very sympathetic, very intelligent, like their father, and like him, promising to be of very handsome presence.—Yes! Yes! Smoke if you will, my General. Don't hesitate."

Cipriano lit a cigarette. From old associations, he was nervous, albeit amused.

"You know all about what I want to do, Father?" said Ramón.

"I don't know all, son of mine, but I know enough. I wouldn't want to hear more. Eh!" he sighed. "It is very sad."

"Not so very sad, Father, if we don't make it sad.—Why make a sad thing out of it, Father? We are in Mexico for the most part Indians. They cannot understand the high Christianity, Father, and the Church knows it. Christianity is a religion of the spirit, and must needs be understood if it is to have any effect. The Indians cannot understand it, any more than the rabbits of the hills."

"Very good! Very good! Son of mine! But we can convey it to them. The rabbits of the hills are in the hands of God."

"No, Father, it is impossible. And without a religion that will connect them with the universe, they will all perish. Only religion
5   will serve: not socialism, nor education, nor anything."

"Thou speakest well," said the Bishop.

"The rabbits of the hills may be in the hands of God, Father. But they are at the mercy of men. The same with Mexico. The people sink heavier and heavier into inertia, and the Church cannot help
10 them, because the Church does not possess the key-word to the Mexican soul."

"Doesn't the Mexican soul know the voice of God?" said the Bishop.

"No, it doesn't. Your dog, your donkey, your servant may know
15 your voice, Father. But if you go out to speak to the birds on the lake, or the deer among the mountains, will they know your voice? Will they wait and listen?"

"Who knows? It is said they waited to listen to the Holy Francis of Assisi."

20   "Now, Father, we must speak to the Mexicans in their own language, and give them the clue-word to their own souls. I shall say *Quetzalcoatl*. If I am wrong, let me perish. But I am not wrong."

The Bishop fidgetted rather restlessly. He didn't want to hear all this. And he did not want to answer. He was impotent anyhow.

25   "Your Church is the Catholic Church, Father?"

"Surely!" said the Bishop.

"And Catholic Church means the Church of All, the Universal Church?"

"Surely, son of mine."

30   "Then why not let it be really catholic? Why call it catholic, when it is not only just one among many churches, but is even hostile to all the rest of the churches? Father, why not let the Catholic Church become really the Universal Church?"

"It is the Universal Church of Christ, my son."

35   "Why not let it be the Universal Church of Mohammed as well: since ultimately, God is One God, but the peoples speak varying languages, and each needs its own prophet to speak with its own tongue. The Universal Church of Christ, and Mohammed, and Buddha, and Quetzalcoatl, and all the others—*that* would be a
40 Catholic Church, Father."

"You speak of things beyond me," said the Bishop, turning his ring.

"Not beyond any man," said Don Ramón. "A Catholic Church is a church of all the religions, a home on earth for all the prophets and the Christs. A big tree under which every man who acknowledges the greater life of the soul, can sit and be refreshed. Isn't *that* the Catholic Church, Father?"

"Alas, my son, I know the Apostolic Church of Christ in Rome, of which I am a humble servant. I do not understand these clever things you are saying to me."

"I am asking you for peace, Father. I am not one who hates the Church of Christ, the *Roman* Catholic Church. But in Mexico I think it has no place. When my heart is not bitter, I am grateful forever to Christ, the Son of God. The affair of the Judases grieves me more than it does you, and the affairs of bloodshed are far bitterer to me."

"I am no innovator, my son, to provoke bloodshed."

"Listen! I am going to remove the holy images from the church at Sayula, with reverence, and with reverence burn them upon the lake. Then I shall put the image of Quetzalcoatl in the church at Sayula."

The Bishop looked up furtively. For some moments he said nothing. But his silence was furtive, cornered.

"Would you dare do that, Don Ramón?" he said.

"Yes! And I shall not be prevented. General Viedma is with me."

The Bishop glanced sideways at Cipriano.

"Certainly," said Cipriano.

"Nevertheless it is illegal," said the Bishop, with acid bitterness.

"What is illegal in Mexico?" said Ramón. "What is weak is illegal. I will not be weak, My Lord."

"Lucky you!" said the Bishop, lifting his shoulders.

There was a break of silence.

"No!" said Ramón. "I come to ask you for peace. Tell the Archbishop what I say. Let him tell the Cardinals and the Pope, that the time has come for a Catholic Church of the Earth, the Catholic Church of All the Sons of Men. The Saviours are more than one, and let us pray they will still be increased. But God is one God, and the Saviours are the Sons of the One God. Let the Tree of the Church spread its branches over all the earth, and shelter the prophets in its shade, as they sit and speak their knowledge of the beyond."

"Are you one of these prophets, Don Ramón?"

"I surely am, Father. And I would speak about Quetzalcoatl in Mexico, and build his Church here."

"Nay! You would invade the Churches of Christ and the Blessed
5 Virgin, I heard you say."

"You know my intentions.—But I do not want to quarrel with the Church of Rome, nor have bloodshed and enmity, Father. Can you not understand me? Should there not be peace between the men who strive down their different ways, to the God-Mystery?"

10 "Once more desecrate the altars! Bring in strange idols. Burn the images of Our Lord and Our Lady, and ask for peace?" said the poor Bishop, who helplessly longed to be left alone.

"All that, Father," said Ramón.

"Son, what can I answer? You are a good man smitten with the
15 madness of pride. Don Cipriano is one more Mexican general. I am the poor, old Bishop of this diocese, faithful servant of the Holy Church, humble child of the Holy Father in Rome. What can I do? What can I answer? Take me out to the cemetery and shoot me at once, General!"

20 "I don't want to," said Cipriano.

"It will end like that," said the Bishop.

"But why?" cried Don Ramón. "Is there no sense in what I say? Cannot you understand?"

"My son, my understanding goes no further than my faith, my
25 duty will allow. I am not a clever man. I live by faith, and my duty to my sacred office. Understand that I do not understand."

"Good-day, Father!" said Ramón, suddenly rising.

"Go with God, my son," said the Bishop, rising and lifting his fingers.

30 "*Adios, Señor!*" said Cipriano, clicking his spurs, and putting his hand on his sword as he turned to the door.

"*Adios, Señor General,*" said the Bishop, darting after them his eyes of old malice, which they could feel in their backs.

"He will say nothing," said Cipriano, as he and Ramón went down
35 the steps. "The old jesuit, he only wants to keep his job and his power, and prevent the heart's beating. I know them. All they treasure, even more than their money, is their centipede power over the frightened people: especially over the women."

"I didn't know you hated them," laughed Ramón.

"Waste no more breath on them, my dear one," said Cipriano. "Go forward, you can walk over broken snakes such as those."

As they went on foot past the post-office square, where the modern scribes at little tables under the arches, sat tapping out letters on their typewriters, for the poor and illiterate, who waited 5 with their few centavos to have their messages turned into florid Castilian, Ramón and Cipriano met with an almost startled respect.

"Why talk to the Bishop?—he doesn't exist any more. I hear his Knights of Cortés had a big dinner the other evening, and it is said—I don't believe it—that they drank oaths in blood to have my 10 life and yours. But I think the oaths of the Catholic Dames* would frighten me more. Why, if a man stops to unfasten his trousers to make water, the Knights of Cortés run for their lives, thinking the pistol is pointed at them.—Don't think about them, Man! Don't try to conciliate them. They will only puff up and become insolent, 15 thinking you are afraid of them. Six soldiers will trample down all that dirt," said the General.

It was the city, and the spirit of the city.

Cipriano had a suite in the big Palace on the Plaza de Armas.*

"If I marry," he said, as they passed into the stone patio, where 20 soldiers stood at attention, "I shall take a house in the colony,* to be more private."

Cipriano in town was amusing. He seemed to exude pride and arrogant authority as he walked about. But his black eyes, glancing above his fine nose and that little goat beard, were not to be laughed 25 at. They seemed to get everything, in the stab of a glance. A demoniacal little fellow.

Chapter XVIII.

Auto-da-Fé.

Ramón saw Carlota and his boys in the city, but it was a rather fruitless meeting. The elder boy was just uncomfortable in the presence [of] his father, but the younger, Cyprian, who was delicate and very intelligent, had a rather lofty air of displeasure with his parent.

"Do you know what they sing, Papa?" he said.

"Not all the things they sing," said Ramón.

"They sing—" the boy hesitated. Then, in his clear young voice, he piped up, to the tune of *La Cucaracha*:*

> Don Ramón don't drink, don't smoke.
> Doña Carlota wishes he would.
> He's going to wear the sky-blue cloak
> That he's stole from the Mother of God.

"No I'm not," said Ramón, smiling. "Mine's got a snake and a bird in the middle, and black zig-zags and a red fringe. You'd better come and see it."

"No Papa! I don't want to."

"Why not?"

"I don't want to be mixed up in this affair. It makes us all look ridiculous."

"But how do you think you look, anyhow, in your striped little sailor suit and your little saintly look? We'd better dress you as the Infant Jesus."

"No Papa! You are in bad taste. One doesn't say those things."

"Now you'll have to confess to a fib. You say one doesn't say those things, when I, who am your father, said them only a moment ago, and you heard me."

"I mean good people don't. Decent people."

"Now you'll have to confess again, for calling your father indecent.—Terrible child!"

The child flushed, and tears rose to his eyes. There was silence for a while.

"So you don't want to come to Jamiltepec?" said Ramón, to his
boys.

"Yes!" said the elder boy, slowly. "I want to come and bathe in the
lake, and have a boat. But—they say it is impossible."

"Why?" 5

"They say you make yourself a *peón*, in your clothes."—The boy
was shy.

"They're very nice clothes, you know. Nicer than those little
breeches of yours."

"They say, also, that you pretend to be the Aztec god 10
Quetzalcoatl."

"Not at all. I only pretend that the Aztec god Quetzalcoatl is
coming back to the Mexicans."

"But, Papa, it is not true."

"How do you know?" 15

"Because it is impossible."

"Why?"

"There never was any Quetzalcoatl, except idols."

"Is there any Jesus, except images?"

"Yes, Papa." 20

"Where?"

"In heaven."

"Then in heaven there is also Quetzalcoatl. And what is in heaven
is capable of coming back to earth. Don't you believe me?"

"I can't." 25

"Then go unbelieving," said the father, laughing at them and
rising to leave them.

"It is very bad that they sing songs about you, and put Mama in:
like about Pancho Villa," said the younger boy. "It hurts me very
much." 30

"Rub it with *Vapor-rub*,* my pet," said Ramón. "Rub it with
Vapor-rub, where it hurts you."

"What a real bad man you are, Papa!"

"What a real good child are you, my son! Isn't that so?"

"I don't know, Papa. I only know you are bad." 35

"Oh! Oh! Is that all they teach thee at thy American school?"*

"Next term," said Ciprianito,* "I want to change my name. I don't
want to be called Carrasco any more. When thou art in the
newspapers, they will laugh at us."

"Oh! Oh! I am laughing at thee *now*, little frog! What name wilt 40

thou choose then? Espina, perhaps. Thou knowest Carrasco is a wild
bush, on the moors in Spain, where we come from. Wilt thou be the
little thorn on the bush? Call thyself Espina, thou art a sprig of the
old tree. *Entonces, Adios! Señor Espina Espinita!*"*

5   "*Adios!*" said the boy abruptly, flushing with rage.

Ramón took a motor-car to Sayula, for there was a made road. But
already the rains were washing it away. The car lurched and bumped
in the great gaps. In one place, a *camión* lay on its back, where it had
overturned.

10   On the flat desert, there were already small smears of water, and
the pink cosmos flowers, and the yellow, were just sprouting their
tufts of buds. The hills in the distance were going opaque, as leaves
came out on the invisible trees and bushes. The earth was coming to
life.

15   Ramón called in Sayula at Kate's house. She was out, but the wild
Concha came scouring across the beach, to fetch her.—"There is
Don Ramón! There is Don Ramón!"

Kate hurried home, with sand in her shoes.

She thought Ramón looked tired, and in his black suit, sinister.

20   "I didn't expect you," she said.

"I am on my way back from town."

He sat very still, with that angry look on his creamy dark face, and
he kept pushing back his black moustache from his closed, angry
lips.

25   "Did you see anybody in town?" she asked.

"I saw Don Cipriano—and Doña Carlota, and my boys."

"Oh how nice for you! Are they quite well?"

"In excellent health, I believe."

She laughed suddenly.

30   "You are still cross," she said. "Is it about the monkeys still."

"Señora," he said, leaning forward, so that his black hair dropped
a little on his brow, "in monkeydom, I don't know who is prince. But
in the kingdom of fools, I believe it is I."

"Why?" she said.

35   And as he did not answer, she added:

"It must be a comfort to be a prince, even of fools."

He looked daggers at her, then burst into a laugh.

"Oh, *Señora mía!* What ails us men, when we are always wanting
to be *good?*"

40   "Are you repenting of it?" she laughed.

"Yes!" he said. "I am a prince of fools! Why have I started this Quetzalcoatl business? Why? Pray tell me why?"

"I suppose you wanted to."

He pondered for a time, pushing up his moustache.

"Perhaps it is better to be a monkey than a fool. I object to being called a monkey, nevertheless. Carlota is a monkey, no more: and my two boys are prize young monkeys in sailor suits. And I am a fool. Yet what is the difference between a fool and a monkey?"

"One wants to be good, and the other is sure he *is* good," said Kate.

"Right!" laughed Ramón. "I want to be good, so I make a fool of myself. They are sure they are always good, so that makes monkeys of them.—Oh, if only the world would blow up like a bomb!"

"It won't!" said Kate.

"True enough.—Ah well!"

He drew himself erect, pulling himself together.

"Do you think, Señora Caterina, you might marry our mutual General?"—Ramón had put himself aside again.

"I? I don't know!" stammered Kate. "I hardly think so."

"He is not sympathetic to you at all?"

"Yes. He is. He is alive, and there is even a certain fascination about him.—But one shouldn't try marrying a man of another race, do you think, even if he were more sympathetic?"

"Ah!" sighed Ramón. "It's no good generalising. It's no good marrying anybody, unless there will be a real fusion somewhere."

"And I feel there wouldn't," said Kate. "I feel he just wants something of me: and perhaps I just want something of him. But he would never meet me. He would never come forward in himself, to meet me. He would come to take something from me, and I should have to let him. And I don't want merely that. I want a man who will come half way, just half way, to meet me."

Don Ramón pondered, and shook his head.

"You are right," he said. "Yet in these matters, one never knows what is half way, nor where it is. A woman who just wants to be taken, and then to cling on, is a parasite. And a man who wants just to take, without giving, is a creature of prey."

"And I'm afraid Don Cipriano might be that," said Kate.

"Possibly," said Ramón. "He is not so with me. But perhaps he would be, if we did not meet—perhaps it is our half way—in some physical belief that is at the very middle of us, and which we recognise in one another. Don't you think there might be that between you and him?"

"I doubt if he'd feel it necessary, with a woman. A woman wouldn't be important enough."

5   Ramón was silent.

"Perhaps!" he said. "With a woman, a man always wants to let himself go. And it is precisely with a woman that he should never let himself go, but stick to his innermost belief, and meet her just there. Because when the innermost belief coincides in them both, if it's 10 physical, there, and then, and nowhere else, they can meet. And it's no good unless there is a meeting. It's no good a man ravishing a woman, and it's absolutely no good a woman ravishing a man. It's a sin, that is. There is such a thing as sin, and that's the centre of it. Men and women keep on ravishing one another. Absurd as it may 15 sound, it is not I who would ravish Carlota. It is she who would ravish me. Strange and absurd and a little shameful, it is true.—Letting oneself go, is either ravishing or being ravished. Oh, if we could only abide by our own souls, and meet in the abiding place.—Señora, I have not a very great respect for myself. Woman and I have failed 20 with one another, and it is a bad failure to have in the middle of oneself."

Kate looked at him in wonder, with a little fear. Why was he confessing to her? Was he going to love her? She almost suspended her breathing. He looked at her with a sort of sorrow on his brow, 25 and in his dark eyes, anger, vexation, wisdom, and a dull pain.

"I am sorry," he went on, "that Carlota and I are as we are with one another. Who am I, even to talk about Quetzalcoatl, when my heart is hollow with anger against the woman I have married and the children she bore me.—We never met in our souls, she and I. At first 30 I loved her, and she wanted me to ravish her. Then after a while a man becomes uneasy. He can't keep on wanting to ravish a woman, the same woman. He has revulsions. Then she loved me, and she wanted to ravish me. And I liked it for a time. But she had revulsions too. The eldest boy is really my boy, when I ravished her. And the 35 youngest is her boy, when she ravished me. See how miserable it is! And now we can never meet, she turns to her crucified Jesus, and I to my uncrucified and uncrucifiable Quetzalcoatl, who at least cannot be ravished."

"And I'm sure you won't make him a ravisher," she said.

40   "Who knows? If I err, it will be on that side. But you know, Señora,

Quetzalcoatl is to me only the symbol of the best a man may be, in the
next days. The universe is a nest of dragons, with a perfectly
unfathomable life-mystery at the centre of it. If I call the mystery the
Morning Star, surely it doesn't matter! A man's blood can't beat in
the abstract. And man is a creature who wins his own creation inch 5
by inch from the nest of the cosmic dragons.* Or else he loses it little
by little, and goes to pieces. Now we are all losing it, in the ravishing
and ravished disintegration. We must pull ourselves together, hard,
both men and women, or we are all lost. We must pull ourselves
together, hard." 10

"But are you a man who needs a woman in his life?" she said.

"I am a man who yearns for the sensual fulfilment of my soul,
Señora," he said. "I am a man who has no belief in abnegation of the
blood desires. I am a man who is always on the verge of taking wives
and concubines to live with me, so deep is my desire for that 15
fulfilment. Except that now I know that it is useless—not momen-
tarily useless, but in the long run—my ravishing a woman with hot
desire. No matter how much she is in love with me and desires me to
ravish her. It is no good, and the very inside of me knows it is no
good. Wine, woman, and song—all that—all that game is up. Our 20
insides won't really have it any more. Yet it is hard to pull ourselves
together."

"So that you really want a woman to be with you?" said Kate.

"Ah Señora! If I could trust myself: and trust her! I am no longer a
young man, who can afford to make mistakes. I am forty-two years 25
old, and I am making my last—and perhaps in truth, my first great
effort as a man. I hope I may perish before I make a big mistake."

"Why should you make a mistake? You needn't."

"I? It is very easy for me to make a mistake. Very easy, on the one
hand, for me to become arrogant and a ravisher. And very easy, on 30
the other hand, for me to deny myself, and make a sort of sacrifice of
my life. Which is being ravished. Easy to let myself, in a certain
sense, be ravished. I did it to a small degree even yesterday, with the
Bishop of Guadalajara. And it is bad. If I had to end my life in a
mistake, Señora, I had rather end it in being a ravisher, than in being 35
ravished. As a hot ravisher, I can still slash and cut at the disease of
the other thing, the horrible pandering and the desire men have to be
ravished, the hateful, ignoble desire they have."

"But why don't you do as you say, stick by the innermost soul that
is in you, and meet a woman there, meet her, as you say, where your 40

two souls coincide in their deepest desire? Not always that horrible unbalance that you call ravishing."

"Why don't I? But which woman can I meet in the body, without that slow degradation of ravishing, or being ravished, setting in? If I marry a Spanish woman or a dark Mexican, she will give herself up to me to be ravished. If I marry a woman of the Anglo-Saxon or any blonde northern stock, she will want to ravish me, with the will of all the ancient white demons. Those that want to be ravished are parasites on the soul, and one has revulsions. Those that want to ravish a man are vampires. And between the two, there is nothing."

"Surely there are *some* really good women?"

"Well, show me them. They are all potential Carlotas or—or—yes, Caterinas. I am sure you ravished your Joachim till he died. No doubt he wanted it: even more than you wanted it. It is not just sex. It lies in the will. Victims and victimisers. The upper classes, craving to be victims to the lower classes: or else craving to make victims of the lower classes. The politicians, craving to make one people victims to another. The Church, with its evil will for turning the people into humble, writhing things that shall crave to be victimised, to be ravished.—I tell you, the earth is a place of shame."

"But if *you* want to be different," said Kate, "surely a few other people do—really."

"It may be," he said, becoming calm. "It may be. I wish I kept myself together better. I must keep myself together, keep myself within the middle place, where I am still. My Morning Star.—Now I am ashamed of having talked like this to you, Señora Caterina."

"Why?" she cried. And for the first time, the flush of hurt and humiliation came into her face.

He saw it at once, and put his hand on hers for a moment.

"No," he said. "I am not ashamed. I am relieved."

She flushed deeply at his touch, and was silent. He rose hastily, to leave, craving to be alone again with his own soul.

"On Sunday," he said, "will you come into the plaza, in the morning, when the drum sounds? Will you come?"

"What for?" she said.

"Well! Come, and you will see."

He was gone in a flash.

There were many soldiers in the village. When she went to the post-office, she saw the men in their cotton uniforms lying about in the entrance to the military station. There must have been fifty or more, little men, not the tall soldiers in slouched hats. These were little, quick, compact men, like Cipriano, and they talked in a strange Indian language, very subdued. They were very rarely seen in the streets. They kept out of sight.

But at night, everyone was requested to be indoors by ten o'clock, and through the darkness Kate heard the patrols of horse-soldiers riding round.

There was an air of excitement and mystery in the place. The parish priest, a rather overbearing, fat man of fifty or so, had preached a famous Saturday evening sermon against Ramón and Quetzalcoatl, forbidding the heathen name to be mentioned, threatening with all the penalties any parishioner who read the Hymns, or even listened.

So of course, he was attacked when he left the church, and had to be rescued by soldiers who were in the doorway. They marched him safely home. But his criada, the old woman who served him, was told by more women than one that the next time the Padre opened his mouth against Quetzalcoatl, he would have a few inches of machete in his fat guts.

So his reverence stayed at home, and a curate officiated.

Practically all the people who came over the lake in boats on Saturdays, went to mass in Sayula church. The great doors stood open all the day. Men as they passed to and fro to the lake, took off their big hats, with a curious cringing gesture, as they went by the gateway of the church. All day long, scattered people were kneeling in the aisles or among the benches, the men kneeling erect, their big hats down by their knees, their curious tall-shaped Indian heads with the thick black hair also erect: only the kneeling legs, close together, humble. The women hooded themselves in their dark rebozos and spread their elbows as they kneeled at a bench, in a slack sort of voluptuousness.

On Saturday night, a great ruddy flickering of many candle-points, away down the dark cavern of the church: and a clustering of dark men's heads, a shuffling of women, a come and go of men arriving from the lake, of men departing to the market. A hush, not exactly of worship, but of a certain voluptuous admiration of the loftiness and glitter, a sensual, almost victimised self-abandon to the god of death, the Crucified streaked with blood, or to the pretty white woman in a blue mantle, with her little doll's face under her crown, Mary, the doll of dolls, Niña of Niñas.

It was not worship. It was a sort of numbness and letting the soul sink uncontrolled. And it was a luxury, after all the week of unwashed dullness in their squalid villages of straw huts. But it irritated Kate.

5 The men got up and tiptoed away in their sandals, crossing themselves front and back, on the navel and on the back of the head, with holy water. And their black eyes shone with a loose, sensuous look. Instead of having gathered themselves together and become graver, stronger, more collected and deep in their own integrity, they
10 emerged only the more loose and sloppy and uncontrolled.

Oh, if there is one thing men need to learn, but the Mexican Indians especially, it is to collect each man his own soul together deep inside him, and to abide by it. The Church, instead of helping men to this, pushes them more and more into a soft, emotional
15 helplessness, with the unpleasant sensuous gratification of feeling themselves victims, victimised, victimised, but at the same time, with the lurking sardonic consciousness that in the end a victim is stronger than the victimiser. In the end, the victims pull down their victimiser, like a pack of hyaenas on an unwary lion. They know it.—
20 Cursed are the falsely meek, for they are inheriting the earth.

On Sunday morning there was early mass at sunrise, another mass at seven o'clock, another at nine, another at eleven. Then there was a little band of violins and cellos, playing old-fashioned dance music: there was, especially early in the morning, a solid mass of peons and
25 women, kneeling on the floor: and a flapping of dusky candles, a smell of the exhaust air of candles, a heavy, rolling fume of incense, and the heavy choir of men's voices, solid, powerful, impressive, from the gallery.

And the people went away in sensuous looseness, which soon
30 turned, in the market, to hate, the old, unfathomable hate which lies at the bottom of the Indian heart, and which always rises black and turbid when they have swayed awhile in sensuous gratification.

The church inside was a dead interior, like all Mexican churches, even the gorgeous Puebla cathedral.* The interior of almost any
35 Mexican church gives the impression of cynical barrenness, cynical meaninglessness, an empty, cynical, mocking shell. The Italian churches are built much in the same style, and yet in them lingers a shadow and stillness of old, mysterious holiness. The hush.

But not in Mexico. The churches outside are impressive. Inside,
40 and it is curious to define it, they are blatant; void of sound and yet

with no hush, simple, and yet completely vulgar, barren, sterile. More barren than a bank or a school-room or an empty concert-hall, less mysterious than any of these. You get a sense of plaster, of mortar, of whitewash, of smeared blue-wash or grey-wash, and of gilt laid on and ready to peel off. Even in the most gorgeous churches, the gilt is hatefully gilt, never golden. Nothing is soft nor mellow.

So the interior of Sayula church: and Kate had often been in. The white exterior was charming, and so valuable in the landscape, with the twin white pagoda-towers peering out of the green willow trees. But inside, it seemed nothing but whitewash, stencilled over with grey scroll-work decorations. The windows were high, and many, letting in the light as into a school-room. Jesus, streaked with blood, was in one of the transepts, and the Virgin, a doll in faded satin, stood startled inside a glass case. There were rag flowers and paper flowers, coarse lace and silver that looked like tin.

Nevertheless, it was quite clean, and very much frequented.

The Month of Mary had gone by, the blue and white paper ribbons were all taken down, the palm-trees in pots were all removed from the aisle, the little girls in white dresses and little crowns of flowers no longer came with posies in their hand, at evening. Curious, the old gentle ceremonials of Europe, how trashy they seem in Mexico, just a cheap sort of charade.

The day of Corpus Christi* came, with high mass and the church full to the doors with kneeling peons, from dawn till noon. Then a feeble little procession of children within the church, because the law forbids religious processions outside. But all, somehow, for nothing. Just so that the people could call it a fiesta, and so have an excuse to be more slack, more sloshy and uncontrolled than ever. The one Mexican desire: to let themselves go in sloppy inertia.

And this was the all-in-all of the religion. Instead of doing as it should, collecting the soul into its own strength and integrity, the religious day left it all the more decomposed and degenerate.

However, the weeks passed, the crowd in the church seemed the same as ever. But the crowd in the church one hour was the crowd of Quetzalcoatl the next hour. Just a sensation.

Till the more socialistic Readers mingled a little anti-clerical bitterness in their reading. And all the peons began to say: Was El Señor a gringo, and the Santísima, was she nothing but a gringuita?—

This provoked retaliation on the part of the priests, first mere admonitions, then at last the loud denunciations and threat of that sermon. Which meant war.

Everybody waited for Saturday. Saturday came, and the church 5 remained shut. Saturday night, the church was dark and closed. Sunday, the church was silent and the doors blank fastened.

Something like consternation spread through the market host. They had nowhere to go!—But among the consternation was a piqued curiosity. Perhaps something exciting was going to happen. 10 Things had happened before. In the revolutions, many of the churches in Mexico have been used for stables and for barracks. And churches are turned into schools, and concert-halls, and cinematograph theatres. The convents and the monasteries are most of them barracks for the rag-tag-and-bobtail soldiers. The world changes, is 15 bound to change.

The second Saturday of the closed church was, as it happened, a big market. Much fruit and stuff had come up the lake, from the south from far distances, even from Colima. There were men with lacquer wooden bowls, and women with glazed pottery. And as 20 usual, men crouching in guard over twenty centavos worth of nauseous tropical plums, or chiles, or mangoes, in tiny pyramids along the roadway.

A crowded market, with the much and the little of the Indians. And the church-doors shut and locked, the church bells silent, even 25 the clock stopped. True, the clock was always stopping. But not with such a final arrest.

No mass, no confession, no little orgy of incense and slack emotion! The low rumble of murmuring tones, the quick, apprehensive glances around. Vendors by the causeway squatted tight, as 30 if to make themselves dense and small, squatting down on their haunches with their knees up to their shoulders, like the Aztec idols. And soldiers in twos and threes sprinkled everywhere. And señoras and señoritas, in their black gauze scarves or mantillas, tripping to the church for mass and shrilling round the gateway of the church, 35 all a-bubble and a-froth of chatter: though they had known quite well the church was shut.

But it was Sunday morning, and something was due to happen.

At about half-past ten, a boat appeared, and men in snow-white clothes got out, one carrying a drum. They marched quickly through 40 the people, under the old trees on the sand, across to the church.

They passed through the broken iron gates into the stone courtyard in front of the church.

At the church-doors, which were still shut, they took off their blouses, and stood in a ring, with dark naked shoulders and the blue-and-black sashes of Quetzalcoatl round their waists.

The drum began to beat, with a powerful, pounding note, as the men stood bareheaded and bare-breasted in a circle outside the church-doors: a strange ring of lustrous, bluey-black heads and dark shoulders, above the snowy white pantaloons. Monotonously the drum beat, on and on. Then the little clay flute with the husky sound wheezed a clear melody.

The whole market pressed densely towards the gateways of the church. But there, soldiers stood guard. And on the inside of the stone yard in front of the church, soldiers quietly guarded the low walls, letting nobody mount. So that outside, under the old willow and pepper trees, in the hot morning sun, the dense crowd stood gazing at the church-doors. They were mostly men in big hats: but some townsmen were there, and some women, and Kate with a parasol lined with dark blue. A close, silent, tense throng under the spangled shade, pressing round the trunks of the palm-trees, climbing on the roots of the pepper trees. And behind were the *camiones* and the motor-cars drawn up.

The drum shuddered and went still, and the earthen flute was silent. The lake could be heard lapping, and a clink of glasses and a sound of chauffeurs' voices at the little cantina-booth. For the rest, the silent breathing of the crowd. Soldiers were quickly distributing a few leaflets among the crowd. A strong, far-carrying male voice began to sing to the softened thud of the drum.

Jesus' Farewell.

Farewell, Farewell, *Despedida*!
The last of my days is gone.
Tomorrow Jesus and Holy Mary
Will be bone.

It is a long, long way
From Mexico to the Pool of Heaven.
Look back the last time, Mary Mother.
Let us call the eleven.

James, and John, and Mark,
Felipe and San Cristóbal,

All my saints, and Anna, Teresa,
Guadalupe whose face is oval.

Come then, now, it is finished for all of us.
Let us all be gone.
5   Follow me now up the ladders of sparks.
Every one.

Joachim, Francis, and Anthony
And many-named María,
Purísima, Refugio, and Soledad*
10   Follow here.

Ho! all my saints and my Virgins
Troop out of your shrines,
After your master, the Crucified:
Bring all your signs.

15   Run up the flames, and with feet on the sparks
Troop into the sky.
Once more following the Master,
Back again now, on high.

Farewell, let all be forgotten
20   In Mexico.
To the pool of peace and forgetting in heaven
We go.

While this was singing, another boat had arrived, and soldiers
made way through the crowd for Ramón, in his white sarape with the
25 blue edges and scarlet fringe, and a young priest of the church in a
black cassock, and six men in dark sarapes with the blue borders of
Quetzalcoatl. This strange procession marched through the crowd
and through the gateways of the yard.

As they approached, the ring of men round the drum opened, and
30 spread into a crescent. Ramón stood tall behind the drum, the six
men in dark sarapes divided and went to the wings of the crescent,
the young, slim priest in a black cassock stood alone, in front of the
crescent, facing the crowd.

He lifted his hand: Ramón took off his hat: all the men in the
35 crowd took off their hats.

The priest turned, met Ramón at the centre of the crescent, and
across the drum handed him the key of the church. Then the priest
waited.

Ramón unlocked the church-doors and flung them open. The men in front of the crowd kneeled down suddenly, seeing the church dark like a cavern, but a trembling blaze of many candles, away, seemingly far down the mysterious darkness, shuddering with dark, rippling flame, like the Presence of the burning bush.

The crowd swayed and rustled, and subsided kneeling. Only here and there a laborer, a chauffeur or a railway man stood erect.

The priest raised his hand a little higher, returning towards the people.

"My children," he said: and as he spoke the lake seemed to rustle; "God the Almighty has called home his Son, and the Holy Mother of the Son. Their days are over in Mexico. They go back to the Father.

> Jesus, the Son of God, bids you farewell.
> Mary, the Mother of God, bids you farewell.
> For the last time they bless you, as they leave you.
> Answer *Adios!*
> Say *Adios!*, my children.

The men in the circle said a deep *Adios!* And from the soldiers, and from the kneeling crowd, a ragged, muttered, strange repeating of *Adios!*, again and again, like a sort of storm.

Suddenly, in a blast, down the darkness of the church into which the kneeling people were staring, the burning bush of candles was gone, there was only darkness. Across the sunshine, lit here and there by a frail light of a taper, was a cave of darkness.

Men in the crowd exclaimed and groaned.

Then the drum softly touched, and two men in the crescent began to sing, in magnificent, terrible voices, the Farewell Hymn again. They were men whom Ramón, or his followers, had found in low drinking dens in Mexico City, men with trained and amazing voices, the powerful Mexican tenor that seemed to tear the earth open. Men whom the "times" have reduced to singing in low city dives. And now they sang with all the terrible desperation that was in them, the hopeless, demonish recklessness.

When they finished, the priest again lifted his hand, and gave the benediction: adding in a quiet voice:

"And now, with all the saints, let me go, saith Jesus. For I go back to my Father which is in heaven, and I lead my Mother in my right hand, home to peace."

He turned and went into the church. Ramón followed. Then
slowly, all the men of the crescent. Overhead the church bell rang a
little while, on the deathly silence. It ceased.

And in a moment, from the depths of the church sounded a drum,
5 with a remote, fearsome thud, and a slow monotony.

The priest, in his white vestments with rich lace, appeared in the
doorway of the church, bearing a tall crucifix. He hesitated, then
came into the sun. The kneeling people clasped their hands.

Candles in the dark church were clustering towards the door,
10 lonely flames. Don Ramón came out of the dark, naked to the waist,
his sarape over one shoulder, bearing the front pole of the great bier
whereon lies, within a glass case, the lifelike, terrible Dead Christ of
Holy Week. A tall, dark man, naked to the waist, held the other end
of the pole on his shoulder. The crowd moaned and crossed
15 themselves. The lifelike Dead Christ seemed really dead, as he
passed the gates. As he entered the crowd, kneeling men and women
lifted sightless faces and flung their arms wide apart, and so
remained, arms rigid and outflung, in an unspeakable ecstasy of fear,
supplication, acknowledgement of death.

20 After the bier of the Dead Christ, a slow procession of men naked
to the waist, carrying litter after litter. First the terrible scourged
Christ, with naked body striped like a tiger with blood. Then the
image of the Saviour of the Sacred Heart, the well-known figure*
from the side altar, with long hair and outstretched hands. Then the
25 image of Jesus of Nazareth, with a crown of thorns.

Then the Virgin with the blue mantle and lace, and the golden
crown. The women began to moan as she emerged rather trashily
into the blazing sunlight. Behind her, in the church, the candles were
one by one going out.

30 Then came brown Saint Anthony of Padua, with a child in his
arms. Then Saint Francis, looking strangely at a cross in his hand.
Then Saint Ann. And last, Saint Joachim. And as he emerged, the
last candles in the dark church went out, there were only open doors
upon a darkness.

35 The images on the shoulders of the brown-skinned men rode
rather childishly out through the blazing sun, into the shadow of
trees. The drum followed last, slowly thudding. On the glass case of
the big Dead Christ the sun flashed with startling flashes, as the
powerful men carrying it turned towards the water. The crowd
40 murmured and swayed on its knees. Women cried: *Purísima!*

Purísima! Don't leave us! and some men ejaculated in strangled anguish, over and over again: *Señor! Señor! Señor!*

But the strange procession made its way slowly under the trees, to the coarse sands, and descended again into the great light towards the lake. There was a little breeze under a blaze of sun. Folded sarapes on naked, soft shoulders swung unevenly, the images rocked and tottered a little. But onwards to the edge of the water went the tall crucifix, then the flashing glass box. And after, came Jesus in a red silk robe, fluttering, then a wooden Jesus all paint and streaks, then Jesus in white with a purple mantle that blew like a kerchief, Mary in lace that fluttered upon stiff white and blue satin. But the saints were only painted: painted wood.

The slim, lace-smocked priest staggered down the sand under the heavy crucifix, which had a white Christ Crucified stretched aloft, facing the lake. By the little wall was a large black *canoa*, sailing-boat, with a broad plank gangway up to her stern. Two barelegged, white-clad men walked by the slim priest, whose white sleeves blew like flags as he slowly climbed the gangway to the ship. Men helped him on board, and he walked away to the prow, where at length he stood the big crucifix, with the Christ still facing outwards.

The ship was open, without deck or hatches, but with fixed tables for the images. Slowly Ramón ascended and descended into the boat, the great glass case was laid down on its rest, the two men could wipe their wet brows and their hot, black hair. Ramón put on his blanket and his hat, against the sun. The boat heaved very slightly. The wind was from the west. The lake was pale and unreal, sun-blinded.

One after another the images rose over the stern of the boat, against the sky, then descended into the vessel, to be set down on their rests, where they rose above the black sides of the *canoa*, in view of the throng on the shore.

It was a strange and tawdry collection of images. And yet, each image had a certain pathos of its own, and a certain touch of horror, as they were grouped together for their last ride, upon the trestle-supports within the vessel. By each image stood the bearers, in hats and sarapes, keeping a steady hand on the poles.

There was a little line of soldiers on the shore, and three motor-boats with soldiers waited by the big *canoa*. The shore was covered with a mass of people. Many row-boats came rowing inquisitively round, like fishes. But none came too near.

Barelegged sailors began to pole the ship from the shore. They leaned heavily on the poles, and walked along the rims of the vessel. Slowly she began to move upon the waters, in the shallows. Slowly, she was leaving the shore, and the throng.

5   Two other sailors swiftly began to hoist the huge, square white sail. Quickly, yet heavily it rose in the air, and took the wind. It had the great sign of Quetzalcoatl, the circling blue snake and the blue eagle upon a yellow field, at the centre, like a great eye.

The wind came from the west, but the boat was steering south-
10 east, for the little Island of the Scorpions, which rose like a small dim hummock from the daze of the lake.* So the sail reached out, and the great eye seemed to be glancing back, at the village with the green willows and the empty white church, the throng on the shore.

Motor-boats circled the huge, slow *canoa*, small boats like insects
15 followed and ranged round at a distance, never coming too close. The running water clucked and spoke, the men by the images steadied the poles with one hand, their hats with the other, the great eye on the sail ever looked back at the land, the sweep of the white canvas sweeping low above the glass case of death, the Christ caked
20 with gore, the images in their fluttering mantles.

On the shore, the people wandered away, or sat on the sands waiting and watching in a sort of dumb patience that was half indifference. The *canoa* grew smaller, more inconspicuous, lapsing into the light, the little boats circled around it like mere dots. The
25 lake tired the eyes with its light.

Away under the trees, in a half silence, a half vacancy, a woman bought a dark water-melon, smashed it open on a stone, and gave the big pinky fragments to her children. In silence, men sprinkled salt on the thick slices of cucumber sold by the woman under the tree. In
30 silence they wandered into the church, past the soldiers on guard at the door.

The church was absolutely dark, save for the light that entered the doorway, and absolutely bare: walls, floor, altar, transepts, all stark bare and empty. The people wandered away again, in silence.

35 It was noon, and a hot day. The *canoa* slowly ranged to the small hummock of the island amid the waters, where lived one family of Indians—fishers, with a few goats and one dry little place where they grew a few beans and heads of maize. For the rest, the island was all dry rock and thorny bushes, and scorpions.

40 The vessel was poled round to the one rocky bay. Slowly she drew

near the island. The motor-boats and the little boats hurried ahead. Already brown, naked men were bathing among the rocks.

The great sail sank, the *canoa* edged up to the rocky shore, men sprang from her into the water, the images were lowered and slowly carried on to the rocks. There they waited for the bearers.   5

Slowly the procession went again up the bank of the dishevelled island, past the couple of huts where a red cock was crowing among the litter, and over to rocks, beyond the bushes, on the far side.

The side facing Sayula was all rock, naked and painful to tread on. In a rocky hollow at the water's edge, tall stones had been put up on   10
end, with iron bars across the top, like a grill. Underneath, a pile of faggots ready; and at the side, a pile of faggots.

The images, the glass box of the great Dead Christ, were laid on the iron bars of the grill, in a pathetic cluster all together. The crucifix was leaned against them. It was noon, the heat and the light   15
were fierce and erect. But already down the lake clouds were pushing up fantastically.

Beyond the water, beyond the glare, the [lake-shore] looked like a mirage, with its trees and villages* and white church-towers.

Men who had come in boats crowded on the rocks of the little   20
amphitheatre. In silence, Ramón kindled shreds of cane and ocote, with a burning glass. Little hasty flames like young snakes arose in the solid sunlight, with vapor of smoke. He set fire to the carefully-arranged pyramid of faggots beneath the grill-table of the images.

There was a crackling,* and a puffing of whitish smoke, the sweet   25
scent of ocote, and orange-red tongues of half-substantial flame were leaping up in the hot white air. Hot breaths blew suddenly, sudden flames gushed up, and the ocote, full of sweet resin, began to roar. The glass of the great box emitted strange, painful yelps as it splintered and fell tinkling. Between the iron bars, brownish flames   30
pushed up among the images, which at once went black. The little vestments of silk and satin withered in a moment to blackness, the caked wounds of paint bubbled black.

The young priest took off his linen vestment, his stole and his chasuble, and with flushed face flung them in the flame. Then he   35
stripped off his black cassock, and emerged in the white cotton of the Men of Quetzalcoatl, his white drawers rolled up to the knee. He threw his cassock in the fire. Someone handed him a big hat, and a white sarape with blue ends.

There was a smell of burning paint, and wool, and ocote. The fire   40 rushed in a dusky mass upon the blackened, flickering images, till nothing was to be seen but a confused bush of smoke and brown-red flame, puthering, reeking, roaring. The flaming crucifix slipped aside, and fell. A man seized it and pushed it into the fire, under the images. Men in a sort of ecstasy threw on more of the heavy, resinous wood, that almost exploded into flame. Rocks cracked and exploded like guns. Everybody drew back from that roaring tree of flame, which rose ever higher and higher, its dark smoke and its sparks unfolding into heaven.

One of the supporting stones burst with a bang, bars of iron and blazing stumps of images tumbled in a confused roar. The glass case had disappeared, but ribbons of iron waved, then curled over red, into the torrent of the sudden fire. Strange rods of iron appeared out of nowhere, protruding from solid red coals.

And soon, all that was left was a fierce glow of red coals of wood, with a medley of half-fused iron.

Ramón stood aside and watched in silence, his dark brow quite expressionless.

Then, when only the last bluish flames flickered out of a tumble of red fire, from the eminence above, rockets began to shoot into the air with a swish, exploding high in the sightless hot blue, with a glimmer of bluish showers, and of gold.

The people from the shore had seen the tree of smoke with its trunk of flame. Now they heard the heavy firing of the rockets, they looked again, exclaiming, half in dismay, half in the joyful lust of destruction:

"*Señor! Señor! La Purísima! La Santísima!*"

The flame and the smoke and the rockets melted as if by miracle, into nothingness, leaving the hot air unblemished. The coals of fire were shovelled and dropped down a steep hole.

As the *canoa* sailed back, the side of the lake, through filmy air, looked brownish and changeless. A cloud was rising in the south-west, from behind the dry, silent mountains, like a vast white tail, like the vast white fleecy tail of some squirrel, that had just dived out of sight behind the mountains. This wild white tail fleeced up and up, to the zenith, straight at the sun. And as the *canoa* spread her sail to tack back, already a delicate film of shadow was over the chalk-white lake.

Only on the low end of the Isle of Scorpions, hot air still quivered.

Ramón returned in one of the motor-boats. Slowly the sky was clouding for the thunder and the rain. The *canoa*, unable to make her way across, was sailing for Tuliapán. The little boats hurried in silence.

They landed before the wind rose. Ramón went and locked the doors of the church.

5

The crowd scattered in the wind, rebozos waving wildly, leaves torn, dust racing. Sayula was empty of God, and at heart, they were glad.

Chapter XIX.

The Attack on Jamiltepec.

Suddenly, nearly all the soldiers disappeared from the village, there was a "rebellion" in Colima. A train had been held up, people killed. And somebody, Generals Fulano and Tulano,* had "pronounced" against the government.

Stir in the air, everybody enjoying those periodical shivers of fear! But for these shivers, everything much the same as usual. The church remained shut up, and dumb. The clock didn't go. Time suddenly fell off, the days walked naked and timeless, in the old, uncounted manner of the past. The strange, old, uncounted, unregistered, unreckoning days of the ancient heathen world.

Kate felt a bit like a mermaid trying to swim in a wrong element. She was swept away in some silent tide, to the old, antediluvian silence, where things moved without contact. She moved and existed without contact. Even the striking of the hours had ceased. As a drowning person sees nothing but the waters, so Kate saw nothing but the face of the timeless waters.

So, of course, she clutched at her straw. She couldn't bear it. She ordered an old, rickety Ford car, to take her bumping out to Jamiltepec, over the ruinous roads, in the afternoon.

The country had gone strange and void, as it does when these "rebellions" start. As if the life-spirit were sucked away, and only some empty, anti-life void remained in the wicked hollow countryside. Though it was not far to Jamiltepec, once outside the village, the chauffeur and his little attendant lad began to get frightened, and to go frog-like with fear.

There is something truly mysterious about the Mexican quality of fear. As if man and woman collapsed and lay wriggling on the ground like broken reptiles, unable to rise. Kate used all her will, against this cringing nonsense.

They arrived without ado at Jamiltepec. The place seemed quiet, but normal. An oxen wagon stood empty in the courtyard. There were no soldiers on guard. They had all been withdrawn, against the rebellion. But several peons were moving round, in a desultory fashion. The day was a fiesta, when not much work was doing. In the

288

houses of the peons, the women were patting tortillas, and preparing hot chile sauce, grinding away on the metates. A fiesta! Only the windmill that pumped up water from the lake was spinning quickly, with a little noise.

Kate drove into the yard in silence, and two mozos with guns and 5
belts of cartridges came to talk in low tones to the chauffeur.

"Is Doña Carlota here?" asked Kate.

"No Señora. The *patrona* is not here."

"Don Ramón?"

"*Sí Señora! Está.*"* 10

Even as she hesitated, rather nervous, Ramón came out of the inner doorway of the courtyard, in his dazzling white clothes.

"I came to see you," said Kate. "I don't know if you'd rather I hadn't. But I can go back in the motor-car."

"No," he said. "I am glad. I was feeling deserted, I don't know 15
why. Let us go upstairs."

"*Patrón!*" said the chauffeur, in a low voice. "Must I stay?"

Ramón said a few words to him. The chauffeur was uneasy, and didn't want to stay. He said he had to be back in Sayula at such and such a time. Excuses, anyhow. But it was evident he wanted to get 20
away.

"Then best let him go," said Ramón to Kate. "You do not mind going home in the boat?"

"I don't want to give you trouble."

"It is least trouble to let this fellow go, and you can leave by boat 25
just whenever you wish to. So we shall all be more free."

Kate paid the chauffeur, and the Ford started rattling. After rattling a while, it moved in a curve round the courtyard, and lurched through the zaguán, disappearing as fast as possible.

Ramón spoke to his two mozos with the guns. They went to the 30
outer doorway, obediently.

"Why do you have to have armed men?" she said.

"Oh, they're afraid of bandits," he said. "Whenever there's a rebellion anywhere, everybody is afraid of bandits. So of course that calls bandits into life." 35

"But where do they come from?" said Kate, as they passed into the inner doorways.

"From the villages," he said, closing the heavy door of that entrance behind him, and putting the heavy iron bars across, from wall to wall. 40

The inner archway was now a little prison, for the strong iron gates at the lake end of the passage were shut fast. She looked through, at the little round pond. It had some blue water-lilies on it. Beyond, the pallid lake seemed almost like a ghost, in the glare of sun.

A servant was sent to the kitchen quarters, Ramón and Kate climbed the stone stairs to the upper terrace. How lonely, stonily lonesome and forlorn the hacienda could feel! The very stone walls could give off emptiness, loneliness, negation.

"But which villages do the bandits come from?" she insisted.

"Any of them. Mostly, they say, from San Pablo or from Ahuajijic."*

"Quite near!" she cried.

"Or from Sayula," he added. "Any of the ordinary men in big hats you see around the plaza, may possibly be bandits, when banditry pays, as a profession, and isn't punished with any particular severity."

"It is hard to believe!" she said.

"It is so obvious!" he said, dropping into one of the rocking-chairs opposite her, and smiling across the onyx table.

"I suppose it is!" she said.

He clapped his hands, and his mozo Martín came up. Ramón ordered something, in a low, subdued tone. The man replied in an even lower, more subdued tone. Then the master and man nodded at one another, and the man departed, his huaraches swishing a little on the terrace.

Ramón had fallen into the low, crushed sort of voice so common in the country, as if everyone were afraid to speak aloud, so they murmured guardedly. This was unusual, and Kate noticed it in him with displeasure. She sat looking past the thick mango trees, whose fruit was changing colour like something gradually growing hot, to the ruffled, pale-brown lake. The mountains of the opposite shore were very dark. Above them lay a heavy, but distant black cloud, out of which lightning flapped suddenly and uneasily.

"Where is Don Cipriano?" she asked.

"Don Cipriano is very much General Viedma at the moment," he replied. "Chasing rebels in the State of Colima."

"Will they be very hard to chase?"

"Probably not. Anyhow Cipriano will enjoy chasing them. He is Zapotec, and most of his men are Zapotecans,* from the hills. They love chasing men who aren't."

"I wondered why he wasn't there on Sunday when you carried away the images," she said. "I think it was an awfully brave thing to do."

"Do you?" he laughed. "It wasn't. It's never half so brave, to carry something off, and destroy it, as to set a new pulse beating." 5

"But you have to destroy those old things, first."

"Those frowsty images—why yes. But it's no good until you've got something else moving, from the inside."

"And have you?"

"I think I have. Don't you?" 10

"Yes," she said, a little doubtful.

"I think I have," he said. "I feel there's a new thing moving inside me."—He was laughing at her, for her hesitation. "Why don't you come and join us?" he added.

"How?" she said. "By being married off to Don Cipriano?" 15

"Not necessarily. Not necessarily. Not necessarily by being married to anybody."

"What are you going to do next?" she said.

"I? I am going to re-open the church, for Quetzalcoatl to come in. But I don't like lonely gods. There should be several of them, I think, 20 for them to be happy together."

"Does one need gods?" she said.

"Why yes. One needs manifestations, it seems to me."

Kate sat in unwilling silence.

"One needs goddesses too. That is also a dilemma," he added, 25 with a laugh.

"How I would *hate*," said Kate, "to have to be a goddess for people."

"For the monkeys?" he said, smiling.

"Yes! Of course." 30

At that moment, he sat erect, listening. There had been a shot, which Kate had heard, but which she had hardly noticed; to her ears, it might have been a motor-car backfiring, or even a motor-boat.

Suddenly, a sharp little volley of shots. 35

Ramón rose swiftly, swift as a great cat, and slammed to the iron door at the top of the stairway, shooting the bars.

"Won't you go into that room?" he said to her, pointing to a dark doorway. "You will be all right there. Just stay a few minutes till I come back." 40

As he spoke, there came a shriek from the courtyard at the back, and a man's death-voice yelled *Patrón!*

Ramón's eyes dilated with terrible anger, the anger of death. His face went pale and strange, as he looked at her without seeing her, the black flame filling his eyes. He had drawn a long-barreled steel revolver from his hip.

Still without seeing her, he strode rapidly, soft and catlike, along the terrace, and leaped up the end stair-case on to the roof. The soft, eternal passion of anger in his limbs.

Kate stood in the doorway of the room, transfixed. The light of day seemed to have darkened before her face.

"*Holá!* You there!" she heard his voice from the roof, in such anger it was almost a laugh, from far away.

For answer, a confused noise from the courtyard, and several shots. The slow, steady answer of shots!

She started as a rushing hiss broke on the air. In terror she waited. Then she saw it was a rocket bursting with a sound like a gun, high over the lake, and emitting a shower of red balls of light.—A signal from Ramón!

Unable to go into the dark room, Kate waited as if smitten to death. Then something stirred deep in her, she flew along the terrace and up the steps to the roof. She realised that she didn't mind dying so long as she died with that man. Not alone.

The roof was glaring with sunshine. It was flat, but its different levels were uneven. She ran straight out into the light, towards the parapet wall, and had nearly come in sight of the gateway of the courtyard below, when something gave a slight smack, and bits of plaster flew in her face and her hair. She turned and fled back like a bee, to the stairway.

The stairs came up in a corner, where there was a little sort of stone turret, square, with stone seats. She sank on one of these seats, looking down in terror at the turn of the stairs. It was a narrow little stone stairway, between the solid stone walls.

She was almost paralysed with shock and with fear. Yet something within her was calm. Leaning and looking out across calm sunshine of the level roof, she could not believe in death.

She saw the white figure and the dark head of Ramón within one of the small square turrets across the roof. The little tower was open, and hardly higher than his head. He was standing in a corner, looking sideways down a loop-hole, perfectly motionless. Snap!

Snap! went his revolver, deliberately. There was a muffled cry below, and a sudden volley of shots.

Ramón stood away from the loop-hole and took off his white blouse, so that it should not betray him. Above his sash was a belt of cartridges. In the shadow of the turret, his body looked curiously 5 dark, rising from the white of his trousers. Again he took his stand quietly at the side of the long, narrow, slanting aperture. He lifted his revolver carefully, and the shots, one, two, three, slow and deliberate, startled her nerves. And again there was a volley of shots from below, and bits of stone and plaster smoking against the sky. Then 10 again, silence, long silence. Kate pressed her hands against her body, as she sat.

The clouds had shifted, the sun shone yellowish. In the heavier light, the mountains beyond the parapet showed a fleece of young green, smoky and beautiful. 15

All was silent. Ramón in the shadow did not move, pressing himself against the wall, and looking down. He commanded, she knew, the big inner doors.

Suddenly, however, he shifted. With his revolver in his hand he stooped and ran, like some terrible cat, the sun gleaming on his 20 naked back as he crouched under the shelter of the thick parapet wall, running along the roof to the corresponding front turret.

This turret was roofless, and it was nearer to Kate, as she sat spell-bound, in a sort of eternity, on the stone seat at the head of the stairs, watching Ramón. He pressed himself against the wall, and 25 lifted his revolver to the slit. And again, one, two, three, four, five, the shots exploded deliberately. Some voice below yelled *Ay-ee! Ay-ee! Ay-ee!*—in yelps of animal pain. A voice was heard shouting command. Ramón kneeled on one knee, re-loading his revolver. Then he struck a match, and again Kate almost started out of her 30 skin, as a rocket rushed ferociously up into the sky, exploded like a gun, and let fall the balls of red flame, that lingered as if loth to die away, in the high, remote air.

She sighed, wondering what it all was. It was death, she knew. But so strange, so vacant. Just these noises of shots! And she could see 35 nothing outside. She wanted to see what was in the courtyard.

Ramón was at his post, pressing himself close to the wall, looking down, with bent head, motionless. There were shots, and a spatter of lead from below. But he did not move. She could not see his face, only part of his back: the proud, heavy, creamy-brown shoulders, the 40

black head bent a little forward, in concentration, the cartridge belt
dropping above his loins, over the white, floppy linen of the trousers.
Still and soft in watchful concentration, almost like silence itself.
Then with soft, diabolic swiftness in his movements, he changed his
5   position, and took aim.

He was utterly unaware of her: even of her existence. Which was
as it should be, no doubt. She sat motionless, waiting. Waiting,
waiting, waiting, in that yellowish sunlight of eternity, with a
certain changeless suspense of stillness inside her. Someone would
10   come from the village. There would be an end. There would be an
end.

At the same time, she started every time he fired, and looked at
him. And she heard his voice saying: "One needs manifestations, it
seems to me." Ah, how she hated the noise of shots.

15   Suddenly she gave a piercing shriek, and in one leap was out of her
retreat. She had seen a black head turning the stairs.

Before she knew it, Ramón jumped past her like a great cat, and
two men clashed in mid-air, as the unseen fellow leaped up from the
stairs. Two men in a crash went down on the floor, a revolver went
20   off, terrible limbs were writhing.

Ramón's revolver was on the floor. But again there was a shot from
the tangled men, and a redness of blood suddenly appearing out of
nowhere, on the white cotton clothing, as the two men twisted and
fought on the floor.

25   They were both big men. Struggling on the ground, they looked
huge. Ramón had the bandit's revolver-hand by the wrist. The
bandit, with a ghastly black face with rolling eyes and sparse
moustache, had got Ramón's naked arm in his white teeth, and was
hanging on, showing his red gums, while with his free hand he was
30   feeling for his knife.

Kate could not believe that the black, ghastly face with the
sightless eyes and biting mouth was conscious. Ramón had him
clasped round the body. The bandit's revolver fell, and the fellow's
loose black hand scrabbled on the concrete, feeling for it. Blood was
35   flowing over his teeth. Yet some blind super-consciousness seemed
to possess him, as if he were a devil, not a man.

His hand nearly touched Ramón's revolver. In horror Kate ran
and snatched the weapon from the warm concrete, running away as
the bandit gave a heave, a great sudden heave of his body, under the
40   body of Ramón. Kate raised the revolver. She hated that horrible

devil under Ramón as she had never hated in her life. Yet she dared not fire.

Ramón shouted something, glancing at her. She could not understand. But she ran round, to be able to shoot the man under Ramón. Even as she ran, the bandit twisted with a great lunge of his body, heaved Ramón up, and with his short free hand got Ramón's own knife from the belt at the groin, and stabbed.

Kate gave a cry! Oh, how she wanted to shoot! She saw the knife strike sideways, slanting in a short jab into Ramón's back. At the same moment there was a stumble on the stairs, and another black-headed man was leaping on to the roof from the turret.

She stiffened her wrist and fired without looking, in a sudden second of pure control. The black head came crashing at her. She recoiled in horror, lifted the revolver and fired again, and missed. But even as it passed her, she saw red blood among the black hairs of that head. It crashed down, the buttocks of the body heaving up, the whole thing twitching and jerking along, the face seeming to grin in a mortal grin.

Glancing from horror to horror, she saw Ramón, his face still as death, blood running down his arm and his back, holding down the head of the bandit by the hair and stabbing him with short stabs in the throat, one, two: while blood shot out like a red projectile, there was a strange sound like a soda-syphon, a ghastly bubbling, one final terrible convulsion from the loins of the stricken man, throwing Ramón off, and Ramón lay twisted, still clutching the man's hair in one hand, the bloody knife in the other, and gazing into the livid, distorted face, in which ferocity seemed to have gone frozen, with a steady, intent, inhuman gaze.

Then, without letting go his victim's hair, he looked up, cautiously. To see Kate's man, with black hair wet with blood, and blood running into his glazed, awful eyes, slowly rising to his knees. It was the strangest face in the world: the high, domed head with blood-soddened hair, blood running in several streams down the narrow, corrugated brow and along the black eyebrows above the glazed, black, numb eyes, in which the last glazing was of ferocity, stranger even than wonder, the glazed and absolute ferocity which the man's last consciousness showed.

It was a long, thin, handsome face, save for those eyes of glazed ferocity, and for the longish white teeth under the sparse moustache.

The man was reduced to his last, blank term of being; a glazed and ghastly ferocity.

Ramón dropped the hair of his victim, whose head dropped sideways with a gaping red throat, and rose to a crouching position.

5 The second bandit was on his knees, but his hand already clasped his knife. Ramón crouched. They were both perfectly still. But Ramón had got his balance, crouching between his feet.

The bandit's black, glazed eyes of blank ferocity took a glint of cunning. He was stretching. He was going to leap to his feet for his 10 stroke.

And even as he leaped, Ramón shot the knife, that was all bright red as a cardinal bird. It flew red like a bird, and the drops of Ramón's handful of blood flew with it, splashing even Kate, who kept her revolver ready, watching near the stairway.

15 The bandit dropped on his knees again, and remained for a moment kneeling as if in prayer, the red pommel of the knife sticking out of his abdomen, from his white trousers. Then he slowly bowed over, doubled up, and went on his face again, once more with his buttocks in the air.

20 Ramón still crouched at attention, almost supernatural, his dark eyes glittering with watchfulness, in pure, savage attentiveness. Then he rose, very smooth and quiet, crossed the bloodstained concrete to the fallen man, picked up the clean, fallen knife that belonged to the fellow, lifted the red-dripping chin, and with one 25 stroke drove the knife into the man's throat. The man subsided with the blow, not even twitching.

Then again, Ramón turned to look at the first man. He gazed a moment attentively. But that horrible black face was dead.

And then Ramón glanced at Kate, as she stood near the stairs with 30 the revolver. His brow was like a boy's, very pure and primitive, and the eyes underneath had a certain primitive, gleaming look of virginity. As men must have been, in the first awful days, with that strange beauty that goes with pristine rudimentariness.

For the most part, he did not recognise her. But there was one 35 remote glint of recognition.

"Are they both dead?" she asked, awestruck.

"*Creo que sí!*"* he replied in Spanish.

He turned to look once more, and to pick up the pistol that lay on the concrete. As he did so, he noticed that his right hand was bright 40 red, with the blood that flowed still down his arm. He wiped it on the

jacket of the dead man. But his trousers on his loins were also
sodden with blood, they stuck red to his hips. He did not notice.

He was like a pristine being, remote in consciousness, and with
far, remote sex.

Curious rattling, bubbling noises still came from the second man, 5
just physical sounds. The first man lay sprawling in a ghastly fashion,
his evil face fixed above a pool of blackening blood.

"Watch the stairs!" said Ramón in Spanish to her, glancing at her
with farouche eyes, from some far remote jungle. Yet still the glint of
recognition sparked furtively out of the darkness. 10

He crept to the turret, and stealthily looked out. Then he crept
back, with the same stealth, and dragged the nearest dead man to the
parapet, raising the body so the head looked over. There was no
sound. Then he raised himself, and peeped over. No sign, no sound.

He looked at the dead body as he let it drop. Then he went to 15
Kate, to look down the stairs.

"You grazed that man with your first shot, you only stunned him I
believe," he said.

"Are there any more?" she asked, shuddering.

"I think they are all gone." 20

He was pale, almost white, with that same pristine clear brow, like
a boy's, a sort of twilight changelessness.

"Are you much hurt?" she said.

"I? No!"—and he put his fingers round to his back, to feel the
slowly welling wound, with his bloody fingers. 25

The afternoon was passing towards yellow, heavy evening.

He went again to look at the terrible face of the first dead man.

"Did you know him?" she said.

He shook his head.

"Not that I am aware," he said. Then: "Good that he is dead. 30
Good that he is dead.—Good that we killed them both."

He looked at her with that glint of savage recognition from
afar.

"Ugh! No! It's terrible!" she said shuddering.

"Good for me that you were there! Good that we killed them 35
between us! Good they are dead."

The heavy, luxurious yellow light from below the clouds gilded the
mountains of evening.* There was the sound of a motor-car honking
its horn.

Ramón went in silence to the parapet, the blood wetting his 40 pantaloons lower and lower, since they stuck to him when he bent down. Rich yellow light flooded the bloodstained roof. There was a terrible smell of blood.

"There is a car coming," he said.

5 She followed, frightened, across the roof.

She saw the hills and lower slopes inland swimming in gold light like lacquer. The black huts of the peons, the lurid leaves of bananas showed up uncannily, the trees green-gold stood up, with boughs of shadow. And away up the road was a puther of dust, then the flash of

10 glass as the automobile turned.

"Stay here," said Ramón, "while I go down."

"Why didn't your peons come and help you?" she said.

"They never do!" he replied. "Unless they are armed on purpose."

15 He went, picked up his blouse and put it on. And immediately the blood came through.

He went down. She listened to his steps. Below, the courtyard was all shadow, and empty, save for two dead white-clothed bodies of men, one near the zaguán, one against a pillar of the shed.

20 The motor-car came sounding its horn wildly all the way between the trees. It lurched into the zaguán. It was full of soldiers, soldiers standing on the running-boards, hanging on.

"Don Ramón! Don Ramón!" shouted the officer, leaping out of the car. "Don Ramón!"—He was thundering at the doors of the

25 inner zaguán.

Why did not Ramón open? Where was he?

She leaned over the parapet and screamed like a wild bird:

"*Viene! Viene Don Ramón! Él viene!*"*

The soldiers all looked up at her. She drew back in terror. Then, in

30 a panic, she turned downstairs, to the terrace. There was blood on the stone stairs, at the bottom, a great pool. And on the terrace near the rocking-chairs, two dead men in a great pool of blood.

One was Ramón! For a moment she went unconscious. Then slowly she crept forward. Ramón had fallen, reeking with blood from

35 his wound, his arms round the body of the other man, who was bleeding too. The second man opened his eyes, wildly, and in a rattling voice, blind and dying, said:

"*Patrón!*"

It was Martín, Ramón's own mozo. He was stiffening and dying in

40 Ramón's arms. And Ramón, lifting him, had made his own wound

gush with blood, and had fainted. He lay like dead. But Kate could
see the faintest pulse in his neck.

She ran blindly down the stairs, and fought to get the great iron
bars from across the door, screaming all the time:

"Come! Somebody! Come to Don Ramón! He will die." 5

A terrified boy and a woman appeared from the kitchen quarters.
The door was opened, just as six horse-soldiers galloped into the
courtyard. The officer leaped from his horse and ran like a hare, his
revolver drawn, his spurs flashing, straight through the doors and up
the stairs, like a madman. When Kate got up the stairs again, the 10
officer was standing with drawn revolver, gazing down at Ramón.

"He is dead?" he said, stupefied, looking at Kate.

"No!" she said. "It is only loss of blood."

The officers lifted Ramón and laid him on the terrace. Then
quickly they got off his blouse. The wound was bleeding thickly in 15
the back.

"We've got to stop this wound," said the lieutenant. "Where is
Pablo?"

Instantly there was a cry for Pablo.

Kate ran into a bedroom for water, and she switched an old linen 20
sheet from the bed. Pablo was a young doctor among the soldiers.
Kate gave him the bowl of water, and the towel, and was tearing the
sheet into bands. Ramón lay naked on the floor, all streaked with
blood. And the light was going.

"Bring light!" said the young doctor. 25

With swift hands he washed the wound, peering with his nose
almost touching it.

"It is not much!" he said.

Kate had prepared bandages and a pad. She crouched to hand
them to the young man. The woman-servant set a lamp with a white 30
shade on the floor by the doctor. He lifted it, peering again at the
wound.

"No!" he said. "It is not much."

Then glancing up at the soldiers who stood motionless, peering
down, the light on their dark faces: 35

"*Té!*" he said, making a gesture.

Quickly the lieutenant took the lamp, holding it over the inert
body, and the doctor, with Kate to help, proceeded to staunch and
bind the wound. And Kate, as she touched the soft, inert flesh of
Ramón, was thinking to herself: This too is he, this silent body! And 40

that face that stabbed the throat of the bandit was he! And that twilit brow, and those remote eyes, like a death-virgin, was he. Even a savage out of the twilight! And the man that knows me, where is he? One among these many men, no more! Oh God! give the man his

5 soul back, into this bloody body. Let the soul come back, or the universe will be cold for me and for many men.

The doctor finished his temporary bandage, looked at the wound in the arm, swiftly wiped the blood off the loins and buttocks and legs, and said:

10 "We must put him in bed. Lift his head."

Quickly Kate lifted the heavy, inert head. The eyes were half open. The doctor pressed the closed lips, under the sparse black moustache. But the teeth were firmly shut.

The doctor shook his head.

15 "Bring a mattress," he said.

The wind was suddenly roaring, the lamp was leaping with a long, smoky needle of flame, inside its chimney. Leaves and dust flew rattling on the terrace, there was a splash of lightning. Ramón's body lay there uncovered and motionless, the bandage was already soaked

20 with blood, under the darkening, leaping light of the lamp.

And again Kate saw, vividly, how the body is the flame of the soul, leaping and sinking upon the invisible wick of the soul. And now the soul, like a wick, seemed spent, the body was a sinking, fading flame.

"Kindle his soul again, oh God!" she cried to herself.

25 All she could see of the naked body was the terrible absence of the living soul of it. All she wanted was for the soul to come back, the eyes to open.

They got him upon the bed and covered him, closing the doors against the wind and the rain. The doctor chafed his brow and hands

30 with cognac. And at length the eyes opened: the soul was there, but standing far back.

For some moments Ramón lay with open eyes, without seeing or moving. Then he stirred a little:

"What's the matter?" he said.

35 "Keep still, Don Ramón," said the doctor, who, with his slim dark hands was even more delicate than a woman. "You have lost much blood. Keep still."

"Where is Martín?"

"He is outside."

40 "How is he?"

"He is dead."

The dark eyes under the black lashes were perfectly steady and changeless. Then came the voice:

"Pity we did not kill them all. Pity we did not kill them all. We have got to kill them all.—Where is the Señora Inglesa?"

"Here she is."

His black eyes looked up at Kate. Then more of his consciousness came back.

"Thank you for my life," he said, closing his eyes. Then: "Put the lamp aside."

Soldiers were tapping at the glass pane, for the lieutenant. A black little fellow entered, wiping the rain from his black face and pushing his thick black hair back.

"There are two more dead on the azotea," he announced to his officer.

The lieutenant rose, and followed him out. Kate too went on to the terrace. In the early darkness the rain was threshing down. A lantern was coming down from the roof; it came along the terrace to the stairs, and after it two soldiers in the pouring rain, carrying a dead body, then behind, two more, with the other body. The huaraches of the soldiers clicked and shuffled on the wet terrace. The dismal cortège went downstairs.

Kate stood on the terrace facing the darkness, while the rain threshed down. She felt uneasy here, in this house of men and of soldiers. She found her way down to the kitchen, where the boy was fanning a charcoal fire, and the woman was crushing tomatoes on the metate, for a sauce.

"Ay, Señora!" cried the woman. "Five men dead, and the *Patrón* wounded to death! Ay! Ay!"

"Seven men dead!" said the boy. "Two on the azotea!"

"Seven men! Seven men!"

Kate sat on her chair, stunned, unable to hear anything but the threshing rain, unable to feel anything more. Two or three peons came in, and two more women, the men wrapped to their noses in their blankets. The women brought *masa*, and began a great clapping of tortillas. The people conversed in low, rapid tones, in the dialect, and Kate could not listen.

At length the rain began to abate. She knew it would leave off suddenly. There was a great sound of water running, gushing, splashing, pouring into the cistern. And she thought to herself: The

rain will wash the blood off the roof and down the spouts into the
cistern. There will be blood in the water.

She looked at her own blood-smeared white frock. She felt chilly.
She rose to go upstairs again, into the dark, empty, masterless house.

5   "Ah, Señora! You are going upstairs? Go, Daniel, carry the
lantern for the Señora!"

The boy lit a candle in a lantern, and Kate returned to the upper
terrace. The light shone out of the room where Ramón was. She
went into the salon and got her hat and her brown shawl. The
10 lieutenant heard her, and came to her quickly, very kindly and
respectful.

"Won't you come in, Señora?" he said, holding the door to the
room where Ramón lay: the guest-room.

Kate went in. Ramón lay on his side, his black, rather thin
15 moustache pushed against the pillow. He was himself.

"It is very unpleasant for you here, Señora Caterina," he said.
"Would you like to go to your house? The lieutenant will send you in
the motor-car."

"Is there nothing I can do here?" she said.

20   "Ah no! Don't stay here! It is too unpleasant for you.—I shall soon
get up, and I shall come to thank you for my life."

He looked at her, into her eyes. And she saw that his soul had
come back to him, and with his soul he saw her and acknowledged
her: though always from the peculiar remoteness that was inevitable
25 in him.

She went downstairs with the young lieutenant.

"Ah, what a horrible affair! They were not bandits, Señora!" said
the young man, with passion. "They didn't come to rob. They came
to murder Don Ramón, you know, Señora! simply to murder Don
30 Ramón. And but for your being here, they would have done it!—Ah,
think of it, Señora! Don Ramón is the most precious man in Mexico.
It is possible that in the world there is not a man like him. And
personally, he hasn't got enemies. As a man among men, he hasn't
got enemies. No Señora. Not one!—But do you know who it will
35 be?—the priests, and the Knights of Cortés."

"Are you sure?" said Kate.

"Sure, Señora!" cried the lieutenant indignantly. "Look! There
are seven men dead. Two were the mozos with guns, watching in the
zaguán. One was Don Ramón's own mozo Martín!—ah, what a
40 faithful man, what a brave one! Never will Don Ramón pardon his

death.—Then moreover, the two men killed on the azotea, and two
men in the courtyard, shot by Don Ramón. Besides these, a man
whom Martín wounded, who fell and broke his leg, so we have got
him.—Come and see them, Señora."

They were down in the wet courtyard. Little fires had been lighted   5
under the sheds, and the little, black, devil-may-care soldiers were
crouching round them, with a bunch of peons in blankets standing
round. Across the courtyard, horses stamped and jingled their
harness. A boy came running with tortillas in a cloth. The dark-faced
little soldiers crouched like animals, sprinkled salt on the tortillas,   10
and devoured them with small, white, strong teeth.

Kate saw the great oxen tied in their sheds, lying down, the
wagons standing inert. And a little crowd of asses was munching
alfalfa in a corner.

The officer marched beside Kate, his spurs sparking in the   15
firelight. He went to the muddy car, that stood in the middle of the
yard: then to his horse. From a saddle-pocket he took an electric
torch, and led Kate across to the end shed.

There he suddenly flashed his light upon seven dead bodies, laid
side by side. The two from the roof were wet. Ramón's dead man lay   20
with his dark, strong breast bare, and his blackish, thick, devilish face
sideways: a big fellow. Kate's man lay rigid. Martín had been stabbed
in the collar bone: he looked as if he were staring at the roof of the
shed. The others were two more peons, and two fellows in black
boots and grey trousers and blue overall jackets. They were all inert   25
and straight and dead, and somehow, a little ridiculous. Perhaps it is
clothing that makes dead people gruesome and absurd. But also, the
grotesque fact that the bodies are vacant, is always present.

"Look!" said the lieutenant, touching a body with his toe. "This is
a chauffeur from Sayula: this is a boatman from Sayula. These two   30
are peons from San Pablo. This man—" the lieutenant kicked the
dead body—"we don't know." It was Ramón's dead man. "But this
man—" he kicked her dead man, with the tall domed head—" is
from Ahuajijic, and he was married to the woman that now lives with
a peon here.—You see, Señora! A chauffeur and a boatman from   35
Sayula—they are Knights-of-Cortés men: and those two peons from
San Pablo are priests' men—These are not bandits. It was an
attempt at assassination. But of course they would have robbed
everything, everything, if they had killed Don Ramón."

Kate was staring at the dead men. Three of them were hand-   40

some: one, the boatman, with a thin line of black beard framing his shapely face, was beautiful. But dead, with the mockery of death in his face. All of them men who had been in the flush of life. Yet dead, they did not even matter. They were gruesome, but it did not matter
5 that they were dead men. They were vacant. Perhaps even in life there had been a certain vacancy, nothingness, in their handsome physique.

For a pure moment, she wished for men who were not handsome as these dark natives were. Even their beauty was suddenly repulsive
10 to her: the dark beauty of half-created, half-evolved things, left in the old, reptile-like smoothness. It made her shudder.

The soul! If only the soul in man, in woman, would speak to her, not always this strange, perverse materialism, or a distorted anima-lism. If only people were souls, and their bodies were gestures from
15 the soul! If one could but forget both bodies and facts, and be present with strong, living souls!

She went across the courtyard, that was littered with horse-droppings, to the car. The lieutenant was choosing the soldiers who should stay behind. The horse-soldiers would stay. A peon on a
20 delicate speckled horse, a flea-bitten roan, came trotting past the soldiers in the zaguán. He had been to Sayula for doctor's stuff, and to give messages to the Jefe.

At last the car, with little soldiers clinging on to it all round, moved slowly out of the courtyard. The lieutenant sat beside Kate. He
25 stopped the car again at the big white barn under the trees, to talk to two soldiers picketed there.

Then they moved slowly on, under the wet trees, in the mud that crackled beneath the wheels, up the avenue to the high-road, where were the little black huts of the peons. Little fires were flapping in
30 front of one or two huts, women were baking tortillas on the flat earthenware plates upon the small wood fires. A woman was going to her hut with a blazing brand, like a torch, to kindle her fire. A few peons in dirty-white clothes squatted silent against the walls of their houses, utterly silent. As the motor-car turned its great glaring
35 head-lights upon the high-road, little sandy pigs with short, curly hair started up squealing, and faces and figures stood out blindly, as in a searchlight.

There was a hut with a wide opening in the black wall, and a grey old man was standing inside. The car stopped for the lieutenant to
40 call to the peons under the wall. They came to the car with their

black eyes glaring and glittering apprehensively. They seemed very much abashed, and humble, answering the lieutenant.

Meanwhile Kate watched a boy buy a drink for one centavo and a piece of rope for three centavos, from the grey old man at the dark hole which was a shop.   5

The car went on, the great lights glaring unnaturally upon the hedges of cactus and mesquite and palo blanco trees, and upon the great pools of water in the road. It was a slow progress.

Chapter XX.

Marriage by Quetzalcoatl.*

Kate hid in her own house, numbed. She could not bear to talk to people. She could not bear even Juana's bubbling discourse. The common threads that bound her to humanity seemed to have snapped. The little human things didn't interest her any more. Her eyes seemed to have gone dark, and blind to individuals. They were all just individuals, like leaves in the dark, making a noise. And she was alone under the trees.

The egg-woman wanted six centavos for an egg.

"And I said to her—I said to her—we buy them at five centavos!" Juana went on.

"Yes!" said Kate. She didn't care whether they were bought at five or fifty, or not bought at all.

She didn't care, she didn't care, she didn't care. She didn't even care about life any more. There was no escaping her own complete indifference. She felt indifferent to everything in the whole world, almost she felt indifferent to death.

"Niña! Niña! Here is the man with the sandals! Look! Look how nicely he has made them for you, Niña! Look what Mexican huaraches the Niña is going to wear!"

She tried them on. The man charged her too much. She looked at him with her remote, indifferent eyes. But she knew, in the world one must live, so she paid him less than he asked, though more than he really would have accepted.

She sat down again in her rocking-chair in the shade of the room. Only to be alone! Only that no-one should speak to her! Only that no-one should come near her! Because in reality her soul and spirit were gone, departed into the middle of some desert, and the effort of reaching across to people to effect an apparent meeting, or contact, was almost more than she could bear.

Never had she been so alone, and so inert, and so utterly without desire: plunged in a wan indifference, like death. Never had she passed her days so blindly, so unknowingly, in stretches of nothingness.

Sometimes, to get away from her household, she sat under a tree by the lake. And there, without knowing it, she let the sun scorch her foot and burn her face inflamed. Juana made a great outcry over her. The foot blistered and swelled, her face was red and painful. But it all seemed to happen merely to her shell. And she was wearily, wanly 5 indifferent.

Only at the very centre of her sometimes a little flame rose, and she knew that what she wanted was for her soul to live. The life of days and facts and happenings was dead on her, and she was like a corpse. But away inside her a little light was burning, the light of her 10 innermost soul. Sometimes it sank and seemed extinct. Then it was there again.

Ramón had lighted it. And once it was lighted the world went hollow and dead, all the world-activities were empty weariness to her. Her soul! Her frail innermost soul! She wanted to live *its* life, 15 not her own life.

The time would come again when she would see Ramón and Cipriano, and the soul that was guttering would kindle again in her, and feel strong. Meanwhile she only felt weak, weak, weak, weak as the dying. She felt that afternoon of bloodshed had blown all their 20 souls into the twilight of death, for the time. But they would come back. They would come back. Nothing to do but to submit, and wait. Wait, with a soul almost dead, and hands and heart of uttermost inert heaviness, indifference.

Ramón had lost much blood. And she, too, in other ways, had 25 been drained of the blood of her body. She felt bloodless and powerless.

But wait, wait, wait, the new blood would come.

One day Cipriano came. She was rocking in her salon, in a cotton housedress, and her face red and rather swollen. She saw him, in 30 uniform, pass by the window. He stood in the doorway on the terrace, a dark, grave, small handsome man.

"Do come in," she said with effort.

Her eyelids felt burnt. He looked at her with his full black eyes, that always had in them so many things she did not understand. She 35 felt she could not look back at him.

"Have you chased all your rebels?" she said.

"For the present," he replied.

He seemed to be watching, watching for something.

"And you didn't get hurt?"   40

"No, I didn't get hurt."

She looked away out of the door, having nothing to say in the world.

"I went to Jamiltepec yesterday evening," he said.

5 "How is Don Ramón?"

"Yes, he is better."

"Quite better?"

"No. Not quite better. But he walks a little."

"Wonderful how people heal."

10 "Yes. We die very easily. But we also come quickly back to life."

"And you? Did you fight the rebels, or didn't they want to fight?"

"Yes, they wanted to. We fought once or twice: not very much."

"Men killed?"

15 "Yes! Some! Not many, no?—Perhaps a hundred. We can never tell, no? Maybe two hundred—"

He waved his hand vaguely.

"But you had the worst rebellion at Jamiltepec, no?" he said suddenly, with heavy Indian gravity, gloom, suddenly settling down.

20 "It didn't last long, but it was rather awful while it did."

"Rather awful, no?—If I had known! I said to Ramón, won't you keep the soldiers?—the guard, no? He said they were not necessary.—But here—you never know, no?"

"Niña!" cried Juana, from the terrace. "Niña! Don Antonio says 25 he is coming to see you."

"Tell him to come tomorrow."

"Already he is on the way!" cried Juana, in helplessness. Don Antonio was Kate's fat landlord: and, of course, Juana's permanent master, more important in her eyes, then, even than Kate.

30 "Here he is!" she cried, and fled.

Kate leaned forward in her chair, to see the stout figure of her landlord on the walk outside the window, taking off his cloth cap and bowing low to her. A cloth cap!—She knew he was a great Fascista, the reactionary Knights of Cortés* held him in great esteem.

35 Kate bowed coldly.

He bowed low again, with the cloth cap.

Kate said not a word.

He stood on one foot, then on the other, and then marched forward up the gravel walk, towards the kitchen quarters, as if he had 40 not seen either Kate or General Viedma. In a few moments he marched back, as if he could not see either Kate or the general, through the open door.

Cipriano looked at the passing stout figure of Don Antonio in a cloth cap as if it were the wind blowing.

"It is my landlord!" said Kate. "I expect he wants to know if I am taking on the house for another three months." 5

"Ramón wanted me to come and see you—to see how you are, no?—and to ask you to come to Jamiltepec. Will you come with me now? The car is here."

"Must I?" said Kate, uneasily. 10

"No. Not unless you wish. Ramón said, not unless you wished. He said, perhaps it would be painful to you, no?—to go to Jamiltepec again—so soon after—"

How curious Cipriano was! He stated things as if they were mere bare facts with no emotional content at all. As for its being painful to 15 Kate to go to Jamiltepec, that meant nothing to him.

"Lucky thing you were there that day, no?" he said. "They might have killed him. Very likely they would! Very likely! Awful, no?"

"They might have killed me too," she said. 20

"Yes! Yes! They might!" he acquiesced.

Curious he was! With a sort of glaze of the ordinary world on top, and underneath a black volcano with hell knows what depths of lava. And talking half-abstractedly from his glazed, top self, the words came out small and quick, and he was always hesitating, and saying: 25 *No?* It wasn't himself at all talking.

"What would you have done if they had killed Ramón?" she said, tentatively.

"I?"—He looked up at her in a black flare of apprehension. The volcano was rousing. "If they had killed him?—" His eyes took on 30 that fixed glare of ferocity, staring her down.

"Would you have cared very much?" she said.

"I? Would I?" he repeated, and the black suspicious look came into his Indian eyes.

"Would it have meant *very* much to you?" 35

He still watched her with a glare of ferocity and suspicion.

"To me!" he said, and he pressed his hand against the buttons of his tunic. "To me Ramón is *more* than life. *More* than life." His eyes seemed to glare and go sightless, as he said it, the ferocity melting in a strange blind, confiding glare, that seemed sightless, either looking 40 inward, or out at the whole vast void of the cosmos, where no vision is left.

"More than anything?" she said.

"Yes!" he replied abstractedly, with a blind nod of the head.

5   Then abruptly he looked at her and said:

"You saved his life."

By this he meant that *therefore*—But she could not understand the therefore.

She went to change, and they set off to Jamiltepec. Cipriano made

10 her a little uneasy, sitting beside him. He made her physically aware of him, of his small but strong and assertive body, with its black currents and storms of desire. The range of him was very limited, really. The great part of his nature was just inert and heavy, unresponsive, limited as a snake or a lizard is limited. But within his

15 own heavy, dark range he had a curious power. Almost she could *see* the black fume of power which he emitted, the dark, heavy vibration of his blood, which cast a spell over her.

As they sat side by side in the motor-car, silent, swaying to the broken road, she could feel the curious tingling heat of his blood,

20 and the heavy power of the *will* that lay unemerged in his blood. She could see again the skies go dark, and the phallic mystery rearing itself like a whirling dark cloud, to the zenith, till it pierced the sombre, twilit zenith: the old, supreme phallic mystery. And herself in the everlasting twilight, a sky above where the sun ran smokily, an

25 earth below where the trees and creatures rose up in blackness, and man strode along naked, dark, half-visible, and suddenly whirled in supreme power, towering like a dark whirlwind column, whirling to pierce the very zenith.

The mystery of the primeval world! She could feel it now in all its

30 shadowy, furious magnificence. She knew now what was the black, glinting look in Cipriano's eyes. She could understand marrying him, now. In the shadowy world where men were visionless, and winds of fury rose up from the earth, Cipriano was still a power. Once you entered his mystery the scale of all things changed, and he

35 became a living male power, undefined, and unconfined. The smallness, the limitations ceased to exist. In his black, glinting eyes the power was limitless, and it was as if, from him, from his body of blood could rise up that pillar of cloud* which swayed and swung, like a rearing serpent or a rising tree, till it swept the zenith, and all the

40 earth below was dark and prone, and consummated. Those small

hands, that little natural tuft of black goat's beard hanging light from his chin, the tilt of his brows and the slight slant of his eyes, the domed Indian head with its thick black hair, they were like symbols to her, of another mystery, the bygone mystery of the twilit, primitive world, where shapes that are small suddenly loom up huge, gigantic 5 on the shadow, and a face like Cipriano's is the face at once of a god and a devil, the undying Pan face. The bygone mystery, that has indeed gone by, but has not passed away. Never shall pass away.

As he sat in silence, casting the old, twilit Pan-power over her, she felt herself submitting, succumbing. He was once more the old 10 dominant male, shadowy, intangible, looming suddenly tall, and covering the sky, making a darkness that was himself and nothing but himself, the Pan male. And she was swooned prone beneath, perfect in her proneness.

It was the ancient phallic mystery, the ancient god-devil of the 15 male Pan. Cipriano unyielding forever, in the ancient twilight, keeping the ancient twilight around him. She understood now his power with his soldiers. He had the old gift of demon-power.

He would never woo: she saw this. When the power of his blood rose in him, the dark aura steamed from him like a cloud pregnant 20 with power, like thunder, and rose like a whirlwind that rises suddenly in the twilight and raises a great pliant column, swaying and leaning with power, clear between heaven and earth.

Ah! and what a mystery of prone submission, on her part, this huge erection would imply! Submission absolute, like the earth 25 under the sky. Beneath an over-arching absolute.

Ah! what a marriage! How terrible! and how complete! With the finality of death, and yet more than death. The arms of the twilit Pan. And the awful, half-intelligible voice from the cloud.

She could conceive now her marriage with Cipriano: the supreme 30 passivity, like the earth below the twilight, consummate in living lifelessness, the sheer solid mystery of passivity. Ah, what an abandon, what an abandon, what an abandon!—of so many things she wanted to abandon.

Cipriano put his hand, with its strange soft warmth and weight, 35 upon her knee, and her soul melted like fused metal.

"*En poco tiempo, verdad?*" he said to her, looking into her eyes with the old, black, glinting look, of power about to consummate itself.

"In a little while, no?"

She looked back at him, wordless. Language had abandoned her, 40

and she leaned silent and helpless in the vast, unspoken twilight of
the Pan world. Her self had abandoned her, and all her day was
gone. Only she said to herself:

"My demon lover!"*

5   Her world could end in many ways, and this was one of them. Back
to the twilight of the ancient Pan world, where the soul of woman was
dumb, to be forever unspoken.

The car had stopped, they had come to Jamiltepec. He looked at
her again, as reluctantly he opened the door. And as he stepped out,
10 she realised again his uniform, his small figure in uniform. She had
lost it entirely. She had only known his face, the face of the supreme
God-demon; with the arching brows and slightly slanting eyes, and
the loose, light tuft of a goat-beard. The Master. The everlasting
Pan.

15   He was looking back at her again, using all his power to prevent
her seeing in him the little general in uniform, in the worldly vision.
And she avoided his eyes, and saw nothing.

They found Ramón sitting in his white clothes in a long chair on
the terrace. He was creamy-brown in his pallor.

20   He saw at once the change in Kate. She had the face of one waking
from the dead, curiously dipped in death, with a tenderness far more
new and vulnerable than a child's. He glanced at Cipriano. Cipriano's face seemed darker than usual, with that secret *hauteur* and
aloofness of the savage. He knew it well.

25   "Are you better?" Kate asked.

"Very nearly!" he said, looking up at her gently. "And you?"

"Yes, I am all right."

"You are?"

"Yes, I think so.—I have felt myself all lost, since that day. Spirit-
30 ually, I mean. Otherwise I am all right.—Are you healing well?"

"Oh yes! I always heal quickly."

"Knives and bullets are horrible things."

"Yes—in the wrong place."

Kate felt rather as if she were coming to, from a swoon, as Ramón
35 spoke to her and looked at her. His eyes, his voice seemed kind.
Kind? The word suddenly was strange to her, she had to try to get its
meaning.

There was no kindness in Cipriano. The god-demon Pan preceded kindness. She wondered if she wanted kindness. She did not
40 know. Everything felt numb.

"I was wondering whether to go to England," she said.

"Again?" said Ramón, with a slight smile. "Away from the bullets and the knives, is that it?"

"Yes!—to get away."—And she sighed deeply.

"No!" said Ramón. "Don't go away. You will find nothing in England."

"But *can* I go on here?"

"Can you help it?"

"I wish I knew what to do."

"How can one know? Something happens inside you, and all your decisions are smoke.—Let happen what will happen."

"I can't *quite* drift as if I had no soul of my own, can I?"

"Sometimes it is best."

There was a pause. Cipriano stayed outside the conversation altogether, in a dusky world of his own, apart and secretly hostile.

"I have been thinking so much about you," she said to Ramón, "and wondering whether it is worth while."

"What?"

"What you are doing: trying to change the religion of these people. If they have any religion to change.—I don't think they are a religious people. They are only superstitious. I have no use for men and women who go crawling down a church aisle on their knees, or holding up their arms for hours. There's something stupid and wrong about it.—They never worship a God. Only some little evil power.—I have been wondering so much if it is worth while giving yourself to them, and exposing yourself to them. It would be horrible if you were really killed. I have seen you *look* dead."

"Now you see me look alive again," he smiled.

But a heavy silence followed.

"I believe Don Cipriano knows them better than you do. I believe he knows best, if it is any good," she said.

"And what does he say?" asked Ramón.

"I say I am Ramón's man," replied Cipriano stubbornly.

Kate looked at him, and mistrusted him. In the long run he was nobody's man. He was that old, masterless Pan-male, that could not even conceive of service: particularly the service of mankind. He saw only glory: the black mystery of glory consummated. And himself like a wind of glory.

"I feel they'll let you down," said Kate to Ramón.

"Maybe! But I shan't let myself down. I do what I believe in.

Possibly I am only the first step round the corner of change. But: ce n'est que le premier pas qui coûte*—Why will you not go round the corner with us? At least it is better than sitting still."

Kate did not answer his question. She sat looking at the mango trees and the lake, and the thought of that afternoon came over her again.

"How did those two men get in: those two bandits on the roof?" she asked wonderingly.

"It was a woman this time: a girl whom Carlota brought here from the Cuna in Mexico, to be a sewing girl and to teach the peons' wives to sew and do little things. She had a little room at the end of the terrace there—" Ramón pointed to the terrace projecting towards the lake, opposite the one where his own room was, and the covered balcony. "She got entangled with one of the peons: a sort of second overseer, called Guillermo. Guillermo had got a wife and four children, but he came to me to say could he change and take Maruca—the sewing girl. I said no, he could stay with his family. And I sent Maruca back to Mexico. But she had had a smattering of education, and thought she was equal to anything. She got messages through to Guillermo, and he ran away and joined her in Mexico, leaving wife and four children here. The wife then went to live with another peon—the blacksmith—whose wife had died and who was supposed to be a good match: a decent fellow.

"One day appeared Guillermo and said: could he come back? I said: not with Maruca. He said he didn't want Maruca, he wanted to come back. His wife was willing to go back to him again with the children. The blacksmith was willing to let her go. I said very well: but he had forfeited his job as sub-overseer, and must be a peon again.

"And he seemed all right—satisfied. But then Maruca came and stayed in Sayula, pretending to make her living as a dressmaker. She was in with the priest: and she got Guillermo again.

"It seems the Knights of Cortés had promised a big reward for the man who would bring in my scalp: secretly, of course. The girl got Guillermo: Guillermo got those two peons, one from San Pablo and one from Ahuajijic: somebody else arranged for the rest.

"The bedroom the girl used to have is that one, on the terrace not far from where the stairs go up to the roof. The bedroom has a lattice window, high up, looking out on the trees. There's a big *laurel de la India* grows outside. It appears the girl climbed on a table and knocked the iron lattice of the window loose, while she was living here, and that Guillermo, by taking a jump from the bough,—a very risky thing, but then he was one of that sort—could land on the window-sill and pull himself into the room.

"Apparently he and the other two men were going to get the scalp and pillage the house before the others could enter. So the first one, the man I killed, climbed the tree, and with a long pole shoved in the lattice of the window, and so got into the room, and up the terrace stairs.

"Martín, my man, who was waiting on the other stairs ready if they tried to blow out the iron door, heard the smash of the window and rushed round just as the second bandit—the one you shot—was crouching on the window-sill to jump down into the room. The window is quite small, and high up.

"Before Martín could do anything the man had jumped down on top of him and stabbed him twice with his machete. Then he took Martín's knife and came up the stairs, when you shot him in the head.

"Martín was on the floor when he saw the hands of a third man gripping through the window. Then the face of Guillermo. Martín got up and gave the hands a slash with the heavy machete, and Guillermo fell smash back down on to the rocks under the wall.

"When I came down, I found Martín lying outside the door of that room. He told me—*They came through there, Patrón. Guillermo was one of them.*

"Guillermo broke his thigh on the rocks, and the soldiers found him. He confessed everything, and said he was sorry, and begged my pardon. He's in the prison hospital now."

"And Maruca?" said Kate.

"They've got her too."

"There will always be a traitor," said Kate gloomily.

"Let us hope there will also be a Caterina," said Ramón.

"But will you go on with it—your Quetzalcoatl?"

"How can I leave off? It's my *métier* now. Why don't you join us? Why don't you help me?"

"How?"

"You will see. Soon you will hear the drums again. Soon the first day of Quetzalcoatl will come. You will see.—Then Cipriano will appear—in the red sarape—and Huitzilopochtli will share the Mexican Olympus with Quetzalcoatl. Then I want a goddess.—"

"But will Don Cipriano be the god Huitzilopochtli?" she asked, taken aback.

"First Man of Huitzilopochtli, as I am First Man of Quetzalcoatl."

5　"Will you?" said Kate to Cipriano. "That horrible Huitzilo-pochtli?"

"Yes Señora!" said Cipriano, with a subtle smile of *hauteur*, the secret savage coming in to his own.

"Not the old Huitzilopochtli—but the new," said Ramón. "And
10　then there must come a goddess: wife or virgin, there must come a goddess. Why not you as the First Woman of—say Itzpapalotl, just for the sound of the name?"

"I!" said Kate. "Never! I should die of shame."

"Shame?" laughed Ramón. "Ah, Señora Caterina, why shame?
15　This is a thing that *must* be done. There *must* be manifestations. We *must* change back to the vision of the living cosmos: we *must*. The oldest Pan is in us, and he will not be denied. In cold blood and in hot blood both, we must make the change. That is how man is made. I accept the *must* from the oldest Pan in my soul, and from the newest
20　*me*. Once a man gathers his whole soul together and arrives at a conclusion, the time of alternatives has gone. I *must*. No more than that. I *am* the First Man of Quetzalcoatl. I am Quetzalcoatl himself, if you like. A manifestation, as well as a man. I accept myself entire, and proceed to make destiny.—Why what else can I do?"

25　Kate was silent. His loss of blood seemed to have washed him curiously fresh again, and he was carried again out of the range of human emotion. A strange sort of categorical imperative!* She saw now his power over Cipriano. It lay in this imperative which he acknowledged in his own soul, and which really was like a messenger
30　from the beyond.

She looked on like a child looking through a railing: rather wistful, and rather frightened.

Ah, the soul! The soul was always flashing and darkening into new shapes, each one strange to the other. She had thought Ramón and
35　she had looked into each other's souls. And now, he was this pale, distant man, with a curious gleam like a messenger from the beyond, in his soul. And he was remote, remote from any woman.

Whereas Cipriano had suddenly opened a new world to her, a world of twilight with the dark, half-visible face of the god-demon
40　Pan, who can never perish, but ever returns upon mankind, from the

shadows. The world of shadows and dark prostration, with the phallic wind rushing through the dark.

Cipriano had to go to the town at the end of the lake, near the State of Colima: to Jaramay.* He was going in a motor-boat with a couple of soldiers. Would Kate go with him? 5

He waited in heavy silence, for her answer.

She said she would. She was desperate. She did not want to be sent back to her own empty dead house.

It was one of those little periods when the rain seems strangled, the air thick with thunder, silent, ponderous thunder latent in the air 10 from day to day, among the thick, heavy sunshine. Kate, in these days in Mexico, felt that between the volcanic violence under the earth, and the electric violence of the air above, men walked dark and incalculable, like demons from another planet.

The wind on the lake seemed fresh, from the west, but it was a 15 running mass of electricity, that burned her face and her eyes and the roots of her hair. When she had wakened in the night and pushed the sheets, heavy sparks fell from her finger-tips. She felt she could not live.

The lake was like some frail milk of thunder: the dark soldiers 20 curled under the awning of the boat, motionless. They seemed dark as lava and sulphur, and full of a dormant, diabolic electricity. Like salamanders. The boatman in the stern, steering, was handsome almost like the man she had killed. But this one had pale greyish eyes, phosphorescent with flecks of silver. 25

Cipriano sat in silence in front of her. He had removed his tunic, and his neck rose almost black from his white shirt. She could see how different his blood was from hers, dark, blackish, like the blood of lizards among hot black rocks. She could feel its changeless surge, holding up his light, bluey-black head as on a fountain. And she 30 could feel her own pride dissolving, going.

She felt he wanted his blood-stream to envelop hers. As if it could possibly be. He was so still, so unnoticing, and the darkness of the nape of his neck was so like invisibility. Yet he was always waiting, waiting, waiting, invisibly and ponderously waiting. 35

She lay under the awning in the heat and light without looking out. The wind made the canvas crackle.

Whether the time was long or short, she knew not. But they were coming to the silent lake-end, where the beach curved round in front of them. It seemed sheer lonely sunlight. 40

But beyond the shingle there were willow trees, and a low
ranch-house. Three anchored *canoas* rode with their black, stiff
lines. There were flat lands, with maize half grown and blowing its
green flags sideways. But all was as if invisible, in the intense hot
5 light.

The warm, thin water ran shallower and shallower, to the reach of
shingle beyond. Black water-fowl bobbed like corks. The motor
stopped. The boat ebbed on. Under the thin water were round
stones, with thin green hair of weed. They would not reach the
10 shore—not by twenty yards.

The soldiers took off their huaraches, rolled their cotton trousers
up their black legs, and got into the water. The tall boatman did the
same, pulling forward the boat. She would go no farther. He
anchored her with a big stone. Then with his uncanny pale eyes,
15 under the black lashes, he asked Kate in a low tone if he could carry
her ashore, offering her his shoulder.

"No no!" she said. "I'll paddle."

And hastily she took off her shoes and stockings and stepped into
the shallow water, holding up her thin skirt of striped silk. The man
20 laughed: so did the soldiers.

The water was almost hot. She went blindly forward, her head
dropped. Cipriano watched her with the silent, heavy, changeless
patience of his race, then when she reached the shingle he came
ashore on the boatman's shoulders.

25 They crossed the hot shingle to the willow trees by the maize-
fields, and sat upon boulders. The lake stretched pale and unreal,
far, far away into the invisible, with dimmed mountains rising on
either side bare and abstract. The *canoas* were black and stiff, their
masts motionless. The white motor-boat rode near. Black birds were
30 bobbing like corks, at this place of the water's end and the world's
end.

A lonely woman went up the shingle with a water-jar on her
shoulder. Hearing a sound, Kate looked, and saw a group of
fishermen holding a conclave in a dug-out hollow by a tree. They
35 saluted, looking at her with black, black eyes. They saluted humbly,
and yet in their black eyes was that ancient remote hardness and
hauteur.

Cipriano had sent the soldiers for horses. It was too hot to walk.

They sat silent in the invisibility of this end of the lake, the great
40 light taking sight away.

"Why am I not the Living Huitzilopochtli?" said Cipriano quietly, looking full at her with his black eyes.

"Do you feel you are?" she said, startled.

"Yes," he replied, in the same low, secret voice. "It is what I feel."

The black eyes looked at her with a rather awful challenge. And the small, dark voice seemed to take all her will away. They sat in silence, and she felt she was fainting, losing her consciousness for ever.

The soldiers came, with a black Arab horse for him: a delicate thing: and for her a donkey on which she could sit sideways. He lifted her into the saddle, where she sat only half conscious. A soldier led the donkey, and they set off, past the long, frail, hanging fishing-nets, that made long filmy festoons, into the lane.

Then out into the sun and the grey-black dust, towards the grey-black, low huts of Jaramay, that lined the wide, desert road.

Jaramay was hot as a lava oven. Black low hut-houses with tiled roofs lined the broken, long, dilapidated street. Broken houses. Blazing sun. A brick pavement all smashed and sun-worn. A dog leading a blind man along the little black walls, on the broken pavement. A few goats. And unspeakable lifelessness, emptiness.

They came to the broken plaza, with sun-decayed church and ragged palm-trees. Emptiness, sun, sun-decay, sun-dilapidation. One man on a dainty Arab horse trotting lightly over the stones, gun behind, big hat making a dark face. For the rest, the waste space of the centre of life.—Curious how dainty the horse looked, and the horseman sitting erect, amid the sun-roasted ruin.

They came to a big building. A few soldiers were drawn up at the entrance. They saluted Cipriano as if they were transfixed, rolling their dark eyes.

Cipriano was down from his horse in a moment. Emitting the dark rays of dangerous power, he found the Jefe all obsequious: a fat man in dirty white clothes. They put their wills entirely in his power.

He asked for a room where his *esposa* could rest. Kate was pale and all her will had left her. He was carrying her on his will.

He accepted a large room with a brick-tiled floor and a large, new brass bed with a coloured cotton cover thrown over it, and with two chairs. The strange, dry, stark emptiness, that looked almost cold in the heat.

"The sun makes you pale. Lie down and rest. I will close the windows," he said.

He closed the shutters till only a darkness remained.

Then in the darkness suddenly, softly he touched her, stroking her hip.

"I said you were my wife," he said, in his small, soft Indian voice.
5 "It is true, isn't it?"

She trembled, and her limbs seemed to fuse like metal melting down. She fused into a molten unconsciousness, her will, her very self gone, leaving her lying in molten life, like a lake of still fire, unconscious of everything save the eternality of the fire in which she
10 was gone. Gone as the burning bush was gone. Gone in the fadeless fire, which has no death. Only the fire can leave *us*, and we can die.

And Cipriano the master of fire. The Living Huitzilopochtli, he had called himself. The living firemaster. The god in the flame: the salamander.

15 One cannot have one's own way, and the way of the gods. It has to be one or the other.

When she went out into the next room, he was sitting alone, waiting for her. He rose quickly, looking at her with black, flashing eyes from which dark flashes of light seemed to play upon her. And
20 he took her hand, to touch her again.

"Will you come to eat at the little restaurant?" he said.

In the uncanny flashing of his eyes she saw a gladness that frightened her a little. His touch on her hand was uncannily soft and inward. His words said nothing: would never say anything. But she
25 turned aside her face, a little afraid of that flashing, primitive gladness, which was so impersonal and beyond her.

Wrapping a big yellow-silk shawl around her, Spanish fashion, against the heat, and taking her white sunshade lined with green, she stepped out with him past the bowing Jefe and the lieutenant, and the
30 saluting soldiers. She shook hands with the Jefe and the lieutenant. They were men of flesh and blood, they understood her presence, and bowed low, looking up at her with flashing eyes. And she knew what it was to be a goddess in the old style, saluted by the real fire in men's eyes, not by their lips.

35 In her big, soft velour hat of jade green, her breast wrapped round with the yellow brocade shawl, she stepped across the sun-eaten plaza, a sort of desert made by man, softly, softly beside her Cipriano, soft as a cat, hiding her face under her green hat and her sunshade, keeping her body secret and elusive. And the soldiers and
40 the officers and clerks of the Jefatura, watching her with fixed black

eyes, saw, not the physical woman herself, but the inaccessible, voluptuous mystery of man's physical consummation.

They ate in the dusky little cavern of a *fonda* kept by a queer old woman with Spanish blood in her veins. Cipriano was very sharp and imperious in his orders, the old woman scuffled and ran in a sort of terror. But she was thrilled to her soul.

Kate was bewildered by the new mystery of her own elusiveness. She was elusive even to herself. Cipriano hardly talked to her at all: which was quite right. She did not want to be talked to, and words addressed straight at her, without the curious soft veiling which these people knew how to put into their voices, speaking only to the unconcerned, third person in her, came at her like blows. Ah, the ugly blows of direct, brutal speech! She had suffered so much from them. Now she wanted this veiled elusiveness in herself, she wanted to be addressed in the third person.*

After the lunch they went to look at the sarapes which were being spun for Ramón. Their two soldiers escorted them a few yards up a broken, sun-wasted wide street of little, low black houses, then knocked at big doors.

Kate entered the grateful shade of the zaguán. In the dark shade of the inner court, or patio, where sun blazed on bananas beyond, was a whole weaver's establishment. A fat, one-eyed man sent a little boy to fetch chairs. But Kate wandered fascinated.

In the zaguán was a great heap of silky white wool, very fine, and in the dark corridor of the patio all the people at work. Two boys with flat square boards bristling with many little wire bristles were carding the white wool into thin films, which they took off the boards in fine rolls like mist, and laid beside the two girls at the end of the shed.

These girls stood by their wheels spinning, standing beside the running wheel, which they set going with one hand, while with the other hand they kept a long, miraculous thread of white wool-yarn dancing at the very tip of the rapidly-spinning spool-needle, the filmy rolls of the carded wool just touching the point of the spool, and at once running out into a long, pure thread of white, which wound itself on to the spool, and another piece of carded wool was attached. One of the girls, a beautiful oval-faced one who smiled shyly at Kate, was very clever. It was almost miraculous the way she touched the spool and drew out the thread of wool almost as fine as sewing cotton.

At the other end of the corridor, under the black shed, were two looms, and two men weaving. They treddled at the wooden tread-looms first with one foot then the other, absorbed and silent, in the shadow of the black mud walls. One man was weaving a brilliant
5   scarlet sarape, very fine, and of the beautiful cochineal red.* It was difficult work. From the pure scarlet centre zig-zags of black and white were running in a sort of whorl, away to the edge, that was pure black. Wonderful to see the man, with small bobbins of fine red yarn, and white yarn, and black, weaving a bit of the ground, weaving the
10 zig-zag of black up to it, and up to that, the zig-zag of white, with deft, dark fingers, quickly adjusting his setting needle, quick as lightning threading his pattern, then bringing down the beam heavily, to press it tight. The sarape was woven on a black warp, long fine threads of black, like a harp. But beautiful beyond words the
15 perfect, delicate scarlet weaving in.

"For whom is that?" said Kate to Cipriano. "For you?"

"Yes," he said. "For me."

The other weaver was weaving a plain white sarape with blue and natural-black ends, throwing the spool of yarn from side to side,
20 between the white harp-strings, pressing down each thread of his woof heavily, with the wooden bar, then treddling to change the long, fine threads of the warp.

In the shadow of the mud shed, the pure colours of the lustrous wool looked mystical, the cardinal scarlet, the pure, silky white, the
25 lovely blue, and the black, gleaming in the shadow of the blackish walls.

The fat man with the one eye brought sarapes, and two boys opened them one by one. There was a new one, white, with close flowers of blue on black stalks, and with green leaves, forming the
30 borders, and at the *boca*, the mouth, where the head went through, a whole lot of little, rainbow-coloured flowers, in a coiling blue circle.

"I love that!" said Kate. "What is that for?"

"It is one of Ramón's: they are Quetzalcoatl's colours, the blue and white and natural black. But this one is for the day of the opening
35 of the flowers, when he brings in the goddess who will come,"* said Cipriano.

Kate was silent with fear.

There were two scarlet sarapes with a diamond at the centre, all black, and a border-pattern of black diamonds.
40 "Are these yours?"

"Well, they are for the messengers of Huitzilopochtli. Those are my colours: scarlet and black. But I myself have white as well, just as Ramón has a fringe of my scarlet."

"Doesn't it make you afraid?" she said to him, looking at him rather blenched. 5

"How make me afraid?"

"To do this. To be the Living Huitzilopochtli," she said.

"I *am* the Living Huitzilopochtli," he said. "When Ramón dares to be the Living Quetzalcoatl, I dare to be the Living Huitzilopochtli. I *am* he.—Am I not?" 10

Kate looked at him, at his dark face with the little hanging tuft of beard, the arched brows, the slightly slanting black eyes. In the round, fierce gaze of his eyes there was a certain silence, like tenderness, for her. But beyond that, an inhuman assurance, which looked far, far beyond her, in the darkness. 15

And she hid her face from him, murmuring:

"I know you are."

"And on the day of flowers," he said, "you too shall come, in a green dress they shall weave you, with blue flowers at the seam, and on your head the new moon of flowers." 20

She hid her face, afraid.

"Come and look at the wools," he said, leading her across the patio to the shade where, on a line, the yarn hung in dripping tresses of colour, scarlet and blue and yellow and green and brown.

"See!" he said. "You shall have a dress of green, that leaves the 25 arms bare, and a white under-dress with blue flowers."

The green was a strong apple-green colour.

Two women under the shed were crouching over big earthenware vessels, which sat over a fire which burned slowly in a hole dug in the ground. They were watching the steaming water. One woman took 30 dried, yellow-brown flowers, and flung them in her water as if she were a witch brewing decoctions. She watched as the flowers rose, watched as they turned softly in the boiling water. Then she threw in a little white powder.

"And on the day of flowers, you too will come. Ah! If Ramón is the 35 centre of a new world, a world of new flowers shall spring up round him, and push the old world back. I call you the First Flower."

They left the courtyard. The soldiers had brought the black Arab stallion for Cipriano, and for her, the donkey on which she could perch sideways, like a peasant woman. So they went through the hot, 40

deserted silence of the mud-brick town, down the lane of deep, dark-grey dust, under vivid green trees that were bursting into flower, again to the silent shore of the lake-end, where the delicate fishing-nets were hung in long lines and blowing in the wind, loop
5   after loop after loop striding above the shingle and blowing delicately in the wind, as away on the low places the green maize was blowing, and the fleecy willows shook like soft green feathers hanging down.

The lake stretched pale and unreal into nowhere: the motor-boat rode near in, the black *canoas* stood motionless a little further out.
10 Two women, tiny as birds, were kneeling on the water's edge, washing.

Kate jumped from her donkey on to the shingle.

"Why not ride through the water to the boat?" said Cipriano.

She looked at the boat, and thought of the donkey stumbling and
15 splashing.

"No," she said. "I will wade again."

He rode his black Arab to the water. It sniffed, and entered with delicate feet into the warm shallows. Then, a little way in, it stood and suddenly started pawing the water, as a horse paws the ground,
20 in the oddest manner possible, very rapidly striking the water with its fore-foot, so that little waves splashed up over its black legs and belly.

But this splashed Cipriano too. He lifted the reins and touched the creature with his spurs. It jumped, and went half-stumbling, half-
25 dancing through the water, prettily, with a splashing noise. Cipriano quieted it, and it waded gingerly on through the shallows of the vast lake, bending its black head down to look, to look in a sort of fascination at the stony bottom, swaying its black tail as it moved its glossy, raven haunches gingerly.
30 Then again it stood still, and suddenly, with a rapid beating of its fore paw, sent the water hollowly splashing up, till its black belly glistened wet like a black serpent, and its legs were shiny wet pillars. And again Cipriano lifted its head and touched it with the spurs, so the delicate creature danced in a churn of water.
35 "Oh, it looks so pretty! It looks so pretty when it paws the water!" cried Kate from the shore. "Why does it do it?"

Cipriano turned in the saddle and looked back at her with the sudden, gay Indian laugh.

"It likes to be wet—who knows?" he said.
40 A soldier hurried wading through the water and took the horse's

bridle. Cipriano dismounted neatly from the stirrup, with a little backward leap into the boat, a real savage horseman. The barefoot soldier leaped into the saddle, and turned the horse to shore. But the black horse, male and wilful, insisted on stopping to paw the waters and splash himself, with a naïve, wilful sort of delight.

"Look! Look!" cried Kate. "It's so pretty."

But the soldier was perching in the saddle drawing up his legs like a monkey, and shouting at the horse. It would wet its fine harness.

He rode the Arab slanting through the water, to where an old woman, sitting in her own silence and almost invisible before, was squatted in the water with brown bare shoulders emerging, lading water from a half gourd-shell over her matted grey head. The horse splashed and danced, the old woman rose with her rag of chemise clinging to her, scolding in a quiet voice and bending forward with her calabash cup, the soldier laughed, the black horse joyfully and excitedly pawed the water and made it splash high up, the soldier shouted again.—But the soldier knew he could make Cipriano responsible for the splashings.

Kate waded slowly to the boat, and stepped in. The water was warm, but the wind was blowing with strong, electric heaviness. Kate quickly dried her feet and legs on her handkerchief, and pulled on her biscuit-coloured silk stockings and brown shoes.

She sat looking back, at the lake-end, the desert of shingle, the blowing, gauzy nets, and beyond them, the black land with green maize standing, a further fleecy green of trees, and the broken lane leading deep into the rows of old trees, where the soldiers from Jaramay were now riding away on the black horse and the donkey. On the right there was a ranch, too: a long, low black building and a cluster of black huts with tiled roofs, empty gardens with reed fences, clumps of banana and willow trees. All in the changeless, heavy light of the afternoon, the long lake reaching into invisibility, between its unreal mountains.

"It is beautiful here!" said Kate. "One could almost live here."

"Ramón says he will make the lake the centre of a new world," said Cipriano.—"We will be the gods of the lake."

"I'm afraid I am just a woman," said Kate.

His black eyes came round at her swiftly.

"What does it mean, just a woman?" he said, quickly, sternly.

She hung her head. What did it mean? What indeed did it mean? Just a woman! She let her soul sink again into the lovely elusiveness where everything is possible, even that oneself is elusive among the gods.

The motor-boat, with waves slapping behind, was running quickly along the brownish pale water. The soldiers, who were in the front, for balance, crouched on the floor with the glazed, stupefied mask-faces of the people when they are sleepy. And soon they were a heap in the bottom of the boat, two little heaps lying in contact.

Cipriano sat behind her, his tunic removed, spreading his white-sleeved arms on the back of his seat. The cartridge belt was heavy on his hips. His face was completely expressionless, staring ahead. The wind blew his black hair on his forehead, and blew his little beard. He met her eyes with a far-off, remote smile, far, far down his black eyes. But it was a wonderful recognition of her.

The boatman in the stern sat tall and straight, watching with pale eyes of shallow, superficial consciousness. The great hat made his face dark, the chin-ribbon fell black against his cheek. Feeling her look at him, he glanced at her as if she were not there.

Turning, she pushed her cushion on to the floor and slid down. Cipriano got up, in the running, heaving boat, and pulled her another seat-cushion. She lay, covering her face with her shawl, while the motor thugged rapidly, the awning rattled with sudden wind, the hurrying waves rose behind, giving the boat a slap and throwing her forward, sending spray sometimes, in the heat and silence of the lake.

Kate lost her consciousness, under her yellow shawl, in the silence of men.

She woke to the sudden stopping of the engine, and sat up. They were near shore: the white towers of San Pablo among near trees. The boatman, wide-eyed, was bending over the engine, abandoning the tiller. The waves pushed the boat slowly round.

"What is it?" said Cipriano.

"More gasoline, Excellency!" said the boatman.

The soldiers woke and sat up.

The breeze had died.

"The water is coming," said Cipriano.

"The rain?" said Kate.

"Yes—" and he pointed with his fine black finger, which was pale on the inside, to where black clouds were rushing up behind the mountains, and in another place farther off, great heavy banks were rising with strange suddenness. The air seemed to be knitting together overhead. Lightning flashed in various places, muffled thunder spoke far away.

Still the boat drifted. There was a smell of gasoline. The man pottered with the engine. The motor started again, only to stop again in a moment.

The man rolled up his trousers and, to Kate's amazement, stepped into the lake, though they were a mile from the shore. The water was not up to his knees. They were on a bank. He slowly pushed the boat before him, wading in the silence.

"How deep is the lake further in?" asked Kate.

"There, Señorita, where the birds with the white breasts are swimming, it is eight and a half metres," he said, pointing as he waded.

"We must make haste," said Cipriano.

"Yes, Excellency!"

The man stepped in again, with his long, handsome brown legs. The motor sputtered. They were under way, running fast. A new chill wind was springing up.

But they rounded a bend, and saw ahead the flat promontory with the dark mango trees, and the pale yellow upper storey of the hacienda house of Jamiltepec rising above the trees. Palm-trees stood motionless, the bougainvillea hung in heavy sheets of magenta colour. Kate could see huts of peons among the trees, and women washing, kneeling on stones at the lake-side where the stream ran in, and a big plantation of bananas just above.

A cool wind was spinning round in the heavens. Black clouds were filling up. Ramón came walking slowly down to the little harbour as they landed.

"The water is coming," he said in Spanish.

"We are in time," said Cipriano.

Ramón looked them both in the face, and knew. Kate, in her new elusiveness, laughed softly.

"There is another flower opened in the garden of Quetzalcoatl," said Cipriano in Spanish.

"Under the red cannas of Huitzilopochtli," said Ramón.

"Yes there, Señor," said Cipriano. "*Pero una florecita tan zarca! Y abrió en mi sombra, amigo.*"

"*Sois hombre de la alta fortuna.*"

"*Verdad!*"*

It was about five in the afternoon. The wind hissed in the leaves, and suddenly the rain was streaming down in a white smoke of power. The ground was a solid white smoke of water, the lake was gone.

"You will have to stay here tonight," said Cipriano to Kate, in
5 Spanish, in the soft, lapping Indian voice.

"But the rain will leave off," she said.

"You will have to stay here," he repeated, in the same Spanish phrase, in a curious voice like a breath of wind.

Kate looked at Ramón, blushing. He looked back at her, she
10 thought, very remote, as if looking at her from far, far away.

"The bride of Huitzilopochtli," he said, with a faint smile.

"Thou, Quetzalcoatl, thou wilt have to marry us," said Cipriano.

"Do you wish it?" said Ramón.

"Yes!" she said. "I want you to marry us, only you."
15 "When the sun goes down," said Ramón.

And he went away to his room. Cipriano showed Kate to her room, then left her and went to Ramón.

The cool water continued to come down, rushing with a smoke of speed down from heaven.

20 As the twilight came through the unceasing rain, a woman-servant brought Kate a sleeveless dress or chemise of white linen, scalloped at the bottom and embroidered with stiff blue flowers upside-down on the black stalks, with two stiff green leaves. In the centre of the flowers was the tiny Bird of Quetzalcoatl.

25 "The *Patrón* asks that you put this on!" said the woman, bringing also a lamp and a little note.

The note was from Ramón, saying in Spanish: Take the dress of the bride of Huitzilopochtli, and put it on, and take off everything but this. Leave no thread nor thing that can touch you from the past.
30 The past is finished. It is the new twilight.

Kate did not quite know how to put on the slip, for it had no sleeves nor arm-holes, but was just a straight slip with a running string. Then she remembered the old Indian way, and tied the string over her left shoulder: rather, slipped the tied string over her left
35 shoulder, leaving her arms and part of her right breast bare, the slip gathered full over her breasts. And she sighed. For it was but a shirt with flowers upturned at the bottom.

Ramón, barefoot, in his white clothes, came for her and took her in silence downstairs into the garden. The zaguán was dark, the rain
40 fell steadily in the twilight, but was abating. All was dark twilight.

Ramón took off his blouse and threw it on the stairs. Then with naked breast he led her into the garden, into the massive rain. Cipriano came forward, barefoot, with naked breast, bareheaded, in the floppy white pantaloons.

They stood barefoot on the earth, that still threw back a white smoke of waters. The rain drenched them in a moment.

"Barefoot on the living earth, with faces to the living rain," said Ramón in Spanish, quietly; "at twilight, between the night and the day; man, and woman, in presence of the unfading star, meet to be perfect in one another. Lift your face, Caterina, and say: *This man is my rain from heaven—*"

Kate lifted her face and shut her eyes in the downpour.

"This man is my rain from heaven," she said.

"This woman is the earth to me—say that, Cipriano," said Ramón, kneeling on one knee and laying his hand flat on the earth.

Cipriano kneeled and laid his hand on the earth.

"This woman is the earth to me," he said.

"I, woman, kiss the feet and the heels of this man, for I will be strength to him, throughout the long twilight of the Morning Star."

Kate kneeled and kissed the feet and heels of Cipriano, and said her say.

"I, man, kiss the brow and the breast of this woman, for I will be her peace and her increase, through the long twilight of the Morning Star."

Cipriano kissed her, and said his say.

Then Ramón put Cipriano's hand over the rain-wet eyes of Kate, and Kate's hand over the rain-wet eyes of Cipriano.

"I, a woman, beneath the darkness of this covering hand, pray to this man to meet me in the heart of the night, and never deny me," said Kate, "but let it be an abiding place between us, for ever."

"I, a man, beneath the darkness of this covering hand, pray to this woman to receive me in the heart of the night, in the abiding place that is between us for ever."

"Man shall betray a woman, and woman shall betray a man," said Ramón, "and it shall be forgiven them, each of them. But if they have met as earth and rain, between day and night, in the hour of the Star: if the man has met the woman with his body and the star of his hope, and the woman has met the man with her body and the star of her yearning, so that a meeting has come to pass, and an abiding place for the two where they are as one star, then shall neither of them betray

the abiding place where the meeting lives like an unsetting star. For
if either betray the abiding place of the two, it shall not be forgiven,
neither by day nor by night nor in the twilight of the star."

The rain was leaving off, the night was dark.

5   "Go and bathe in the warm water, which is peace between us all.
And put oil on your bodies, which is the stillness of the Morning Star.
Anoint even the soles of your feet, and the roots of your hair."*

Kate went up to her room and found a big earthenware bath with
steaming water, and big towels. Also, in a beautiful little bowl, oil,
10 and a soft bit of white wool.

She bathed her rain-wet body in the warm water, dried, and
anointed herself with the clear oil, that was clear as water. It was soft,
and had a faint perfume, and was grateful to the skin. She rubbed all
her body, even among her hair and under her feet, till she glowed
15 softly.

Then she put on another of the slips with the inverted blue
flowers, that had been laid on the bed for her, and over that, a dress
of green, hand woven wool, made of two pieces joined openly
together down the sides, showing a bit of the white, full under-dress,
20 and fastened on the left shoulder. There was a stiff flower, blue, on a
black stem, with two black leaves, embroidered at the bottom, at each
side. And her white slip showed a bit at the breast, and hung below
the green skirt, showing the blue flowers.

It was strange and primitive, but beautiful. She pushed her feet
25 into the plaited green huaraches. But she wanted a belt. She tied a
piece of ribbon round her waist.

A mozo tapped to say supper was ready.

Laughing rather shyly, she went along to the salon.

Ramón and Cipriano were both waiting, in silence, in their white
30 clothes. Cipriano had his red sarape loosely thrown over his
shoulders.

"So!" said Cipriano, coming forward. "The bride of Huitzilopochtli, like a green morning. But Huitzilopochtli will put on your
sash, and you will put on his shoes, so that he shall never leave you,
35 and you shall be always in his spell."

Cipriano tied round her waist a narrow woolen sash of white wool,
with white, terraced towers upon a red and black ground. And she
stooped and put on his small, dark feet the huaraches of woven red
strips of leather, with a black cross on the toes.

40 "One more little gift," said Ramón.

He made Kate put over Cipriano's head a blue cord bearing a little symbol of Quetzalcoatl, the snake in silver and the bird in blue turquoise. Cipriano put over her head the same symbol, but in gold, with a bird in black dull jet, and hanging on a red cord.

"There!" said Ramón. "That is the symbol of Quetzalcoatl, the Morning Star. Remember the marriage is the meeting-ground, and the meeting-ground is the star. If there be no star, no meeting-ground, no true coming together of man with the woman, into a wholeness, there is no marriage. And if there is no marriage, there is nothing but an agitation. If there is no honorable meeting of man with woman and woman with man, there is no good thing come to pass.—But if the meeting come to pass, then whosoever betrays the abiding place, which is the meeting-ground, which is that which lives like a star between day and night, between the dark of woman and the dawn of man, between man's night and woman's morning, shall never be forgiven, neither here nor in the hereafter. For man is frail and woman is frail, and none can draw the line down which another shall walk. But the star that is between two people and is their meeting-ground shall not be betrayed.

"And the star that is between three people, and is their meeting-ground, shall not be betrayed.

"And the star that is between all men and all women, and between all the children of men, shall not be betrayed.

"Whosoever betrays another man, betrays a man like himself, a fragment. For if there is no star between a man and a man, or even a man and a wife, there is nothing. But whosoever betrays the star that is between him and another man, betrays all, and all is lost to the traitor.

"Where there is no star and no abiding place, nothing is, so nothing can be lost—"

Chapter XXI.

The Opening of the Church.

Kate went back to her house in Sayula, and Cipriano went back to his command in the city.

5   "Will you not come with me?" he said. "Shall we not make a civil marriage, and live in the same house together?"*

"No," she said. "I am married to you by Quetzalcoatl, no other. I will be your wife in the world of Quetzalcoatl, no other. And if the star has risen between us, we will watch it."

10   Conflicting feelings played in his dark eyes. He could not bear even to be the least bit thwarted. Then the strong, rather distant look came back.

"It is very good," he said. "It is the best."

And he went away without looking back.

15   Kate returned to her house, to her servants and her rocking-chair. Inside herself she kept very still and almost thoughtless, taking no count of time. What was going to unfold must unfold of itself.

She no longer feared the nights, when she was shut alone in her darkness. But she feared the days a little. She shrank so mortally 20 from contact.

She opened her bedroom window one morning, and looked down to the lake. The sun had come, and queer blotty shadows were on the hills beyond the water. Way down at the water's edge a woman was pouring water from a calabash bowl over a statuesque pig, dipping 25 rapidly and assiduously. The little group was seen in silhouette against the pale, dun lake.

But impossible to stand at her open window looking on the little lane. An old man suddenly appeared from nowhere, offering her a leaf full of tiny fish, charales, like splinters of glass, for ten centavos, 30 and a girl was unfolding three eggs from the ragged corner of her rebozo, thrusting them imploringly forward to Kate. An old woman was shambling up: with a sad story, Kate knew. She fled from her window and the importunity.

At the same instant, the sound that always made her heart stand 35 still woke on the invisible air. It was the sound of drums, of tom-toms

332

rapidly beaten. The same sound she had heard in the distance, in the tropical dusk of Ceylon, from the temples at sunset. The sound she had heard from the edge of the forests in the north, when the Red Indians were dancing by the fire. The sound that wakes dark, ancient echoes in the heart of every man, the thud of the primeval world.

Two drums were violently throbbing against one another. Then gradually they were slowing down, in a peculiar uneven rhythm, till at last there was only left one slow, continual, monotonous note, like a great drop of darkness falling heavily, continually, dripping in the bright morning.

The re-evoked past is frightening, and if it be re-evoked to overwhelm the present, it is fiendish. Kate felt a real terror of the sound of a tom-tom. It seemed to beat straight on her solar plexus, to make her sick.

She went to her window. Across the lane rose a tall garden-wall of adobe brick, and above that, the sun on the tops of the orange trees, deep gold. Beyond the orange garden rose three tall, handsome, shaggy palm-trees, side by side on slim stems. And from the very top of the two outer palms, rose the twin tips of the church-towers. She had noticed it so often: the two ironwork Greek crosses seeming to stand on the mops of the palms.

Now in an instant she saw the glitter of the symbol of Quetzalcoatl in the places where the cross had been: two circular suns, with the dark bird at the centre. The gold of the suns—or the serpents— flashed new in the light of the sun, the bird lifted its wings dark in outline within the circle.

Then again the two drums were speeding up, beating against one another with the peculiar uneven savage rhythm, which at first seems no rhythm, and then seems to contain a summons almost sinister in its power, acting on the helpless blood direct. Kate felt her hands flutter on her wrists, in fear. Almost, too, she could hear the heart of Cipriano beating: her husband in Quetzalcoatl.

"Listen, Niña! Listen, Niña!" came Juana's frightened voice from the verandah.

Kate went to the verandah. Ezequiel had rolled up his mattress and was hitching up his pants. It was Sunday morning, when he sometimes lay on after sunrise. His thick black hair stood up, his dark face was blank with sleep, but in his quiet aloofness and in his slightly bowed head Kate could see the secret satisfaction he took in the barbarous sound of the drums.

"It comes from the church!" said Juana.

Kate caught the other woman's black, reptilian eyes unexpectedly. Usually, she forgot that Juana was dark, and different. For days she would not realise it. Till suddenly she met that black, void look with the glint in it, and she started inwardly, involuntarily asking herself: Does she hate me?

Or was it only the unspeakable difference in blood?

Now, in the dark glitter which Juana showed her for one moment, Kate read fear, and triumph, and a slow, savage, nonchalant defiance. Something very inhuman.

"What does it mean?" Kate said to her.

"It means, Niña, that they won't ring the bells any more. They have taken the bells away, and they beat the drums in the church. Listen! Listen!"

The drums were shuddering rapidly again.

Kate and Juana went across to the open window.

"Look! Niña! The Eye of the Other One! No more crosses on the church. It is the Eye of the Other One. Look! how it shines! How nice!"

"It means," said Ezequiel's breaking young voice, which was just turning deep, "that it is the church of Quetzalcoatl. Now it is the temple of Quetzalcoatl: our own god."

He was evidently a staunch Man of Quetzalcoatl.

"Think of it!" murmured Juana, in an awed voice. She seemed like a heap of darkness low at Kate's side.

Then again she glanced up, and the eyes of the two women met for a moment.

"See the Niña's eyes of the sun!" cried Juana, laying her hand on Kate's arm. Kate's eyes were a sort of hazel, changing, grey-gold, flickering at the moment with wonder, and a touch of fear and dismay. Juana sounded triumphant.

A man in a white sarape, with the blue and black borders, suddenly appeared at the window, lifting his hat, on which was the sign of Quetzalcoatl, and pushing a little card through the window.

The card said: Come to the church when you hear the one big drum: about seven o'clock.—It was signed with the sign of Quetzalcoatl.

"Very well!" said Kate. "I will come."

It was a quarter to seven already. Outside the room was the noise of Juana sweeping the verandah. Kate put on a white dress and a yellow hat, and a long string of pale-coloured topaz that glimmered with yellow and mauve.

The earth was all damp with rain, the leaves were all fresh and tropical thick, yet many old leaves were on the ground, beaten down.

"Niña! You are going out already! Wait! Wait! The coffee. Concha! quick!"

There was a running of bare feet, the children bringing cup and plate and sweet buns and sugar, the mother hastily limping with the coffee. Ezequiel came striding along the walk, lifting his hat. He went down to the servants' quarters.

"Ezequiel says—!" Juana came crying. When suddenly a soft, slack thud seemed to make a hole in the air, leaving a gap behind it. *Thud!—Thud!—Thud!—*rather slowly. It was the big drum, irresistible.

Kate rose at once from her coffee.

"I am going to the church," she said.

"Yes Niña—Ezequiel says—I am coming, Niña—"

And Juana scuttled away, to get her black rebozo.

The man in the white sarape with the blue and black ends was waiting by the gate. He lifted his hat, and walked behind Kate and Juana.

"He is following us!" whispered Juana.

Kate drew her yellow shawl around her shoulders.

It was Sunday morning, sailing-boats lined the water's edge, with their black hulls. But the beach was empty. As the great drum let fall its slow, bellowing note, the last people were running towards the church.

In front of the church was a great throng of natives, the men with their dark sarapes, or their red blankets over their shoulders: the nights of rain were cold: and their hats in their hands. The high, dark Indian heads!—Women in blue rebozos were pressing among. The big drum slowly, slackly exploded its note from the church-tower. Kate had her heart in her mouth.

In the middle of the crowd, a double row of men in the scarlet sarapes of Huitzilopochtli with the black diamond on the shoulders, stood with rifles, holding open a lane through the crowd.

"Pass!" said her guard to her. And Kate entered the lane of scarlet and black sarapes, going slow and dazed between watchful black eyes of the men. Her guard followed her. But Juana had been turned back.

Kate looked at her feet, and stumbled. Then she looked up.

In the gateway of the yard before the church stood a brilliant figure in a sarape whose zig-zag whorls of scarlet, white, and black ran curving, dazzling, to the black shoulders: above which was the face of Cipriano, calm, superb, with the little black beard and the arching brows. He lifted his hand to her in salute.

Behind him, stretching from the gateway to the closed door of the church, was a double row of the guard of Quetzalcoatl, in their white blankets with the blue and black borders.

"What shall I do?" said Kate.

"Stand here with me a moment," said Cipriano, in the gateway.

It was no easy thing to do, to face all those dark faces and black, glittering eyes. After all, she was a gringuita, and she felt it. A sacrifice? Was she a sacrifice? She hung her head, under her yellow hat, and watched the string of topaz twinkling and shaking its delicate, bog-watery colours against her white dress. Joachim had given it her. He had had it made up for her, the string, in Cornwall. So far away! In another world, in another life, in another era! Now she was condemned to go through these strange ordeals, like a victim.

The big drum overhead ceased, and suddenly the little drums broke like a shower of hail on the air, and as suddenly ceased.

In low, deep, inward voices, the guard of Quetzalcoatl began to speak, in heavy unison:

"*Oye! Oye! Oye! Oye!*"*

The small, inset door within the heavy doors of the church opened and Don Ramón stepped through. In his white clothes, wearing the Quetzalcoatl sarape, he stood at the head of his two rows of guards, until there was a silence. Then he raised his naked right arm.

"What is God, we shall never know!" he said, in a strong voice, to all the people.

The guard of Quetzalcoatl turned to the people, thrusting up their right arm.

"What is God, we shall never know!" they repeated.

Then again, in the crowd, the words were re-echoed by the guard of Huitzilopochtli.

After which there fell a dead silence, in which Kate was aware of a forest of black eyes glistening with white fire.

But the Sons of God come and go.
They come from beyond the Morning Star:
And thither they return, from the land of men.

It was again the solemn, powerful voice of Ramón. Kate looked at
his face: it was creamy-brown in its pallor, but changeless in 5
expression, and seemed to be sending a change over the crowd,
removing them from their vulgar complacency.

The guard of Quetzalcoatl turned again to the crowd, and
repeated Ramón's words to the crowd.

Mary and Jesus have left you, and gone to the place of 10
    renewal.
And Quetzalcoatl has come. He is here.
He is your lord.

With his words, Ramón was able to put the power of his heavy,
strong will over the people. The crowd began to fuse under his 15
influence. As he gazed back at all the black eyes, his eyes seemed to
have no expression, save that they seemed to be seeing the heart of all
darkness in front of him, where his unknowable God-mystery lived
and moved.

Those that follow me, must cross the mountains of the sky, 20
And pass the houses of the stars by night.
They shall find me only in the Morning Star.

But those that will not follow, must not peep.
Peeping, they will lose their sight, and lingering, they will fall
    very lame— 25

He stood a moment in silence, gazing with dark brows at the
crowd. Then he dropped his arm, and turned. The big doors of the
church opened, revealing a dim interior. Ramón entered the church
alone. Inside the church, the drum began to beat. The guard of
Quetzalcoatl slowly filed into the dim interior, the scarlet guard of 30
Huitzilopochtli filed into the yard of the church, taking the place of
the guard of Quetzalcoatl. Cipriano remained in the gateway of the
churchyard. His voice rang out clear and military.

"Hear me, people. You may enter the house of Quetzalcoatl. Men
must go to the right and left, and remove their shoes, and stand erect. 35
To the new God no man shall kneel.

"Women must go down the centre, and cover their faces. And
they may sit upon the floor.

"But men must stand erect.

"Pass now, those who dare."

Kate went with Cipriano into the church.

It was all different, the floor was black and polished, the walls were
5 in stripes of colour, the place seemed dark. Two files of the
white-clad Men of Quetzalcoatl stood in a long avenue down the
centre of the church.

"This way," said one of the Men of Quetzalcoatl, in a low voice,
drawing her into the centre, between the motionless files of men.

10 She went alone and afraid over the polished black floor, covering
her face with her yellow shawl. The pillars of the nave were dark
green, like trees rising to a deep-blue roof. The walls were vertically
striped in bars of black and white and vermilion and yellow and
green, with the windows between rich with deep-blue and crimson
15 and black glass, having specks of light. A strange maze, the
windows.

The daylight came only from small windows, high up under the
deep-blue roof, where the stripes of the walls had run into a maze of
green, like banana leaves. Below, the church was all dark, and rich
20 with hard colour.

Kate went forward to the front, near the altar steps. High at the
back of the chancel, above where the altar had been, burned a small
but intense bluey-white light, and just below and in front of the light
stood a huge dark figure, a strange looming block, apparently carved
25 in wood. It was a naked man, carved archaic and rather flat, holding
his right arm over his head, and on the right arm balanced a carved
wooden eagle with outspread wings whose upper surface gleamed
with gold, near the light, whose under surface was black shadow.
Round the heavy left leg of the man-image was carved a serpent, also
30 glimmering gold, and its golden head rested in the hand of the
figure, near the thigh. The face of the figure was dark.

This great dark statue loomed stiff like a pillar, rather frightening*
in the white-lit blue chancel.

At the foot of the statue was a stone altar with a small fire of ocote
35 wood burning. And on a low throne by the altar sat Ramón.

People were beginning to fill into the church. Kate heard the
strange sound of the naked feet of the men on the black, polished
floor, the white figures stole forward towards the altar steps, the dark
faces gazing round in wonder, men crossing themselves involunta-
40 rily. Throngs of men slowly flooded in, and women came half

running, to crouch on the floor and cover their faces. Kate crouched down too.

A file of the Men of Quetzalcoatl came and stood along the foot of the altar steps, like a fence with a gap in the middle, facing the people. Beyond the gap was the flickering altar, and Ramón.

Ramón rose to his feet. The Men of Quetzalcoatl turned to face him, and shot up their naked right arms, in the gesture of the statue. Ramón lifted his arm, so his blanket fell in towards his shoulder, revealing the naked side and the blue sash.

"All men salute Quetzalcoatl!" said a clear voice in command.

The scarlet Men of Huitzilopochtli were threading among the men of the congregation, pulling the kneeling ones to their feet, causing all to thrust up their right arm, palm flat to heaven, face uplifted, body erect and tense. It was the statue receiving the eagle.

So that around the low dark shrubs of the crouching women stood a forest of erect, upthrusting men, powerful and tense with inexplicable passion. It was a forest of dark wrists and hands up-pressing, with the striped wall vibrating above, and higher, the maze of green going to the little, iron-barred windows that stood open, letting in the light and air of the roof.

"I am the Living Quetzalcoatl," came the solemn, impassive voice of Ramón.

I am the Son of the Morning Star, and child of the deeps.
No man knows my Father, and I know Him not.*
My Father is deep within the deeps, whence He sent me
    forth.
He sends the eagle of silence down on wide wings
To lean over my head and my neck and my breast
And fill them strong with strength of wings.
He sends the serpent of power up my feet and my loins
So that strength wells up in me like water in hot springs.
But midmost shines as the Morning Star midmost shines
Between night and day, my Soul-star in me,
Which is my Father whom I know not.

I tell you, the day should not turn into glory,
And the night should not turn deep,
Save for the morning and evening star, upon which they turn.

Night turns upon me, and Day, who am the star between.

Between your breast and belly is a star.

If it be not there
You are empty gourd-shells filled with dust and wind.

When you walk, the star walks with you, between your breast
    and your belly.
5   When you sleep, it softly shines.
When you speak true and brave, it is bright on your lips and
    your teeth.
When you lift your hands in courage and bravery, its glow is
    clear in your palms.
10   When you turn to your wives as brave men turn to their
    women
The Morning Star and the Evening Star shine together.
For man is the Morning Star.
And woman is the Star of Evening.

15   I tell you, you are not men alone.
The star of the beyond is within you.

But have you seen a dead man, how his star has gone out of
    him?
So the star will go out of you, even as a woman will leave a
20   man if his warmth never warms her,
Should you say: *I have no star. I am no star.*

So it will leave you, and you will hang like a gourd on the vine
    of life
With nothing but rind:
25   Waiting for the rats of the dark to come and gnaw your
    inside.

Do you hear the rats of the darkness gnawing at your inside?
Till you are as empty as rat-gnawed pomegranates hanging
    hollow on the Tree of Life?

30   If the star shone, they dare not, they could not.
If you were men with the Morning Star.
If the star shone within you
No rat of the dark dared gnaw you.

But I am Quetzalcoatl, of the Morning Star.
35   I am the Living Quetzalcoatl.
And you are men who should be men of the Morning Star.
See you be not rat-gnawed gourds.

I am Quetzalcoatl of the eagle and the snake.
The earth and air.
Of the Morning Star.
I am Lord of the Two Ways—

The drum began to beat, the Men of Quetzalcoatl suddenly took 5
off their sarapes, and Ramón did the same. They were now men
naked to the waist. The eight men from the altar steps filed up to the
altar where the fire burned, and one by one kindled tall green
candles, which burned with a clear light. They ranged themselves on
either side the chancel, holding the lights high, so that the wooden 10
face of the image glowed as if alive, and the eyes of silver and jet
flashed most curiously.

"A man shall take the wine of his spirit and the blood of his heart,
the oil of his belly and the seed of his loins, and offer them first to
the Morning Star," said Ramón, in a loud voice, turning to the 15
people.

Four men came to him. One put a blue crown with the bird on his
brow, one put a red belt round his breast, another put a yellow belt
round his middle, and the last fastened a white belt round his loins.
Then the first one pressed a small glass bowl to Ramón's brow, and 20
in the bowl was white liquid like bright water. The next touched a
bowl to the breast, and the red shook in the bowl. At the navel the
man touched a bowl with yellow fluid, and at the loins, a bowl with
something dark. They held them all to the light.*

Then one by one they poured them into a silver mixing-bowl that 25
Ramón held between his hands.

"For save the Unknown God pours His Spirit* over my head and
His fire into my heart, and sends His power like a fountain of oil into
my belly, and His lightning like a hot spring into my loins, I am not. I
am nothing. I am a dead gourd. 30

"And save I take the wine of my spirit and the red of my heart, the
strength of my belly and the power of my loins, and mingle them all
together, and kindle them to the Morning Star, I betray my body, I
betray my soul, I betray my spirit and my God who is Unknown.

"Fourfold is man. But the star is one star. And one man is but one 35
star."

He took the silver mixing-bowl and slowly circled it between his
hands, in the act of mixing.

Then he turned his back to the people, and lifted the bowl high up,
between his hands, as if offering it to the image. 40

Then suddenly he threw the contents of the bowl into the altar fire.

There was a soft puff of explosion, a blue flame leaped high into the air, followed by a yellow flame, and then a rose-red smoke. In
5 three successive instants the faces of the men inside the chancel were lit bluish, then gold, then dusky red. And in the same moment Ramón had turned to the people and shot up his hand.

"Salute Quetzalcoatl!" cried a voice, and men began to thrust up their arms, when another voice came moaning strangely:
10 "No! Ah no! Ah no!"—the voice rose in a hysterical cry.

It came from among the crouching women, who glanced round in fear, to see a woman in black, kneeling on the floor, her black scarf falling back from her lifted face, thrusting up her white hands to the Madonna, in the old gesture.
15 "No! No! It is not permitted!" shrieked the voice. "Lord! Lord! Lord Jesus! Holy Virgin! Prevent him! Prevent him!"

The voice sank again to a moan, the white hands clutched the breast, and the woman in black began to work her way forward on her knees, through the throng of women who pressed aside to make
20 her way, towards the altar steps. She came with her head lowered, working her way on her knees, and moaning low prayers of supplication.

Kate felt her blood run cold. Crouching near the altar steps, she looked round. And she knew, by the shape of the head bent in the
25 black scarf, it was Carlota creeping along on her knees to the altar steps.

The whole church was frozen in horror. "Saviour! Saviour! Jesus! Oh Holy Virgin!" Carlota was moaning to herself as she crawled along.
30 It seemed hours before she reached the altar steps. Ramón still stood below the great Quetzalcoatl image with arm upflung.

Carlota crouched black at the altar steps and flung up her white hands and her white face in the frenzy of the old way.

"Lord! Lord!" she cried, in a strange ecstatic voice that froze
35 Kate's bowels with horror: "Jesus! Jesus! Jesus! Jesus! Jesus! Jesus!"

Carlota strangled in her ecstasy. And all the while, Ramón, the Living Quetzalcoatl, stood before the flickering altar with naked arm upraised, looking with dark, inalterable eyes down upon the woman.
40 Throes and convulsions tortured the body of Carlota. She gazed

sightlessly upwards. Then came her voice, in the mysterious rhapsody of prayer:

"Lord! Lord! Forgive!

"God of love, forgive! He knows not what he does.

"Lord! Lord Jesus! Make an end. Make an end, Lord of the world, Christ of the Cross, make an end. Have mercy on him, Father. Have pity on him!

"Oh, take his life from him now, now, that his soul may not die."

Her voice had gathered strength till it rang out metallic and terrible:

"Almighty God, take his life from him, and save his soul."

And in the silence after that cry her hands seemed to flicker in the air like flames of death.

"The Omnipotent," came the voice of Ramón, speaking quietly, as if to her, "is with me, and I serve Omnipotence!"

She remained with her white clasped hands upraised, her white arms and her white face showing mystical, like onyx, from her thin black dress. She was absolutely rigid. And Ramón, with his arm too upraised, looked down on her abstractedly, his black brows a little contracted.

A strong convulsion seized her body. She became tense again, making inarticulate noises. Then another convulsion seized her. Once more she recovered herself, and thrust up her clenched hands in frenzy. A third convulsion seized her as if from below, and she fell with a strangling moan in a heap on the altar steps.

Kate had risen suddenly and run to her, to lift her up. She found her stiff, with a little froth on her discoloured lips, and fixed, glazed eyes.

Kate looked up in consternation at Ramón. He had dropped his arm, and stood with his hands against his thighs, like a statue. But he remained with his wide, absorbed dark eyes watching without any change. He met Kate's glance of dismay, and his eyes quickly glanced, like lightning, for Cipriano. Then he looked back at Carlota, across a changeless distance. Not a muscle of his face moved. And Kate could see that his heart had died in its connection with Carlota, his heart was quite quite dead in him; out of the deathly vacancy he watched his wife. Only his brows frowned a little, from his smooth, male forehead. His old connections were broken. She could hear him say: *There is no star between me and Carlota.*—And how terribly true it was!

Cipriano came quickly, switched off his brilliant sarape, wrapped it round the poor, stiff figure, and picking up the burden lightly, walked with it through the lane of women to the door, and out into the brilliant sun, Kate following. And as she followed, she heard the slow, deep voice of Ramón:

I am the Living Quetzalcoatl.
Naked I come from out of the deep
From the place which I call my Father,
Naked have I travelled the long way round
From heaven, past the sleeping sons of God.

Out of the depths of the sky, I came like an eagle.
Out of the bowels of earth like a snake.

All things that lift in the lift of living between earth and sky,
   know me.

But I am the inward star invisible.
And the star is the lamp in the hand of the Unknown Mover.

Beyond me is a Lord who is terrible, and wonderful, and dark
   to me forever.
Yet I have lain in his loins, ere he begot me in mother space.

Now I am alone on earth, and this is mine.
The roots are mine, down the dark, moist path of the snake.
And the branches are mine, in the paths of the sky and the
   bird.
But the spark of me that is me is more than mine own.

And the feet of men, and the hands of the women know me.
And knees and thighs and loins, and the bowels of strength
   and seed are lit with me.
The snake of my left hand out of the darkness is kissing your
   feet with his mouth of caressive fire,
And putting his strength in your heels and ankles, his flame
   in your knees and your legs and your loins, his circle of rest
   in your belly.
For I am Quetzalcoatl, the feathered snake,
And I am not with you till my serpent has coiled his circle of
   rest in your belly.

And I, Quetzalcoatl, the eagle of the air, am brushing your
   faces with vision.

I am fanning your breasts with my breath.
And building my nest of peace in your bones.

I am Quetzalcoatl, of the Two Ways.

Kate lingered to hear the end of this hymn. Cipriano also had 5
lingered in the porch, with the strange figure in the brilliant sarape in
his arms. His eyes met Kate's. In his black glance was a sort of
homage, to the mystery of the Two Ways: a sort of secret. And Kate
was uneasy.

They crossed quickly under the trees to the hotel, which was very 10
near, and Carlota was laid in bed. A soldier had gone already to find a
doctor: they sent also for a priest.

Kate sat by the bed. Carlota lay on the bed, making small, horrible
moaning noises. The drums outside on the church-roof started to
roll, in a savage, complicated rhythm. Kate went to the window and 15
looked out. People were streaming dazzled from the church.

And then, from the church-roof, came the powerful singing of
men's voices, fanning like a dark eagle in the bright air: a deep,
relentless chanting, with an undertone of passionate assurance. She
went to the window to look. She could see the men on the 20
church-roof, the people swarming down below. And the roll of that
relentless chanting, with its undertone of exultance in power and life,
rolled through the air like an invisible dark presence.

Cipriano came in again, glancing at Carlota and at Kate.

"They are singing the Song of Welcome to Quetzalcoatl," said he. 25

"Is that it?" said Kate. "What are the words?"

"I will find you a song-sheet," he said.

He stood beside her, putting the spell of his presence over her.
And she still struggled a little, as if she were drowning. When she
wasn't drowning, she wanted to drown. But when it actually came, 30
she fought for her old footing.

There was a crying noise from Carlota. Kate hurried to the
bed.

"Where am I?" said the white-faced, awful, deathly-looking
woman. 35

"You are resting in bed," said Kate. "Don't trouble."

"Where was I?" came Carlota's voice.

"Perhaps the sun gave you a touch of sunstroke," said Kate.

Carlota closed her eyes.

Then suddenly outside the noise of drums rolled again, a powerful 40 sound. And outside in the sunshine life seemed to be rolling in powerful waves.

Carlota started, and opened her eyes.

"What is that noise?"

5   "It is a fiesta," said Kate.

"Ramón has murdered me, and lost his own soul," said Carlota. "He has murdered me, and lost his own soul. He is a murderer, and one of the damned. The man I married! The man I married! A murderer among the damned!"

10   It was evident she no longer heard the sounds outside.

Cipriano could not bear the sound of her voice. He came quickly to the side of the bed.

"Doña Carlota!" he said, looking down at her dulled hazel eyes, that were fixed and unseeing: "Do not die with wrong words on your

15   lips. If you are murdered, you have murdered yourself. You were never married to Ramón. You were married to your own way."

He spoke fiercely, avengingly.

"Ah!" said the dying woman. "Ah! I never married Ramón. No! I never married him! How could I? He was not what I would have him

20   be. How could I marry him?—Ah! I thought I married him. Ah! I am so glad I didn't—so glad."

"You are glad! You are glad!" said Cipriano in anger, angry with the very ghost of the woman, talking to the ghost. "You are glad because you never poured the wine of your body into the mixing-

25   bowl! Yet in your day you have drunk the wine of his body and been soothed with his oil. You are glad you kept yours back. You are glad you kept back the wine of your body and the secret oil of your soul? That you gave only the water of your charity?—I tell you the water of charity, the hissing water of the spirit is bitter at last in the mouth and

30   in the breast and in the belly, it puts out the fire. You would have put out the fire, Doña Carlota.—But you cannot. You shall not. You have been charitable and compassionless to the man you called your own. So you have put out your own fire."

"Who is talking?" said the ghost of Carlota.

35   "I, Cipriano Viedma, am talking."

"The oil and the wine! The oil and the wine and the bread! They are the sacrament! They are the body and the blessing of God! Where is the priest? I want the sacrament. Where is the priest? I want to confess, and take the sacrament, and have the peace of God," said

40   the ghost of Carlota.

"The priest is coming.—But you can take no sacrament, unless you give it. The oil and the wine and the bread! They are not for the priest to give. They are to be poured into the mixing-bowl, which Ramón calls the cup of the star. If you pour neither oil nor wine into the mixing-bowl, from the mixing-bowl you cannot drink. So you have no sacrament." 5

"The sacrament! The bread!" said the ghost of Carlota.

"There is no bread. There is no body without blood and oil, as Shylock found out."*

"A murderer, lost among the damned!" murmured Carlota. "The father of my children! The husband of my body! Ah no! It is better for me to call to the Holy Virgin, and die." 10

"Call then, and die!" said Cipriano.

"My children!" murmured Carlota.

"It is well you must leave them. With your beggar's bowl of charity you have stolen their oil and their wine as well. It is good for you to steal from them no more, you stale virgin, you spinster, you born widow, you weeping mother, you impeccable wife, you just woman. You stole the very sunshine out of the sky and the sap out of the earth. Because back again, what did you pour? Only the water of dead dilution into the mixing-bowl of life, you thief. Oh die!—die!—die! Die and be a thousand times dead! Do nothing but utterly die!" 15 20

Doña Carlota had relapsed into unconsciousness: even her ghost refused to hear. Cipriano flung his sinisterly-flaming sarape over his shoulders and his face, over his nose, till only his black, glittering eyes were visible as he blew out of the room. 25

Kate sat by the window, and laughed a little. The primeval woman inside her laughed to herself, for she had known all the time about the two thieves on the Cross with Jesus: the bullying, marauding thief of the male in his own rights, and the much more subtle, cold, sly, charitable thief of the woman in *her* own rights, forever chanting her beggar's whine about the love of God and the God of pity.* 30

But Kate, too, was a modern woman and a woman in her own rights. So she sat on with Carlota. And when the doctor came, she accepted the obsequiousness of the man as part of her rights. And when the priest came, she accepted the obsequiousness from him, just the same, as part of her woman's rights. These two ministers of love, what were they for, but to be obsequious to her? As for herself, she could hardly be called a thief, and a sneak-thief of the world's 35 40

virility, when these men came forcing their obsequiousness upon
her, whining to her to take it and relieve them of the responsibility of
their own manhood. No, if women are thieves, it is only because men
want to be thieved from. If women thieve the world's virility, it is only
5 because men want to have it thieved, since for men to be responsible
for their own manhood seems to be the last thing men want.

So Kate sat on in the room of the dying Carlota, smiling a little
cynically. Outside she heard the roll of the tom-toms and the deep
chanting of the Men of Quetzalcoatl. Beyond, under the trees, in the
10 smoothed, cleared space before the church, she saw the half-naked
men dancing in a circle, to the drum: the round dance. Then later,
dancing a religious dance of the return of Quetzalcoatl. It was the
old, barefooted, absorbed dancing of the Indians, the dance of
downward-sinking absorption. It was the dance of these people too,
15 just the same: the dance of the Aztecs and Zapotecs and the
Huicholes, just the same in essence, indigenous to America: the
curious, silent, absorbed dance of the softly-beating feet and ankles,
the body coming down softly, but with deep weight, upon powerful
knees and ankles, to the tread of the earth, as when a male bird treads
20 the hen. And women softly stepping in unison.

And Kate, listening to the drums and the full-throated singing,
and watching the rich, soft bodies in the dance, thought to herself a
little sceptically: Yes! For these it is easier. But all the white men, of
the dominant race, what are they doing at this moment?

25 In the afternoon there was a great dance of the *Welcome to
Quetzalcoatl*. Kate could only see a little of it, in front of the church.

The drums beat vigorously all the time, the dance wound
strangely to the water's edge. Kate heard afterwards that the
procession of women with baskets on their heads, filled with bread
30 and fruits all wrapped in leaves, went down to the shore and loaded
the boats. Then dancers and all got into the boats and *canoas*, and
rowed to the island.

They made a feast on the island, and learned the dance of the
Welcome to Quetzalcoatl, which they would dance every year on that
35 day. And they learned the Song of the *Welcome to Quetzalcoatl*, which
later on Cipriano brought to Kate, as she sat in that dim room with
the unconscious woman, who made small, terrible, mechanical
noises.

The doctor came hastening, and the priest came after a while.
40 Neither could do anything. They came in the afternoon again, and

Kate walked out and wandered on the half-deserted beach, looking at the flock of boats drawing near the island, and feeling that life was a more terrible issue even than death. One could die and have done. But living was never done, it could never be finished, and the responsibility could never be shifted.

She went back again to the sick room, and with the aid of a woman she undressed poor Carlota and put a night dress on her. Another doctor came from the city. But the sick woman was dying. And Kate was alone with her again.

The men, where were they?

The business of living? Were they really gone about the great business of living, abandoning her here to this business of dying?

It was nightfall before she heard the drums returning. And again that deep, full, almost martial singing of men, savage and remote, to the sound of the drum. Perhaps after all life would conquer again, and men would be men, so that women could be women. Till men are men indeed, women have no hope to be women. She knew that fatally enough.

Cipriano came to her, smelling of sun and sweat, his face darkly glowing, his eyes flashing. He glanced at the bed, at the unconscious woman, at the medicine bottles.

"What do they say?" he asked.

"The doctors think she may come round."

"She will die," he said.

Then he went with her to the window.

"See!" he said. "This is what they are singing."

It was the song-sheet of the *Welcome to Quetzalcoatl*.

Welcome to Quetzalcoatl.

We are not wasted. We are not left out.
Quetzalcoatl has come!
There is nothing more to ask for.
Quetzalcoatl has come!

He threw the Fish in the boat.
The cock rose,* and crew over the waters.
The naked one climbed in.
Quetzalcoatl has come!

Quetzalcoatl loves the shade of trees.
Give him trees! Call back the trees!

We are like trees, tall and rustling.
Quetzalcoatl is among the trees.

Do not tell me my face is shining.
Quetzalcoatl has come!
Over my head his noiseless eagle
Fans a flame.

Tie my spotted shoes for dancing,
The snake has kissed my heel.
Like a volcano my hips are moving
With fire, and my throat is full.

Blue daylight sinks in my hair.
The star comes out between the two
Wonders, shines out of everywhere,
Saying without speech: Look you!

Ah Quetzalcoatl!
Put sleep as black as beauty in the secret of my belly.
Put star-oil over me.
Call me a man.

Even as she read, she could hear the people outside singing it, as
the [clay] flutes* unthreaded the melody time after time. This strange
dumb people of Mexico was opening its voice at last. It was as if a
stone had been rolled off them all, and she heard their voice for the
first time, deep, wild, with a certain exultance and menace.

The naked one climbed in.
Quetzalcoatl has come!

She could hear the curious defiance and exultance in the men's
voices. Then a woman's voice, clear almost as a star itself, went up
the road at the verse:

Blue daylight sinks in my hair.
The star comes out between the two
Wonders. . . .

Strange! The people had opened hearts at last. They had rolled
the stone of their heaviness away, a new world had begun. Kate was
frightened. It was dusk. She laid her hand on Cipriano's knee, lost.
And he leaned and put his dark hand against her cheek, breathing
silently.

"Today," he said softly, "we have done well."

She felt for his hand. All was so dark. But oh, so deep, so deep and beyond her, the vast, soft, living heat! So beyond her!

> Put sleep as black as beauty in the secret of my belly.
> Put star-oil over me. 5

She could almost feel her soul appealing to Cipriano for this sacrament.

They sat side by side in darkness, as the night fell, and he held his hand loosely on hers. Outside, the people were still singing. Some were dancing round the drum. On the church-towers, where the 10 bells had been, there were fires flickering, and white forms of men, the noise of a heavy drum, then again, the chant. In the yard before the church-doors a fire was blazing, and Men of Huitzilopochtli stood watching two of their men, naked save for a breech-cloth and the scarlet feathers on their head, dancing the old spear-dance, 15 whooping challenge in the firelight.

Ramón came in, in his white clothes. He pulled off his big hat, and stood looking down at Carlota. She no longer made noises, and her eyes were turned up horribly, showing the whites. Ramón closed his eyes a moment, and turned away, saying nothing. He came to the 20 window, where Cipriano still sat in his impenetrable but living silence, that satisfied where all speech had failed, holding Kate's hand loosely. Nor did he let go her hand.

Ramón looked out, at the fires in the church-towers, the fire before the church-doors, the little fires on the beach by the lake, and 25 the figures of men in white, the figures of women in dark rebozos, with full white skirts, the two naked dancers, the standing crowd, the occasional scarlet sarapes of Huitzilopochtli, the white and blue of Quetzalcoatl, the creeping away of a motor-car, the running of boys, the men clustering round the drum, to sing. 30

"It is life," he said, "which is the mystery. Death is hardly mysterious in comparison."

There was a knocking. The doctor had come again, and a sister to nurse the dying woman. Softly the sister paced round the room and bent over her charge. 35

Cipriano and Kate went away in a boat over the dark lake, away from all the fires and the noise, into the deep darkness of the lake beyond, to Jamiltepec. Kate felt she wanted to be covered with deep and living darkness, the deeps where Cipriano could lay her.

Put sleep as black as beauty in the secret of my belly.
Put star-oil over me.

And Cipriano, as he sat in the boat with her, felt the inward sun
rise darkly in him, diffusing through him; and felt the mysterious
5 flower of her woman's femaleness slowly opening to him, as a
sea-anemone opens deep under the sea, with infinite soft fleshliness.
The hardness of self-will was gone, and the soft anemone of her
deeps blossomed for him of itself, far down under the tides.

Ramón remained behind in the hotel, in the impenetrable sanc-
10 tuary of his own stillness. Carlota remained unconscious. There was
a consultation of doctors: to no effect. She died at dawn, before her
boys could arrive from Mexico; as a *canoa* was putting off from the
shore with a little breeze, and the passengers were singing the Song
of *Welcome to Quetzalcoatl*, unexpectedly, upon the pale water.

Chapter XXII.

The Living Huitzilopochtli.

They buried Doña Carlota in Sayula, and Kate, though a woman, went also to the funeral.* Don Ramón followed the coffin, in his white clothes and big hat with the Quetzalcoatl sign. His boys went with him: and there were many strangers, men, in black.

The boys looked odd young shoots, in their black suits with short breeches and bare knees. They were both round-faced and creamy-brown in complexion, both had a touch of fairness. The elder, Pedro, was more like Don Ramón: but his hair was softer, more fluffy than his father's, with a hint of brown. He was sulky and awkward, and kept his head ducked. The younger boy, Cyprian, had the fluffy, upstanding brown hair and the startled hazel eyes of his mother.

They had come in a motor-car with their aunt, from Guadalajara, and were returning straight to town. In her will, the mother had named guardians in place of the father, stating that the father would consent. And her considerable fortune she had left in trust for the boys. But the father was one of the trustees.

Ramón sat in his room in the hotel, overlooking the lake, and his two boys sat on the cane settee opposite him.

"What do you want to do, my sons?" said Ramón. "To go back with your Aunt Margarita, and return to school in the United States?"

The boys remained a while in sulky silence.

"Yes!" said Cyprian at last, his brown hair seeming to fluff up with indignation. "That is what our mother wished us to do. So, of course, we shall do it."

"Very well!" said Ramón quietly. "But remember I am your father, and my door, and my arms, and my heart will always be open to you, when you come."

The elder boy shuffled with his feet, and muttered, without looking up:

"We cannot come, Papa!"

"Why not, child?"

353

The boy looked up at him with brown eyes as challenging as his own.

"You, Papa, you call yourself the Living Quetzalcoatl?"

"Yes."

"But, Papa, our father is called Ramón Carrasco."

"It is also true," said Ramón smiling.

"We," said Pedro, rather heavily, "are not the children of the Living Quetzalcoatl, Papa. We are called Carrasco y de Lara."

"Good names both," said Ramón.

"Never," said the young Cyprian, his eyes flashing, "never can we love you, Papa. You are our enemy. You killed our mother."

"No, no!" said Ramón. "That you must not say. Your mother sought her own death."

"Mama loved you much, much, much!" cried Cyprian, the tears rising to his eyes. "Always she loved you and prayed for you—" He began to cry.

"And I, my son?" said Ramón.

"You hated her and killed her! Oh Mama! Mama! Oh Mama! I want my mother!" he wept.

"Come to me, little one!" said Ramón softly, holding out his hands.

"No!" cried Cyprian, stamping his foot and flashing his eyes through his tears. "No! No!"

The elder boy hung his head and was crying too. Ramón had the little, perplexed frown of pain on his brow. He looked from side to side, as if for some issue. Then he gathered himself together.

"Listen, my sons," he said. "You also will be men: it will not be long. While you are little boys, you are neither men nor women. But soon, the change will come, and you will have to be men. And then you will know that a man must be a man. When his soul tells him to do a thing, he must do it. When you are men, you must listen carefully to your own souls, and be sure to be true. Be true to your own souls: there is nothing else for a man to do."

"Je m'en fiche de ton âme, mon père!"* said Cyprian, with one of his flashes into French. It was a language he often spoke with his mother.

"That you may, my boy," said Ramón. "But I may not."

"Papa!" put in the elder boy. "Is your soul different from Mama's soul?"

"Who knows?" said Ramón. "I understand it differently."

"Because Mama always prayed for your soul."

"And I, in my way, pray for hers, child. If her soul comes back to me, I will take it into my heart."

"Mama's soul," said Cyprian, "will go straight into Paradise."

"Who knows, child! Perhaps the paradise for the souls of the dead is the hearts of the living."* 5

"I don't understand what you say."

"It is possible," said Ramón, "that even now the only paradise for the soul of your mother is in my heart."

The two boys stared at him with open eyes. 10

"Never will I believe that," said Cyprian.

"Or it may be in *thy* heart," said Ramón. "Hast thou a place in *thy* heart for the soul of thy mother?"

The young Cyprian stared with bewildered hazel eyes.

"The soul of my mother goes direct to Paradise, because she is a 15 saint," he asserted flatly.

"Which paradise, my son?"

"The only one. Where God is."

"And where is that?"

There was a pause. 20

"In the sky," said Cyprian, stubbornly.

"It is very far—and very empty.—But I believe, my son, that the hearts of living men are the very middle of the sky. And there God is: and Paradise: inside the hearts of living men and women. And there the souls of the dead come to rest, there, at the very centre, where 25 the blood turns and returns: that is where the dead sleep best."

There was a very blank pause.

"And wilt thou go on saying thou art the Living Quetzalcoatl?" said Cyprian.

"Surely! And when you are a little older, perhaps you will come to 30 me and say it too."

"Never! Thou hast killed our mother, and we shall hate thee. When we are men we ought to kill thee."

"Nay, that is bombast, child! Why wilt thou listen only to servants and priests and people of that sort? Are they not thy inferiors, since 35 thou art my son, and thy mother's son? Why dost thou take the talk of servants and inferiors into thy mouth? Hast thou no room for the speech of brave men?—Thou wilt not kill me, neither will thy brother. For I would not allow you, even if you wished it. And you do not wish it. Talk no more of this empty lackey-talk to me, Cyprian, 40 for I will not hear it. Art thou already a little lackey, or a priest? Come, thou art vulgar. Thou art a little vulgarian. We had better speak English: or thy French. Castilian is too good a language to turn into this currish talk."

5   Ramón rose and went to the window to look out at the lake. The drums on the church were sounding for mid-day, when every man should glance at the sun, and stand silent with a little prayer:

> The sun has climbed the hill, the day is on the downward
>   slope.
> 10 Between the morning and the afternoon, stand I here with my
>   soul, and lift it up.
> My soul is heavy with sunshine, and steeped with strength.
> The sunbeams have filled me like a honeycomb,
> It is the moment of fulness,
> 15 And the top of the morning.

Ramón turned and repeated the Mid-day Verse to his boys. They listened in confused silence.

"Come!" he said. "Why are you confused? If I talked to you about your new boots, or ten pesos, you would not be confused. But if I 20 speak of the sun and your own souls filled from the sun like honeycombs, you sulk. You had better go back to your school in America, to learn to be business men. You had better say to everybody: Oh no! we have no father! Our mother died, but we never had a father. We are children of an immaculate conception, so we 25 should make excellent business men."

"I shall be a priest," said Cyprian.

"And I a doctor," said Pedro.

"Very good! Very good! *Shall-be* is far from *am*, and tomorrow is another day. Come to me when your heart tells you to come. You are 30 my little boys, whatever you say, and I shall stroke your hair and laugh at you. Come! Come here!"

He looked at them, and they dared not refuse to obey, his power was so much greater than theirs.

He took his eldest son in his arms and stroked his head.

35   "There!" he said. "Thou art my eldest son, and I am thy father, who calls himself the Living Quetzalcoatl. When they say: Is it thy father who calls himself the Living Quetzalcoatl?—say to them: Yes, he is my father. And when they ask you what you think of such a father, say: I am young, and I do not understand him yet. But I do not

judge my father without understanding him.—Wilt thou say that, my boy, Pedro, my son?"—And Ramón stroked the boy's hair with the gentleness and tenderness which filled the child with a sort of awe.

"Yes, Papa! I will say that," said the boy, relieved.

"It is well," said Ramón, laying his hand on the child's head for a moment, like a blessing.

Then he turned to the younger son.

"Come then," he said, "and let me stroke thy upstanding hair."

"If I love thee, I cannot love Mama!" said Cyprian.

"Nay, is thy heart so narrow? Love not at all, if it makes thee petty."

"But I do not want to come to thee, Papa."

"Then stay away, my son, and come when thou dost want it."

"I do not think thou lovest me, Papa."

"Nay, when thou art an obstinate monkey, I love thee not. But when thy real manhood comes upon thee, and thou art brave and daring, rather than rash and impudent, then thou wilt be lovable. How can I love thee if thou art not lovable?"

"Mama always loved me."

"She called thee her own. I do not call thee mine own. Thou art thyself. When thou art lovable, I can love thee. When thou art rash and impudent, nay, I cannot. The mill will not spin when the wind does not blow."

The boys went away. Ramón watched them as they stood in their black clothes and bare knees upon the jetty, and his heart yearned over them.

"Ah the poor little devils!" he said to himself. And then:

"But I can do no more than keep my soul like a castle for them, to be a stronghold to them when they need it—if ever they do."

These days Kate often sat by the lake-shore, in the early light of the morning. Between the rains, the day came very clear, she could see every wrinkle in the great hills opposite, and the fold, or pass, through which a river came, away at Tuliapán, was so vivid to her she felt she had walked it. The red birds looked as if rains had freshened even their poppy-buds, and in the morning frogs were whirring.

But the world was somehow different: all different. No jangle of bells from the church, no striking of the clock. The clock was taken away.

And instead, the drums. At dawn, the heavy drum rolling its sound

on the air. Then the sound of the Dawn-Verse chanted from the
tower, in a strong man's voice:

> The dark is dividing, the sun is coming past the wall.
> Day is at hand.
> Lift your hand, say Farewell! say Welcome!
> Then be silent.
> Let the darkness leave you, let the light come into you,
> Man in the twilight.

The voice, and the great drum ceased. And in the dawn the men
who had risen stood silent, with arm uplifted, in the moment of
change, the women covered their faces and bent their heads. All was
changeless still for the moment of change.

Then the light drum rattled swiftly, as the first sparkle of the
bright sun flashed in sheer light from the crest of the great hills. The
day had begun. People of the world moved on their way.

At about nine o'clock the light drum rattled quickly, and the voice
in the tower cried:

"Half way! Half way up the slope of the morning!"

There was the heavy drum at noon, the light drum again at about
three o'clock, with the cry:

"Half way! Half way down the slope of afternoon."

And at sunset again, the great drum rolling, and the voice crying:

> Leave off! Leave off! Leave off!
> Lift your hand, say Farewell! say Welcome!
> Man in the twilight.
> The sun is in the outer porch, cry to him: Thanks! Oh
>   Thanks!
> Then be silent.
> You belong to the night.

And again in the sunset everywhere men stood with lifted faces
and hand, and women covered their faces and stood with bowed
heads, all was changeless still for the moment of change.

Then the lighter drums suddenly beat, and people moved on into
the night.

The world was different, different. The drums seemed to leave
the air soft and vulnerable, as if it were alive. Above all, if it could be
prevented, Ramón would have no strike of metal on metal, during
the moments of change.

Metal for resistance.
Drums for the beating heart.
The heart ceases not.

This was one of Ramón's little verses.

Strange, the change that was taking place in the world. Always the air had a softer, more velvety silence, it seemed alive. And there were no hours. Dawn and noon and sunset, mid-morning, or the upslope middle, and mid-afternoon, or the downslope middle, this was the day, with the watches of the night. They began to call the four watches of the day the watch of the rabbit, the watch of the hawk, the watch of the turkey-buzzard and the watch of the deer. And the four quarters of the night were the watch of the frog, the watch of the fire-fly, the watch of the fish, the watch of the squirrel.

"I shall come for you," wrote Cipriano to her, "when the deer is thrusting his last foot towards the forest."

That meant, she knew, in the last quarter of the hours of the deer: something after five o'clock.

It was as if, from Ramón and Cipriano, from Jamiltepec and the lake region, a new world was unfolding, unrolling, as softly and subtly as twilight falling and removing the clutter of day. It was a soft, twilit newness slowly spreading and penetrating the world, even into the cities. Now, even in the cities the blue sarapes of Quetzalcoatl were seen, and the drums were heard at the Hours, casting a strange mesh of twilight over the clash of bells and the clash of traffic. Even in the Capital the big drum rolled again, and men, even men in city clothes would stand still with uplifted faces and arm upstretched, listening for the Noon-Verse, which they knew in their hearts, and trying not to hear the clash of metal.

Metal for resistance.
Drums for the beating heart.

But it was a world of metal, and a world of resistance. Cipriano, strangely powerful with the soldiers, in spite of the hatred he aroused in other officials, was for meeting metal with metal. For getting Montes to declare: The religion of Quetzalcoatl is the religion of Mexico, official and declared.—Then backing up the declaration with the army.

But no! no! said Ramón. Let it spread of itself. And wait awhile, till you can be declared the Living Huitzilopochtli, and your men can have the red and black blanket, with the snake-curve. Then perhaps we can have the open wedding with Caterina, and she will be a mother among the gods.—

All the time, Ramón tried as far as possible to avoid arousing resistance and hate. He wrote open letters to the clergy, saying:

5　"Who am I, that I should be enemy of the One Church! I am catholic of catholics. I would have One Church of all the world, with Rome for the Central City, if Rome wish.

"But different peoples must have different Saviours, as they have different speech and different colour. The final mystery is one

10　mystery. But the manifestations are many.

"God must come to Mexico in a blanket and in huaraches, else he is no god of the Mexicans, they cannot know him. Naked, all men are but men. But the touch, the look, the word that goes from one naked man to another is the mystery of living. We live by manifest-

15　ations.

"And men are fragile, and fragments, and strangely grouped in their fragmentariness. The invisible God has done it to us, darkened some faces and whitened others, and grouped us in groups, even as the zopilote is a bird, and the parrot of the hot lands is a bird, and the

20　little oriole is a bird. But the angel of the zopilotes must be a zopilote, and the angel of the parrots a parrot. And to one, the dead carcase will ever smell good; to the other, the fruit.

"Priests who will come to me do not forsake either faith or God. They change their manner of speech and vestments, as the peon calls

25　with one cry to the oxen, and with another cry to the mules. Each responds to its own call in its own way—"

To the socialists and agitators he wrote:

"What do you want? Would you make all men as you are? And when every peon in Mexico wears an American suit of clothes and

30　shiny black shoes, and looks for life in the newspaper and for his manhood to the government, will you be satisfied? Did the government, then, give you your manhood, that you expect it to give it to these others?

"It is time to forget. It is time to put away the grudge and the pity.

35　No man was ever the better for being pitied, and every man is the worse for a grudge.

"We can do nothing with life, except live it.

"Let us seek life where it is to be found. And having found it, life will solve the problems. But every time we deny the living life, in

40　order to solve a problem, we cause ten problems to spring up where was one before. Solving the problems of the people, we lose the people in a poisonous forest of problems.

"Life makes, and moulds, and changes the problem. The problem will always be there, and will always be different. So nothing can be solved, even by life and living, for life dissolves and resolves, solving it leaves alone.

"Therefore we turn to life: and from the clock to the sun and the stars, and from metal to membrane.

"This way we hope the problem will dissolve, since it can never be solved. When men seek life first, they will not seek land nor gold. The lands will lie on the lap of the gods, where men lie. And if the old communal system comes back, and the village and the land are one, it will be very good. For truly, no man can possess lands.

"But when we are deep in a bog, it is no use attempting to gallop. We can only wade out with toil. And in our haste to have a child, it is no good tearing the babe from the womb.

"Seek life, and life will bring the change.

"Seek life itself, even pause at dawn and at sunset, and life will come back into us and prompt us through the transitions.

"Lay forcible hands on nothing, only be ready to resist, if forcible hands should be laid on you. For the new shoots of life are tender, and better ten deaths than that they should be torn or trampled down by the bullies of the world. When it comes to fighting for the tender shoots of life, fight as the jaguar fights for her young, as the she-bear for her cubs.

"That which is life is vulnerable, only metal is invulnerable. Fight for the vulnerable unfolding of life. But for that, fight never to yield."

Cipriano, too, was always speaking to his soldiers, always with the same cry:

"We are men! We are fighters!

"But what can we do?

"Shall we march to simple death?

"No! No! We must march to life.

"The gringos are here. We have let them come. We must let them stay, for we cannot drive them out. With guns and swords and bayonets we can never drive them out, for they have a thousand where we have one. And if they come in peace, let them stay in peace.

"But we have not lost Mexico yet. We have not lost each other.

"We are the blood of America. We are the blood of Montezuma.

"What is my hand for? Is it to turn the handle of a machine alone?

"My hand is to salute the God of Mexicans, beyond the sky.

"My hand is to touch the hand of a brave man.

"My hand is to hold a gun.

5 "My hand is to make the corn grow out of the ground.

"What are my knees for?

"My knees are to hold me proud and erect.

"My knees are for marching on my way.

"My knees are the knees of a man.

10 "Our god is Quetzalcoatl of the blue sky, and Huitzilopochtli red at the gates, watching.

"Our gods hate a kneeling man. They shout *Ho! Erect!*

"Then what can we do?

"Wait!

15 "I am a man, naked inside my clothes as you are.

"Am I a big man? Am I a tall and powerful man, from Tlaxcala, for example?

"I am not. I am little. I am from the south. I am small.

"Yet am I not your general?

20 "Why?

"Why am I a general, and you only soldiers?

"I will tell you.

"I found the other strength.

"There are two strengths: the strength which is the strength of 25 oxen and mules and iron, of machines and guns, and of men who cannot get the second strength.

"Then there is the second strength. It is the strength you want. And you can get it, whether you are small or big. It is the strength that comes from behind the sun. And you can get it: you can get it 30 here—!" he struck his breast—"and here!" he struck his belly— "and here!" he struck his loins. "The strength that comes from back of the sun."

When Cipriano was roused, his eyes flashed, and it was as if dark feathers, like pinions, were starting out of him, out of his shoulders 35 and back, as if these dark pinions clashed and flashed like a roused eagle. His men seemed to see him, as by second sight, with the demonish clashing and dashing of wings, like an old god. And they murmured, their eyes flashing:

"It is Cipriano! It is he! We are Ciprianistas, we are his children."

40 "We are men! We are men!" cried Cipriano.

"But listen. There are two kinds of men. There are men with the second strength, and men without it.

"When the first gringos came, we lost our second strength. And the padres taught us: Submit! Submit!

"The gringos had got the second strength!   5

"How?

"Like cunning ones, they stole it on the sly. They kept very still, like a tarantula in his hole. Then when neither sun nor moon nor stars knew he was there, Biff!—the tarantula sprang across, and bit, and left the poison and sucked the secret.*   10

"So they got the secrets of the air and the water, and they got the secrets out of the earth. So the metals were theirs, and they made guns and machines and ships, and they made trains and telegrams and radio.

"Why? Why did they make all these things? How could they do it?   15

"Because, by cunning, they had got the secret of the second strength, which comes from behind the sun.

"And we had to be slaves, because we had only got the first strength, we had lost the second strength.

"Now we are getting it back. We have found our way again, to the   20
secret sun behind the sun. There sat Quetzalcoatl, and at last Don Ramón found him. There sits the red Huitzilopochtli, and *I* have found him. For *I* have found the second strength.

"When he comes, all you who strive shall find the second strength.

"And when you have it, where will you feel it?   25

"Not here! (and he struck his forehead) Not where the cunning gringos have it, in the head, and in their books. Not we. We are men, we are not spiders.

"We shall have it here! (he struck his breast) and here! (he struck his belly) and here! (he struck his loins).   30

"Are we men? Can we not get the second strength?

"Can we not? Have we lost it forever?

"I say no! Quetzalcoatl is among us. I have found the red Huitzilopochtli. The second strength!

"When you walk or sit, when you work or lie down, when you eat   35
or sleep, think of the second strength, that you must have it.

"Be very quiet. It is shy as a bird in a dark tree.

"Be very clean, clean in your bodies and your clothes. It is like a star, that will not shine in dirt.

"Be very brave, and do not drink till you are drunk, nor soil   40 yourself with bad women, nor steal. Because a drunken man has lost his second strength, and a man loses his strength in bad women, and a thief is a coward, and the red Huitzilopochtli hates a coward.

"Try! Try for the second strength. When we have it, the others will lose it."

Cipriano struggled hard with his army. The curse of any army is the having nothing to do. Cipriano made all his men cook and wash for themselves, clean and paint the barracks, make a great garden to grow vegetables, and plant trees wherever there was water. And he himself took a passionate interest in what they did. A dirty tunic, a sore foot, a badly-made huarache did not escape him. But even when they cooked their meals he went among them.

"Give me something to eat," he would say. "Give me an enchilada!"

Then he praised the cooking, or said it was bad.

Like all savages, they liked doing small things. And like most Mexicans, once they were a little sure of what they were doing, they loved doing it well.

Cipriano was determined to get some discipline into them. Discipline is what Mexico needs, and what the whole world needs. But it is the discipline from the inside that matters. The machine discipline, from the outside, breaks down.

He had the wild Indians from the north beat their drums in the barracks' yard, and start the old dances again. The dance, the dance which has meaning, is a deep discipline in itself. The old Indians of the north still have the secret of animistic dancing. They dance to gain power: power over the *living* forces or potencies of the earth. And these dances need intense dark concentration, and immense endurance.

Cipriano encouraged the dances more than anything. He learned them himself, with curious passion. The shield and spear dance, the knife dance, the dance of ambush and the surprise dance, he learned them in the savage villages of the north, and he danced them in the barracks' yard,* by the bonfire, at night, when the great doors were shut.

Then, naked save for a black breech-cloth, his body smeared with oil and red earth-powder,* he would face some heavy naked Indian and with shield and spear dance the dance of the two warriors, champions in the midst of the dense ring of soldiers. And the silent, rhythmic concentration of this duel in subtlety and rapidity kept the feet softly beating with the drum, the naked body suave and subtle, circling with suave, primitive stealth, then crouching and leaping like a panther, with the spear poised, to a clash of shields, parting again with the crowing yell of defiance and exultance.

In this dance, no-one was more suave and sudden than Cipriano. He could swerve along the ground with bent, naked back, as invisible as a lynx, circling round his opponent, his feet beating and his suave body subtly lilting to the drum. Then in a flash he was in the air, his spear pointing down at the collar-bone of his enemy and gliding over his shoulder, as the opponent swerved under, and the war-yell resounded. The soldiers in the deep circle watched fascinated, uttering the old low cries.

And as the dance went on, Cipriano felt his strength increase and surge inside him. When all his limbs were glistening with sweat, and his spirit was at last satisfied, he was at once tired and surcharged with extraordinary power. Then he would throw his scarlet and dark sarape round him, and motion other men to fight, giving his spear and shield to another officer or soldier, going himself to sit down on the ground and watch, by the firelight. And then he felt his limbs and his whole body immense with power, he felt the black mystery of power go out of him over all his soldiers. And he sat there imperturbable, in silence, holding all those black-eyed men in the splendour of his own, silent self. His own dark consciousness seemed to radiate through their flesh and their bones, they were conscious, not through themselves but through him. And as a man's instinct is to shield his own head, so their instinct was to shield Cipriano, for he was the most precious part of themselves to them. It was in him they were supreme, they got their splendour from his power and their greatest consciousness was his consciousness diffusing them.

"I am not of myself," he would say to them. "I am of the red Huitzilopochtli and the power from behind the sun. And you are not of yourselves. Of yourselves you are nothing. You are of me, my men."

He encouraged them to dance naked, with the breech-cloth, to rub themselves with the red earth-powder, over the oil.

"This is the oil of the stars. Rub it well into your limbs, and you will be strong as the starry sky. This is the red blood of volcanoes. Rub yourselves with it, you will have the power of the fire of the volcanoes, from the centre of the earth."

He encouraged them to dance the silent, concentrated dances to the drum, to dance for hours, gathering power and strength.

"If you know how to tread the dance, you can tread deeper and deeper till you touch the middle of the earth with your foot. And when you touch the middle of the earth, you will have such power in your belly and your breast, no man will be able to overcome you. Get the second strength. Get it, get it out of the earth, get it from behind the sun. Get the second strength."

He made long, rapid marches across the wild Mexican country, and through the mountains, moving light and swift. He liked to have his men camping in the open, with no tents: but the watch set, and the stars overhead. He pursued the bandits with swift movements. He stripped his captives and tied them up. But if it seemed a brave man, he would swear him in. If it seemed to him a knave, a treacherous cur, he stabbed him to the heart, saying:

"I am the red Huitzilopochtli, of the knife."

Already he had got his own small, picked body of men out of the ignominious drab uniform, dressed in white with the scarlet sash and the scarlet ankle cords, and carrying the good, red and black sarape. And his men must be clean. On the march they would stop by some river, with the order for every man to strip and wash, and wash his clothing. Then the men, dark and ruddy, moved about naked, while the white clothing of strong white cotton dried on the earth. They moved on again glittering with the peculiar whiteness of cotton clothes in Mexico, gun at their backs, sarape and small pack on their backs, wearing the heavy straw hats with the scarlet crowns on their heads.

"They must move!" he said to his officers. "They must learn again to move swiftly and untiringly, with the old power. They must not lie about. In the sleep hours, let them sleep. In the waking, let them work, or march, or drill, or dance."

He divided his regiment up into little companies of a hundred each, with a centurion and a sergeant in command. Each company of a hundred must learn to act in perfect unison, freely and flexibly. "Perfect your hundred," Cipriano insisted, "and I will perfect your thousands and your tens of thousands."*

"Listen!" he said. "For us, no trench and cannon warfare. My men are no cannon-fodder, nor trench-dung. Where cannon are, we move away. Our hundreds break up, and we attack where the cannon are not. That we are swift, that we are silent, that we have no

burdens, and that the second strength is in us: that is all. We intend
to put up no battle-front, but to attack at our own moment, and at a
thousand points."

And always he re-iterated:

"If you can get the power from the heart of the earth, and the   5
power from behind the sun: if you can summon the power of the red
Huitzilopochtli into you, nobody can conquer you. Get the second
strength."

Ramón was pressing Cipriano now openly to assume the Living
Huitzilopochtli.   10

"Come!" he said. "It is time you let General Viedma be swallowed
up in the red Huitzilopochtli. Don't you think?"

"If I know what it means," said Cipriano.

They were sitting on the mats in Ramón's room, in the heat before
the rain came, towards the end of the rainy season.   15

"Stand up!" said Ramón.

Cipriano stood up at once, with that soft, startling alertness in his
movement.

Ramón came quietly to him, placed one of his hands over
Cipriano's eyes, and one over the back of his head. Cipriano waited, 20
in the dark, living warmth, his head in the circle of Ramón's hands.
And slowly the darkness began to move upon a centre in Cipriano's
consciousness, to a centre that plunges into the bottomless depth,
like sleep.

"Cipriano?"—the voice sounded so far off.   25

"Yes."

"Is it dark?"

"It is dark."

"Is it alive? Is the darkness alive?"

"Surely it is alive."   30

"Who lives?"

"I."

"Where?"

"I know not. In the living darkness."

Ramón then bound Cipriano's eyes and head with a strip of black   35
fur. Then again, with a warm, soft pressure, he pressed one naked
hand over Cipriano's naked breast, and one between his shoulders.
Cipriano stood in profound darkness, erect and silent.

"Cipriano?"

"Yes."   40

"Is it dark in your heart?"

"It is coming dark."

Ramón felt the thud of the man's heart slowly slackening. In Cipriano, another circle of darkness had started slowly to revolve, from his heart. It swung in widening rounds, like a greater sleep.

"Is it dark?"

"It is dark."

"Who lives?"

"I."

Ramón bound Cipriano's arms at his sides, with a belt of fur round the breast. Then he put his one hand over the navel, his other hand in the small of the other man's back, pressing with slow, warm, powerful pressure.

"Cipriano?"

"Yes."

The voice and the answer were going farther and farther away.

"Is it dark?"

"No my Lord."

Ramón knelt and pressed his arms close round Cipriano's waist, pressing his black head against his side. And Cipriano began to feel as if his mind, his head were melting away in the darkness, like a pearl in black wine,* the other circle of sleep began to swing, vast. And he was a man without a head, moving like a dark wind over the face of the dark waters.

"Is it perfect?"

"It is perfect."

"Who lives?"

"Who—!"

Cipriano no longer knew.

Ramón bound him fast round the middle, then, pressing his head against the hip, folded the arms round Cipriano's loins, closing with his hands the secret places.

"Cipriano?"

"Yes."

"Is it all dark?"

But Cipriano could not answer. The last circle was sweeping round, and the breath upon the waters was sinking into the waters, there was no more utterance. Ramón knelt with pressed head and arms and hands, for some moments still. Then he bound the loins, binding the wrists to the hips.

Cipriano stood rigid and motionless. Ramón clasped the two knees with his hands, till they were warm, and he felt them dark and asleep like two living stones, or two eggs. Then swiftly he bound them together, and grasped the ankles, as one might grasp the base of a young tree as it emerges from the earth. Crouching on the earth, he gripped them in an intense grip, resting his head on the feet. The moments passed, and both men were unconscious.

Then Ramón bound the ankles, lifted Cipriano suddenly, with a sleep-moving softness, laid him on the skin of a big mountain lion,* which was spread upon the blankets, threw over him the red and black sarape of Huitzilopochtli, and lay down at his feet, holding Cipriano's feet to his own abdomen.

And both men passed into perfect unconsciousness, Cipriano within the womb of undisturbed creation, Ramón in the death sleep.

How long they were both dark, they never knew. It was twilight. Ramón was suddenly aroused by the jerking of Cipriano's feet. He sat up, and took the blanket off Cipriano's face.

"Is it night?" said Cipriano.

"Almost night," said Ramón.

Silence followed, while Ramón unfastened the bonds, beginning at the feet. Before he unbound the eyes, he closed the window, so the room was almost dark. Then he unfastened the last binding, and Cipriano sat up, looking, then suddenly covering his eyes.

"Make it quite dark!" he said.

Ramón closed the shutters, and the room was complete night. Then he returned and sat on the mats by Cipriano. Cipriano was asleep again. After a while, Ramón left him.

He did not see him again till dawn. Then Ramón found him going down to the lake, to swim. The two men swam together, while the sun rose. With the rain, the lake was colder. They went to the house to rub oil in their limbs.

Cipriano looked at Ramón with black eyes which seemed to be looking at all space.

"I went far," he said.

"To where there is no beyond?" said Ramón.

"Yes, there."

And in a moment or two, Cipriano was wrapped in his blanket again, and asleep.

He did not wake till the afternoon. Then he ate, and took a boat, and rowed down the lake to Kate. He found her at home. She was surprised to see him, in his white clothes and with his sarape of Huitzilopochtli.

"I am going to be the Living Huitzilopochtli," he said.

5 "Are you? When? Does it feel queer?"—Kate was afraid of his eyes, they seemed inhuman.

"On Thursday. The day of Huitzilopochtli is to be Thursday. Won't you sit beside me, and be wife of me when I am a god?"

"But do you feel you *are* a god?" she asked, querulous.

10 He turned his eyes on her strangely.

"I have been," he said. "And I have come back. But I belong there, where I went."

"Where?"

"Where there is no beyond, and the darkness sinks into the water, 15 and waking and sleeping are one thing."

"No," said Kate, afraid. "I never understood mystical things. They make me uneasy."

"Is it mystical when I come in to you?"

"No," said Kate. "Surely that is physical."

20 "So is the other, only further.—Won't you be the bride of Huitzilopochtli?" he asked again.

"Not so soon," said Kate.

"Not so soon!" he re-echoed.

There was a pause.

25 "Will you come back with me to Jamiltepec now?" he asked.

"Not now," she said.

"Why not now?"

"Oh, I don't know.—You treat me as if I had no life of my own," she said. "But I have."

30 "A life of your own? Who gave it you? Where did you get it?"

"I don't know. But I have got it. And I must live it. I can't be just swallowed up."

"Why, Malintzi?" he said, giving her a name.* "Why can't you?"

"Be just swallowed up?" she said. "Well, I just can't."

35 "I am the Living Huitzilopochtli," he said. "And I am swallowed up. I thought, so could you be, Malintzi."

"No! Not quite!" she said.

"Not quite! Not quite! Not now! Not just now! How often you say *Not*, today!—I must go back to Ramón."

40 "Yes. Go back to him. You only care about him, and your Living

Quetzalcoatls and your Living Huitzilopochtli.—I am only a woman."

"No, Malintzi, you are more. You are more than Kate, you are Malintzi."

"I am not! I am only Kate, and I am only a woman. I mistrust all 5 that other stuff."

"I am more than just a man, Malintzi.—Don't you see that?"

"No!" said Kate. "I don't see it. Why *should* you be more than just a man?"

"Because I am the Living Huitzilopochtli. Didn't I tell you? 10 You've got dust in your mouth today, Malintzi."

He went away, leaving her rocking in anger on her terrace, in love again with her old self, and hostile to the new thing. She was thinking of London and Paris and New York, and all the people there.

"Oh!" she cried to herself, stifling. "For heaven's sake let me get 15 out of this, and back to simple human people. I loathe the very sound of Quetzalcoatl and Huitzilopochtli. I would die rather than be mixed up in it any more. Horrible, really, both Ramón and Cipriano. And they want to put it over me, with their high-flown bunk, and their Malintzi. Malintzi! I am Kate Forrester, really. I am neither 20 Kate Leslie nor Kate Tylor. I am sick of these men putting names over me. I was born Kate Forrester, and I shall die Kate Forrester. I want to go home. Loathsome, really, to be called Malintzi.—I've had it put over me."

Chapter XXIII.

Huitzilopochtli's Night.

They had the Huitzilopochtli ceremony at night, in the wide yard in front of the church. The guard of Huitzilopochtli, in sarapes of black, red and yellow stripes, striped like tigers or wasps, stood holding torches of blazing ocote. A tall bonfire was built, but unkindled, in the centre of the yard.

In the towers where the bells had been, fires were blazing and the heavy drum of Huitzilopochtli went rolling its deep, sinister notes.* It had been sounding all the while since the sun went down.

The crowd gathered under the trees, outside the gates in front of the church. The church-doors were closed.

There was a bang of four firework cannons exploding simultaneously, then four rockets shot up into the sky, leaning in the four directions, and exploding in showers of red, green, white and yellow.

The church-doors opened, and Cipriano appeared, in his brilliant sarape of Huitzilopochtli, and with three green parrot feathers erect on his brow. He was carrying a torch. He stooped and lit the big bonfire, then plucked out four blazing brands, and tossed them to four of his men, who stood waiting, naked save for their black breech-cloths. The men caught the brands as they flew, and ran in the four directions, to kindle the four bonfires that waited, one in each corner of the yard.

The guard had taken off their blankets and blouses, and were naked to the red sash. The lighter drum began to beat for the dance, and the dance began, the half-naked men throwing their blazing torches whirling in the air, catching them as they came down, dancing all the while. Cipriano, in the centre, threw up brand after brand from the fire.

Now that he was stripped of his blanket, his body was seen painted in horizontal bars of red and black, while from his mouth went a thin green line, and from his eyes a band of yellow.*

The five fires, built hollow of little towers of ocote faggots, sent pure flame in a rush up to the dark sky, illuminating the dancing men, who sang in deep voices as they danced.

The fires rushed rapidly upwards in flame. The drum beat without ceasing. And the Men of Huitzilopochtli danced on, like demons. Meanwhile the crowd sat in the old Indian silence, their black eyes glittering in the firelight. And gradually the fires began to die down, the white façade of the church, that had danced also to the yellow flames, began to go bluish above, merging into the night, rose-coloured below, behind the dark shapes that danced to the sinking fires.

Suddenly the dance ceased, the men threw their sarapes around them, and sat down. Little ocote fires upon the cane tripods flickered here and there, in a silence that lasted for some minutes. Then the drum sounded, and a man began to sing, in a clear, defiant voice, the *First Song of Huitzilopochtli.**

> I am Huitzilopochtli,
> The Red Huitzilopochtli,
> The blood-red.
>
> I am Huitzilopochtli
> Yellow of the sun,
> Sun in the blood.
>
> I am Huitzilopochtli
> White of the bone,
> Bone in the blood.
>
> I am Huitzilopochtli
> With a blade of grass between my teeth.
>
> I am Huitzilopochtli, sitting in the dark,
> With my redness staining the body of the dark.
>
> I watch by the fire.
> I wait behind men.
>
> In the stillness of my night
> The cactus sharpens his thorn.
> The grass feels with his roots for the other sun.
>
> Deeper than the roots of the mango tree
> Down in the centre of the earth
> Is the yellow, serpent-yellow shining of my sun.*
>
> Oh beware of him!
> Oh beware of me!

Who runs athwart my serpent-flame
Gets bitten and must die.

I am the sleeping and waking
Of the anger of the manhood of men.
5   I am the leaping and quaking
Of fire bent back again.

The song came to an end. There was a pause. Then all the Men of Huitzilopochtli took it up again, changing the "I" into "He."

He is Huitzilopochtli,
10   The Red Huitzilopochtli,
The blood-red.

He is Huitzilopochtli
Yellow of the sun,
Sun in the blood.

15   He is Huitzilopochtli
White as bone,
Bone in the blood.

He is Huitzilopochtli
With a blade of green grass between his teeth.

20   He is Huitzilopochtli, sitting in the dark,
With his redness staining the body of the night.

He is watching by the fire.
Waiting behind men.

In the stillness of his night
25   Cactuses sharpen their thorns.
Grass feels downwards with his roots.

Deeper than the roots of the mango tree
Down in the centre of the earth
Shines the yellow, serpent-yellow shining of his sun.

30   Oh men, take care, take care!
Take care of him and it.
Nor run aslant his rays.
Who is bitten, dies.

He is Huitzilopochtli, sleeping or waking
35   Serpent in the bellies of men.
Huitzilopochtli, leaping and quaking
Fire of the passion of men.

The big fires had all died down. Only the little flames on the tripods lit up the scene with a ruddy glow. The guard withdrew to the outer wall of the yard, holding bayonets erect. The big drum was going alone, slowly.

The yard was now a clear space, with the glowing red heaps of the bonfires, and the ocote flames flapping. And now was seen a platform erected against the white wall of the church.

In the silence the big doors of the church opened, and Cipriano came out, in his bright sarape, holding in his hand a bunch of black leaves, or feathers, and with a tuft of scarlet feathers, black-tipped, rising from the back of his head. He mounted the platform and stood facing the crowd, the light of a torch on his face and on the brilliant feathers that rose like flames from the back of his head.

After him came a strange procession: a peon in floppy white clothes, led prisoner between two of the guards of Huitzilopochtli, who wore their sarapes with red and black and yellow and white and green stripes: then another peon prisoner: then another: in all, five, the fifth one tall, limping, and with a red cross painted on the breast of his white jacket. Last of all came a woman, prisoner likewise between two guards, her hair flowing loose, over a red tunic.

They mounted the platform. The peons, prisoners, were placed in a row, their guards behind them. The limping peon was apart, with his two guards behind him: the woman again was apart, her two guards behind her.

The big drum ceased, and a bugle rang out, a long, loud triumphant note, repeated three times. Then the kettle-drums, or the small tom-toms like kettle-drums, rattled fierce as hail.

Cipriano lifted his hand, and there was silence.

Out of the silence he began to speak, in his short, martial sentences:

> Man that is man is more than a man.
> No man is man till he is more than a man.
> Till the power is in him
> Which is not his own.

> The power is in me from behind the sun,
> And from middle-earth.
> I am Huitzilopochtli.
> I am dark as the sunless under-earth,
> And yellow as the fire that consumes,

And white as bone,
And red as blood.

But I touched the hand of Quetzalcoatl.
And between our fingers rose a blade of green grass.
5　　I touched the hand of Quetzalcoatl.

Lo! I am lord of the watches of the night*
And the dream of the night rises from me like a red feather.

I am the watcher, and master of the dream.

In the dream of the night I see the grey dogs prowling,
10　　Prowling to devour the dream.

In the night the soul of a coward creeps out of him
Like a grey dog whose mouth is foul with rabies,
Creeping among the sleeping and the dreaming, who are
　　　lapped in my dark,
15　　And in whom the dream sits up like a rabbit, lifting long ears
　　　tipped with night,
On the dream-slopes browsing like a deer in the dusk.

In the night I see the grey dogs creeping, out of the sleeping
　　men
20　　Who are cowards, who are liars, who are traitors, who have
　　　no dreams
That prick their ears like a rabbit, or browse in the dark like
　　　deer,
But whose dreams are dogs, grey dogs with yellow mouths.

25　　From the liars, from the thieves, from the false and
　　　treacherous and mean
I see the grey dogs creeping out, where my deer are browsing
　　　in the dark.
Then I take my knife, and throw it upon the grey dog.
30　　And lo! it sticks between the ribs of a man!
The house of the grey dog!

Beware! Beware!
Of the men and the women who walk among you,
You know not how many are houses of grey dogs.
35　　Men that seem harmless, women with fair words,
Maybe they kennel the grey dog.

The drums began to beat, and the singer began to sing, clear and pure:

The Song of the Grey Dog.

When you sleep and know it not
The grey dog creeps among you.   5
In your sleep, you twist, your soul hurts you.
The grey dog is chewing your entrails.

Then call on Huitzilopochtli:
The grey dog caught me at the cross-roads
As I went down the road of sleep   10
And crossed the road of the uneasy.

The grey dog leapt at my entrails.
Huitzilopochtli, call him off.
Lo! the Great One answers. *Track him down!*
Kill him in his unclean house.   15

Down the road of the uneasy
You track the grey dog home
To his house in the heart of a traitor,
A thief, a murderer of dreams.

And you kill him there with one stroke,   20
Crying: *Huitzilopochtli, is this well done?*
That your sleep be not as a cemetery
Where dogs creep unclean.

The song ceased, and there was silence. Then Cipriano beckoned to the men to bring forward the peon with the red cross painted on 25 his front and back. He limped forward.

Cipriano: What man is that, limping?
Guards: It is Guillermo, overseer of Don Ramón, who betrayed Don Ramón, his master.
Cipriano: Why does he limp?   30
Guards: He fell from the window on to the rocks.
Cipriano: What made him wish to betray his master?
Guards: His heart is a grey dog, and a woman, a grey bitch, enticed him forth.
Cipriano: What woman enticed the grey dog forth?   35
The guards came forward with the woman:
Guards: This woman, Maruca, my Lord, with the grey bitch heart.

Cipriano: Is it she, indeed?

Guards: It is she.

Cipriano: The grey dog, and the grey bitch, we kill, for their
mouths are yellow with poison. Is it well, Men of Huitzilo-
5   pochtli?

Guards: It is very well, my Lord.

The guards stripped the peon Guillermo of his white clothes,
leaving him naked, in a grey loin-cloth, with a grey-white cross
painted on his naked breast. The woman too had a grey-white cross
10 painted on her body. She stood in a short petticoat of grey wool.

Cipriano: The grey dog, and the grey bitch shall run no more
about the world. We will bury their bodies in quick-lime, till
their souls are eaten, and their bodies, and nothing is left. For
lime is the thirsty bone that swallows even a soul and is not
15   slaked.—Bind them with the grey cords, put ash on their
heads.

The guard quickly obeyed. The prisoners, ash-grey, gazed with
black, glittering eyes, making not a sound. A guard stood behind
each of them. Cipriano gave a sign, and quick as lightning the guards
20 had got the throats of the two victims in a grey cloth, and with a sharp
jerk had broken their necks, lifting them backwards in one
movement. The grey cloths they tied hard and tight round the
throats, laying the twitching bodies on the floor.

Cipriano turned to the crowd:

25   The Lords of Life are the Masters of Death.
Blue is the breath of Quetzalcoatl.
Red is Huitzilopochtli's blood.
But the grey dog belongs to the ash of the world.

The Lords of Life are the Masters of Death.
30   Dead are the grey dogs.
Living are the Lords of Life.
Blue is the deep sky and the deep water.
Red is the blood and the fire.
Yellow is the flame.
35   The bone is white and alive.
The hair of night is dark over our faces.

But the grey dogs are among the ashes.

The Lords of Life are the Masters of Death.

Then he turned once more, to the other, imprisoned peons.

Cipriano: Who are these four?

Guards: Four who came to kill Don Ramón.

Cipriano: Four men, against one man?

Guards: They were more than four, my Lord.

Cipriano: When many men come against one, what is the name
of the many?

Guards: Cowards, my Lord.

Cipriano: Cowards it is. They are less than men. Men that are
less than men are not good enough for the light of the sun. If
men that are men will live, men that are less than men must
be put away, lest they multiply too much. Men that are more
than men have the judgment of men that are less than
men.—Shall they die?

Guards: They shall surely die, my Lord.

Cipriano: Yet my hand has touched the hand of Quetzalcoatl,
and among the black leaves one sprung green, with the colour
of Malintzi.

An attendant came and lifted Cipriano's sarape over his head,
leaving his body bare to the waist. The guards likewise took off their
sarapes.

Cipriano lifted up his fist, in which he held a little tuft of black
feathers, or leaves. Then he said slowly:

Huitzilopochtli gives the black blade of death.
Take it bravely.
Take death bravely.
Go bravely across the border, admitting your mistake.

Determine to go on and on, till you enter the Morning Star.
Quetzalcoatl will show you the way.
Malintzi of the green dress will open the door.
In the fountain you will lie down.

If you reach the fountain, and lie down
And the fountain covers your face, forever,
You will have departed forever from your mistake.

And the man that is more than a man in you
Will wake at last from the clean forgetting
And stand up, and look about him,
Ready again for the business of being a man.

But Huitzilopochtli touched the hand of Quetzalcoatl
And one green leaf sprang among the black.
The green leaf of Malintzi
Who pardons once, and no more.*

5　　Cipriano turned to the four peons. He held out his fist with the four black twigs, to the first. This first one, a little man, peered at the sprigs curiously.

"There is no green one," he said sceptically.

"Good!" said Cipriano. "Then receive a black."

10　And he handed him a black leaf.

"I knew it," said the man, and he threw the leaf away with contempt and defiance.

The second man drew a black leaf. He stood gazing at it, as if fascinated, turning it round.

15　The third man drew a leaf whose lower half was green.

"See!" said Cipriano. "The green leaf of Malintzi!"

And he handed the last black leaf to the last man.

"Have I got to die?" said the last man.

"Yes."

20　"I don't want to die, *Patrón*."

"You played with death, and it has sprung upon you."

The eyes of the three men were blindfolded with black cloths, their blouses and pantaloons were taken away. Cipriano took a bright, thin dagger.

25　"The Lords of Life are Masters of Death," he said in a loud, clear voice.

And swift as lightning he stabbed the blindfolded men to the heart, with three swift, heavy stabs. Then he lifted the red dagger and threw it down.

30　"The Lords of Life are Masters of Death," he repeated.

The guards lifted the bleeding bodies one by one, and carried them into the church. There remained only the one prisoner, with the green leaf.

"Put the green leaf of Malintzi between his brows; for Malintzi 35　pardons once, and no more," said Cipriano.

"Yes, my Lord!" replied the guard.

And they led the man away into the church.

Cipriano followed, the last of his guard after him.

In a few minutes the drums began to beat, and men came slowly streaming into the church. Women were not admitted. All the interior was hung with red and black banners. At the side of the chancel was a new idol: a heavy, seated figure of Huitzilopochtli, done in black lava stone. And round him burned twelve red candles. The idol held the bunch of black strips, or leaves in his hand. And at 5 his feet lay the five dead bodies.

The fire on the altar was flickering high, to the dark statue of Quetzalcoatl. On his little throne Ramón sat, wearing his blue and white colours of Quetzalcoatl. There was another corresponding throne next him, but it was empty. Six of the guard of Quetzalcoatl 10 stood by Ramón: but Huitzilopochtli's side of the chancel was empty save for the dead.

The hard drums of Huitzilopochtli were beating incessantly outside, with a noise like madness. Inside was the soft roll of the drum of Quetzalcoatl. And the men from the crowd outside 15 thronged slowly in, between the guard of Quetzalcoatl.

A flute sounded the summons to close the doors. The drums of Quetzalcoatl ceased, and from the towers was heard again the wild bugle of Huitzilopochtli.

Then down the centre of the church, in silence, barefoot, came 20 the procession of Huitzilopochtli, naked save for the black loin-cloths and the paint, and the scarlet feathers of the head-dresses. Cipriano had his face painted with a white jaw, a thin band of green stretched from his mouth, a band of black across his nose, yellow from his eyes, and scarlet on his brow. One green feather rose from 25 his forehead, and behind his head a beautiful head-dress of scarlet feathers. A band of red was painted round his breast, yellow round his middle. The rest was ash-grey.

After him came his guard, their faces red, black and white, their bodies painted as Cipriano's, and a scarlet feather rising from the 30 back of their heads. The hard, dry drum of Huitzilopochtli beat monotonously.

As the Living Huitzilopochtli came near the altar steps, the Living Quetzalcoatl rose and came to meet him. The two saluted, each covering his eyes with his left hand for a moment, then touching 35 fingers with the right hand.

Cipriano stood before the statue of Huitzilopochtli, dipped his hand in a stone bowl, and giving the loud cry or whoop of Huitzilopochtli, lifted up his red hand. His guard uttered the loud cry, and quickly filed past, each man dipping his hand and raising his 40

wet, red fist. The hard drums of Huitzilopochtli rattled like madness
in the church, then fell suddenly silent.

    Ramón: Why is your hand red, Huitzilopochtli, my brother?

    Cipriano: It is the blood of the treacherous, Oh Quetzalcoatl.

5   Ramón: What have they betrayed?

    Cipriano: The yellow sun, and the heart of darkness; the hearts
of men, and the buds of women. While they lived, the
Morning Star could not be seen.

    Ramón: And are they verily dead?

10   Cipriano: Verily dead, my Lord.

    Ramón: Their blood is shed?

    Cipriano: Yes, my Lord, save that the grey dogs shed no blood.
Two died the bloodless death of the grey dogs, three died in
blood.

15   Ramón: Give me the blood of the three, my brother Huitzilopochtli, to sprinkle the fire.

    Cipriano brought the stone bowl, and the little bunch of black
leaves from Huitzilopochtli's idol. Ramón slowly, gently sprinkled a
little blood on the fire, with the black leaves.

20   Ramón: Darkness, drink the blood of expiation.

    Sun, swallow up the blood of expiation.

    Rise, Morning Star, between the divided sea.

    He gave back the bowl and the leaves to Huitzilopochtli, who
placed them by the black idol.

25   Ramón: Thou who didst take the lives of the three,
Huitzilopochtli, my brother, what wilt thou do with the
souls?

    Cipriano: Even give them to thee, my Lord, Quetzalcoatl, my
Lord of the Morning Star.

30   Ramón: Yea, give them to me and I will wrap them in my breath
and send them the longest journey, to the sleep and the far
awakening.

    Cipriano: My Lord is Lord of Two Ways.

    The naked, painted guard of Huitzilopochtli came and carried the

35 dead bodies of the three stabbed men, carried them on red biers, and
laid them at the foot of the Quetzalcoatl statue.

    Ramón: Lo, there is a long way to go, past the sun to the gate of
the Morning Star. And if the sun is angry, he strikes swifter
than a jaguar, and the whirr of the winds is like an angry
eagle, and the upper waters strike in wrath like silver-

coloured snakes. Ah, three souls, make peace now with the sun and winds and waters, and go in courage, with the breath of Quetzalcoatl around you like a cloak. Fear not and shrink not and fail not: but come to the end of the longest journey, and let the fountain cover your face. So shall all at length be 5 made new.

When he had spoken to the dead, Ramón took incense and threw it on the fire, so clouds of blue smoke arose. Then with a censer he swung the blue smoke over the dead. Then he unfolded three blue cloths, and covered the dead. Then the guards of Quetzalcoatl lifted 10 the biers, and the flute of Quetzalcoatl sounded.

"Salute the Morning Star!" cried Ramón, turning to the light beyond the statue of Quetzalcoatl, and throwing up his right arm in the Quetzalcoatl prayer. Every man turned to the light and threw up his arm in the passion. And the silence of the Morning Star filled the 15 church.

The drum of Quetzalcoatl sounded: the guards slowly moved away with the three blue-wrapped dead.

Then came the voice of the Living Huitzilopochtli:

Upon the dead grey dogs the face of Quetzalcoatl cannot look. 20
Upon the corpses of grey dogs rises no Morning Star. But the
fire of corpses shall consume them.

There was a sharp rattle of the dry drums of Huitzilopochtli. Ramón remained with his back to the church, his arm upraised to the Morning Star. And the guard of Huitzilopochtli lifted the strangled 25 bodies, laid them on biers, covered them with grey cloths, and bore them away.

The bugle of Huitzilopochtli sounded.

Cipriano: The dead are on their way. Quetzalcoatl helps them
on the longest journey.—But the grey dogs sleep within the 30
quick-lime, in the slow corpse-fire.—It is finished.

Ramón dropped his arm and turned to the church. All men dropped their hands. The soft drums of Quetzalcoatl sounded, mingling with the hard drums of Huitzilopochtli. Then both guards began to sing together: 35

Huitzilopochtli's Watch.

Red Huitzilopochtli
Keeps day and night apart.

Huitzilopochtli the golden
Guards life from death, and death from life.

No grey dogs, cowards, pass him.
No spotted traitors crawl by.
5   False fair ones cannot slip through
Past him, from the one to the other.

Brave men have peace at nightfall,
True men look up at the dawn,
Men in their manhood walk out
10   Into blue day, past Huitzilopochtli.

Red Huitzilopochtli
Is the purifier.

Black Huitzilopochtli
Is doom.

15   Huitzilopochtli golden
Is the liberating fire.

White Huitzilopochtli
Is washed bone.

Green Huitzilopochtli
20   Is Malintzi's blade of grass.

At the beginning of each stanza, the guard of Huitzilopochtli
struck their left palm with their scarlet right fist, and the drums gave
a great crash, a terrific splash of noise. When the song ended, the
drums gradually died down, like subsiding thunder, leaving the
25   hearts of men re-echoing.

Ramón: Why is your hand so red, Huitzilopochtli?
Cipriano: With blood of slain men, Brother.
Ramón: Must it always be red?
Cipriano: Till green-robed Malintzi brings her water-bowl.
30   The bugle and the flute both sounded. The guard of Huitzilopochtli put out the red candles, one by one, the guard of Quetzalcoatl
extinguished the blue candles. The church was dark, save for the
small, but fierce blue-white light beyond the Quetzalcoatl statue,
and the red smouldering on the altar.
35   Ramón began slowly to speak:

The dead are on their journey, the way is dark.
There is only the Morning Star

Beyond the white of whiteness,
Beyond the blackness of black,
Beyond spoken day,
Beyond the unspoken passion of night,
The light which is fed from two vessels   5
From the black oil and the white
Shines at the gate.

A gate to the innermost place
Where the Breath and the Fountain commingle.
Where the dead are living, and the living are dead.   10
The deeps that life cannot fathom,
Whence knowing trickles in myriad streams.
The Source and the End, of which we know
Only that it is, and its life is our life and our death.

All men cover their eyes   15
Before the unseen.
All men be lost in silence,
Within the noiseless.

The church was utterly still, all men standing with a hand pressed
over their eyes.   20
Till there was one note of a silver gong, and the green candles of
Malintzi were being lighted in the altar place.—Ramón's voice was
heard again:

Light the green candles of Malintzi
Like a tree in new leaf.   25
The rain of blood is fallen, is gone into the earth.

The dead have gone the long journey
Beyond the star.
Huitzilopochtli has thrown his black mantle
To those who would sleep.   30

When the blue wind of Quetzalcoatl
Waves softly,
When the water of Malintzi falls
Making a greenness:

Count the red grains of the Huitzilopochtli   35
Fire in your hearts, Oh men.
And blow the ash away.

For the living live,
And the dead die.
But the fingers of all touch the fingers of all
In the Morning Star.

Chapter XXIV.

Malintzi.

When the women were shut out of the church, Kate went home gloomy and uneasy. The executions shocked and depressed her. She knew that Ramón and Cipriano did deliberately what they did: they believed in their deeds, they acted with all their conscience. And as men, probably they were right.

But they seemed nothing but men. When Cipriano said: *Man that is man is more than a man*, he seemed to be driving the male significance to its utmost, and beyond, into a sort of demonism. It seemed to her all terrible *will*, the exertion of pure, awful will.

And deep in her soul came a revulsion against this manifestation of pure will. It was fascinating also. There was something dark and lustrous and fascinating to her in Cipriano, and in Ramón. The black, relentless power, even passion of the will in men! The strange sombre, lustrous beauty of it! She knew herself under the spell.

At the same time, as is so often the case with any spell, it did not bind her completely. She was spell-bound, but not utterly acquiescent. In one corner of her soul was revulsion and a touch of nausea.

Ramón and Cipriano no doubt were right for themselves, for their people and country. But for herself, ultimately, ultimately she belonged elsewhere. Not to this terrible, natural *will* which seemed to beat its wings in the very air of the American continent. Always will, will, will, without remorse or relenting. This was America to her: all the Americas. Sheer will!

The Will of God! She began to understand that once fearsome phrase. At the centre of all things, a dark, momentous Will sending out its terrific rays and vibrations, like some vast octopus. And at the other end of the vibration, men, created men, erect in the dark potency, answering Will with will, like gods or demons.

It was wonderful too. But where was woman, in this terrible interchange of will? Truly only a subservient, instrumental thing: the soft stone on which the man sharpened the knife of his relentless volition: the soft lode-stone to magnetise his blade of steel and keep all its molecules alive in the electric flow.

Ah yes, it was wonderful. It was, as Ramón said, a manifestation, a manifestation of the Godhead. But to the Godhead as a sheer and
5 awful Will she could not respond.

Joachim, letting himself be bled to death for people who would profit nothing by his sacrifice, he was the other extreme. The black and magnificent pride of will which comes out of the volcanic earth of Mexico had been unknown to him. He was one of the white,
10 self-sacrificing gods. Hence her bitterness. And hence, naturally, the spell of beauty and lustrous satisfaction which Cipriano could cast over her—She was in love with him, when he was with her; in his arms, she was quite gone in his spell. She was the deep, slumbrous lode-stone which set all his bones glittering with the energy of
15 relentless pride—And she herself derived a great gratification in the embrace, a sense of passive, downward-sinking power, profound.

Yet she could not be purely this, this thing of sheer reciprocity. Surely, though her woman's nature was reciprocal to his male, surely it was more than that! Surely he and she were not two potent and
20 reciprocal currents between which the Morning Star flashed like a spark out of nowhere. Surely this was not it? Surely she had one tiny Morning Star inside her, which was herself, her own very soul and star-self!

But he would never admit this. The tiny star of her very self he
25 would never see. To him, she was but the answer to his call, the sheath for his blade, the cloud to his lightning, the earth to his rain, the fuel to his fire.

Alone, she was nothing. Only as the pure female corresponding to his pure male, did she signify.
30 As an isolated individual, she had little or no significance. As a woman on her own, she was repulsive, and even evil, to him. She was not real till she was reciprocal.

To a great extent this was true, and she knew it. To a great extent, the same was true of him, and without her to give him the power, he
35 too would not achieve his own manhood and meaning. With her or without her, he would be beyond ordinary men, because the power was in him. But failing her, he would never make his ultimate achievement, he would never be whole. He would be chiefly an instrument.
40 He knew this too: though perhaps not well enough. He would

strive to keep her, to have her, for his own fulfilment. He would not let her go.

But that little star of her own single self, would he ever recognise that? Nay, did he even recognise any single star of his own being? Did he not conceive of himself as a power and a potency on the face of the earth, an embodied will, like a rushing dark wind? And hence, inevitably, she was but the stone of rest to his potency, his bed of sleep, the cave and lair of his male will.

What else? To him there was nothing else. The star, Don Ramón's Morning Star, was something that sprung between him and her and hung shining, the strange third thing that was both of them and neither of them, between his night and her day.

Was it true? Was she nothing, nothing, by herself? And he, alone, failing his last manhood, without her was he nothing, or next to nothing? As a fig tree which grows up, but never comes to flower.

Was this thing true, the same of both of them?—that alone, they were next to nothing? Each of them, separate, next to nothing. Apart in a sort of grey, mechanical twilight, without a star?

And together, in strange reciprocity, flashing darkly till the Morning Star rose between them?

He would say to her, as Ramón had said of Carlota:

"Soul! No, you have no soul of your own. You have at best only half a soul. It takes a man and a woman together to make a soul. The soul is the Morning Star, emerging from the two. One alone cannot have a soul."

This Ramón said. And she knew it conveyed what Cipriano really felt. Cipriano could not see Kate as a being by herself. And if he lived a thousand more years, he would never see her as such. He would see her only as reciprocal to himself. As the balance of him, and the correspondence on the other side of heaven.

"Let the Morning Star rise between us," he would say. "Alone you are nothing, and I am *manqué*. But together we are the wings of the Morning."*

Was it true? Was this the final answer to man's assertion of individuality?

Was it true? And was it her sacred duty to sit beside him in the green dress of Malintzi, in the church, the goddess admitting her halfness? Her halfness! Was there no star of the single soul? Was that all an illusion?

Was the individual an illusion? Man, any man, every man, by

himself just a fragment, knowing no Morning Star? And every woman the same; by herself, starless and fragmentary. Even in relation to the innermost God, still fragmentary and unblest.

Was it true, that the gate was the Morning Star, the only entrance to the Innermost? And the Morning Star rises between the two, and between the many, but never from one alone.

And was a man but a dark and arrowy will, and woman the bow from which the arrow is shot? The bow without the arrow was as nothing, and the arrow without the bow only a short-range dart, ineffectual?

Poor Kate, it was hard to have to reflect this. It meant a submission she had never made. It meant the death of her individual self. It meant abandoning so much, even her own very foundations. For she had believed truly that every man and every woman alike was founded on the individual.

Now, must she admit that the individual was an illusion and a falsification?—There was no such animal. Except in the mechanical world. In the world of machines, the individual machine is effectual. The individual, like the perfect being, does not and cannot exist, in the vivid world. We are all fragments. And at the best, halves. The only whole thing is the Morning Star. Which can only rise between two: or between many.

And men can only meet in the light of the Morning Star.

She thought again of Cipriano and the executions, and she covered her hands over her face. Was this the knife to which she must be sheath? Was it such a star of power and relentlessness that must rise between her and him? Him naked and painted, with his soldiers, dancing and sweating and shouting among them. Herself unseen and nowhere!

As she sat rocking in her terrible loneliness and misgiving, she heard the drums on the towers, and the sound of rockets. She went to the gate. Over the church, in the night sky, hung a spangling cloud of red and blue fire, the colours of Huitzilopochtli and Quetzalcoatl. The night of Huitzilopochtli would be over. The sky was dark again, and there were all the stars, beyond, far, far beyond where the spangling had been.

She went indoors again, to retire. The servants had all run out to see the rockets. Ezequiel would be in with the men in church.

She heard footsteps on the gravel walk, and suddenly Cipriano stood in the doorway, in his white clothes. He took off his hat, quickly. His black eyes were sparkling, almost blazing to her, with a flashing of light such as she had never seen. There were still smears of paint on his face. In the blazing of his eyes he seemed to be smiling to her, but in a dazzling, childish way.

"Malintzi," he said to her in Spanish. "Oh come! Come and put 5 on the green dress. I cannot be the Living Huitzilopochtli, without a bride. I cannot be it, Malintzi!"

He stood before her flickering and flashing and strangely young, vulnerable, as young and boyish as flame. She saw that when the fire came free in him, he would be like this always, flickering, flashing 10 with a flame of virgin youth. Now, not will at all. Sensitive as a boy. And calling her only with his boyish flame. The living, flickering, fiery *Wish*. This was first. The *Will* she had seen was subsidiary and instrumental, the *Wish* in armour.

She had been so used to fighting for her own soul with individual- 15 istic men, that for a moment she felt old, and uncertain. The strange, flashing vulnerability in him, the nakedness of the living Wish, disconcerted her. She was used to men who had themselves well in hand, and were seeking their own ends as individuals.

"Where do you want me to come?" she said. 20

"To the church," he said. "It is mine tonight, I am Huitzilopoch-tli: but I cannot be it alone," he added with quick, wistful, watchful smile, as if all his flesh were flickering with delicate fire.

Kate wrapped herself in a dark tartan shawl and went with him. He stepped quickly, in the short, Indian way. The night was very 25 dark. Down on the beach some fireworks were flaring, and the people were all watching.

They entered the yard of the church from the back, by the priest's little gate. Soldiers were already rolled up in their blankets, sleeping under the wall. Cipriano opened the little vestry door. Kate passed in 30 to the darkness. He followed, lighting a candle.

"My soldiers know I am watching tonight in the church," he said. "They will keep guard."

The body of the church was quite dark, but the bluish white light burned above the statue of Quetzalcoatl, giving not much light. 35

Cipriano lifted his candle to the black statue of Huitzilopochtli. Then he turned to Kate, his black eyes flashing.

"I am Huitzilopochtli, Malintzi," he said in his low, Indian Spanish. "But I cannot be it without you. Stay with me, Malintzi. Say you are the bride of the Living Huitzilopochtli." 40

"Yes!" she replied. "I say it."

Convulsive flames of joy and triumph seemed to go over his face. He lit two candles in front of Huitzilopochtli.

"Come!" he said. "And put on the green dress."

5 He took her to the vestry, where were many folded sarapes, and the silver bowl and other implements of the church, and left her while she put on the dress of Malintzi she had worn when Ramón married them.

When she stepped out, she found Cipriano naked and in his 10 paint, before the statue of Huitzilopochtli, on a rug of jaguar skins.*

"I am the Living Huitzilopochtli," he murmured to her, in a sort of ecstasy.

"You are Malintzi," he said. "The bride of Huitzilopochtli."

15 The convulsion of exultance went over his face. He took her hand in his left hand, and they stood facing the bluish light.

"Cover your face!" he said to her.

They covered their faces in the salute.

"Now salute Quetzalcoatl."—And he flung up his arm. She held 20 out her left hand, in the woman's salute.

Then they turned to the statue of Huitzilopochtli.

"Salute Huitzilopochtli!" he said, bringing his right fist down with a smash in the palm of his left hand. But this was the male salute. He taught her to press her hands together in front of her breast, then 25 shoot them out towards the idol.

Then he put a little lamp of earthenware between the feet of Huitzilopochtli. From the right knee of the idol he took a little black vessel of oil, making her take a little white vessel from the god's left knee.

30 "Now," he said, "together we fill the lamp."

And together they poured the oil from their little pitchers, into the saucer-shaped lamp.

"Now together we light it," he said.

He took one of the two candles burning before the black idol, she 35 took the other, and with the flames dripping and leaping together, they kindled the floating wick of the lamp. It burned in a round blue bud, then rose higher.

"Blow out your candle," he said. "It is our Morning Star."

They blew out the two candles. It was almost dark now, with the 40 slow light, like a snow-drop, of their united lives floating between the feet of Huitzilopochtli, and the everlasting light burning small and bluish beyond the statue of Quetzalcoatl.

At the foot of the altar, beside the chair of Huitzilopochtli, a third chair was placed.

"Sit in your throne of Malintzi," he said to her.

They sat side by side, his hand holding her hand, in complete silence, looking down the dark church. He had placed tufts of greenish flowers, like thin, greenish lilac, above her chair, and their perfume was like a dream, strong, overpoweringly sweet on the darkness.

Strange how naïve he was! He was not like Ramón, rather ponderous and deliberate in his ceremonials. Cipriano, in his own little deeds tonight with her, was naïve like a child. She could hardly look at that bud of light which he said meant their united lives, without a catch at her heart. It burned so soft and round, and he had such an implicit, childish satisfaction in its symbol. It all gave him a certain wild, childish joy. The strange convulsions like flames of joy and gratification went over his face!

"Ah God!" she thought. "There are more ways than one of becoming like a little child."*

The flaminess and the magnificence of the beginning: this was what Cipriano wanted to bring to his marriage. The reeling, powerful perfume of those invisible green flowers, that the peons call *buena de noche*: good by night.*

Strange—that which he brought to marriage was something flamey and unabashed, forever virginal. Not, as she had always known in men, yearning and seeking his own ends. Naïvely bringing his flame to her flame.

As she sat in that darkened church in the intense perfume of flowers, in the seat of Malintzi, watching the bud of her life united with his, between the feet of the idol, and feeling his dark hand softly holding her own, with the soft, deep Indian heat, she felt her own childhood coming back on her. The years seemed to be reeling away in great circles, falling away from her.

Leaving her sitting there like a girl in her first adolescence. The Living Huitzilopochtli! Ah, easily he was the Living Huitzilopochtli. More than anything. More than Cipriano, more than a male man, he was the Living Huitzilopochtli. And she was the goddess bride, Malintzi of the green dress.

Ah yes, it was childish. But it was actually so. She was perhaps fourteen years old, and he was fifteen. And he was the young Huitzilopochtli, and she was the bride Malintzi, the bride-girl. She had seen it. When the flame came up in him and licked him all over, he was young and vulnerable as a boy of fifteen, and he would always be so, even when he was seventy.

And this was her bridegroom. Here at least he was not a *will*. When he came clothed in his own free flame, it was not *will* that clothed him. Let him be a general, an executioner, what he liked, in the world. The flame of their united lives was a naked bud of flame. Their marriage was a young, vulnerable flame.

So he sat in silence on his throne, holding her hand in silence, till the years reeled away from her in fleeing circles, and she sat, as every real woman can sit, no matter at what age, a girl again, and for him, a virgin. He held her hand in silence, till she was Malintzi, and virgin for him, and when they looked at one another, and their eyes met, the two flames rippled in oneness. She closed her eyes, and was dark.

Then later, when she opened her eyes and saw the bud of flame just above her, and the black idol invisibly crouching, she heard his strange voice, the voice of a boy hissing in naïve ecstasy, in Spanish:

"*Miel! Miel de Malintzi!*—Honey of Malintzi!"

And she pressed him to her breast, convulsively. His innermost flame was always virginal, it was always the first time. And it made her again always a virgin girl. She could feel their two flames flowing together.

How else, she said to herself, is one to begin again, save by re-finding one's virginity? And when one finds one's virginity, one realises one is among the gods. He is of the gods, and so am I. Why should I judge him!

So, when she thought of him and his soldiers, tales of swift cruelty she had heard of him: when she remembered his stabbing the three helpless peons, she thought: Why should I judge him? He is of the gods. And when he comes to me he lays his pure, quick flame to mine, and every time I am a young girl again, and every time he takes the flower of my virginity, and I his. It leaves me insouciante like a young girl. What do I care if he kills people? His flame is young and clean. He is Huitzilopochtli, and I am Malintzi. What do I care, what Cipriano Viedma does or doesn't do? Or even what Kate Leslie does or doesn't do!

Chapter XXV.

Teresa.

Ramón somewhat surprised Kate by marrying again, a couple of months or so after the death of Doña Carlota. The new bride was a young woman of about twenty-eight, called Teresa. There was a very quiet civil wedding, and Ramón brought his new wife to Jamiltepec.

He had known her since she was a child, for she was the daughter of the famous hacienda of Las Yemas, some twelve miles inland from Jamiltepec. Don Tomás, her father, had been a staunch friend of the Carrascos.

But Don Tomás had died a year ago, leaving the large, flourishing tequila hacienda to his three children, to be administrated by Teresa. Teresa was the youngest. Her two brothers had reverted to the usual wasteful, spendthrift, brutal Mexican way. Therefore Don Tomás, in order to save the hacienda from their destructive hands, had especially appointed Teresa *administradora*, and had got the brothers' consent to this. After all, they were shiftless neer-do-wells, and had never shown the slightest desire to help in the rather burdensome business of managing a large tequila hacienda, during their father's life-time. Teresa had been the one. And during her father's illness the whole charge had devolved on her, while her brothers wasted themselves and their substance in the squashy prostitution-living of Mexicans of their class, away in the cities.

No sooner was the father dead, however, and Teresa in charge, than home came the two brothers, big with their intention to be hacendados. By simple brute force they ousted their sister, gave orders over her head, jeered at her, and in crushing her united for once with each other. They were putting her back into her place as a woman: that is to say, back into a secluded sort of prostitution, to which, in their eyes, women belonged.

But they were bullies, and as bullies, cowards. And like so many Mexicans of that class, soft and suicidal towards themselves. They made friends with judges and generals. They rode about in resplendent charro dress, and had motor-loads of rather doubtful visitors.

Against their soft, sensuous brutality Teresa could do nothing,

395

and she knew it. They were all soft and sensual, or sensuous, handsome in their way, open-handed, careless, but bullies, with no fear at the middle of them.

"Make yourself desirable, and get a husband for yourself," they
5 said to her.

In their eyes, her greatest crime was that she did not make herself desirable to men of their sort. That she had never had a man, that she was not married, made her almost repulsive to them. What was woman for, but for loose, soft, prostitutional sex?

10 "Do you want to wear the trousers?" they jeered at her. "No, Señorita! Not while there are two men on the place, you are not going to wear the trousers. No, Señorita! The trousers, the men wear them. The women keep under their petticoats that which they are women for."

15 Teresa was used to these insults. But they made her soul burn.

"You, do you want to be an American woman?" they said to her. "Go off to America, then, and bob your hair and wear breeches. Buy a ranch there, and get a husband to take your orders. Go!"

She went to her lawyers, but they held up their hands. And she
20 went to Ramón, whom she had known since she was a child.

It would have meant a hopeless and ruinous law-suit, to get the brothers ejected from the hacienda. It would have meant the rapid ruin of the estate. Ramón instead asked Teresa to marry him, and he carefully arranged her dowry, so that she should always have her own
25 provision.

"It is a country where men despise sex, and live for it," said Ramón. "Which is just suicide."

Ramón came with his wife, to see Kate. Teresa was rather small, pale, with a lot of loose black hair and big, wide black eyes. Yet in her
30 quiet bearing and her well-closed mouth there was an air of independence and authority. She had suffered great humiliation at the hands of her brothers, there was still a certain wanness round her eyes, the remains of tears of anger and helpless indignation, and the bitterness of insulted sex. But now she loved Ramón, with a wild,
35 virgin loyalty. That too was evident. He had saved her sex from the insult, restored it to her in its pride and its beauty. And in return, she felt an almost fierce reverence for him.

But with Kate she was shy and rather distant: a little afraid of the travelled, experienced, rather assertive white-skinned woman, the
40 woman of the other race. She sat in Kate's salon in her simple white

dress with a black gauze rebozo, her brown hands motionless in her lap, her dark neck erect, her dark, slender, well-shaped cheek averted. She seemed, Kate thought, rather like a little sempstress.

But Kate was reckoning without that strange quiescent power of authority which Teresa also possessed, in her slight, dark body. And without the black, flashing glances which rested on her from time to time, from Teresa's eyes, full of searching fierceness and fiery misgiving. A fiery soul, in such a demure, slight, dark body.— Sometimes a muted word came from her mouth, and a constrained smile moved her lips. But her burning eyes never changed. She did not even look at Ramón.

"How much do you charge per word, Chica?" he asked her, with a sort of soft fondness.

Then her dark eyes flashed at him, and her mouth gave a little smile. It was evident she was hopelessly in love with him, in a sort of trance or muse of love. And she maintained such a cold sort of blankness towards Kate.

"She despises me," thought Kate, "because I can't be in love as she is."

And for one second Kate envied Teresa. The next second, she despised her. "The harem type—"

Well, it was Ramón's nature to be a sort of Sultan. He looked very handsome in his white clothes, very serene and pasha-like in his assurance, yet at the same time, soft, pleasant, something boyish also in his physical well-being. In his soft yet rather pasha-like way, he was mixing a cocktail, of gin and vermouth and lime. Teresa watched him from the corner of her eye. And at the same time, she watched Kate, the potential enemy, the woman who talked with men on their own plane.

Kate rose to get spoons. At the same moment, he stepped back from the low table where he was squeezing a lime, so that he came into slight collision with her. And Kate noticed again, how quick and subtle was his physical evasion of her, the soft, almost liquid, hot quickness of his sliding out of contact with her. His natural voluptuousness avoided her as a flame leans away from a draught.

She flushed slightly. And Teresa saw the quick flush under the fair, warm-white skin, the leap of yellow light, almost like anger, into Kate's grey-hazel eyes. The moment of evasion of two different blood-streams.

And Teresa rose and went to Ramón's side, bending over and

looking in the tumblers, asking, with that curious affected childishness of dark women:

"What do you put in?"

"Look!" said Ramón. And with the same curious male childishness of dark men, he was explaining the cocktail to her, giving her a little gin in a spoon, to taste.

"It is an impure tequila," she said naïvely.

"At eight pesos a bottle?" he laughed.

"So much! It is much!"

She looked into his eyes for a second, and saw all his face go darker, warmer, as if his flesh were fusing soft towards her. Her small head poised the prouder. She had got him back.

"Harem tricks!" said Kate to herself. And she was somewhat impatient, seeing the big, portentous Ramón enveloped in the toils of this little dark thing. She resented being made so conscious of his physical presence, his full, male body inside his thin white clothes, the strong, yet soft shoulders, the full, rich male thighs. It was as if she herself, also, being in the presence of this Sultan, should succumb as part of the harem.

What a curious will the little dark woman had! What a subtle female power inside her rather skinny body! She had the power to make him into a big, golden full glory of a man. Whilst she herself became almost inconspicuous, save for her big black eyes lit with a tigerish power.

Kate watched in wonder. She herself had known men who made her feel a queen, who made her feel as if the sky rested on her bosom and her head was among the stars. She knew what it was to rise grander and grander, till she filled the universe with her womanhood.

Now she saw the opposite taking place. This little bit of a black-eyed woman had an almost uncanny power, to make Ramón great and gorgeous in the flesh, whilst she herself became inconspicuous, almost *invisible*, save for her great black eyes. Like a sultan, he was, like a full golden fruit in the sun, with a strange and magnificent presence, glamour. And then, by some mysterious power in her dark little body, the skinny Teresa held him most completely.

And this was what Ramón wanted. And it made Kate angry, angry. The big, fluid male, gleaming, was somewhat repulsive to her. And the tense little female with her pale-dark face, wan under her great, intense black eyes, having all her female being tense in an effort to exalt this big glistening man, this enraged Kate. She could not bear the glistening smile in Ramón's dark eyes, a sort of pasha satisfaction. And she could not bear the erect, tense little figure of the dark woman, using her power in this way.

This hidden, secretive power of the dark female! Kate called it harem, and self-prostitution. But was it?—Yes, surely it was the *slave* approach. Surely she wanted nothing but sex from him, like a prostitute! The ancient mystery of the female power, which consists in glorifying the blood-male.

Was it right? Kate asked herself. Wasn't it degrading for a woman? And didn't it make the man either soft and sensuous, or else hatefully autocratic?

Yet Kate herself had convinced herself of one thing, finally: that the clue to all living and to all moving-on into new living lay in the vivid blood-relation between man and woman. A man and a woman in their togetherness were the clue to all present living and future possibility. Out of this clue of togetherness between a man and a woman, the whole of the new life arose. It was the quick of the whole.

And the togetherness needed a balance. Surely it needed a balance! And did not this Teresa throw herself entirely into the male balance, so that all the weight was on the man's side?

Ramón had not wanted Kate. Ramón had got what he wanted— this black little creature, who was so servile to him and so haughty in her own power. Ramón had never wanted Kate: except as a friend, a clever friend. As a woman, no!—He wanted this little viper of a Teresa.

Cipriano wanted Kate. The little general, the strutting little soldier, he wanted Kate: just for moments. He did not really want to marry her. He wanted the moments, no more. She was to give him his moments, and then he was off again, to his army, to his men. It was what he wanted.

It was what she wanted, too. Her life was her own! It was not her métier to be fanning the blood in a man, to make him almighty and blood-glamorous. Her life was her own!

She rose and went to her bedroom to look for a book she had promised Ramón. She could not bear the sight of him in love with Teresa any longer. The heavy, mindless smile on his face, the curious glisten of his eyes, and the strange, heavy, lordly *aplomb* of his body affected her like a madness. She wanted to run.

This was what they were, these people! Savages, with the impossible fluid flesh of savages, and that savage way of dissolving into an awful black mass of desire. Emerging with the male conceit and haughtiness swelling his blood and making him feel endless. While
5   his eyes glistened with a haughty blackness.

The trouble was, that the power of the world, which she had known until now only in the eyes of blue-eyed men, who made queens of their women—even if they hated them for it in the end—was now fading in the blue eyes, and dawning in the black. In
10 Ramón's eyes at this moment was a steady, alien gleam of pride, and daring, and power, which she knew was masterly. The same was in Cipriano's quick looks. The power of the world was dying in the blond men, their bravery and their supremacy was leaving them, going into the eyes of the dark men, who were rousing at last.

15 Joachim, the eager, clever, fierce, sensitive genius, who could look into her soul, and laugh into her soul, with his blue eyes: he had died under her eyes. And her children were not even his children.

If she could have fanned his blood as Teresa now fanned the blood of Ramón, he would never have died.

20 But it was impossible. Every dog has his day. And every race.

Teresa came tapping timidly.

"May I come?"

"Do!" said Kate, rising from her knees and leaving little piles of books all round her book-trunk.

25 It was a fairly large room, with doors opening on to the patio and the sun-hard garden, smooth mango trees rising like elephants' trunks out of the ground, green grass after the rains, chickens beneath the ragged banana leaves. A red bird splashed in the basin of water, opening and shutting brown wings above his pure scarlet,
30 vivid.

But Teresa looked at the room, not out of doors. She smelt the smell of cigarettes, and saw the many cigarette stumps in the agate tray by the bed. She saw the littered books, the scattered jewellery, the brilliant New-Mexican rugs on the floor, the Persian curtain
35 hung behind the bed, the handsome, coloured bed-cover, the dresses of dark silk and bright velvet flung over a trunk, the folded shawls with their long fringe, the scattered shoes, white, grey, pale-brown, dark-brown, black, on the floor, the tall Chinese candlesticks. The room of a woman who lived her own life, for her
40 own self.

Teresa was repelled, uneasy, and fascinated.

"How nice this is!" she said, touching the glowing bed-cover.

"A friend made it for me, in England."

Teresa looked with wonder at everything, especially at the tangle of jewellery on the dressing table.

"Don't you like those red stones!" said Kate, kneeling again to put the books back, and looking at the brown neck bent absorbedly over the jewels. Thin shoulders with a soft, dark skin, in a bit of a white dress! And loosely-folded masses of black hair held by tortoise-shell pins.—An insignificant little thing, humble, Kate thought to herself.

But she knew really that Teresa was neither insignificant nor humble. Under that soft brown skin, and in that stooping female spine was a strange old power to call up the blood in a man, and glorify it, and, in some way, keep it for herself.

On the sewing-table was a length of fine India muslin which Kate had bought in India, and did not know what to do with. It was a sort of yellow-peach colour, beautiful, but it did not suit Kate. Teresa was fingering the gold-thread selvedge.

"It is not organdie?" she said.

"No, muslin. Hand-made muslin from India—Why don't you take it. It doesn't suit me. It would be perfect for you."

She rose and held the fabric against Teresa's dark neck, pointing to the mirror. Teresa saw the warm-yellow muslin upon herself, and her eyes flashed.

"No!" she said. "I couldn't take it."

"Why not? It doesn't suit me. I've had it lying about for a year now, and was wondering whether to cut it up for curtains. Do have it."

Kate could be imperious, almost cruel in her giving.

"I can't take it from you!"

"Of course you can!"

Ramón appeared in the doorway, glancing round the room, and at the two women.

"Look!" said Teresa, rather confused. "The Señora wants to give me this India muslin."—She turned to him shyly, with the fabric held to her throat.

"You look very well in it," he said, his eyes resting on her.

"The Señora ought not to give it me."

"The Señora would not give it you unless she wished to."

"Then!" said Teresa to Kate. "Many thanks! But many thanks!"

"It is nothing," said Kate.

"But Ramón says it suits me."

"Yes, doesn't it suit her!" cried Kate to him. "It was made in India for someone as dark as she is. It *does* suit her!"

"Very pretty!" said Ramón.

5 He had glanced round the room, at the different attractive things from different parts of the world, and at the cigarette ends in the agate bowl: the rather weary luxury and disorder, and the touch of barrenness, of a woman living her own life.

She did not know what he was thinking. But to herself she
10 thought: This is the man I defended on that roof. This is the man who lay with a hole in his back, naked and unconscious under the lamp. He didn't look like a Sultan then.

Teresa must have divined something of her thought, for she said, looking at Ramón:

15 "Señora! But for you Ramón would have been killed. Always I think of it."

"Don't think of it," said Kate. "Something else would have happened.—Anyhow it wasn't I, it was destiny."

"Ah, but you were the destiny!" said Teresa.

20 "Now there is a hostess, won't you come and stay some time at Jamiltepec?" said Ramón.

"Oh do! Do come!" cried Teresa.

"But do you really want me?" said Kate, incredulous.

"Yes! Yes!" cried Teresa.

25 "She needs a woman-friend," said Ramón gently.

"Yes, I do!" she cried. "I have never had a true, *true* woman-friend: only when I was at school and we were girls."

Kate doubted very much her own capacity for being a *true*, true woman-friend to Teresa. She wondered what the two of them saw in
30 her. As what did they see her?

"Yes, I should like to come for a few days," she replied.

"Oh yes!" cried Teresa. "When will you come?"

The day was agreed.

"And we will write the Song of Malintzi," said Ramón.

35 "Don't do that!" cried Kate quickly.

He looked at her, in his slow, wondering way. He could make her feel, at moments, as if she were a sort of child: and as if he were a ghost.

Kate went to Jamiltepec, and before the two women knew it,
40 almost, they were making dresses for Teresa, cutting up the

pineapple-coloured muslin. Poor Teresa, for a bride she had a scanty wardrobe: nothing but her rather pathetic black dresses that somehow made her look poor, and a few old white dresses. She had lived for her father—who had a good library of Mexicana and was all his life writing a history of the State of Jalisco—and for the hacienda. And it was her proud boast that Las Yemas was the only hacienda within a hundred miles range, which had not been smashed at all during the revolutions that followed the flight of Porfirio Díaz.

Teresa had a good deal of the nun in her. But that was because she was deeply passionate, and deep passion tends to hide within itself, rather than expose itself to vulgar contact.

So Kate pinned the muslin over the brown shoulders, wondering again at the strange, uncanny softness of the dark skin, the heaviness of the black hair. Teresa's family, the Romeros, had been in Mexico since the early days of the Conquest.*

Teresa wanted long sleeves.

"My arms are so thin!" she murmured, hiding her slender brown arms with a sort of shame. "They are not beautiful like yours."

Kate was a strong, full-developed woman of forty, with round, strong white arms.

"No!" she said to Teresa. "Your arms are not thin: they are exactly right for your figure, and pretty and young and brown."

"But make the sleeves long, to the wrist," pleaded Teresa.

And Kate did so, realising it became the other woman's nature better.

"The men here don't like little thin women," said Teresa, wistfully.

"One doesn't care what *the men* like," said Kate. "Do you think Don Ramón wishes you were a plump partridge?"

Teresa looked at her with a smile in her dark, big, bright eyes, that were so quick, and in many ways so unseeing.

"Who knows!" she said.—And in her quick, mischievous smile it was evident she would like also, sometimes, to be a plump partridge.

Kate now saw more of the hacienda life than she had done before. When Ramón was at home, he consulted his overseer, or *administrador*, every morning. But already Teresa was taking this work off his hands. She would see to the estate.

Ramón was a good deal absent, either in Mexico or in Guadalajara, or even away in Sonora.* He was already famous and notorious throughout the country, his name was a name to conjure with. But

underneath the rather ready hero-worship of the Mexicans, Kate
somehow felt their latent grudging. Perhaps they took more satisfaction in ultimately destroying their heroes, than in temporarily
raising them high. The real perfect moment was when the hero was
5	downed.

And to Kate, sceptic as she was, it seemed much more likely that
they were sharpening the machete to stick in Ramón's heart, when
he got a bit too big for them, than anything else. Though to be sure
there was Cipriano to reckon with. And Cipriano was a little devil
10	whom they quite rightly feared. And Cipriano, for once, was faith-
ful. He was, to himself, Huitzilopochtli, and to this he would maintain a demonish faith. He was Huitzilopochtli, Ramón was Quetzalcoatl. To Cipriano this was a plain and living fact. And he kept his
army keen as a knife. Even the President would not care to run
15	counter to Cipriano. And the President was a brave man too.

"One day," he said, "we will put Quetzalcoatl in Puebla Cathedral, and Huitzilopochtli in Mexico Cathedral, and Malintzi in
Guadalupe.* The day will come, Ramón."

"We will see that it comes," Ramón replied.

20	But Ramón and Montes suffered alike from the deep, devilish
animosity the country sent out in silence against them. It was the
same, whoever was in power: the Mexicans seemed to steam with
invisible, grudging hate, the hate of demons foiled in their own
souls, whose only motive is to foil everything, everybody, in the
25	everlasting hell of cramped frustration.

This was the dragon of Mexico, that Ramón had to fight.
Montes, the President, had it to fight the same. And it shattered his
health. Cipriano also had it up against him. But he succeeded best.
With his drums, with his dances round the fire, with his soldiers
30	kept keen as knives he drew real support from his men, he grew
stronger and more brilliant.

Ramón also, at home in his own district, felt the power flow into
him from his people. He was their chief, and by his effort and his
power he had almost overcome their ancient, fathomless resistance.
35	Almost he had *awed* them back into the soft mystery of living, awed
them until the tension of their resistant, malevolent wills relaxed. At
home, he would feel his strength upon him.

But away from home, and particularly in the city of Mexico, he
felt himself bled, bled, bled by the subtle, hidden malevolence of
40	the Mexicans, and the ugly negation of the greedy, mechanical

foreigners, birds of prey forever alighting in the cosmopolitan capital.

While Ramón was away, Kate stayed with Teresa. The two women had this in common, that they felt it was better to stand faithfully behind a really brave man, than to push forward into the ranks of cheap and obtrusive women. And this united them. A certain deep, ultimate faithfulness in each woman, to her own man who needed her fidelity, kept Kate and Teresa kindred to one another.

The rainy season had almost passed, though throughout September and even in October occasional heavy downpours fell. But the wonderful Mexican autumn, like a strange, inverted spring was upon the land. The waste places bloomed with pink and white cosmos, the strange wild trees flowered in a ghostly way, forests of small sunflowers shone in the sun, the sky was a pure, pure blue, the floods of sunshine lay tempered on the land, that in part was flooded with water, from the heavy rains.

The lake was very full, strange and uneasy, and it had washed up a bank of the wicked water-hyacinth along all its shores. The wild-fowl were coming from the north, clouds of wild ducks like dust in the high air, sprinkling the water like weeds. Many, many wild-fowl, grebe, cranes, and white gulls of the inland seas, so that the northern mystery seemed to have blown so far south. There was a smell of water in the land, and a sense of soothing. For Kate firmly believed that part of the horror of the Mexican people came from the unsoothed dryness of the land and the untempered crudity of the flat-edged sunshine. If only there could be a softening of water in the air, and a haze above trees, the unspoken and unspeakable malevolence would die out of the human hearts.

Kate rode out often with Teresa to see the fields. The sugar cane in the inner valley was vivid green, and rising tall, tall. The peons were beginning to cut it with their sword-like machetes, filling the bullock wagons, to haul the cane to the factory in Sayula. On the dry hill-slopes the spikey tequila plant—a sort of maguey—flourished in its iron wickedness. Low wild cactuses put forth rose-like blossoms, wonderful and beautiful for such sinister plants. The beans were gathered from the bean-fields, some gourds and squashes still sprawled their uncanny weight across the land. Red chiles hung on withering plants, red tomatoes sank to the earth. Some maize still reared its flags, there was still young corn to eat on the cob. The

banana crop was small, the apples and the guavas were nearly all gathered. The children came in with the little wild yellow tejocote apples, for making preserves. Teresa was making preserves, even with the late figs and peaches. On the trees, the ponderous mango
5 trees, some fruit was again orange-yellow and ripe, but the most still hung in strings, heavy and greenish and dropping like the testes of bulls.

It was autumn in Mexico, with wild duck on the waters, and hunters with guns, and small wild doves in the trees. Autumn in
10 Mexico, and the coming of the dry season, with the sky going higher and higher, pure pale blue, the sunset arriving with a strange flare of crystal yellow light. With the coffee berries turning red on the straggling bushes under the trees, and bougainvillea in the strong light glowing with a glow of magenta colour so deep you could
15 plunge your arms deep in it. With a few humming-birds in the sunshine, and the fish in the waters gone wild, and the flies, that steamed black in the first rains, now passing away again.

Teresa attended to everything, and Kate helped. Whether it was a sick peon in one of the little houses, or the hosts of bees from the
20 hives under the mangoes, or the yellow, yellow bees-wax to be made into little bowl-fuls, or the preserves, or the garden, or the calves, or the bit of butter and the little fresh cheeses made of strands of curd, or the turkeys to be overlooked: she saw to it along with Teresa. And she wondered at the steady, urgent, efficient *will* which had to be
25 exerted all the time. Everything was kept going by a heavy exertion of will. If once the will of the master broke, everything would break, and ruin would overtake the place almost at once. No real relaxation, ever. Always the sombre, insistent will.

Ramón arrived home one evening in November, from a long
30 journey to Sonora. He had come overland from Tepic, and twice had been stopped by floods.* The rains, so late, were very unusual. He was tired and remote-seeming. Kate's heart stood still a moment as she thought: He goes so remote, as if he might go away altogether into death.

35 It was cloudy again, with lightning beating about on the horizons. But all was very still. She said Goodnight! early, and wandered down her own side of the terrace, to the look-out at the end, which looked on to the lake. Everything was dark, save for the intermittent pallor of lightning.
40 And she was startled to see, in a gleam of lightning, Teresa sitting

with her back to the wall of the open terrace, Ramón lying with his head in her lap, while she slowly pushed her fingers through his thick black hair. They were as silent as the night.

Kate gave a startled murmur and said:

"I'm so sorry! I didn't know you were here."

"I wanted to be under the sky!" said Ramón, heaving himself to rise.

"Oh *don't* move!" said Kate. "It was stupid of me to come here. You are tired."

"Yes," he said, sinking again. "I am tired. These people make me feel I have a hole in the middle of me. So I have come back to Teresa."

"Yes!" said Kate. "One isn't the Living Quetzalcoatl for nothing. Of course they eat holes in you.—Really, is it worth it?—To give yourself to be eaten away by them."

"It must be so," he said. "The change has to be made. And some man has to make it.—I sometimes wish it wasn't I."

"So do I wish it. So does Teresa. One wonders if it isn't better to be just a man," said Kate.

But Teresa said nothing.

"One does what one must. And after all, one is always just a man," he said. "And if one has wounds—à la guerre comme à la guerre!"*

His voice came out of the darkness like a ghost.

"Ah!" sighed Kate. "It makes one wonder what a man is, that he must needs expose himself to the horrors of all the other people."

There was silence for a moment.

"Man is a column of blood, with a voice in it," he said. "And when the voice is still, and he is only a column of blood, he is better."

She went away to her room sadly, hearing the sound of infinite exhaustion in his voice. As if he had a hole, a wound in the middle of him. She could almost feel it, in her own bowels.

And if, with his efforts, he killed himself?—Then she and Cipriano would come apart, and it would be all finished.

Ah, why should a man have to make these efforts on behalf of a beastly, malevolent people who weren't worth it! Better let the world come to an end, if that was what it wanted.

She thought of Teresa soothing him, soothing him and saying nothing. And him like a great helpless wounded thing! It was rather horrible really. Herself, she would have to expostulate, she would have to try to prevent him. Why should men damage themselves with

this useless struggling and fighting, and then come home to their
women to be restored!

To Kate, the fight simply wasn't worth one wound. Let the beastly
world of man come to an end, if that was its destiny, as soon as
5 possible. Without lifting a finger to prevent it.—Live one's own
precious life, that was given but once, and let the rest go its own
hellish way.

She would have *had* to try to prevent Ramón from giving himself
to destruction this way. She was willing for him to be ten Living
10 Quetzalcoatls. But not to expose himself to the devilish malevolence
of people.

Yet he would do it. Even as Joachim had done. And Teresa, with
her silence and her infinitely soft administering, she would heal him
far better than Kate, with her expostulation and her opposition.

15 "Ah!" said Kate to herself. "I'm glad Cipriano is a soldier, and
doesn't get wounds in his *soul*."

At the same time, she knew that without Ramón, Cipriano was just
an instrument, and not ultimately interesting to her.

In the morning, Teresa appeared alone to breakfast. She seemed
20 very calm, hiding her emotions in her odd, brown, proud little way.

"How is Ramón?" said Kate.

"He is sleeping," said Teresa.

"Good! He seemed to me almost done up, last night."

"Yes."—The black eyes looked at Kate, wide with unshed tears
25 and courage, and a beautiful deep, remote light.

"I *don't* believe in a man's sacrificing himself in this way," said
Kate. "And I *don't*."

Teresa still looked her full in the eyes.

"Ah!" she said. "He doesn't sacrifice himself. He feels he must do
30 as he does. And if he must, I must help him."

"But then you are sacrificing yourself to *him*, and I don't believe in
that either," said Kate.

"Oh no!" replied Teresa quickly, and a little flush burned in her
cheek, and her dark eyes flashed. "I am not sacrificing myself to
35 Ramón. If I can give him—sleep—when he needs it—that is not
sacrifice. It is—" She did not finish, but her eyes flashed, and the
flush burned darker.

"It is love, I know," said Kate. "But it exhausts you too."

"It is not simply love," flashed Teresa proudly. "I might have
40 loved more than one man: many men are lovable. But Ramón!—my

soul is with Ramón.—" The tears rose to her eyes. "I do not want to talk about it," she said, rising. "But you must not touch me there, and judge me."

She hurried out of the room, leaving Kate somewhat dismayed. Kate sighed, thinking of going home.

But in an hour Teresa appeared again, putting her cool, soft, snake-like little hand on Kate's arm.

"I am sorry if I was rude," she said.

"No," said Kate. "Apparently it is I who am wrong."

"Yes, I think you are," said Teresa. "You think there is only love. Love is only such a little bit."

"And what is the rest?"

"How can I tell you if you do not know?—But do you think Ramón is no more to me than a lover?"

"A husband!" said Kate.

"Ah!"—Teresa put her head aside with an odd impatience. "Those little words! Those little words! Nor either a husband.—He is my life!"

"Surely it is better for one to live one's own life!"

"No! It is like seed. It is no good till it is given. I know. I kept my own life for a long time. As you keep it longer, it dies. And I tried to give it to God. But I couldn't, quite.—Then they told me, if I married Ramón and had any part in the Quetzalcoatl heresy, my soul would be damned.—But something made me know it was not true. I even knew he needed my soul.—Ah Señora—" a subtle smile came on Teresa's pale face—"I have lost my soul to Ramón. What more can I say!"

"And what about his soul?"

"It comes home to me—*here!*"—She put her hand over her womb.

Kate was silent for a time.

"And if he betrays you?" she said.

"Ah Señora!" said Teresa. "Ramón is not just a lover. He is a brave man, and he doesn't betray his own blood. And it is his soul that comes home to me.—And I would struggle to my last breath to give him sleep, when he came home to me with his soul, and needed it," she flashed. Then she added, murmuring to herself: "No, thank God! I have not got a life of my own! I have been able to give it to a man who is more than a man, as they say in their Quetzalcoatl language. And now it needn't die inside me, like a bird in a cage.—Oh yes, Señora! If he goes to Sinaloa and the west coast, my soul goes with him and takes part in it all. It does not let him go alone. And he does not forget that he has my soul with him. I know it.—No, Señora! You must not criticise me or pity me."

5   "Still!" said Kate. "It still seems to me it would be better for each one to keep her own soul, and be responsible for it."

"If it were possible!" said Teresa. "But you can no more keep your own soul inside you for yourself, without its dying, than you can keep the seed of your womb. Until a man gives you his seed, the seed

10 of your womb is nothing. And the man's seed is nothing to him.—And until you give your soul to a man, and he takes it, your soul is nothing to you.—And when a man has taken your whole soul—Ah, do not talk to me about betraying. A man only betrays because he has been given *a part*, and not the whole. And a woman

15 only betrays because only the part has been taken from her, and not the whole. That is all about betrayal. I know.—But when the whole is given, and taken, betrayal can't exist. What I am to Ramón, I am. And what he is to me, he is. I do not care *what* he does. If he is away from me, he does as he wishes. So long as he will always keep safe

20 what I am to him."

Kate did not like having to learn lessons from this little waif of a Teresa. Kate was a woman of the world, handsome and experienced. She was accustomed to homage. Other women usually had a slight fear of her, for she was powerful and ruthless in her own way.

25   Teresa also feared her a little, as a woman of the world. But as an intrinsic woman, not at all. Trenched inside her own fierce and proud little soul, Teresa looked on Kate as on one of those women of the outside world, who make a very splendid show, but who are not so sure of the real secret of womanhood, and the innermost power.

30 All Kate's handsome, ruthless female power was second-rate to Teresa, compared with her own quiet, deep passion of connection with Ramón.

Yes, Kate was accustomed to looking on other women as inferiors. In her own line, they usually were her inferiors. But the tables were

35 suddenly turned. Even as, in her soul, she knew Ramón to be a greater man than Cipriano, suddenly she had to question herself, whether Teresa was not a greater woman than she.

Teresa! A greater woman than Kate? What a blow! Surely it was impossible!

40   Yet there it was. Ramón had wanted to marry Teresa, not Kate.

And the flame of his marriage with Teresa she saw both in his eyes and in Teresa's. A flame that was not in Kate's eyes.

Kate's marriage with Cipriano was curious and momentary. When Cipriano was away, Kate was her old individual self. Only when Cipriano was present, and then only sometimes, did the connection overwhelm her.

When Teresa turned and looked at her with this certain flame, touched with indignation, Kate quailed. Perhaps for the first time in her life she quailed and felt abashed: repentant.

Kate even knew that Teresa felt a little repugnance for her: for the foreign white woman who talked as cleverly as a man and who never gave her soul: who did not believe in giving her soul. All these well-dressed, beautiful women from America or England, Europe, they all kept their souls for themselves, in a sort of purse, as it were.

Teresa was determined that Kate should leave off treating her, very, very indefinably, as an inferior. It was how all the foreign women treated the Mexican women. Because the foreign women were their own mistresses! They even tried to be condescending to Ramón.

But Ramón! He could look at them and make them feel small, feel really nothing, in spite of all their money and their experience and their air of belonging to the ruling races. The ruling races! Wait! Ramón was a challenge to all that. Let those rule who can.

"You did not sleep well?" Teresa said to Kate.

"Not very well," said Kate.

"No, you look as if you had not slept very well.—Under your eyes."

Kate smoothed the skin under her eyes, querulously.

"One gets that look in Mexico," she said. "It's not an easy country to keep your youth in.—You are looking well."

"Yes, I am very well."

Teresa had a new, soft bloom on her dark skin, something frail and tender, which she did not want to have to defend against another woman.

"I think I will go home now Ramón has come," said Kate.

"Oh, why? Do you wish to?"

"I think I'd better."

"Then I will go with you to Sayula. In the boat, no?"

Kate put her few things together. She had slept badly. The night had been black, black, with something of horror in it. As when the

bandits had attacked Ramón.—She could see the scar in his back, in
the night. And the drumming crash of falling water, menacing and
horrible, seemed to keep up for hours.

In her soul, Kate felt Teresa's contempt for her way of wifehood.

5   "I have been married, too," Kate had said. "To a very exceptional
man, whom I *loved*."

"Ah yes!" said Teresa. "And he died."

"He wanted to die."

"Ah yes! He wanted to die."

10   "I did my level best to prevent him from wearing himself out."

"Ah yes, to prevent him."

"What else could I have done?" flashed Kate in anger.

"If you could have given him your life, he would not even have
wanted to die."

15   "I *did* give him my life. I loved him—ah, you will never
know.—But he didn't *want* my soul. He believed I should keep a soul
of my own."

"Ah yes, men are like that, when they are merely men. When a
man is *warm* and brave—then he wants the woman to give him her
20   soul, and he keeps it in *his* womb, so he is more than a mere man, a
single man. I know it. I know where my soul is. It is in Ramón's
womb, the womb of a man, just as his seed is in my womb, the womb
of a woman. He is a man, and a column of blood. I am a woman, and
a valley of blood. I shall not contradict him. How can I? My soul is
25   inside him, and I am far from contradicting him when he is trying
with all his might to do something that *he* knows about. He won't die,
and they won't kill him. No! The stream flows into him from the
heart of the world: and from me.—I tell you, because you saved his
life, and therefore we belong to the same thing, you and I and
30   he—and Cipriano. But you should not misjudge me. That other way
of women, where a woman keeps her own soul—ah, what is it but
weariness!"

"And the men?"

"Ah! if there are men whose souls are warm and brave, how they
35   comfort one's womb, Caterina!"

Kate hung her head, stubborn and angry at being put down from
her eminence.—The slave morale! she said to herself. The miserable old trick of a woman living just for the sake of a man. Only living
to send her soul with him, inside his precious body! And to carry his
40   precious seed in her own womb! Herself, apart from this, nothing.

Kate wanted to make her indignation thorough, but she did not quite succeed. Somewhere, secretly and angrily, she envied Teresa her dark eyes with the flame in them and their savage assurance. She envied her her serpent-delicate fingers. And above all, she envied her, with repining, the comfort of a living man permanent in her womb. And the secret, savage indomitable pride in her own womanhood, that rose from this.

In the warm morning after rain, the frogs were whirring frantically. Across the lake, the mountains were blue-black, and little pieces of white, fluffy vapor wandered low across the trees. Clouds were along the mountain-tops, making a level sky-line of whitish softness the whole length of the range. On the lovely, fawn-coloured water, one sail was blowing.

"It is like Europe—like the Tyrol today," said Kate wistfully.

"Do you love Europe very much?" asked Teresa.

"Yes, I think I love it."

"And must you go back to it?"

"I think so. Soon! To my mother and my children."

"Do they want you very much?"

"Yes!" said Kate, rather hesitant. Then she added: "Not *very* much, really. But I want them."

"What for?—I mean," Teresa added, "do you long for them?"

"Sometimes," said Kate, the tears coming to her eyes.

The boat rowed on in silence.

"And Cipriano?" Teresa asked timidly.

"Ah!" said Kate shortly. "He is such a stranger to me."

Teresa was silent for some moments.

"I think a man is always a stranger to a woman," said Teresa. "Why should it not be so?"

"But you," said Kate, "haven't any children."

"Ramón has.—And he says: 'I cast my bread upon the waters.* It is my children too. And if they return to me after many days, I shall be glad.'—Is it not the same for you?"

"Not quite!" said Kate. "I am a woman. I am not a man."

"I, if I have children," said Teresa, "I shall try to cast my bread upon the waters, so my children come to me that way. I hope I shall. I hope I shall not try to fish them out of life for myself, with a net. I have a very great fear of love. It is so personal. Let each bird fly with its own wings, and each fish swim its own course.—Morning brings more than love. And I want to be true to the morning."

Chapter XXVI.

Kate is a Wife.

Kate was glad to get back to her own house, and to be more or less alone. She felt a great change was being worked in her, and if it worked too violently, she would die. It was the end of something, and the beginning of something, far, far inside her: in her soul and womb. The men, Ramón and Cipriano, caused the change, and Mexico. Because the time had come.—Nevertheless, if what was happening happened too rapidly, or violently, she felt she would die. So, from time to time she had to withdraw from contact, to be alone.

She would sit alone for hours on the shore, under a green willow tree that hung its curtains of pale-green fronds, on the beach. The lake was much fuller and higher up the shore, softer, more mysterious. There was a smell of the piles of water-hyacinth decaying at the water's edges. Distance seemed farther away. The near conical hills were dotted with green bushes, like a Japanese drawing. Bullock wagons with solid wheels came rolling to the village, high with sugar cane, drawn by eight oxen with ponderous heads and slowly swinging horns, while a peon walked in front, with the guiding-stick on the cross-beam of the yoke. So slow, so massive, yet with such slight control!

She had a strange feeling, in Mexico, of the old prehistoric humanity, the dark-eyed humanity of the days, perhaps, before the glacial period. When the world was colder, and the seas emptier, and all the land-formation was different. When the waters of the world were piled in stupendous glaciers on the high places, and high, high upon the poles. When great plains stretched away to the oceans, and countries rose above the oceans, like Atlantis and the lost continents of Polynesia, so that seas were only great lakes, and the soft, dark-eyed people of that world could walk around the globe. Then there was a mysterious, hot-blooded, soft-footed humanity with a strange civilisation of its own.*

Till the glaciers melted, and drove the peoples to the high places, like the lofty plateaux of Mexico, separated them into cut-off nations.

Sometimes, in America, the shadow of that old pre-Flood world was so strong, that the day of historic humanity would melt out of Kate's consciousness, and she would begin to approximate to the old mode of consciousness, the old, dark will, the unconcern for death, the subtle, dark consciousness, non-cerebral, but vertebrate. When   5
the mind and the power of man was in his blood and his back-bone, and there was the strange, dark inter-communication between man and man and man and beast, from the powerful spine.

The Mexicans were still this. That which is aboriginal in America still belongs to the way of the world before the Flood, before the   10
mental-spiritual world came into being. In America, therefore, the mental-spiritual life of white people suddenly flourishes like a great weed let loose in virgin soil. Probably it will as quickly wither. A great death come. And after that, the living result will be a new germ, a new conception of human life, that will arise from the fusion of the   15
old blood-and-vertebrate consciousness with the white man's present mental-spiritual consciousness. The sinking of both beings, into a new being.*

Kate was more Irish than anything, and the almost deathly mysticism of the aboriginal Celtic or Iberian peoples lay at the   20
bottom of her soul. It was a residue of memory, something that lives on from the pre-Flood world, and cannot be killed. Something older, and more everlastingly potent, than our would-be fair-and-square world.

She knew more or less what Ramón was trying to effect: this   25
fusion! She knew what it was that made Cipriano more significant to her than all her past, her husbands and her children. It was the leap of the old, antediluvian blood-male into unison with her. And for this, without her knowing, her innermost blood had been thudding all the time.   30

Ireland would not and could not forget that other old, dark, sumptuous living. The Tuatha De Danaan might be under the western sea. But they are under the living blood too, never quite to be silenced. Now they have to come forth again, to a new connection. And the scientific, fair-and-square Europe has to mate once more   35
with the old giants.

But the change, Kate felt, must not come on her too soon and too suddenly, or it would rupture her and she would die. The old way has its horror. The heavy-footed, *à terre* spirit of aboriginal Mexico could be so horrible to her, as to make her wicked. The slow,   40

indomitable kind of existing and persisting, without hope or élan, which is in the aboriginal American, sometimes made her feel she would go mad. The sullen will persisting over the slow, dark centuries, counting the individual existence a trifle! A tenacity of
5 demons, less than human. And a sudden ferocity, a sudden lust of death rousing incalculable and terrible.

People who never really changed. Men who were not faithful to life, to the living actuality. Faithful to some dark necessity out of the past. The actual present suddenly collapsing in the souls of the men
10 and the women, and the old, black, volcanic lava bursting up in violence, followed by a lava-rock indifference.

The hope! The hope! Would it ever be possible to revive the hope in these black souls, and achieve the marriage which is the only step to the new world of man?

15 But meanwhile, a strange, almost torn nausea would come over Kate, and she felt she must go away, to spare herself. The strange, reptilian insistence of her very servants: *Blood is one blood. We are all of one blood-stream.* Something aboriginal and tribal, and almost worse than death to the white individual. Out of the dark eyes and
20 the powerful spines of these people, all the time the unknown assertion: *The blood is one blood.* It was a strange, overbearing insistence, a claim of blood-unison.

Kate was of a proud old family. She had been brought up with the English, Germanic idea of the *intrinsic* superiority of the hereditary
25 aristocrat. Her blood was different from the common blood, another, finer fluid.

But in Mexico, none of this. Her criada Juana, the *aguador* who carried the water, the boatman who rowed her on the lake, all looked at her with one look in their eyes: *The blood is one blood. In the blood,*
30 *you and I are undifferentiated.* She saw it in their eyes, she heard it in their words, it tinged their deference and their mockery. And sometimes it made her feel physically sick: this overbearing blood-familiarity.

And sometimes, when she tried to hold herself up, in the proud
35 old assertion: *My blood is my own. Noli me tangere,** she would see the terrible ancient hatred in their eyes, the hatred which leads them to atrocities and fearful maimings.

They would defer to her spirit, her knowledge, her understanding. They would give her deference, and a sort of grudging reverence for
40 this. She belonged to the ruling races, the clever ones. But back

again they demanded her acquiescence to the primeval assertion: *The blood is one blood. We are one blood.* It was the assertion that swept away all individualism, and left her immersed, drowned in the grand sea of the living blood, in immediate contact with all these men and all these women.

To this she must submit. Or they would persist in the slow revenge.

And she could not submit, off-hand. It had to be a slow, organic process. Anything sudden or violent would destroy her.

Now she understood Ramón's assertion: Man is a column of blood: Woman is a valley of blood. It was the primeval oneness of mankind, the opposite of the oneness of the Spirit.

But Kate had always looked upon her blood as absolutely her own, her individual own. Her spirit she shared, in the spirit she communed. But her blood stayed by her in individuality.

Now she was confronted by the other great assertion: The blood is one blood.—It meant a strange, marginless death of her individual self.

Now she understood why Ramón and Cipriano wore the white clothes and the sandals, and were naked, or half-naked, as living gods. It was the acquiescence in the primitive assertion. It was the renewal of the old, terrible bond of the blood-unison of man, which made blood-sacrifice so potent a factor of life. The blood of the individual is given back to the great blood-being, the god, the nation, the tribe.

Now she understood the strange unison she could always feel between Ramón and his men, and Cipriano and his men. It was the soft, quaking, deep communion of blood-oneness. Sometimes it made her feel sick. Sometimes it made her revolt. But it was the power she could not get beyond.

Because, admitting his blood-unison, Ramón at the same time claimed a supremacy, even a godliness. He was a man, as the lowest of his peons was a man. At the same time, rising from the same pool of blood, from the same roots of manhood as they, and being, as they were, a man of the pulsing blood, he was still something more. Not in the blood nor in the spirit lay his individuality and his supremacy, his godhead. But in a star within him, an inexplicable star which rose out of the dark sea and shone between the flood and the great sky. The mysterious star which unites the vast universal blood with the universal breath of the spirit, and shines between them both.

Not the rider on the white horse: nor the rider on the red.* That which is beyond the riders and the horses, the inexplicable mystery of the star whence no horseman comes and to which no horseman can arrive. The star which is a man's innermost clue, which rules the
5 power of the blood on the one hand, and the power of the spirit on the other.

For this, the only thing which is supreme above all power in a man, and at the same time, is power; which far transcends knowledge; the strange star between the sky and the waters of the first cosmos: this is
10 man's divinity.

And some men are not divine at all. They have only faculties. They are slaves, or they should be slaves.

But many a man has his own spark of divinity, and has it quenched, blown out by the winds of force or ground out of him by
15 machines.

And when the spirit and the blood in man begin to go asunder, bringing the great death, most stars die out.

Only the man of a great star, a great divinity, can bring the opposites together again, in a new unison.

20 And this was Ramón, and this was his great effort: to bring the great opposites into contact and into unison again. And this is the god-power in man. By this power you shall know the god in a man. By none other.

Ramón was a man as the least of his peons was a man, with the
25 beating heart and the secret loins and the lips closed on the same secret of manhood. And he was human as Kate was human, with the same yearning of the spirit, for pure knowledge and communion, the soul in the greatness of its comprehending.

But only he had that starry power for bringing together the two
30 great human impulses to a point of fusion, for being the bird between the vast wings of the dual created power to which man has access and in which man has his being. The Morning Star, between the breath of dawn and the deeps of the dark.

Men had tried to murder him with knives. Carlota would have
35 murdered him with her spirit. Each half separately wanted to commit the murder of him.

But he kept himself beyond. He was the Living Quetzalcoatl, and the tiny sparkle of a star was rising in his own men, in his own woman.

40 The star between the two wings of power: that alone was divinity in a man, and final manhood.

Kate had a message from Cipriano to say he was coming out to stay in the Villa Aragón . The Villa Aragón was the chief house on the lake, in small but rather beautiful grounds with tufts of palm-trees and heavy hedges of jasmine, a garden kept always green by constant watering. The house was built rather like a little castle, absurd, yet its deep, spacious verandahs opening on to the slopes and knolls of the tree-clustered garden, above the lake, were pleasant.

Cipriano arrived very pleased, his black eyes shining with the boyish look. He wanted Kate to marry him, go through the Mexican civil marriage, and instal herself in the Villa Aragón. She hesitated. She knew she must go back to Europe, to England and Ireland, very soon. The necessity was imperative. The sense of menace that Mexico put over her, and the feeling of inner nausea, was becoming too much to bear. She felt she could not stand it, unless she went away to relax for a time.

This she told to Cipriano. And his face fell.

"It doesn't matter to me very much whether I marry or not, before I go," she said. "But I must go soon—soon."

"How soon?"

"By January."

His face lightened again.

"Then marry me before you go," he said. "Next week."

She agreed, with curious indifference, and he, his eyes flashing again like a boy's, moved quickly, to make the necessary legal preparations.

She did not care whether she married or not. In one essential sense, she had married Cipriano already. He was first and foremost a soldier, swift to come to her, and swift to go. She would always be a good deal alone.

And him alone, just as a man and a soldier, she could marry easily enough. It was this terrible Mexico that frightened her with a sense of doom.

The Quetzalcoatl movement had spread in the country, but sinisterly. The Archbishop had declared against it, Ramón and Cipriano and their adherents were excommunicated. An attempt had been made to assassinate Montes.

The adherents of Quetzalcoatl in the Capital had made the Church of San Juan Bautista, which was called the Church of the Black Saviour,* their Metropolitan House of Quetzalcoatl. The Archbishop, a choleric man, had summoned his fervent followers, to march in procession to this Church of San Juan, now called the

House of Quetzalcoatl, and seize it and restore it to the Catholic Church. The government, knowing it would have to fight sooner or later, arrested the Archbishop and broke up the procession after some bloodshed.

5   Then a kind of war began. The Knights of Cortés brought out their famous hidden stores of arms, not very impressive, after all, and a clerical mob, headed by a fanatical priest, surged into the Zócalo. Montes had the guns turned on them. But it looked like the beginnings of a religious war. In the streets the white and blue

10 sarapes of Quetzalcoatl and the scarlet and black sarapes of Huitzilopochtli were seen in bands, marching to the sound of tom-toms, and holding up the curious round banners, made of feather-work, of Quetzalcoatl, and the tall scarlet signs of Huitzilopochtli, long poles with the soft club of scarlet feathers at the top, tufted with a black

15 point.*—In the churches, the priests were still inflaming the orthodox to a holy war. In the streets, priests who had gone over to Quetzalcoatl were haranguing the crowd.

It was a wild moment. In Zacatecas General Narciso Beltrán had declared against Montes and for the Church.* But Cipriano with his

20 Huitzilopochtli soldiers had attacked with such swiftness and ferocity, Beltrán was taken and shot, his army disappeared.

Then Montes declared the old Church illegal in Mexico, and caused a law to be passed, making the religion of Quetzalcoatl the national religion of the Republic. All churches were closed. All

25 priests were compelled to take an oath of allegiance to the Republic, or condemned to exile. The armies of Huitzilopochtli and the white and blue sarapes of Quetzalcoatl appeared in all the towns and villages of the Republic. Ramón labored ceaselessly. Cipriano appeared in unexpected flashes, in unexpected places. He managed

30 to rouse the most discontented states, Veracruz, Tamaulipas, Yucatán, to a sort of religious frenzy. Strange baptisms took place in the sea, and scarlet and black towers of Huitzilopochtli rose along the shores.

The whole country was thrilling with a new thing, with a release of

35 new energy. But there was a sense of violence and crudity in it all, a touch of horror.

The Archbishop was deported, no more priests were seen in the streets. Only the white and blue and earth-coloured sarapes of Quetzalcoatl, and the scarlet and black of Huitzilopochtli, were seen

40 among the crowds. There was a great sense of release, almost of exuberance.

This is why Cipriano came to Kate with those black, flashing, boyish eyes. He was in a strange state of triumph. Kate was frightened, and she felt curiously hollow. Even the queer, new, flashing triumph and the sense of a new thing on the face of the earth could not quite save her. She belonged too much to the old world of Europe, she could not, could not make herself over so quickly. But she felt that if she could go back to Ireland, and let her life and her body *pause* for a time, then she could come back and take her share.

For it was not her spirit alone which was changing, it was her body, and the constitution of her very blood. She could feel it, the terrible katabolism and metabolism in her blood, changing her even as a creature, changing her to another creature.

And if it went too fast, she would die.

So, she was legally married to Cipriano, and she went to live with him in the Villa Aragón, for a month. After a month, she would sail away, alone, to Ireland. He agreed too.

It was strange, to be married to him. He made her go all vague and quiet, as if she sank away heavy and still, away from the surface of life, and lay deep in the underlife. The strange, heavy, *positive* passivity. For the first time in her life she felt absolutely at rest. And talk, and thought, had become trivial, superficial to her: as the ripples on the surface of the lake are as nothing, to the creatures that live away below in the unwavering deeps.

In her soul, she was still and proud. If only her body had not suffered the unbearable nausea of change. She had sunk to a final rest, within a great, opened-out cosmos. The universe had opened out to her new and vast, and she had sunk to the deep bed of pure rest. She had become almost like Teresa in sureness.

Yet the process of change within her blood was terrible to her.

Cipriano was happy, in his curious Indian way. His eyes kept that flashing, black, dilated look of a boy looking newly on a strange, almost uncanny wonder of life. He did not look very definitely at Kate, or even take much definite notice of her. He did not like talking to her, in any serious way. When she wanted to talk seriously, he flashed a cautious dark look at her, and went away.

He was aware of things that she herself was hardly conscious of. Chiefly, of the curious irritant quality of talk. And this he avoided. Curious as it may seem, he made her aware of her own old desire for frictional, irritant sensation. She realised how all her old love had been frictional, charged with the fire of irritation and the spasms of frictional voluptuousness.

Cipriano, curiously, by refusing to share any of this with her, made it become external to her. Her strange, seething feminine will and desire subsided in her and swept away, leaving her soft and powerfully potent, like the hots springs of water that gushed up so noiseless, so soft, yet so powerful, with a sort of secret potency.

She realised, almost with wonder, the death in her of the Aphrodite of the foam: the seething, frictional, ecstatic Aphrodite.* By a swift dark instinct, Cipriano drew away from this in her. When, in their love, it came back on her, the seething electric female ecstasy, which knows such spasms of delirium, he recoiled from her. It was what she used to call her "satisfaction." She had loved Joachim for this, that again, and again, and again he could give her this orgiastic "satisfaction," in spasms that made her cry aloud.

But Cipriano would not. By a dark and powerful instinct he drew away from her as soon as this desire rose again in her, for the white ecstasy of frictional satisfaction, the throes of Aphrodite of the foam. She could see that to him, it was repulsive. He just removed himself, dark and unchangeable, away from her.

And she, as she lay, would realise the worthlessness of this foam-effervescence, its strange externality to her. It seemed to come upon her from without, not from within. And succeeding the first moment of disappointment, when this sort of "satisfaction" was denied her, came the knowledge that she did not really want it, that it was really nauseous to her.

And he, in his dark, hot silence would bring her back to the new, soft, heavy, hot flow, when she was like a fountain gushing noiseless and with urgent softness from the volcanic deeps. Then she was open to him soft and hot, yet gushing with a noiseless soft power. And there was no such thing as conscious "satisfaction." What happened was dark and untellable. So different from the beak-like friction of Aphrodite of the foam, the friction which flares out in circles of phosphorescent ecstasy, to the last wild spasm which utters the involuntary cry, like a death-cry, the final love-cry. This she had known, and known to the end, with Joachim. And now this too was removed from her. What she had with Cipriano was curiously beyond her knowing: so deep and hot and flowing, as it were subterranean. She had to yield before *it*. She could not grip it into one final spasm of white ecstasy which was like sheer knowing.

And as it was in the love-act, so it was with him. She could not *know* him. When she tried to know him, something went slack in her,

and she had to leave off. She had to let be. She had to leave him, dark
and hot and potent, along with the things that *are*, but are not known.
The presence. And the stranger. This he was always to her.

There was hardly anything to say to him. And there was no
personal intimacy. He kept his privacy round him like a cloak, and
left her immune within her own privacy. He was a stranger to her,
she to him. He accepted the fact absolutely, as if nothing else were
possible. She, sometimes, felt it strange. She had so craved for
intimacy, *insisted* on intimacy.

Now she found herself accepting him finally and forever as the
stranger in whose presence she lived. It was his impersonal presence
which enveloped her. She lived in his aura, and he, she knew, lived in
hers, with nothing said, and no personal or spiritual intimacy
whatever. A mindless communion of the blood.

Therefore, when he had to go away, it did not matter so very
much. His presence was something he left with her, and he took her
presence along with him. And somehow, there was no need for
emotions.

He had to leave early one morning, for Mexico. The dawn came
perfect and clear. The sun was not yet on the lake, but it caught the
mountains beyond Tuliapán, and they shone magically distinct, as if
some magic light were focussed on them. The green furrows of the
mountain-sides were as if in her own hand. Two white gulls, flying,
suddenly got the light, and glittered. But the full, soft, noiseless dun
lake was pallid unlit.

She thought of the sea. The Pacific was not very far away. The sea
seemed to have retreated entirely out of her consciousness. Yet she
knew she needed its breath again.

Cipriano was going down to bathe. She saw him walk out on the
masonry of the square basin which was their own tiny harbour. He
threw off his wrap and stood dark in silhouette against the pale, unlit
water. How dark he was! Dark as a Malay. Curious that his body was
as dark, almost, as his face. And with that strange archaic fulness of
physique, with the full chest and the full, yet beautiful buttocks of
men on old Greek coins.

He dropped off the edge of the masonry and waded out in the dim,
soft, uncanny water. And at that moment the light tipped over the
edge of the mountain and spilled gold upon the surface of the lake.
And instantly he was red as fire. The sunshine was not red, the sun
was too high for that. It was golden with morning. But as it flushed

along the surface of the lake it caught the body of Cipriano and he
was red as fire, as a piece of pure fire.

The Sons of the Morning!* The column of blood! A red Indian.
She looked at him in wonder, as he moved pure red and luminous
5 further into the lake, unconscious. As if on fire!

The Sons of the Morning! She let her effort at knowing slip away
from her once more, and remained without effort, within the
communion.

It was his race, too. She had noticed before how the natives shone
10 pure red when morning or evening light caught them, rather level.
As fires they stood in the water. The Red Indians.

He went away, with his man, on horseback. And she watched him
ride over the brow of the road, sitting dark and still on his silky, roan
horse. He loved a red horse. And there was a curious motionlessness
15 about him as he rode horseback, an old, male pride, and at the same
time the half-ghostly, dark invisibility of the Indian, sitting close
upon the horse as if he and it belonged to one birth.

He was gone, and for a while she felt the old nostalgia for his
presence. Not for him, exactly. Not even to see him or touch him or
20 speak to him. Only to feel him about.

Then quickly she recovered. She adjusted herself to the presence
he left behind with her. As soon as he had *really* gone, and the act of
going was over, his presence came back to her.

She walked a little while by the shore, beyond the breakwater-
25 wall. She loved to be alone: a great deal alone, with a garden and the
lake and the morning.

"I am like Teresa, really," she said to herself.

Suddenly before her she saw a long, dark soft rope, lying over a
pale boulder. But her soul was softly alert, at once. It was a snake,
30 with a subtle pattern along its soft dark back, lying there over a big
stone, with its head sunk down to earth.

It felt her presence, too, for suddenly, with incredible soft
quickness, it contracted itself down the boulder, and she saw it
entering a little gap in the bottom of the wet wall.

35 The hole was not very big. And as it entered it quickly looked
back, poising its little, dark, wicked, pointed head, and flickering a
dark tongue. Then it passed on, slowly easing its dark length into the
hole.

When it had all gone in, Kate could see the last fold still, and the
40 flat little head resting on the fold, like the devil with his chin on his

arms, looking out of a loop-hole. So the wicked sparks of the eyes looked out at her, from within the recess. Watching out of its own invisibility.

So she wondered over it, as it lay in its hidden places. At all the unseen things in the hidden places of the earth. And she wondered if 5 it was disappointed at not being able to rise higher in creation: to be able to run on four feet, and not keep its belly on the ground.

Perhaps not! Perhaps it had its own peace. She felt a certain reconciliation between herself and it.

Chapter XXVII.

Here!*

She and Teresa visited one another along the lake. There was a kinship and a gentleness between them, especially now Kate was
5 going away for a while.

There was a certain autumnal purity and lull on the lake. The moisture still lingered, the bushes on the wild hills were green in puffs. Sunlight lay in a rich gleam on the mountains, and shadows were deep and velvety. The green almost covered the rocks and the
10 pinkish land. Bright green the sugar cane, red the ploughed earth, dark the trees, with white specks of villages here and there. And over the wild places, a sprinkle of bushes, then stark grey rock still coming out.

The sky was very high and pure. In the morning came the sound of
15 drums, and on the motionless, crystal air the cry for the pauses of the day. And always the day seemed to be pausing and unfolding again to the greater mystery. The universe seemed to have opened vast and soft and delicate with life.

There was something curiously soothing even in the full, pale,
20 dove-brown water of the lake. A boat was coming over, with its sail hollowed out like a shell, pearly white, and its sharp black canoe-beak slipping past the water. It looked like the boat of Dionysos coming with a message, and the vine sprouting.*

Kate could hardly remember now the dry, rigid pallor of the heat,
25 when the whole earth seemed to crepitate viciously with dry malevolence: like memory gone dry and sterile, hellish.

Ramón and Teresa came along the lake, and rowed into the basin. It was a morning when the shadows on the mountains were almost corn-flower blue.

30 "Yet you must go away?" Ramón said to her.

"For a little while. You don't think I am Lot's wife,* do you?"

"No!" laughed Ramón. "I think you're Cipriano's."

"I am really. But I want to go back for a little while."

"Ah yes! Better go, and then come again.—Tell them in your
35 Ireland to do as we have done here."

"But how?"

426

"Let them find themselves again, and their own universe, and their own gods. Let them substantiate their own mysteries. The Irish have been so wordy about their far-off heroes and green days of the heroic gods. Now tell them to substantiate them, as we have tried to substantiate Quetzalcoatl and Huitzilopochtli." 5

"I will tell them," she said. "If there is anybody to listen."

"Yes!" he said.

He watched the white sail* blowing nearer.

"But why do you go away?" he asked her, after a silence.

"You don't care, do you?" she said. 10

There was a dead pause.

"Yes, I care," he said.

"But why?"

Again it was some time before he answered.

"You are one of us, we need you," he said. 15

"Even when I don't do anything?—and when I get a bit bored with living Quetzalcoatls—and the rest, and wish for a simple Don Ramón?" she replied.

He laughed suddenly.

"What is a simple Don Ramón?" he said. "A simple Don Ramón 20 has a living Quetzalcoatl inside him. But you help all the same."

"You go ahead so grandly, one would not think you needed help: especially from a mere woman who—who after all is only the wife of your friend."

They were sitting on a bench under a red-flowering poinsettia 25 whose huge scarlet petal-leaves spread out like sharp plumes.

"The wife of my friend!" he said. "What could you be better?"

"Of course," she said, more than equivocal.

He was leaning his arms on his knees, and looking out to the lake, abstract, and remote. There was a certain worn look on his face, and 30 the vulnerability which always caught at Kate's heart. She realised again the isolation and the deadly strain his effort towards a new way of life put upon him. Yet he had to do it.

This again gave her a feeling of helplessness, a woman's utter helplessness with a man who goes out to the beyond. She had to stifle 35 her resentment, and her dislike of his "abstract" efforts.

"Do you feel awfully sure of yourself?" she said.

"Sure of myself?" he re-echoed. "No! Any day I may die and disappear from the face of the earth. I not only know it, I *feel* it. So why should I be sure of *myself*?" 40

"Why should you die?" she said.

"Why should anybody ever die?—even Carlota!"

"Ah!—her hour had come!"

"Can you set one's hour as one sets an alarm clock?"

Kate paused.

"And if you're not sure of yourself, what are you sure of?" she challenged.

He looked at her with dark eyes which she could not understand.

"I am sure—sure—" his voice tailed off into vagueness, his face seemed to go grey and peaked, as a dead man's, only his eyes watched her blackly, like a ghost's. Again she was confronted with the suffering ghost of the man. And she was a woman, powerless before this suffering ghost which was still in the flesh.

"You don't think you are wrong, do you?" she asked, in cold distress.

"No! I am not wrong. Only maybe I can't hold out," he said.

"And then what?" she said, coldly.

"I shall go my way, alone." There seemed to be nothing left of him but the black, ghostly eyes that gazed on her. He began to speak Spanish.

"It hurts me in my soul, as if I were dying," he said.

"But why?" she cried. "You are not ill?"

"I feel as if my soul were coming undone."

"Then don't let it," she cried, in fear and repulsion.

But he only gazed with those fixed, blank eyes. A sudden deep stillness came over her: a sense of power in herself.

"You should forget for a time," she said gently, compassionately laying her hand on his. What was the good of trying to understand him or wrestle with him? She was a woman. He was a man, and—and—and therefore not quite real. Not true to life.

He roused himself suddenly from her touch, as if he had come awake, and he looked at her with keen, proud eyes. Her motherly touch had roused him like a sting.

"Yes!" he said. "It is true!"

"Of course it is!" she replied. "If you want to be so—so abstract and Quetzalcoatlian, then bury your head sometimes, like an ostrich in the sand, and forget."

"So!" he said, smiling. "You are angry again!"

"It's not so simple," she said. "There is a conflict in me. And you won't let me go away for a time."

"We can't even prevent you," he said.

"Yes, but you are against my going—you don't let me go in peace."

"Why must you go?" he said.

"I must," she said. "I must go back to my children, and my mother."

"It is a necessity in you?" he said.

"Yes!"

The moment she had admitted the necessity, she realised it was a certain duplicity in herself. It was as if she had two selves: one, a new one, which belonged to Cipriano and to Ramón, and which was her sensitive, desirous self: the other hard and finished, accomplished, belonging to her mother, her children, England, her whole past. This old accomplished self was curiously invulnerable and insentient, curiously hard and "free." In it, she was an individual and her own mistress. The other self was vulnerable, and organically connected with Cipriano, even with Ramón and Teresa, and so was not "free" at all.

She was aware of a duality in herself, and she suffered from it. She could not definitely commit herself, either to the old way of life, or to the new. She reacted from both. The old was a prison, and she loathed it. But in the new way she was not her own mistress at all, and her egoistic will recoiled.

"That's just it!" she said. "It *is* a necessity in me, and you want to prevent me."

"No! No!" said Ramón. "I hope not."

"Yes! You put a weight on me, and paralyse me, to prevent me from going," she said.

"We must not do that," he said. "We must leave you, and not come near you for a time, if you feel it is so."

"Why? Why can't you be friendly? Why can't you be *with* me in my going? Why can't you *want* me to go, since I must go?"

He looked at her with dispassionate eyes.

"I can't do that," he said. "I don't believe in your going. It is a turning back: there is something renegade in it.—But we are all complicated. And if you *feel* you must go back for a time, go! It isn't terribly important. You have chosen, really. I am not afraid for you."

It was a great relief to her to hear this: because she was terribly afraid for herself. She could never be sure, never be *whole* in her connection with Cipriano and Ramón. Yet she said, mocking slightly:

"Why *should* you be afraid for me?"

"Aren't you sometimes afraid for yourself?" he asked.

"Never!" she said. "I'm absolutely sure about myself."

5 They had been sitting in the garden of the Villa Aragón, under the poinsettia tree with the huge scarlet petal-leaves, like soft red quill feathers. The morning was becoming hot. The lake had gone still, with the fallen wind. Everything was still. Save the long scarlet of the poinsettia.

Christmas was coming! The poinsettia reminded Kate of it.

10 Christmas! Holly-berries! England! Presents! Food!—If she hurried, she could be in England for Christmas. It felt so safe, so familiar, so normal, the thought of Christmas at home, in England, with her mother. And all the exciting things she could tell to the people at home! And all the exciting gossip she could hear! In the

15 distance, it looked very attractive.—She still had a qualm as to what the actual return would be like.

"One can have too much of a good thing," she said to Ramón.

"What good thing in particular?" he asked her.

"Oh—Quetzalcoatl and all that!" she said. "One can have too

20 much of it."

"It may be," he said, rising and going quietly away; so quietly, he was gone before she knew. And when she realised he had gone like that, she flushed with anger. But she sat on under the poinsettia tree, in the hot, still November sun, looking with anger at the hedge

25 of jasmine, with its pure white flowers, and its sere, withered flowers, and its pinkish buds among the dark leaves. Where had she heard something about jasmine? "And the jasmine flowers between us!"

Oh! how tired she was of all that!

30 Teresa came down the garden slope.

"You are still sitting here?" she exclaimed.

"Where else should I be?" Kate answered.

"I don't know.—Ramón has gone to Sayula, to see the Jefe. He wouldn't wait for us, to come with us in the boat."

35 "I suppose he was in a hurry," said Kate.

"How fine these nochebuenas* are!" said Teresa looking at the brilliant spread of the red poinsettias.

"They are your Christmas flower, aren't they?" said Kate.

"Yes—the flowers of the Nochebuena—"

40 "How awful, Christmas with hibiscus and poinsettia! It makes me

long to see mistletoe among the oranges, in a fruiterer's shop in Hampstead."

"Why that?" laughed Teresa.

"Oh!" Kate sighed petulantly. "To get back to simple life. To see the buses rolling on the mud in Piccadilly, on Christmas Eve, and the wet pavements crowded with people under the brilliant shops."

"Is that life, to you?" asked Teresa.

"Yes! Without all this abstraction, and *will*. Life is good enough for me if I am allowed to live and be myself."

"It is time Cipriano should come home," said Teresa.

But this made Kate rise from her seat, with sudden impatience. She would not have this thing put over her! She would break free, and show them!

She went with Teresa to the village. The air seemed mysteriously alive, with a new Breath. But Kate felt out of it. The two women sat under a tree on the beach at Sayula, talking a little, and watching the full expanse of the dove-pale lake.

A black boat with a red-painted roof and a tall mast was moored to the low breakwater-wall, which rose about a yard high, from the shallow water. On the wall stood loose little groups of white-clad men, looking into the black belly of the ship. And perched immobile in silhouette against the lake, was a black-and-white cow, and a huge monolithic black-and-white bull. The whole silhouette frieze motionless, against the far water that was coloured brown like turtle doves.

It was near, yet seemed strange and remote. Two peons fixed a plank gangway up to the side of the boat. Then they began to shove the cow towards it. She pawed the new broad planks tentatively. Then, with that slow Mexican indifference, she lumbered unwillingly on to the gangway. They edged her slowly to the end, where she looked down into the boat. And at last, she dropped neatly into the hold.

Now the group of men broke into motion, for the huge and spangled bull. A tall old Mexican, in fawn, skin-tight trousers and little leather jacket, and a huge felt hat heavily embroidered with silver, gently took the ring in the bull's nose, gently lifted the wedge of the bull's head, so the great soft throat was uplifted. A peon behind put his head down, and with all his might began shoving the mighty, living flanks of the bull. The slim-legged, high-hatted old Mexican pulled evenly at the nose-ring. And with a calm and weighty poise, the bull stepped along the crest of the wall, delicately and impassively, to the plank gangway. There he stopped.

The peons began to re-group. The one behind, with his red sash tied so determinedly over his white hips, ceased to shove, the slim-legged Mexican let go the ring.

Then two peons passed a rope loosely round the haunches of the bull. The high-hatted farmer stepped on to the planks, and took the nose-ring again, very gently. He pulled softly. The bull lifted its head, but held back. It struck the planks with an unwilling foot. Then it stood, spangled with black on its whiteness, like a piece of the sky, immobile.

The farmer pulled once more at the ring. Two men were pulling the rope, pressing in the flanks of the immovable, passive, spangled monster. Two peons, at the back, with their heads down and their red-sashed, flexible loins thrust out behind, shoved with all their strength in the soft flanks of the mighty creature.

And all was utterly noiseless and changeless; against the fulness of the pale lake, this silent, monumental group of life.

Then the bull stepped slowly, imperturbably, yet against its will, on to the loose planks, and was edged slowly along, to the brink of the boat. There he waited.

He stood huge and silvery, dappled like the sky, with black snake-markings down his haunches, looming massive above the red roof of the *canoa*. How would he ever duck to that roof, and drop under, into the darkness of the ship?

He lowered his head, and looked into the hold. The men behind shoved his living flanks. He took no heed, but lowered his head and looked again. The men pushed with all their might, in the dense Mexican silence.

Slowly, carefully, the bull crouched himself, made himself small, and with a quick, massive little movement dropped his forefeet down into the body of the boat, leaving his huge hind-quarters heaved up behind. There was a shuffle and a little stagger down below, then the soft thud as his hind-feet leaped down. He had gone.

The planks were taken away. A peon ran to unfasten the mooring-rope from the stones of the shore. There was a strange thudding of soft feet within the belly of the boat. Men in the water were pushing the ship's black stern, to push her off. But she was heavy. Slowly, casually they pulled the stones from under her flat bottom, and flung them aside. Slowly she edged, swayed, moved a little, and was afloat.

The men climbed in. The two peons on the ship's rims were poling her out, pressing their poles and walking heavily till they reached the stern, then lifting their poles and running to the high prow. She slid slowly out, on to the lake.

Then quickly they hoisted the wide white sail. The sail thrust up her horn and curved in a whorl to the wind. The ship was going across the waters, with her massive, sky-spangled cargo of life invisible.

All so still and soft and remote.

"And will Ramón want you to sit beside him in the church as the bride of Quetzalcoatl—with some strange name?" Kate asked of Teresa.

"I don't know," said Teresa. "Later, he says, when the time comes for them to have a goddess."

"And will you mind?"

"For myself, I am afraid of it. But I understand why Ramón wants it. He says it is accepting the greater responsibility of one's existence. And I think that is true. If there is God in me, and God as woman, then I must accept this part of myself also, and put on the green dress, and be for the time the God-woman, since it is true of me also. I think it is true. Ramón says we must make it manifest. When I think of my brothers, I know we must. So I shall think of the God that beats invisible, like the heart of all the world. So when I have to wear the green dress, and sit before all the people in the church, I shall look away to the heart of all the world, and try to be my sacred self, because it is necessary, and the right thing to do. It is right. I would not do it if I thought it was not right."

"But I thought the green dress was for the bride of Huitzilopochtli!" said Kate.

"Ah yes!" Teresa caught herself up. "Mine is the black dress with the white edges, and the red clouds."

"Would you rather have the green?" Kate asked. "Have it if you would. I am going away."

Teresa glanced up at her quickly.

"The green is for the wife of Huitzilopochtli," she said, as if numbed.

"I can't see that it matters," said Kate.

Teresa looked at her with quick, dark eyes.

"Different men must have different wives," she said. "Cipriano would never want a wife like me."

"And different women must have different husbands," said

Kate. "Ramón would always be too abstract and overbearing for me."

Teresa flushed slowly, looking down at the ground.

"Ramón needs far too much submission from a woman, to please me," Kate added. "He takes too much upon himself."

Teresa looked up quickly, and raised her head proudly, showing her brownish throat like a rearing, crested snake.

"How do you know that Ramón needs submission from a woman?" she said. "How do you know? He has not asked any submission from you.—And you are wrong. He does not ask submission from me. He wants me to give myself gently to him. And then he gives himself back to me far more gently than I give myself to him. Because a man like that is more gentle than a woman. He is not like Cipriano. Cipriano is a soldier. But Ramón is gentle. You are mistaken in what you say."

Kate laughed a little.

"And you are a soldier among women, fighting all the time," Teresa continued. "I am not such. But some women must be soldiers in their spirit, and they need soldier husbands. That is why you are Malintzi, and your dress is green. You would always fight. You would fight with yourself, if you were alone in the world."

It was very still by the lake. They were waiting for Ramón.

A man was stripping palm-stalks, squatting in silence under a tree, in his white clothes, his black head bent forward. Then he went to wet his long strips in the lake, returning with them dangling.

Then he sat down again, and deftly, silently, with the dark, childlike absorption of the people, took up his work. He was mending a chair-bottom. When Kate watched him, he glanced up with a flash of black eyes, saluting her. And she felt a strange power surge in her limbs, from the flash of living recognition and deference in his eyes. As if his deference were a sort of flame of life, rich in him when he saw her.

A roan horse speckled with white was racing prancing along the shore, neighing frantically. His mane flowed in the wind, his feet struck the pebbles as he ran, and again he opened his long nose and neighed anxiously. Away up the shore he ran. What had he lost?

A peon had driven a high-wheeled wagon, drawn by four mules, deep into the lake, till the water was above the high axles of the wheels, almost touching the bed of the cart. It looked like a dark square boat drawn by four soft, dark sea-horses which slowly waved their long dark ears like leaves, while the peon, in white with his big hat proudly balanced, stood erect. The mules deep in the water stepped gently, curving to the shore.

It was winter, but like spring by the lake. White-and-yellow calves, new and silky, were skipping, butting up their rear ends, lifting their tails, trotting side by side down to the water, to sniff at it suspiciously.

In the shadow of a great tree a mother-ass was tethered, and her foal lay in the shadow, a little thing black as ink, curled up, with fluffy head erect and great black ears spreading up, like some jet-black hare full of witch-craft.

"How many days?" called Kate to the peon, who had come out of the straw hut.

He gave her the flash of his dark eyes, in a sort of joy of deference. And she felt her breast surge with living pride.

"Last night, *Patrona*!" he smiled in answer.

"So new! So new! He doesn't get up. Can't he?"

The peon went round, put his arm under the foal, and lifted it to its feet. There it straddled on high, in amaze, upon its black legs like bent hair-pins.

"How nice it is!" cried Kate in delight, and the peon laughed at her with a soft, grateful flame, touched with reverence.

The ink-black ass-foal did not understand standing up. It rocked on its four loose legs, and wondered. Then it hobbled a few steps, to smell at some green, growing maize. It smelled and smelled and smelled, as if all the dark æons were stirring awake in its nostrils.

Then it turned, and looked with its bushy-velvet face straight at Kate, and put out a pink tongue at her. She laughed aloud. It stood wondering, dazed. Then it put out its tongue again. She laughed at it. It gave an awkward little skip, which surprised its own self very much. Then it ventured forward again, and all unexpectedly even to itself, exploded into another little skip.

"Already it dances!" cried Kate. "And it came into the world only last night."

"Yes, already it dances!" re-iterated the peon.

After be-thinking itself for a time, the ass-foal walked uncertainly towards the mother. She was a well-liking grey-and-brown she-ass, rather glossy and self-assured. The ass-foal straight found the udder, and was drinking.

Glancing up, Kate met again the peon's eyes, with their black, full flame of life heavy with knowledge and with a curious re-assurance.

The black foal, the mother, the drinking, the new life, the mystery of the shadowy battle-field of creation: and the adoration of the full-breasted, glorious woman beyond him: all this seemed in the primitive black eyes of the man.

5   "*Adios!*" said Kate to him, lingeringly.

"*Adios Patrona!*" he replied, suddenly lifting his hand high, in the Quetzalcoatl salute.

She walked across the beach to the jetty, feeling the life surging vivid and resistant within her. "It is sex," she said to herself. "How
10   wonderful sex can be, when men keep it powerful and sacred, and it fills the world! Like sunshine through and through one!—But I'm not going to submit, even there. Why should one give in, to anything!"

Ramón was coming down towards the boat, the blue symbol of
15   Quetzalcoatl in his hat. And at that moment the drums began to sound for mid-day, and there came the mid-day call, clear and distinct, from the tower. All the men on the shore stood erect, and shot up their right hands to the sky. The women spread both palms to the light. Everything was motionless, save the moving animals.

20   Then Ramón went on to the boat, the men saluting him with the Quetzalcoatl salute as he came near.

"It is wonderful, really," said Kate, as they rowed over the water, "how—how splendid one can feel in this country! As if one were still genuinely of the nobility."

25   "Aren't you?" he said.

"Yes, I am. But everywhere else it is denied. Only here one feels the full force of one's nobility. The natives still worship it."

"At moments," said Ramón. "Later, they will murder you and violate you, for having worshipped you."

30   "Is it inevitable?" she said flippantly.

"I think so," he replied. "If you lived here alone in Sayula, and queened it for a time, you would get yourself murdered—or worse—by the people who had worshipped you."

"I don't think so," she said.

35   "I know," he replied.

"Why?" she said, obstinate.

"Unless one gets one's nobility from the gods and turns to the middle of the sky for one's power, one will be murdered at last."

"I do get my nobility that way," she said.

40   But she did not quite believe it. And she made up her mind still more definitely, to go away.

She wrote to Mexico City, and engaged a berth from Veracruz to
Southampton: she would sail on the last day of November.* Cipriano
came home on the seventeenth, and she told him what she had done.
He looked at her with his head a little on one side, with a queer,
boyish judiciousness, but she could not tell at all what he felt.   5

"You are going already?" he said in Spanish.

And then she knew, at last, that he was offended. When he was
offended he never spoke English at all, but spoke Spanish just as if
he were addressing another Mexican.

"Yes," she said. "On the 30th."   10

"And when do you come back?" he asked.

"*Quién sabe!*—Who knows!" she retorted.

He let his black eyes rest on her face for some minutes, watching
her, unchanging and incomprehensible. He was thinking, superficially, that if he liked, he could use the law and have her prevented   15
from leaving the country—or even from leaving Sayula—since she
was legally married to him. There was the old fixity of Indian anger,
glinting fixed and relentless in the depths of his eyes. And then the
almost invisible change in his face, as the hidden emotion sank down
and the stoic indifference, the emotionlessness of centuries, and the   20
stoic kind of tolerance came over him. She could almost feel the
waves of successive shadow and coldness go through his blood, his
mind hardly aware at all. And again a fear of losing his contact
melted her heart. It was somehow, to her, beautiful, to feel shadows,
and cold gleams, and a hardness like stone, then the strange heavy   25
inertia of the tropical mid-day, the stupor of the sun, moving upon
him while he stood motionless, watching her. In the end it was that
weird, sultry, tropical stupor of the hot hours, a heat-swoon of sheer
indifference.

"*Como quieres tú!*" he said. "As you wish."   30

And she knew he had already released her, in the dark, sultry
stupor of his blood. He would make no further effort after her. This
also was the doom of his race.

He took a boat and went down to Jamiltepec, to Ramón: as she
knew he would.   35

She was alone, as usual. It occurred to her, that she herself willed
this aloneness. She could not relax and be with these people. She
could not relax and be with anybody. She always had to recoil upon
her own individuality, as a cat does.

Sex, sexual correspondence, did it matter so very much to her? It   40
might have mattered more, if she had not had it. But she had had

it—and very finally and consummately, with Cipriano. So she knew all about it. It was as if she had conquered another territory, another field of life. The conqueress! And now she would retire to the lair of her own individuality, with the prey.

5   Suddenly, she saw herself as men often saw her: the great cat, with its spasms of voluptuousness and its life-long lustful enjoyment of its own isolated individuality. Voluptuously to enjoy a contact. Then with a lustful feline gratification, to break the contact, and roam alone in a sense of power. Each time, to seize a sort of power, purring
10   upon her own isolated individuality.

She knew so many women like that. They played with love and intimacy as a cat with a mouse. In the end, they quickly ate up the love-mouse, then trotted off with a full belly and a voluptuous sense of power.

15   Only sometimes, the love-mouse refused to be digested, and there was life-long dyspepsia. Or, like Cipriano, turned into a sort of serpent, that reared and looked at her with glittering eyes, then slid away into the void, leaving her blank, the sense of power gone out of her.

20   Another thing, she had observed, with a touch of horror. One after the other, her women "friends," the powerful love-women at the age of forty, forty-five, fifty, they lost all their charm and allure, and turned into real grimalkins, greyish, avid, and horrifying, prowling around looking for prey that became scarcer and scarcer. As human
25   beings, they went to pieces. And they remained these grey-ribbed grimalkins, dressed in elegant clothes, the grimalkin howl even passing into their smart chatter.

Kate was a wise woman, wise enough to take a lesson.

It is all very well for a woman to cultivate her ego, her individual-
30   ity. It is all very well for her to despise love, or to love love as a cat loves a mouse, that it plays with as long as possible, before devouring it to vivify her own individuality and voluptuously fill the belly of her own ego. "Woman has suffered far more from the suppression of her ego than from sex suppression," says a woman writer, and it may well
35   be true. But look, only look at the modern women of fifty and fifty-five, those who have cultivated their ego to the top of their bent! Usually, they are grimalkins to fill one with pity or with repulsion.

Kate knew all this. And as she sat alone in her villa, she remembered it again. She had had her fling, even here in Mexico.
40   And these men would let her go again. She was no prisoner. She could carry off any spoil she had captured.

And then what! To sit in a London drawing-room, and add another to all the grimalkins? To let the peculiar grimalkin-grimace come on her face, the most weird grimalkin-twang come into her voice? Horror! Of all the horrors, perhaps the grimalkin women, her contemporaries, were the most repellant to her. Even the horrid old tom-cat men of the civilised roof gutters, did not fill her with such sickly dread.

"No!" she said to herself. "My ego and my individuality are not worth *that* ghastly price. I'd better abandon some of my ego, and sink some of my individuality, rather than go like that."

After all, when Cipriano touched her caressively, all her body flowered. That was the greater sex, that could fill all the world with lustre, and which she dared not think about, its power was so much greater than her own will. But on the other hand when she spread the wings of her own ego, and sent forth her own spirit, the world could look very wonderful to her, when she was alone. But after a while, the wonder faded, and a sort of jealous emptiness set in.

"I must have both," she said to herself. "I must not recoil against Cipriano and Ramón, they make my blood blossom in my body. I say they are limited. But then one must be limited. If one tries to be unlimited, one becomes horrible. Without Cipriano to touch me and limit me and submerge my will, I shall become a horrible, elderly female. I ought to *want* to be limited. I ought to be *glad* if a man will limit me with a strong will and a warm touch. Because what I call my greatness, and the vastness of the Lord behind me, lets me fall through a hollow floor of nothingness, once there is no man's hand there, to hold me warm and limited. Ah yes! Rather than become elderly and a bit grisly, I will make my submission; as far as I need, and no further."

She called a man-servant, and set off down the lake in a row-boat. It was a very lovely November morning, the world had not yet gone dry again. In the sharp folds of the steep mountain slopes to the north-east, the shadows were pure corn-flower blue. Below was the lingering delicacy of green, already drying. The lake was full still, but subsided, and the water-hyacinth had drifted away. Birds flew low in the stillness. It was very full and still, in the strong, hot light. Some maize-fields showed sere stubble, but the palo-blanco flowers were out, and the mesquite bushes were frail green, and there were wafts of perfume from the little yellow flower-balls, like cassia.

"Why should I go away!" said Kate. "Why should I see the buses on the mud of Piccadilly, on Christmas Eve, and the crowds of

people on the wet pavements, under the big shops like great caves of
light? I may as well stay here, where my soul is less dreary. I shall
have to tell Ramón I am sorry for the things I said. I won't carp at
them. After all, there is another kind of vastness here, with the sound
5 of drums, and the cry of Quetzalcoatl."

Already she could see the yellow and reddish, tower-like upper
storey of Jamiltepec, and the rich, deep fall of magenta bougainvillea,
from the high wall, with the pale spraying of plumbago flowers, and
many loose creamy-coloured roses.

10 "*Están tocando!*"* said her boatman quietly, looking up at her with
dark, pregnant eyes.

He had heard already the sound of the light drum, at Jamiltepec.
The boat rowed softly: and there came a sound of a man's voice
singing in the morning.

15 Her boatman lifted an oar, as a signal to the house. And as the boat
rounded the curve into the basin, a man-servant in white clothes
came running down to the little jetty. In the changeless sunshine was
a scent, perhaps of datura and of roses, and an eternal Mexican
silence, which the noise of the drum, and the voice of singing, did not
20 disturb.

"Is Don Cipriano here?" asked Kate.

"*Está!*" murmured the man, with a slight motion towards
Ramón's balcony, whence the singing came. "Shall I say you have
come?"

25 He did not lift his voice above the murmur.

"No!" said Kate. "I shall sit here in the garden a while, before I
come up."

"Then I will leave open the door," said the man, "and you can
come up when you will."

30 Kate sat on a seat under a big tree. A creeping plant, with great
snake-like cords and big sulphur-and-brown trumpet flowers hung
above. She listened to the singing. It was Ramón, teaching one of the
singers.

Ramón had not a very good voice. He sang quietly, as if to the
35 inner air, with very beautiful, simple expression. But Kate could not
catch the words.

"*Ya?*" said Ramón, when he had finished.

"*Ya, Patrón!*"* said the man, the singer.

And he began, in his strong, pure voice that caught at the very
40 bowels, to sing another of the Hymns.

My way is not thy way, and thine is not mine.
But come, before we part
Let us separately go to the Morning Star,
And meet there.

I do not point you to my road, nor yet   5
Call: Oh come!
But the Star is the same for both of us,
Winsome.

The good ghost of me goes down the distance
To the Holy Ghost.   10
Oh you, in the tent of the cloven flame*
Meet me, you I like most.

Each man his own way forever, but towards
The hoverer between;
Who opens his flame like a tent-flap,   15
As we slip in unseen.

A man cannot tread like a woman,
Nor a woman step out like a man.
The ghost of each through the leaves of shadow
Moves as it can.   20

But the Morning Star and the Evening Star
Pitch tents of flame
Where we foregather like gypsies, none knowing
How the other came.

I ask for nothing except to slip   25
In the tent of the Holy Ghost
And be there in the house of the cloven flame,
Guest of the Host.

Be with me there, my woman
Be bodily there.   30
Then let the flame wrap round us
Like a snare.

Be there along with me, oh men!
Reach across the hearth,
And laugh with me while the woman rests   35
For all we are worth.

The man had sung this hymn over several times, halting and forgetting, his pure, burning voice faltering out; then the low, rather husky voice of Ramón, with a subtler intensity, coming in, as if heard from the centre of a shell; then again the sudden ripping sound of the
5   true singer's tenor, going like a flame through the blood.

Her mozo, a man-servant, had followed her into the garden, and sat at a distance on his heels, under a tree, with his back to the trunk, like a crouching shadow clothed in white. His toes spread dark and hard, in his open huaraches, and the black braid of his hat-string
10 hung against his dark cheek. For the rest he was pure white, the white cotton tight on his thighs.

When the singing had finished above, and the drum was silent, and even the voices speaking in low tones, were silent, her mozo looked up at Kate, with his black hat-string dangling at his chin, his
15 black eyes shining, and a timid sort of smile on his face.

"*Está muy bien, Patrona?*" he said shyly. "It is good, isn't it, Mistress?"

"It is very good," she replied, with the infallible echo. But there were conflicting feelings in her breast, and the man knew it.

20 He looked so young, when he smiled that gay, shy, excited little smile. Something of the eternal child in him. But a child that could harden in an instant into a savage man, revengeful and brutal. And a man always fully sex-alive, for the moment innocent in the fulness of sex, not in the absence. And Kate thought to herself, as she had
25 thought before, that there were more ways than one of "becoming again as a little child."

But the man had a sharp, watchful look in the corner of his eye: to see if she were feeling some covert hostility. He wanted her to acquiesce in the hymn, in the drum, in the whole mood. Like a child
30 he wanted her to acquiesce. But if she were going to be hostile, he would be quick to be first in the hostility. Her hostile judgment would make a pure enemy of him.

Ah, all men were alike!

At that moment the man stood up, with soft suddenness, and she
35 heard Cipriano's voice from the balcony above:

"What is it, Lupe?"

"*Está la Patrona,*" answered the servant.

Kate rose to her feet and looked up. She saw the head and the naked shoulders of Cipriano above the parapet of the balcony.
40 "I will come up," she said.

And slowly she went through the great iron gates into the passage-way. Lupe, following, bolted the doors behind her.

On the terrace above she found Ramón and Cipriano both with their upper bodies naked, waiting for her in silence. She was embarrassed.

"I wanted to hear the new hymn," she said.

"And how does it seem to you?" said Ramón, in Spanish.

"I like it," she said.

"Let us sit down," said Ramón, still in Spanish. He and she sat in the cane rocking-chairs: Cipriano stood by the wall of the terrace.

She had come to make a sort of submission: to say she didn't want to go away. But finding them both in the thick of their Quetzalcoatl mood, with their manly breasts uncovered, she was not very eager to begin. They made her feel like an intruder. She did not pause to realise that she *was* one.

"We don't meet in your Morning Star, apparently, do we!" she said, mocking, but with a slight quaver.

A deeper silence seemed suddenly to hold the two men.

"And I suppose a woman is really *de trop*, even there, when two men are together."

But she faltered a bit in the saying. Cipriano, she knew, was baffled and stung when she taunted him.

Ramón answered her, with the gentleness that could come straight out of his heart: but still in Spanish:

"Why, Cousin,* what is it?"

Her lip quivered, as she suddenly said:

"I don't really want to go away from you."

Ramón looked swiftly at Cipriano, then said:

"I know you don't."

But the gentle protective tone of his voice only made Kate rebel again. She brimmed over with sudden tears, crying:

"You don't really want me."

"Yes, I want you!—*Verdad! Verdad!*"* exclaimed Cipriano, in his low, secret, almost muttering voice.

And even amid her tears, Kate was thinking to herself: *What a fraud I am! I know all the time it is I who don't altogether want them. I want myself to myself. But I can fool them so that they shan't find out.*

For she heard the hot, phallic passion in Cipriano's voice.

Then came the voice of Ramón, like a chill:

"It is you who don't want," he said, in English this time. "You needn't commit yourself to *us*. Listen to your own best desire."

"And if it tells me to go away?" she flashed, defiant through the end of her tears.

"Then go! Oh certainly go!"

5   Suddenly her tears came afresh.

"I knew you didn't really want me," she wept.

Then Cipriano's voice said, with a hot, furtive softness of persuasion:

"You are not his! He would not tell you!"

10   "That is very true," said Ramón. "Don't listen to me!"

He spoke in Spanish. And Kate glanced up sharply through her tears, to see him going quietly, but swiftly, away.

She wiped her face, suddenly calm. Then she looked with wet eyes at Cipriano. He was standing erect and alert, like a little fighting

15   male, and his eyes glowed back and uncannily as he met her wet, limpid glance.

Yes, she was a bit afraid of him too, with his inhuman black eyes.

"You don't want me to go, do you?" she pleaded.

A slow, almost foolish smile came over his face, and his body was

20   slightly convulsed. Then came his soft-tongued Indian speech, as if all his mouth were soft, saying in Spanish, but with the "r" sound almost lost:

"*Yo! Yo!*"—his eyebrows lifted with queer mock surprise, and a little convulsion went through his body again. "*Te quiero mucho!*[*]

25   *Mucho te quiero! Mucho! Mucho!* I like you very much! Very much!"

It sounded so soft, so soft-tongued, of the soft, wet, hot blood, that she shivered a little.

"You won't let me go!" she said to him.

EXPLANATORY NOTES

EXPLANATORY NOTES

7:2 **Beginnings of a Bull-fight.** DHL, Frieda, Witter Bynner and Willard ('Spud') Johnson attended a bull-fight on Easter Sunday, 1 April 1923, which served as the model for this one. Owen Rhys is based on Bynner and Villiers on Johnson. See also Bynner 19–60; *D. H. Lawrence: Letters to Thomas and Adele Seltzer*, ed. Gerald M. Lacy (Santa Barbara, 1976), pp. 87–8; Calderón de la Barca 77–9; Clark 25–32.

7:11 **Kate.** Something of Frieda is evident in Kate Leslie's character, though many of her feelings were DHL's. His first attempt at an 'American novel' was based on the experiences of Mabel Dodge Luhan: see 'The Wilful Woman', in *St. Mawr and Other Stories*, ed. Brian Finney (Cambridge, 1983), pp. 197–203. DHL learned of Mabel Sterne's marriage to Tony Luhan, her Indian lover, a week before he began 'Q'. See *Letters*, iv. 439, 442.

7:25 **Toreo ... Chapultepec.** The *Toreo* was the main bull-ring of Mexico City in DHL's day. He wrote '*Torero*', which means 'bull-fighter' ... The Bosque de Chapultepec is a large park, one of the chief features of Mexico City. The name is of Nahuatl origin – Hill of the Grasshopper.

11:2 **the President would attend.** The President of Mexico from 1920 to 1924 was Álvaro Obregón (1880–1928). Bynner (p. 48) reports that he was expected at the bull-fight on Easter Sunday but failed to appear.

11:6 **the Authorities' section.** The *autoridades* at a bull-fight, the judges of the event, have special seating, though political dignitaries may sometimes sit in the same section.

11:19 **Música ... mal tono.** 'Music already paid for is not well played'. An expression in Mexico and the American Southwest warning against removing the incentive before the work is done. The more usual form is *música pagada hace mal son*: 'music already paid for sounds flat'. The irony in the crowd's demand depends on the dual meaning of *música*: 'band' as well as 'music'.

12:10 **a Polish bolshevist fellow** Bynner (p. 54) says that this was 'a middle-aged Polish professor of psychology ... from some American university'.

12:14 **Muy bien ...muy bien!"** 'Very well, sir, very well!'

15:16 **one of the horsemen with lances** The first horsemen to enter the ring (14:10–11) are customarily the *alguaciles* (constables), who ask permission of the *autoridades* for the event to begin. DHL does not clearly distinguish between the ceremonial riders and those with lances in the present passage, who are *picadores*. These are one of the three sorts of *toreros*, the other two being *banderilleros* and *matadores*. The function of the *picador*, and of the *banderillero* by different means, is

447

to weaken with his lance the powerful shoulder muscles of the bull, preparing him for the kill by the *matador*, the aristocrat of *toreros*. DHL's term *toreador*, which he applies only to *matadores*, is an old-fashioned word for *torero*. DHL reinforced his repugnance for bull-fighting by reading. Terry gives a brief account (pp. xcvii–cxii), and according to Bynner (p. 55), DHL read further than this.

15:25 **Don Quixote ... four Spanish horsemen of the Apocalypse!** Don Quixote names his mount by enlarging the word *rocín*, 'nag', to Rocinante, thus dubbing him the greatest nag in the world ... *The Four Horsemen of the Apocalypse (Los cuatro jinetes del Apocalypsis)* is by the Spanish novelist Vicente Blasco Ibáñez (1867–1928). An English translation of this First World War novel (New York, 1918) was for a time at the top of the American best-seller list. See also Revelation vi. 1–8.

17:13 **the great Mithraic beast.** The Bull was to Mithraism what the Lamb is to Christianity. Cf. *Apocalypse and the Writings on Revelation*, ed. Mara Kalnins (Cambridge, 1980), p. 99. The Persian god Mithras was mediator between mankind and the unknowable god of light, who created the Bull. Mithras grasped the horns of the Bull, only to be carried far through the cosmos before subduing the creature and shutting him in a cave. He soon escaped, however, with Mithras in pursuit. On overtaking the Bull, Mithras was ordered by the supreme deity to sacrifice him. From the blood of the Bull sprang up all the life on earth. Some modern scholars argue that the bull-fight is the present-day equivalent of such ancient sacrificial rites. See also note on 249:3.

19:26 **Orpheus looking back into hell,** Orpheus lost Eurydice by looking back to see if she was following him out of Hades.

21:6 *A Ver que Sale.* 'Let's see what happens' (literally, 'what comes out'). The *pulquerías* of Mexico City often had fanciful names. See also 48:3, Terry lxxxii–lxxxv and Glossary.

21:20 *Con permiso!* 'With (your) permission!', i.e. 'Excuse me!'

21:25 **"General Viedma! Don Cipriano!"** See note on 30:4.

22:1 **a yellow taxi.** Like those of the Yellow Cab Company in the USA, these cabs were operated by licensed drivers. The most common cars for hire in Mexico City were the jitneys, or dilapidated Fords, sometimes operated by questionable characters; see 8:1 and 47:39ff.

22:28 **Hotel San Remo.** This hotel is modelled on the Monte Carlo, Avenida Uruguay, where the Lawrences stayed during their first visit to Mexico City. Their arrival, like Kate's, was mentioned in a newspaper (see Clark 25–6). They also at first tried more luxurious quarters, staying for two days at the Hotel Regis, which Terry (p. 235) lists as one of the 'largest and most modern' in the city. He does not mention the Monte Carlo.

22:33 **my cousin and Mr Thompson?"** No Mr Thompson appears in either version of the novel. As he is associated with Owen Rhys, the name may at one time have been intended for Bud Villiers.

22:36   **Señor Ramón Carrasco."** See note on 30:4.

24:2   **Sanborn's,** This well-known eating place is described in Terry (p. 326) as 'at once a rendezvous for visiting travellers and a sort of social centre for the best American and Mexican elements in the capital'. It is located in the House of Tiles on Avenida Madero.

25:2   **Tea-party in Tlacolula.** In this chapter and the two following, DHL conflates details of his first three visits to Mexico City: March–April 1923, November 1923 and October–November 1924.

26:39   **GREAT ...** *seven* **BULLS—"** Accounts in *Excelsior*, 2 April 1923, disagree as to how good this bull-fight was. A Mexican commentator called it a 'success'. According to an article signed 'Juanito' on the English page, it was 'unexciting'. But each kill is reported in detail, with emphasis on how 'horseflesh suffered' in the ring. The number of bulls killed may be wrong: ordinarily, six bulls are sent into the arena in a bull-fight.

27:12   **chief toreador ... a fat cigar.** Two Spanish *toreros* participated in this bull-fight: Manuel Mejías and José García. The other *matador* was a Mexican, Juan Silveti, whom Bynner (p. 54) identifies as the one described here; he was never seen without 'a large cigar in his mouth' (Barnaby Conrad, *Encyclopedia of Bullfighting*, Boston, 1961).

28:23   **Argus.** In Greek mythology, Argus was a giant with a hundred eyes, some of them always awake.

29:40   **Mrs Norris ... village of Tlacolula.** The original for Mrs Norris was the anthropologist Zelia Maria Magdalena Nuttall (1858–1933). American by birth, she was largely educated in Europe and spent much of her life abroad. She made lasting contributions to the study of the Aztec codices, one of which bears her name. One of DHL's sources for Mexican indigenous material was her theoretical work *The Fundamental Principles of Old and New World Civilizations*. See *Letters*, iv. 421; letters to Zelia Nuttall, 12 April 1925; to Willard Johnson, ?25 and 29 October 1924 ... Tlacolula is the actual Coyoacán, a suburb on the s. side of Mexico City. DHL often borrows a place-name from another part of Mexico to fictionalise a locality; Tlacolula is a district near Oaxaca.

30:4   **Don Ramón Carrasco and General Viedma.** Ramón may owe something to several Mexicans DHL had met or heard of, such as José Vasconcelos (1881–1959), Mexico's first Minister of Education. His autobiography, *A Mexican Ulysses* (Indiana, 1963), tells against the probability, along with such writings of his as 'Quetzalcoatl' (*Atenea*, no. 23, Universidad de Concepción, Chile, 1929, pp. 450–3). His ideas on an 'Indian revival' were very different from DHL's. See also note on 52:10. The careers of other Mexican leaders suggest points of contact with Ramón: for instance, Manuel Gamio (1883–1960); see note on 66:20 and Ross Parmenter, *Lawrence in Oaxaca: A Quest for the Novelist in Mexico* (Salt Lake City, 1984), pp. 277–80, 292–3. The character and career of Emiliano Zapata (1873–1919) may be reflected in the character of Cipriano Viedma, and so may the life of Benito Juárez (see note on 65:15). See Clark 29–30. President Plutarco Elías Calles (1877–1945), dictator of Mexico from 1924 to 1934, and General Joaquín Amaro (1889–1952), his Secretary of War, must together have looked rather like

Ramón and Cipriano. Amaro was of pure Indian extraction and humble origins. His mastery of strategy and skill in reforming the army are like the talents attributed to Cipriano. A probable source for the fictional names is *Don Quixote*. Sansón Carrasco first appears in Part II, chapter III of that novel. Two brothers with the surname Pérez de Viedma enter the action for a time, the first appearing in Part II, chapter XXXVII.

30:22 **Pullman ... El Paso,** The Lawrences travelled by Pullman from Ciudad Juárez (across the Border from El Paso, Texas) to Mexico City, 21–3 March 1923. The Pullman sleeping-car was named after its inventor, George Mortimer Pullman (1831–97).

31:19 **the volcanoes** The two giant peaks at the eastern edge of the Valley of Mexico: Ixtaccihuatl (White Woman) and Popocatepetl (Smoking Mountain). See 49:15ff. For a description of Popocatepetl in a lighter vein, see DHL's revision of 'See Mexico After, by Luis Q.' (Luis Quintanilla), reprinted in *Phoenix* 111–16.

31:28 **Xochimilco or Tlalpam.** The first is a resort, well watered with many flowers, s. of Mexico City. For Tlalpam, see note on 60:19.

32:19 **house of the Conquistadores,** Zelia Nuttall's house in Coyoacán was called the Casa Alvarado, having belonged originally to Pedro de Alvarado (1495?–1541), a key figure in the Conquest.

33:40 **Garfield Spence ... letter of introduction."** DHL had in mind Lincoln Steffens (1866–1936), who had sent him a letter of introduction to the University Club of Mexico City. Steffens was a writer and lecturer active in the cause of radical political reform, with great hopes for the Mexican and the Russian Revolutions. See *Autobiography of Lincoln Steffens* (New York, 1931), and DHL's letter of thanks to him (*Letters*, iv. 410). For Frieda's report of the event behind this episode, see Lacy, *Seltzer*, p. 88. Cf. Bynner 22–3.

34:32 **new President ... into office.** The inauguration of Plutarco Elías Calles (Tomás Montes in the novel) took place not in the spring but on 1 December 1924. In a letter to A. D. Hawk, 29 October 1924, DHL wrote: 'Everybody on the qui vive, uncertain as to what will happen when Calles gets in'. See also note on 36:11.

36:2 **Street Sweepers Band ... the ship!"** According to the *New York Times*, when President-elect Calles arrived in New York, on 27 October 1924, he was welcomed by dignitaries, business leaders and the US Army Band. His ties with organized labour were strong in the USA as well as in his own country. See note on 43:2.

36:11 **The latest rumour ... the inauguration."** There were fears in late 1924 that General Ángel Flores (1883–1926), whom Calles had defeated in the Presidential election, would start a rebellion near the date of Calles' inauguration. The uprising never occurred, and according to Flores, was not planned. See letter to William Hawk, 14 November 1924.

36:22 **Laboristas** The *Laborista* party was the political arm of the Confederación Regional Obrera Mexicana. This labour union, formed in 1918, was larger and more powerful by 1924 than stated here. Its head, Luis Morones (1890–1964), became Secretary of Industry, Commerce and Labour in the Calles cabinet.

Bynner (p. 22) says that DHL met Morones. See letter to George Conway, 10 June 1925.

36:24 gringos ... gachupines. *Gringos* are white citizens of the USA; *gringuitos* are any other white foreigners; see 103:8–9, 148:40–149:2 and 224:8–34 ... Spaniards (*gachupines*) were deeply unpopular in Mexico during this revolutionary period, having been identified since colonial days with economic exploitation; the derogatory term has been in use since at least the 17th century.

36:31 *Buenos Días* ... *algo?* 'Good day! Sir! Come in! Do you want something?'

36:39 Twenty pesos ... ten minutes work. The Federación Obrera de Progreso, an organisation of dockworkers, regulated all such labour for a time, forcing very high wages.

37:15 National Museum [37:3] ... walked out. DHL based this on his own experience, according to Dorothy Brett (*Lawrence and Brett: A Friendship*, Philadelphia, 1933, pp. 164–5). In 'the patio where the stones are' (37:4), the Aztec Sunstone would have been on exhibition. See notes on 80:2 and 120:24.

37:18 Méjico In Peninsular Spanish, 'México' is spelled with a 'j'. DHL employs this spelling to stress the imported nature of much of the patriotism.

37:20 Mixcoac Fictitious name for Oaxaca, perhaps an echo of Mixcoatl, the name of an Aztec hero, meaning 'Cloud Serpent'.

37:30 *Señor Fulano* The Spanish equivalent of Mr John Doe (the average citizen).

37:40 the Virgin of Guadalupe An apparition of the Virgin Mary reportedly seen by the Indian Juan Diego on the hill of Tepeyac n.e. of Mexico City in 1531. See notes on 227:18 and 262:4.

38:2 A man up [37:19] ... it's Mexico." The story echoes DHL's views of politics in Oaxaca: 'I called on the Governor of the State, in the Palace ... Only it's all just crazy. Tomorrow he asked me to go out to the opening of a road into the hills. The road isn't begun yet. That's why *we* open it'; and 'Fancy even a Zapotec Indian, when he becomes governor, is only a fellow in a Sunday suit grinning and scheming' (letters to John Middleton Murry, 15 and 17 November 1924).

39:17 Ajusco!" Extinct volcano of 12,800 feet, located s. of Mexico City on the way to Cuernavaca; see note on 183:25.

40:40 Not *Viva* ... *Vamos! Viva!*" 'Not Long Live Christ the King! but Long Live Death the King! Let's go! Viva!' *Viva Cristo Rey* was the battle cry of the militant Catholic faction in Mexico, much opposed to the Revolution. See note on 247:28.

42:13 *Senōra mía,*" My dear lady'.

42:19 *Open Sesame!*" From *Arabian Nights* (15th century); a robber chieftain's command for a cave in the rocks to open, overheard by Ali Baba and later used by him to gain possession of the robbers' hoard.

42:30 **that article ... *Excelsior?***" Hope is modelled on Boyden Sparkes (1890–1954), a newspaperman reporting on agrarian reform in Mexico for the *New York Tribune*. Two articles of his were published in translation in *Excelsior*. In the first, 31 March 1923, Sparkes describes the devastation of the State of Morelos by agrarian troubles. In the second, 1 April 1923, he argues that the agrarian laws are unworkable, pointing out that the land from the haciendas was sometimes turned over to the peons with crops ready to harvest, which they had no resources to gather, and maintaining that through laziness, ignorance or lack of equipment the peons would let the land lie idle. According to Sparkes, agricultural production dropped by twenty-five per cent between 1921 and 1922.

43:2 **socialists and *sinvergüenzas*** ('shameless individuals'). Labour leaders from the USA, including Samuel Gompers, President of the American Federation of Labor and a supporter of Calles, attended his inauguration. Two days later (3 December 1924) a convention of the Pan-American Federation of Labor opened in Mexico City.

43:23 **San Juan de Letrán and Madero.** A principal intersection in the heart of Mexico City.

44:11 **Lexington Avenue:** A main thoroughfare in New York City.

45:2 **obsidian."** A black volcanic glass which can be chipped to a razor edge. It was of great cultic significance in Mexico. See Spence 27–33.

46:29 **the Zócalo,"** The great square at the centre of Mexico City, also called the Plaza de la Constitución, site of the Cathedral and the National Palace. It was also the heart of the Aztec city of Tenochtitlan, with the *teocalli* (temple) where the Cathedral now is.

48:12 **No presto ... troppo presto!"** (Italian) 'Not fast. Too fast. You're going too fast!' – except that 'no' should read 'non'.

49:35 **jaguar spotted with night.** The passage contains echoes of ancient Mesoamerican beliefs. In the *Codex Borgia* the god Tepeyollotl – Heart of the Mountain or of the Earth – is depicted as a jaguar. A related image in 'Corasmin and the Parrots', *Mornings in Mexico* (1927), concerns the destruction of the world at the end of one of the Aztec cycles by a monstrous jaguar. Cf. Bynner 42–3. See also note on 123:5.

50:2 **dragon of the Aztecs ... the Toltecs** Mesoamerican mythology taught that the earth had been fashioned from the body of a monster of chaos. See Spence 40, 113–14 and Appendix I below. The Aztecs, whose rise and fall occurred between 1325 and 1521, were the last inheritors of the religion of Anáhuac. They were preceded, with an interval of turbulence between, by the Toltecs (*c.* 750–1000 AD), a culture in some ways more highly developed than that of the Aztecs. Most scholars of DHL's time thought of Teotihuacán as the home of the Toltecs, not realizing that Tula, a little farther n. of Mexico City, had been their seat and that the Teotihuacanos had flourished before the Toltecs. See notes on 58:36 and 79:26. Cf. Bynner 24.

50:17 ***Muera!* Death [50:10] ... its own mystery.** The Mexican preoccupation with death has often been traced to indigenous sources and seen as a prime determinant of the national character. See Octavio Paz, *The Labyrinth of Solitude*, trans. Lysander Kemp (New York, 1961), especially the chapter 'The Day of the Dead'. See 106:17–19 and notes on 58:36, 109:7 and 261:39. The *Grito* (shout) at 50:8 alludes to Padre Hidalgo's shout of revolt against Spain in 1810. The Fiesta del Grito is still celebrated on 15 September, with a ceremonial shout from the President of Mexico and local leaders. See Paz, p. 47 and Frances Toor, *A Treasury of Mexican Folkways* (New York, 1947), pp. 234–5.

50:24　**a huge old church … white tiles,** The former church of San Agustín, which housed the National Library.

50:35　*consummatum est* 'It is finished'; Vulgate version of Christ's last words on the Cross, as recorded in John xix. 30.

51:10　**a young Mexican** Bynner thought this character, García, was a combination of the painter Miguel Covarrubias (1902–57) – whom DHL met in April 1923 – and a 'youthful professor' (p. 30). Luis Quintanilla (1900–80) may have contributed to the composite figure, and even, perhaps, Jean Charlot (see note on 53:35). DHL did not meet Quintanilla until late 1924, but García does not appear in 'Q'. See Nehls, ii. 368–70.

52:10　**The University [52:6] … my boys!** In 1921, Vasconcelos put Diego Rivera (1886–1957) and a group of young associates to work on a mural in the auditorium of the National Preparatory School (the 'University'). 'Ribera' (52:14), already well known as a painter of cubist tendencies, had lived and worked in Europe before coming home to contribute to social reform in the Revolution. His fame resulted from application of modernist techniques to native Mexican themes. By March–April 1923, when DHL toured the Preparatory School, several murals were in progress. For an incident concerning DHL and Vasconcelos, and its aftermath, see Bynner 26–31, Nehls, ii. 227–31 and Vasconcelos' three-part review of Bynner in *Novedades* (Mexico City), 28 December 1951–4 January 1952.

52:38　**épater le bourgeois.** 'To shock the middle-class person' (French).

53:1　**old Jesuit convent** Kate passes from the older part of the National Preparatory School to the former Colegio de San Ildefonso, founded by the Jesuits but later made an annexe to the School.

53:35　**by another man [53:3] … of the poor.** DHL uses two of his own visits to fashion Kate's. José Clemente Orozco (1883–1949) began his murals in the San Ildefonso courtyard in July 1923, but he did not take up subjects like those described here until later on, when he underwent a radical change of style. The mural that DHL refers to, 'Los Ricos' (The Rich), dates according to most sources from 1924. The only occasion when DHL could have seen this mural and still have drawn on it for his novel was October–November 1924. He wrote the pages describing Kate's visit in late November or in December. For accounts by one of the artists involved concerning DHL's responses to the murals, see Jean Charlot, *The Mexican Mural Renaissance, 1920–1925* (New Haven, 1963), pp. 119, 152, 160–1, 237–8.

54:13　*casus belli* 'Occasion for war' (Latin): event or situation used to justify a conflict.

56:8 **cards with the corners turned down.** Calling cards were sometimes carried in by a servant, while the caller waited in a conveyance outside. If the caller left the card in person, he would turn down the upper right-hand corner.

56:14 *Universal* Like *Excelsior*, an important daily newspaper in Mexico City.

56:18 **The Gods ... to Mexico.** Mythological sources and analogues are treated in the notes below and in Appendix I. Although this account is offered as a translation from a newspaper in Spanish, the style seems to imitate Terry. The account in 'Q' (p. 50) is short, recounting only that a man rises naked from the water, appropriates clothing, announces that he has been speaking with Quetzalcoatl under the lake and disappears.

56:20 **Lake of Sayula,** Lake Chapala, Jalisco. DHL borrowed the fictional name from a lake and a village 25 miles s.w. of Lake Chapala.

56:27 **Montezuma,** Montezuma II (1466–1520), emperor of the Aztecs, overthrown by the Spaniards in the Conquest.

56:31 **little images ... not yet altogether forgotten.** One legend relates that the early Chapala inhabitants were descended from the Toltecs; see Antonio de Alba, *Chapala* (Guadalajara, 1954), p. 15. They made tiny clay vessels (*ollitas*), deposited in them a drop of their own blood taken from the ear and threw the vessels into the lake as offerings to the gods. Early Christian missionaries thought the Indians expected to gain immortality by this ritual. Some Indians still follow the tradition in this century. See de Alba, pp. 23–5 and also Spence 24. The place-name 'Chapala' may have come from that of the chief god of the lake (*Enciclopedia de México*, México, D. F., 1970, ii. 1185). Fray Antonio Tello, writing in the 17th century, says that while each neighbourhood along the lake in ancient times had its own god, the people also worshipped, with bonfires, dancing and human sacrifice, a more powerful god whom Tello identifies as 'Huitzilopoch', but also calls him by a local name meaning 'hidden god'. His image stood near the hot springs of Chapala; see *Crónica miscelanea de la Sancta Provincia de Xalisco* (Guadalajara, 1945), libro ii, pp. 195–6, and the Guadalajara edition of 1968, libro iv, pp. 75–6.

56:39 **His face ... like gold.** A ritual with close parallels to DHL's invented apparition is found in Adolf Bandelier's *The Gilded Man* (New York, 1893), pp. 14–15, which DHL had read.

57:10 **Quetzalcoatl and Tlaloc,** The hero-god and the rain god of ancient central Mexico. Tlaloc never appears in the novel. See notes on 58:36 and 62:10 and Appendix I.

57:14 **I have come ... their own home—** The Aztecs' expectation of Quetzalcoatl's return contributed to their defeat. The Spaniards turned out not to be the awaited deity and his followers, but anticipation of a second coming of the indigenous god did not die out. This hope has taken many forms and has had a great effect on attitudes and events in Mexican history. See Jacques Lafaye, *Quetzalcoatl and Guadalupe: The Formation of the Mexican National Consciousness, 1531–1815* (Chicago, 1976). See also Spence 119, 124, 141 and Terry 304–5, 496, 519–21.

57:31 **four little men ... water.** Stories of Quetzalcoatl's departure into exile often mention four companions, who are in some versions dwarfs. See Spence 126 and Caso 41–2. See also note on 202:1.

57:35 *The bath ... to come.* A fire to symbolise rebirth was associated with various ancient Mexican beliefs and practices: for example, Aztec infants were quickly swept over hearth flames as a form of baptism. See note on 120:32.

58:4 **eminent historian and archaeologist,** In 'Q' (p. 154) Ramón is said to have written a history of Mexico, but little is made in the published novel of his standing as a scholar. DHL does not make clear whether Ramón instigated the occurrence just reported or who the mysterious figure is. See 103:14ff. In 'Q' Ramón states (p. 247) that he read of the incident in the newspaper, and its origin is left a mystery.

58:36 **The name Quetzalcoatl [58:19] ... and vindictiveness?** DHL touches here on most of the traditional attributes of Quetzalcoatl, with elaborations of his own. For his response to Quetzalcoatl as an 'American' god, see 'Au Revoir, U.S.A.' (*Phoenix* 104–6). It was a tradition in Anáhuac that Quetzalcoatl had discouraged human sacrifice, though the Aztecs practised it on a large scale. Two variant legends of his departure were current in ancient times, and some confusion between a god Quetzalcoatl and a priest-king Quetzalcoatl has long been evident. The god was an ancient one, undergoing changes of name and function in later cultures. See Miguel León-Portilla, *Aztec Thought and Culture*, trans. Jack Emory Davis (Oklahoma, 1963). See also Spence 117–45 and Nuttall 67–71 *et passim*. According to William York Tindall (*D. H. Lawrence and Susan His Cow*, New York 1939, p. 114), DHL had read Alexandre de Humboldt, *Vues des Cordillères et Monuments des Peuples Indigènes de l'Amérique* (Paris, 1810). What DHL has to say of Quetzalcoatl suggests that he also may have read Eduard Seler. See Seler, ii. 668–705 and iv. 3–156.

59:9 **Ye must be born again.** John iii. 7 (AV).

59:22 **a peace that passes understanding.** Cf. Philippians iv. 7 ['... the peace of God, which passeth all understanding ...'].

60:19 **The house ... at Tlalpam.** Tlalpán is a southern suburb of Mexico City, between Coyoacán and Xochimilco. DHL went to dinner there at the home of the British Consul-General on 17 November 1923. See *Letters*, iv. 534, 536 and Knud Merrild, *A Poet and Two Painters* (1938), p. 350. Between versions of his novel, DHL moved the scene of the fictional dinner-party from Coyoacán to 'Tlalpam', and perhaps incorporated elements of the November visit into the extensive revision.

60:27 **Owen's kicking ... whole porcupine.** Cf. 'it is hard for thee to kick against the pricks', Acts ix. 5 (AV), and 'Ye blind guides, which strain at a gnat, and swallow a camel', Matthew xxiii. 24 (AV).

60:31 **an Ossianic goddess,** A deity from a cycle of ancient Celtic literature (*c.* 3rd century AD), now more commonly known as the Fenian cycle.

62:10 *Huitzilopochtli ... Tlaloc!* Huitzilopochtli was the chief tribal god of the Aztecs, and led them to the Lake of Mexico. See Spence 66–91 ... Tlaloc, as the chief god of rain, was of such importance that his shrine on the summit of the great temple of the Aztecs was matched only by that of Huitzilopochtli. See Spence 234–56.

62:11 **Mani padma Om!** Often written *Om Mani Padme Hūm* ('Hail to the Jewel of the Lotus'). This is a Buddhist *mantra*, a magical formula utilising the occult power of sound; from Edwin Arnold, *The Light of Asia* (1879), viii. 289. See *The Letters of D. H. Lawrence*, ed. James T. Boulton (Cambridge, 1979), i. 46.

62:14 **Itzpapalotl! Tezcatlipoca!** At the same time a butterfly and an obsidian knife, Itzpapalotl was one of the several paradoxical forms of the Great Mother, maternal yet devouring. Originally a hunting goddess of the savage northern tribes, the Chichimecs, in the Aztec pantheon she was the double of Xochiquetzal (Precious Flower), a virgin deity who once lived in Tamoanchan, the Aztec Eden, which she lost, like Eve, by eating forbidden fruit. See Spence 223–8 and notes on 236:8 and 370:33. Tezcatlipoca's name derives from the obsidian mirror that Aztec seers used in divination. He was a great sorcerer, both sustaining and dangerous to mankind. In nearly every role he is pictured as in conflict with Quetzalcoatl. See Spence 91–116 and Appendix I.

62:38 **Porfirio Díaz** (1830–1915), dictator of Mexico from 1876 to 1911, when he was driven into exile in France.

63:2 **in sixty years there will be no Mexicans:** The census of 1910 gave the population of Mexico as 15,160,369, an increase of 11% since 1900. The next census was delayed until 1921, when the figure was 14,334,780, a decrease of 5.4%. García's figures are exaggerated, and now seem ironic, since Mexico has one of the fastest-growing populations in the world.

63:22 **angelito** [63:18] ... **walls of death.** See 'The Mozo', *Mornings in Mexico* and note on 261:39.

64:7 **Tlaxcalan Indians** A small, fiercely independent Nahuatl tribe of a mountainous region east of Tenochtitlan, the Tlaxcalans were never conquered by the Aztecs. After initial resistance to the Spaniards, they became loyal allies.

64:40 **Mexicans of mixed blood** [64:19] ... **you expect?"** These discussions of the racial history of Mexico embody fundamental issues long present and revived by the Revolution. DHL found them in his reading, and doubtless in talk heard during his stays in Mexico City. He broadened his knowledge of such matters between drafts of this novel; neither these ideas nor the guests expounding them appear in 'Q'. For a contemporary evaluation of these issues, see Ernest Gruening, *Mexico and Its Heritage* (New York, 1928), pp. 69–88.

65:15 **Benito Juárez,** Zapotec Indian (1806–72) orphaned at the age of three and unofficially adopted by an ecclesiastic and his mistress. Cipriano's early life has parallels with that of Juárez. As President of Mexico (1858–72), Juárez was a constitutional democrat; by defeating Maximilian he ended a European attempt to impose a monarchy. His reforms brought the beginnings of social and economic progress to Mexico; they were suppressed by his successor, Porfirio Díaz.

65:25 **turkey in black sauce.** *Mole* sauce, a favourite in Mexico, largely made from deep red *chile* and chocolate; hence the colour.

66:20   your serious-minded men. If DHL had a particular man in mind, it was most likely Manuel Gamio. The two carried on a brief correspondence in 1924, and Gamio sent DHL one of his books, probably *Forjando Patria* [*Forging a Nation*] (Mexico, 1916). Gamio was at that time Director of Archaeology for the Mexican Department of Agriculture. An intended meeting never took place, and DHL's letters to Gamio have disappeared. See letters to Thomas Seltzer, 18 May 1924 and Willard Johnson, ?25 October 1924. See also Nehls, ii. 351, 366–8; Clark 36–7.

68:19   Like the flowers ... any smell." See note on 393:24.

68:32   Bishop Severn ... Oaxaca. Cipriano's benefactor in 'Q' is a rich Englishwoman. For the Bishop, DHL possibly used as a model Father Edward Rickards (1876–1950) of Oaxaca, English but Mexican-born, from whom DHL rented his house in Oaxaca and whose charity was legendary in the region. See Nehls, ii. 365-6, 377-8. DHL may also have made use of what he had heard about Gregorio Gillow, first archbishop of Oaxaca (1841–1922); see Parmenter, *Lawrence in Oaxaca*, pp. 26–7, 35–7.

71:25   babyish figure ... Santa María de la Soledad, The statue of the Virgin of Sorrows is the chief treasure of the 17th-century Church and Convent of La Soledad in Oaxaca. She is patroness of the city and venerated by the Indians of the region. One of the principal ceremonies in her honour is a procession seeking her intercession for abundant rains.

72:2   To Stay ... To Stay. DHL first entitled this chapter 'The Lake' in MS (p. 121); for intermediate versions, see Textual apparatus.

73:7   put his wine ... old wine-skin, See Matthew ix. 17 (RV).

75:21   a bunch of black-tarnished swords The symbolic portrayal of several *pulque* gods in Anáhuac culture displayed parallels between the obsidian knife of sacrifice and the blade-like leaves of the agave plant. See Spence 285–99, especially pp. 292–3.

76:9   They were [76:4] ... pervades the whole. Gamio stresses the same differences and similarities among the Indians of Mexico. See especially the chapter 'Perjuicios sobre la raza indígena y su historia' ('Prejudices against the indigenous race and its history') in *Forjando Patria*.

78:9   great negative pull ... the world? Cf. the two versions of 'Eagle in New Mexico' (*Complete Poems* 372–4, 780–3), and also the two versions of 'The Spirit of Place' in *Symbolic Meaning* and *Studies*.

78:13   Europe. At this point in TS DHL deleted a long passage found in the Textual apparatus: the excision covered six lines at the end of p. 90 of TS, all of pp. 91–3, which he removed and discarded, and four lines at the top of p. 95. He did no renumbering to fill the gap left by the removal of pages.

78:15   Moloch-worshippers, Moloch was a Canaanite god whose worship often threatened that of Yahweh among the Israelites. Children, especially the firstborn, were sacrificed to him.

79:13 Cortés Hernán Cortés (1485–1547), Spanish adventurer who with a small army invaded Mexico in 1519 and by 1521 had destroyed the Aztec empire.

79:26 The ponderous pyramids ... and pure The Pyramid of the Sun, the Pyramid of the Moon and the Temple of Quetzalcoatl, in that order, are the largest ruins at Teotihuacán. The carved facade of this last is banded with the feathered bodies of snakes from which giant heads with fangs displayed protrude at intervals. DHL visited Teotihuacán shortly after his first arrival in Mexico. See 'Au Revoir, U.S.A.' and Bynner 24.

79:33 Cholula ... and fascination. This city s.e. of the capital was a centre of Quetzalcoatl worship. His chief temple stood on the pyramid of Cholula, a largely artificial hill where worship of various kinds has been carried on since time immemorial. Today a church dedicated to La Virgen de los Remedios occupies the site. See Terry 518–21. DHL had read the work that Terry quotes: William Hickling Prescott, *History of the Conquest of Mexico* (New York, 1843). Both in Prescott and in his source, Bernal Díaz (ch. LXXXIII), DHL had read of the great slaughter of the Cholulans by the Spaniards in this market-place in 1519.

79:35 Mitla ... terrible gusts. Although this ruin, which DHL visited during his stay in Oaxaca, is in the Mixtec–Zapotec region, it received its modern name from a Nahuatl word meaning 'city of the dead'. See Brett, *Lawrence and Brett*, pp. 182–4; Terry 540–1; and Toor, *Treasury of Mexican Folkways*, p. 191.

80:2 knife of sacrifice ... the world? At the centre of the Aztec Sunstone is the face of the sun god, Tonatiuh, whose downward-protruding tongue represents the obsidian knife of sacrifice.

80:29 dark forest ... of America. In the 1919 version of 'Fenimore Cooper's Leatherstocking Novels', DHL treated the destruction and renewal of the American wilderness in similar terms. See *Symbolic Meaning* 93–111.

81:2 The Lake. The journey in this chapter and the next is based on one DHL took just before he started writing 'Q'. In a 'last effort' to find a house in Mexico, before sailing for Europe or returning to the United States, he left Frieda, Bynner and Johnson in Mexico City and took the train for Jalisco, on 27 April 1923, to look at Lake Chapala, intending to send for the others if he liked it. See Merrild, *Poet and Two Painters*, p. 293, *Letters*, iv. 433 and Bynner 59–60,79–82. The fictional Ixtlahuacan where Kate descends from the train is the actual Ocotlán, Orilla is El Fuerte and Sayula is Chapala. The hotel where Kate goes was called the Hotel Ribera Castellanos. See Terry 151–9.

81:15 Ah no ... yellow teeth. DHL's introduction to Edward Dahlberg's *Bottom Dogs* (1929) comments on the question that troubles Kate here (*Phoenix* 267–73).

82:40 a new governor. No such passage occurs in 'Q' and no 'new' governor entered office in this state when Calles became President. Governor José Guadalupe Zuno had been inaugurated on 1 March 1923. He held office until 23 March 1926, when he was removed for derelictions of duty and political miscalculations. See Gruening, *Mexico and Its Heritage*, pp. 440ff. Zuno was never a strong Calles supporter, though he took measures against Catholics. See note on 113:11.

83:34 rancheros ... hats stitched with silver. As distinct from *hacendados*, *rancheros* are independent cattlemen of moderate means. These are wearing the typical *charro* dress, which was becoming popular among amateur ranchers and others. See Toor, *Treasury of Mexican Folkways*, pp. 285ff.

84:17 Tacuba, All states of the text read 'Tacubaya', not 'Tacuba'. However, 'Tacuba' was pencilled in as a correction in the right-hand margin of galley 28. The handwriting resembles DHL's but is not so characteristic as to be positively identifiable. 'Tacuba' has been accepted nonetheless, since DHL was nearly always exact when he employed an actual place-name, and the railroad w. from Mexico City toward Lake Chapala ran through Tacuba, on the northern outskirts of the Capital, not through Tacubaya on the southern outskirts.

87:5 Ópalos! Mexico is one of the world's largest producers of opals.

89:39 Kate looked ... buff water, The G compositor set the first line of the following paragraph instead of the proper line and then repeated it where it belonged. To correct the repetition DHL revised without reference to TS; his original version has been restored (see Textual apparatus).

91:35 till the Morning Star rises." Quetzalcoatl in pre-Columbian symbolism was identified with the planet Venus as both Morning and Evening Star. Cf. 2 Peter i. 19. In 'Q' this god is once said to have become a star (p. 205), but no Morning Star symbolism as such appears in that version.

92:37 little river Anapo: A river that rises in the Monti Iblei of southeastern Sicily and enters the Ionian Sea at Siracusa.

93:35 a scylla and a charybdis ... in its flight. The monster Scylla and the whirlpool Charybdis which jointly threatened mariners in the Straits of Messina. To this classical myth DHL has added that of the thunderbird from American Indian lore.

95:16 skeletons of gods that cannot die. In Mesoamerican belief, bone was the stuff of immortality. See Appendix I. In another myth Quetzalcoatl died and went through a period of afterlife as 'bones' before rising as the Morning Star. See Spence 132. Bone as the substance of immortality is a part of the esoteric tradition as well. See *Blavatsky*, ii. 15–21 and also note on 123:18.

97:10 turkey-cock [97:5] ... his plumage. Cf. the poem 'Turkey-Cock', (*Complete Poems* 369–72), written in the autumn of 1920; see also 372:8–10.

97:40 The lymphatic ... somebody said. In 'Q' a similar remark is attributed to Owen Rhys, who in that version of the novel accompanies Kate to Sayula. But in Bynner (p. 181), the metaphor is said to have been DHL's.

98:2 the Lake. The typescript from which G was set – TS – up to the end of chap. v was the work of Dorothy Brett (see Introduction, pp. xxxiii–xxxv); the same machine was used for a few pages of chap. XXVII. Brett also produced chap. VI and the first six pages of VII, in both a ribbon and a carbon copy, on which DHL made minor revisions. These fragments of chaps. VI and VII have been designated

TS1, the ribbon copy, and TCC1, the carbon copy. Variations sometimes occur between DHL's revisions on TS1 and TCC1, and sometimes between them and the TSR text; these are recorded in the Textual apparatus after the main entry (with *R* added to designate DHL's changes). Readings from TSR1 and TCCR1 have been recorded even when identical to those of TSR, as evidence of DHL's procedure in revising. But unless otherwise noted TCCR1 agrees with TSR1.

98:5   Nice ... Mentone of the country.   See Terry 155, where similar terms are employed.

98:7   **Don Porfirio ... half-a-crown.**   See Appendix III. Before decimalisation there were twenty shillings in a British pound and twelve pennies in a shilling. A 'half-crown' was two shillings and sixpence, the equivalent of 55 American cents at the average exchange rate of 1924.

98:11   **a feeble new start**   Some semblance of political order and some attempts at economic recovery began in Mexico during Obregón's presidency.

101:10   **Towards the end [98:21] ... the others.**   Bynner reports that this episode was based on an experience of Winfield Scott, an American who had lived for several years in Mexico, though DHL introduced fictional variations. After the ordeal, Scott moved to Chapala. In 1923 he was manager there of the Hotel Arzapalo, where Bynner and Johnson stayed while they and the Lawrences were living in Chapala. See Bynner 124–7.

102:9   **United States to intervene.**   A few wealthy Mexicans may have favoured American intervention during the Revolution, but most were utterly opposed. Intervention was occasionally debated in Washington; Veracruz was briefly occupied in 1914, and an unsuccessful punitive expedition was mounted against Pancho Villa in northern Mexico in 1916–17.

105:13   **the hot springs, the church,**   The hot springs are probably those at Agua Caliente; the church is most likely the one at San Pedro Itzicán.

105:22   **the island ... and prison.**   The Isla de Mezcala, sometimes called El Presidio from the fortress that later became a prison. See Terry 156–7.

108:3   **Tuliapán**   The actual Tizapán, a village on the s. shore of Lake Chapala.

108:34   **Great Breath.**   A term from Theosophical symbolism. See Blavatsky, i. 2, where the Great Breath is equated with supreme life, 'eternal, invisible, yet Omnipresent, without beginning or end, yet periodical in its regular manifestations'. Quetzalcoatl was created, according to one account, by the breath of the supreme deity. See Spence 36.

109:7   **between the bluish ribs ... the earth.**   The heart of the earth or the mountains might be envisioned as a devouring jaguar or a skeletal death god in lore known to DHL; but he also knew less aggressive terrestrial heart symbolism; see Nuttall 71–2, Spence 332–5 and Gamio, *Forjando Patria*, pp. 160–1. See also 'Taos' (*Phoenix* 100).

109:21   **stone, cool, dark house [109:17] ... mango trees.**   This house is modelled on 307 Zaragoza Street (then number 4), where the Lawrences lived in Chapala in May and June 1923 and where DHL wrote 'Q'.

109:23 **a Mexican Juana ... one son.** This character and her children are based on the Lawrences' maid in Chapala, Isabel Medina, and her family. This mention of only one son is an oversight, since two sons soon appear in the narrative.

110:1 *No, Niña, no hay másn***" '**No, Mistress [literally, 'child'], there isn't any more'.

111:4 *Qué ... bonita!***" '**How pretty! How pretty, Mistress! Look how pretty!'

112:23 **The railway ... fought with extinction.** This enterprise was in operation from 1920 to 1926. See Bynner 89–90, de Alba, *Chapala*, p. 121 and opp. p. 144.

112:30 **One hope, one faith, one destiny:** Cf. Ephesians iv. 5: 'One Lord, one faith, one baptism'; also Kate Brownlee Sherwood (1841–1914): 'One heart, one hope, one destiny'.

113:11 **loose great floppy drawers** *Calzones*. For a fuller account of this controversy, see Bynner 119–21. Governor Zuno of Jalisco apparently intervened in favour of the peons.

113:23 *Cinco de Espadas! Rey de Copas!* 'Five of Swords! King of Cups!' – equivalent to Spades and Hearts. The other two suits of the Spanish pack of cards are Bastos (Clubs) and Oros (coins), i.e. Diamonds.

115:8 **Fifis [115:3] ... sacrificed to some Mexican god ... sacrificial calves** The sacrifice of bull calves among the Israelites (Leviticus i. 3ff. and viii. 1ff.) always called for an animal without blemish. In human sacrifice among the ancient Mexicans, several different ceremonies required the victim to be pampered for as much as a year before the offering. See Spence 97–102 and also Nehls, ii. 522.

115:20 **tan brogue bands.** Bands of leather decorated by patterns of perforation.

117:34 **Red Indians ... religious significance,** From 1922 to 1924, DHL gathered many impressions from Southwestern Indian ceremony which were transformed and woven into the novel. See 'Pan in America', 'Indians and an Englishman', 'Taos' and 'New Mexico' (*Phoenix* 22–31, 92–9, 100–3, 141–7) and the Southwestern sketches of *Mornings in Mexico*. Cf. also ['Autobiographical Fragment'] (*Phoenix* 817–36) and the music DHL wrote for *David*. In 'Q' the ceremonial music is largely that of guitars and other modern Mexican instruments, with drums introduced only in the last third of the manuscript. The flute played here, later said to be of clay, is similar to a Mexican *chirimía*. None of the Indian music DHL heard in the Southwest includes that instrument, but it is still used in Mexican native dances, some of which DHL attended. See Bynner 119 and Nehls, ii. 240.

118:22 **turquoise ornament ... stone in the centre.** Many Indians of the Southwest and Mexico use turquoise as a ceremonial stone. In ancient Mexico it was part of the class, including jade, designated *chalchihuitl* (green stone), and connected with the worship of several deities, Quetzalcoatl among them. See Spence 25–7. The goddess of water and consort of the rain god Tlaloc was Chalchiuhtlicue (Jade Skirt), some of whose attributes figure in Kate's apotheosis.

The Tlaxcalans worshipped this goddess in the form of their highest mountain, a peak which today is called Malinche. See note on 370:33.

118:40 **This eagle ... an eye.** DHL drew the design of an eagle enclosed in a circular snake which was stamped on the front cover of the first American edition (A1). The story of the 'Mexican emblem' (118:35), from the national flag, goes back to the founding of Tenochtitlan. Both Spence (pp. 320–1) and Nuttall (pp. 12–14) take up the solar and stellar symbolism of the eye. See also Clark 104, 131–3 and Blavatsky, ii. 298. DHL certainly had the Aztec Sunstone in mind as well. See Caso 32–3 and Seler, iv. 46–9.

119:8 **place of the west [119:1] ... the winds are born.** Quetzalcoatl's departure and expected return had always been associated with the east, but his identification with the planet Venus also gave him Evening Star attributes, and as the god Kukulkan of the Maya he arrived from the west. The seat of the most ancient of the Aztec gods was in the west (Spence 223). The creation of mankind in Tamoanchan, with the aid of Quetzalcoatl, took place in the west. The details of this poem and of the prose 'myth' beginning on 122:35 shows that DHL retained the framework of the Quetzalcoatl myth. The god's journey in defeat to the Gulf Coast and his departure and promised return are associated with old age and the need for rejuvenation: in a fountain of youth (Spence 141). For Quetzalcoatl's struggle with Tezcatlipoca, the god of the old way, and other significant parallels from the mythology, see Appendix I. See also Seler, iv. 6, 41, 54, 62. See Spence 175, 189, 200 and 314 for hymns that may have influenced DHL, and Caso 76 for a later translation of one of these.

119:27 **while Jesus passed ... womb of refreshment.** This journey echoes that of Quetzalcoatl and the return of the warriors to the sun after death and other journeys of the Aztec dead. See Spence 61–4, 302–3.

119:29 **sandals of the Saviour** Sandals were an important item of ritual dress among the Aztecs, as the elaborately carved footwear of surviving religious statuary attests. Bernal Díaz says that the sandals of Montezuma had soles of gold and were decorated with precious stones (ii. 41). See also 330:37–9.

120:2 **My bride between the seas** Anáhuac, the Nahuatl name for central Mexico, means 'land between the seas'. (The line just above this one, 120:1, is a single-line stanza.)

120:24 **yellow sun ... dazzling motion.** A design that may have contributed to the concept of this flag, sometimes called 'the wheel of the winds', is to be found in Spence opp. p. 118. Brett incorporated the whole figure that includes this design in her dust jacket, used on A1. Nuttall (pp. 13, 54) takes up the symbol of the black sun in ancient Mexican culture. DHL may also have seen a reproduction of the *manta del sol negro* (cloth of the black sun) described and drawn on p. 6 of the *Codex Magliabecchiano*, a variation of the Cross and Circle motif which had long fascinated him. See 'The Two Principles', *Symbolic Meaning*. See also Blavatsky, ii. 536ff.; Seler, v. 145; Clark 129–32.

120:32 **two ocote torches ... long cane tripod,** For 'ocote', see Glossary. This ceremonial use of fire, like that of the rain-welcoming ritual (193:35ff.), both new to this version of the novel, clearly owes much to the sacred nature of fire as DHL had observed it among Indians of the American Southwest. The symbolism also suggests the lighting of the new fire at the end of an Aztec solar cycle and the fires dedicated to various ancient gods. See Spence 268–84, 303–5, and Brundage 26–7. For other mythical events pertaining to fire, including the creation of a new sun and purification of a deity by fire, see Seler, iv. 38–64.

122:41 **one of the gods ... the water,** Creation myths centring upon lakes are common in the American Indian lore that DHL was familiar with. Nuttall (p. 133) describes an example from the Incas, in which demi-gods rose from Lake Titicaca and founded Cuzco, 'navel of the world'. Taos Indians believe they were created by Father Sun, then entered this world through a lake. Dispute with the United States government over control of their sacred lake in the mountains above Taos Pueblo was part of the Indian lands controversy DHL heard about when he first arrived in New Mexico. See 'Certain Americans and an Englishman' (*Phoenix II* 238–43).

123:5 **swallow it** The greater sun swallowing the lesser sun echoes the Nahuatl cosmogony of the 'suns' or ages. Cf. 'Corasmin and the Parrots', *Mornings in Mexico*. Cf. Humboldt, *Vues des Cordillères*, pp. 242–3, and Seler, 'Mexicans, Ancient', *Encyclopedia of Religion and Ethics*, ed. James Hastings. DHL saw an eclipse of the sun in southern California on 11 September 1923. See *Letters*, iv. 498 and Nehls, ii. 257–9.

123:13 **Come! Come ... sweet water!** Cf. Isaiah lv. 1.

123:18 **drunk too ... dry enough?** See the fragments of Heraclitus and discussion of them in John Burnet, *Early Greek Philosophy* (1907). Cf. *Women in Love*, chap. xiv. The human soul is said to be a harmony or a balance of wet and dry, fire and water. There is also a probable allusion to Ezekiel xxxvii. 1–14.

125:10 **greatest of the great suns ... my womb,** It was fundamental to Aztec mythology that the supreme creative power was dual, male and female. See Appendix I and Spence 146–52.

127:5 **Verbum Sat.** From *verbum sapienti sat est*: 'A word to the wise is sufficient' (Latin).

129:32 **It was she ... shy snatching.** Among several American Indian tribes it is customary for the woman to ask the man to dance.

130:2 **The inner circle ... was closing.** Reminiscent of the round dance among American Indians. See ['Autobiographical Fragment'] (*Phoenix* 832) and 'Indians and Entertainment', *Mornings in Mexico*.

131:18 **waters over the earth ... waters under the earth,** Cf. Genesis i. 6–7 and Exodus xx. 4.

134:27 *Nieve! Nieve!,* Literally 'snow', the common term for ice cream in central Mexico.

134:31 **the Jefe** The *jefe político* (political chief), the political leader of a district, appointed by the central government.

135:5 **But even Humboldt ... fierce eyes.** While DHL may have taken this observation directly from some work (passage not located) of Alexander von Humboldt (1769–1859), German explorer and statesman, he probably came across it in Calderón de la Barca, which he read in 1923. See Bynner 43, 117–18. See also 76:18–20.

137:19 **old Pan ... evil forms of consciousness,** 'The Last Laugh', 'The Overtone', and 'Pan in America' (written not long before DHL began this version of the novel) take quite different views of Pan and his influence.

138:17 **She dozed** [136:33] **... a wreck.** The attempted break-in is modelled on DHL's own experience in his Chapala house. See *Letters*, iv. 442 and Bynner 160–3. DHL began to write 'Q' two days after the incident, and Kate's terror of the Mexican night is described in it, but he made no fictional use of the attempted break-in until he wrote the second version.

138:22 *Mire!"* Literally 'Look!' Often employed to call attention with the force of 'Just think!' or 'My God!'

138:26 **The other señora** This character is never mentioned again. DHL may have been alluding to Dorothy Brett, who stayed at a hotel in Oaxaca in 1924–5 while the Lawrences lived in a house.

138:28 *Entonces! Entonces,* 'Then! Then'.

140:16 *à terre,* Literally 'at the level of the earth', with the sense of 'common' or 'ignoble' (French).

141:31 *No hay!* 'There isn't any', the standard Spanish phrase for being out of anything. Cf. 'Walk to Huayapa', *Mornings in Mexico.*

141:37 **Eggs ... *rancheros?*** Rural dish prepared by frying or scrambling eggs and adding a sauce of *chiles* and tomatoes.

142:37 **centavos.** The Mexican peso during this period was worth fifty cents in US currency, each *centavo* thus amounting to half an American cent.

142:40 *Entonces ... memoria!* 'And then! And then! After that! Ah, Mistress, my memory is terrible!'

144:29 **a black Fascista shirt,** In 'Q' (p. 216) Jesús's shirt is black but has nothing political about it. See also note on 308:34.

145:14 **the socialist government ... the village.** In pre-Conquest days a clan or a village possessed a portion of land, an *ejido*, whose use could be passed from father to son but which could never be owned by an individual. Under pressure from such movements as Zapata's and Villa's, the revolutionary leaders wrote agrarian reform based on the old *ejido* system into the Constitution of 1917, and Obregón restored a little land to the Indians. The Calles administration was just beginning to set up more extensive redistribution of land from some of the big haciendas at the time when DHL was rewriting his novel. No such situation as the present one is described in 'Q'. Ramón favours something like the *ejido* system, in 'Q' as well as in the published novel. See 'Q' 311, Appendix III and note on 42:30.

149:18 **Ezequiel had worked** [149:14] **... bitter disappointment.** Cf. Bynner 94–5.

151:21 **Men and women** [151:18] **... and taken.** Cf. 'The Theatre', *Twilight in Italy* (1916).

155:7 **reddish-and-yellow ... the lake.** The original of Ramón's *hacienda* dwelling was the villa of El Manglar ('The Mango Grove'), which had belonged to Porfirio Díaz's brother before the Revolution; see Bynner 90–1, Clark 34–5 and plates IX and X. DHL apparently took the *hacienda* name, 'Jamiltepec' (159:1), from a village in the s.w. part of the state of Oaxaca. In 'Q' the property is called Las Yemas; see 395:8.

156:38 **Cuna ... Carmelite sisters.** DHL borrowed much of his information about this institution from Calderón de la Barca 434–5, 446–8.

163:1 *Hermoso ... bonito!"* 'Beautiful – yes! Yes, pretty!'

164:37 **Pancho Villa ... Don Ramón.** For information on General Francisco Villa's role in the Revolution, see Appendix III. Neither this contrast nor any other parallel is drawn between the fictional leader and the real-life one in 'Q'. By the time DHL began his Mexican novel, the feats which had made Pancho Villa a popular hero were in the past. He was living in retirement when assassinated on 20 July 1923, about three weeks before 'Q' was finished.

165:8 **vanity of vanities,** Cf. Ecclesiastes i. 2.

168:2 **Count Tolstoy ... Señor Moujik?"** Although an aristocrat by birth and upbringing, Leo Tolstoy (1828–1910) was an advocate of the liberation and education of the Russian serfs; he wore the blouse of the *moujik*, the peasant, worked in the fields and learned shoemaking.

169:2 **Lords of the Day and Night.** DHL's reason for choosing this title becomes clear in the poem beginning at 177:30, and in Ramón's declaration (178:33ff.). In the Aztec solar calendar there was a god or 'lord' for each day, each week and nearly every division of time, including every 'hour' of the day and the night; see Spence 268, 359–70. DHL imposes his own variations at 359: 9–13.

173:40 **Ramón paused ... the loom.** Johnson tells of DHL designing his own sarape to be woven in Jocotepec, at the w. end of Lake Chapala, a village known for its weavers. See Nehls, ii. 235–6 and also letter to Johnson, ?25 October 1924, Bynner 94–5 and Terry 529–30.

175:3 **blue eyes filled with white,** See note on 118:40. Stellar symbolism in Aztec imagery was often expressed by an eye, either open or half-closed.

175:26 **birds that fly in one consciousness.** Cf. ['Autobiographical Fragment'] (*Phoenix* 832).

175:35 **there is only Now,"** For a full development of the present moment as the ultimate reality, see 'Poetry of the Present' (*Complete Poems* 181–6).

176:10 *I Am!* Cf. Exodus iii. 13–14.

179:33 **the burning bush between us.** See Exodus iii. 1–6, also 176:10 and 281:5.

181:2 **The First Waters.** In MS, chap. XII extends through the ceremonial welcome of the first rains, including what becomes chap. XIII in *The Plumed Serpent*. DHL made the division in TSR; see note on 190:2.

182:36　**how Salome had looked at John.**　In Oscar Wilde's *Salome* (1893), the daughter of Herodias says to John the Baptist, 'Thy mouth is like a band of scarlet on a tower of ivory. It is like a pomegranate cut in twain with a knife of ivory. The pomegranate flowers that blossom in the gardens of Tyre, and are redder than roses, are not so red'. Cf. Mark vi. 14–29 and Matthew xiv. 1–12.

183:25　*Mexico means Below this!*"　The Director of the Mexican National Archives told Frances Calderón de la Barca's husband that 'Mexico in Indian means "below this", alluding to the population who, according to tradition, are buried beneath the *Pedregal*' (*Life in Mexico*, p. 409). The etymology is doubtful, but folk belief in a buried race came about after Mt Ajusco erupted some two thousand years ago, covering several ancient villages and forming the lava-rock area near Mexico City known as the *Pedregal*. Spence reports another local tradition that the Toltecs live on beneath the ground (pp. 208–12). In 'Q', Ramón uses the phrase 'below this' with mystical overtones (p. 137), invoking the 'children of wrath who among themselves have a tenderness like the morning, and a faith that is not catholic nor protestant, but of the alive blood, which is dark and below this' (p. 140). DHL scribbled 'Below This' on a flyleaf of one of his composition books (Roberts E313c) as a possible title for the novel. He did not call the work 'Quetzalcoatl' until he had written more than eighty per cent of the first draft.

184:29　**The curse of Eve**　Cf. Genesis iii. 16.

184:32　**Daughter of Eve, of greedy vision,**　According to tradition, Satan took on the form of the prelapsarian serpent in order to appeal to Eve's eye for beauty; see *Paradise Lost*, Book IX, 495–531.

187:33　**The meek ... to prophecy.**　See Matthew v. 5.

189:2　**It is the sin ... sin of men.**　Pride, the sin of Satan, is the greatest of the Seven Deadly Sins. See Romans xii. 16.

190:2　**The First Rain.**　There is in 'Q' a description of the start of the rainy season, based on DHL's experience of that important event in arid Mexico, but no ceremony of the revived religion is linked with a rain cult. Between versions of the novel DHL attended a spring corn dance at Santo Domingo and the Hopi snake dance; see 'Dance of the Sprouting Corn' and 'The Hopi Snake Dance', *Mornings in Mexico*. He may have been influenced by Spence, who says of the Aztec hymns: 'In several of these chants we assuredly arrive at the whole significance of Mexican religion, which in its essence and as seen at the Conquest period, was nothing more than a vastly elaborated rain-cult, similar in its general tendency to that still prevalent among the Pueblo tribes of New Mexico and Arizona' (p. 11). See also Spence 22–7.

190:14　**Secretary, and President**　If Ramón were to become Montes' Secretario de Gobernación, the highest official of the presidential cabinet, he would probably succeed as President when Montes left office, as Calles had done after serving in the same post under Obregón.

190:35　**honest in his convictions.**"　Cf. DHL's reference to 'the present government' (Obregón's) as 'good idealists and sensible' (*Letters*, iv. 432). See also Bynner 26 and Nehls, ii. 384.

193:27   *Ya ... Ya!*" 'Now, Master?' ... 'Now!'

193:34   *Viene ... Patrón.*" 'Is the rain coming?' ... 'I think it is, Master'.

195:25   **Someone will** [195:14] ... **Shall I!** Imitative of the hymn 'Shall you? Shall I?' (1887) by James McGranahan (1840–1907) in *Sacred Songs and Solos*, compiled by Ira D. Sankey (1889). DHL knew many such hymns from chapel in his youth. Cf. 'Hymns in a Man's Life' (*Phoenix II* 597–601). This hymn echoes the parable of the Wise and Foolish Virgins.

198:29   **Bird of** [198:16] ... **swoop!**" In 'The Hopi Snake Dance', *Mornings in Mexico*, DHL discusses the snake as a messenger to the rain-giving powers. The chant may also owe something to a Navajo rain prayer. See Clark 108–10.

201:20   **juggernaut car ... the outside world.** 'Juggernaut' comes from one of the names of Krishna, *jagannath*, a Hindi word meaning 'lord of the world'. Worshippers would throw themselves beneath the wheels of the giant car carrying the image of the god.

202:1   **Down came ... vessel had broken.** Cf. Tlaloc's dwarf-like assistants breaking great vessels to send rain to the earth. See Spence 49, 242–3.

203:28   *cuando ... perder?*" 'When it begins to rot?'

205:21   *Quién ... rester,*" 'Who knows! That remains to be seen.' 'And will continue so to remain' (Spanish, French).

209:10   **the white Anti-Christ** For the great evil figure prophesied to precede the Second Coming of Christ, see 1 John ii. 18–22 and iv. 1–3. Cf. Matthew xxiv. 1–24.

210:19   **out of ... and sucklings,**" Psalm viii. 2 (Book of Common Prayer).

212:23   *Verdad! Verdad!*" Literally 'truth'. Here the expression means approximately 'Have you really!' At 221:32 the meaning is approximately 'Are you not?'

214:32   **Pío Baroja novel ... stets verneint!** DHL read the novel *César o Nada* (1910) by Pío Baroja (1872–1956) while writing 'Q'. See *Letters*, iv. 452 ... 'I am the spirit that eternally denies' (German): Mephistopheles' identification of himself in Goethe's *Faust*, Part I, line 1338.

223:27   **fire rose** [223:19] ... **of darkness.** This passage echoes the myth of Quetzalcoatl's departure from Tula and his journey eastward. See Appendix I. When he immolated himself on Mt Orizaba – in another account, on the shore – his ashes rose to become birds of beautiful plumage. In a fragment of ancient poetry, the immolation ends thus:

> When the pyre had ceased to burn,
> Quetzalcoatl's heart came forth,
> Went up to heaven, and entered there.
> And the ancient ones say
> It was converted to the morning star ...

See Miguel León-Portilla, *Pre-Columbian Literatures of Mexico*, trans. Grace Lobanov and the author (Oklahoma, 1969), p. 42. See also Terry 496.

224:14 **feet of the Niña ... Santísima!** Santísima means 'Most Holy'. Some Mexican folk hymns speak of kissing the Virgin's feet or the soles of her feet.

225:21 **I travelled the longest journey.** A long and arduous journey awaited the souls of the Aztec dead, who at one place crossed the Plain of the Wind of Knives. These journeys were believed to imitate Quetzalcoatl's quest to the realm of the dead for assistance in creating mankind. See Spence 61–4; Caso 25, 58–65; León-Portilla, *Pre-Columbian Literatures*, p. 58; Seler, i. 618–67.

225:33 **the four winds ... the six.** See Appendix I, Spence 57–60 and Caso 10–11.

226:33 **his beak ... like a dragon.** See DHL's poem 'Humming-Bird' (*Complete Poems* 372).

227:18 **my mother ... in the moon.** The Virgin of Guadalupe, chief image of Mary in Mexico, stands on a crescent moon. Cf. the woman who has the moon under her feet in Revelation xii. In ancient Mexican mythology, the moon could be male or female, and in either case was a rival of the sun. See Spence 85–7, 308–9 and note on 233:24.

229:8 **Tlapaltepec [229:5] ... San Cristóbal** One place-name is real: San Cristóbal Zapotitlán, on the s.w. shore of Lake Chapala; others are distortions of real names: Jaramay – Jamay (though the location of 'Jaramay' is that of Jocotepec – see 317:4; Cuxcueco – Tuxcueco; Tuliapán – Tizapán. Cf. note on 81:2. Tlapaltepec appears to be a cross between Tlaquepaque and Jocotepec, villages in the locality. For a contrasting reponse to Mexican markets, written while DHL was in the midst of rewriting this novel, see 'Market Day', *Mornings in Mexico*.

233:24 **But the moonshine [233:12] ... said she.** The moon had many maleficent attributes in ancient Anáhuac. As Coyolxauhqui, sister of Huitzilopoch-tli, the moon led the stars in battle against him as the morning sun. He cut her in pieces and left her head on top of a hill, which may suggest for the moon a skull image. Tlazolteotl, goddess of filth and of sex as well, was sometimes worshipped in lunar form. See Spence 308–10 and Brundage 42, 138–9, 162–3.

233:31 **The corner ... excrement.** This sentence was excised in final proofs for E1, apparently not by DHL but by an editor or printer after a copy of these proofs were sent to Knopf. The sentence does appear in A1.

234:7 **Qué Niña!** 'What (a) Mistress!'

234:16 **Navajo women ... soul into it.** The explanation may have been a misunderstanding of a practice among Navajo weavers, but the story has been widely repeated.

236:8 **Itzpapalotl ... to herself.** Itzpapalotl (Obsidian Knife Butterfly), like many of the Aztec deities, filled conflicting roles. In one she was the knife of sacrifice itself, in another the terrifying and insatiable Earth Mother. But she was the double, also, of Xochiquetzal (Precious Flower), the lovely virgin who once presided over the lost paradise of Tamoanchan. Many of the legends about Xochiquetzal, in one of which she is the wife of Tlaloc the rain god, make her a beneficent fertility goddess. See notes on 62:14 and 370:33. See also Spence 223–8 and Brundage 159–62.

238:25   **cactus vegetable,** Tender young pads from the prickly pear are cleaned of thorns, cut up and cooked. In Spanish the vegetable is called *nopalitos.*

242:3   **sour milk rotten with thunder,** Cf. the folk belief that thunder causes milk to go sour.

243:36   *Muy chiquitas!*" 'Very small!'

245:4   **ruttled** An uncommon variant of 'rattled' (*A New English Dictionary on Historical Principles*, ed. Sir James A. H. Murray and others, 10 vols, 1884–1928).

247:2   **the Bishop.** The 'Bishop' of Guadalajara would have been an Arch-bishop. Francisco Orozco y Jiménez (1864–1936) was appointed in 1913. Law-rence gives his character the matrilineal segment of the name (247:25), but not the temperament of the real-life Archbishop, who was more like the 'Archbishop of Mexico' in this novel (262:17). Orozco y Jiménez challenged the authority of Governor Zuno of Jalisco, encouraged resistance to the government after the Cristero Rebellion and was expelled from the country in 1931.

247:5   **a "rebellion."** See note on 288:5.

247:8   **Knights of Cortés** In 'Q', DHL called this order the Knights of Columbus, the Catholic fraternity founded in 1882, whose original purpose of opposing the Masons extended in Mexico to resisting governmental control of the Church. Many of the members participated in the Cristero Rebellion.

247:28   **a 'national' church.** Conservative Catholics were uneasy from the first about Calles' presidency; during the Obregón administration most of them had supported de la Huerta in his rebellion. In the months when DHL was at work on *The Plumed Serpent* in Oaxaca, feelings were building up toward the eruption of the Cristero Rebellion in 1926. As for a 'national' church, DHL may have known something of the Mexican Catholic Apostolic Church, a schismatic body which rejected papal supremacy and clerical celibacy, and which had Calles' support in its defiance of the Roman Church. The schismatics, under the leadership of Patriarch José Joaquín Pérez, seized a Catholic church in Mexico City on 21 February 1925. The movement was never widespread, though vestiges of it remained for a few years. See Jean A. Meyer, *The Cristero Rebellion*, trans. Richard Southern (Cambridge, 1976), pp. 33–7.

248:28   **Natural Aristocrats of the World** Cf. the 'Foreword' DHL wrote in the autumn of 1921 for *Fantasia of the Unconscious* (1922).

249:3   **Thor and [248:34] ... of Freya,** Thor was the Teutonic god of thunder and war, from whose name we derive Thursday, the day on which Cipriano is installed as Huitzilopochtli (370:7). Wotan (Odin or Woden) was the principal god of some Germanic tribes, though below Thor in other pantheons. He taught mankind the secrets of better living, and he was the guide of the dead. Human sacrifices were offered to Wotan. In Norse lore Igdrasil was the universe seen as a prodigious ash-tree whose roots constituted the underworld and whose branches formed the sky. 'Druidic world ... mistletoe': the prophet-priests of the ancient Celts, the Druids, held mistletoe in veneration, and cut it from the sacred oak with a golden sickle. The Tuatha de Danaan (People of the Goddess Dana, people of faery) in mythic times wrested Ireland from the Fomorians, a preceding race of demi-gods; see 415:32. 'Hermes ... Mediterranean': Hermes was the herald and messenger of the Olympian gods, and also the guide of travellers. 'Ashtaroth to Tunis': Ashtaroth was one form of the name Astarte, the Great Mother worshipped under various titles in the Mediterranean. The inhabitants of Carthage, in what is now Tunisia, revered her as the protectress of their city. Cf. *Sea and Sardinia*, chap. II. 'Brahma unbroken to India': Brahma is both the supreme all-pervasive divine essence and the creator within the Hindu trinity, of which the other two are Vishnu the preserver and Shiva the destroyer. The supreme Brahma brought forth the lesser deity out of himself, thus breaking his completeness. 'oldest of dragons to China': serving at the command of the August Person of Jade, who created humanity, the four Dragon-Kings of the Chinese cosmos ruled the four seas and shared out the rain to each quarter of the globe. 'First Woman of Freya': in some versions of Teutonic myth, Freya was the wife of Wotan and queen of the Valkyries. It was she who welcomed into Valhalla the heroes slain in battle.

250:36 *monos y no más?"* 'Monkeys and nothing more?'

252:37 **the crime against the Holy Ghost.** See Matthew xii. 31–2.

253:29 **Judas figures ... Easter time.** See note on 262:4.

255:26 *Monos ... Affen!* 'We are monkeys. – You [familiar] are all monkeys!' (German).

255:34 *Vamos ... Vamos!"* 'Come! Let us make fools of ourselves! ... Come! Come!' The verb form happens to repeat the Spanish for 'monkey'. In MS (p. 459) the phrase reads 'Let the monkeys play at monkeyshines'.

256:3 *Mucho ... calor!"* 'It is very hot, Mistress! Very hot!'

258:8 **The dragon of ... the world.** Apocalyptic and Dantesque echoes in this poem may obscure others from lesser-known sources. The dragon suggests the fire-snakes which form the outer perimeter of the Aztec Sunstone. The dead may have been suggested by the *tzitzimime*, the sky demons of Aztec cosmogony, as the host of stars were held to be, who would descend in the last days to devour mankind. See Spence 324–6. But DHL had knowledge of these from other sources, possibly Seler. For his identification of the stars with the dead and speculation on the sky 'dragons', see Seler, iv. 27, 82–4.

258:40 **salamanders, in fire.** The popular belief that salamanders will not burn dates from early times. Aristotle states that the creature not only walks through fire but can quench it. The small amphibian with this supposed immunity has its name from a mythical reptile. In esoteric lore the creatures who inhabit the sphere of fire are called salamanders.

260:12 **the sign of the dragon,** This sign is not mentioned elsewhere in the novel.

261:32 **Punch ... harlequin.** The grotesque Punch probably descended from some demonic original ... The harlequin, the comic character in black domino mask and multicoloured tights, has been identified as the modern form of a demon known in medieval and earlier lore.

261:39 **the days of the dead** 1 November is the Feast of All Saints, 2 November the Feast of All Souls. 1 November is celebrated in Mexico as *El Día de los Angelitos* (Day of the Little Angels) (cf. 63:16–20), when the souls of children return; while 2 November (El Día de los Muertos – Day of the Dead) is set aside for the return of adult souls. Food and marigolds, the flower of the dead, are taken to family graves and a vigil is kept there all night. Sugar skulls and toy skeletons are sold in great quantitites. DHL was in Mexico at this season in 1924. Bynner (pp. 41–2) records DHL's feelings about the Day of the Dead.

262:4 **the scandal of the Holy Images** Several attacks were made on churches by anti-Catholic activists during the Obregón administration; the gravest was a bomb explosion near the high altar of the Basílica de Guadalupe. The famous image of the Virgin was unharmed. Another suggestion may have arisen from a practice at some of the Easter fiestas in which Judas tries to enter the church but is repelled. See Bynner 45–7.

262:18 **expulsion of all foreign priests ... Archbishop ... an Italian.** See 420:22ff. Obregón expelled an Italian Archbishop, a papal envoy to Mexico, in January 1923. Calles deported all foreign priests in February 1926. Attitudes and actions ascribed to Montes by DHL are close to those of Calles. A British diplomat described Calles' attitude in 1926 in words which could refer to Ramón: Calles approached 'the religious question in an apocalyptic and mystic spirit' (Meyer, *Cristero Rebellion*, p. 44).

267:11 **the Catholic Dames** The *Damas Católicas* were an influential and conservative association, the female counterpart of the Knights of Columbus.

267:19 **Palace ... Plaza de Armas.** The 17th-century Palacio de Gobierno, on the n. side of the plaza at the centre of Guadalajara, also called the Plaza de la Constitución and the Plaza Mayor.

267:21 **a house in the colony,** Districts of Mexican cities are often called *colonias*. Cipriano may be speaking of the Colonia Reforma, a wealthy residential district of Guadalajara.

268:11 *La Cucaracha*: A revolutionary ballad about the misadventures of a cockroach during the struggle. Satirical commentary on political figures often circulated as verses of this song. Each revolutionary group had its favourite ballad: 'La Cucaracha' was preferred by the followers of Pancho Villa.

269:31 *Vapor-rub,* A salve for cuts, colds and minor ailments.

269:36 **teach thee at thy American school?"** The shift in the presumed Spanish from formal address (the *usted* form) to familiar (*tu*) suggests that Ramón has been speaking in a teasing manner with his sons up to this point. In normal conversation a child would address his father as *usted* and the father would use *tu*.

269:37 **Ciprianito,** Diminutive of Cipriano.

270:4 **Carrasco ... *Espinita!"** *Carrasco* applies to several kinds of trees and shrubs. The Spanish translates as 'Well, goodbye! Mr Thorn Littlethorn!'

273:6 **nest of the cosmic dragons.** Cf. 'The Hopi Snake Dance', *Mornings in Mexico*.

276:34 **the gorgeous Puebla cathedral.** One of the best examples in Mexico of Spanish Renaissance architecture, designed by Juan de Herrera (*c.*1530–97), architect of the Escorial.

277:24 **Month of Mary [277:18] ... day of Corpus Christi** May is the month of the Virgin ... Corpus Christi, the first Thursday after Trinity Sunday, fell on 31 May in 1923, during DHL's residence in Chapala. See *Letters*, iv. 450–2.

280:9 **James, and John [279:38] ... Soledad** St James (Santiago), San Juan, San Marcos, San Felipe el Apóstol and San Cristóbal (St Christopher) are favourite saints in the Spanish-speaking world. Santiago is the patron saint of Spain, and San Cristóbal the special protector of voyagers and explorers. St Ann and St Joachim were the parents of the Virgin, according to tradition. St Teresa of Ávila (1515–82) was the reformer of the Order of Carmelite nuns and close associate of St John of the Cross. St Francis is probably the popular Francis Xavier (1506–52), often portrayed holding a cross (282:31). St Anthony of Padua (1195–1231) is a popular saint with wonder-working powers. María de la Purísima Concepción (Mary of the Immaculate Conception) is still one of the most venerated images in the parish church of Chapala. The title 'Refugio' belongs to the Virgin in her role as the refuge of sinners, and the title 'Soledad' presents her as the Sorrowing Mother.

282:23 **Sacred Heart, the well-known figure** Another prized image of the Chapala parish church. In later years the church was dedicated to the Sacred Heart.

284:11 **Island of the Scorpions ... the lake.** The Isla de los Alacranes is a real island in the Lake of Chapala.

285:19 **the [lake-shore] ... and villages** DHL revised TS (chap. XVIII, p. 31) to read: 'the village looked like a mirage, with its trees and villages ...' The mistake was not corrected in proof.

285:25 **There was a crackling,** This burning of images may reflect the Aztec practice of despatching messengers to the sun through sacrifice, as well as the new-fire ceremony at the close of an Aztec solar cycle.

288:5 **"rebellion" in Colima ... Generals Fulano and Tulano,** There appears to be no historical original for this rebellion. The only uprising of consequence during DHL's association with Mexico was the de la Huerta rebellion (see Appendix III) ... Fulano is analogous to 'John Doe', and Tulano is DHL's echoic repetition.

289:10 **Está." '**He is here.'

290:11 **San Pablo ... Ahuajijic."** The first may be San Juan Cosalá, a few miles w. of Chapala on the lake shore ... Ahuajijic is the actual Ajijic.

290:39 **He is Zapotec ... his men are Zapotecans,** Cipriano and his soldiers have acquired some of the attributes DHL admired in the Zapotecs of Oaxaca. See 'The Mozo', *Mornings in Mexico*. DHL wrote of the Zapotecs as 'small but proud Indians' (letter to Quintanilla, 11 November 1924) and as 'quite fierce' (letter to Murry, 15 November 1924). But in this letter, and in another to Murry two days later, he also spoke of them as adopting the scheming ways of Mexican politicians; see note on 38:2. See also letter to William Hawk, 14 November 1924.

296:37 *Creo que sí!*" 'I think so!'

297:38 **of evening.** At this point in 'Q' (pp. 281–2), Kate dips a forefinger in the blood of the slain conspirator, at Ramón's command, and lifts her hand to offer the blood to the sinking sun.

298:28 *Viene... viene!*" 'He is coming! Don Ramón is coming! He is coming!'

306:2 **Marriage by Quetzalcoatl.** Nuttall argues that during a period of history 'when the Aztec race was jointly governed by a priest, personifying the heaven, and a priestess, "his wife and sister," who personified the earth, some form of sacred marriage rite must have been annually performed' at the start of the rainy season (pp. 101–2).

308:34 **a great Fascista, the reactionary Knights of Cortés** DHL's assumption that Fascist organizations existed in Mexico at this time, and that the Italian Black Shirt was their emblem (144:29), is premature. Fascist influence was just beginning to be felt. Calles had a certain sympathy with Mussolini, fostered by his trip to Europe in 1924, and he imitated some of Mussolini's methods. On the other hand, Antonio Díaz Soto y Gama, leader of the National Agrarian Party, accused the de la Huertistas of being fascists, with their Church and conservative support. Organized Fascist groups, the most prominent being the Gold Shirts, appeared in the early 1930s.

310:38 **pillar of cloud** See Exodus xiii. 21–2 and xiv. 19–20.

312:4 **My demon lover!"** Cf. Coleridge, 'Kubla Khan' (1798), l. 16.

314:2 **ce n'est... qui coûte** 'It is only the first step which is difficult' (French).

316:27 **categorical imperative!** The principle of behaviour recommended by Immanuel Kant: 'Act only on that maxim through which you can at the same time will that it should become a universal law' (*Fundamental Principles of the Metaphysic of Morals*, 1785).

317:4 **near the State of Colima: to Jaramay.** While DHL plainly envisages Jocotepec at the w. end of Lake Chapala as his fictional Jaramay, the town is in reality a long way from the State of Colima.

321:15 **to be addressed in the third person.** Probably an allusion to the use in Spanish formal address of the *usted* construction. While this is not third person as such, it is a shortening of *vuestra merced* – Your Grace – and might be taken as an 'elusive' manner of addressing a superior.

322:5 **the beautiful cochineal red.** A colour worn by the Aztec nobility. The dye is made from the dried bodies of a small insect gathered mainly from the prickly pear.

322:35 **the opening of the flowers ... the goddess who will come,"** This passage, in conjunction with others to the end of the chapter, is a notable example of DHL's synthesis of material from Spence (see pp. 147–96 and 223–8). None of this flower symbolism appears in 'Q'. Kate as 'First Flower' (323:37) assimilates qualities of many fertility deities. Xochiquetzal was the goddess of flowers, but also the wife either of Tlaloc the rain god or of Cinteotl the maize god; she was a companion of the sun, with her dwelling in Tamoanchan, the source of maize. Aztec syncretism went on to identify her as the female of the original progenitor pair of deities, Tonacacihuatl, and also with Chicomecoatl, another goddess of maize and sister of Tlaloc. Itzpapalotl too had flower and maize attributes. Tlazolteotl, severally the mother of the gods, the goddess of love, of the moon and even of excrement, was militant like Kate, with a battle of flowers and phallic rites preceding the sacrifice of a victim at one of her festivals. She was impregnated by Huitzilopochtli, who thus fathered Cinteotl. (Cf. DHL's comments on her in 'The Mozo', *Mornings in Mexico*.) For details of Kate's costume borrowed from Pueblo sources, see DHL's drawing of Santo Domingo dancers, in *The Letters of D. H. Lawrence*, ed. Aldous Huxley (1932), opp. p. 636 and 'Dance of the Sprouting Corn', *Mornings in Mexico*. See also 433:23ff.

327:39   **Pero una ... Verdad!"** 'But such a fair little flower! And it bloomed in my shade, my friend.' 'You are a very lucky man!' 'Yes indeed!' A probable play on words: *zarco* refers to a 'fair-skinned' or a 'white' person; in reference to eyes and objects in nature it means 'light blue' or 'clear blue' – Kate has hazel eyes (81:29). DHL appears to be alluding to the light race / dark race contrast and also to the blue flowers in Kate's wedding dress (328:22).

330:7   **Anoint ... your hair."** Spence refers to a ritual hair-washing in the worship of an Aztec god (p. 216). Among other American Indian tribes, for example the Hopi, this ritual is a step in the marriage ceremony.

332:6   **a civil marriage ... same house together?"** In Mexico two marriage ceremonies take place, one in the church and one required by civil law to make the union legal. Kate and Cipriano have so far spoken only their 'church' vows.

336:27   **Oye ... Oye!"** 'Hear ye! Hear ye! Hear ye! Hear ye!'

338:32   **a strange looming** [338:24] **... rather frightening** While the statue appears to be entirely of DHL's own imagining, it is reminiscent of a description in Bernal Díaz (chap. XCII) of the statues crowning the great temple in Tenochtitlan.

339:24   **No man ... Him not.** A reversal of Jesus' claims in the Gospel of John, e.g. 'As the Father knoweth me, even so know I the Father' (x. 15, AV).

341:24   **A man** [341:13] **... the light.** A synthesis of traditional and imagined elements, the traditional stemming both from European and native American lore. Allusion to the four humours is likely. For more of DHL's fascination with this and other facets of the symbolism of four, see *Apocalypse*, ed. Kalnins, pp. 101–49. Four is the most sacred number among American Indians. Each of the four directions has its sacred colour, though the colour of a specific direction varies from tribe to tribe and from one myth to another within a tribe. See Caso 10–11, 64–5, 85. DHL's blue, red, yellow and white, which he originally wrote in MS as blue, gold, red and black, are repeated later in the Huitzilopochtli ceremony, except that blue becomes green (372:15), which is Kate's colour, in order to unite the colour symbolism of the deified couple.

341:27   **the Unknown God pours His Spirit** Cf. Acts ii. 17–18.

347:9   **no body without blood ... Shylock found out."** See *The Merchant of Venice*, IV. i. 299–312.

347:33 **the two thieves** [347:30] ... **God of Pity.** Mark xv. 27, Luke xxiii. 39–43. In TSR, DHL struck out some paragraphs which had prepared for these images; see Textual apparatus 347:17, 18 and 22.

349:34 **the Fish ... The cock rose,** For a TSR excision which illuminates this passage, see Textual apparatus entry for 348:32.

350:20 **[clay] flutes** DHL wrote 'reed-flutes' in MS (p. 627). He probably had in mind the *chirimía*, a clay flute from pre-Conquest days still played at Mexican fiestas.

353:4 **Kate ... went also to the funeral.** Many cultures, besides Latin America, share the practice – apparently based on a belief that women cannot bear so much grief – that they attend the funeral mass but do not accompany the men to the burial.

354:34 **Je m'en ... mon père!"** 'I don't give a damn about your soul, father!' (French).

355:6 **paradise ... hearts of the living."** DHL's attraction to this belief goes back at least to 1912. See 'Everlasting Flowers: For a Dead Mother' (*Complete Poems* 226–7).

363:10 **the tarantula sprang ... the secret.** Cf. Nietzsche, *Thus Spake Zarathustra* (1883), chap. XXIX.

364:34 **The shield and spear dance ... in the barracks' yard,** Some of these dances are analogous to those discussed in 'Indians and Entertainment', *Mornings in Mexico*.

364:37 **Then, naked ... red earth-powder,** Body paints made of earth pigments and plant substances confer ceremonial powers. In Indian pueblos divided by the moiety system into the Summer or Squash People and the Winter or Turquoise People, the bare torsos of the Squash-People male dancers are painted with an orange-coloured ochre.

366:36 **your thousands and your tens of thousands."** See 1 Samuel xviii. 6–8, and DHL's play *David*, Scenes IX and X.

368:22 **like a pearl in black wine,** Powdered pearl suspended in liquid is believed in many parts of the world to have magical or curative powers.

369:9 **mountain lion,** The mountain lion (American puma) had little if any sacred significance in Aztec belief, but see DHL's poem 'Mountain Lion' (*Complete Poems* 401–2).

370:33 **Malintzi ... giving her a name.** No such goddess existed in the Aztec pantheon, but the name has a curious history in Mexican lore. The Indian mistress of Cortés took the name Marina when she was baptised and was thereafter known as Doña Marina. She served as interpreter between Cortés and the Indian leaders. In Nahuatl her name was pronounced 'Malin', –tzin being added as a suffix of respect. Montezuma, as Bernal Díaz heard him, always addressed Cortés himself as Malinche. In this form the word found its way into Mexican folklore with a number of meanings. Doña Marina herself as 'Malinche' has always been seen both as the mother of the Mexican race and the betrayer of her own people to the

Spaniards. The painter Orozco saw her as the Mexican Eve, portraying her and Cortés in a mural as the progenitors of the Mexican race; Octavio Paz explores her relation to the Mexican temperament in the chapter 'Sons of La Malinche', in *The Labyrinth of Solitude*. Terry (p. 497) translates the name as 'sorceress', which is not strictly correct, but Malinche has been identified with La Llorona, the dangerous ghost who weeps in the night at crossroads for her lost children. Since Kate is to be 'First Woman' of a new race, the name is fitting for her elevated status, with the appropriate reversal that in this second 'Conquest' the woman is European and the man 'Red Indian'. At Taos pueblo a *matachín* dance that employs a *malinche* is sometimes held during Christmas. DHL may have been acquainted with another legend of Doña Marina: that she was born on a day whose sign was one of the combinations of *malinalli* (grass) and that she chose the Christian name Marina to stay close to her indigenous name. In 'Q', Cipriano offers the clearest exposition of Kate's divine function. She is to be the 'living Malinchi, the white goddess, the mother of rain', that is, the 'mother of gentle rain, which Mexico needs, not our heavy, breaking Tlaloc rain' (p. 313).

372:9 **the heavy drum … sinister notes.** Cf. 'Turkey-Cock' (*Complete Poems* 369–72) and Bernal Díaz, chap. CLII.

372:32 **painted in … band of yellow.** Bands of colour identify many Aztec deities in the codices. For instance, Xiuhtecuhtli, the Fire God, was often painted with a yellow countenance, and one of his hymns was entitled 'Song of the Yellow-faced'. See Spence 270–3. In this same section of Spence, Xiuhtecuhtli exhibits most of the characteristics attributed to Cipriano here, such as 'Lord of the Four Quarters', and, through the colour green, 'Master of the Grass'. The green parrot feathers suggest also the sacred green feathers of the quetzal bird. Huitzilopochtli was a rain god in that he presided over the beginning of the wet season. See Spence 367.

373:13 *First Song of Huitzilopochtli.* Much of this poem stands as DHL wrote it in 'Q', before he had read Spence, but some nuances appear to have their source in this author, in his discussion of Huitzilopochtli and that of Tezcatlipoca. See Spence 65–116. León-Portilla notes that the 'song of Huitzilopochtli' was 'one of the most important hymns in the Aztec religious cult', and says that it was 'chanted in the form of a dialogue' (*Pre-Columbian Literatures*, pp. 64–5).

373:34 **serpent-yellow shining of my sun.** Huitzilopochtli's weapon in slaying his sister the moon and his brothers the stars was a fire-serpent. See Spence 76ff. and 211.

376:6 **lord of the watches of the night** According to Spence, quoting Seler, Huitzilopochtli, in the form of Xiuhtecuhtli the Fire God, was lord of the first hour of the night (365).

380:4 **Malintzi … no more.** The role of Malintzi as confessor in this poem is reminiscent of the Aztec practice of confession. Tlazolteotl presided over the individual's confession of sins, which was allowed him only once in a lifetime. See Spence 165–6.

389:33 **the wings of the Morning."** Psalm cxxxix. 9.

392:11 **a rug of jaguar skins.** Cf. the jaguar-skin coverings for the seats of Huitzilopochtli and Xochiquetzal in Spence 67, 188. See Brundage 83–4 for the night-time symbolism of this animal.

393:20 **becoming like a little child."** Cf. Mark x. 14–15 and Luke xviii. 15–17 ['as a little child'] and Matthew xviii. 3–4 ['become as little children']. See also 442:26.

393:24 *buena de noche*: **good by night.** No such name for this flower has been located. DHL may have misheard *reina de noche* ('queen of night') and confused it with *huele de noche* ('fragrant by night'), widespread common names sometimes applied in different regions to the same flower. He probably had the French *belle de nuit* in mind. See Bynner 148 and 'The Flying-Fish' in *St. Mawr*, ed. Finney, p. 207.

403:15 **the Romeros ... early days of the Conquest.** DHL may have noted in Bernal Díaz that one Alonso Romero fought with Cortés and later became a rich resident of Veracruz (chaps. XLII and CCV).

403:39 **Ramón was ... away in Sonora.** Northern Mexico was the source of the greatest revolutionary ferment and produced most revolutionary leaders. Coahuila was the home of Madero and Carranza, and Chihuahua of Pancho Villa, but by DHL's time men from Sonora were prominent, especially Obregón, Calles and de la Huerta.

404:18 **Quetzalcoatl in Puebla ... Malintzi in Guadalupe.** Cholula, just outside Puebla, was a centre of Quetzalcoatl worship. The Cathedral of Puebla is the greatest modern religious monument in the area. See Terry 518–21. The great *teocalli*, the supreme temple of the Aztecs, with Huitzilopochtli as their tribal god, once stood on the site now occupied by the Cathedral in Mexico City. To restore a goddess such as Malintzi to the Basílica de Guadalupe would be to reverse the action of the Christians. The apparition of the dark Virgin of Guadalupe on the hill of Tepeyac in 1531 took place where an indigenous goddess had been worshipped. Father Sahagún, recorder of much data on the religion that his own replaced, says that this goddess was the highest female deity of the ancient Mexicans, called Cihuacoatl (Serpent Woman) and also Tonantzin (Our Mother).

406:31 **overland from Tepic ... stopped by floods.** In the autumn of 1923, accompanied by the Danish artist Kai Götzsche, DHL made a similar arduous journey down the west coast of Mexico. See *Letters*, iv. 502–15.

407:22 **à la ... à la guerre!"** 'One must take what comes' (French).

413:31 **I cast my bread upon the waters.** Ecclesiastes xi. 1 ['Cast thy bread ...'].

414:32 **the old prehistoric humanity [414:22] ... its own.** DHL took seriously the myth of Atlantis and of Lemuria, a sunken Pacific continent. See 'Foreword' to *Fantasia of the Unconscious*. His knowledge of the theories concerning these places came from several sources: Spence in *The Problem of Atlantis* (1924) and *The Problem of Lemuria* (1933); and Blavatsky. Nuttall touches on the topic (p. 446). In the present passage DHL follows part of the argument of Thomas Belt in *The Naturalist in Nicaragua* (1874), which hypothesises that a vast volume of the earth's water was once trapped in glaciers and that mean sea level was as much as a thousand feet lower than it is today. Belt speculates that both Atlantis and a Pacific continent existed and that the Nahuatl-speaking peoples migrated to Mexico from the latter.

415:18 **The Mexicans** [415:9] ... **new being.** The imaginative concept of a fusion between the inheritors of an antediluvian consciousness and later humanity begins with reference to the New World in the early versions of DHL's American literature essays, in particular the essay on Cooper's Leatherstocking novels.

416:35 *Noli me tangere,* 'Touch me not' John xx. 17 (Vulgate).

418:1 **the rider on the white horse ... the red.** See Revelation vi. 1–4, and also *Apocalypse*, ed. Kalnins, pp. 101–5.

419:39 **San Juan Bautista ... Black Saviour,** Whether DHL had a specific church in mind is uncertain, but this incident of the 'Black Saviour' relates to a tradition in Mesoamerican Catholicism relevant to any concept of a native revival. Besides the dark-skinned Virgin of Guadalupe, several other holy images of the region are distinctly Indian in colouring. Several dark Christs are worshipped along the coast of Mexico below Veracruz, in an area where in pre-Conquest times a god called Ixtlilton (The Black One) was worshipped. Perhaps the most famous Cristo Negro of Mesoamerica is in Esquipulas, Guatemala, whose cult probably continues that of a black rain god or a black Tezcatlipoca among the Maya. Many Mexican Indians make pilgrimages to this shrine. During DHL's time, a replica of this Cristo was venerated in a church in San Juan Bautista (now Villa Hermosa), Tabasco. Frieda also reports having seen a black Christ during the Lawrences' stay in Mexico; see *"Not I, But the Wind ..."* (Santa Fe, 1934), p. 156.

420:15 **curious round banners ... a black point.** The Aztecs had feather flags; see Clark 131. The description given here is reminiscent of the life-pole carried by dancers at Pueblo Indian festivals.

420:19 **General Narciso Beltrán ... for the Church.** Certain generals did join in the Cristero Rebellion in 1926, but no military leader has been identified as a model for Beltrán.

422:7 **She realised ... ecstatic Aphrodite.** One of DHL's favourite analogies for clitoral orgasm was the foam-born Aphrodite, best known from Botticelli's painting.

424:3 **The Sons of the Morning!** Cf. Isaiah xiv. 12, where Lucifer is called 'son of the morning', and note on 91:35.

426:2 **Here!** The last chapter of the novel was the only one DHL did not entitle, even in final proofs, until Secker asked him to do so. He replied by postcard from Baden Baden on 12 November 1925: 'Call the last chapter just *Here!*' See L. D. Clark, 'D. H. Lawrence and the American Indian,' *D. H. Lawrence Review*, ix (Fall 1976), 316.

426:23 **the boat of Dionysos ... the vine sprouting.** Dionysus as a boy was kidnapped by pirates, and as they sailed away the ship stopped suddenly in mid-ocean and vines began to wind up the mast. The bewildered pirates leaped into the sea and became dolphins. DHL is recalling an illustration he had seen early in 1916, of Dionysus in a boat 'with a white sail and the mast a tree with grapes, sailing over a yellow sea, with dark, keen, joyful fish' (*The Letters of D. H. Lawrence*, ed. George Zytaruk and James T. Boulton, Cambridge, 1981, ii. 517 and n. 2).

426:31 **Lot's wife,** See Genesis xix. 15–26.

427:8 **white sail** From here to 431:14, the TS pages were done on DHL's machine, as were the first five chapters and the fragments of VI and VII; see Introduction, pp. xxxiii–xxxv and note on 98:2. Apparently DHL completely rewrote these pages and had his new text typed – or possibly typed it himself – and discarded the original typed pp. 3–9; these were replaced by pp. 3–9, 9a–9c. However, in final proofs for E1, DHL again revised heavily from 428:34 to 430:4. Then, through 433:17 all states of the text are extant, including the TS pages from the Curtis Brown typing, up to 433:1, where about two and a third pages of TS are again from DHL's machine; no MS text is extant for the portion from 433:17 to 434:22. All texts appear again from 434:22 to 436:23, the Curtis Brown typing with the others except for the last few lines of the passage. From 436:18 to the end of the novel the Curtis Brown typing was all discarded in favour of the later TS text, and the MS text was completely rejected, though not destroyed, for a total rewriting from 436:23 to the close of the book. The complexity of this textual history is reflected in the Textual apparatus entries for this chapter.

430:36 **nochebuenas** The *flor de Nochebuena* ('flower of Christmas Eve') is named for the time of year when it blooms. Its English name *poinsettia* derives from Joel R. Poinsett, US Ambassador to Mexico in the early 19th century, who sent the first seeds to the USA in 1828. See also 'Market Day', *Mornings in Mexico*.

437:2 **a berth from Veracruz ... last day of November.** DHL had sailed from Veracruz for Southampton on 22 November 1923. (At the end of 'Q', Kate is in Chapala packing to leave for Europe.)

440:10 **Están tocando!"** 'They are playing!'

440:38 **Ya? ... Ya, Patrón!"** Literally 'already', this word serves a number of colloquial purposes. In this instance the English counterpart would be 'All right?' or 'Do you understand?' and the affirmative reply is a declarative repetition of the same word.

441:11 **Holy Ghost ... the cloven flame** See Acts ii. 1–4.

443:25 **Cousin,** This is not a Spanish usage but an English one, now uncommon: 'a term of intimacy, friendship, or familiarity' (*A New English Dictionary*, ed. Murray).

443:33 **Verdad! Verdad!"** The force of the expression here is 'Yes! Yes!'

444:24 **Te quiero mucho!** 'I love you!'

GLOSSARY OF SELECTED SPANISH TERMS

adobe: Bricks moulded of mud and straw and dried in the sun, the native building material of Hispanic North America.

aguador: Water-carrier. In Mexican towns without running water an *aguador* carries water for hire or sells it in the streets.

aguardiente: Literally 'burning water'. Brandy or any other strong distilled spirits, such as *tequila* or *mescal* (q.v.).

alameda: A grove or ornamental planting of *álamos*, in English 'cottonwoods'. A boulevard or plaza is often so named in Hispanic America.

ambiente: Environment or surroundings.

azotea: A flat roof.

bagre: Catfish.

banderillero: The *torero* who places in the shoulder muscles of the bull the *banderillas*, short darts so called from the streamers, 'little flags', on the shaft.

bote: A bucket or can of almost any size.

cajeta: A viscous Mexican candy whose main ingredient is browned milk, so named for the 'little, round box' of thin wood in which it is packed. The best-known variety is produced in Celaya.

calabacita: A squash or sometimes a gourd, literally 'little pumpkin'.

caldo: Any thick soup or stew.

camote: Sweet potato or yam.

canoa: Although the cognate of English 'canoe', the term in the Lake Chapala region is applied to a large partially covered wooden boat with a tall mast and single sail.

cargador: Anyone handling cargo; stevedore, longshoreman.

centavo: Equivalent to English 'penny' or American 'cent', one hundredth part of a peso. It was worth half an American cent.

charales: Plural of *charal*, a tiny almost translucent fish abundant in Lake Chapala and prized as a delicacy.

charro: A horseman of the ranching regions of Mexico whose costume of tight-fitting jacket, trousers and large hat is elaborately decorated with braid and silver conchos.

chica: Feminine form of *chico*, small. Common designation for young girls.

chile: Hot peppers of several varieties much eaten in Hispanic America, and also meat dishes prepared with this pepper. The usual English spelling is 'chili'.

criada: A female servant.

cuartelazo: Also '*cuartelada*', a military conspiracy to overthrow a government, said to be planned in a *cuartel*, barracks, and ordinarily initiated with a pronouncement.

despedida: A farewell.

dueña: Mistress of a household or owner of a business establishment, also a chaperone of young girls.

dulce: Sweet, both adjective and noun, including the designation for candy or sometimes for dessert.

enchilada: Mexican dish of meat or cheese wrapped in a corn tortilla and baked in a chile sauce.

esposa: Wife.

fifí: Mexican popular term for an idle and foppish young man.

fonda: Inn or hotel.

fresno: Ash-tree.

gachupín: A derogatory name for Spaniards in Mexican Spanish. See note on 36:24.

hacendado/hacienda: The proprietor and his large, sometimes vast, estate. Chief target of the agrarian laws and as a class scorned by the revolutionaries.

huaraches: Sandals of braided leather, the common footwear of Mexican peasants.

Jefe/Jefatura: In full *Jefe político*, the chief political officer of a region, appointed by the central government, and the headquarters from which he operates.

machete: A long heavy knife used for cutting vegetation or as a weapon.

mantilla: A lacy scarf worn over the head and shoulders.

masa: A dough of corn meal, water, and a little limestone, from which *tortillas* are made.

mescal: Also spelled '*mezcal*', a liquor distilled from the harvested core of several varieties of agave. See also *tequila*.

mesquite: A thorny deciduous tree of arid America, with acacia-like leaves and bearing long pods of bean-like seeds.

metate: A large flat stone with a slight concavity on which corn is ground or vegetables pulped by grating with a small stone held in the hand.

mozo: A male servant usually employed in menial tasks.

música: Not only music in the general sense but also a band such as a military band.

nopal: The prickly pear cactus common in arid America. The tender young pads are dethorned, sliced and cooked as a vegetable, called *nopalitos*.

norte: North, but also a strong cold north wind, like 'norther' in American English.

novedades: Novelties.

obrero: Worker.

ocote: A pitch pine widely used to make torches in Mexico.

palo blanco: Literally 'white stick'; in northern Mexico 'white wood', and also called *palo dulce*: sweet wood. A bush with white sweet-smelling flowers hanging in clusters.

patrón/patrona: The master and mistress of a household with servants, or the proprietor or manager of any business establishment.

pelado: 'Peeled' or in any sense barren of cover, applied with distaste to the peasant class in Mexico.

peso: The Mexican unit of currency, consisting of one hundred centavos. In the 1920s the peso was worth 50c. (USA).

petate: A straw mat for the floor, used as a bed among the peons.

picador: The mounted *torero* who goads the bull by pricking his shoulder muscles with a lance.

pitahaya: The soft pulpy fruit of a giant cactus growing in the desert parts of northern Mexico.

planta: Used in both senses as in English: an electric plant or any green plant.

poncho: Sometimes a synonym for *sarape*, but usually a similar blanket-like cloak from South America.

portal: Not used quite as the English 'portal', more nearly like 'arcade'. The plural is *portales*.

pulque/pulquería: A fermented drink and the bar where it is served. A liquid called *agua miel*, honey-water, is drawn by suction from the centre of an agave plant, then allowed to ferment.

real: From the word for 'royal', a coin in Spanish colonial times but in the 20th century one-eighth of a *peso*, for which no coin exists: the same as the American 'bit', one-eighth of a dollar, also not represented by an actual coin.

reina: Queen.

tamales: Plural of *tamal*. Typically a dish made by moulding a mush-like corn dough around chile meat, wrapping the roll in a corn shuck and steaming it.

té: Tea.

tejocote: A medium-sized tree of the rose family with rough bark and thorny branches, whose round greenish-yellow fruit is eaten raw or used in jam.

tepache: A lightly fermented drink of pineapple, sugar and water.

tequila: A liquor distilled from the harvested cores of *Agave tequilana Weber*, mostly in the Mexican State of Jalisco. See also *mescal*.

toreador: An obsolete word for *torero*.

tortilla: A flat bread made by patting dough into round cakes and cooking them on a griddle.

tostón: A Mexican coin equal to fifty *centavos*, half a *peso*.

zaguán: A long entry-way or vestibule.

zapote: A medium-sized tree of the *saptacea* family, with a greenish-yellow fruit whose flesh is creamy and sweet.

zopilote: Buzzard or vulture.

TEXTUAL APPARATUS

TEXTUAL APPARATUS

The following symbols are used to distinguish states of the text:

MS = Autograph manuscript
TS = Typescript
TSR = Typescript revision by DHL
G = Galley proofs, first English edition
E1 = First English edition
A1 = First American edition

All subsequent editions in DHL's lifetime reproduced *E1* and *A1*.

For chapter VI and the first part of chapter VII (up to 116:29), substantive variants from a fragment of superseded typescript have been recorded; see note on 98:2. These readings follow all other variants. The following symbols are employed for this fragment:

TS1 = Typescript fragment
TSR1 = Ribbon copy typescript revision by DHL
TCCR1 = Carbon copy typescript revision by DHL

The following symbols are used editorially:

Ed. = Editor
Om. = Omitted
P = New paragraph
/ = Line or page break resulting in a punctuation, hyphenation or spelling error, and also for a line break in poetry
~ = Repeated word in recording an accidental variant

The apparatus records variants for all parts of the text retained into the published work and for shorter passages rejected in *TS* or *G*. Readings adopted from the base-text (*MS*) appear within the square bracket with no symbol, unless the same variant recurs in a later text, in which case both source-symbols appear. When a reading later than *MS* has been preferred, it appears with its source-symbol within the square bracket; rejected readings follow the bracket in chronological order, with their first source recorded. Unless otherwise noted, a reading continues throughout the subsequent states of the text.

In order to reduce the difficulty of tracing DHL's revisions, some passages rejected in *TS* or *G* (e.g. 427:9) are printed with variants internally recorded inside braces and, if the entry is more than 300 words, in a column extending to the left-hand margin. When variants occur in revisions which replace these passages, they are indicated by the note '*see also following entries to* . . .'.

7:2 Bull-fight] BULL-FIGHT *E1*
Bull-Fight *A1*

7:7 continent] Continent *TS*

7:24 *camiones Ed.*] *camions MS*
Camions *TS*

7:24 *Toreo Ed.*] *Torero MS see notes*

7:28 Oh] ~, *G*

7:34 he more than anybody] more
than anybody *TS* more than
anybody he *TSR*

8:1 car *TSR*] taxi *MS*

8:14 life] Life *TS*

8:15 took] took the *TS*

8:15 entrance] ~, *G*

8:21 on. *P* "Feeling] ~. "Feeling *G*

8:24 yet] *Om. TS*

8:24 the lout] he *TS* the fellow *TSR*

8:27 counter-slips] counter-/ slips
TS counterslips *G*

8:30 beetle-trap] beetle trap *TS*

8:39 thrilling! *MS, A1*] ~, *G*

9:13 mottled *TSR*] sat on *MS*

9:14 below *TSR*] below our party
MS

9:14 sanded; *TSR*] ~, *MS*

9:16 pairs] a pair *A1*

9:18 Shade,'] ~' *TS*

9:19 amphitheatre *TSR*] concrete
amphitheatre *MS*

9:27 still *TSR*] still it *MS*

9:30 the audience *TSR*] it *MS*

9:35 marshmallows *TSR*] candy *MS*

10:2 skimming meteor-like] ~, ~,
G

10:2 moment,] ~ *G*

10:17 knee] knees *TS*

10:18 definite] definitely *TS*

10:22 but] and *TS*

10:24 said *TSR*] came *MS*

10:29 a] tae *TS* the *TSR*

10:29 will] would *G*

10:33 bands *TSR*] band *MS*

10:36 These musicians *TSR*] They
MS

10:36 dark-grey] dark grey *TS*

10:40 *música Ed.*] "musica" *MS*

11:2 But] But the *TS*

11:8 impending:] ~; *TS*

11:9 crowd] crowds *TS*

11:10 bands, *TSR*] bands were *MS*

11:10 still *TSR*] and they *MS*

11:12 *La música! La música! Ed.*] La
musica! La musica! *MS*

11:13 The] the *TS*

11:17 *their TSR*] their *MS*

11:18 present *TSR*] there *MS*

11:19 *Música pagada toca mal tono Ed.*]
Musica pagada toca mal tono
MS Musica...tono TSR

11:21 *La música! La música! Ed.*] La
musica! La musica! *MS La
musica! La musica! TSR La
musica! La musica! G*

11:21 violent:] ~. *TS*

11:22 *La música! Ed.*] La musica!
MS La musica! TSR La musica!
G

11:23 yell: the *TSR*] ~. The *MS*

11:24 City! *TSR*] ~. *MS*

11:27 good! *TSR*] ~. *MS*

11:33 *Música pagada toca mal tono Ed.*]
Musica pagada toca mal tono
MS Musica ... tono G

11:35 half-past *TS*] half past *MS*

11:36 unknown] given *TS*

12:8 her] the *TS*

12:10 bolshevist *TSR*] *Om. MS*

12:14 *Muy bien, Señor, muy bien! G*]
Muy bien, señor, muy bien!
MS Muy ... Señor ... bien!
TSR

12:22 off?] ~. *A1*

12:25 Mexicans] Mexican *G*

12:34 *off*] off *TS*

12:35 emphatically] ~, *G*

13:7 re-iterated] reiterated *A1*

13:10 Oh home] ~, ~ *G*

13:10 Oh land] ~, ~ *TS*

13:17 sodden] sudden *G*

13:17 had] had had *TS*

13:19 pale] white *TS*

13:20 shoulder] shoulders *TS*

13:26 glared *TSR*] looked *MS*

13:28 *en famille TSR*] intimate *MS*

13:31 *not TSR*] not *MS*

13:32 there.— *TSR*] ~. *MS*

13:32 how] how to *TS*
14:8 Mexican] ~, *G*
14:10 uniforms *E1*] uniform *MS*
14:18 salutes] salut *TS* salute *TSR*
14:19 disgust. In] ~. *P* In *TS*
14:21 tortoise-shell *TSR*] tortoiseshell *MS*
14:26 effeminate-looking] effeminate looking *TS*
14:34 Then there] There *TS*
14:34 *Ah!*] AH! *TS* Ah! *G*
15:5 take the leap *TSR*] vault over *MS*
15:6 went,] ~ *TS*
15:9 arena *TSR*] open arena *MS*
15:10 enquiring *Ed.*] inquiring *MS* inquiringly *TS*
15:22 pole:] ~; *G*
15:24 Oh shades] O shades *G*
15:24 Quixote! *TSR*] ~. *MS*
15:25 Apocalypse! *TSR*] ~. *MS*
16:1 So,] ~ *G*
16:6 cherished *TSR*] had *MS*
16:7 shoulder] shoulders *TS*
16:12 bowels! *TSR*] ~. *MS*
16:21 across] over *TS*
16:22 *Life! Ed.*] *Life*! *MS* Life! *TS*
16:23 England!] ~. *TS*
16:33 red] real *TS*
16:36 repelled *TSR*] horror-struck *MS*
16:36 amazement, *TSR*] ~ *MS*
16:41 awful:] ~, *TS*
17:2 anyhow?] ~! *TS*
17:8 foolish *TSR*] flimsy *MS*
17:19 *men TSR*] men *MS*
17:23 of *TSR*] of for *MS*
17:24 bull-fight] bull-fights *TS*
17:25 and] of *A1*
17:26 toreadors] toreador *A1*
17:28 slanting] *Om. TS*
17:31 swaying] swinging *TS*
17:38 amused, now ... for safety. *TSR*] amused. *MS*
18:16 delivered] delivered the *TS*
18:18 upward] upwards *TS*
18:23 toreadors,] ~ *TS*
18:26 exit] ~, *TS*

18:30 gangway,] ~ *TS*
19:2 feet,] ~ *TS*
19:3 watch *TSR*] see *MS*
19:5 that] *Om. TS*
19:8 spell-bound *MS, A1*] spell-/bound *TS* spellbound *G*
19:10 round] *Om. TS*
19:13 exit-tunnel *TS*] exit tunnel *MS*
19:14 fluttered] flustered *TS*
19:16 cried] said *TS*
19:20 The scene ... national insult. *TSR*] *Om. MS*
19:22 hurriedly *TSR*] *Om. MS*
19:24 I can't ... stink. *TSR*] *Om. MS*
19:29 spattered] sputtered *TS*
19:30 drops *TSR*] drops now *MS*
19:31 shelter; *TSR*] ~, *MS*
19:34 more?] ~. *TS* ~! *TSR*
19:35 diarrhœa! *TSR*] ~, *MS, A1* ~ *TS, G*
20:2 free! *TSR*] ~. *MS*
20:26 mass] man *TS* men *E1*
20:38 soft,] ~ *TS*
21:1 ricketty] rickety *TS*
21:2 pinky-white] pink-white *G*
21:3 road] *Om. TS* street *E1*
21:6 named: *TSR*] ~ *MS*
21:9 debonnaire *Ed.*] debonnair *MS* debonair *TS*
21:14 A little *TSR*] An *MS*
21:15 was *TSR*] was rather *MS*
21:16 *impériale Ed.*] imperial *MS*
21:21 contact *TSR*] the crowd *MS*
21:22 a] the *TS*
21:23 that,] ~ *TS*
21:26 brittle *TSR*] certain *MS*
21:35 half savage ... deprecating. *TSR*] a bit shy and farouche. *MS* half-savage ... deprecating. *G*
22:8 Yes.] ~ *TS* ~! *TSR*
22:14 is! *TSR*] ~, *MS*
22:15 Yes,] ~ *TS*
22:15 general. There] ~. *P* There *G*
22:18 American] Americans *TS*
22:20 newspaper *TSR*] paper *MS*
22:21 here—] ~ *TS*

22:25 hostility, under ... reputation. *TSR*] haughtiness. *MS*

22:32 del *TSR*] de *MS*

22:38 And *TSR*] When *MS*

23:1 some of *TSR*] *Om. MS*

23:2 awful! *TSR*] ~. *MS*

23:3 prostitution *TSR*] low-down prostitution *MS*

23:4 it is] its *TS* it's *TSR*

23:7 Well—" he said—] ~," ~ ~, *G*

23:7 unfortunate—] ~, *TS*

23:15 blank *TSR*] bitter *MS*

23:16 and] and an *TS*

23:17 naïve *MS*, *A1*] naive *G*

23:19 here] here now *TS*

23:21 Well—!] ~— *TS* ~, *G*

23:23 shrinking.] ~, *TS*

23:24 wait—] ~, *G*

23:30 very] *Om. TS*

23:38 Remo,] ~. *TS*

23:38 del Perú— *Ed.*] de Peru— *MS* de Peru, *G*

24:6 with] *Om. TS*

24:11 aggressive:] ~; *G*

24:11 nervousness *TSR*] shyness *MS*

24:12 gloom *TSR*] sadness *MS*

24:14 which perhaps *TSR*] which *MS* which, perhaps, *G*

24:15 warmth! Perhaps! *TSR*] warmth. *MS*

24:16 had] *Om. TS*

24:18 huge *TSR*] huge black *MS*

25:2 Tea-party] Tea-Party *E1* Tea-Party *A1*

25:3 half-past *TS*] half past *MS*

25:5 And,] ~ *TS*

25:9 shortcake *A1*] short-cake *MS*

25:10 Oh] ~, *G*

25:14 But] but *G*

25:15 The] the *G*

25:27 all] *Om. TS*

25:32 him—] ~. *G*

25:33 those *TSR*] those eunuch *MS*

25:34 another] see another *TS*

26:3 still,] ~ *TS*

26:4 plucky.] pretty. *TS* pretty. Really very plucky. *TSR*

26:5 They,] ~ *G*

26:7 behave!] ~. *TS*

26:10 being] *Om. TS*

26:10 I wish I] I ~ I *TS*

26:12 Well—!] ~! *G*

26:12 uneasily.] ~, *G*

26:27 for even] even for *TS*

26:30 life! *TSR*] ~. *MS*

26:36 has] had *G*

26:36 bellyful] bellyfull *A1*

26:39 *seven TSR*] seven *MS*

26:39 BULLS—] ~. *G*

27:3 calves—] ~, *G*

27:3 come] gone *A1*

27:4 gone—] ~.— *TS* ~. *G*

27:8 eyes, like a debauch. *TSR*] eyes. *MS*

27:23 added] asked *TS*

27:25 Well,] ~ *TS*

27:26 *after TSR*] after *MS*

27:26 gift. "Oh,] ~. *P* "Oh, *TS* ~. *P* "Oh *G*

27:31 said, *TSR*] ~ *MS*

27:31 can!—] ~! *TS*

27:35 lovers—] ~. *G*

27:39 *could*] could *TS*

28:4 just] first *TS*

28:10 heavy,] ~ *TS*

28:16 then,] ~ *TS*

28:30 eyes:] eye *TS* eyes, *TSR*

28:31 walked *TSR*] came *MS*

28:35 dinner—] ~. *G*

28:35 you—] ~. *G* ~? *A1*

28:39 it.—You *TSR*] ~—you *MS* ~. You *G*

29:13 so] not so *G*

29:16 came,] ~ *TS*

29:22 so often *TSR*] always *MS*

29:30 Owen, in ... voice. *TSR*] Owen hollowly. *MS*

29:33 *And* the ... dead laugh. *TSR*] And don't forget the youth. That's another," laughed Owen. *MS* And the ... laugh. *G*

29:35 snirt] snort *G*

29:35 amusement *TSR*] laughter *MS*

29:38 Capital] capital *TS*

30:1 Ye-es] Yes *G*

30:7 now,] now, my *TS*

30:9 "Thank ... to." *P* She] She *TS* Kate *TSR*

30:10 general:] ~; *TS*

30:12 bird-like *Ed.*] birdlike *MS*

30:12 with the] with *TS*

30:13 *impériale Ed.*] impérial *MS* imperial *TS*

30:15 yet cocky *TSR*] quiet, yet aggressive *MS*

30:17 intonations] intonation *TS*

30:17 eyes! *P* Till ... minute, she ... herself: to ... it. *P* He *TSR*] eyes! *P* He *MS* eyes ... minute she ... herself, to ... it. He *G*

30:28 tall,] ~ *TS*

30:29 reddened,] ~ *TS*

30:34 Ladies] ladies' *G*

30:37 had *TSR*] *Om. MS*

31:1 clamoring] clamouring *TS*

31:2 platforms] platform *TS*

31:2 this] the *TS*

31:5 people, in ... elsewhere. *TSR*] people in Mexico. *MS*

31:8 asks] ~, *TS*

31:10 avoided. *TSR*] avoided, as one avoids burglars and pickpockets. *MS*

31:20 flat *TSR*] ~, *MS*

31:22 welted] wetted *TS*

31:26 it.] *Om. TS* it! *TSR*

31:28 car-lines *TSR*] railway *MS*

31:29 outside *TSR*] beside *MS*

31:29 lines *TSR*] train-lines *MS*

31:29 the asphalt *TSR*] the road *MS*

31:31 big straw *TSR*] big, broken *MS*

31:32 dust-track] dust-tracks *TS*

31:34 traffic:] ~; *G*

31:36 outside-seeming *TSR*] hopeless-seeming *MS*

31:40 motionless, black-and-white] motionless-black-and-white *G* motionless black-and-white *A1*

31:40 cattle *TSR*] patched cattle *MS*

32:1 field *TSR*] plain *MS*

32:4 fruits *E1*] ~, *MS*

32:6 pink-and-yellow *TSR*] pink and yellow *MS*

32:9 doors,] ~: *G*

32:15 there] ~, *G*

32:18 a] *Om. TS*

32:23 jet-like *TSR*] black, jet-like *MS*

32:23 stair-case *Ed.*] staircase *MS* staircase, *TSR*

32:23 and] *Om. TS*

32:30 feet,] ~ *TS*

32:32 years,] ~. *G*

32:34 you—?] ~? *G*

32:35 Conquistador *Ed.*] conquistador *MS*

32:36 herself,] ~ *TS*

32:38 grey *TSR*] blackened *MS*

32:39 voice, hammered ... metal, was slow, distinct, and with a peculiar] voice hammered ...peculiar *TS* voice hammered ... metal, with a slow, distinct, peculiar *TSR*

33:3 expression] experience *TS*

33:12 number; *TSR*] ~, *MS*

33:15 little] *Om. TS*

33:17 sitting-room *TSR*] sitting room *MS*

33:17 three] *Om. TS*

33:19 crêpe-de-chine *TSR*] crêpe de chine *MS*

33:20 black] *Om. TS*

33:22 Middle-West *Ed.*] middle-west *MS*

33:31 Judge:] ~; *G*

33:36 *I*] I *TS*

34:1 Spence?"—*TSR*] ~?" *MS*, *G*

34:2 Why the] ~, ~ *A1*

34:2 a *TSR*] a rank *MS*

34:2 Why he] ~, ~ *A1*

34:6 clear,] ~ *A1*

34:13 jade—!] ~! *G*

34:14 stone itself ... stone *TSR*] colours ... tints *MS*

34:15 quality of it— *TSR*] white and grey rose and mauve— *MS* quality of it. *G* quality of it! *E1*

34:16 wonderful—!] ~! *TS*

34:27 known Mexico before] known it Mexico before *TS* known it before! Mexico before *TSR*

34:28 revolutions] revolution *G*

34:30 rumour *TSR*] rumor *MS*

34:32 office *TSR*] power *MS*

34:35 Labor *Ed.*] Labour *MS, G* labour *TS*

34:36 Rhys *TSR*] Owen *MS*

35:2 Well] ~, *G*

35:3 walls?] ~!? *TS* ~!?— *TSR* ~?— *G*

35:6 Why, *TSR*] ~ *MS*

35:6 hear such a thing?] hear of a thing? *TS* hear of such a thing! *TSR, E1* hear of such a thing, *G*

35:7 Labor President *Ed.*] Labour president *MS* Labour President *G*

35:21 barren *TSR*] helpless *MS*

35:28 a] A *G*

35:32 Presidents *G*] presidents *MS*

36:1 Sweepers] ~' *G*

36:2 Sweepers] ~' *G*

36:3 But you] And you *TS* You *TSR*

36:5 and] and to *G*

36:6 Sweepers] ~' *G*

36:10 Ayala] Angala *TS* Angulo *TSR*

36:12 possible? *TSR*] ~, *MS*

36:12 Kate. "When *TSR*] ~, "when *MS, E1* ~; "when *G*

36:15 Judge. "He's] ~, "He's *TS* ~, "he's *G*

36:16 Party, *Ed.*] party, *MS* Party! *TS*

36:16 Owen, almost at bay. *TSR*] Owen. *MS*

36:22 Laboristas] Laborites *TS* Labourites *G*

36:23 up] *Om. TS*

36:23 Hotel *TSR*] Hotel de *MS*

36:24 gachupines] Gachupines *TS*

36:24 hotel *TS*] Hotel *MS*

36:27 funny] ~, *G*

36:28 and] *Om. A1*

36:29 bench] hard bench *TS*

36:35 seems to overcome *TSR*] overcomes *MS*

36:36 Mexico *TSR*] Mexico today *MS*

36:37 fright:] ~; *G*

36:39 minutes] ~' *G*

37:8 Yes] yes *G*

37:12 at me] at *TS Om. TSR*

37:13 Museum] ~, *G*

37:17 When they *TSR*] If they could *MS*

37:18 Méjico *Ed.*] Mejico *MS* Mexico *TS*

37:20 Mixcoac ... Mixcoac] Mexcoac ... Méxcoac *TS* Mexcoatl ... Méxcoatl *TSR* Mixcoatl ... Mixcoatl *G*

37:21 Well] ~, *G*

37:24 *haven't*] *have TS*

37:27 *gentlemen! G*] *gentleman. MS gentlemen! TSR*

37:27 *Governor TSR*] *governor MS*

37:29 *Governor TSR*] *governor MS*

37:34 *Querido TSR*] *Mirabal MS*

37:35 *so-and-so TSR*] *so and so MS*

37:36 *right? G*] ~. *MS* ~? *TSR*

37:36 *thanks! G*] ~. *MS* ~! *TSR*

38:1 expect *TSR*] think *MS*

38:4 Kate. "It's] ~, "It's *TS* ~, "it's *G*

38:5 alone—] ~. *TS*

38:6 Well!] ~, *G*

38:10 things. They] things. They seem to want the ugly things They *TS* things ... things. They *G*

38:10 *want*] want *A1*

38:12 stir it] stir *TS*

38:14 *is*] is *G*

38:24 gone—] ~ *TS* ~, *TSR*

38:24 to go to *TSR*] in them *MS*

38:29 you—] ~. *G*

38:37 her shoulders *TSR*] herself *MS*

38:38 to *TSR*] on to *MS*

39:4 Yes,] ~ *TS*

39:5 possessor—] ~. *G*

39:7 bell-flower] bell-flowers *TS*

39:9 are] *Om. TS*

39:13 pearly] pearl *TS*

39:21 grimacing,] ~ *TS*

39:22 bâton *TSR*] batôn *MS*

39:24 General] general *G*

39:24 expressionless] ~, *G*

39:28 English, that ... parrot talking. *TSR*] English. *MS*

39:31 automatic] automatically *TS*

40:1 deal,] ~ *TS*

40:9 not—] ~, *G*

40:15 asked] added *TS*

40:16 but with ... mockery *TSR*] timorously *MS*

40:17 resistant *TSR*] old *MS*

40:21 hats, *TSR*] ~ *MS*

40:25 calculating *TSR*] puzzled *MS*

40:30 quite matter of fact *TSR*] troubled, resentful *MS*

40:34 rich and] rich *TS* heavy *TSR*

40:36 *Other!* If I ... revolutions, I]
Other! I ... revolutions, I *TS*
Other! I ... revolutions, and I
TSR Other! I ... revolutions, and I *G*

40:40 *Viva!!*] ~!! *TS* ~! *G*

41:1 knowing,] ~ *TS*

41:6 a] *Om. TS*

41:6 Mexican—,] ~— *TS, E1* ~, *G*

41:11 Conquistador *TS*] conquistador *MS*

41:12 eyes,] eye *TS* eyes *E1*

41:12 pince-nez *E1*] spectacles *MS*

41:14 Stately *TSR*] Huge *MS*

41:17 or Señor] *Om. G*

41:22 *Don Cipriano*] Don Cipriano *TS*

41:26 little,] ~ *TS*

41:27 foot-man] footman *TS*

41:36 Cipriano] ~, *G*

41:36 hand] ~, *G*

42:2 society, British ... social world]
society *TS* society, she watched people *TSR*

42:7 *real*] ~, *G*

42:9 Ah] ~, *G*

42:11 *tostón TSR*] *tostino MS* tostón *G*

42:13 *Señora mía Ed.*] Señora mia *MS*

42:16 them!] ~? *A1*

42:26 quietly] quickly *TS*

42:27 seed] Seed *TS*

42:28 shut."—And *TSR*] ~," and *MS* ~." And *G*

42:30 read] see *TS*

42:33 *only*] only *TS*

42:38 things *TSR*] anything *MS*

43:1 socialists and *singvergüenzas*]
Socialists and Sinvergüenzas *G*

43:3 pince-nez *G*] pince nez *MS*

43:8 irritated] irritable *TS*

43:16 way, how] ~. How *TS* ~! How *TSR*

43:17 ankle? *TSR*] ~. *MS*

43:19 *so*] so *A1*

43:22 Why,] ~ *TS*

44:11 Avenue:] ~; *G*

44:18 are] were *A1*

44:18 diseases *TSR*] evils *MS*

44:18 today,] to-day— *G*

44:19 Americanism:] ~; *G*

44:34 "Why," said ... at it."] *Om. TS*

45:4 jade,] ~ *TS*

45:13 tint. White] ~— white *G*

45:16 Black, oh] ~. Oh *TS* ~? Oh *TSR*

45:17 *Only green jade TSR*] Only green jade *MS*

45:19 stone] ~, *G*

45:20 of] *Om. TS*

45:25 General *TS*] general *MS*

45:28 side] ~, *G*

45:28 reddish-and-yellow *TSR*] reddish and yellow *MS*

45:31 yellow,] ~ *TS*

45:34 were suspended *TSR*] hung *MS* were suspended, *G*

46:11 Capital] capital *TS*

46:14 was night] was already night *TS*

46:18 dear! *TSR*] ~. *MS*

46:18 much! Well! I'll see! *TSR*] ~. ~, ~ ~. *MS*

46:22 out?] ~! *TS*

46:23 Kate, peering into the dark. *P* It
Ed.] Kate. *P* It *MS* Kate. It *TS*
Kate, peering ... dark. It *TSR*

46:30 tram, *TSR*] ~ *MS*

46:30 baby-faced] ~, *G*

46:37 'em] them *TS*

47:1 hate] ~, *G*

47:3 moment] time *TS*

47:3   bright] *Om. G*
47:4   dragon-like *TSR*] dragon like *MS*
47:4   walls] wall *TS*
47:8   baby-faced] ~, *G*
47:12 class; *TSR*] ~, *MS*
47:14 Goodnight] goodnight *G*
47:15 know:] ~; *G*
47:17 commonplace *Ed.*] common-place *MS*
47:24 that] the *TS*
47:24 Middle-West *TS*] Middle-west *MS*
47:25 whiteness— —!] ~...! *G*
47:30 he ... he] He ... He *G*
47:33 That] The *TS*
47:33 Middle-West *TS*] Middle West *MS*
48:3   "The *pulquería ... Día ...* apprehensive laugh. *Ed.*] *Om. MS* "The *pulqueria ... Dia ...* laugh. *TSR*
48:11 Chauffeur] chauffeur *G*
48:20 tea-party] teaparty *TS* tea party *G*
49:6   side] side there *TS*
49:7   was] *Om. TS*
49:13 James *TSR*] *Om. MS*
49:17 under heaven *TSR*] in the under heavens *MS*
49:19 Ixtaccihuatl, the White Woman, *TSR*] Popocatepetl *MS*
49:20 Popocatepetl *G*] Ixtaccihuatl, the White Woman *MS* Popo-catépetl *TSR*
49:23 this] their *TS*
49:24 mountains *TSR*] monsters *MS*
49:35 low,] ~ *TS*
50:4   steam] stream *A1*
50:4   of] of a *TS* of an *G*
50:8   *Odio.*] ~— *G*
50:8   Mexican] Mexicano *TS*
50:9   hate.— *TSR*] ~. *MS, G*
50:10 *Viva TSR*] Viva *MS*
50:11 Death] death *G*
50:12 forever] for ever *G*
50:16 has *E1*] had *MS*

50:20 across, *TSR*] ~ *MS*
50:20 sudden] ~, *G*
50:22 barrel] barred *A1*
50:27 pecked] perched *TS*
50:32 old *TSR*] odd *MS*
50:32 no! *TSR*] ~. *MS*
50:33 undertow] undertone *TS*
50:39 page,] ~ *TS*   ·
51:3   bright] ~, *G*
51:10 University *Ed.*] university *MS*
51:12 *camiones Ed.*] camions *MS*
51:15 crêpe-de-chine *Ed.*] crêpe de chine *MS* crêpe de Chine *A1*
51:16 hustle] bustle *TS*
51:25 lifting,] ~ *TS*
51:25 small,] ~ *TS*
51:28 small,] ~ *TS*
51:35 clothes, the] clothes, the the *TS* clothes, and the *G*
51:36 Something serpent-like ... and appealing.] *Om. TS*
51:39 contrast] ~, *G*
52:2   two or three *TSR*] ten *MS*
52:5   seemed] seem *TS*
52:5   little] *Om. TS*
52:6   that had been *TSR*] *Om. MS*
52:9   and of] and *G*
52:10 young.—Go *TSR*] ~: go *MS* ~, go *TS* ~. Go *G*
52:11 then] ~, *E1*
52:14 Ribera's] Riberas' *G*
52:16 craft. *TSR*] craft. He could put his simplified forms together till they had an almost cumula-tive symbolic significance, almost like picture-writing with the meaning not too evident. There was beauty, too, and a certain pathos. *MS*
52:19 social *TSR*] mental *MS*
52:22 capitalism *G*] capitalisms *MS*
52:24 half-an-hour *TSR*] half an hour *MS*
52:26 a profound unbelief *TSR*] an incompleteness *MS*
52:27 Liberty] liberty *G*
52:28 Progress] progress *G*
52:28 Socialism] socialism *G*

52:29   him. *TSR*] him. *P* The inarticulate people of today are victims both ways. They are indeed victims of exploitation. But they are also victims of the mental sympathisers. The exploiter wastes their physical life to a certain degree. But the mental sympathiser damages their very spirit. *P* If there is sympathy, it must be sympathy of the blood, the tenderness and the anger of the blood bringing forth its own wisdom: far, far different from the ideal wisdom of materialistic and "educational" socialism. *MS*

52:30   University *G*] university *MS*

52:31   smartly] *Om. TS*

52:31   their *TSR*] with *MS*

52:32   deliberate youth-and-eagerness *TSR, E1*] "conscious" youth and eagerness *MS* deliberate, youth-and-eagerness *G*

52:34   amiability *G*] aimiability *MS*

52:39   *épatisme, Ed.*] épatism *MS* épatis *TS* épatisme, *TSR ~A1*

52:40   *épatant le bourgeois Ed.*] épatant le bourgeois *MS*

52:40   *épateurs Ed.*] épateurs *MS*

53:1   convent] ~, *G*

53:3   these] they *TS*

53:4   merely repelled *TSR*] speechless *MS*

53:5   but *TSR*] and *MS*

53:6   as shocking] so shocking *TS*

53:6   are] were *TS*

53:7   Strident *TSR*] Hideous *MS*

53:7   Capitalist,] ~ *G*

53:9   patio] patios *TS*

53:10   the *TSR*] a *MS*

53:10   balance *TSR*] gentleness *MS*

53:11   misdemeanour. *TSR*] shame of vulgarity. *P* Because the spirit behind them is gross hate. In the frescoes of the university there is hate too, but it is ideal hate. In these caricatures there is hate gross and vulgar. *MS*

53:13   therefore *TSR*] but *MS*

53:19   government] Government *G*

53:21   soft, petulant, *TSR*] charming *MS* soft, petulant *G*

53:21   liked him *TSR*] liked him very much *MS*

53:26   They defeat ... ends. *TSR*] *Om. MS*

53:30   ugly, no?"— *Ed.*] ~, No?" *MS* ~, No?"— *TSR* ~. No?" *G*

53:31   Kate. "These ... at all *TSR*] Kate. "They are no longer human. They are no longer true. They are *too* repulsive *MS* Kate, "these ... all *G*

53:35   poor. "That] ~. *P* "That *TS*

53:36   Who is ... certain balance *TSR*] But you can't fix all your attention on just that," said Kate. "You have to remain human *MS*

53:39   keep a balance *TSR*] remain human *MS*

53:40   balanced *TSR*] human *MS*

54:2   *more*] more *G*

54:2   human—] ~, *G*

54:18   Mexicans] Mexican *TS*

54:19   half-Spaniards] half Spaniards *TS*

54:19   asserting *TSR*] *Om. MS*

54:20   nothing else. *E1*] nothing else. There are fifteen million people in Mexico. Twelve million are absolutely silent, helpless, and hopeless. You other few pose as Mexico, pose as Saviours, and all you care about is your own selves: either your own ideas and gas, or else about money. It's all silly spiteful hate, hate, hate all the time, from your Hidalgo and your miserable Benito Juarez down to you yourself. And you call that Mexico! There *is* no Mexico, save the dumb, dark-faced, helpless millions whom you just use as a stick to beat one another with. *MS* nothing else … Mexic pose … spiteful hate, hate all … another with. *TS* nothing else … and hopeless, and getting wickeder. You … Mexicans pose … own self-assertion: either … save the devilish, dark-faced millions … use as a weapon, from time to time. *TSR* nothing else … Mexicans, pose … weapon from … time. *G*

54:29　taxi] ~, *G*
54:30　stupid] ~, *G*
54:33　such] such a *TS*
54:34　anger] ~, *G*
54:39　frustration, because … was frustrated] frustration *TS* frustration, frustration of life *TSR*
55:9　done.] ~?. *TS* ~? *G*
55:13　I too … I too] ~, ~, … ~, ~, *G*
55:15　I too] ~, ~, *G*
55:15　it] *Om. TS*
55:18　But I] ~ ~, *G*
55:28　flushed,] ~ *G*
55:35　those] these *G*
55:36　*everything!*"—] ~!" *TS* ~!" *G*
55:38　so—] ~. *G*
56:2　natural gay] natural grey *TS* natural soft, sensuous *TSR* natural, soft, sensuous *G*
56:2　flow] ~, *G*
56:9　dinner,] ~ *G*
56:12　difficulty: the] ~. The *TS*
56:24　groups] ~, *G*
56:24　water-fowl] ~, *G*
56:27　lake *G*] Lake *MS*
56:36　labors *Ed.*] labours *MS*
57:9　Why] '~ *TSR*
57:10　gods *G*] Gods *MS*
57:13　you,] ~ *G*
57:14　home— *Ed.*] ~—" *MS* ~—' *TSR* ~.' *G*
57:17　and *TSR*] and then *MS*
57:22　labors *Ed.*] labours *MS*

57:25　shadow] shadows *TS*
57:27　replied:] ~; *G*
57:27　No] ~, *A1*
57:29　room or cellar] ~, ~ ~, *G*
57:30　men] ~, *G*
57:30　children] ~, *G*
57:33　sweet-smelling *TS*] sweet smelling *MS*
57:37　besides] beside *TS*
58:2　accuse him of] arrest him for *TS*
58:6　spot,] ~ *TS*
58:7　Meanwhile] ~, *G*
58:10　outrage] ~, *G*
58:11　was] was at the *G*
58:19　Quetzalcoatl too] ~, ~, *G*
58:20　high] high up *TS*
58:22　Quetzalcoatl is … Serpent, so *TSR*] Quetzalcoatl, the Feathered Serpent, *MS*
58:25　fair-faced,] ~ *TS*
58:29　Mexico,] ~ *TS*
58:36　deities] deity *TS*
58:36　vindictiveness? *TSR*] ~. *MS*
58:38　Irish *TSR*] Celtic *MS*
58:39　god] God *TS*
58:40　god] God *TS*
59:1　god grows] Gods grows *TS* gods grow *G*
59:1　him] them *TSR*
59:2　sweeps] sways *TS*
59:24　Life] life *G*
59:24　tea-parties,] tea-part *TS* tea-party, *TSR*
59:25　enjoyments,] enjoyments; like *TS*, *A1* enjoyments, like *E1*
59:26　effusions] effusion *TS*
59:26　Life] life *G*
59:32　Life] life *G*
59:33　degenerated] degenerate *TS*
60:1　this] the *TS*
60:1　death-rattles] ~, *G*
60:2　feel as … she could] *Om. TS*
60:12　vile] *Om. TS*
60:19　way] *Om. TS*
60:27　porcupine *TSR*] hedgehog *MS*
60:31　an Ossianic *TSR*] a Norse *MS*
60:38　night flowers] nightflowers *TS*

60:40 night-flower] nightflower *TS*
61:6 dinner jacket] dinner-jacket *G*
61:12 those] these *G*
61:13 plaintive,] ~ *TS*
61:20 in an] in in *TS* in *TSR*
61:26 the] a *G*
61:29 interesting? *TSR*] ~. *MS*
61:32 *word?*] ~! *TS* ~! *G*
61:35 Mirabal *MS, A1*] Mirabel *G*
61:37 Mexico:] Mexicoo: *TS* Mexico? *TSR*
61:37 gods?"—] ~!" *TS* ~?" *TSR*
62:8 gods! *TSR*] ~. *MS*
62:8 think the] ~ *the A1*
62:9 *Huitzilopochtli*] Huitzilpochtli *TS*
62:10 *Tlaloc*] Tlaloc *TS*
62:12 *Itzpapalotl! Ed.*] *Itzpapalotl! MS* Itzpapalotl! *TS*
62:13 *Itzpapalotl! Tezcatlipoca! Ed.*] ~! *Teczcatlipocâ! MS* Itzpapalotl! Tezcatlipocá! *TS*
62:16 *Jahveh*] *Jehovah TS*
62:31 half-aggressive] half aggressive *TS*
62:35 is—"] ~ *TS* ~." *TSR*
63:25 man-servant *Ed.*] manservant *MS*
63:27 Toussaint] ~, *G*
63:28 seems *TSR*] seemed *MS*
63:32 own lives] lives *TS*
63:34 Naturally] ~, *G*
63:36 what for] for what *TS*
64:1 percent] per cent. *G*
64:2 Indians] Indian *TS*
64:3 Spaniards] Spaniard *TS*
64:4 real] *Om. TS*
64:5 Now] ~, *G*
64:8 Mirabal *MS, A1*] Mirabel *G*
64:9 myself] ~, *TS*
64:10 well! Now ... French blood,] well *TS* well! Now you mix blood of the same *race, TSR* well! Now ... same race, *G*
64:12 of] *Om. TS*
64:14 Now] ~, *G*
64:24 half-breed,] ~ *TS*

64:26 in and we] in an we *TS* in. We *TSR*
64:29 all] *Om. TS*
64:31 soul, or *TSR*] ~. Or *MS*
65:4 the] that *G*
65:12 pure blooded,] pure-blooded, but *TS* pure-blooded, and *TSR*
65:20 No] ~, *G*
65:22 us?] ~! *TS*
65:27 chile *Ed.*] chili *MS* chili, *G*
65:34 anywhere] anyhow *TS*
65:36 with a ... about nothing,] *Om. TS*
65:37 terrible,] *Om. TS*
65:38 alive."] ~," *TS* ~!" *G*
65:39 then] ~, *G*
65:40 care.] care. They don't care. *TS*
66:3 chile] chili *TS*
66:10 God, *TSR*] God, his passionate repose in a woman whom he trusts with his soul, *MS*
66:11 at] in *TS*
66:13 absolutely true ... [66:24] of despair. *G*] absolutely true. *P* But look at the other side.—At {side. At *TS*} the moment of coition, all a man's selfishness, his greediness, his brutality, {his callousness, *TSR*} his coldness, can come to a crisis then. And that is how it has been between the Spaniards and the Indians. Even that brave, cold, selfish Cortés began that very way, {that way, *TS*} and so it went on. And what can you expect of their descendants? {descendants! *TS*} Nothing but what you get. *P* You speak of the Indians. How are they? I will tell you. They have hot blood, and they put all the belief that is left to them in the moment of coition. They are not selfish, greedily eating the woman. They don't care for a woman unless she cares for them. They don't want her unless she wants them. The old instinct of the sacredness of that desire on both sides is still with them. It is not, as with white men and women, {woman, *TS*} a

case of capture, where the man captures the woman and puts something over her; or else, more {her, more *TS*; her, or, more *TSR*} often, the woman captures the man and eats his soul. That is the bad part of white people: the moment of coition. Either it is a fight, or it is a victim being eaten by the other one: the soul eaten out, as it is eaten out of prostitutes and of American men. The women eating the soul out of men, or the men eating the soul out of women. *P* Now let me say, the Indians are not like that. That is why they are still beautiful to look at. When the man and woman come together, each brings a gift of fire to the other. Their blood is still potent with the life fire, and the woman hands her torch to the man, the man hands his torch to the woman, and the fire leaps in both of them. *P* So far {far, *TS*} so good. But what more? There is more necessary. The man must feel he can hand on the life-fire, on and on, in the world. And the woman must feel she can hand it on, in her children, in her service to her man. {to the man. *TS*} *P* And what happens? The man is hopeless about his life fire. He cannot bring it into consciousness and activity. He does not know what his gods want of him, and he cannot find out. Serving the white man's gods makes him feel empty, kills his fire. There is nothing to be done, and so he does nothing, except know that death is his only way back to his gods. He is filled with fatality and hopelessness, and real carelessness. He really doesn't care, not about anything. *P* Then sometimes he turns obscene, full of obscene hate— *MS*

66:28 who have *TSR*] of *MS*
66:31 hope in anything *TSR*] what we call intelligence *MS*
66:36 declamation] declaration *TS*
66:37 wine. *TSR*] ~, *MS*
66:38 watched and directed *TSR*]

watching and directing *MS*
67:7 face,] ~ *TS*
67:8 felt,] ~ *TS*
67:17 light,] ~ *TS*
67:29 black as black] black as black as *TS* black, as black as *G*
67:33 that] that Don *TS*
67:34 at] *Om. TS* to *TSR*
67:36 between] between them *G*
67:38 menacing *TSR*] terrible *MS*
68:4 the] this *TS*
68:6 his hand through *TSR*] deep enough *MS*
68:7 verandah, *TSR*] ~ *MS*
68:9 yucca] Yucca *G*
68:10 *laurel de la India Ed.*] Laurel de India *MS*
68:16 falling,] ~ *TS*
68:16 else *TSR*] so real, so positive *MS*
68:35 rich] ~, *G*
68:35 Revolution *Ed.*] revolution *MS*
68:37 Revolution *Ed.*] revolution *MS*
69:3 hands.] hand *TS* hand. *TSR*
69:4 three,] three *TS* three or *G*
69:5 hands] ~, *A1*
69:9 Well] ~, *G*
69:15 god-father *TS*] godfather *MS*
69:18 priests—] ~. *G*
69:26 better—] ~, *G*
69:28 saints] Saints *TS*
69:30 mysterious. Everything ... strange and] *Om. TS*
69:32 then,] ~ *TS*
69:34 was—] ~, *G*
69:37 Revolution *Ed.*] revolution *MS*
69:40 revolutions] revolution *TS*
70:13 Bishop's *Ed.*] bishop's *MS*
70:18 James *TSR*] *Om. MS*
70:28 just] *Om. TS*
70:32 good] ~, *G*
71:1 Ireland.] ~? *A1*
71:7 *you*] *Om. TS*
71:14 hadn't—"] ~." *G* ~——" *A1*
71:29 ducked,] ~ *TS*
71:29 a] her *TS*
71:35 down] down again *TS*

72:2 To Stay ... To Stay *Ed.*] To Be or Not To Be *MS* To Be ... to Be *TS* To Stay ... to Stay *TSR*

72:11 in] on *A1*

73:7 wine-skin, it] ~. it *TS* ~. It *TSR*

73:11 God that gives *TSR*] invisible powers that give *MS*

73:13 God of ... [75:11] stiff-backed men, *TSR*] will be invisible gods. {God. *TSR*} The will of our living gods {god *TSR*} is liberty to us, nothing else. Free will, Liberty so-called, is a slavery to circumstances, and {circumstances and *TS*} it is a torture of ennui. And free Mexico, instead of being enslaved to the church, is enslaved to vulgar greedy individual ambition, and to shoddy militarism. {militarism, and socialistic materialism. *TSR*} Liberty is just a change of chains." *P* Kate had suffered the bitter disillusion of Ireland. Now it was the blacker disillusion of Mexico that faced her. *P* To her, Mexico meant the dark-faced men in cotton clothes and big hats: the peasants, the peons, the pelados, the Indians. Those pale-faced Mexicans of the capital, those hacendados and ranch-owners in tight trousers, with their weak, soft faces, pale victims of their own feebleness, they were not Mexico to her. Mexico was just the mass of the peons, the peon class. *P* She thought again of these peons, *MS see also following entries to 75:5*

73:14 colonial-ecclesiastical *TSR*] colonial, ecclesiastical *G* colonial ecclesiastical *A1*

73:17 Liberty *TSR*] liberty *G*

73:17 chains— *TSR*] ~. *G*

73:29 *God TSR*] God *A1*

73:30 sentimentalism, *TSR*] ~ *G*

73:36 himself— *TSR*] ~, *G*

74:8 *Will TSR*] *will G*

74:10 repulsive, *TSR*] ~ *G*

74:12 God *TSR*] god *G*

74:20 appetite?— *TSR*] ~? *G*

74:23 *will TSR*] will *G*

74:25 me.— *TSR*] ~— *G*

74:35 the God *E1*] God *TSR*

74:36 is the *E1*] is *TSR*

74:36 And the *E1*] And *TSR*, *A1*

74:36 God gives *E1*] ~, ~ *TSR*, *A1*

74:39 more— *TSR*] ~. *G*

74:39 off, *TSR*] ~ *G*

75:4 clothes and *TSR*] clothes, *G*

75:5 natives! *TSR*] ~. *G*

75:19 grape] dark grape *TS*

75:19 has malted *G*] had malted *MS*

75:21 a *TSR*] Om. *MS*

75:24 *Agua miel! Pulque! G*] Agua miel! Pulque! *MS Agua miel! Pulque! TSR*

75:28 these] those *TS*

75:29 fire-waters,] ~ *TS*

75:29 chile] chili *TS*

75:32 sugar cane *Ed.*] sugar-cane *MS*

75:33 *peón Ed.*] peón *MS*

75:33 wide] white *G*

75:40 queer-looking] ~, *A1*

76:10 floppy white] ~, ~, *G*

76:13 spine,] ~ *TS*

76:16 skin] skins *A1*

76:16 heads] ~, *G*

76:17 gleams *TSR*] gleamed *MS*

76:18 look *TSR*] looked *MS*

76:18 have *TSR*] had *MS*

76:19 sudden] ~, *G*

76:19 you smile *TSR*] you smiled *MS*

76:21 remember too] ~, ~, *G*

76:39 down] ~, *TS*

77:11 lice:] ~; *G*

77:13 woman's shoulder:] woman *TS* woman's shoulder; *TSR* woman's shoulder, *G*

77:16 insolence! *TSR*] ~. *MS*

77:17 been:] ~; *G*
77:26 *No TSR*] No *MS*
77:27 and even African *Yes TSR*] Yes *MS*
77:31 destruction?] ~! *TS*
77:34 living, spontaneous creature *TSR*] living, creative soul *MS* living spontaneous creature *G*
77:37 continent] continents *A1*
78:2 god *TSR*] creative *MS* God *G*
78:3 where the ... itself "free," *TSR*] Om. *MS*
78:6 godless democracy ... of materialism. *TSR*] of eternal, demonish, energetic negation? *MS* Godless ... materialism. *G*
78:8 Americas] Americans *TS*
78:13 Europe. *G*] Europe. *P* Owen, what was he doing? With his poetry, and his very secure income, and his socialism, what did he amount to? A parlour socialist, of which there are so many in America. Why? What did he want? *P* She felt it very vividly. He wanted to destroy the soul out of life, by {life by *TS*} preserving the shells of living human beings. He hated the old divinity of man, the old divine authority which is in the soul of every living man, and which the soul of every living man gratefully recognises. Every living woman too. She knew this since Joachim's death. If she was looking for anything positive in her life now, it was for the old divine authority which used to fill the souls of passionate, true men, and which all the tendency of the modern democratic world is to pull down and destroy. The old heroic soul, that serves the god which is its life, and bows before this god alone. The soul that yields to the divine authority, and which is in turn imbued with the same. *P* This she was still seeking for. Not for a man personally. But for a man who could reach the divine flame, and pass it on. Pass on the cup of fire and timeless peace. Her woman's soul was weary,

aching, vacant. She wanted again to be given to the living god. *P* And Owen, she knew, hated her for this desire. He hated her because she felt a natural ridicule of his unheroic attitude. A parlour socialist! A playboy of the western world. Play-boying, and nothing else. What was there here for a woman? *P* What was more, his soft, heavy, play-boying hatred of the divine inspiration which carries with it a divine authority. He hated religion in any form, even the simple instinct of religion. He liked aestheticism because it was a toy to play with. *P* The hollow, grinding gap of negation that was the middle of him! Yet in this way he was a good fellow, superficially kind and good-natured. But at the middle of him, the grinding void of negation, grinding against any sort of positivity. *P* Grinding to destroy the old god-power in man, the old god-authority— Grinding, grinding to reduce the living, creative quick to dust. Then grinding on and on, with mechanical benevolent insistence, to keep all the shells of human beings alive. The great American benevolence! Preserve life, preserve all life, but only when the soul has been killed out of it, and it is automatic harmless. *P* The great, hideous American activity! Democracy! *P* Owen, snapping little Kodak pictures, putting together bits of automatic poetry, or writing little pseudo-snappy articles on saving the poor from oppression, in his hotel bedroom. Owen exploring the Thieves Market, and raking everywhere to buy things that people in the United States hadn't got and might envy him for having. Raking, raking, raking to get some old blanket or some old pearl. Collecting, they call it. Junking! Owen hating the capitalist with eye-rolling hatred, and joining hands with syphilitic socialists, scum like the Pole of infamous memory, in order to save Mexico. Owen thrilled to the marrow by the fact that Mexico was at last getting a real representative government, a Labour government to represent the Indians, save the mark! Owen hating with spider-like hate the old authority of Europe, yet spouting European tenets in Mexico, European socialism for Mexican Indians, the quicker to Americanise them and blank them out into the European nullity. *P* The playboy with the hopeless void of indifference and gnawing dreariness scooping out the middle of him, till soon there would be nothing in him at all. Emptier than a gourd rattle. Yet still rattling about a Labour government "representing" the People of Mexico. As if Mexico had such a thing as a People! The gap growing wider and wider. The void where the soul should be. Till surely he would have to cave in on his own emptiness. *P* Young Villiers, the American of the younger generation, almost worse. He hadn't even the incentive of Socialism or labour sympathies. He didn't have any sympathies at all, except with himself. And not by any means so easy to amuse. Like the Mexican who scrapes and cauterises his inside with tequila and red pepper, Villiers needed something pretty scorching before he got a sensation off it. And with the toughness of his American will, he was all the time hardening his own shell to be able scoop (*sic*) sensations closer and closer up to it. Scooping away with a bird-like scraping, getting a frictional sensation. The younger generation. *P* In the centre of his eye, a strange, arching, conscious void, conscious of its own will-to-emptiness. Usually this will basked half veiled, like a snake with its head down. But sometimes its will-to-emptiness became positive, the apathy uncoiled in a sort of ghastly frenzy. *P* The gap, the horrible gap! The triumph of empti-

ness! The god-spark and the creative authority cast out, and sensation clawing and scraping at the inner walls of the emptiness! Americans! The bottomless pit! *P* With the Mexicans it was a dark hollow with a strong, dark flame of life flowing round it. And this was the problem. Was the dark flame of life to concentrate into a pure strong core of being and of creative triumph, in the Mexican soul, or was it a flame wheeling on the void of the bottomless pit, forever? *P* The bottomless pit! Everything in the white man's world going over with a slow, soft slide, over the brink, in a rattle of sensational nullity. Over the edge of the bottomless pit that has opened like a fissure in the white man's soul, and now gapes insatiable. Down which the white man's world will slide into oblivion. Caved in on an inner emptiness, the god-power, the god-authority betrayed with Judas kisses, and so departed, leaving man pithed, a hole where his core should be. *P* The white man's world caving in and slithering with a slow soft slithering down the void which has appeared at the centre of the white man's soul. The void of denial of the gods of being. When we deny the gods of being, they depart, and their place in us is an insatiable emptiness, that can swallow the cosmos. *P* But the Mexicans! In one way so attractive, in the other so repellant. The old, reptilian centre-lessness. Was it the black void of a soul not yet created, yearning for creation? Or the raging, powerful void of positive destruction? *P* Those old Aztecs, with their horrible religion and their unnatural, nauseating religious festivals—was it just an inevitable Moloch worship? Worship of the black maw of anti-creation, all fangs and claws and basilisk eyes? Was this the American truth, for ever and ever? *MS*

78:16 acknowledgement] acknow-
ledgment *G*
78:17 them] *Om. TS*
78:18 reckless] careless *TS*
78:25 void: were *TSR*] ~. Were *MS*
78:26 so many *TSR*] the *MS*
78:28 of a man] of man man *TS* of a
man in a man *TSR*
78:32 men] man *TS*
78:33 god] God *G*
78:40 revolution-broken] revolution
broken *G*
79:2 pinnacle] pinnacles and *TS*
79:10 buildings] building *TS*
79:13 Ah the] All the *TS* The *TSR*
79:14 race, unless ... new inspiration, *TSR*] race *MS*
79:25 Snake] snake *G*
79:31 pressure,] ~ *TS*
79:31 Down-sinking *TSR*] Down
sinking *MS*
79:32 market-place *TSR*] market
place *MS*
79:34 arid] *Om. TS*
79:37 fascination but] ~, ~ *TS*
79:37 repellance] repellence *A1*
80:1 meaning?] ~! *TS*
80:2 world? *TSR*] ~. *MS*
80:3 vindictive *TSR*] stone-edged
MS
80:4 smite to] smite *TS*
80:8 boys] ~, *G*
80:26 alive,] ~ *TS*
80:26 shoots. And] ~. *P* And *TS* ~. *P*
"And *G*
80:32 again—] ~. *G*
81:6 alone,] ~ *TS*
81:17 government] Government *G*
81:27 so] *Om. TS*
81:32 black] back *A1*
81:35 Madonnas] Madonna *TS*
82:3 knelt: with ... again. But *TSR*]
knelt. And *MS*
82:5 power. His *TSR*] power. All his
MS
82:6 barbarian consciousness *TSR*]
energy *MS*
82:11 her, she] ~. She *G*

82:22 certain *TSR*] certain fierce *MS*
82:22 *hauteur*] hauteur *TS*
82:26 real *TSR*] dragon of *MS*
82:27 real *TSR*] dragon of *MS*
82:28 real *TSR*] dragon of *MS*
82:31 You can *TSR*] Do *MS*
82:33 an] a *A1*
82:38 Near! *TSR*] Not far. *MS*
82:39 going *TSR*] going to be transferred *MS*
82:40 governor] Governor *G*
83:6 at the ... and desirous *TSR*]
perplexed *MS*
83:10 nowadays, *TSR*] ~ *MS*
83:15 any] any other *TS*
83:22 Yes,] ~. *G*
83:22 Of course! We] of course we
TS of course, we *G*
83:24 peace!] ~.! *TS* ~. *G*
83:27 on] *Om. TS* by *TSR*
83:32 quietly] quickly *TS*
83:33 rancheros, *TSR*] rancheros *MS*
ranchers, *G*
83:35 a *MS, A1*] *Om. G*
83:40 green-plush *TSR*] green plush
MS
84:10 *sensibilité, TSR*] ~ *MS*
84:10 with *TSR*] with simple *MS*
84:17 Tacuba *Ed.*] Tacubaya *MS see
notes*
84:23 lifted] uplifted *TS*
84:25 in and out] in-and-out *TS*
84:28 earthern] earth *TS* earthenware *TSR*
84:29 sauce:] ~; *G*
84:30 the women *TSR*] they *MS*
84:40 cook the] cook *TS*
85:1 second-class *TSR*] second
class *MS*
85:1 first-class *TSR*] first class *MS*
85:2 second-class *Ed.*] second class
MS
85:2 jam full] jam-full *G*
85:5 beneath *TSR*] under *MS*
85:6 again] *Om. TS*
85:10 uniforms *TSR*] uniform *MS*
85:11 look-out *TSR*] look out
MS

85:15 A sort of demon-world. *TSR*]
    Om. MS

85:16 no-one] no one *G*

85:22 and] *Om. TS*

85:26 shadow,] ~. *TS* ~; *TSR*

85:29 rows *TSR*] lines *MS*

85:33 darkness] dark *TS*

85:35 attendants] attendant *TS*

85:38 charge, *TSR*] ~ *MS*

86:1 smoking room] smoking-room
    G

86:3 half-past *TSR*] half past *MS*

86:5 States—] ~. *G*

86:10 noises] noise *TS*

86:15 will or] *Om. TS*

86:20 a] tha *TS* the *G*

86:20 dark in] in dark *TS*

86:21 ruddy] red *A1*

86:32 she saw eyes *TSR*] the eyes
    glaring *MS*

86:33 sudden *TSR*] the sudden *MS*

86:35 The platform … was all *Ed.*]
    Under the pullman all was *MS*
    Under the Pullman all was *TS*
    The platform below the
    Pullman all was *TSR*

86:37 sweetmeat] sweetmeats *TS*

86:39 She *TSR*] But she *MS*

86:39 Pullman *TSR*] pullman *MS*

87:2 Pullman *TSR*] pullman *MS*

87:6 softly *TSR*] *Om. MS*

87:9 saloon *TSR*] pullman *MS*

87:11 complete *TSR*] deep *MS*

87:18 handfuls *MS*, *A1*] handfulls *G*

87:22 lambs, *TSR*] ~ *MS*

87:25 *lirio Ed.*] lirio *MS*

87:25 water-hyacinth *Ed.*] water hya-
    cinth *MS*

87:30 she gazed at the *G*] the *MS* she
    gazed at *TSR*

87:32 remote lifelessness *TSR*]
    general forlornness *MS*

87:33 yard *TSR*] approach *MS*

87:34 stones] ~, *G*

87:37 *Adonde? Ed.*] Adonde? *MS*

88:5 The strange … of life! *TSR*]
    Om. MS

88:7 subduedly] suddenly *TS*

88:9 the] *Om. A1*

88:11 vacuous, *TSR*] *Om. MS*

88:12 The human life *TSR*] Morning
    MS

88:14 plaza] ~, *G*

88:17 women] ~, *G*

88:18 *portales Ed.*] portales *MS*

88:20 stopped,] ~ *TS*

88:25 far-gone *TSR*] dreary *MS*

88:27 life ebbing … ruin *TSR*]
    collapse and delapidation *MS*

88:28 to a *TSR*] a *MS*

88:31 Each one *TSR*] They all *MS*

88:31 his *TSR*] their *MS*

88:34 yes! The hotel] ~; The Hotel
    G

89:2 cripple,] ~ *TS*

89:5 full-flowing] fuller-flowing *TS*

89:10 willow trees *Ed.*] willow-trees
    MS

89:14 laughed,] ~ *TS*

89:15 felt *TSR*] knew *MS*

89:21 water-fowl *TSR*] water fowl
    MS

89:21 swiftly *TSR*] happily *MS*

89:24 moistness] the moistness *A1*

89:25 pepper trees] pepper-trees
    TSR

89:30 head] ~, *G*

89:32 Señorita *TSR*] señorita *MS*

89:38 Kate looked … stream of] On
    the flat near the river a peon,
    perched on the rump of *G* The
    boat moved slowly, in the hush
    of departed night, upon the *E1*
    see notes

89:40 willow trees] willow-trees *TS*

89:40 edge *TSR*] water *MS*

90:1 green foliage *TSR*] *Om.*
    MS

90:5 glistened] glistered *TS*

90:5 ochreous *G*] pinky buff *MS*
    ochreous, *TSR*

90:8 the flat] a flat *G*

90:11 pepper trees *Ed.*] pepper-trees
    MS

90:11 light-and-shade *TSR*] light and
    shade *MS*

90:12 after, in *G*] ~. In *MS* ~ In *TS* ~, In *TSR*

90:28 she watched *TSR*] *Om. MS*

90:29 men] ~, *G*

90:38 boatman *TS*] boat-man *MS*

90:38 him] ~, *G*

90:40 it.] ~! *TS*

91:7 boatman *G*] boat-man *MS*

91:15 Gods] gods *G*

91:26 If you ... the lake!— *TSR*] It's a case of making enemies, *MS*

91:33 said, with ... Star rises. *TSR*] muttered. "Leave it to the morning star. *MS*

91:39 which] ~, *TSR*

91:40 realised as] realise as *TS* realised, was *TSR*

92:2 face too] ~, ~, *G*

92:7 *We will ... Star rises? TSR*] *Leave it to the morning-star? MS* 'We will wait till the Morning Star rises?' *G*

92:9 slowly:] ~. *TS*

92:14 Señorita *TSR*] señorita *MS*

92:15 you?—] ~? *G*

92:22 morning star *G*] morning-star *MS*

92:24 Señorita *TSR*] señorita *MS*

92:33 Yes] ~, *G*

92:33 Señorita! *TSR*] señorita. *MS*

92:33 sailing-boats *Ed.*] sailing boats *MS*

92:34 canal—] ~. *G*

93:1 green, in ... country *TSR*] green *MS*

93:4 winding] ~, *G*

93:11 of] in *TS*

93:13 tough *TSR*] inane, tough *MS*

93:14 toughness *TSR*] inanity *MS*

93:23 Shoal water *MS, TSR*] Shoals water *TS* Shoal-water *G*

93:25 stretch of water] stretch of *TS* desert of water *TSR*

93:25 blue] ~, *G*

93:33 scylla ... charybdis] Scylla ... Charybdis *A1*

93:33 small,] ~ *TS*

93:38 evening star *Ed.*] evening-star *MS*

93:40 vast hollow] ~, ~, *G* ~, ~ *E1*

94:1 morning star *Ed.*] morning-star *MS*

94:1 the watcher] the watches *TS* that watches *TSR*

94:6 jokes *TSR*] vulgarism *MS*

94:10 another *TSR*] a *MS*

94:11 breeze *TSR*] wind *MS*

94:12 *petates*] petates *TS*

94:13 barelegged *Ed.*] bare-legged *MS*

94:18 outcropping,] ~ *TS*

94:23 pepper trees *Ed.*] pepper-trees *MS*

94:25 in *TSR*] upon *MS*

94:26 landing-place] ~, *G*

94:26 and] and a *TS*

94:26 in the distance *TSR*] approaching *MS*

94:27 someone *TSR*] a man *MS*

94:27 was *TSR*] *Om. MS*

94:34 crusted *TSR*] crusted a little *MS*

94:34 lake-deposit] lake deposit *TS*

94:36 Ollita *MS, A1*] Olitta *G* Ollitta *E1*

94:37 Señorita *TSR*] señorita *MS*

94:39 No] ~, *G*

94:39 Señorita *TSR*] señorita *MS*

94:40 sometimes *TSR*] *Om. MS*

95:4 animal. The ... also an] *Om. TS*

95:6 coyote," he said.] coyote!" *TS*

95:9 old] old *TS*

95:13 casseroles,] ~ *TS*

95:13 water." *P* And] ~." And *TS*

95:17 stage:] ~; *G*

95:21 trousers,] ~ *A1*

95:21 mozo *Ed.*] *mozo MS*

95:22 her] the *TS*

95:23 *Adios, Señorita! Ed.*] Adios, señorita! *MS* Adios, Señorita! *TSR*

95:36 been long] long been *TS*

95:36 place! *TSR*] ~. *MS*

95:37 not in] not *TS*

95:40 dining-room *A1*] dining room *MS* dining-/ room *G*

96:4 a dozen *TSR*] ten *MS*

96:8 Capital *Ed.*] capital *MS*

96:12 pepper trees *Ed.*] pepper-trees *MS*

96:13 drooped] dropped *TS*

96:13 birds,] ~ *TS*

96:14 poppy buds] poppy-buds *TS*

96:15 pepper-beads] pepper-heads *G*

96:20 organ cactus *Ed.*] organ-cactus *MS*

96:23 lingering] ~, *G*

96:30 mood] moods *TS*

96:31 morning star *Ed.*] morning-star *MS*

96:31 intermediate *TSR*] interregnum *MS*

96:39 look] look out *TS*

96:41 bulks *TSR*] chunks *MS*

96:41 organ cactus *Ed.*] organ-cactus *MS*

97:3 sun! *TSR*] ~. *MS*

97:9 chuffed] chuffed, *G* he chuffed, *A1*

97:11 pale-earth, *TSR*] ~ *MS*

97:12 rose *TSR*] *Om. MS*

97:13 dim-seeming] dim-seeing *TS*

97:18 or dived, *TSR*] *Om. MS*

97:19 in:] ~; *G*

97:34 rode *TSR*] *Om. MS*

97:39 flimsy and] and *TS Om. TSR*

For entries 98:3–116:29, see introductory note to Textual apparatus, and Explanatory note on 98:2.

98:3 Lake-side *TSR, TSR1*] Lake *MS*

98:4 was] *Om. A1*

98:7 half-a-crown.—But ... is said, especially ... enemies. *Ed.*] half-a-crown. *MS* half-a-crown.—But ... is said. *TSR* half-a-crown. But ... is said. *G* half-a-crown. But ... is said, especially ... enemies. *E1* half-

a-crown.—But probably this also is untrue. *TSR1*

98:10 Paradise] paradise *G*

98:11 brick-work] brickwork *G*

98:21 year] ~, *G*

98:22 hotel:] ~, *G*

98:26 bag:] ~, *G*

98:33 *Don't ... noise!* *Ed.*] *Don't ... noise! MS* "*Don't ... noise!*" *TS* "*Don't ... noise!*" *G*

99:7 want? *MS, A1*] ~, *TS*

99:9 Oh] ~, *G*

99:10 the money *TSR*] it *MS*

99:12 sincerity:] ~; *TS*

99:19 Good! *TSR*] ~. *MS*

99:23 Now] ~, *G*

99:23 bandits *TS, TSR1*] blankets *MS*

99:34 organ cactus *MS, G*] organcactus *TS* organ-cactus *A1*

99:36 going] ~, *TS*

100:4 anywhere!— *TSR*] ~.— *MS* ~! *G*

100:6 them? *TSR*] ~. *MS*

100:8 central *TSR, TSR1*] *Om. MS*

100:12 cactus *TSR, TSR1*] bush *MS*

100:15 on] in *G*

100:21 *Perdóneme ... me!* *Ed.*] *Perdoneme ... me! MS* "*Perdoneme ... me!*" *TS* "*Perdoneme ... me!*" *G*

100:24 downslope] down-/ slope *G* down-slope *A1*

100:26 barefoot] ~, *G*

100:39 and to *TSR*] and *MS*

101:5 fourteen *TSR*] fourteen great *MS*

101:6 bed] ~, *G*

101:9 Michoacán: *Ed.*] Michoacan: *MS* Michoacan; *TS*

101:11 re-opened] re-/ opened *G* reopened *A1*

101:20 wrote] went *A1*

101:24 latent] latest *TS*

101:27 day:] ~; *TS*

101:29 Now] ~, *G*

101:36 their spoke in the wheel *TSR*, *TCCR1*] a whole fist in the pie *MS* their ... into ... wheel *TSR1*

101:36 of *TSR*, *TCCR1*] of the *MS*

101:37 catchwords, to catch *TSR*, *TSR1*] catchwords which sentimental reformers supply them with, to save *MS*

101:37 poor. *TSR*] poor. The sincere socialists, who prepare the pious phrases to save the poor, are just the catspaws for pulling the chestnuts out of the fire for the scoundrels. *MS*

101:38 is *TSR*] is really *MS*

101:40 socialism. *TSR*] socialism. But it's like the plague in the Middle Ages, and I suppose it serves the same purposes. It kills off the people and manures the soil: no more: except it fattens and bloats a set of scoundrels—for a while. *MS*

102:1 no-one] no one *G*

102:1 it?] ~, *TS*

102:3 away? *MS*, *A1*] ~, *TS* ~. *G*

102:6 violating his wife on the bed,] *Om. TS1* violating his wife *TSR1*

102:10 Americans:] ~; *TS*

102:14 Patria:] Patria; *TS* patria; *G*

102:17 *honour.*] honour; *TS*

102:20 the very *TSR*] "~ ~" *MS*

102:20 "Labor!" and "*socialism!*" *TSR*] Labor! and *socialism!* *MS* Labor! and *socialism!* *TS* "Labour" and "*Socialism!*" *G*

102:20 rant] sort *TS*

102:21 her. *TSR*] her. *P* "The Spaniards came here for gold, and they found the natives stinking with blood-sacrifice. Ever since then, everybody has come here for gold, money pure and simple: and the natives still want the smell of blood. They've got to have it. That's all there is to it." *MS*

102:22 Men] men *G*

102:25 bolshevists *Ed.*] Bolshevists *MS*

102:25 socialism *G*] Socialism *MS*

102:32 these] those *TS*

103:4 anything, except *TSR*] anything to *MS* anything but *TSR1*

103:8 gringuita *Ed.*] gringito *MS* gringita *E1*

103:9 los ... los *TSR*, *TSR1*] the ... the *MS*

103:10 *peón Ed.*] peón *MS* peon *TS*

103:10 *caballero*] caballero *TS*

103:17 feel:] ~; *TS*

103:22 slushy *TSR*, *TSR1*] dry *MS*

103:23 spiritualism. *TSR*] spiritualism. The pride, the dignity, the *nobility* of life had collapsed. *MS*

103:24 but so without any] was entirely without *TSR1*

103:26 wonder. *TSR*] wonder. Their half-nakedness had no mystery in it, their stark-nakedness even less. They were as neat, as pretty as things made in a shop. And as empty of the unknown. *MS* wonder ... had no charm, no mystery, in ... unknown. *TSR1* wonder ... no charm, no mystery in ... unknown. *TCCR1*

103:27 Europe. *TSR*] Europe. Life was such a paltry thing there. The United States were even worse, more like manufactured goods, the people. People all like manufactured goods: from different factories, at different prices, but all of 'em, all of 'em, every one of 'em factory made. That, to her, was the United States. *MS*

103:28 And no!—she *TSR*] No, she *MS* And no! She *G*

103:29 an] a *TS* a defeated *TSR1*

103:36 he too] ~, ~, *G*

103:36 widdershins. When he ... he was] *Om. TS*

103:39 mechanical connections. *TSR*] widdershins connections, the widdershins people. *MS*

104:2 Even] Every *G*

104:2 did] ~, *G*

104:6 wrong *TSR*] widdershins *MS*

104:7 that life ... was fathomless *TSR*] good. Their flow was good, and rich, and it was with the sun, not against it *MS* that life was big, vast, and death was fathomless *TSR1* that life was big, and death was fathomless *TCCR1*

104:8 them. But ... out, sometimes, if men are not machines *TSR*] them, if they were driven widdershins, or caught by the cog-wheels of rapacity or lust, the widdershins mechanism of money. But after all, this was exceptional. And even then, it showed that they were not widdershins-mechanical, as the Americans are, and as the Europeans are rapidly becoming. Even their widdershins was passionate, not mechnical. *MS* them. But ... out, if man is not a machine. *TSR1* them. But ... out, if one is not a machine. *TCCR1*

104:13 mechanical widdershins] mechanical widdershin *TS* mechanical *TSR1*

104:19 unknown people] the unknown *TSR1*

104:20 mechanical *TSR, TSR1*] widdershins *MS* widdershim *TS*

104:22 stress *TSR*] lilt *MS*

104:22 stars,] ~ *TS*

104:29 above. *TSR, TSR1*] above. *P* And at the same time, the soft-touching, sunwise souls knocking at the big doors, and coming quietly {quickly *TS*} in

for a little while, to stay a while and then go again. *P* But not the busy cog-wheel people! To keep doors shut to them, fast shut. *MS*

104:37 man-servant *TS*] manservant *MS*

105:3 *let the ... for me TSR*] *the beauty of the world MS the livingness of the world TSR1*

105:4 *man's automatism TSR*] *the world's worldliness MS* the world's automatism *TSR1*

105:9 up on *TSR*] up *MS* up in *TSR1*

105:10 specks:] ~; *TS*

105:15 precipitous] ~, *G*

105:26 repellant] repellent *A1*

105:28 fishermen lived *G, TSR1*] fisherman *MS* fisherman lived *TSR* fishermen *TS1*

105:30 government] Government *G*

105:35 labored *Ed.*] laboured *MS*

106:10 perished inert] going corrupt *TSR1*

106:12 swarms] ~, *G*

106:16 non-integrate. *TSR*] non-integrate. *P* The morbid will *not-to-believe.* The horror of that which is only partially existent and partially created, fighting rabidly to preserve its own amorphousness from the living urge into being. The awful sight of apes, possessing and glimpsing one mystery beyond them, sex, glutting themselves in utter depravity of the mystery, in the baboon-like will not-to-believe in anything, not even the clear voice of their own senses. *MS*

106:32 them. They] ~, they *G*

107:1 fulness *TSR, TSR1*] Holy Ghost *MS*

107:4 other presence *TSR*] Life-presence *MS*

107:5 life-breath *G*] Life-breath *MS*

107:7 before:] ~; *TS*

107:14 *honour TSR, TSR1*] *nobility MS*
107:15 look,] ~; *TS*
107:16 recognition *TSR*] gratitude *MS*
107:22 him:] ~; *TS*
107:25 unbroken *TSR*] proud *MS* unquenched *TSR1*
107:28 They can receive the gift of grace, *TSR*] They have the ... grace, *MS* It is good, since I can draw the strange power of grace from the air, *TSR1*
107:29 they] the men *TSR1*
107:31 fulness *MS, A1*] fullness *G*
108:1   The vessel *TSR*] She *MS* The steamer *TSR1*
108:3   Tuliapán *TSR*] Teotitlan *MS* Tuliapan *TSR1*
108:6   Sayula:] ~; *G*
108:7   trees:] ~; *TS*
108:12 sand:] ~; *TS*
108:13 pepper trees *Ed.*] pepper-trees *MS*
108:15 trees:] ~; *TS*
108:17 which] ~, *G*
108:17 letters] ~, *G*
108:35 And then ... demons.—But ... believe they ... than anything *TSR*] But they want to come to the communion of grace, that they can become true men *MS* And then ... demons. But ... believe, they ... anything *G* And they are demonish. But surely they want to come ... men *TSR1*
108:40 air,] ~ *A1*
109:8   wanted:] ~; *TS*
109:17 it:] ~; *TS*
109:18 verandah:] ~; *TS*
109:19 out *TSR, TSR1*] out on *MS*
109:24 dining-room *G*] dining room *MS*
109:28 whose low, barred window opened *TSR*] *Om. MS*
109:30 her *TSR, TSR1*] *Om. MS*
109:32 do:] ~; *TS*
109:33 thing *TSR*] blessing *MS* world *TSR1*

109:37 with] with a *A1*
109:38 hair] ~, *G*
109:39 'n' *TSR*] n *MS* "n" *G*
110:1   *No ... másn Ed.*] No, Niña, no hay masn *MS No ... masn TSR*
110:2   *Child*] *child G*
110:3   honorable] honourable *G*
110:8   criada *Ed.*] *criarda MS* criada *TSR, TSR1*
110:10 reckless:] ~; *TS*
110:19 *Child*] child *G*
110:20 note *TSR*] touch *MS*
110:29 chairs exactly] chairs, exactly *E1* chairs, and *TSR1*
110:30 cane settee] settee *TSR1*
110:37 face to face] face-to-face *G*
110:38 María *Ed.*] Carmen *MS* Maria *TSR, TSR1*
111:4   *Qué bonita! Qué ... Niña! ... qué bonita! Ed.*] Qué bonita! Qué bonita, Niña! Mire que bonita! *MS Que bonita! Que ... Niña! ... que bonita! TSR Que bonita! Que ... Niña! ... que bonita! G*
112:3   resort:] ~; *TS*
112:3   has] has a *A1*
112:5   there] these *TS*
112:7   outlying *Ed.*] out-lying *MS*
112:13 life-time] life-/ time *G* lifetime *A1*
112:16 Bolshevists somehow] ~, ~, *G*
112:19 compartments *TSR*] coaches *MS*
112:20 engines, *TSR*] ~ *MS*
112:20 seems *E1*] seem *MS*
112:21 logical *TSR*] malignant *MS* fated *TSR1*
112:23 extinction *TSR, TSR1*] death *MS*
112:28 called] the latter called *TSR1*
112:29 *camiones Ed.*] camions *MS*
112:30 destiny:] ~; *TS*
112:30 *camión Ed.*] camion *MS*
113:1   street] streets *TS*
113:1   *camiones Ed.*] camions *MS*
113:11 drawers] pantaloons *TSR1*

113:17 o'clock: *Ed.*] oclock: *MS* o'clock; *TS*
113:18 work.— *TSR*] ~— *MS* ~. *G*
113:20 women,] women, and *G*
113:26 sweetmeat *Ed.*] sweet-meat *MS*
113:27 pavement, *TSR*] ~ *MS*
113:29 woman in ... a man] woman *TS1* man or a *woman TSR1*
113:32 cents] ~' *G*
113:33 sell:] ~; *TS*
113:34 pyramid:] ~; *TS*
114:1 swan song] swansong *TS*
114:3 range:] ~; *TS*
114:7 food-booths] food booths *G*
114:8 blind:] ~; *TS*
114:10 in] ~, *G*
114:16 movement:] ~; *TS*
114:19 barelegged *Ed.*] bare-legged *MS*
114:23 hotel] ~, *G*
114:30 *camiones Ed.*] camions *MS*
114:32 face-powder *Ed.*] face powder *MS*
114:36 make-up,] ~; *TS*
115:3 flappers:] ~; *TS*
115:7 twelvemonth:] ~; *G*
115:25 females,] ~; *TS*
115:36 heavy] ~, *G*
115:36 balance] ~, *G*
115:38 might, *TSR*] ~ *MS*
115:40 black, heavy *TSR*] nocturnal *MS*
115:40 sang froid] sang-froid *G*
116:4 invisible opposition *TSR*] rocks *MS*
116:8 there] ~, *TS*
116:15 flannel-trouser *TSR*] flannel trouser *MS*
116:16 gave in] gave *TS1* gave way *TSR1*
116:19 the Spirit] ~ spirit *TS*
116:19 is Spirit] ~ spirit *G*
116:20 Spirit] spirit *G*
116:22 Spirit] spirit *G*
116:24 Soul] soul *G*
116:25 Spirit] spirit *G*

116:28 Spirit] spirit *G*
116:29 Spirit] spirit *G*

For above entries (from 98:3), see introductory note to Textual apparatus, and Explanatory note on 98:2.

116:34 table, *TSR*] ~ *MS*
116:39 young] younger *A1*
116:40 day:] ~; *TS*
117:4 *petates Ed.*] petates *MS*
117:9 heavy potency *TSR*] dark power *MS*
117:12 *canoas Ed.*] canoas *MS*
117:13 sail, *TSR*] ~ *MS*
117:36 enquiringly] inquiringly *TS*
118:3 Yes. It] ~, It *TS* ~, it *G*
118:8 Still] ~, *G*
118:13 bougainvillea *TS*] bougain-villæa *MS*
118:24 blue-and-dark edges, *TSR*] blue and dark edges *MS*
118:34 mouth:] ~; *TS*
118:35 a nopal] an opal *A1*
118:36 beak and claws *TSR*] talons *MS* cactus *TS*
119:13 fading, / Was] ~, was *TS*
119:15 bird:] ~; *TS*
119:18 *moon Ed.*] Moon *MS*
119:23 sun] Sun *TS*
119:29 Saviour *G*] saviour *MS*
120:30 watching the *TSR*] with *MS*
120:31 torches, which ... cane tripod *TSR*] torches in iron torch-sockets *MS*
121:1 too] ~, *G*
121:4 the ground at *TSR*] *Om. MS*
121:9 women *TSR*] women both *MS*
121:13 lit-up *TSR*] lit up *MS*
121:16 a] the *G*
121:17 feet *TSR*] seat *MS*
121:21 forward: *MS, A1*] ~; *TS*
121:28 mouth:] ~; *TS*
121:40 still:] ~; *TS*
122:11 life. *TSR*] life. Here, she felt, was life itself, powerful, subtle, repellant. *MS*

122:11 Repellant   ...   Repellant]
        Repellent ... Repellent *A1*
122:15 deep *TSR*] red *MS*
122:19 mankind! *TSR*] ~. *MS*
122:24 old:] ~; *TS*
122:29 heavier, *TSR*] Om. *MS*
123:6   Is it time *Ed.*] *Is it time MS*
123:17 into] with *A1*
123:35 a dead coyote's head *E1*] dead
        flower-cups *MS*
124:21 a cross] the Cross *TS*
124:40 What is ... forever ... cross ...
        of bone? *Ed.*] What is ...
        forever ... Cross ... bone? *MS*
        What is ... forever ... Cross ...
        bone? [TSR has in italic] What is
        ... for ever ... Cross ... bone? G
125:5   Is it ... mother ... old bone ...
        beyond redeem? *Ed.*] Is it ...
        mother ... dry bone ...
        redeem? *MS Is it ... mother ...*
        old bone ... redeem? TSR [TSR
        has in italic] *Is it ... Mother ...*
        old bone ... redeem? G
125:9   his mother] His Mother *G*
125:10 my] My *G*
125:14 men. Jesus] ~. *P* "Jesus *TS*
125:19 rush] rushing *A1*
125:21 Dawn Star *Ed.*] dawn-star *MS*
        down-star *G*
125:31 men] ~, *G*
125:37 "*Bienvenido! ... Adios!*" *Ed.*]
        [*MS* has in roman]
125:38 And the ... *Adios!*" *Ed.*] And
        ... "Bienvenido! Adios! Bien-
        venido! Adios!" *MS Om. TS*
126:3   "*Bienvenido! ... Adios-n! Ed.*]
        [*MS* has in roman]
126:4   natural,] ~ *TS*
126:4   'n.'] 'n'. *TS* "n." *G*
126:5   intensive *E1*] syncopated *MS*
126:9   old] Old *G*
127:6   My bride ... herself: Quezal-
        coatl! *TSR*] "They are taking
        away from me my strenuous-
        ness and my onwardness. They
        are stripping me of hope and
        fear. They are throwing change

away, like small money that is
too troublesome. Keeping the
indivisible piece of gold.
Change is cheap money, to be
thrown to paupers. The gold
itself never changes, and
cannot be broken up. I am
weary of small change." *MS*
Om. E1
127:12 other] ~, *TS*
127:19 In the ... I, Quetzalcoatl. *TSR*]
        Om. MS, E1
127:27 away *TSR*] way *MS*
128:6   blackish-and-blue *TSR*] black-
        ish and blue *MS*
128:20 Who sleeps ... Who sleeps ...
        wake] [*TSR* has in italic]
128:23 snake;] ~: *TS*
128:25 iron, *TS*] ~ *MS*
128:28 world—] ~. *TS*
128:30 sha-all] sha-ll *G*
128:31 earth—] ~. *G*
128:34 foam] foom *TS* form *TSR*
129:9   circle,] ~ *TS*
129:14 fire] fired *G* fires *A1*
129:27 fulness] fullness *TS*
130:19 nearness] ~, *G*
130:28 untrammeled] untrammelled *G*
130:31 and,] ~ *G*
130:35 sun *A1*] ~, *MS*
131:6   transcendent *MS, A1*] tran-
        scendant *G*
131:7   had] has *TS*
131:26 of] of the *TS*
131:31 dawn star *Ed.*] dawn-star *MS*
132:13 smile,] ~ *TS*
132:26 have to sink in to this mystery.]
        have ... into ... mystery. *G* not
        look at her watch. She would
        lay her watch face down to hide
        its phosphorous figures. She
        would not be timed. *A1*
132:27 lake-shore *Ed.*] lake shore *MS*
132:29 hulks] bulks *TS*
132:29 sailing-*canoas Ed.*]   sailing-
        canoas *MS* sailing-canoes *TS*
132:30 night.] ~! *TS*
132:32 phosphorus] phosphorous *A1*

133:11 where *TSR*] where all *MS*
133:28 most countries *TSR*] Mexico *MS*
134:2 fear, *TSR*] ~ *MS*
134:4 half-intelligent] half intelligent *TS*
134:16 terror-struck *TSR*] terror struck *MS* terror-stricken *A1*
134:27 *Nieve!*,] ~! *TS* ~! *G*
134:28 seats] streets *G*
134:35 some *TSR*] some poisonous *MS*
134:36 evil,] ~; *TS*
134:40 breath *TSR*] lust *MS*
135:1 country, *TSR*] ~ *MS*
135:11 limpid] limp *A1*
135:12 naïveté *MS, A1*] naiveté *TS*
135:19 integrity,] ~ *TS*
135:21 serpent *TSR*] octopus *MS*
135:27 heavy,] ~ *TS*
135:30 the *TSR*] his *MS*
135:31 a man arrives *TSR*] he comes *MS*
135:35 So,] ~ *A1*
135:35 men, unable] ~, ~ *G*
135:36 serpent *TSR*] octopus *MS*
136:1 *supreme*] supreme *TS*
136:7 Past] past *G*
136:8 redeemer] Redeemer *G*
136:12 *quo*. *E1*] *quo*. *P* When man ceases to fight his way out, out into a new world of being; when he becomes like a miner in the underground, then the ancient dominion of the metals re-asserts itself in his consciousness. The primeval saturnine age of the metals reaps him back again, and his lust is for the virgins of the rocks, for gold and silver. It is man {is a man *G*} buried again, entombed in a bygone underworld, where gold itself is the sun and the flower of creation, and silver a virgin daughter. Then man falls under the spell of the old supreme, he worships gold. Evil is the collapse backwards into old, out-lived forms. And men collapse far, far back, to the age of Saturn, when gold was the first blossom and iron the stuff {the bone *TSR*} of life. *P* In the collapse backwards into the subterranean forms, there is a lust of hatred of the above-world forms. In the collapse backwards, the great thirsty, spell-bound lust of gold, or even of silver, starts automatically the lust of murder. The two things work almost simultaneously. *P* And this explains revolutions. All violent, real revolutions, like the French and Russian, arise from a feebleness in the higher state, the reins slip, the horses bolt downhill. The populace is the lower being, and it rushes downhill. It rushes back into the plutonic underworld, mad, mad to possess itself of the world's gold and treasure. And with the mad lust for the gold automatically arises the mad lust to murder those who have been masters of {superior to the *TSR*} gold, the leaders in the overhead world. *P* So a Mexican, overcome by the sight of a few pesos, may in lust stab and stab and stab his victim, again and again. So great nations, fallen into the lust for wealth, which is the only recognised {recognized *TS* recognised *G*} power in the underworld: it is the kingdom of gold: {gold; *TS*} will break out in a lust of war. Fair words will always be invented to cover foul deeds. But a murder, and a bloody revolution perhaps can never be lived down. *P* It is strange that men will give bread, meat, and life itself for bits of silver and gold. The Standard! The Idol forever. The plutonic underworld. *P* So now Kate felt the heavy horror of evil in the air, life falling back into old, horrible forms, horrible to the life which has passed beyond those forms. The sudden panic lust of gold, with murder in the second stroke. *P* The heavy horror of Mexico, the same the Spaniards felt when they smelt the stench of rotten human blood around the pyramids of Huitzilopochtli. It darkened the air. Because already,

the life-hope was dead, there was an instinct of death-worship in the Aztecs. And the gentle hopelessness of Montezuma was the counterpart of the lust of tearing out the heart of life. *The hearts of men are changeable*, says the old chronicler {Chronicler *TS*} who fought with Cortes and knew the Indians for many years: *but particularly the hearts of the Indians.*—{Indians. *TS*} Changing from gentle, extreme, almost hopeless love, to a vindictive diabolism.—{diabolism. *G*} The human being without any true centre. *MS*

136:16 absolutely *MS,A1*] absolute *TS*
136:19 rabble—] ~ *TS* ~; *TSR*
136:38 panel-space *TSR*] shutter *MS*
137:14 myself? *TSR*] ~. *MS*
137:23 really had the power *TSR*] was really evil *MS*
137:26 reassured *Ed.*] re-assured *MS*
137:34 dining-room *G*] dining room *MS*
137:34 on to] on *TS*
138:14 balls] ~, *G*
138:19 "How ... Niña?" *TSR*] ~ ... ~? *MS*
138:24 window-shutter] window shutter *TS*
138:30 door. Jesúsn ... outside your] *Om. TS*
138:33 Ah] ~, *G*
138:35 it, *TSR*] ~ *MS*
138:36 No] ~, *G*
138:37 mid-day—] ~. *G*
138:38 mid-day *G*] mid day *MS*
138:38 wild] ~, *G*
138:39 half savage *E1*] very simple *MS*
139:2 Kate *TSR*] her *MS*
139:6 old,] ~ *TS*
139:6 long-barreled] long-barrelled *G*
139:10 *Pst! Pst! G*] Pst! Pst! *MS Pst! Pst! TSR*
139:12 some thing] something *TS*
139:14 And] ~, *A1*
139:14 if *A1*] If *MS*
139:22 other-world] other world *TS*

140:2 las] la *TS*
140:3 her] the *TS*
140:6 shy] ~, *G*
140:6 bird-like *G*] birdlike *MS*
140:7 *absorb*] absorb *TS*
140:12 heavy,] ~ *A1*
140:23 viscous] vicious *TS*
140:23 fear, and wonder,] ~ ~ ~ *TS*
140:27 becoming *TSR*] *Om. MS*
141:3 earth,] ~ *TS*
141:7 *cared*] cared *TS*
141:8 *she TSR*] she *MS*
141:9 brooms] broom *TS*
141:16 *aguador Ed.*] aquador *MS* aquador *A1*
141:19 wonder:] ~; *TS*
141:20 an *MS, E1*] no *TSR*
141:25 Niña?—*TSR*] Niña? *Está durmiendo*—*MS* Niña. *G* Niña? *A1*
141:28 dressing gown *Ed.*] dressing-gown *MS*
141:30 *aguador Ed.*] aquador *MS* aquador *A1*
141:32 *aguador Ed.*] aquador *MS* aquador *A1*
141:33 shutters,] ~ *TS*
141:37 *rancheros Ed.*] rancheros *MS*
142:8 No Niña! *TSR*] ~ ~. *MS* ~, ~! *G*
142:11 fruit,] ~ *TS*
142:14 Oh] ~, *G*
142:31 sun,] ~ *TS*
142:35 Silently appears an *TSR*] An *MS*
142:36 *patrona Ed.*] patrona *MS*
142:37 right? Where] ~? *P* Where *A1*
143:5 is it] it is *A1*
143:9 am! *Ed.*] ~. *MS* ~? *TSR*
143:12 yes!"—] ~!" *TS*
143:15 *Mire! ... perejil ... centavo Ed.*] Mire! Niña! Compré perjil a un centavo *MS*
143:19 dining-room *G*] dining room *MS*
143:22 window-hole] window hole *TS*
143:24 school!—] ~! *TS*
143:25 No!— *TSR*] ~, *MS*

143:25 window-hole *Ed.*] window hole *MS*

143:28 earthenware] earthen-/ ware *TS* earthen-ware *A1*

143:29 raw] new *TS*

143:30 the palm of] *Om. TS*

143:32 *Clap! ... Clap! Ed.*] Clap! Clap! Clap! Clap! Clap! Clap! *MS*

143:32 *Clap!*—it *Ed.*] Clap!—~ *MS* Clap! ~ *TS* Clap!. It *G*

143:34 window-hole] window hole *TS*

143:35 mid-day *G*] midday *MS* mid-/ day *TS*

143:36 window-hole *Ed.*] window hole *MS*

143:40 mid-day *G*] midday *MS*

144:11 calabacitas *TSR*] calabasitas *MS*

144:12 *dulce*] dulce *TS*

144:19 lake,] ~ *TS*

144:26 half-past *Ed.*] half past *MS*

144:28 low] *Om. A1*

144:31 little] *Om. A1*

145:12 socialist government] Socialist Government *G*

145:14 stones *MS, A1*] stone *TS*

145:17 unnatural *TSR*] dead *MS*

145:21 in his barbarism *TSR*] really *MS*

145:38 rag] rags *TS*

145:40 stupefied *A1*] stupified *MS*

146:8 working,] ~ *A1*

146:21 naïve *A1*] naïve, *MS* naive, *TS* naive *E1*

146:25 out] *Om. TS*

146:29 beach:] ~; *G*

146:35 lie] be *TS*

147:14 continent] Continent *TS*

147:19 feet!] ~. *TS*

147:23 peculiar] ~, *G*

147:27 Guadalajara:] ~— *TS*

148:15 proud] ~, *TS*

148:19 engulph] engulf *TS*

148:28 break *TSR*] break it *MS*

148:28 No] ~, *TS*

148:28 *didn't*] didn't *TS*

148:29 No] ~, *A1*

148:33 leadership: who] ~. Who *TS*

148:38 lined,] ~ *TS*

148:40 *Usted ... gringuitos ... todo Ed.*] Usted sabe, Niña, los gringos, los gringitos llevan todo *MS*

148:40 You] you *TS*

148:41 gringos *Ed.*] *gringos MS*

148:41 gringuitos *Ed.*] *gringitos MS*

148:41 everything————] ~ ... *G*

149:1 gringos *Ed.*] *gringos MS*

149:2 gringuitos *Ed.*] *gringitos MS*

149:6 Niña!] ~, *G*

149:8 Niña—!] ~! *TS*

149:12 would] could *TS*

149:25 *I*] I *TS*

149:30 hurt—] ~. *TS*

149:34 amiable *G*] aimiable *MS*

149:40 quiet, *MS, A1*] ~ *TS*

149:41 cleansed] cleaned *TS*

150:1 flitting] ~, *G*

150:1 coming-and-going] coming and going *TS*

150:2 clap-clap-clapping] clap—clap—clapping *TS*

150:3 metate *TSR*] petate *MS*

150:4 well—] ~. *TS*

150:4 Jesús *TSR*] Jesus *MS*

150:5 all! *TSR*] ~. *MS*

150:5 *fun*] fun *TS*

150:8 all, *TSR*] ~ *MS*

150:16 the family *TSR*] them *MS*

150:16 vagaries *TSR*] flights *MS*

150:18 At *TSR*] But at *MS*

150:22 eggs] ~, *TS*

150:23 dining table *Ed.*] dining-table *MS*

150:29 *insouciance*] insouciance *G*

150:36 suddenly,] ~ *TS*

150:39 even] *Om. TS*

151:6 of] if *G*

151:6 something] something was *A1*

151:6 his *TSR*] *Om. MS* her *TS*

151:16 heads,] ~ *TS*

151:30 if] *Om. A1*

152:10 and] or *G*

152:11 street-corner] street-/ corner *TS* street corner *G*

152:14 motionless] ~, *G*

152:28 litter] a litter *G*

152:31 human male *TSR*] specimen *MS*

152:33 unconscious *E1*] indifferent *MS*

152:39 band *MS, A1*] brand *TS*

153:7 day] day there *G*

153:11 twenty-two *TS*] twenty two *MS*

153:28 mid-day *Ed.*] mid day *MS* midday *TS, A1* mid-/ day *G*

153:29 evening:] ~; *TS*

153:31 kitchen-hole *Ed.*] kitchen hole *MS*

153:39 know how to put even] even know how to put *TS*

154:9 relatives] relative *TS*

154:10 money: he] ~. He *MS*

154:15 knife,] ~ *TS*

154:19 *good*] Good *TS*

155:5 reddish-and-yellow *TSR*] reddish-and yellow *MS* reddish and yellow *TS*

155:7 mango-grove *Ed.*] mango grove *MS*

155:7 trees] ~, *G*

155:8 lake] ~, *G*

155:11 had had *TSR*] had *MS*

155:12 government] Government *G*

155:14 lake-shore *Ed.*] lake shore *MS*

155:22 Kate.] ~? *A1*

155:23 woman] ~, *G*

155:26 stout, *TS*] ~; *MS*

156:5 *will TSR*] pain *MS*

156:8 he] she *A1*

156:14 Men *Ed.*] men *MS*

156:25 Oh] ~, *TS*

156:25 well; *TSR*] ~: *MS*

156:25 is the] ~, ~ *E1*

156:26 delicate—] ~. *G*

156:28 at] in *A1*

156:28 Here—! Here] ~—here *TS*

156:35 Kate.] ~; *TS*

156:37 foundlings] ~' *G*

157:4 seemed, *TSR*] seemed as if *MS*

157:23 dress-makers] dressmakers *TS, A1* dress-/ makers *G*

157:30 victim:] ~; *TS*

157:36 eagerness] ~, *TS*

158:11 god-father *Ed.*] godfather *MS*

158:14 general?] ~, *A1*

158:16 general:] ~; *TS*

158:19 oh] ~, *G*

158:29 Men *TSR*] men *MS*

158:33 Men *G*] men *MS*

158:33 Quetzalcoatl,] ~— *TS*

158:34 say—] ~, *G*

159:9 already] ~, *G*

159:9 possible] ~, *G*

159:16 landscape:] ~; *TS*

159:18 lake-shore *Ed.*] lake shore *MS*

159:27 half-naked *Ed.*] half naked *MS*

159:38 out] ~, *G*

159:40 wiggly] wriggly *TS*

160:4 their shoulders ... colour,] *Om. TS*

160:15 itself dry *TSR*] *Om. MS*

160:37 *Jamiltepec, Señorita ... Ramón! Ed.*] Jamiltepec, señorita. La hacienda de Don Ramón! *MS* Jamiltepec, Señorita ... Ramon! *TSR*

161:1 how] How *TS*

161:6 No] ~, *TS*

161:11 willow trees *Ed.*] willow-trees *MS*

161:14 path] patch *TS*

161:38 ox wagons *Ed.*] ox-wagons *MS*

162:5 zaguán or passage *Ed.*] zaguán *MS* Zaguan *TS* Zaguan or passage *TSR* zaguan or passage *G*

162:13 entrance-way *Ed.*] entrance way *MS*

162:33 sailing-*canoa Ed.*] sailing canoe *MS*

162:38 San] *Om. A1*

163:1 *Hermoso ... bonito! Ed.*] Hermoso—si! Si, bonito! *MS*

163:7 cloisters] cloister *A1*

163:8 neglected formal *TSR*] untidy *MS*

163:12 with a] with *TS*

163:24 whitewashed, *Ed.*] whitewashed; *MS* white-/ washed; *G* white-washed; *A1*

163:24 furniture, *Ed.*] ~; *MS*

163:25 garden-arbor] garden-arbour *G*

163:31 out-of-doors *Ed.*] out of doors *MS*

164:13 talk] *talk TS*

164:29 But] ~, *G*

164:30 possible!] ~. *G*

164:36 pug-faced,] ~ *TS*

165:1 be very] ~ ~, *G*

165:4 humility? *A1*] ~. *MS*

165:5 pride?— *Ed.*] ~.— *MS* ~. *G* ~? *A1*

165:5 his *Ed.*] His *MS*

165:13 Ah] ~, *G*

165:23 go] *Om. TS* be *G*

165:25 held] held I've held *TS* held, I've held *G*

165:34 died, and *E1*] died. *MS* died, *TS*

166:9 Ah—!] ~! *G*

166:13 him—"] ~"— *TS* ~." *G*

166:32 Virgin:] ~! *G*

166:39 God, and] ~. And *TS*

166:40 him] Him *G*

167:12 bitter—!] ~! *G*

167:20 *peones Ed.*] peóns *MS* peons *TS*

167:24 woolen] woollen *G*

167:27 red,] ~ *TS*

167:28 woolen] woollen *G*

167:37 joint *TSR*] place *MS*

168:1 *peón Ed.*] peon *MS*

168:1 *Señor Peón Ed.*] Señor Peon *MS*

168:1 *Señor Moujik Ed.*] Señor Moujik *MS*

168:9 And in ... another world] It was evident that Ramon was thinking in another world, in the silence *TS*

168:10 stillness] silence *A1*

168:37 Oh] ~, *G*

168:38 leave *TSR*] leave with *MS*

169:11 upright *G*] ~, *MS*

169:12 brain] ~, *G*

169:19 other strength *TSR*] strength of the beyond *MS*

169:32 and threw *TSR*] then threw *MS*

170:2 front. *P* He] ~. He *TS*

170:13 ox wagon *Ed.*] ox-wagon *MS*

170:18 round] around *G*

170:30 *patrón TSR*] patron *MS*

170:33 *Patrón TSR*] Patron *MS*

170:35 smith *TSR*] man *MS*

170:35 tongs *G*] tongues *MS*

170:35 tongue-shaped *TSR*] tongue shaped *MS*

170:36 Ramón *TSR*] Don Ramón *MS*

170:36 it] it for *A1*

170:37 smith *TSR*] man *MS*

171:2 *Patrón TSR*] Patrón *MS*

171:28 Ah] ~, *G*

171:32 Carlota. "Will] ~, "will *G*

171:33 boat! *TSR*] ~. *MS* ~? *G*

171:33 Martín] Martin *TS*

171:38 This!] ~? *G*

172:2 Carlota? *TSR*] ~. *MS*

172:6 I!] ~? *G*

172:10 Oh] ~, *TS*

172:38 blouse-shirt] blouse-skirt *TS*

173:15 peace *TSR*] nobility *MS*

173:24 *Adios! Ed.*] Adios! *MS*

173:25 *Adios Ed.*] Adios *MS* Adios, *G*

173:25 *Señor! Ed.*] señor! *MS*

173:28 its *E1*] with its *MS*

173:39 Señor] *Señor TSR*

174:18 stair-case] staircase *G*

174:21 Martín] Martin *TS*

174:25 still *TSR*] perfect *MS*

174:28 tom-tom, *TSR*] ~ *MS*

174:29 face *TSR*] face serene and *MS*

175:29 turned] ~, *G*

175:30 daytime voices *TSR*] voices *MS*

175:33 face *TSR*] face proud and *MS*

175:39 plasm *E1*] plasm of the Only One *MS*

176:2 heaving] hearing *TS* wearing *TSR*

176:3 yesterday] ~, *G*

176:22 *I Am Ed.*] I Am *MS*

176:24 *I Am Ed.*] I Am *MS*

176:26 *I Am! I Am! Ed.*] I Am! I Am! *MS*

176:33 On] In *TS*

176:35 *I Am Ed.*] I Am *MS*

177:6 *I Am Ed.*] I Am *MS*

177:9 *I Am Ed.*] I Am *MS*

177:23 Now, and] ~ ~ *TS*

177:23 *I Am Ed.*] I Am *MS*
177:25 bullock wagon *Ed.*] bullock-wagon *MS*
178:9 multitudes] multitude *A1*
178:10 waving *TSR*] wave *MS*
178:17 and] and the *TS*
178:23 Between] Between the *A1*
178:35 of the day, and lords] *Om. TS*
179:25 pomegranate:] ~; *TS*
179:31 Snake] snake *TS*
179:32 and *TSR*] and the *MS*
180:4 space] *Om. A1*
180:8 thine.] ~! *TS*
180:19 Ah! *TSR*] ~, *MS*
180:26 Lo] ~, *G*
181:10 separateness *E1*] loneliness *MS*
181:13 laboring *Ed.*] labouring *MS*
181:16 him] them *G*
181:29 uniform, *TSR, E1*] ~ *MS,G*
182:5 *Qué tal? Ed.*] Qué tal? *MS* Que tal? *TS*
182:6 *Bien! Muy Bien! Ed.*] Bien! Muy bien! *MS*
182:8 *himself*] ~, *TS*
182:29 deep-chested] deep chested *TS*
182:37 had,] ~; *E1*
182:38 undressed.] ~! *G*
183:9 Sailing-boats *Ed.*] Sailing boats *MS*
183:12 sperm-like] spum-like *TS* spume-like *TSR*
183:14 church-towers] church towers *TS*
183:22 brown. Like] ~, like *TS*
183:25 *Mexico E1*] Mexico *MS*
183:25 *Below*] *below G*
183:26 rocking-chair *Ed.*] rocking chair *MS*
183:28 tea-cup] tea-cups *G*
184:8 and his] and *A1*
184:8 narcotic,] ~ *A1*
184:10 if] *Om. A1*
184:13 powerful,] ~ *A1*
184:33 eyes—!] ~! *G*
184:36 break-water *Ed.*] breakwater *MS, A1* break-/ water *G*
184:39 charales *Ed.*] *charales MS*
185:23 Oh no] ~, ~ *G*

185:23 Doña] *Om. TS*
185:23 Oh yes] ~, ~ *G*
185:26 Ah] ~, *G*
185:27 Ah] ~, *G*
185:32 fair] far *G* good *E1*
185:34 Now do] No wo *TS* Now would *TSR*
185:34 asked,] ~ *TS*
186:7 quiet] ~, *TS*
186:37 involuntary,] ~ *TS*
186:39 of the] *Om. TS*
187:4 marry,] ~. *TS*
187:34 No] ~. *TS*
187:34 No] ~, *G*
187:36 *what*] what *TS*
187:36 she said] said she *TS*
187:38 changeful *TSR*] kindly *TS*
188:11 blond *TSR*] *Om. MS*
188:22 Oh] ~, *G*
188:23 in to] into *G*
188:28 strange *E1*] false *MS*
188:32 Ah] ~, *G*
189:8 Ah] ~, *G*
189:17 fume,] ~ *TS*
189:24 high-road] highroad *G*
189:30 in to] into *G*
189:32 rowed disconsolate] ~ ~, *TS* ~, ~, *E1*
190:1 Chapter XIII ... Rain. *TSR*] *Om. MS*
190:7 Ramón—] ~. *TS*
190:23 him *G*] *Om. MS*
190:25 Don] '~ *G*
190:34 street." *MS, A1*] ~.'" *G*
191:1 Secretary,] ~ *G*
191:6 me,] ~ *G*
191:9 also of] also *G*
192:6 wouldn't *MS, A1*] Wouldn't *TS*
192:20 went] walked *G*
192:37 upstairs,] ~ *G*
192:40 say. *P* He] ~. He *G*
193:25 Martín *Ed.*] Guisleno *MS* Martin *E1*
193:26 *Ya, Patrón A1*] Ya, Patrón *MS* Ya, Patron *TSR*
193:27 *Ya TSR*] Ya *MS*
193:30 *Patrón A1*] Patrón *MS* Patron *TS*

193:33 *Viene el agua TSR*] Vienen las
aguas *MS Vene el agua G*

193:34 *Creo que sí, Patrón Ed.*] Creo
que sí, Patrón *MS Creo que sì,
Patrón TSR*

193:36 *petates Ed.*] petates *MS*

193:37 Martín *Ed.*] Guisleno *MS*
Martin *A1*

193:38 cane, *E1*] ~ *MS*

193:39 cord, *E1*] ~ *MS*

194:3 up] *Om. G*

194:5 Martín *Ed.*] Guisleno *MS*
Martin *A1*

194:7 firelight *Ed.*] fire-light *MS*

194:18 from the house *TSR*] running
too *MS*

194:20 zig-zags *Ed.*] zigzags *MS*

194:25 into] in *G*

194:26 all] *Om. TS*

194:30 standing,] ~ *G*

194:38 coming *TSR*] running *MS*

195:5 of the house *TSR*] *Om. MS*

195:9 poppy-petal *TSR*] sealing-wax
MS

195:12 outside, *TSR*] ~ *MS*

195:16 man *TSR*] throng *MS*

195:20 heart's *TSR*] soul's *MS*

195:25 you!] ~? *G*

195:25 I!] ~? *G*

195:27 the] *Om. G*

195:31 came *TSR*] ran *MS*

196:3 away] way *A1*

196:8 Come] come *A1*

196:8 Snake *TSR*] snake *MS*

196:8 fire of] fire at *A1*

196:17 *peones Ed.*] peóns *MS* peons *TS*

196:33 your] you *G*

196:39 Arre *Ed.*] Harreh *MS Harreh G*

196:39 Burro] *Burro G*

197:16 growing,] ~ *G*

197:16 Mexico—] ~. *TS*

197:28 looking] looking up *G*

197:31 "Up!] "~ *G*

198:11 Yet you] You you *TS* You *G*

198:16 all] *Om. TS*

198:21 in, *TSR*] ~ *MS*

198:22 settle] Settle *G*

198:24 clouds,] ~; *TS*

198:26 blue] the blue *G*

198:27 neck *TSR*] wings *MS*

198:38 faces *E1*] heads *MS*

199:3 Don] *Om. TS*

199:7 Morning Star *Ed.*] Morning-
star *MS*

199:13 you, the star] you, the stars
TS

199:16 Morning Star *Ed.*] Morning-
Star *MS* Morning-star *G*

199:24 far-flying] far-lying *G*

199:33 Dawn Star *Ed.*] Dawn-Star *MS*

200:6 sons] Sons *TS*

200:6 men] Men *G*

200:13 like yesterday *TSR*] *Om. MS*

200:18 zopilote] Zopilote *TS* Xopilote
G

200:21 god] God *G*

200:21 coming, Quetzalcoatl,] ~. ~,
TS ~. ~ *G*

200:22 shadow] shadows *TS*

200:28 houses] homes *TS*

200:30 Men *E1*] men *MS, A1*

200:38 fabrics *E1*] silk *MS* fabric *A1*

201:1 ghosts *E1*] sheep *MS*

201:5 Martín *Ed.*] Guisleno *MS*
Martin *E1*

201:13 violence *TSR*] great violence
MS

201:17 street-lamp] streetlamp *TS*
streeet lamp *G* street lamp
A1

202:13 rocking-chairs *Ed.*] rocking
chairs *MS*

202:17 Ah] ~, *G*

202:22 comes—] ~. *TS*

202:29 barefoot] barefooted *G*

202:30 women-servants *TSR*] women
servants *MS*

202:36 us *TSR*] Mexico *MS*

203:4 What am] '~ ~ *G*

203:4 here?"] ~?'" *G*

203:6 English English] English *TS*
good English *TSR*

203:18 last] least *A1*

203:23 deadened!] ~? *G*

203:28 *cuando … perder? Ed.*] cuando
se echa a perder? *MS*

203:31 don't know ... do think *TSR*]
think he is rather terrible, and
{terrible and *TS*} rather splendid. I do think that something
inside oneself *believes* him:
some old, old, old part of
oneself, that one had mislaid.
Perhaps it is Irish.—But I do
think, as well, *MS*

204:9 belief,] ~ *G*

204:12 god-father *Ed.*] godfather *MS*

204:26 little *TSR*] little bantam of a
MS

204:30 thoughts] ~, *G*

205:3 *peones Ed.*] peóns *MS* peons *TS*

205:11 *à l'américaine TSR*] à l'américaine *MS*

205:15 you?—keep] ~? Keep *TS*

205:20 *Quién sabe! Ed.*] Quien sabe!
MS

205:21 à] a *TS*

206:34 slow] ~, *TS*

206:34 change,] ~ *G*

207:1 Liberty] liberty *TS*

207:7 Christ] ~, *TS*

207:13 unforeseen *MS*, *A1*] unforseen
G

207:14 the white ... to do *TSR*] all
white America does *MS*

207:19 love-will *Ed.*] love will *MS* lost
will *TS*

207:40 And] ~, *G*

208:6 Life *TSR*] America *MS*

208:13 replied;] ~, *G*

208:39 doing!] ~? *G*

209:5 And He *TS*] And he *MS*

209:9 Mexico,—] ~—*A1*

209:9 hasn't;] ~— *G*

209:10 charity *Ed.*] Charity *MS*

209:11 reform, *TSR*] ~ *MS*

209:14 all] *Om. TS*

209:15 so-forth] so forth *G*

209:20 reason,] ~ *G*

209:26 merely,] ~ *G*

209:30 Ah] ~, *G*

209:37 good *E1*] ridiculous *MS*

209:39 *assert*] assert *TS*

210:1 whole] *Om. A1*

210:11 *Instinctively*] Instinctively *TS*

210:12 Is] '~ *G*

210:15 it."] ~.'" *G*

210:17 gramophones *MS*, *A1*] grama-
phones *TS*, *E1*

210:19 believe—] ~ *TS*

210:19 sucklings, *G*] ~ *MS* ~. *TS*

210:22 gramophones *MS*, *A1*] grama-
phones *G*

210:28 door:] ~. *TS*

210:29 away!"] ~," *G*

210:29 smell *TSR*] gangrene *MS*

211:10 Ah,] ~ *G*

211:18 her] the *TS*

211:19 modern life *TSR*] the American
continent *MS*

211:20 flippant *TSR*] *Om. MS*

211:21 modern *TSR*] American *MS*

211:21 cry "Niña! Niña!"] ~— "~!
~! *TS* ~.—~! ~! *G*

211:32 caressive,] ~ *TS*

211:33 with] was *TS*

211:36 Niña!"—] ~!" *TS*

212:6 mockery, issuing from *TSR*]
mockery of *MS*

212:7 against *TSR*] for *MS*

212:10 downwards] downward *TS*

212:11 *there*] there *G*

212:14 say: *TSR*] ~ *MS*

212:15 camote! *E1*] ~. *MS*

212:17 of the] of her *TS*

212:19 true?] ~! *TS*

212:23 *Verdad! Verdad! Ed.*] Verdad!
Verdad! *MS*

212:25:gringos ... gringos *Ed.*] *gringos
... gringos MS*

213:6 dingy-looking *TSR*] dingy
looking *MS*

213:17 dark-green] dark green *TS*

213:32 quietly] quickly *TS*

213:37 glotzing] glozing *A1*

214:8 lake-front *Ed.*] lake front *MS*

214:10 Rose-red *Ed.*] Rose red *MS*

214:16 harebells] hare-/ bells *G* harebells *A1*

214:26 lines] lies *G*

214:26 zig-zags *Ed.*] zigzags *MS*

214:29 felt *Ed.*] *Om. MS*

215:3 left *TSR*] ~, *MS*
215:9 glare. *P* She] ~. She *G*
215:12 years *MS, AI*] ~' *G*
215:13 which *TSR*] with *MS*
215:13 round-faced *G*] round faced *MS* round-/ faced *TSR*
215:16 little-man's] little man's *TS*
215:19 got,] ~? *AI*
216:10 fibre string] fibre-string *TS*
216:39 faces, *TSR*] ~ *MS*
217:2 say:] ~ *G*
217:21 hat,] ~ *TS*
217:21 trousers,] ~ *G*
217:24 stiff-shouldered *MS, AI*] stiff-shoulder *G*
217:29 at] *Om. G*
218:1 great] ~, *TS*
218:9 good! *TSR*] ~. *MS*
218:12 interfere! *TSR*] ~. *MS*
218:13 sulky-faced *TSR*] sulky faced *MS*
218:14 apprehension—] ~. *TS*
218:16 twin-towers *Ed.*] twin towers *MS*
218:19 after] after the *TS*
218:20 animal,] ~ *TS*
218:38 Gringos] gringos *TS*
219:8 wreck *EI*] wreak *MS, AI*
219:17 mud bricks] mud-bricks *TS*
220:4 half-past *TSR*] half past *MS*
220:14 not? *TSR*] ~. *MS*
220:34 cuentas *Ed.*] *cuentas MS*
221:2 secret,] ~ *G*
221:5 rocking-chair *Ed.*] rocking chair *MS*
221:19 recognised] recognized *TS*
221:32 Niña. You] ~, you *TS*
222:9 beginning? *AI*] ~. *MS*
222:20 said: My *TS*] ~: *P* "My *MS* ~: 'My *TSR*
222:21 cross] Cross *TS*
222:24 Mexico.] ~.' *TSR*
222:32 Mexico? *G*] ~. *MS*
222:37 Mexico!] ~. *TS*
223:9 mother *Ed.*] Mother *MS*
223:32 Christians—] ~. *TS*
224:8 el] El *TS*
224:9 his *Ed.*] His *MS*

224:13 his *Ed.*] His *MS*
224:17 Mary, *MS, AI*] ~ *TS*
224:17 gringuita, *Ed.*] gringita, *MS* gringita. *G*
224:19 She *Ed.*] she *MS*
224:23 sea] Sea *TS*
224:25 gringuito ... gringuito *Ed.*] gringito ... gringito *MS* Gringito ... Gringito *G*
224:31 himself *Ed.*] Himself *MS*
224:31 gringo] Gringo *TS*
224:34 gringo] Gringo *G*
225:2 his *Ed.*] His *MS*
225:8 *Quién sabe! Ed.*] Quien sabe! *MS*
225:14 barking,] ~ *TS*
225:18 Second *Ed.*] second *MS*
225:23 sun] Sun *TS*
225:28 *This is ... and slowly TSR*] [*MS* has in roman]
225:36 *He is dead ... but unrelinquished TSR*] He is dead ... but unrelinquished *MS*
226:6 all] *Om. TS*
226:11 No-one] No one *TS*
226:13 Lo] So *TS*
226:29 now] new *G*
226:34 wanting] waiting *TS*
226:38 *moon] Moon TS*
227:19 art *AI*] are *MS*
227:21 Oh] ~, *AI*
227:22 mother *Ed.*] Mother *MS*
227:23 churches] Churches. *TS*
227:24 strength, *MS, AI*] ~ *G*
227:26 woman] ~, *G*
227:28 despair] despairs *TS*
227:32 Oh] ~, *G*
227:33 serpent-silent] serpent—silent *TS*
227:40 the lord] The ~ *TS*
228:6 And] ~, *AI*
229:3 *canoas Ed.*] canoas *MS* canoes *G*
229:7 Yemas] Zemas *TS*
229:8 boat-loads *Ed.*] boat-/ loads *MS* boatloads *TS*
229:13 on Saturdays, *TSR*] *Om. MS*

229:17 melons dark-green *TSR*] *Om.* MS

229:22 donkeys] *Om. TS* asses *TSR*

229:28 her] the *TS*

229:34 pays] pays for *A1*

230:1 barefoot] ~, *G*

230:3 even] ever *TS*

230:7 walnuts; *TSR*] ~, *MS*

230:9 pearl-white *TSR*] pearl white *MS*

230:17 men] men were *G*

230:36 will:] ~; *TS*

230:39 men *TSR*] men who *MS*

231:5 invisibly] invincibly *A1*

231:6 wanted,] ~ *TS*

231:11 looped hats *MS, A1*] looped-hats *TS*

231:26 thick] rich *TS*

231:26 ground! *TSR*] ~. *MS*

231:37 *peón Ed.*] peón *MS* peon *TS*

232:1 slim] ~, *G*

232:5 rapidly-emptying *TSR*] rapidly emptying *MS*

232:16 pistol-firer *TSR*] pistol firer *MS*

232:18 pistol,] ~ *TS*

232:27 General *E1*] general *MS*

232:38 lake-shore *Ed.*] lake shore *MS*

232:38 mountains,] mountain *TS*

233:17 moon *MS, A1*] Moon *TS*

233:23 moon! *E1*] ~, *MS*

233:30 The corner ... human excrement. *MS, A1*] *Om. E1 see notes*

233:34 pip!—pip!—pip!] pip!-pip! *TS*

233:39 Yes! *TSR*] ~. *MS*

234:6 round] *Om. G*

234:7 *Qué Niña! Qué Niña! Ed.*] *Que Niña! Que Niña! MS Que Niña! Que Niña! A1*

234:7 as] As *TS*

234:8 life? *E1*] ~. *MS*

234:25 finished. It] ~ it *TS*

234:29 answered:] ~. *TS*

235:4 her] ~, *A1*

235:13 me.— *MS, A1*] ~—*G* ~. *E1*

235:24 *really*] really *TS*

236:1 sharp,] ~ *G*

236:9 her!] ~? *TS*

236:22 repellant *E1*] devilish *MS* repellent *A1*

236:36 on] On *TS*

236:39 him *A1*] it *MS*

237:7 —not] Not *TS*

237:7 eh?"—] ~?" *TS*

237:11 No!] ~!— *TS*

237:14 tomorrow—] ~, *TS* to-morrow, *A1*

237:18 Men] men *TS*

237:37 awoke] woke *A1*

238:4 cross,] ~ *TS*

238:8 green-watered] green watered *G*

238:10 of feet] of the feet *G*

238:35 Oh no] ~, No *TS* ~, no *A1*

238:36 crape] crepe *TS* crêpe *A1*

238:39 young] *Om. G*

239:7 shadow. Concha ... "*Está muy flaco!* He ... thin." *Ed.*] shadow. *P* "He is very thin!" said Juana, of the cockerel. *MS* shadow. Concha ... "Está muy flaco! He ... thin." *TSR*

239:18 *Está muy flaco! Ed.*] Está muy flojo! *MS* Está muy flaco! *TSR*

239:18 still *TSR*] *Om. MS*

239:20 scraggy *TSR*] flaccid *MS*

239:24 *flaco TSR*] *flojo MS*

240:3 brother!] ~, *A1*

240:3 images.] ~, *TS*

240:16 Wondering,] ~ *G*

240:16 her—] ~ *TS* ~, *G*

240:17 ruins] truins *TS* trains *TSR*

240:33 Quetzalcoatl ... *Holálá, Mexicanos! Ed.*] Quetzalcoatl ... Holàlà, Mexicanos! *MS Om. TS*

241:4 till it *TSR*] till *MS*

241:7 Stone of Change *Ed.*] stone of change *MS*

241:13 *Are there ... you awake*] Are there two of you awake *TS*

241:15 First Man *Ed.*] first man *MS*

241:16 laughing.] ~? *TS*

241:17 *Holálá, TSR*] *Holàlà, MS Holálá A1*

241:25 skin:] ~; *TS*
242:6 name *Ed.*] Name *MS*
242:22 Of these] Of those *G*
242:25 that *MS, A1*] than *E1*
242:28 money-vermin] money vermin *G*
242:33 every one] everyone *G*
242:34 world *TSR*] cosmos *MS*
243:9 and again, and again,] and again, *TS*
243:27 water,] ~ *TS*
243:28 fishing-nets *Ed.*] fishing nets *MS*
243:36 *Muy chiquitas! Ed.*] Muy chiquitas! *MS*
243:37 tradesman. "Do] ~: "do *TS* ~; "do *TSR*
244:15 *aguador Ed.*] aguador *MS* aquador *TS*
244:20 shadow] shadows *G*
244:20 silence, a] silence, *G*
245:4 ruttled] rattled *TS*
245:10 *canoa Ed.*] canoe *MS* canoe, *G*
245:11 mast] ~, *A1*
245:12 roof; *TSR*] ~, *MS* ~ *TS*
245:27 darkness:] ~; *TS*
246:3 still] *Om. A1*
246:5 back] *Om. TS*
246:6 motor-boat *G*] motor boat *MS*
247:8 Cortés *Ed.*] Columbus *MS* Cortes *TSR*
247:15 things, *TSR*] things, Cipriano, *MS*
247:35 Maybe! *TSR*] ~. *MS*
247:35 legend, *TSR*] ~ *MS*
248:9 said,] ~ *G*
248:13 that we know *TSR*] don't you think *MS*
248:16 Programmes:] ~. *G*
248:18 tree. *E1*] tree. The United States is a negation. *MS*
248:18 like *TSR*] like vast *MS*
248:24 hummingbird *Ed.*] humming bird *MS*
248:26 nation into ... And even] nation *TS* nation; and even *TSR*
248:27 then,] ~ *G*

249:11 apart:] ~; *TS*
249:11 and they] and *TS*
249:24 directions] direction *A1*
249:36 oftener? *TSR*] ~. *MS*
250:1 people; *TSR*] people, and *MS*
250:4 Army?— *TSR*] ~? *MS*
250:5 laughed *TSR*] laughed loudly *MS*
250:6 masses of *E1*] *Om. MS*
250:6 But these ... people *E1*] I have detested and despised them for years *MS*
250:10 goodnight] good-night *G*
250:25 feeling,] ~ *G*
250:30 *Puros monos! ... puras monerías Ed.*] Puras monas! ... Y lo que hacen, puras monerias *MS*
250:36 *monos ... más Ed.*] monos y no mas *MS* monos ... mas *TSR monas ... mas E1*
250:37 No *TSR*] Yes *MS*
250:37 angry with ... partly *TSR*] terribly angry. "I'm afraid so *MS*
250:39 then," he added, "what] ~," ~ ~. "What *TS* ~!" ~ ~.—"What *TSR*
251:1 Ah] ~, *G*
251:3 go too near even to a rosebush,] go to a rose-bush, *TS* go to a rose-bush, to be intimate with it, *TSR*
251:13 time:] ~; *TS*
251:24 the] a *A1*
251:25 antagonism *TSR*] hate *MS*
251:34 loved, *TSR*] ~ *MS*
251:35 a certain *E1*] violent *MS*
252:10 him too] ~, ~, *G*
252:13 disaster:] ~; *TS*
252:16 different:] ~; *TS*
252:16 His soul ... or other *TSR*] With a certain delicate cool atmosphere of silence. Even passion moving in silence, in a certain loneliness, darkly *MS*
252:23 loneliness:] ~; *TS*
252:27 anything] everything *TS*
252:36 violation] ~, *G*
253:4 our selves] ourselves *TS*

253:15 strained] restrained *G*

253:21 perfect *E1*] perfected *MS* perfectd *G*

253:28 papier-mâché *MS, A1*] papier-mache *TS* papier-maché *TSR*

253:31 general] General *TS*

253:36 life:] ~; *TS*

253:37 his God ... Then afterwards, *TSR*] the Morning Star, and *MS*

254:1 requires] required *TS*

254:3 places:] ~; *TS*

254:6 moment:— *TSR*] ~: *MS*

254:10 I have ... holiness *TSR*] *I am MS*

254:15 glad I should be of *TSR*] I could enjoy *MS*

254:22 round] around *G*

254:35 reproachfulness: an ... certain resentment. *TSR*] reproachfulness. *MS*

255:4 *impériale Ed.*] *impérial MS imperial TS*

255:6 hostility *TSR*] hate *MS*

255:8 stand, *TSR*] stand, but *MS*

255:9 all,] ~ *G*

255:26 *Señora mía ... Monos somos Ed.*] Señora mia ... Monos somos *MS*

255:30 enough:] ~; *TS*

255:34 priest? *E1*] priest? *Que jueguen los monos a las monerias! MS*

255:39 collected,] ~; *TS*

255:39 Alonso,] ~ *G*

256:3 *Mucho ... calor! Ed.*] Mucho calor, Niña! Mucho calor! *MS*

256:9 lirio] Lirio *G*

256:14 Mexico] ~. *TS*

256:15 *Who are ... and why? TSR*] [*MS* has in roman]

256:22 *What ... want? TSR*] What then do they want? *MS*

256:23 mountains, *TSR*] ~ *MS*

256:33 ones! *TSR*] ~. *MS*

256:34 *And you ... you do? TSR*] And you, Mexicans and peons, what do you do? *MS*

256:38 *Do you love them then? TSR*] Do you love them then? *MS*

257:5 *I see ... the country TSR*] I see dark things rushing across the country *MS*

257:6 trains] ~, *A1*

257:6 *camiones Ed.*] camions *MS*

257:7 *camiones Ed.*] camions *MS*

257:8 *peón Ed.*] peón *MS* peon *TS*

257:9 *camión Ed.*] camion *MS*

257:13 *cine Ed.*] cine *MS*

257:21 Oh] ~, *G*

257:29 Oh] ~, *G*

257:32 fire-waters] fire-water *A1*

257:33 of] of the *A1*

257:35 Oh] ~, *G*

258:6 sleep:] ~; *TS*

258:24 There are ... at you.] *Om. TS*

258:30 again, *TSR*] ~ *MS*

258:33 you:] ~; *TS*

259:2 motion *TSR*] steam *MS*

260:15 train:] ~; *TS*

260:15 Capital] capital *TS*

260:20 Readers who *Ed.*] readers ~ *MS*

260:37 barred with ... dark sarapes] *Om. TS*

261:4 races, *TSR*] ~ *MS*

261:5 people:] ~; *TS*

261:11 and an *Ed.*] and and *MS* and *TS*

261:14 market-places *G*] market places *MS*

261:15 little,] ~ *A1*

261:19 I] "~ *G*

261:20 again.] ~." *G*

261:27 papier-mâché *TSR*] papier-maché *MS*

261:28 lifelike *A1*] life-like *MS* life-/like *G*

261:31 up-turned] up-/ turned *G* upturned *A1*

261:34 Mexican:] ~; *TS*

261:37 skeleton,] Skeleton, *TS*

261:38 horseback, *TSR*] ~ *MS*

261:40 Saturday] Saturdays *A1*

262:7 gingerly:] ~; *TS*

262:8 priests] priest *TS*

262:8 church bells *G*] churchbells *MS*

262:16 Church *Ed.*] church *MS*

262:17 the expulsion of *TSR*] expelling *MS*

262:24 military,] ~ *G*

262:31 city] City *TS*

262:36 *Señor General TSR*] Señor General *MS*

263:11 Gentlemen! *TSR*] ~. *MS*

263:16 Honours!] ~. *G*

263:27 father, and] ~; ~, *G*

264:5 serve:] ~; *TS*

264:12 soul *MS*, *A1*] Soul *TS*

264:12 voice] Voice *TS*

264:13 Bishop. *P* "No ... may know] Bishop know *TS* Bishop. *P* "Your own children may know *TSR*

264:18 Francis *Ed.*] Francisco *MS*

264:23 fidgetted] fidgeted *A1*

264:32 churches? *G*] ~. *MS*

264:33 Universal *A1*] universal *MS*

264:35 well:] ~; *TS*

265:6 soul,] ~ *G*

265:18 church *G*] Church *MS*

265:19 burn *TSR*] sacrifice *MS*

265:29 My Lord *E1*] Monsignor *MS* my Lord *A1*

266:9 ways,] ~ *G*

266:16 poor,] ~ *G*

266:25 duty will] ~, ~ *G*

266:30 *Adios Señor! Ed.*] Adios Señor! *MS* Adios, Señor! *G*

266:32 *Adios, Señor General Ed.*] Adios, Señor General *MS*

266:35 jesuit] Jesuit *A1*

266:36 and prevent ... beating *E1*] his creeping, putrid power *MS* his creeping, centipede power *TSR*

266:37 centipede *TSR*] mangy *MS*

266:38 people:] ~; *TS*

267:4 arches,] ~ *G*

267:5 typewriters,] ~ *G*

267:12 Why, *TSR*] ~ *MS*

267:14 Man] man *G*

268:2 Auto-da-Fé *Ed.*] Auto da Fe. *MS* Auto da fe *E1* Auto Da Fé *A1*

268:5 [of] *Ed.*] *Om. MS* with *TS*

268:8 Papa] papa *G*

268:13 wishes] wished *TS*

268:16 No] ~, *G*

268:17 zig-zags *Ed.*] zigzags *MS*

268:19 No Papa] ~, papa *G*

268:26 No Papa] ~, papa *G*

269:6 *peón Ed.*] peón *MS* peon *TS*

269:14 Papa] papa *G*

269:20 Papa] papa *G*

269:28 Mama] mama *G*

269:28 in:] ~; *TS*

269:33 Papa] papa *G*

269:34 son! *E1*] ~? *MS*

269:35 Papa] papa *G*

270:4 *Entonces ... Espinita! Ed.*] Entonces, Adios! Señor Espina Espinita! *MS*

270:5 *Adios! Ed.*] Adios! *MS*

270:8 *camión Ed.*] camion *MS*

270:19 and] ~, *G*

270:26 boys." *Ed.*] ~.' *MS* ~!" *TS*

270:27 Oh] ~, *G*

270:30 still.] ~? *TS*

270:38 *Señora mía! Ed.*] Señora mia! *MS*

271:1 said *E1*] said fiercely *MS*

271:6 more:] ~; *TS*

271:9 One wants ... be good, so] One wants to be good, and the other is sure he *is* good, so *TS* Quien sabe?" said Kate. *P* "One wants to be good, and the other is sure he *is* good. So *TSR*

271:15 Ah] ~, *G*

271:19 I?] ~— *G*

271:27 me:] ~; *TS*

271:28 in] *Om. G*

271:29 me,] ~ *TS*

271:31 half way ... half way] half-way ... half-way *G*

271:33 Yet] ~, *G*

271:34 half way] half-way *G*

271:39 half way *Ed.*] half-way *MS*

271:40 physical *TSR*] central *MS*

272:8 go,] go. And it is precisely with a woman that he should never let himself go, *TS* go. It is ... himself go, *TSR*

272:9 if it's physical, *TSR*] *Om. MS*

272:23 love her? *TSR*] ~ ~. *MS*

272:36 meet,] ~; *G*

273:9 lost.] ~— *TS* ~.— *G*

273:16 fulfilment *TSR*] gratification *MS*

273:16 it] *Om. TS*

273:24 Ah] ~, *G*

273:24 myself:] ~; *TS*

273:28 needn't. *Ed.*] ~? *MS*

274:7 blonde] blond *A1*

274:14 it:] ~; *TS*

274:16 classes:] ~; *TS*

274:19 things that shall crave *TSR*] things, craving *MS*

275:14 So] ~, *G*

275:17 women *E1*] men *MS*

275:17 Padre] padre *G*

275:28 erect:] ~; *TS*

275:33 church:] ~; *TS*

275:39 mantle, with her *TSR*] mantle and *MS*

276:16 time,] ~ *G*

276:19 hyaenas] hyænas *G*

276:23 cellos'] '~ *G*

276:23 music:] ~; *TS*

276:25 floor:] ~; *TS*

277:2 school-room] schoolroom *A1*

277:4 grey-wash,] ~; *TS*

277:8 church: *Ed.*] Church: *MS* Church; *TS* church; *G*

277:13 school-room *Ed.*] schoolroom *MS*

277:19 palm-trees *Ed.*] palm trees *MS*

277:30 desire:] ~; *TS*

277:38 say: Was] ~; was *TS* ~: was *G*

277:38 El] *Om. A1*

278:12 concert-halls *Ed.*] concert halls *MS*

278:20 centavos] ~' *A1*

278:21 chiles] chilies *A1*

278:24 church-doors] church doors *G*

278:24 church bells *G*] church-bells *MS*

278:29 squatted *E1*] squatting *MS, A1*

278:30 squatting] squatted *A1*

278:32 señoras *Ed.*] Señoras *MS*

278:33 señoritas *Ed.*] Señoritas *MS*

278:35 a-bubble and a-froth] a bubble and a froth *TS*

278:35 chatter:] ~; *TS*

279:3 church-doors] church doors *G*

279:7 bareheaded *Ed.*] bare-headed *MS*

279:8 church-doors:] church-doors; *TS* church doors; *G*

279:8 bluey-black *TSR*] bluey black *MS*

279:10 clay *TSR*] wooden *MS*

279:10 husky *TSR*] reedy *MS*

279:17 church-doors] church doors *G*

279:17 hats:] ~; *TS*

279:20 palm-trees *Ed.*] palm trees *MS*

279:22 *camiones Ed.*] camions *MS*

279:23 earthen flute *TSR*] reed-flute *MS*

279:26 crowd. Soldiers] crowd— soldiers *TS* crowd.—Soldiers *TSR*

280:2 oval. *Ed.*] ~ *MS* ~, *A1*

280:3 us.] ~, *A1*

280:5 sparks.] ~, *G*

280:7 Joachim *Ed.*] Joaquin *MS*

280:13 Crucified:] ~; *TS*

280:15 on the *TSR*] of *MS*

280:17 Master, *TSR*] ~ *MS*

280:22 We *TSR*] Let us *MS*

280:34 hand:] ~; *TS*

280:34 hat:] ~; *TS*

280:36 and] ~, *G*

280:37 drum] ~, *TS*

281:1 church-doors] church doors *G*

281:3 candles, *TSR*] ~ *MS*

281:5 rippling] ripping *A1*

281:5 of *TSR*] in *MS*

281:6 subsided] ~, *G*

281:8 returning] re-/ turning *TS* re-turning *G*

281:10 said:] ~; *TS*

281:11 his] His *G*

281:18 *Adios!,*] ~! *G*

281:19 *Adios TSR*] Adios *MS*

281:21 *Adios!,*] ~! *G*
281:22 blast, *TSR*] blast, far *MS*
281:22 of the church *TSR*] *Om. MS*
281:24 only *TSR*] a gulf of *MS*
281:25 cave *TSR*] a terrible vault *MS*
281:28 Hymn *TSR*] hymn *MS*
281:32 low *TSR*] ~, *MS*
281:35 they] they had *A1*
281:36 benediction:] ~; *TS*
281:37 me] Me *G*
282:12 Dead *Ed.*] dead *MS*
282:15 Dead *TSR*] dead *MS*
282:16 he] He *TSR*
282:19 acknowledgement] acknow-
    ledgment *A1*
282:25 thorns *Ed.*] Thorns *MS*
282:32 Ann *Ed.*] Anna *MS*
282:32 last] at last *A1*
282:32 Joachim *Ed.*] Joaquin *MS*
282:36 through *TSR*] of *MS*
282:38 Dead *TSR*] dead *MS*
282:40 *Purísima! Purísima ... us Ed.*]
    Purisima! Purisima! Don't
    leave us *MS Purisma! Purisma
    ... us TSR*
283:2 *Señor! Señor! Señor! TSR*]
    Señor! Señor! Senor! *MS*
283:9 then a wooden *TSR*] *Om. MS*
283:10 then *TSR*] *Om. MS*
283:12 painted:] ~; *TS*
283:15 sailing-boat *Ed.*] sailing boat
    MS
283:16 barelegged] bare-legged *G*
283:17 white-clad *TSR*] white clad *MS*
283:17 blew *TSR*] waved *MS*
283:20 crucifix] Crucifix *A1*
283:21 deck] decks *A1*
283:30 *canoa G*] canoa *MS*
283:32 each image had ... its *TSR*]
    they had all ... their *MS*
283:38 motor-boats *G*] motorboats
    MS
283:38 *canoa G*] canoa *MS*
284:1 Barelegged] Bare-legged *G*
284:2 rims] rim *A1*
284:10 Scorpions, *TSR*] ~ *MS*
284:11 daze] haze *G*
284:14 *canoa Ed.*] canoe *MS*

284:18 the sweep ... white canvas
    TSR] *Om. MS*
284:23 *canoa Ed.*] canoe *MS*
284:27 bought] brought *A1*
284:29 slices] slice *TS*
284:33 bare:] ~; *TS*
285:3 The great sail sank, the *G*] The
    MS The great sail sank, The
    TSR
285:6 again] *Om. A1*
285:7 huts] ~, *G*
285:15 leaned] laid *A1*
285:18 [lake-shore] looked *Ed.*]
    village, *MS* village looked *TSR*
    see notes
285:19 church-towers] church towers
    G
285:37 Men *Ed.*] men *MS*
285:37 Quetzalcoatl, his ... the knee.
    TSR] Quetzalcoatl. *MS*
286:1 dusky *TSR*] *Om. MS*
286:3 flame] flames *G*
286:24 rockets *TSR*] rocks *MS*
286:27 *Señor! Señor ... Santísima!
    Ed.*] Señor! Señor! La Puri-
    sima! La Santisima! *MS*
286:36 *canoa G*] canoa *MS*
286:39 Isle *Ed.*] isle *MS*
286:39 quivered *TSR*] wavered *MS*
287:7 and] ~, *G*
288:20 ricketty] rickety *A1*
288:21 roads,] ~ *G*
288:24 void] ~, *TS*
289:8 *patrona Ed.*] patrona *MS*
289:10 *Sí Señora! Está Ed.*] Si Señora!
    Està *MS*
289:17 *Patrón! Ed.*] Patron! *MS*
    Patròn! *TSR Patrón! A1*
289:32 said] asked *A1*
290:3 of] of the *G*
290:22 something, *TSR*] ~ *MS*
290:24 one another] each other *A1*
290:27 were] was *A1*
290:29 mango trees *Ed.*] mango-trees
    MS
291:7 why] ~, *G*
291:16 by] *Om. A1*
291:18 said] asked *A1*

291:23 me." *P* Kate] ~." Kate *A1*
291:33 backfiring] back-/ firing *G* back-firing *A1*
291:37 stairway *Ed.*] stair-way *MS*
292:2 *Patrón TSR*] *Patron MS*
292:7 catlike,] ~*TS*
292:8 stair-case] stair-/ case *TS* staircase *G*
292:12 *Holá! Ed.*] Holà! *MS, TSR* Hola! *TS*
292:29 bee,] ~ *G*
292:40 Snap! Snap!] Snap! *TS*
293:28 *Ay-ee!— Ed.*] ~!— *MS* ~! *TS*
293:32 flame,] ~ *TS*
293:40 back:] ~; *TS*
294:1 cartridge belt *Ed.*] cartridge-belt *MS*
294:4 he *TSR*] as he *MS*
294:6 her:] ~; *TS*
294:39 of] to *A1*
294:40 horrible] terrible *A1*
295:13 at] to *A1*
295:22 two:] ~, *TS*
295:22 projectile,] ~; *G*
295:27 distorted] disordered *A1*
295:31 running] running down *G*
295:32 world:] ~; *TS*
296:4 gaping *TSR*] ghastly, gaping *MS*
296:21 with *TSR*] with supernatural *MS*
296:22 bloodstained *Ed.*] blood-stained *MS*
296:31 primitive,] ~ *TS*
296:37 *Creo que sí Ed.*] Creo que si *MS* Creo que si *G*
297:3 being *E1*] savage *MS*
297:13 so] as *TS* till *E1*
297:21 clear *E1*] savage *MS*
297:23 said] asked *A1*
297:24 No!"—] ~!" *TS*
297:24 round to] round *A1*
297:24 feel] feel of *A1*
297:30 Then:] ~; *TS*
297:32 savage *E1*] *Om. MS*
298:2 bloodstained] blood-/ stained *TS* blood-stained *A1*
298:15 picked up ... put] picking up

his blouse and put *G* picking up his blouse and putting *E1*
298:28 *Viene! ... Él viene! Ed.*] Viene! Viene Don Ramon! El viene! *MS*
298:30 turned *TSR*] flew *MS*
298:33 One *TSR*] It *MS*
298:38 *Patrón A1*] Patron *MS* Patron *TSR*
299:6 a] *Om. A1*
299:35 faces: *MS, A1*] ~. *TS*
299:36 *Té TSR*] Té *MS*
300:2 death-virgin *E1*] boy-savage *MS*
300:2 he. *E1*] he. And this is he. And the man who laughs at me is he, and the man who looks at me in torment, because Carlota torments him, and the proud, still man who is so alone, and the stern man who burned the images, and the man Cipriano loves, and the Patron whom Martin worshipped! Ah God! So many men. *MS* he. And the man ... men. *TS* he ... *Patrón* ... men. *G*
300:18 lightning.] ~, *A1*
300:30 opened:] ~; *TS*
300:33 little:] ~. *TS*
300:35 who,] ~ *TS*
301:7 black] dark *A1*
301:16 to] *Om. A1*
301:18 roof;] ~: *G*
301:24 and of] and *A1*
301:28 *Patrón TSR*] Patron *MS*
301:35 *masa Ed.*] masa *MS*
302:13 lay:] ~; *TS*
302:24 her:] ~; *TS*
302:27 Ah,] ~ *A1*
302:35 be?—] ~? *TS*
303:1 the two] two *A1*
303:17 yard:] ~; *TS*
303:22 sideways:] ~; *TS*
303:23 bone:] ~; *TS*
303:30 Sayula:] ~; *TS*

303:36 Knights-of-Cortés   *Ed.*]
       Knights' of Cortes   *MS*
       Knights-of-Cortes *TSR*
303:36 men:] ~; *TS*
303:37 men—] ~. *G*
303:40 handsome:] ~; *TS*
304:10 her:] ~; *TS*
304:28 high-road] highroad *G*
304:31 plates] ~, *TS*
304:35 high-road] highroad *G*
305:5 hole] ~, *G*
306:23 knew, *E1*] ~ *MS*
306:27 no-one] no one *G*
306:28 no-one] no one *G*
306:33 desire:] ~; *TS*
307:15 frail] ~, *G*
307:26 her] the *TS*
307:32 small] ~, *G*
308:13 twice:] ~; *TS*
308:16 hundred—] ~. *TS*
308:19 gloom, *TSR*] ~ *MS*
308:28 landlord:] ~; *TS*
309:1 general] General *TS*
309:25 hesitating, and] hesitating, was
       A1
309:26 *No TSR*] No *MS*
310:23 zenith:] ~; *TS*
311:1 goat's] goats' *TS*
311:8 Never shall pass away. *TSR*]
       Om. MS
311:19 woo:] ~; *TS*
311:19 this. *TSR*] this. He would take.
       MS
311:20 the dark ... steamed ... and
       rose *TSR*] he would see no
       resistance, no obstacle, it
       would be *MS* the dark ...
       streamed ... rose *G*
311:24 submission, on her part, *TSR*]
       submission *MS*
311:30 Cipriano:] ~; *TS*
311:37 *En ... verdad? Ed.*] En poco
       tiempo, verdad? *MS*
312:3 herself: *TSR*] ~, *MS*
312:6 Pan world *G*] Pan-world *MS*
312:12 God-demon] god-demon *TS*
312:31 Oh] ~, *G*
313:19 doing:] ~; *TS*

313:36 service:] ~; *TS*
313:37 glory:] ~; *TS*
314:2 coûte *Ed.*] coute *MS*
314:7 in:] ~; *TS*
314:9 time:] ~; *TS*
314:14 peons:] ~; *TS*
314:23 match:] ~; *TS*
314:24 Guillermo] ~, *G*
314:25 said:] ~; *TS* ~ *G*
314:27 well:] ~; *TS*
314:32 priest:] ~; *TS*
314:34 scalp:] ~; *TS*
314:35 Pablo *TSR*] Pedro *MS*
314:36 Ahuajijic:] ~; *TS*
314:39 *laurel de la India Ed.*] laurel de
       India *MS laurel de India TSR*
315:2 bough,—] ~— *G*
315:8 of *TSR*] and *MS*
315:10 stairs] ~, *G*
315:24 *They came ... Patrón ... of them*
       Ed.] They came through there,
       Patron. Guillermo was one of
       them *MS They came ... Patron*
       ... them TSR
316:7 Yes] ~, *G*
316:7 *hauteur Ed.*] hauteur *MS*
316:8 in to] into *G*
316:10 goddess:] ~; *TS*
316:11 you] ~, *G*
316:13 I!] ~? *G*
316:15 There *must*] ~ must *TS*
316:16 cosmos:] ~; *TS*
316:24 Why] ~, *G*
316:31 railing:] ~; *TS*
316:36 distant   *TSR*]   laughing
       MS
316:36 gleam] ~, *G*
316:39 twilight] ~, *G*
316:40 mankind,] ~ *G*
317:4 Colima:] Colina; *TS* Colima;
       E1
317:5 him? *G*] ~. *MS*
317:6 waited] ~, *G*
317:8 empty] ~, *G*
317:9 seems *TSR*] seemed *MS*
317:11 Kate, *TSR*] ~ *MS*
317:20 thunder:] ~; *TS*
317:31 could] would *TS*

318:1 willow trees G] willow-trees MS

318:7 water-fowl TSR] water fowl MS

318:15 Kate TSR] her MS

318:17 No] ~, G

318:20 laughed:] ~; TS

318:22 silent,] ~ A1

318:25 willow trees Ed.] willow-trees MS

318:27 invisible, TSR] ~ MS

318:28 side] ~, G

318:28 *canoas* G] canoas MS

318:29 motor-boat G] motor boat MS

318:37 *hauteur A1*] hauteur MS

319:1 Living Ed.] living MS

319:9 him:] ~; TS

319:10 thing:] ~; TS

319:10 donkey] ~, G

319:11 half conscious] half-conscious G

319:12 fishing-nets Ed.] fishingnets MS fishing nets G

319:22 palm-trees Ed.] palm trees MS

319:23 Arab G] arab MS

319:31 obsequious:] ~; TS

320:2 darkness] ~, G

320:10 Gone as ... was gone.] Om. TS

320:11 *us TSR*] us MS

320:13 flame:] ~; TS

320:24 nothing:] ~; TS

320:25 primitive E1] rather awful MS

320:28 green MS, E1] blue TSR

320:35 her breast TSR] Om. MS

321:8 all:] ~; TS

321:23 wandered] ~, G

321:30 wheels] ~, G

321:37 one] ~, G

322:2 tread-looms] ~, G

322:3 foot] foot and G

322:5 of TSR] Om. MS

322:6 zig-zags Ed.] zigzags MS

322:8 yarn,] Om. TS

322:10 zig-zag] zigzag G

322:10 and] ~, G

322:10 zig-zag] zigzag G

322:13 heavily,] ~ G

322:17 me.] ~! TS

322:33 Ramón's:] Ramon's; TS

323:7 Living Ed.] living MS

323:8 Living Ed.] living MS

323:9 Living ... Living Ed.] living ... living MS

323:18 you too] ~, ~, G

323:24 brown TSR] rose MS

323:30 woman] Om. TS

323:31 yellow-brown TSR] yellow brown MS

323:35 flowers, you too] ~ ~, ~, G

323:39 her, the donkey] ~ ~ ~, G

324:4 fishing-nets] fishing nets G

324:5 after loop after loop] after loop G

324:8 nowhere:] ~; TS

324:28 bottom, TSR] bottom, and MS

324:31 fore paw] fore-paw G

325:5 naïve] naive TS

325:7 saddle] ~, G

325:11 squatted TSR] seated MS

325:11 lading] ladling G

325:15 cup,] ~; G

325:22 biscuit-coloured TSR, A1] biscuit coloured MS, G

325:24 and] ~, G

325:28 too:] ~; TS

325:35 —"We Ed.] —~ MS ~ TS "~ TSR

326:9 cartridge belt] cartridge-belt G

326:13 But it ... of her. TSR] Om. MS

326:21 thugged] chugged G

326:28 shore:] ~; TS

326:39 farther] further A1

327:6 trousers] ~, G

327:17 sputtered] spluttered G

327:20 mango trees Ed.] mango-trees MS

327:20 storey] story TS

327:24 lake-side A1] lake side MS

327:36 Yes] ~, G

327:36 *Pero una ... zarca ... amigo Ed.*] Pero una florecita tan zarco! Y abrió en mi sombra, amigo MS Pero ... zarca ... amigo TSR

327:38 *Sois hombre ... fortuna Ed.*] Seis hombre de la alta fortuna MS

327:39 *Verdad! Ed.*] Creo que si! *MS*
Verdad! *E1*
328:20 woman-servant *TSR*] woman
servant *MS*
328:23 stalks, *TSR*] ~ *MS*
328:25 *Patrón Ed.*] Patrón *MS* Patron
TS
328:25 on!" *TSR*] ~?" *MS* ~, *TS*
328:27 Take] "~ *G*
328:30 twilight.] ~." *G*
328:32 with a] of *A1*
328:34 shoulder:] ~; *TS*
329:7 with *TSR*] with lifted *MS*
329:11 *heaven*—] ~. *TS*
329:14 that, *G*] ~ *MS*
329:29 me, *G*] ~; *MS*
329:30 Kate, "but] ~. "But *TS*
329:36 Star:] ~; *TS*
330:11 rain-wet *TSR*] rain wet *MS*
330:11 dried,] ~ *TS*
330:17 that,] ~ *G*
330:18 hand woven] handwoven *TS*
hand-woven *G*
330:19 under-dress *G*] under dress
MS
330:36 woolen] woollen *G*
330:36 white *TSR*] red *MS*
330:37 red *TSR*] green *MS*
331:10 honorable] honourable *G*
331:12 pass.—But ... pass, then *TSR*]
pass. And *MS* pass. But ...
then *G*
331:30 lost—] ~. *TS*
332:7 am *TSR*] am to be *MS*
332:7 other *TSR*] more *MS*
332:8 other *TSR*] more *MS*
332:23 hills *E1*] lake *MS*
332:32 up:] up] *TS* up *TSR*
333:2 temples] temple *TS*
333:16 orange trees] orange-trees *A1*
333:18 palm-trees *Ed.*] palm trees *MS*
333:19 church-towers *Ed.*] church
towers *MS*
333:20 often:] ~; *TS*
333:20 Greek *TSR*] Latin *MS*
333:23 been:] ~; *TS*
333:32 beating:] ~; *TS*
333:38 and in] and *TS*

334:1 church *Ed.*] Church *MS*
334:6 Does ... me?] "~ ... ~?" *G*
334:18 Eye *G*] eye *MS*
334:18 how] How *G*
334:22 Quetzalcoatl:] ~; *TS*
334:22 god] God *G*
334:37 drum:] ~; *TS*
335:15 *Thud!—Thud!—Thud!*]
Thud!—Thud!—Thud! *G*
335:28 bellowing *TSR*] thudding *MS*
335:31 shoulders:] ~; *TS*
335:32 cold:] ~; *TS*
336:6 shoulders:] ~; *TS*
336:7 superb *E1*] inscrutable *MS*
336:9 closed *TSR*] *Om. MS*
336:10 white] *Om. TS*
336:27 *Oye! Oye! Oye! Oye! Ed.*] Oye!
Oye! Oye! Oye! *P* "Hear thou!
Hear thou!" *MS* Oye! ... Oye!
E1
336:32 we *E1*] you *MS, A1*
336:34 guard] Guard *TS*
336:36 we *A1*] you *MS*
336:37 guard] Guard *TS*
337:2 Star:] ~; *TS*
337:5 face:] ~; *TS*
337:6 a change *TSR*] volts of power
MS
337:8 guard] Guard *TS*
337:25 lame—] ~. *TS*
338:6 Men *Ed.*] men *MS*
338:6 avenue *TSR*] line *MS*
338:8 Men *Ed.*] men *MS*
338:9 centre,] ~ *TS*
338:12 deep-blue *Ed.*] deep blue *MS*
deep, blue *TS*
338:13 white and] white *G* white, *A1*
338:14 deep-blue *Ed.*] deep blue *MS*
338:18 deep-blue *Ed.*] deep blue *MS*
338:29 of the man-image *TSR*] *Om.*
MS
338:34 ocote wood *Ed.*] ocote-wood
MS
338:36 fill] file *G*
339:3 Men *Ed.*] men *MS*
339:6 Men *Ed.*] men *MS*
339:7 statue.] ~, *G*
339:10 Quetzalcoatl! *TSR*] ~, *MS*

339:11 Men *Ed.*] men *MS*
339:21 Living *Ed.*] living *MS*
339:27 wide *Ed.*] still *MS*
339:28 lean over *Ed.*] croon on *MS*
339:29 of wings *E1*] *Om. MS*
339:32 Star ... shines *E1*] ~ ... Shines *MS*
339:33 me] one *TS*
339:37 star] stars *TS*
340:6 brave] true *E1*
340:8 bravery *E1*] strength *MS*
340:20 her,] ~. *E1*
340:21 *I ... star. I ... star. Ed.*] I have no star. I am no star. *MS* I ... star; I ... star. *TS I ... star, I ... star. E1 I ... star, I ... star, A1*
340:24 rind: *E1*] weight. *MS*
340:29 Tree *TSR*] tree *MS*
340:35 Living *Ed.*] living *MS*
341:4 Ways—] ~——*A1*
341:5 Men *Ed.*] men *MS*
341:7 altar steps *Ed.*] altar-steps *MS*, *A1* altar-/ steps *G*
341:20 one *A1*] one they *MS*
341:20 Ramón's *Ed.*] his *MS* Ramon's *TSR*
341:21 in the bowl was ... water *TSR*] into the bowl, from the bird, flowed the purplish wine *MS* with the bowl ... wine *TS*
341:21 touched a *TSR*] pressed the *MS*
341:22 shook in the bowl *TSR*] liquid flowed in *MS*
341:23 touched a bowl with *TSR*] took the *MS*
341:23 loins, a ... dark *TSR*] loins, the white *MS* loins a ... dark *G*
341:27 God *TSR*] Father *MS*
341:27 and His] and *TS*
341:28 His power] his ~ *TS*
341:34 God *TSR*] Father *MS*
341:34 is *TSR*] is the *MS*
342:14 Madonna, in ... gesture. *TSR*] Madonna. *MS*
342:25 Carlota] ~, *TS*
342:28 Oh] O *A1*
342:32 her] the *TS*

342:38 Living *Ed.*] living *MS*
343:6 Cross *Ed.*] cross *MS*
343:10 terrible:] ~. *TS*
343:14 The *E1*] The God *MS*
343:14 speaking quietly ... serve Omnipotence! *E1*] "is with me, and I die not. *MS* speaking quietly, as if to her, "is with me, and I with Him. I stay with my God! *TSR*
343:26 run] ran *TS*
343:31 absorbed *E1*] proud *MS*
343:36 heart *E1*] old heart *MS*
343:36 quite quite] ~, ~ *G*
343:36 dead in him; out ... his wife *E1*] dead, his wife was unreal to him, a sort of spectral thing *MS* dead in him, out ... wife *A1*
343:39 *There is ... Carlota TSR*] There is no star between me and Carlota *MS*
344:4 sun,] ~; *TS*
344:4 she heard *TS*] he heard *MS*
344:12 earth] the earth *G*
344:14 know me *E1*] are mine *MS*
344:17 and wonderful, *TSR*] *Om. MS*
344:19 mother] Mother *TS*
344:21 down] down to *A1*
344:23 bird.] ~, *TS*
344:25 of the] of *A1*
344:25 know me *E1*] are mine *MS*
344:27 lit with me *E1*] mine *MS*
344:28 left hand *Ed.*] left-hand *MS*
344:28 kissing] hissing *A1*
344:29 fire, *TSR*] ~ *MS*
344:37 vision *E1*] daylight *MS*
345:8 Ways:] ~; *TS*
345:12 doctor:] ~; *TS*
345:18 air:] ~; *TS*
345:18 deep,] ~ *G*
345:22 exultance *E1*] joy *MS*
345:25 Song] song *TS*
346:6 Ramón has *Ed.*] Ramon his *MS* Ramon he's *TS* Ramon, he's *TSR* Ramón, he's *G*
346:16 way *E1*] will *MS*
346:24 body *E1*] body nor the heavy oil of your soul *MS*

346:26 back.] ~? *TS*

346:27 soul? *TSR*] soul? You are glad that you kept them to yourself? *MS*

346:29 spirit] ~, *A1*

346:31 not. *TSR*] not. You can only put out your own, with the thin water of your charity, and the cold breath of your will. You have put out your own fire. *MS*

346:32 have been *E1*] are *MS*

346:32 compassionless to *E1*] compassionless. Above all you have been charitable and compassionless to *MS*

347:3 mixing-bowl *G*] mixing bowl *MS*

347:13 Cipriano. *E1*] Cipriano. "You have borne the fatherless children of your own denial, you virgin. You have given your unnourishing body as a wafer, the oil and the wine held back, you spinster. You have given the thin love of your will and your spirit, and you have stolen the oil and wine of a man, you natural widow. Now call and die! For you are one of the two theives crucified on each side of the cross. One was the righteous charity-theif, and that is you, you woman in her own rights. And the other was the robber with a cudgel, the man in his own rights. And the three of you crucify together. It is well. Die then. Die!" *MS* Cipriano ... the manless children ... thieves ... charity-thief, and that is you." *TSR* Cipriano ... nourishing body ... you." *G*

347:15 them. *TSR*] them, theif. *MS*

347:17 stale *TSR*] theif, *Om. MS*

347:18 just *TSR*] gallant *MS*

347:18 woman. *TSR*] woman in her own rights. You gallant woman—you theif! You strong, true wife—you theif! You devoted mother—you theif! *MS*

347:20 earth. *TSR*] earth, you theif! *MS*

347:22 dead! *TSR*] dead, you theif of theives, you woman in her own rights, you sneak-theif, theiving the oil and wine of the world's virility, and pouring dead, waste water back into the mixing-bowl. Oh die! die! die! *MS*

347:24 unconsciousness: *Ed.*] unconscious: *MS* unconscious; *TS* unconsciousness; *TSR*

347:30 Jesus:] ~; *TS*

348:3 manhood *TSR*] virility *MS*

348:6 manhood *TSR*] virility *MS*

348:9 Men *Ed.*] men *MS*

348:11 drum:] ~; *TS*

348:13 Indians *E1*] old Red Indians *MS*

348:14 downward-sinking *E1*] down-ward sinking *MS* downward sinking *G*

348:16 America:] ~; *TS*

348:21 drums] ~, *G*

348:23 For these ... this moment *E1*] They are trying very hard to learn to be men again, in the old way, to be responsible for their own virility, and to know what to do with it. But will they succeed *MS*

348:25 In *TSR*] She thought of the Red Indians in America: {America; *TS*} even worse than white men, impotent to contain the flame of their own virility, impotent to direct it and to make the world great with its fire. Even worse than the men of the white world, creeping around and asking the women to take their virility from them, for the love of love. *P* The wine and the oil of the world's virility! Much need women had to steal it, when all men crept round like prostitutes, asking the women for an opportunity wherein they could let their virility leak into her, the woman. These leaky vessels of virility calling women theives! {thieves! *TSR*} It was nothing but the croaking of cracked vessels, as they dripped their content into the female bowl: {bowl; *TS*} or failing that, into their newspapers and books and speech! *P* Oil and wine of a woman's soul and body, to be poured into the mixing-bowl. Much oil and wine the men poured into any mixing-bowl. {mixing-bowl! *TSR*} They just leaked at large, {large; *TS*} and then had a grievance. Let men stop leaking in their virile bodies, and woman might feel she could pour out her oil and her wine again. Meanwhile she retained them, and poured her waste water of pity, charity or licentiousness {charity and licentiousness, *TSR*} quite freely. *P* In *MS*

348:25 *Welcome to Quetzalcoatl Ed.*] Welcome of Quetzalcoatl *MS* *Welcome of Quetzalcoatl TSR*

348:26 church. *TSR*] church. There were women in short black tunics with red and green embroidered stiff flowers, and tiaras of blue, with the eye of Quetzalcoatl on their heads. They danced barefoot, bare-legged behind the men, holding boughs of green in their hand. And the men, naked and smeared with oil, wearing kilts of white with an end of blue and red and black

embroidery, and long sashes with the stiff cloud-terrace embroidery in blue and black and red, with long fringe, swaying at the side, and boots of spotted fur, danced with the seed-rattle in the left hand and a bough of pine-tree in their right. *MS*

348:31 *canoas G*] canoas *MS*

348:32 island. *TSR*] island. As they neared the rocky tip of the island, which they must pass, they heard the sound of singing from a little cave. Then the first boat drew near, and Ramon rose glistening from the water. He threw a fish and a live cock into the boat, climbed in, and was rowed to the landing place. After him, as the boats rowed up, always a man rose out of the water, and threw a fish and a live fowl into the boat, then climbed in. *MS*

348:34 *Welcome to Quetzalcoatl Ed.*] welcome of Quetzalcoatl *MS* *Welcome of Quetzalcoatl TSR*

348:35 *Welcome to Quetzalcoatl, Ed.*] Welcome of Quetzalcoatl, *MS* Welcome of Quetzalcoatl; *TS*

348:39 hastening *E1*] in the morning *MS*

348:39 after a while *E1*] in the morning *MS*

349:6 sick room] sick-room *G*

349:9 night dress] night-/ dress *TS* nightdress *A1*

349:27 song-sheet *Ed.*] Song-sheet *MS*

349:27 *Welcome to Quetzalcoatl TSR*] Welcome to Quetzalcoatl *MS*

349:33 threw] drew *A1*

349:37 shade] shades *A1*

350:4 *come! G*] ~. *MS*

350:6 a *TSR*] his *MS*

350:9 moving] ~. *A1*

350:15 Ah] ~, *G*

350:20 [clay] flutes *Ed.*] reed-flutes *MS*
350:32 opened hearts *E1*] let go *MS*
350:35 hand *E1*] cheek *MS*
351:4 as black] so black *TS*
351:8 his hand loosely on *E1*] her hand softly in *MS* his hand softly in *TS*
351:13 church-doors] church doors *G*
351:13 Men *Ed.*] men *MS*
351:23 loosely *E1*] softly *MS*
351:24 church-towers *Ed.*] church towers *MS*
351:25 church-doors] church doors *G*
351:25 lake,] ~; *TS*
351:28 white and *E1*] *Om. MS*
351:29 motor-car *G*] motor car *MS*
352:1 *Put sleep ... over me E1*] [*MS*, *A1* have in roman]
352:3 And Cipriano ... [352:8] the tides. *E1*] *Om. MS*
352:11 doctors:] ~: *TS*
352:14 *Welcome to Quetzalcoatl Ed.*] Welcome to Quetzalcoatl *MS*
353:6 him:] ~; *TS*
353:9 creamy-brown *A1*] creamy brown *MS*
353:10 Ramón: *Ed.*] Ramon: *MS* Ramon; *TS* Ramón; *G*
353:34 Papa] papa *G*
354:3 Papa] papa *G*
354:3 the *A1*] The *MS*
354:5 Papa] papa *G*
354:6 Ramón *Ed.*] Ramon *MS* Ramón, *G*
354:8 Papa] papa *G*
354:8 called] *Om. TS*
354:11 Papa] papa *G*
354:18 Oh Mama ... Oh Mama] ~, mama ... ~, mama *G*
354:27 men:] ~; *TS*
354:33 souls:] ~; *TS*
354:34 père *A1*] Papa *MS* Père *TSR* perè *G*
354:38 Mama's] mama's *G*
355:1 Mama] mama *G*
355:5 paradise *Ed.*] Paradise *MS*
355:8 paradise] Paradise *G*

355:17 paradise *Ed.*] Paradise *MS*
355:22 far—] ~ *TS*
355:23 is:] ~; *TS*
355:24 Paradise:] ~; *TS*
355:26 returns:] ~; *TS*
355:40 Cyprian *G*] Cipriano *MS*
356:3 English:] ~; *TS*
356:6 mid-day *Ed.*] midday *MS*
356:7 prayer:] ~. *TS*
356:16 Mid-day] midday *A1*
356:16 Verse *Ed.*] verse *MS*
356:23 Oh] ~, *G*
356:28 *Shall-be ... am TSR*] Shall-be ... am *MS*
356:35 art] are *A1*
356:36 the *Ed.*] The *MS*
356:36 Is] '~ *G*
356:37 the *Ed.*] The *MS*
356:37 Quetzalcoatl?—] ~?'— *G*
356:37 Yes] '~ *G*
356:38 father.] ~.' *G*
356:39 I am] '~ ~ *G*
357:1 father without understanding him.— *Ed.*] father.— *MS* father. *TS* father ... him'. *E1*
357:5 Papa] papa *G*
357:10 Mama] mama *G*
357:13 Papa] papa *G*
357:15 Papa] papa *G*
357:19 art] are *A1*
357:28 Ah] ~, *G*
357:30 it—if ever they do. *TSR*] it. *MS*
357:31 lake-shore *Ed.*] lake shore *MS*
357:37 different:] ~; *TS*
357:37 jangle] jingle *TS*
358:26 Oh Thanks] ~, Thanks *G* ~, thanks *A1*
358:36 if it ... Ramón ... on metal *Ed.*] if it ... Ramon ... on metal *MS* if metal on metal *TS* no clang of metal on metal *TSR* no clang of metal *A1*
359:7 upslope] up-slope *G*
359:8 downslope *Ed.*] down-slope *MS*
359:16 deer:] ~; *TS*
359:25 Capital] capital *G*
359:26 clothes] ~, *G*

359:27 Noon-Verse *Ed.*] Noon-verse
        MS noon-verse *TS*
359:32 aroused] roused *A1*
359:34 religion *Ed.*] Religion *MS*
359:38 Living *Ed.*] living *MS*
360:5 Church!] ~? *G*
360:6 catholic] catholics *A1*
360:12 he ... god] He ... God *G*
360:12 him] Him *G*
360:22 good; *TSR*] ~, *MS*
360:33 others? *TSR*] ~. *MS*
360:38 And] ~, *G*
361:7 life:] ~; *TS*
361:9 dissolve, since ... solved. *E1*]
        dissolve. *MS*
361:16 good *E1*] good our *MS*
361:23 bullies *E1*] knaves *MS*
362:1 a *MS*, *A1*] *Om. TS*
362:12 *Ho! Erect! G*] Ho! Erect! *MS*
        Ho! Erect! *TSR*
362:18 small.] ~— *TS*
362:24 strengths:] ~; *TS*
362:29 it:] ~; *TS*
362:30 here—!"] ~!"— *G*
362:31 here!" ... here!"] ~!"— ...
        ~!"— *G*
362:33 if *E1*] if great *MS*
362:37 clashing] ~, *A1*
363:5 strength! *G*] ~? *MS*
363:9 Biff!— *TSR*] ~! *MS*
363:20 again,] ~ *TS*
363:21 secret sun *TSR*] secret *MS*
363:26 here! (and] ~!"—— *G*
363:26 forehead) Not] ~. "~ *G*
363:29 here! (he] ~! (He *TS* ~!"—he
        G
363:29 breast) and *TS*] ~.) ~ *MS*
        ~—"~ *G*
363:29 here! (he] ~! (He *TS* ~!"—he
        G
363:30 belly) and] ~—"~ *G*
363:30 here! (he] ~!" (He *TS*
        ~!"—he *G*
363:30 loins). *Ed.*] ~) *MS* ~. *G*
363:31 strength? *P* "Can *Ed.*] ~? *P*
        Can *MS* ~? Can *TS*
364:11 badly-made *TSR*] badly made
        MS

364:16 And] ~, *G*
364:24 barracks' yard] barrack's yard
        TS barracks-yard *G*
364:27 power:] ~; *G*
364:34 barracks' yard] barrack's yard
        TS barracks-yard *G*
365:4 crowing] crowning *A1*
365:5 no-one *Ed.*] no one *MS*
365:11 watched] ~, *G*
365:17 round] around *TS*
365:22 the] *Om. A1*
365:26 their] that *G*
365:28 supreme, they] ~. They *TS*
365:37 limbs,] ~ *TS*
365:38 volcanoes *MS*, *A1*] volcanos *G*
365:39 yourselves] yourself *A1*
366:11 tents:] ~; *A1*
366:19 good,] ~ *A1*
366:24 again] ~, *G*
367:4 re-iterated *Ed.*] reiterated *MS*
367:6 sun:] ~; *TS*
367:9 Living] living *TS*
367:14 mats] mast *A1*
367:19 quietly] quickly *TS*
367:20 eyes, and ... Ramón's ... bot-
        tomless depth *Ed.*] eyes, and ...
        Ramon's ... bottomless depth
        MS consciousness, to a centre
        that plunges into the bottom-
        less depths *TS* eyes, closing
        them. Ramon stood behind
        Cipriano, who remained
        motionless in the warm dark,
        his consciousness reeling in
        strange concentric waves,
        towards a centre where it sud-
        denly plunges into the bottom-
        less deeps *TSR* eyes, closing ...
        Ramón ... deeps *G*
367:34 living *TSR*] warm *MS*
368:16 were] *Om. G*
368:18 No] ~, *G*
369:9 mountain lion] mountain-lion
        TS
370:4 Living] living *TS*
370:8 a] as *A1*
370:14 water *E1*] sea *MS*
370:35 Living] living *TS*

370:36 could you] you could *A1*
370:37 quite!] ~? *G*
370:38 Not now!] *Om. A1*
370:40 Living Quetzalcoatls] living Quetzalcoatls *TS* living Quetzalcoatl *G*
371:1 Living *Ed.*] living *MS*
371:10 Living] living *TS*
371:18 Horrible, *TSR*] Horrible bounders, *MS*
371:24 me." *E1*] me." *P* Cipriano, rowing home, said to himself: *P* "I opened my breast like a bird over the dark waters. Then I became a breath. Then I passed away in the waters, and the waters passed away in me.—I wish I had Malintzi, to be the sea beneath me now, now I am come back. I wish I had her in her god-self, for I feel my god-self upon me now, seeking for its mate in the god-self.—But {god-self. But *TS*} she says she has her own life to live—whatever that may mean!" *MS*
372:12 church-doors *Ed.*] church doors *MS*
372:16 church-doors *Ed.*] church doors *MS*
372:20 waiting, *TSR*] ~ *MS*
372:22 bonfires *G*] bon-fires *MS*
372:22 waited, *TSR*] ~ *MS*
373:2 Men *Ed.*] men *MS*
373:3 sat *TSR*] sat on, *MS*
373:5 façade *G*] facade *MS*
373:13 *First Song of Huitzilopochtli. TSR*] First Song of Huitzilo-pochtli. *MS First ... Huitzilopochtli*: *G*
373:17 Huitzilopochtli] ~, *G*
373:18 sun, *G*] ~ *MS*
373:20 Huitzilopochtli] ~, *G*
373:23 Huitzilopochtli] ~, *G*
373:25 dark, *Ed.*] ~. *MS*
373:26 body *TSR*] mantle *MS*
373:30 thorn. *G*] ~ *MS*

373:35 Oh] ~, *G*
373:36 Oh] ~, *G*
374:6 bent *E1*] turning *MS*
374:7 Men] men *TS*
374:9 Huitzilopochtli, *G*] ~ *MS*
374:10 Huitzilopochtli, *G*] ~ *MS*
374:12 Huitzilopochtli] ~, *G*
374:15 Huitzilopochtli] ~, *G*
374:16 as] of the *G*
374:16 bone, *G*] ~ *MS*
374:18 Huitzilopochtli] ~, *G*
374:21 body *TSR*] mantle *MS*
374:29 his] the *TS*
374:30 Oh] ~, *G*
374:32 Nor *TSR*] Never *MS*
374:37 Fire of ... of men *E1*] And shaking with fire in his den *MS* And shaking fire of the passion of men *TSR*
375:6 bonfires *G*] bon-fires *MS*
375:15 Huitzilopochtli,] ~: *TS*
375:19 woman, prisoner] ~, ~, *TS* woman-prisoner, *TSR*
375:20 over *TSR*] dressed in *MS*
375:30 sentences: *G*] ~. *MS*
375:32 No man] No more *A1*
375:33 him *TSR*] ~. *MS*
375:34 Which is not his own *TSR*] The power from the beyond *MS*
375:35 sun, *TSR*] ~ *MS*
375:36 middle-earth *Ed.*] middle earth *MS*
376:9 prowling,] ~. *TS*
376:17 dream-slopes *TSR*] dream steps *MS*
376:24 dogs, grey dogs with *TSR*] grey dogs with poisonous *MS*
376:33 you,] ~. *TS*
377:1 beat,] ~ *TS*
377:2 pure: *G*] ~ *MS*
377:10 of] to *A1*
377:24 Cipriano *TSR*] Ramon *MS*
377:25 red *Ed.*] black *MS*
377:36 woman:] ~. *TS*
378:4 poison. *Ed.*] rabies poison? *MS* poison? *TSR*
378:4 Men] men *TS*
378:9 woman too] ~, ~, *G*

378:13 eaten, *TSR*] ~ *MS*
378:17 guard] guards *G*
378:34 flame. *TS*] ~ *MS*
378:35 alive. *TS*] ~ *MS*
378:36 faces. *TS*] ~ *MS*
379:1 Then] ~, *A1*
379:23 leaves. Then ... slowly: *TSR*] leaves. *MS* leaves. *P* Then ... slowly: *G*
379:31 down. *TS*] ~ *MS*
380:7 sprigs] springs *TS* leaves *TSR*
380:11 he] *Om. A1*
380:16 Malintzi!" *TSR*] ~." *MS* ~. *TS*
380:20 *Patrón TSR*] Patron *MS*
380:21 played with *E1*] asked for *MS*
380:21 has sprung upon *E1*] is given *MS*
380:25 Death *G*] death *MS*
380:39 beat,] ~ *TS*
381:20 barefoot *MS, A1*] bare-/ foot *TS* bare-foot *G*
381:31 heads *Ed.*] head *MS*
382:6 sun,] ~ *TS*
382:7 buds *E1*] lips *MS*
382:18 gently] ~, *TS*
382:26 souls? *TSR*] ~. *MS*
382:32 Lord of Two Ways *Ed.*] lord of two ways *MS*
382:36 Lo] So *TS* "So *TSR*
382:37 angry,] ~ *TS*
383:4 not:] ~; *G*
383:6 new.] ~." *TSR*
383:10 cloths,] ~ *TS*
384:3 grey dogs *Ed.*] grey-dogs *MS*
384:4 by.] ~, *TS*
384:8 look up *E1*] dare look *MS*
384:21 guard] Guard *TS*
384:27 Brother. *E1*] ~? *MS* ~! *A1*
384:35 Ramón began ... speak: *Ed.*] Ramon: *MS* Ramon began ... speak: *TSR*
384:37 Star] ~. *TS*
385:3 day, *TSR*] ~ *MS*
385:4 night, *TSR*] ~ *MS*
385:7 at the *E1*] as a *MS*
385:9 Fountain] Fountains *TS*
385:9 commingle.] ~ *TS* ~, *TSR*

385:11 life *TSR*] knowing *MS*
385:12 Whence knowing ... streams.] *Om. G*
385:13 Source] source *A1*
385:14 it is *TSR*] it lives *MS*
385:15 men *TSR*] men must *MS*
385:17 men *TSR*] men must *MS*
385:21 gong *TSR*] bell *MS*
385:22 place.—Ramón's ... again *G*] place. *P* Ramon *MS* place.—Ramon's ... again *TSR*
385:24 Light] Like *G*
385:25 a] a new *A1*
385:26 into *TSR*] in *MS*
385:35 grains] drains *A1*
387:4 uneasy *TSR*] angry *MS*
387:8 *Man that ... a man TSR*] Man that is man is more than a man *MS*
387:10 into] with *TS*
387:16 strange] ~, *TS*
388:1 lode-stone] lode-/ stone *G* lodestone *A1*
388:5 not *TSR*] not quite *MS*
388:5 respond. *TSR*] respond. For this continent, for America, and perhaps for the Americans of all races, it was true. But for herself—even as a Celt, it was not pure truth. As a Celt she knew the old and extreme fascination of the gorgeous, lustrous, terrible will-mystery. But the years of Europe had put other things into her soul. But she could not quite acquiesce. *MS* respond. For this Continent ... acquiesce. *TS*
388:12 her—] ~. *TS*
388:12 when he was with her; *E1*] truly. And *MS*
388:13 spell. *E1*] spell. She was herself the unspeakably soft stone on which he sharpened the knife of his will. *MS* She was herself unspeakably ... will. *TS*
388:14 lode-stone] lode-/ stone *G* lodestone *E1*

388:15 pride—] ~. *TS*
388:16 profound. *E1*] profound. She
was the sheath of the knife. *MS*
388:18 reciprocal *E1*] almost purely
reciprocal *MS*
388:19 it was more than that *E1*] there
was a little more *MS*
388:25 him,] ~ *TS*
388:30 As an ... repulsive, and ... was
reciprocal *E1*] Set her {Let her
TS} alone, apart from him, and
she was fuel with no fire to
kindle it, a bonfire piled ready,
and never lit, wasting only to
dust *MS* As an ... repulsive
and ... reciprocal *A1*
388:34 same was true of him *E1*]
reverse was also true *MS*
388:35 own manhood and *E1*] last and
ultimate *MS*
388:38 achievement, he ... instrument. *E1*] achievement. *MS*
389:3 recognise] recognize *TS*
389:4 recognise] recognize *TS*
389:8 male *E1*] rushing dark *MS*
389:9 star, Don Ramón's Morning
Star, *Ed.*] star ... Ramon's
Star, *MS* star. Don Ramon's
Morning Star, *TS* star. Don
Ramon's Morning Star *TSR*
star! Don Ramón's Morning
Star *E1*
389:13 herself? *MS*, *E1*] ~. *G*, *A1*
389:14 manhood *E1*] accomplishment
MS
389:15 fig *E1*] *Om. MS*
389:16 true, *TSR*] ~ *MS*
389:23 make a *E1*] make a perfect *MS*
389:29 balance of ... of heaven *E1*]
sheath and the sharpening-
stone for his sheer will *MS*
389:33 Morning *E1*] Morning Star
MS
390:2 in] in the *G*
390:3 innermost] utmost *A1*
390:6 between the many, but *TSR*]
Om. MS
390:11 hard *TSR*] terrible *MS*

390:17 Except in ... is effectual. *E1*]
Om. MS
390:19 exist, in the vivid world. *E1*]
exist. *MS*
390:22 two: or between many. *TSR*]
two. *MS*
390:26 power *E1*] electric will *MS*
390:37 had *E1*] were *MS*
391:5 Oh] ~, *G*
391:7 Malintzi! *TSR*] ~. *MS*
391:8 her] ~, *G*
391:12 The living ... instrumental, the
Wish in armour. *E1*] *Om. MS*
The ... instrumental. *TSR*
391:17 the nakedness ... Wish *TSR*]
like a boy's *MS*
391:21 tonight,] tonight. *TS* to-night.
G
391:21 am *E1*] am the Living *MS* am
the *A1*
391:22 alone *E1*] without a bride
MS
391:22 wistful, watchful *TSR*] vulnerable *MS*
391:26 flaring] flaming *TS*
391:30 in to] into *G*
391:38 am *E1*] am the Living *MS* am
the *A1*
391:38 Indian *E1*] hurried *MS*
391:39 Stay with me *E1*] Be my bride
MS
392:1 replied.] ~, *TS*
392:1 I] I will *A1*
392:4 And put] put *TS* Put *G*
392:9 out,] ~ *TS*
392:12 Living *Ed.*] living *MS*
392:12 her,] ~ *TS*
392:14 You are *TSR*] I am *MS*
392:14 he *TSR*] she *MS*
392:14 of *E1*] of the Living *MS*
392:15 exultance *E1*] joy *MS*
393:11 naïve *MS*, *A1*] naive *TS*
393:12 Cipriano,] ~ *TS*
393:13 naïve *MS*, *A1*] naive *TS*
393:18 went *TSR*] that went *MS*
393:19 Ah] ~, *TS*
393:21 the beginning *TSR*] childhood
MS

393:24 *buena de TSR*] *bueno de MS*
buena del *A1*

393:26 flamey] flamy *A1*

393:26 unabashed *TSR*] boyish *MS*

393:27 yearning and *TSR*] merely *MS*

393:27 his] her *A1*

393:27 Naïvely *MS, A1*] Naïvely *G*

393:36 the Living] ~ living *TS*

393:38 Living] living *TSR*

393:40 Ah] ~, *G*

393:40 perhaps *TSR*] only *MS*

394:6 least] last *G*

394:7 free *E1*] fulness of *MS*

394:15 looked at ... eyes met *TSR*]
put their cheeks together *MS*

394:16 She closed ... dark. *TSR*] *Om.*
MS

394:19 naïve *MS, A1*] naive *TS*

394:20 *Miel! ... Malintzi! Ed.*] Miel!
Miel de Malintzi! *MS*

394:27 realises *MS, A1*] realizes *TS*

394:28 him! *TSR*] ~. *MS*

394:32 quick flame to *E1*] young flame
beside *MS* fierce flame to *TSR*

394:34 insouciante] insouciant *G*

395:17 neer-do-wells] ne'er-do-wells
A1

395:29 woman:] ~— *G*

395:31 and] ~, *G*

396:2 no fear ... of them *E1*] no
integrity *MS* fear ... them *A1*

396:11 Señorita *TSR*] señorita *MS*

396:12 No, Señorita *G*] ~ señorita *MS*

396:34 Ramón, *Ed.*] Ramon, *MS*
Ramon *TS* Ramón *G*

396:35 virgin *E1*] fierce *MS*

396:35 That too] ~, ~, *G*

396:37 reverence for *E1*] gratitude to
MS belief in *TSR*

397:26 cocktail,] ~ *TS*

397:34 his] *Om. TS*

398:7 naïvely *MS, A1*] naively *TS*

398:18 the] *Om. A1*

398:20 subtle *TSR*] dark *MS*

398:21 body! *TSR*] ~. *MS*

398:22 glory *E1*] moon *MS* leopard
TSR

398:23 lit with *TSR*] full of *MS*

398:34 fruit in the sun *E1*] moon in the
sky *MS* panther in the sun *TSR*

399:1 intense] ~, *TS*

399:3 in *TSR*] on *MS*

399:3 satisfaction *TSR*] foolishness
MS

399:16 and woman] and women *A1*

399:17 their] this *TS*

399:22 side? *E1*] side? *P* Kate asked
herself about Cipriano. "If I really
married him and lived with him," she
said, "this is what he would bring me to:
or try to. I should have to spend my life
fanning his blood to greatness, and
keeping him blood-faithful. And he
would come and go like the lord of
everything." *P* From Joachim she had
had mental and nerve faithfulness.
Mental faithfulness! Nerve faithfulness!—this to Cipriano would mean
nothing. To Joachim it had been everything. Cipriano would want the kindled
blood, and herself to fan it into flame.
Like a slave! *P* Ah {Ah, *G*} no! She
must keep her own life separate. *P* Her
first husband had made her into a
queen. He had been a sort of slave to
fan her into female queenliness and
overbearing. But there had been a
certain abjectness about him, that slave
touch, which she could not bear. *P*
Now, was she to be the slave, as the
wheel went round? *P* Never! *P* Her first
husband had been blood-faithful to
her, like a slave full of lust. And she had
become a queen, with the lust-slaves
running to her feet. *P* This she had had
to break. So it was Joachim, with the
intimacy and the understanding and the
nervous sympathy and exaltation, which
led to his bloodless death. As if his
blood had died in him. *P* Now it was
Cipriano. But Cipriano was only
moments {moments *TS*} in her life,
nothing consecutive. Her life was
somehow still in Europe, in England.
This was just moments. She would
leave Cipriano. She could not spend

her life fanning his blood and keeping him blood-faithful. Ah {Ah, *G*} no! It was not her metier. *P* She had not done it even with Joachim. *P* If she had, Joachim would not have died.—This too {This, too, *G*} was up against her. *MS*

399:23 Kate *E1*] her *MS*
399:28 strutting *E1*] devilish *MS*
399:33 wanted,] ~ *G*
399:34 métier *TSR*] metier *MS*
400:5 blackness. *TSR*] blackness, as if the man were dissolving into a black, thick liquid. *MS*
400:11 daring *TSR*] courage *MS*
400:11 masterly *TSR*] indomitable *MS*
400:20 day.] ~— *TS* ~.— *G*
400:24 her] the *TS*
400:26 mango trees *Ed.*] mango-trees *MS*
400:32 cigarettes,] ~ *TS*
400:35 bed-cover] bedcover *G*
401:5 dressing table] dressing-table *G*
401:7 absorbedly *MS, A1*] absolvedly *TS*
401:8 shoulders] ~, *G*
401:9 loosely-folded] loosely folded *TS*
401:20 India—] ~.— *G*
401:21 it.] ~? *A1*
401:21 for] on *A1*
401:34 shyly, *TSR*] *Om. MS*
401:37 it] it to *TS*
401:39 Many thanks! *TSR*] ~ ~. *MS*
402:3 her!] ~. *TS*
402:22 Oh] ~, *G*
402:26 woman-friend *G*] woman friend *MS*
402:32 Oh] ~, *G*
402:37 child:] ~ *TS*
403:1 pineapple-coloured *TSR*] pineapple coloured *MS*
403:6 hacienda] ~, *G*
403:24 realising *MS, A1*] realizing *TS*
403:30 big,] ~ *TS*
403:33 also, sometimes, *TSR*] also *MS*

403:35 *administrador Ed.*] administrador *MS* administrator *G*
403:39 notorious *TSR*] infamous *MS*
404:5 downed *E1*] *crêvé MS crève G*
404:8 Though ... sure] ~, ... ~, *G*
404:14 care *TSR*] dare *MS*
404:16 Cathedral *G*] cathedral *MS*
404:17 Cathedral, *MS, A1*] ~ *TS*
404:30 men, he] ~. He *TS*
404:34 resistance *TSR*] malevolence *MS*
404:38 city *TSR*] evil city *MS*
404:39 hidden malevolence ... capital *E1*] hidden, but almost inhuman malevolence the Mexicans poured out against him. It seemed almost to eat holes in him, at the solar plexis. And he had to drive on with sheer will *MS* hidden, but inhuman ... will *TSR*
405:12 spring] ~, *G*
405:13 white *E1*] white and yellow *MS*
405:19 water-hyacinth] water-hyacinths *TS*
405:21 wild-fowl *Ed.*] wild fowl *MS*
405:30 sugar cane *Ed.*] sugar-cane *MS, A1* suger-cane *G*
405:33 bullock wagons] bullock-wagons *G*
405:34 spikey] spiky *A1*
405:38 chiles] chilies *A1*
406:1 apples and ... gathered. The] *Om. TS*
406:5 again *E1*] already *MS*
406:5 orange-yellow *TSR*] orange yellow *MS*
406:13 straggling] struggling *TS*
406:15 humming-birds] humming-/birds *TS* hummingbirds *G*
406:16 wild, and] wild, *A1*
406:16 flies, *TSR*] ~ *MS*
406:21 bowl-fuls] bowlfuls *G*
406:36 Goodnight!] goodnight! *TS* good-night; *G* good-night *E1*
407:8 Oh] ~, *G*
407:11 me. *E1*] me: and I might fall down it. *MS*

407:16 said. *E1*] said, wearily. *MS* said
  wearily. *TS*
407:21 always just a man *E1*] not dead
  yet *MS*
409:22 has wounds ... guerre! *E1*] has
  big invisible wounds—one has
  someone to heal them—*MS*
  has big ... has help to heal
  them. *TSR*
407:32 Then she and] Then she said
  TS Then, she said, *TSR*
407:38 helpless] ~, *G*
407:39 horrible] ~, *G*
408:16 *soul TSR*] soul *MS*
408:27 *don't TSR*] don't *MS*
408:29 must do as he does *E1*] must
  MS
408:33 Oh] ~, *G*
408:40 my soul ... Ramón.—" *Ed.*]
  Ramon has taken my soul.—"
  MS Ramon has ... my soul."—
  TS my soul ... Ramon."—
  TSR My soul ... Ramón."— *G*
409:18 life! *TSR*] soul-keeper. *MS* life.
  G
409:19 live *TSR*] keep *MS*
409:19 life *TSR*] soul *MS*
409:21 life *TSR*] soul *MS*
409:25 Ah] ~, *G*
409:26 lost *TSR*] given *MS*
409:26 Ramón. *Ed.*] Ramon. *MS*
  Ramon— *TS* Ramón.— *G*
409:27 say! *TSR*] ~. *MS*
409:33 Ah] ~, *G*
409:34 blood *E1*] soul *MS*
409:38 life *TSR*] soul *MS*
410:1 Oh] ~, *G*
410:13 soul— *MS, A1*] ~.— *G*
410:17 What I ... Ramón ... care *what*
  ... to him. *Ed.*] him. It is gone
  beyond. It is Ramon's Morning
  Star. *MS* What ... Ramon ...
  him. *TSR* What ... Ramón ...
  care what ... him. *G*
410:28 are not so sure of *TSR*] have
  lost *MS*
410:30 second-rate *TSR*] really trivial
  MS

410:31 connection *TSR*] creation *MS*
410:34 In her ... her inferiors.] *Om.*
  TS
411:3 Kate's marriage ... [411:6]
  overwhelm her. *E1*] *Om. MS*
411:24 well] *Om. MS*
411:40 black, with] ~ ~ *A1*
412:5 married,] ~ *TS*
412:7 Ah] ~, *G*
412:9 Ah] ~, *G*
412:10 wearing himself out. *E1*] killing
  himself. *MS*
412:11 Ah] ~, *G*
412:13 life *TSR*] soul *MS*
412:15 life *TSR*] soul *MS*
412:15 ah] oh *TS*
412:18 Ah] ~, *G*
412:18 men. *E1*] men. When they are
  coldly brave. *MS*
412:24 blood. *E1*] blood. And over us
  is his Quetzalcoatl star.
  Because of the star over us, he
  is Quetzalcoatl, and more than
  a man. *MS*
412:26 *he TSR*] only he *MS*
412:30 should *E1*] shall *MS*
412:31 women *E1*] womanhood *MS*
412:39 body!] ~. *TS*
412:40 own] *Om. TS*
413:7 that *TSR*] *Om. MS*
413:8 after] after the *G*
413:9 blue-black] blue black *TS*
413:10 vapor *Ed.*] vapour *MS*
413:12 lovely] lonely *TS*
413:22 them? *TS*] ~. *MS*
413:28 I think a *E1*] A *MS*
413:29 Why ... so? *E1*] A life-stranger.
  Ramon will be a stranger to me
  all my life. I know it. I yield to
  the stranger that he is to me.—I
  should not like him to be as a
  brother, or a friend. He is so
  much more to me, as a
  stranger. *MS* A ... me. I ...
  or as a friend ... stranger. *TS*
413:32 is *TSR*] is for *MS*
413:34 woman.] ~, *TS*
413:38 personal *TSR*] protective *MS*

413:39 Morning brings ... the morning. *E1*] But the star is above us all. And I want to be true to the star I know, even before I love my own children, whom I cannot know. If I am true to the star, the star will shine upon my children. And that will be better even than a mother's love. *MS* But the Star ... star. I know ... love. *TS*

414:3 glad *E1*] glad always *MS*

414:8 Nevertheless,] ~ *TS*

414:16 Bullock wagons *Ed.*] Bullock-wagons *MS*

414:21 control! *E1*] control! *P* Many donkeys and mother-donkeys with long-legged foals wandered across the beach, eating leaves and bits, the foals, all legs and ears, flicking themselves into a sudden staccato gallop and ducking at the she-asses, to drink. Two bull-calves were having a real earnest fight, tails uplifted. A group of young sows went grunting their soft, obstinate way, and a demon of a young black ram persistently tormented them, sniffing at their rear, and butting them with his horns, so that they ran away squealing with pig's expostulation. Till one sow at last turned with a rush and a grab, and the young ram went off helter-skelter, with his flat horns, and his thick tail flopping between his legs. *P* All the animals seemed to roam oddly on their own. And most of them were entire: not many were castrated. Kate used to say that all the animals in Mexico seemed cowed, broken. But it was not really so. They wandered their own silent and obstinate way, subdued, but not broken. They had their own heavy way of life. And the donkeys were very queer, running at one another, nipping, then kicking out: and then running away as if they had forgotten: then suddenly remembering, and running towards one another in the wierdest way, necks out- stretched, mouths open, to bray.— Then the peon was sure to throw stones at them, to stop them braying. *P* The people were always throwing stones: at the cattle, at the pigs, at one another. If a mother was angry with a girl, she immediately stooped to pick up a stone: and *whizz!* {*whizz! G*} she {She *TS*} threw viciously at the child. But always so as just to miss. Aiming just to miss. The same when the boys threw stones at one another: aiming just to miss. And the stones the men threw so fiercely at the cattle almost always skimmed just over the animal's back, and by its thud on the earth, startled the creature. The animals knew perfectly well the peon's intention. It was a heavy, subdued recognition of *will*. *P* Kate was always amused at the women who came with their pig on a string, down to the lake for the creature to drink. The cunning, obstinate pig almost always escaped. After it went the woman, stopping and viciously throwing stones. The pig skipped away with little squeals, per- fectly well aware of the woman's inten- tions. And like the obstinate demon it was, it would rush into peoples {people's *TS*} gardens, or away to the plaza. Till the village policemen—two together—would suddenly, silently appear {appears *TS*} to seize it: for pigs were forbidden the freedom of the street. *P* Then another scene: so differ- ent in feeling, so exactly the same in circumstance as in Sicily. But the woman muted, angry, frightened: the two sort of policemen {two so-called policemen *TSR*} quiet, insidious, with a cautious menace and a strange heavy, wary sort of overbearing: always {over- bearing always *TS*} sending for more witnesses, and insisting with a quiet, demonish malevolence. The woman becoming more sullen, and the strange shadow of vengeance, of the thrust of a heavy knife, in the future, darkening the

air. Everything with a sinister suggestion. *P* It weighed down on Kate, and
she wanted to go home, to Europe, to
Ireland. England she mistrusted with a
profound mistrust. England's tolerance seemed to hide a peculiar
unpleasant rottenness. A sense of
uncleaness, inward decay. This was
how the thought of England affected
her. Ireland {rottenness. Ireland *TSR*}
was almost another Mexico. But
Ireland was not so heavy, heavy,
heavy, black, sinister, and lava-heavy.
MS

414:22 prehistoric *A1*] pre-historic
        MS pre- historic *G*
414:27 and countries ... oceans,] *Om.*
        TS
414:29 only *TSR*] only like *MS*
414:32 civilisation] civilization *TS*
415:3   consciousness,] ∼; *A1*
415:7   between man and man] ∼ ∼ ∼
        ∼, *A1*
415:11 In America, therefore, *TSR*]
        And this is the way of the
        American continent. There,
        MS
415:13 Probably *TSR*] But *MS*
415:14 death *TSR*] death will *MS*
415:19 deathly *TSR*] sinister *MS*
415:20 peoples] people *TS*
415:33 blood] ∼, *G*
415:35 scientific *E1*] charming *MS*
416:1   existing *TSR*] waiting *MS*
416:11 violence *TSR*] horror *MS*
416:12 revive the hope in *E1*] restore
        the hope to *MS*
416:17 servants:] ∼. *TS*
416:24 English, Germanic] English-
        Germanic *G*
416:27 *aguador Ed.*] aguador *MS*
        aquador *TS*
416:29 eyes:] ∼. *TS*
416:40 She belonged ... clever ones.
        TSR] *Om. MS*
417:12 Spirit] spirit *TS*
417:28 quaking, deep *TSR*] subtle,
        cat-like *MS*

418:14 ground out ... machines *E1*]
        extinguished by the waters of
        fury, or starved out by the
        sterile failure to marry the
        spirit and the blood *MS*
418:22 a] *Om. G*
418:27 communion *TSR*] understand-
        ing *MS*
418:31 dual created] dual-created *G*
418:37 Living *Ed.*] living *MS*
419:24 boy's,] ∼ *A1*
419:32 doom. *E1*] doom. She believed
        in Ramon {Ramón *G*} and
        Cipriano, and in what they
        were doing. In fact these two
        men seemed to her like one
        firm, green island in a world of
        quaking bogs. The gods were
        with them: and she was with
        them herself. But beyond
        Ramon {Ramón *G*} and Cipri-
        ano and the strange firm reality
        they represented, was the wide
        and frightening menace of
        America. She felt she must go
        away, or the strain and the
        nausea would kill her. *MS*
        doom ... firm, bushy island ...
        of aboriginal America ... her.
        TSR
419:37 Capital *Ed.*] capital *MS*
419:40 followers,] ∼ *TS*
420:4   some *TSR*] much *MS*
420:6   not very impressive, after all,
        TSR] *Om. MS*
420:7   mob,] ∼ *TS*
420:7   Zócalo *TSR*] Zocalo *MS*
420:28 labored *TS*] laboured *MS, G*
420:30 states] States *TS*
420:32 scarlet ... towers] scarlet ...
        tower *TS* a scarlet ... tower
        TSR
421:2   a *MS, A1*] *Om. TS*
421:9   body *E1*] very body *MS*
421:19 underlife. The] ∼. *P* The *G*
421:21 thought, *TSR*] ∼ *MS*
421:24 still and proud *E1*] happy *MS*
421:24 her body] the body *TS*

421:25 She had *E1*] Or rather, she was not exactly happy: she had, rather, *MS*

421:28 She had ... in sureness. *E1*] *Om. MS*

421:35 cautious] ~, *G*

421:39 realised *MS, A1*] realized *TS*

422:2 strange,] ~ *TS*

422:6 realised *MS, A1*] realized *TS*

422:10 recoiled *E1*] drew away *MS*

422:19 realise *MS, A1*] realize *TS*

422:35 her. *TSR*] her. And she was changed again to a soft, hot spring of inner waters, gushing noiselessly and beyond knowing, in the dark. *MS*

422:36 flowing, *TSR*] ~ *MS*

422:37 subterranean *TSR*] beyond her *MS*

422:37 it] it *G*

423:13 or spiritual *TSR*] *Om. MS*

423:14 A mindless ... the blood. *TSR*] *Om. MS*

423:23 mountain-sides] mountain-/sides *G* mountain sides *A1*

423:25 pallid] ~, *G*

423:36 of the] of *TS*

424:3 Sons of the Morning *G*] sons of the morning *MS*

424:3 red] Red *G*

424:8 communion *TSR*] presence *MS*

424:11 fires *E1*] flames *MS*

424:11 Indians] Indian *TS*

424:15 an] and *A1*

424:24 breakwater-wall *Ed.*] break-water wall *MS* break-/water wall *G* breakwater wall *A1*

424:26 morning. *P* "I ... to herself. *E1*] morning. *MS* morning. "I ... herself. *A1*

424:34 wet] *Om. G*

425:7 not *TSR*] *Om. MS*

426:2 Here! *A1*] *Om. MS* HERE! *E1 see notes*

426:11 trees,] ~ *G*

426:24 dry,] ~ *TS*

427:9 "But why ... [430:3] about myself." *E1*] "Tell them," he said, "the centre of the cosmos is alive, and terribly alive. But not with any personal god. A centre of life like some watchful octopus, that throws its arms out studded with stars and suns: and we on one of the stars. *P* Tell them the only gods are men. That terrible being of the Innermost casts out rays and circles of creation, and creation casts back an answer, which is food for the One at the centre. The One casts us out like a question, and we, at the far end of the ray, have to cast back the answer. If we cannot give the answer, the answer *I am*, to the One at the centre, then the One curves his rays round us and drags us back out of creation into oblivion. *P* Tell your people that: it is old wisdom. There is the Old One at the centre of all the cosmos, who pulses out the unknown questions and demands. And we, and all created things, have to pulse back our substantial answer. The answer is: *I am*. Men that can answer, are gods. Men that cannot answer, are dragged into oblivion like dead dogs. *P* And all life consists in this: the demand from the Only One, and the answer from us. Between his demand and our answer the suns spin on their pivots, the worlds balance themselves with their moons. It all happens within the vast rush of the demand, and the backward sweep of our answer. *P* If we cannot answer, our sun will break on its pivot, the fires inside the earth will burst forth, or go cold, the waters over the earth will not come to us. There are no laws outside the demand and the answer. *P* It is the rhythm of the answer which has set the sun spinning and made waters and winds to travel; metals to lie still under our feet. Waters, and winds, and metals are all alive within the question and the answer. *P* And we, men, at the end of the vivid rays of question, we have the first responsibility for the answer. If we fail, our world fails. If men fail to give the answer, in their own substantial creation, our world will break, our earth will burst, our metals will be gone. *P* Our world can end. It can never grow worn-out and stale, and collapse for lack of anything, save the courage of men. But it can utterly collapse and disappear. There is no such thing as wearing out of the worlds, for the worlds are alive. But living, they must breathe the great Breath, and make the living *geste* of answer. When the supreme courage of men, the life-courage, the hot courage, collapses, our world collapses. *P* The One gives us the Breath and the question. We have to create the *geste* and the answer. The flowers seem perfect answerers. The animals and birds seem perfect answerers. But man, man is the coward, the bungler, the conceited fool, the ape with too many tricks. Man is the ape with too many tricks. *P* But the Breath, and the demand, never cease to come. The ape neither breathes nor answers. The Breath passes into the earth, and will burst the bowels of the earth with fire, so the globe of apes is shattered. *P* Tell them of man's responsibility. Tell them of his doom. All the tricks of all the apes avail not a straw. The great Breath never ceases to blow, and what it does not create, it destroys. And now it is blowing destruction on the world of man-apes. *P* Tell them to breathe the Breath, and find the answer. *P* Because I, when I say I am the Living Quetzal-coatl, do no more than make plain my acceptance of my last responsibility, as a man, towards the inscrutable and unescapable One of the centre." *P* Kate always trembled a little when Ramon became passionate in his earnestness. It was almost more than she could bear. *P* Yet in her own woman's way she understood what he meant. That the great First Cause was like a dragon coiled at the very centre of all the cosmos, and peeping out, like her snake. Utterly incomprehensible and non-human, the great, coiling serpent of the everlasting First Cause watching, and lashing, and breathing forth. Breathing forth waves of fire and life, living fire and living moisture, away, away to the bounds of the cosmos. And drawing back the breath of creation. *P* And the living moisture and the living fire were sent forth also to a goal: the goal of substantial existence. Reaching a certain point in their out-rushing, they swirled to a pivot, many pivots, and the worlds began. The world of waters must send back waters to the First Cause, and the world of fire must send back fire. Fire comes in a living, uncreated breath: goes back in a wavering of created flame. Water comes breathing lovely and invisible from the Wonder-dragon at the centre of the cosmos: steals back misty and thoughtful, as created substance. Fires cannot die, and waters cannot perish, because all the time they come invisibly from the deeps of all the cosmos, and differently, having moved substantial in the created worlds, they return. *P* The First Cause is alive: and being alive, must be nourished. It is the first and last of laws. *P* Substantial creation sends back to the coiled First Cause the essential nourishment. Fires flaming on earth, waters misting up, metals rusting: it is all the return, the gift back again. *P* But the dragon of the First Cause sent out Breath after Breath, in strange circles. He breathed the waters in the first Breath, and away in the cosmos waters rolled and distilled into blue drops, and Ocean, then started the return, mistily, happily. *P* In the second Breath he breathed the elemental fire, away in the cosmos fire rolled and tumbled into drops, till stars awoke, and suns, and the light shone, and the heat wavered back again, in strange nourishment, to the nostrils of the First Cause. *P* And the living waters passing the living fire, make the rainbow in their conjunction. *P* The dragon breathed again, and among the tumble of fire and waters, between the suns and moons of the cosmos, substance came, the earths. Then the metals flowered yellow and white and ruddy, and exhaled their first delicate exhalation back to the Innermost. And the Innermost drank the taste of the metals. *P* So breath by breath, till the flowers came, and at the point of creation within the cosmos, they rose up, revealed and manifest, and in their manifestation they said to the First Cause: Lo, I am! So the First Cause thrilled with joy, and drank the breath of flowers back again, and was nourished, and said: Go on forever, saying to me, *I am*. So the little seeds rolled up inside the fading flowers. *P* Then amid all the flying, living Breaths, on the rush of a new Breath came a new whirling centre, and insects were alive. They took wings, and the flutter of their wings was the answer-cry, *I am*. Then the dragon laughed, and tasted honey. *P* And a new Breath came, and the reptiles appeared, then another Breath, quickly and out in our part of the cosmos humming-birds glittered at the flowers. Shadowy birds began to sing. Our part of the cosmos rang with the answer: I am! I am! *P* This was a glorious morning in the cosmos. *P* But there came a long day, and the great unease grew in the dragon. The answer was not enough, the nourishment was not enough. Heavy with unease, he withheld his breath, and the fires did not flow, the waters began to fall inert and freeze, the worlds began to crack. And the unease lasted, and the birds died, and the lizards lay down and died,

and the worlds froze. *P* Then, in the last warm marshes, a last slow Breath focussed the waters and fires, and flower-plasm and snake-plasm and bird-plasm, and from the mud a wondering animal rose motherless and fatherless, shook himself, looked around with pain and pleasure, and said *I am*! *P* So the answer was given, and the dragon sighed with relief. He sent his Breath in great gusts, and floods came, and whales gambolled for the first time in the water. *P* So on and on, through the days and the cataclysms of Creation, till man arrives. And upon man devolves the great responsibility, to give the answer, and send back the offering. *P* And still man fails, for the answer is not in him. He cannot say: *I am*, because even now, he is-not. And the offering he sends back, smoke of factories and crackle of electricity, abnegation and inventions, is not enough. The dragon stirs with unease, and holds back his Breath. The fires do not flow, and the waters do not come to us. The worlds shake on their pivots. The great death is imminent. *P* There is no hope for us, save to give the answer and to make the life-offering. The multitudes are already doomed. *P* The sense of doom, the vision into the beyond, the sense of responsibility to the inner dragon, stayed with Kate all the time. So that the scenes of the day were like mirage, through the wavering of which she could see the terrible hinterland, to the cosmic centre, where the dragon is. *MS* "But why ... like a sting. [428:32] *P* "Still!" he said. "*C'est mon affaire.*" *P* "Of course it is!" she replied. "If you want to be so—so abstract, and Quetzalcoatlian, and then bury your head in the lap of a Teresa, like an ostrich in the sand when he has brought his enemies upon him, then of course it is your affair!" *P* "So!" he said, smiling. "So! Am I abstract?" *P* "What else? Life, just living, is not good enough for you. You want to parade something from your own will. And it is not enough for you to be a man, a real man. You dress yourself up as a God, with your Quetzalcoatl, and think you monopolise the Godhead. Do you think you and Cipriano, you two men, can make a goddess of me, with your *Malintzi*? I like your cheek. I am more than all your Malintzis and Quetzalcoatls, when I am just myself." *P* "So! So! Another declaration of Independence! But what is it that you are, when you are *just yourself?*" *P* "More than I should be if I let you rig me out as *your* Malintzi. Do you think that I, Kate Forrester, am not ten times as real and important as any Malintzi, or any living Quetzalcoatl either?" *P* "No! Frankly, I don't. Kate Forrester without any Malintzi, and with no Quetzalcoatl, or Huitzilopochtli in her life seems to me—I won't say just like anybody else—but with just a common destiny, a vulgar destiny; embedded in the rest of vulgar people." *P* Kate paused, baffled. Then she retorted: *P* "It may *seem* to you so, but it isn't so. Of course, if you refuse to recognise in me what I am, and the real Lord that is behind me, of course it will seem to you that I am embedded in the vulgar destiny. But {destiny, but *G*} my destiny is my own, for all that. And it is no smaller than your destiny. And in my opinion it is more real—more alive. Because I am a woman.—You make a Quetzalcoatlish abstraction of yourself, then bury {then you bury *G*} your head in the lap of a Teresa—and you seem to me so limited, so limited, with no great space round you. Just like a man—a mere man—who thinks he is being his greatest when he is being abstract, and asserting his will over life.—I have the greatest respect for you when you are just Ramon. But when you are the Living Quetzalcoatl {Quatzalcoatl, *G*} you seem to me a—a conceited boy, like a vain, self-conscious, posing boy of nineteen." *P* He watched her in silence, with a slow, ironical smile on his face. *P* "So!" he said at length. "So! We are judged! Out of the mouth of Woman the Mother." *P* "No!" said Kate. "You needn't turn me into another abstraction. I am just myself." *P* "If we knew that that meant." *P* "*I* know!" she cried. "It is enough for me, that *I* know what I am. You don't know, because you don't want to. That is why I am going away." *P* "*Adios!*" he said. *P* She flushed suddenly. *P* "Oh! I know you want to get rid of me!" she cried. "I am in your way, with this Quetzalcoatl stunt of yours. But I am going!—I have given in to you for a time. But I can't keep it up. And why should I?—Religion!—{Religion— *G*} Religion! I can't feel any real religion behind you. There is no *fervour*, no purity. It is all male will." *P* "I don't want fervour and purity," he said. *P* "There is no God behind you, except your own tuppenny male will," she said. "The Lord that is behind me is much greater—vaster. You are all so tight and limited. I *do* think you and Cipriano are wonderful, in some ways. But I can conceive of a much higher type than either of you." *P* "We must be grateful for the small mercies of your good opinion," he said. "But I must be allowed to add, that for myself—and I believe the same is true of Cipriano—I look on your 'higher types' with an unconquerable disgust. I don't care for 'heights',—especially Gothic." *P* "And I don't care what words you put on me—Gothic or baroque. What do I care about your words! I know what I *feel*—and that is enough for me." *P* "You have felt many things, contradictory things, too, in {things, in *G*} the course of your life. You have even 'felt' Huitzilopochtli and Quetzalcoatl—and felt them deeply." *P* "No!" she cried. "Not deeply. It has been an experience—but not very deep. I know something better, really." *P* "What is it?" *P* "Just life! And being oneself." "Which self?" *P* "I am myself. You may not know whether you have any self or not. But I know that I am myself." *P* "But which self? The one that came trailing over from England to America?—and trailing down to Mexico with your cousin Owen?—and becoming hysterical at a bull-fight, and being driven to Sanborn's for tea and strawberry shortcake?" *P* For a moment, she wondered at his good memory, and was flattered. Then she retorted. *P* "Yes! Even that self is better than if I let myself be tricked out as Malintzi or Itzpapalotl, or some such thing that I don't believe in." *P* "It is very good!" he said in Spanish. "It is very good. Go with God! With your own particular God!" *P* "That is what I shall do," she said. "I am not afraid."

TS see also following entries to 429:30

427:15 one of ... you *E1*] *Om. MS* a help, after all *TS*

427:17 Quetzalcoatls— *E1*] *Om. MS* Quetzalcoatl, *TS* Quetzalcoatls, *TSR*

427:21 all the same *E1*] *Om. MS* by your presence *TS*

427:30 worn look *E1*] *Om. MS* weariness *TS*

427:31 realised *A1*] *Om. MS* realized *TS*

428:15 I can't hold *E1*] *Om. MS* my life will not last *TS*

428:25 her: *TS*] *Om. MS* ~; *G*

428:26 forget for a time *E1*] *Om. MS* go to sleep *TS*

428:35 sometimes, *E1*] *Om. MS* ~ *A1*

429:1 but you *E1*] *Om. MS* but *A1*

429:9 selves: *E1*] *Om. MS* ~, *A1*

429:30 Why? *E1*] *Om. MS* ~! *A1*

430:7 long *E1*] *Om. MS* strange *TS*

430:14 In the ... be like *E1*] *Om. MS* Why strain oneself after faceless gods and beating hearts! Something in her own heart felt alive and self-sufficient *TS*

430:19 Quetzalcoatl *E1*] *Om. MS* God *TS*

430:22 realised *G*] *Om. MS* realized *TS*

430:29 Oh *E1*] *Om. MS* Pah *TS*

430:37 of the *TS*] *Om. MS* of *A1*

431:4 simple life *E1*] *Om. MS* normal *TS*

431:5 buses *TS*] *Om. MS* '~ *G*

431:7 life *E1*] *Om. MS* normal *TS*

431:8 "Yes! Without ... Cipriano should *E1*] *Om. MS* "I suppose it is. It is what I'm used to." *P* "You want Cipriano to *TS*

431:11 impatience. She ... show them! *E1*] *Om. MS* contemptuous impatience. What! was she to go on submitting to this: that she was the mere female. Was the individual woman in her to be so insulted? *TS* contemptuous ... this, that ... insulted. *G*

431:15 But Kate ... of it. *TSR*] *Om. MS*

431:16 on the ... Sayula *TSR*] *Om. MS*

431:21 ship. And *TSR*, *E1*] ship, and *MS* ship. A *G*

431:22 was *TSR*] *Om. MS*

431:24 brown like *TSR*] as *MS*

431:27 up to the side *TSR*] down to the hold *MS*

431:28 tentatively. Then *Ed.*] ~, Then *MS* ~, then *TS*

431:33 huge *E1*] vast *MS*

431:35 leather jacket *TSR*] skin jacket *MS* skin-jacket *TS*

431:36 wedge *E1*] heavy, short wedge *MS* heavy short wedge *TS*

431:39 high-hatted] high hatted *G*

432:17 changeless; *TSR*] ~, *MS*

432:17 fulness] fullness *TS*

432:23 snake-markings] snake markings *TS*

432:36 mooring-rope] mooring rope
TS

433:16 why] that *TS*

433:18 And I ... [434:15] you say."
TS] So I tell him, I will do as he
wishes. I belong to him chiefly.
And if I must sit before the
people as his god-wife as well
as his human wife, I will do it. I
tell him I shall sit with my head
bent down, hiding my face, and
hiding my hands in my lap, but
he says it will do.—Yes, if I am
Ramon's wife, I am the bride of
Quetzalcoatl too, whatever
name he gives me. Though it is
hard for me.—For you it would
be different." *P* "Why?" said
Kate. *P* "You are a woman for
all the people in the world. So
Ramon says. I am a woman for
one man only." *P* "You don't
think I am a wife, as you are?" *P*
"Not as I am, because you are
so much stronger in the world
than I. You are a woman in the
eyes of all people. It is your
race. I am a woman in the
shadow of a man." *P* "You
don't think I could ever be a
perfect wife?" *P* "Ah! Yes, to
another man. There are many
men who don't want a wife like
me. There are men who want
who can hold her own, and
fight the woman's battle. Cipriano is a soldier, and you too are
like a soldier among women.
People would always turn to
look at you: and most people
would be a little afraid of you,
after the first. Ramon says you
are the real wife of Huitzilopochtli, and he hopes you will
come back and sit beside
Cipriano, in the green dress.

He says he will make your
statue standing looking out
into the people as if you were
searching them—" *MS see
also following entries to* 434:5

433:25 self, because ... do. It is right. I
E1] self, not the more trivial
sleves that I am as well. It is
right. I *TS* self because ... do. I
A1

433:28 bride *Ed.*] Bride *TS*

433:38 quick *E1*] wide *TS*

434:1 abstract *E1*] didactic *TS*

434:3 slowly *E1*] darkly *TS*

434:5 "He takes ... himself." *E1*]
Om. *TS*

434:17 "And you ... the world. *TSR*]
"I am as frightened, really, as
you," she said. *P* "It is different," Teresa replied, shaking
her head. "You have a fighting
soul. *MS*

434:27 people, took up his work. He
E1] people, he *MS* people. He
TSR

434:28 chair-bottom] chair bottom
TS

434:37 wagon, *TSR*] ~ *MS*

435:4 winter *E1*] autumn *MS*

435:4 White-and-yellow] White and
yellow *TS*

435:11 peon, *TSR*] ~ *MS*

435:15 *Patrona TSR*] patrona *MS*

435:16 up. Can't] ~, can't *TS*

435:17 foal,] ~ *G*

435:18 high, *TSR*] ~ *MS*

435:21 grateful *TSR*] ~, *MS*

435:25 æons] aeons *TS*

435:34 re-iterated] reiterated *TS*

435:35 be-thinking] bethinking *TS*

435:40 knowledge *TSR*] reverence
MS

436:2 creation: and ... glorious
woman *TSR*] creation, the joy
in a leader, and in a woman
leading *MS* creation; and ...
woman *G*

436:5 *Adios! Ed.*] Adios! *MS*

436:6 *Adios Patrona! Ed.*] Adios patrona! *MS* Adios Patrona! *TSR, A1* Adios, Patrona! *E1*

436:8 surging vivid ... world! Like ... [436:13] to anything!" *E1*] surging dark and powerful within her. She *felt* godly. *MS* surging vivid and resistant within her. *TSR* surging vivid ... world! like ... anything! *A1*

436:23 splendid one ... [444:28] to him. *TS*] *noble* it makes one feel." *P* He laughed. *P* "No nobler than one is," he said. *P* "But the people are so wonderful. They make me feel noble, like the growing maize: as if they watered my roots." *P* "If you can give man his reverence back, he will be more grateful for that than for everything. It is the flow of life. If the life flows in, what does anything else matter. And if man or woman can restore the life-flow, to the people from whom it has been cut off, then that man or woman will be the gods and aristocrats of that people." *P* "I was born an aristocrat, and I always *felt* an aristocrat," said Kate. "But I never knew till now what it was to feel it move in me like life." *P* "Ah Señora, aristocracy is not a static thing. Aristocracy also is a flow, a living flow. If we can bring back the Living Breath to the earth, then the people will give us glory again. Jesus brought back the Living Breath with self-sacrifice, and had his need of glory. That is over. We have now to bring back the Breath, and take the glory: in the name of our manhood and our womanhood." *P* There was always, in the eyes of Ramon, something which was never said, and which perhaps never could be said, and before which Kate just bowed her head. *P* She stayed a few days at Jamiltepec, before Cipriano returned and she departed: for go she must. *P* "You don't think I am wrong, to go?" she said. *P* "No no! You are like Persephone. You must go between two worlds." *P* "I know the greater world is here," she said, wavering. *P* "therefore you will never abandon it. No, Caterina, go to your Europe. Tell them their Day of Salvation is over: the Via Crucis is travelled and finished: the serpent has flung his fold round the Cross again. The Spirit has flown the great flight, and alighted once more in the throat of the dragon. The Son of Man steps down from the Cross: because that is finished: *Consummatum est.*" *P* "Then why must I go?" she said. *P* "Go! Tell them the Cross is a Tree again, and they may eat the fruit if they can reach the branches. Tell them the snake coils in peace round the ankle of Eve, and she no longer tries to bruise his head. The fruit of Knowledge is digested. Now we can plant the core." *P* "But I shall never remember," she laughed. *P* "It doesn't matter," he said. "Tell them the body is the cup, and man is a column of blood, and woman a valley of blood, and the spirit trembles in the wine. Tell them man's supreme mystery is being in the flesh. When man is no longer in the flesh he is no longer man. The dragon drinks him up. Tell them the body is the manifestation and the flame, and the spirit in the body has a house and a tent of flame, which is more than she, for it lives where she cannot. *P* Tell them to kneel no more, but to stand erect as a flame stands, among the heavens. *P* Tell them to look at the canals of the sky, with all the far-off water-lilies, and laugh with confidence. *P* Tell them our feet are upon the mountains, we are sons of the morning, and the morning-star is on our foreheads. *P* Tell them the maize is man-high in Mexico, but the bull is angry, and is treading down the green wheat. *P* Tell them the serpent has slid into the cup, and the throat of the volcano is yellow as the sun. *P* Tell them blood is flowing into the mixing-bowl, and the eagle is striking at the moon with angry talons. *P* Tell them the Wheel of the Æon has turned, and Quetzalcoatl is delivering the maiden from the dragon. *P* Tell them the rider on the white horse has passed on, down the road of tombs. *P* Tell them Huitzilopochtli is calling: Lift up your heads, oh ye gates! *P* Tell them the fish has swum into the shadow, and the pole of the earth has shifted. *P* Tell them the serpent is desire, and they must put up his image in gold. Else they are all lost. *P* Tell them to spin the wine to a vortex, before they drink. *P* Tell them the mistletoe hides its tufts beneath the apple-blossom, and in winter emerges in berries. *P* Tell them the acorns stand in the sky, before they fall like a shower. *P* Tell them anything, or tell them nothing, what does it matter! Tell them it is all a joke, and their symbols are pretty play-things, and they are all great-god Peter-Pans. *P* Tell them what they want to hear, that they are the cutest ever. *P* Then come back, and leave them to it. *MS see also following entries to* 444:28

436:37 Unless one ... believe it. *E1*] They wouldn't see at all that famous Lord of yours, that you say is behind you. They would worship the 'mere woman' that you are, and on her they would be revenged." *P* "I don't believe it," she said. *P* But she did believe it. *TS*

437:3 seventeenth *E1*] Seventeenth *TS*

437:4 queer, *TS*] ~ *G*

437:11 come *TS, E1*] came *G, A1*

437:12 *Quién sabe! Ed.*] Quien sabe! *TS*

437:23 fear of ... contact *E1*] tenderness *TS*

437:24 heart. It *TS*] ~. *P* It *G*

437:25 stone *E1*] frost *TS*

437:26 mid-day *G*] midday *TS*

437:26 sun *E1*] Sun *TS, A1*

437:30 *Como quieres tú! Ed.*] Como quieres tu, *TS* Como quieres tu! *E1*

437:31 released *E1*] forgotten *TS*

438:5 men often *E1*] Ramon and Cipriano *TS*

438:6 life-long *Ed.*] lifelong *TS*

438:7 own isolated *Ed.*] own isolated, isolated *TS*

438:13 love-mouse *Ed.*] love mouse *TS*

438:13 with *TS*] into *A1*

438:15 sometimes, *TS*] ~ *G*

438:15 refused to ... life-long dyspepsia *E1*] turned into a dangerous grey rat, that might even whip the love-pussy *TS* refused ... lifelong dyspepsia *A1*

438:16 turned *E1*] Om. *TS*

438:21 love-women *TS*] ~, *E1*

438:25 beings, *TS*] ~ *G*

438:33 ego. "Woman *TS*] ~. *P* "Woman *G*

438:35 women *TS*] woman *A1*

439:5 repellant *TS*] repellent *A1*

439:12 That was ... lustre, and ... hand when *E1*] And when *TS* That ... lustre and ... hand, when *A1*

439:36 still, *TS*] ~ *A1*

439:40 buses *TS*] '~ *G*

440:2 dreary *E1*] tense *TS*

440:7 storey *Ed.*] story *TS*

440:10 *Están tocando! Ed.*] Estan tocando! *TS*

440:12 heard already *TS*] already heard *A1*

440:22 *Está! Ed.*] Esta! *TS* Està! *E1*

440:31 flowers *TS*] ~, *E1*

440:37 *Ya? Ed.*] Ya? *TS*

440:38 *Ya, Patrón! Ed.*] Ya, Patron! *TS*

441:3 separately *E1*] ~, *TS*

441:7 same *E1*] Same *TS*

441:17 woman, *E1*] ~. *TS*

441:29 woman *TS*] ~, *A1*

441:35 me *TS*] ~, *A1*

441:35 rests *TS*] ~.*A1*

442:16 *Está muy bien, Patrona? Ed.*]
Esta muy bien, Patrona? *TS*

442:19 breast, *G*] ~. *TS*

442:33 alike! *E1*] alike! She thought
sourly to herself. *TS*

442:37 *Está la Patrona Ed.*] Esta la
Patrona *TS* Està la Patrona
E1

443:7 said *TS*] asked *A1*

443:16 your *E1*] the *TS*

443:19 a woman ... even there ... are
together. *E1*] the terrace of
Jamiltepec isn't sanctified
enough ground for two such—
such wonderful beings? *TS* a
... even here ... together. *A1*

443:29 I know you don't *E1*] No!
Never leave us *TS*

443:30 voice *E1*] ~, *TS*

443:33 *Verdad! Verdad! Ed.*] Verdad!
Verdad! *TS*

443:35 herself: *G*] ~; *TS*

444:1 best desire *E1*] Holy Ghost *TS*

444:4 Oh *TS*] ~, *A1*

444:8 persuasion *E1*] hate *TS*

444:9 He would not *E1*] It is not for
him to *TS*

444:10 listen *E1*] *listen TS*

444:21 "r" *E1*] 'r' *TS*

444:28 You won't ... to him *E1*] Le
gueux m'a plantee la!" she said
to herself, in the words of an
old song *TS*

In this edition the following compound words are hyphenated at the end of a line;
the hyphenated form should be retained in quotation.

7:9	bull-fights	103:36	factory-made
8:26	concrete-and-iron	108:15	palm-trees
8:27	counter-slips	116:15	flannel-trouser
9:9	rain-coat	131:11	non-individual
30:40	meal-stop	139:6	long-barreled
31:3	window-pane	141:12	half-amusing
31:7	face-powder	155:5	reddish-and-yellow
31:27	fenced-in	157:20	Spanish-Mexicans
43:8	fellow-countryman	157:22	house-servants
47:24	Middle-West	160:4	orange-brown
50:28	tower-stumps	183:17	poppy-buds
55:4	serpent-like	189:18	salmon-red
57:33	sweet-smelling	193:39	three-pronged
58:25	fair-faced	215:2	ruddy-dark
59:24	tea-parties	215:13	stiff-backed
61:1	tropical-scented	218:13	sulky-faced
73:25	would-be-cocksure	231:23	motor-car
78:14	death-worshippers	232:5	rapidly-emptying
79:37	four-square	238:14	semi-frenzied
88:31	motor-boat	238:23	chopped-up
89:39	water-hyacinth	252:5	white-flowering
90:16	turkey-buzzards	275:32	candle-points
92:18	semi-abstraction	283:34	trestle-supports
92:25	semi-transparent	284:9	south-east
95:39	ranch-house	285:23	carefully-arranged
96:2	up-to-date	286:32	south-west
97:1	ground-squirrels	291:33	motor-boat
97:13	dim-seeming	295:32	blood-soddened

304:17 horse-droppings
318:25 maize-fields
319:12 fishing-nets
322:2 tread-looms
324:24 half-dancing
326:8 white-sleeved
331:7 meeting-ground
331:20 meeting-ground

346:24 mixing-bowl
381:21 loin-cloths
382:39 silver-coloured
402:26 woman-friend
405:19 wild-fowl
416:32 blood-familiarity
424:24 breakwater-wall
426:21 canoe-beak

APPENDIXES

Appendix I

A sketch of Aztec mythology

The Aztecs believed that the universe was destined to exist through five ages, each beginning with the birth of a new sun, which had to be fed on human blood, and each ending with the destruction of that sun. The supreme power of their cosmos was Ometeotl, exalted in the highest heaven yet invoked as Lord of the Close Vicinity. He was also said to dwell in Tamoanchan, the Aztec Paradise in the west, or at the navel of the earth, which was not only a centre but a 'direction' too, the first of the five sacred directions and source of the other four. Ultimately Ometeotl, whose name translates as Two-God, was the male–female duality addressed as Lord and Lady of Sustenance, origin and support of all creation.

From Ometeotl four sons came forth empowered to create the universe: Red Tezcatlipoca, Black Tezcatlipoca, Huitzilopochtli and Quetzalcoatl. Since Huitzilopochtli was often thought of as a form of Tezcatlipoca, the order reduces itself to a pair of gods, who existed as rivals. Each of the ages they created began with a battle for dominance, the victory alternating from one age to the next. In the best known version of the myth, Tezcatlipoca took possession of the sky as the first sun, the 'sun' of the jaguar, beast of earth and darkness. In the half-light of that epoch, the earth could produce only defective giants, and when in time Quetzalcoatl knocked his rival from the sky with his staff, Tezcatlipoca turned into a jaguar and devoured them. Then Quetzalcoatl became the second sun, the 'sun' of the wind, and remained in the sky until Tezcatlipoca in turn struck him down, and great hurricanes came to sweep away the world and transform the humans of that age into monkeys. Now Tezcatlipoca was in the ascendant again, and he transformed the rain god Tlaloc into the third sun. But the myth presents this as the age of fire, because Quetzalcoatl called down a rain of fire to destroy the world, transforming the human survivors into birds. Quetzalcoatl now chose the sister of Tlaloc, Chal-chiuhtlicue, as the fourth sun, the 'sun' of water, which ended with floods so enormous that the waters of the sky merged with the earth, and mankind was transformed into fish. Then for once Quetzalcoatl and Tezcatlipoca united their strength, in order to lift the sky to its proper height and prepare for a new age.

The first four ages had embodied the four elements, the four outreaching directions and four sacred colours. The fifth sun, as the Aztecs' own and the final age of the world, was designated not by a concrete entity but as the 'sun of movement': motion as a symbolic concept and also as earthquake, that ultimate motion which was to bring the world to annihilation. To recreate the sun for the fifth time, all the gods assembled at Teotihuacán, 'place of the gods' – a ruin even in Aztec days – and decided that one of their number must sacrifice himself in the great fire they had built. Two gods volunteered, the nobler and bolder of whom drew back at the last instant while the other, a diseased god who welcomed the purifying flame, leaped in. The hesitant god, now ashamed, jumped in after him. Both blazed up and vanished. Shortly the sick god was resurrected as the sun, with the other volunteer close behind as the moon. But then the new sun refused to move till all the other gods had sacrificed themselves. Once they had complied, the sun of the last age began his journey up the sky.

No doubt this host of immolated gods was the stars, which the sun consumes each day as he rises. Only the Morning Star, in this myth, dared to defy the great luminary, but even he had to submit in the end. Elsewhere in Aztec lore, the sun and the planet Venus exist by identity rather than opposition, as though the Evening Star descending toward the sun and the Morning Star preceding him out of the womb of night were alter egos of the sun. Venus as the Morning Star was one of the transformations of the ubiquitous Quetzalcoatl, and the Evening Star was his double, Xolotl.

With the fifth age now in progress, the earth had to be peopled so that the gods might have creatures to serve them. For this purpose the gods gathered at Tamoanchan, the Paradise which in some tales is the place of Aztec origin. Since they could not produce humans without bones, the stuff of immortality, they sent Quetzalcoatl and Xolotl to the underworld to petition Mictlantecuhtli, lord of the dead, for bones of a former race. He did not refuse outright but he demanded that Quetzalcoatl first accomplish a seemingly impossible task. When Quetzalcoatl met the challenge and was on his way back to Tamoanchan with the bones, Mictlantecuhtli pursued and overcame him and took back most of the precious substance. But Quetzalcoatl managed to reach Tamoanchan with a few fragments, which the mother goddess ground up and placed in a sacred bowl. When Quetzalcoatl drew blood from his penis to drop on the substance, and the other gods did likewise, a man and a woman arose from the bowl. To provide them with food Quetzalcoatl stole maize from a guardian deity and taught them how to cultivate it. He went on to instruct them in the skills to live by, among other things inventing the calendar. He even brought the forbidden *pulque* to earth to ease for mankind the burden of mortality.

Another origin myth, which includes the creation of the lesser gods as well as men, begins with Star Skirt, the Great Mother. She gave birth to a flint knife, the destructive-creative instrument of human sacrifice. It fell to the earth at Chicomoztoc, the place of seven caves in the west which alternates with Tamoanchan as the point of Aztec origin. From this knife sprang up a multitude of gods, again unquestionably the stars, yet dwelling on earth and in need of human servitors. In this myth also, on the advice of Star Skirt, the gods sent to the underworld for bones with which to fashion a new humanity. Xolotl alone undertook the mission this time, and what happened on the journey parallels the events of the Tamoanchan version.

In one variant of the myth Quetzalcoatl and Tezcatlipoca cooperated not to separate earth and sky, but to create them out of chaos. For this they made use of Cipactli, a monster wallowing in the eternal waters. The two gods took the shape of serpents, and coiling themselves around Cipactli squeezed her in two pieces. One half they elevated as the sky and the other they transformed into the earth, making trees from her hair, flowers from her skin, flowing water from her mouth and eyes, and mountains from her shoulders.

The Aztecs made no claim to know when the last age would end. The cataclysm would come, beyond even the knowledge of the gods, at the close of some fifty-two-year cycle, a measure of time psychologically comparable to our century. On the last night of each such period, all fires in the kingdom were allowed to die. Then priests impersonating the great gods led a procession to the Hill of the Star, south of Tenochtitlan, to await the crucial hour. If the constellation we call the Pleiades continued westward after passing the zenith, then the world was safe from annihilation for at least another fifty-two years. The priests then celebrated by tearing the heart out of a captive warrior and building a fire in the cavity of his body. From here by torches, first to the Temple of Huitzilopochtli in the city, and thence to every Aztec hearth, the new fire was disseminated, signifying continuance of the sun.

The Aztecs adopted most of their deities from the long-established traditions of Anáhuac when they arrived as barbarians from the north, though adapting their own tribal gods in some cases to fit new concepts of national destiny. Quetzalcoatl was inherited from older Mesoamerican culture, and Huitzilopochtli was originally a tribal deity.

Quetzalcoatl appears in many guises. Even his name has two possible translations: 'Plumed Serpent' or 'Precious Twin'. His manifestations did not end with those of cosmic creator, the brightest of the star warriors, and culture hero. He was the god of the wind too, and by extension, of breath, of life itself. It was said also that he made the world and all mankind, not only the original human couple but each separate child in the womb. He thus approached, though he never quite usurped, the supreme power of Ometeotl. Yet, despite his near omnipotence, Quetzalcoatl was the only Aztec deity to possess a distinctly human identity, with a compassion and a fallibility which make him the most appealing of Aztec gods. Still he shared the frightful traits of the whole Aztec pantheon. He was a sky dragon of terrifying proportions. And while in this role he was the giver of waters, he was also the bringer of hurricane winds. As Xolotl, his twin or demonic opposite, he was portrayed as a hulking animal, patron of twins and monstrous births. When the sun refused to budge at the start of the fifth age without the blood of the gods, Xolotl put them all to the knife, Quetzalcoatl with the rest, and then stabbed himself.

Quetzalcoatl was a composite of an historical figure, a priest-king of the Toltecs, and the god this man served. The confusion is such that in the myths human and divine actions are attributed to him indiscriminately. As a god, he was of early provenance and had accumulated many ancient identities. The historical Quetzalcoatl sought a radical reform of devotion to the god, with fasting and sexual abstinence. He engaged in penitential rites such as ablutions and letting blood from his own body. But he taught that his god rejected human sacrifice, desiring only that of birds and flowers. Missionaries and travelling merchants carried the new doctrine to distant parts of Mexico, leading to the adoption of Quetzalcoatl by the Maya, under the name of Kukulkan. The legend came into being that the reign of Quetzalcoatl in Tula, city of the Toltecs, was a golden age, with a great plenitude of nature and such peace and happiness among the people as the world had never known.

Then Quetzalcoatl's old enemy Tezcatlipoca arrived on the scene, in the guise of a sorcerer, scheming to drive out the pious ruler and re-establish the cult of human sacrifice. Tezcatlipoca held a smoking mirror up to Quetzalcoatl, which showed his face as hideously deformed, deeply sinful for all his claims of righteousness. Then Tezcatlipoca tricked him into drinking *pulque*, which he had always forbidden himself to do, and when he became intoxicated his enemy lured him into bed with his own sister.

Self-condemned for his weakness, Quetzalcoatl left Tula broken and lamenting, and the paradisal land faded into ordinary reality. He passed slowly through the Valley of Mexico, over the volcanoes and on to the east coast, heading for the mythical land of Tlapallan. All stages of his journey found their way into legend, the most famous of which was a long stay at Cholula, which became his holy city and a place of pilgrimage from all over central Mexico. Two conflicting accounts bring his sojourn in Meso-america to a close. One relates that when he reached the seashore he threw himself upon a pyre and was consumed, or else he climbed the volcano Mount Orizaba (Citlaltepetl: 'Hill of the Star') and leaped in. After a short time which he spent in the underworld, his heart rose as the Morning Star. The alternative legend relates that Quetzalcoatl sailed away on a raft of serpents, promising to return one day and re-establish his dominion over the land.

After the Conquest, Quetzalcoatl took on new identities. Some Spaniards were certain he originated in the Old World. He alone among the Aztec deities was pictured with a beard – beards being scanty among American Indians. Saint Thomas the Apostle – also known as Thomas Didymus, the Twin – had been sent to preach the Gospel in India, and these were the Indies. Quetzalcoatl must therefore have been Saint Thomas. Other theories identified him as a Christian missionary of the fourth or fifth century, from the Continent by one account, from Ireland by another.

Huitzilopochtli had been with the Mexican Aztecs for a long time, absorbing attributes or whole identities of other gods as the circumstances of his worshippers changed. He roused the Aztecs in their homeland of Aztlán – where the Seven Caves and Paradise were located – and guided them to their imperial destiny in the Valley of Mexico, delivering oracles to drive them on when they showed signs of weakening. By our calendar the departure took place about 1168 AD. At one critical point in the journey, near Tula, the Aztecs built a dam in obedience to a command from Huitzilopochtli, creating a huge lake out of whose waters arose Coatepec (Serpent Mountain). Here the Aztecs settled and lived in utopian ease till Huitzilopochtli broke the dam and forced his reluctant charges to continue their quest.

When the Aztecs became dominant and attempted to trace their spiritual ancestry to the Toltecs, Coatepec was said to be the birthplace of Huitzilopochtli. As the story went, Coatlicue the Earth Goddess, after giving birth to the moon and stars, retired to an isolated temple on Coatepec. One day as she was sweeping, a ball of feathers came floating past her through the air. Taking hold of it and putting it under her skirt for safekeeping, she discovered soon afterwards that she was pregnant. The moon and stars were so scandalised to hear of this that they threatened to kill their mother. But Huitzilopochtli assured her from the womb that he was more than a match for all his siblings. When the attack came, headed by his pernicious sister the Moon – which in Aztec lore could be either male or female – Huitzilopochtli sprang from his mother's body full-grown and armed with a serpent of fire, with which he slew all the other celestial beings. From all appearances this is another mythical account of the ascent of the sun from the underworld to conquer the darkness by destroying the rulers of night. Huitzilopochtli retained much of this solar orientation at his fullest development, but he was never a personification of the sun. He is best described as the genius of the Aztec people.

Huitzilopochtli had revealed to his people that they were to establish their city at the place where they discovered an eagle perched on a giant prickly pear cactus. When they reached the Valley of Mexico, the last of the Nahuatl tribes to arrive, Huitzilopochtli watched over them through many hardships, even enslavement by some of their neighbours, for over fifty years. One significant event toward the founding of Tenochtitlan occurred when they were living at Chapultepec. One of their number, a sorcerer by the name of Copil, had turned on his own people and was preparing to assist in an enemy assault when he was apprehended and sacrificed and his heart thrown into the Lake of Mexico. When the Aztecs were at length driven to seek out a territory of their own in the lakeside marshes, considered worthless by the other tribes, Huitzilopochtli led them toward the spot where the heart of Copil had fallen. According to one version of the legend, as the Aztecs penetrated this inhospitable terrain, they decided to send two of their priests ahead to explore. These two had not gone far when they saw the long-awaited omen, and the prickly pear on which the eagle sat had sprung from the heart of Copil. By some accounts, the eagle had his wings spread to the sun, by others he was holding a snake in his claws, and by still others he clutched a bird of bright plumage – a hint, perhaps, of a plumed serpent. As the two priests approached, they saw that the water all around this spot was as green as emerald, and when they reached it they were stricken with awe. All of a sudden one of them disappeared into the bright water. The other hurried back to the rest of the tribe to report what had happened, and all that night and into the next day they waited in fear and amazement. But then as suddenly as he had vanished the missing priest reappeared and recounted his strange adventure. All this time he had been under the water in the presence of Tlaloc, the god of the earth – more specifically, the god of the lake, for as we know, this was the rain god. Tlaloc had told the priest that Huitzilopochtli was his son, and that he was glad to welcome him and his followers, for this was indeed the spot they were to make the centre of their realm. So here the Aztecs built Tenochtitlan, locating their great temple just where they saw the eagle on the cactus. The summit of this temple, the heart of the Aztec empire, was shared by statues of Tlaloc and Huitzilopochtli, Quetzalcoatl having his own temple nearby.

Appendix II

Cultural periods in the Valley of Mexico

1500–200 BC	Various formative cultures
200 BC	Founding of Teotihuacán
700 AD	End of decline and destruction of Teotihuacán
700–900 AD	Transitional cultures
900–1200 AD	Toltec dominance, from the city of Tula
1200–1300 AD	Invasion of northern tribes, largely Mexica (Nahuatl)
1325 AD	Founding of Tenochtitlan (site of Mexico City)
1400–1521 AD	Aztec Empire

Dates are approximate.

Appendix III

Mexican historical events relevant to *The Plumed Serpent*

In 1519 a few hundred Spanish adventurers led by Hernán Cortés invaded the domains of the Mexican Aztecs. By 1521 they had completed their conquest, assisted by the Aztecs' enemies, especially the Tlaxcalans, and also by the native belief that Cortés was an emissary of Quetzalcoatl, if not the god himself, who had long been expected to return from the east and resume control of the land from which he had been driven centuries before.

After the Conquest, the Spanish King set up an *encomienda* system, through which colonial masters were to provide for the material and spiritual welfare of the Indians; but the plan led to their enslavement, and it was eventually abandoned. Still, in one way or another, Spanish overlords and the Catholic Church continued to take over Indian land, much of which had been held in communal ownership by tribal custom: the *ejido* system. Those who worked the land for the Spanish became serfs, *peones*. Redress for their wrongs was nearly unobtainable; no one of native birth, even if purely Spanish, was permitted to hold office. All government officials had to be Peninsular-born.

In a struggle that lasted from 1810 to 1821, the Mexican people won their independence from Spain, but even so they achieved little political or economic emancipation. The Catholic Church retained its wealth and privileges, and opposing factions of the native Mexican ruling class kept the country in a state of constant revolution. The first advances towards democracy came when the Liberals, under Benito Juárez, began the Reform Movement, from which emerged the Constitution of 1857. The chief aim of the Reform Laws was to abolish *fueros*, the right of the clergy to be tried in ecclesiastical courts, even for capital offences, and to break up the vast holdings of the Church for redistribution among the rural poor, mostly of Indian stock. After a few years of open warfare between Liberals and Conservatives, Juárez became President in 1861, only to be driven out by the French, who in 1864 succeeded in enthroning the Habsburg Maximilian and his wife Carlota as Emperor and Empress of Mexico. When the United States compelled France to withdraw her troops in 1867, Maximilian was soon defeated and executed by the Liberals, and Juárez brought his fugitive government back to the Capital. Re-elected in 1871, he died in 1872, before he could bring about widespread enforcement of the Reform Laws. In time, through various legal manoeuvres, most of the land that had been expropriated from the Church was absorbed by the big *haciendas*.

Porfirio Díaz, a Liberal general prominent in the overthrow of Maximilian, opposed Juárez in the election of 1871 and afterwards led an unsuccessful rebellion. But when Juárez's less able successor attempted to stay in office for another term in 1876, Díaz rebelled again and this time gathered enough support in the Mexican Congress to have himself made President. Then in 1880, in what seemed to be the beginnings of democracy, Díaz surrendered the Presidency to another man, but he turned out to be so corrupt and incompetent that Díaz easily won re-election in 1884 and remained in office until 1911.

During the Díaz regime, which governed by lavish favours to supporters, unlimited privilege to foreign capital and brutal suppression of opposition, Mexico saw a great expansion of exports, some industrial growth and a treasury surplus for the first time in history. But all this was a thin surface over poverty and misery among the peons and the growing population of industrial workers. When Díaz spoke of tolerating opposition in the election of 1910, Francisco I. Madero came forward to run against him. When the challenge began to appear serious, Díaz had his opponent arrested but then made the mistake of releasing him on bail. Madero promptly issued a declaration of rebellion, which was enough to bring the national discontent to a boil. By May 1911 the country was in tumult everywhere, and Porfiro Díaz was forced to resign and go into exile.

President for less than two years, Madero never ceased to have trouble from agrarians like Emiliano Zapata on the one hand, and reactionaries on the other. In February 1913 Victoriano Huerta, Madero's most trusted general, succeeded by intrigue in having himself appointed President, imprisoned Madero and the Vice-President, and had them murdered. Even though soon repudiated by the other Revolutionary leaders, Huerta managed to stay in power until July 1914 by terrorizing or assassinating his opponents.

In order to oust Huerta, Venustiano Carranza of Coahuila proposed an alliance of the leading Constitutionalists: Pancho Villa of Chihuahua, Álvaro Obregón of Sonora, Emiliano Zapata of Morelos, with himself as First Chief. Obregón accepted the arrangement and Villa cooperated as far as it suited him, while Zapata warily kept his distance. As their separate armies moved south toward Mexico City, a breach soon developed between Villa and Carranza, and later between Villa and Obregón, but a measure of unity endured long enough to bring about the primary goal: the resignation and departure into exile of Victoriano Huerta.

Rivalries now flared, and all attempts to settle them proved in vain. Carranza and Villa became the chief contestants for national control, with Obregón in Carranza's camp and Zapata siding with Villa but unwilling to risk his forces beyond his stronghold south of the Capital. Retreats and advances with sporadic battles went on for many months, but all the while the power of Carranza and Obregón increased and that of Villa declined, particularly after his crushing defeat by Obregón at Celaya in April 1915. At length the victors called a convention and succeeded in framing the Constitution of 1917 to express the ideals of the Revolution, not only by reaffirming the Laws of Reform, now including a ban on foreign priests, but also by formulating new principles for agrarian reform, recovery of natural resources from foreign hands, and improvement of the condition of labour.

The struggle to put the provisions of this Constitution into effect went on for years. Carranza was elected President in March 1917. After serving briefly in the new government, Obregón returned to private life in Sonora, and Villa went on marauding like a bandit chief. Zapata resisted Carranza almost from the start, finding him no more anxious to reapportion land than many a predecessor. Open war soon developed, and for a while the total devotion of the Morelos population to Zapata frustrated Carranza's attempts to destroy him. It was only by elaborate treachery, in April 1919, that Zapata was at last lured into a trap and shot down.

Carranza soon began stifling all opposition, while economic conditions worsened and corruption in his government ran wild. When he moved to impose a successor of his own choosing, Obregón protested, and after barely escaping Carranza's vengeance, he pronounced against the government, with the support of Plutarco Elías Calles and Adolfo de la Huerta – not to be confused with Victoriano Huerta.

In May 1920, with most of the other revolutionaries now against him, Carranza and a few adherents took a special train from the Capital to Veracruz with all the state treasure they could carry. When the train came under attack, Carranza and his staff fled on horseback, only to be captured by a bandit 'general', who had Carranza murdered. In June the triumphant Sonora faction appointed de la Huerta as provisional President to serve out Carranza's term. During his six months in office, de la Huerta managed to pacify the still active Zapata faction and to negotiate the retirement of Villa by awarding him a great *hacienda* in Chihuahua and an honour guard.

In the Presidential election of September 1920, Obregón readily defeated the other candidates and was inaugurated on the first day of December. During his administration, he made cautious moves to put into effect some of the provisions of the Constitution of 1917, but even his limited redistribution of land and his encouragement of trade unions raised a cry of bolshevism in some quarters. In fact, his labour policies brought the ruthless Luis Morones to power. In appointing José Vasconcelos as Minister of Education, Obregón did much toward bringing a semblance of free public education to Mexico, and Vasconcelos' sponsorship of murals for public buildings brought about, through such artists as Rivera and Orozco, Mexico's greatest modern cultural achievement, the Mexican Renaissance in painting. In addition to other accomplishments, Obregón paid off some of the claims for damage to foreign property during the revolutions, and he resumed payments on the foreign debt.

When Lawrence first visited Mexico, in the spring of 1923, with Obregón over half-way through his term in office and re-election forbidden by the new Constitution, the question of a successor was in the air. No one doubted that the man would be one of Obregón's old Sonora cronies, Calles or de la Huerta. When Obregón chose Calles, supporters of de la Huerta raised the old cry of 'imposition'. Villa made a few ominous noises about coming out of retirement, but this danger was cut short when he was assassinated in July 1923 – shortly after Lawrence ended his first Mexican stay. Whether Villa's death was to be attributed to enemies at home or to Obregón has never been established.

A rebellion led by de la Huerta gathered headway through the year 1923, erupting in a brief and bloody conflict in December. The decisive battle was fought near Ocotlán (Lawrence's Ixtlahuacan) at the eastern end of Lake Chapala, in February 1924. Mopping-up operations continued into the spring, but de la Huerta managed to escape to the United States.

The Presidential campaign, with Calles as the real candidate and General Ángel Flores as a token opponent, continued into the election of July 1924. Once his victory was official, Calles went on a tour of western Europe, talking with heads of state, then visiting the United States on his way home, where he conferred with President Coolidge. He was inaugurated on 1 December 1924 for a four-year term, during which he carried on policies begun by Obregón but applied them with more vigour, stepping up the still lagging agrarian reforms. Arriving in Mexico City shortly before Calles was to be inaugurated, Lawrence made use of the talk that surrounded anticipation of that event, with Calles as 'Montes', the possibility of rebellion by a disgruntled general (the real-life Ángel Flores), and much else having to do with Calles' politics. All connections between real figures or events and those of Lawrence's fiction are identified in the Explanatory notes.

Appendix IV

Maps

Mexico
Lake Chapala (with actual place-names in bold and fictional in parentheses)

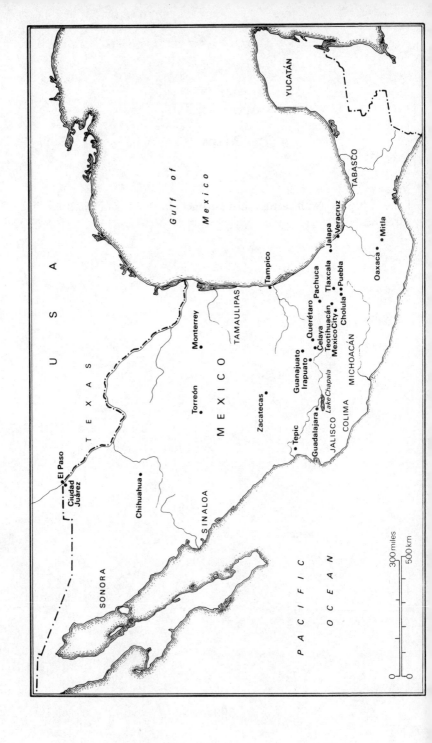

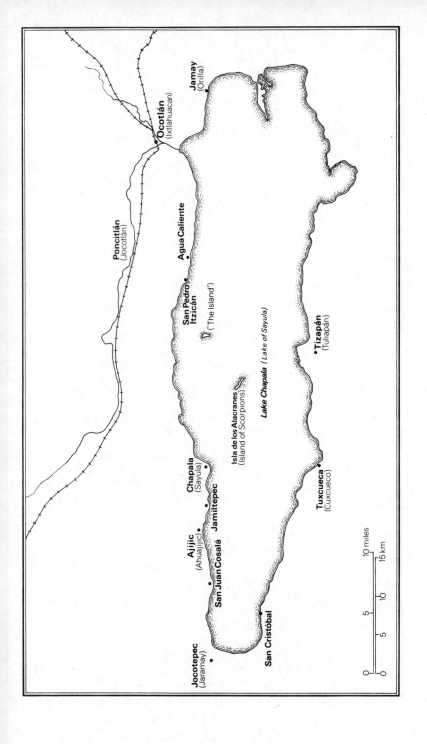

Poncitlán
(Jocotlán)

Ocotlán
(Ixtlahuacan)

Jamay
(Orilla)

Agua Caliente

San Pedro
Itzicán

('The Island')

Isla de los Alacranes
(Island of Scorpions)

Lake Chapala (Lake of Sayula)

Tizapán
(Tuliapán)

Chapala
(Sayula)

Jamiltepec

Ajijic
(Ahuajijic)

San Juan Cosalá

Tuxcueca
(Cuxcueco)

Jocotepec
(Jaramay)

San Cristóbal

0   5   10 miles
0   5   10   15 km